45¢

**The
Political
Imagination**

The
Political
Imagination

Dialogues in politics and political behavior

Edgar Litt *University of Wisconsin, Milwaukee*

SCOTT, FORESMAN AND COMPANY *Glenview, Illinois*

Atlanta *Dallas* *Palo Alto* *Oakland N.J.*

Contents

Part I

**The Rise and
Fall of
Political Myths**   1

Part II

Political Ideology: Motive, Weapon, Rationalization

Part III

Political Resources: The Open Society and Its Friends

Part IV

**Political Institutions:
Modern and
Comparative**

Part V

**Public Policies:
A Reader's Guide
to Education
and Politics**   427

A. THE POLITICS OF EDUCATION

B. EDUCATION AND ITS PUBLICS

Introduction

The major emphasis of *The Political Imagination* is on the cultural framework of politics — the set of beliefs, norms, and behaviors that underlie the complex developments of public life. The neophyte is introduced to the political landscape along this path for several reasons. First, the literature about politics should be judged by classic yardsticks. One of the common characteristics of enduring contributions — such as those of Lasswell, Mosca, and Neumann, which are reproduced in these pages — is that they are written from the perspective of their society and its historical and cultural base. Second, a cultural approach to politics, with its emphasis on myths and ideology, contributes to an intellectual dialogue. Theories are not proposed or tested in vacuums; they are significantly affected by the political and social currents impinging on their authors. Third, a broad cultural approach encourages the interaction of theory and empirical research that is the heart of an intellectual discipline. Political scientists work at many levels: some coin grand theory, others speculate critically about political tendencies, and others attempt to test propositions through empirical research. All these efforts are meaningful, but only if there is a common thread — a meaningful discourse between theorist and researcher, between abstract thought and pragmatic policies. From this discourse the student will learn about the varieties of knowledge that contribute to our political understanding.

A fourth consideration that guided the preparation of this reader is the relationship of political inquiry to the social sciences. The best of political inquiry has been firmly rooted in the development of the social sciences as a whole; that development in turn, has been influenced by the intellectual milieu of American society. This reader is organized in such a manner as to relate the advances of empiricism to the classic questions scholars have asked about the purposes of political life, the nature of political power and man, and the evolution of public policies.

These, then, are some of the considerations that have guided the preparation of this reader. The selections deal with subjects appealing to behavioralists and humanists, to those with an interest in the conscious course of political processes and institutions, and to those who are most attracted to the political subconscious expressed in myths and ideas — the cultural and psychic fabrics that clothe politics. But the main purpose is to nourish inquisitive minds with a broad, critical analysis of political life.

The plan of *The Political Imagination* is quite simple. The book begins with selections that will increase the student's awareness of the free-floating and often contradictory segments of political thought he brings to the classroom. We first analyze the "cheer-words" of modern man — equality, fraternity, freedom. Then, after grounding our inquiry in the nature and application of political myths in Part I, we turn in Part II to the study of coherent ideologies that have shaped political systems throughout the world. Here we also critically assess the contemporary's tendency to understand his past better than his present, and we wonder if organized belief systems (or ideologies) are truly remnants of the past. This issue is debated, and then some suggestions of modern ideologies are offered for consideration and debate.

Part III attempts to do two things: first, to illustrate the transformation of the average man from a pawn of ordained political powers to an actual or potential participant in his society; and, second, to draw from some of the best empirical research of the last decade some prerequisites of democratic political systems.

Part IV presents a sample of political institutions and processes in American and non-American systems. It also focuses attention on a perennial topic of political analysis — the new forces and men who have risen to power within the framework of the eighteenth-century constitution that still provides the formal definition of institutional power in the United States. Then, rather than offering a hodgepodge of excerpts about politics in other lands, Part IV presents the heart of a concrete debate on what constitutes "comparison" in systematic political studies.

To conclude, Part V concentrates on one crucial area of public policy: education. Any policy area is the focus of a multiplicity of political conflicts and public goals; this is most evident when readings are coordinated to reveal the diverse facets of educational politics. In addition, a concentration on one set of policies enables the student to apply other readings to an analysis of this problem. It encourages the shuttling between abstract and specific, theory and research, that is the heart of developing political knowledge and the wisdom to apply that knowledge as teachers and citizens.

Several pedagogical considerations have guided the editor's labors. First, this reader avoids presenting snippets of articles and books, because the student must have enough of an author's thesis to make an intelligent evaluation. The editor also has refrained from a "great books" approach, predicated on the mistaken notion that only authors who lived a century ago are classical. It is the problems under analysis that determine importance, and this relevance handled skillfully and meaningfully determines classical political inquiry.

Two major efforts have gone into the selection of readings. One is to relate general theory, criticism, or speculation and specific empirical or case studies. For instance, the historical role of equality in American politics advanced through De Tocqueville and Shils leads to Lane's judgments, based on depth interviewing, about the limitations of equality as a political goal in the mind of the American common man. Second, insofar as possible the book has been organized to convey the import of dialogue and debate in intellectual and scholarly writings on politics. This is done overtly in the Bell-Aiken debate on the end of ideology in Part II and in the discussion of Neumann's approach to the nature of comparative politics in Part IV. Elsewhere, as in the short introductions preceding selections about ideology and democratic resources, the editor has tried to sketch the intellectual and political context of the topics under discussion; in this way the readings are related to the real views and problems of politically engaged men.

In conclusion, it is our hope that this collection will have a derivative benefit, one that directly affects the instructor of introductory courses and, through him, the students he meets several times a week. The bridging of the interests of undergraduate teaching and academic research is not an easy task. Aware of this situation, and attempting to labor under it, the editor has endeavored to pique the student's appetite for serious research and to further the instructor's effort to fuse the two realms of scholarship and teaching. Most bright undergraduates are not interested in mulling over the finer points of recent Ph.D. dissertations, although most recent Ph.D.'s are, or should be, interested in stimulating the political interests of sophomore neophytes. Together they may find in these pages some light to brighten the path to political truth for both scientist and student, scholar and inquiring youngster, too often separated by the chasms of time and learning.

Part I

The Rise
and Fall of
Political Myths

Political myths are fundamental beliefs or assumptions about the political nature of society. More important than their truth or falsity is the fact that they determine the distribution of economic, social, and political power. Myths have guided almost every political society, and they have been most effective when taken for granted by the citizenry. During most of the history of the Western world the political order has been based on myths such as the supernatural doctrine ordaining the divine right of kings and the doctrine ordaining division of the clerical and secular realms.

Political myths are operative when the fundamental social and political systems are regarded as both natural and legitimate — when men obey because nearly all of them see public life through essentially the same eyes. Those who offer critical appraisals of the dominant system may be regarded as political heretics and treated accordingly. To deny the political postulates of the slavery and plantation systems of the antebellum American South, to challenge the political system based on laissez-faire economics (as the Keynesians did when they advocated the government's positive role in the political economy), or to deny the basic assumptions about contemporary American democracy have been, in their respective eras, critical acts. At most times and in most places, a majority have looked uncritically at their own political environments. The Greeks, for example, could see no alternative to the polity of city-states, and thus they resisted the internationalism of Alexander the Great.

One of the virtues of social science—and one of the reasons it is the first scholarly effort to be disrupted in totalitarian systems—is its analysis of political myths. To untangle the web of politics in our society means to confront our primary political myths; and this process, like all efforts at self-analysis, may be painful, for we have a vested interest in the ongoing political order. In that prototype of modern societies, the American political system, we are guided by an enduring Constitution and nurtured by the premises of equality, fraternity, and freedom; yet we need to dissect these primary assumptions of our polity, because criticism is the heart of political inquiry. Moreover, if myths lack concrete meaning, they may become fossilized; and that is the signal for invasion by alien ideologies or the growth of countermyths born in alienation and designed to supplant the old order.

---

1. Political Myths

To develop an inquiry, succinct definitions are useful. In the first selection that follows, Harold Lasswell and Abraham Kaplan provide us with a cogent and useful vocabulary for the exploration of political myths. Note especially their emphasis on the functions of myths within a political system and the direct ratio between a myth's pervasiveness and the scope of political power behind it.

One key aspect of a political myth is its description of and justification for a particular method of securing political power. The theory of a ruling class as propounded by the twentieth-century Italian political scientist Gaetano Mosca maintains that a dominant political stratum creates and sustains myths or formulas to justify its position. In his essay, Mosca describes both the essence of political power and the symbols that are advanced to sustain power.

Another aspect of all political myths is the definition of the goal or purpose of political action. The doctrine of progress in human affairs, for instance, fitted nicely with the aspirations of the bourgeoisie emerging from the constraints of feudalism and mercantilism. Progress is now the goal of much political and social action. R. G. Collingwood discusses the meaning of progress *both as a law of nature and as a creation of historians and suggests that it, too, has become a political myth that is subject to critical analysis and, perhaps, revision.*

A GRAMMAR OF POLITICS

HAROLD D. LASSWELL AND ABRAHAM KAPLAN

DF. The *political myth* is the pattern of the basic political symbols current in a society.

The basic symbols are those having a bearing on the social structure, not merely on some one particular power relationship or practice. They formulate the most general perspectives concerning interpersonal relations in the society; specific power facts are responded to in these perspectives. The political myth ·consists of the political perspectives most firmly accepted.

> *The whole body of beliefs existing in any given age may generally be traced to certain fundamental assumptions which at the time, whether they be actually true or false, are believed by the mass of the world to be true with such confidence that they hardly appear to bear the character of assumptions.*[1]

The political myth comprises these "fundamental assumptions" about political affairs. It consists of the symbols invoked not only to explain but also to justify specific power practices.

The term "myth" is not to be interpreted as necessarily imputing a fictional, false, or irrational character to the symbols — though . . . such an imputation is often correct. . . . [W]e characterize symbols in terms of their functioning, not directly by their properties.

The present concept is close to a number of others which have played an important part in the classical literature: Marx's "ideology," Sorel's "myth," Mosca's "political formula," Pareto's "derivations," Mannheim's "ideology" and "utopia," and others. . . .

DF. The *political doctrine* is the part of the political myth that formulates basic expectations and demands; the *miranda,* the part consisting of basic symbols of sentiment and identification.

The political doctrine consists of the basic expectations and demands concerning power relations and practices in the society. Merriam refers to these as "credenda" — things to be believed — as distinguished from the "miranda" — things to be admired:

> *The credenda of power . . . contain the reasons which oblige the intellect to give assent to the continuance of authority. And this*

[1]A. V. Dicey, *Law and Public Opinion* (New York: Macmillan, 1926), p. 20.

From *Power and Society* (New Haven: Yale University Press, 1950), pp. 116–125. Title supplied by the editor.

> *assent may be due to government in general, or to particular holders*
> *of power, or to the special system of authority in vogue at any given*
> *moment in a particular unit of power.*[2]

The political doctrine is authoritatively set forth in constitutions (especially preambles), charters, formal declarations, and so on.

Frequently political theory serves chiefly to embody political doctrine. No clear separation is made between hypotheses of political science and the demands and expectations of political philosophy. Political theory is normatively ambiguous to a high degree—statements purporting to be scientific generalizations often serve instead to express and justify political preferences. Rousseau's remark, "I always feel happy, whenever I meditate on governments, always to discover in my researches new reasons for loving that of my country," is suggestive, to say the least. The matter is forcibly put by Merriam in the view that theories of the state "have been in large measure justifications or rationalizations of groups in power or seeking power—the special pleadings of races, religions, classes, in behalf of their special situation."[3] Theories of the state have often been, in short, enunciations of political doctrine.

In the same way, legal and economic theories have often served as formulations of political doctrine, apart from whatever scientific purport they may have had. Indeed, scientific propositions in the strict sense may at the same time be functioning as political symbols, and especially is this true of the social sciences. As Louis Wirth has pointed out, "Every assertion of a 'fact' about the social world touches the interests of some individual or group."[4] This need not impugn the objectivity of the assertion, but calls attention to its possible functioning in the political process as well as the process of inquiry.

Another important component of the political myth, embodying (at least in its latent content) many elements of political doctrine, are the various elaborations of social norms, the theories of what is right, good, proper—symbols included in what Pareto calls "derivations." Mill observed in his essay on liberty that "wherever there is an ascendant class, a large portion of the morality of the country emanates from its class interests, and its feelings of class superiority." And not only does it "emanate" from the social structure, but it may serve also to formulate fundamental justifications for that structure. A similar relation between standards of taste and the social structure has been emphasized by Veblen and others.

The miranda are the symbols of sentiment and identification in the political myth. They are those whose function is to arouse admira-

---

[2]C. E. Merriam, *Political Power* (New York: McGraw-Hill, 1934), p. 113.

[3]C. E. Merriam, *New Aspects of Politics*, 2d ed. (Chicago: University of Chicago Press, 1931), p. xiv.

[4]In the introduction to K. Mannheim, *Ideology and Utopia* (New York: Harcourt, Brace, 1936), p. xvii.

tion and enthusiasm, setting forth and strengthening faiths and loyalties. They not only arouse emotions indulgent to the social structure, but also heighten awareness of the sharing of these emotions by others, thereby promoting mutual identification and providing a basis for solidarity.

> *The emblem or shibboleth not only calls the attention of an individual who sees or hears it to the object or fact that it symbolizes, and awakens in him certain feelings; it also fixes his attention upon the feelings that it arouses and the conduct that it incites in others. The emotions and conduct of others, of which he is thus made aware, at once begin to act upon himself as an influence that merges with the original effect of the emblem or shibboleth.*[5]

Flags and anthems, ceremonials and demonstrations, group heroes and the legends surrounding them—these exemplify the importance of miranda in the political process.

PROP. The content of the political doctrine is determined by its political function rather than by the matters of fact which it purports to describe.

That is, the content of the political doctrine is determined by its role in the political process, not in the process of inquiry. It consists of political, not scientific symbols, with characteristics appropriate to their function. Their purport is primarily valuative and incitive, not informative.

Hence it comes about that, as Russell has observed, "Beliefs which have been successful in inspiring respect for the existing distribution of power have usually been such as cannot stand against intellectual criticism."[6] But it is to be added that "intellectual criticism" finds its most fruitful application to scientific discourse. We need no more expect political discourse to withstand it than the discourse of poetry or prayer. (We are speaking, of course, of political doctrine, not political science.) Whether a statement is true or false, validly or invalidly deduced from others, and so on, are questions important only with regard to those statements whose successful functioning requires these characteristics. There is a considerable tendency to misunderstand semantics as requiring of all symbols the properties essential to scientific discourse. The mistake is made of supposing that symbols lacking these properties are to be rejected as "nonsense" rather than analyzed in terms of functions other than that of conveying knowledge.

[5] F. H. Giddings, *Inductive Sociology* (New York: Macmillan, 1901), p. 138.
[6] B. Russell, *Power* (New York: W. W. Norton, 1938), p. 98.

The importance of avoiding this misconception, as applied to political doctrines, has been emphasized by Mosca, among others: Although they

> *do not correspond to scientific truths, that does not mean that they are mere quackeries invented to trick the masses into obedience. They answer a real need in man's social nature; and this need, so universally felt, of knowing that one is governed not on the basis of mere material or intellectual force, but on the basis of a moral principle, has beyond any doubt a practical and real importance.*[7]

This need has a "practical and real importance" for those exercising power as well as for those subject to it. Continued reliance on violence only has obvious disadvantages for the powerful; and scientific discourse is often inexpedient and ineffective. Rousseau discusses the point fully:

> *There are a thousand kinds of ideas which it is impossible to translate into the language of the people. Views very general and objects very remote are alike beyond its reach; and each individual, approving of no other plan of government than that which promotes his own interests, does not readily perceive the benefits that he is to derive from the continual deprivations which good laws impose . . . Since the legislator cannot employ either force or reasoning, he must needs have recourse to an authority of a different order, which can compel without violence and persuade without convincing. It is this which in all ages has constrained the founders of nations to resort to the intervention of heaven. . . .*[8]

The preceding discussion is in no way to be construed as a defense of falsehood and distortion as a political technique. It is rather an insistence that a clear understanding of political doctrine requires its interpretation in terms of other categories and standards than those appropriate to the analysis of a scientific account of political structures and practices. It is not to our present purpose to make value judgments of the characteristics typically exhibited by political doctrines. What is being asserted is simply that the symbols have certain nonscientific (not necessarily *unscientific*) characteristics, and that these are derivative from the functions they perform.

PROP. Maintenance of power depends on adherence in the domain of power to the political doctrine under which the power is being exercised.

[7]G. Mosca, *Ruling Class* (New York: McGraw-Hill, 1939), p. 71.
[8]J. J. Rousseau, *Social Contract*, II, 7.

The hypothesis calls attention to the inadequacy of violence alone as a stable base for the possession and exercise of power. Merriam observes:

> *No power could stand if it relied upon violence alone, for force is not strong enough to maintain itself against the accidents of rivalry and discontent. The might that makes right must be a different might from that of the right arm. It must be a might deep-rooted in emotion, embedded in feelings and aspiration, in morality, in sage maxims, in forms of rationalization among the higher levels of cultural groups.*[9]

Or, as Rousseau puts it more simply, "The strongest man is never strong enough to be always master, unless he transforms his power into right and obedience into duty." And Hobbes still more concisely: "Even the tyrant must sleep."

This transformation from might to right is effected by the political doctrine. Power distributed and exercised in accord with the political doctrine is right, and submission to it is a duty. Outside of or contrary to the doctrine, power is "tyranny," and not only does not obligate submission, but may even obligate resistance. The political doctrine thus provides the key symbols and unquestioned axioms on which the justification of the social structure rests. This is essentially the function attributed to it by Mosca:

> *Ruling classes do not justify their power exclusively by* de facto *possession of it, but try to find a moral and legal basis for it, representing it as the logical and necessary consequence of doctrines and beliefs that are generally recognized and accepted. . . . The majority of a people consents to a given governmental system solely because the system is based upon religious or philosophical beliefs that are universally accepted by them. The amount of consent depends upon the extent to which, and the ardor with which, the class that is ruled believes in the political formula by which the ruling class justifies its rule.*[10]

PROP. Dependence of a power structure on acceptance of the political doctrine varies inversely with the weight and scope of the power in question.

The inadequacy of violence as a stable base for the exercise of power is, of course, not an absolute, but depends on certain features of the power situation. The hypothesis directs attention to two of these fea-

---

[9]Merriam, *Political Power*, p. 102.
[10]Mosca, *op. cit.*, pp. 70 and 97.

tures. Where the power in question is of great weight—approaching absolutism—dependence on doctrine is less than it otherwise would be. For even if opposition did arise, it would be, by hypothesis, relatively powerless. Conversely, dependence on doctrine is greatest where power is shared to a considerable extent. But even in the extreme case of absolutism, there is still a political doctrine and exercise of power in accord with it. "Even in despotic states we never see arbitrary power raised to the height of a principle. Even the despot is regarded as acting according to the requirements of justice."[11] Political doctrine not only serves to keep the domain in subjection; it also provides self-justification for the power holders.

Similarly, power of great scope—one approaching totalitarianism —is less dependent on acceptance of the political doctrine than otherwise. For the greater the scope of power, the greater the control exercised by the powerful over what will be accepted. The function of propaganda in stabilizing a totalitarian regime, to mention only the most direct technique, is a commonplace. Where power is so limited in scope as to exclude control over symbols, accepted doctrine must be relied upon to minimize the threat from conflicting power holders.

DF. The *ideology* is the political myth functioning to preserve the social structure; the *utopia*, to supplant it.

The terms are taken over from Mannheim;[12] a utopia as here defined need not be "utopian" in the sense of either impracticability or perfection. We call a pattern of political symbols a utopia if their function in the political process is to induce fundamental changes in power relationships or practices; an ideology, if they serve to maintain the given power patterns. Thus counterrevolutionary symbols are as utopian in the present sense as those of a revolutionary movement, and with the seizure of power utopian symbols become ideology. There is not involved here any concept of direction of social change, or any standard of valuation of social structures.

The definitions are based on the way the symbols function, not on characteristics of the symbols themselves. Symbols functioning at one time as utopias may at another serve as ideology, as indeed usually happens in the case of successful revolution—utopian symbols are retained regardless of their increasing divergence from the power facts. And the same individual symbols may simultaneously appear as elements in both an ideology and a utopia (for example, "Americanism" in the slogan "Communism is twentieth century Americanism"). As with other symbol categories previously introduced, the classification

[11]N. M. Korkunov, *General Theory of Law* (New York: Macmillan, 1922), p. 141.
[12]Mannheim, *op. cit.*

cannot be made in abstraction from the concrete situation in which the symbols function.

PROP. In a society with a stable social structure, the ideology is a matter of consensus, not opinion.

That is, the ideology is noncontroversial; disagreements occur only in regard to "applications" of the ideological principles to specific cases. The degree to which the ideology *is* a subject of disagreement and debate may be taken as an index of instability of the social structure supported by the ideology. Under conditions of stability, elaboration of the ideology is in the direction of ceremonialization and glorifications, not explanation and justification.

Spontaneous (nonpropaganda) formulations of the ideology will be frequent and highly elaborated if the ideology is widely and intensely adhered to. Manipulated expressions of ideological faith and loyalty indicate the existence of at least strong predispositions to bring the ideology into question.

> *A well-established ideology perpetuates itself with little planned propaganda by those whom it benefits most. When thought is taken about ways and means of sowing conviction, conviction has already languished, the basic outlook of society has decayed, or a new, triumphant outlook has not yet gripped the loyalties of old and young.*[13]

PROP. Uniformity of ideology—in formulation, promulgation, and acceptance—is a function of other perspectives and of nonsymbolic ("material") uniformities.

The perspectives adopted by persons in given situations depend not merely on the symbols brought to their focus of attention, but also on the relation of these symbols to the predispositions and practices already adopted, both elements varying with the material situation. From the viewpoint of the power holders, the ideology put forward will clearly depend on the base values of their power, on the principles of recruitment to power position, on the characteristic power practices, and in general on the relations of the power holders to their domain.

Thus changes in the division of labor or other nonsymbolic conditions will effect changes in ideology. Conversely, it is difficult to impose a uniform ideology where the conditions set up heterogeneous predispositions and practices.

[13]H. D. Lasswell, *Politics: Who Gets What, When, How* (New York: McGraw-Hill, 1936), pp. 29–30.

> *A common culture cannot be created merely by desiring it. It rests upon economic foundations. It is incompatible with the existence of too violent a contrast between the economic standards and educational opportunities of different classes . . . .*[14]

PROP. Every utopia is elaborated into a political doctrine.

Opposition to a social structure is never formulated as a demand merely for the substitution of one set of power holders for another (though this may indeed be the latent content of the demand). It is formulated, rather, in terms of a new "principle" of political organization. A different basis for power is put forward, with concomitant differences in power practices, and only incidentally, as it were, changes in personnel. Michels has been especially concerned with the utopian elaboration of political doctrine:

> *In the modern life of the classes and of the nations, moral considerations have become an accessory, a necessary fiction. Every government endeavours to support its power by a general ethical principle. The political forms in which the various social movements become crystallized also assume a philanthropic mask. There is not a single one among the young class-parties which fails, before starting on its march for the conquest of power, to declare solemnly to the world that its aim is to redeem, not so much itself as the whole of humanity, from the yoke of a tyrannical minority, and to substitute for the old and inequitable regime a new reign of justice.*[15]

The doctrine brought forward by the utopia need not always be a new one, however. Opposition may take the form of alleging that the social structure actually obtaining deviates in fact from the doctrine invoked to justify it, and that a change in the social structure is demanded by that doctrine itself. This is a technique to which Pareto, among others, has called attention:

> *Assailants of the social order, the better to destroy it, try to take advantage of the forces engendered by that order and therefore make every effort to show that acts which are undoubtedly acts of revolt are legal and therefore ought not to and cannot be punished by the defenders of the order.*[16]

Even in such cases, the actual transformation of the social structure involves also changes in the political doctrine. A utopia does not consist

[14]R. H. Tawney, *Equality* (New York: Harcourt, Brace, 1931), p. 41.
[15]R. Michels, *Political Parties* (New York: Hearst's International Library, 1915), p. 15.
[16]V. Pareto, *Mind and Society* (New York: Harcourt, Brace, 1935), par. 1879.

simply of rival miranda, though it may begin with such symbols, and certainly will include them; demands and expectations are elaborated to make explicit a justification of the proposed changes in the social structure.

THE FINAL VERSION OF THE THEORY OF THE RULING CLASS

GAETANO MOSCA

The two traditional classifications of the forms of government are those of Aristotle and Montesquieu. The former distinguished between monarchies, aristocracies, and democracies, depending on whether sovereign power was vested in a single person, a restricted class, or in the totality of the citizens. Montesquieu defined as despotic those regimes in which the power of the sovereign was unrestrained by any custom, local or class privilege, or his own law; a monarchy, he said, was a state in which the ruler was subject to those restraints, and all organizations with non-hereditary heads of state he labeled as republics of the democratic or aristocratic type, depending on whether sovereignty belonged to all or only a part of the citizens.

These classifications have this common defect, that they are based on observation of a single moment in the evolution of political organisms. In the case of Aristotle, the model was the Greek polis of the fifth and fourth centuries B.C.; Montesquieu considered only the conditions which existed in the Europe of his time, when Venice, Genoa, and Switzerland did not have a hereditary chief of state, when France was governed by a monarchy which to a certain extent was limited by custom, a relatively independent judiciary, and by the privileges of the upper classes and the corporations, and Turkey was ruled by a unique despot who, apparently, did as he pleased. Between the lines, the author of *The Spirit of the Laws* let it be known that his ideal was the tempered monarchy as it existed at the time in England.

The other, more important, defect of the two traditional classifications is the superficiality of the criteria on which they are based. They take into account the formal rather than the really substantial differences between the various political organisms. Speaking of Montesquieu, it is not difficult to prove that there is more dissimilarity between the governments he calls republics than between some of them and certain monarchies. For instance, the United States has today surely less in common with the French Republic than the latter has with the Kingdom of Belgium; it is hardly necessary to mention the great differences between the republics of our time and those of medieval times or of antiquity. If we consider Aristotle's scheme, we see at once that it is quite impos-

Reprinted from *The Myth of the Ruling Class* by James Meisel by permission of The University of Michigan Press and Messrs. Laterzo. Copyright © by the University of Michigan, 1958.

sible for one man to rule over millions of subjects without the assistance of a hierarchy of officials or a ruling class, and equally impossible
for a democracy to function without a co-ordinating and directing body
which again will be an organized minority, another ruling class.

Today a whole new method of political analysis attempts to draw
attention to that very fact; its major purpose is to study the formation
and organization of that ruling stratum which in Italy is by now generally known by the name of *political class* — an expression which together
with the term *elite*, used by Pareto, begins to find international acceptance.

To be exact, the method is not altogether new, for the importance of, and the need for, a ruling class had already been intuitively
recognized in isolated instances in antiquity, and later by such men as
Machiavelli, Guicciardini, and Rousseau. Even more authors had that
intuition in the nineteenth century, foremost among whom was Saint-
Simon. But it was only toward the end of that century and afterwards
that the new vision became diffused.

One of the first results of the new method was the notion of what,
since 1883, has been known as the *political formula*, meaning that in
all societies, be their level ever so mediocre, the ruling class will justify
its power by appealing to some sentiment or credence generally accepted
in that period and by that society, such as the presumed Popular or
Divine Will, the notion of a distinct nationality or Chosen People,
traditional loyalty toward a dynasty, or confidence in a man of exceptional qualities. . . .

Any indication that a political formula has become "dated," that
the faith in its principles has become shaky, that the ardent sentiments
which once inspired it have begun to cool down is a sign that serious
transformations of the ruling class are imminent. The French revolution came when the great majority of Frenchmen ceased to believe in
the divine right of kings, and the Russian revolution broke out when
virtually the whole intelligentsia, and perhaps also the majority of the
Russian workers and peasants, had stopped believing that the Tsar
had received the right from God to govern Holy Russia autocratically.

Vice versa, when a political formula is in harmony with the mentality of the epoch and in tune with the prevailing sentiments of the
nation, its utility is undeniable: it often serves as a check on the power
of the ruler and ennobles somewhat the subjection of the ruled, making
it appear less the result of merely brute coercion.

Given the fact that a ruling class is necessary to the functioning of
all political organisms, it is evident that the study of political phenomena
must focus upon the examination of the various ways in which the ruling
class is formed and organized.

As concerns organization, one may say that, up to now, three types
existed: the feudal, the bureaucratic, and the third, less frequent but

with an impressive intellectual heritage and quite important in its times, the Greek-Italian city-state.

The system which, in accord with the historical tradition, we call feudal is the simplest and most primitive of the three. It is also the least satisfactory because it rarely succeeds in co-ordinating all the forces of a people in pursuit of one and the same end, in peace or war. Its main characteristic is the fragmentation of the state into small parts, in each of which the representative of the supreme lord appropriates to himself all sovereign powers. That is what happened in medieval Europe when the baron was at the same time the military chief and the chief civil magistrate and also had the right to levy taxes and all kinds of tributes in his fief.

The result was to make each part of the state so independent of the center that complete secession became relatively easy. Accordingly, the unity of any feudal state and the cohesion between its component parts could be maintained only when the central organ was administered by a superior ruler of enough prestige and energy to overawe the local chieftain, or else when the national sentiment was sufficiently developed to hinder the dismemberment of the state, as was the case in Japan prior to the *Tokugawa Shoguns* early in the eighteenth century.

The bureaucratic system is characterized by the fact that the governmental functions are distributed not geographically but according to their nature. The military tasks thus become separated from the administrative-judicial duties, and these from financial operations. Each attribute of sovereignty is now entrusted to as many special hierarchies of officeholders, each of which receives its impulse from the central organ of the state. With the various activities of government distributed among different persons, the action of the small group which presides over the state becomes much more efficient and secure; conversely, there is little chance for any part to break away and achieve independence from the state.

The ancient oriental monarchies and the Mohammedan states usually retained a feudal character. In contrast, we can find in ancient Egypt traces of an evolution toward state bureaucracy. Bureaucratization can be likewise ascertained during the happier periods of Chinese civilization, although the provincial governors retained great power. Even greater was the independence of the Persian satraps, and there is no doubt that excessive local independence was one of the main causes of the, relatively rapid, dissolution of the Caliphate of Baghdad and of the Moghul empire.

The transition from the feudal to the bureaucratic stage is usually quite slow. A typical example is the development of France, where the struggle between central monarchy and feudalism lasted almost seven centuries, from Hugh Capet to Louis XIV. Disintegration of a bureaucratic state is rarer than the dissolution of a feudal organism, but when it happens, as for instance in the case of the Western Roman Empire in the fifth century A.D., the collapse is likely to be more complete and more enduring than that of a feudal system, and the breakdown of the political machinery will be accompanied by a change of the moral forces and by the deterioration of the economic strength which that society had previously enjoyed.

. . . [Certain] characteristics distinguished the old city-states of Greece and Rome from the two other types of government—characteristics which can also be discovered in the medieval communes rising throughout Western Europe after 1000 A.D. In these as in the old city-states the ruling class was, at least in appearance, very large, including (given the short tenure and the fast rotation of all public offices) a good-sized portion of the citizenry. In fact, however, the important offices were almost always controlled by the members of a certain number of illustrious families. That was particularly so in Rome; in Greece the democratic current triumphed in imposing absolute equality on all the citizens, but the accompanying civil wars, and the spoliation of the rich that went with them, prepared the ground for the formation of tight oligarchies, which in turn produced the tyrant.

In the medieval commune, too, the most important offices were as a rule reserved for the heads of the major craft guilds or, as in Venice, for a certain number of distinguished families. Where such a power concentration in a limited group did not occur, the commune almost invariably gave way to a *signoria*, the equivalent of the ancient tyranny.

It is a well-known fact that hardly ever did the old polis or the medieval commune manage to extend its boundaries and at the same time keep intact the principles on which the state was based. Only the political wisdom of Rome could partly overcome that difficulty, but when her dominion had expanded to all corners of the Mediterranean, even Rome was finally forced to adopt a bureaucratic form of government.

Still, the strength and the resilience of the city-state in an emergency surpassed by far the limitations of its size. Thus Athens, after having lost all but a few of the forty thousand men sent on the ill-fated Sicilian expedition, remained strong enough to withstand the Peloponnesian League for almost another decade. Rome's immense losses did not prevent her from winning the first and second Punic wars, and Pisa, which in the thirteenth century never had more than eighty thousand inhabitants, suffered no less than five thousand casualties and eleven thousand prisoners in the battle of La Meloria alone. The Athenian, Florentine, Venetian contributions to the arts and sciences are too well known to require more than a brief mention.

The intellectual influence exerted by this form of government was, in conjunction with some other factors, favorable to the evolution of that type of social and political organization which may be called liberal, in distinction from that other type which may be labeled autocratic.

The main characteristic of the liberal system consists in the fact that in it power is transmitted from the bottom to the top. That is, the functionaries are elected by the citizens who subsequently are expected to obey them, whereas in the autocratic system the supreme chief appoints his immediate aides who in turn appoint the lower officials.

The last-named system was in force in the old oriental monarchies, the Moslem states, the Roman and Byzantine empires and, with certain limitations, also in the Western European monarchies from the sixteenth to the early nineteenth century. As examples of the liberal regime we may list, in addition to the ancient city-states and medieval communes, the various republican governments and parliamentary monarchies, although they may as well be classified as a mixed type, since their bureaucracies, which control a good part of the effective power, are almost always recruited along autocratic lines.

In general, the autocratic regimes may be said to have a greater staying power than the liberal regimes. The organism of the latter is so delicate that it will function only under suitable conditions, preferably in periods of economic prosperity and of great intellectual flowering. It would be naive to assume that the regimes called liberal are actually based, as their political formula claims, on the explicit consent of the popular majority. . . . [T]he electoral contest takes place between organized minorities controlling the disorganized majority of voters, who may choose between a small number of candidates presented by those minorities.

Still, the necessity to make a bid for the allegiance of the vast, unorganized majority obliges each of those groups to adapt itself, if only in appearance, to the thoughts and sentiments prevailing among the masses. That necessity sometimes enables liberal regimes to display an amazing vigor, but it has also the effect of forcing the ruling class to play up to the great majority of people who are less aware of the true interests of the society. And that is why the greatest threat to liberal institutions comes from the extension of the suffrage to the most uncultured strata of the population.

Even more important than the examination of the various types of ruling class organization is the study of the various methods by which ruling classes are recruited. What criteria are they using to admit some individuals while keeping out the rest?

The predominant criterion, all but indispensable to the formation of a ruling class, is the ability to rule. It is, as Saint-Simon already knew, the sum of all the personal characteristics most appropriate to the direction of a certain people in a certain period. Add to it the will to rule and the conviction of possessing the right qualities — qualities which undergo continuous change as the conditions of each people in intellectual, moral, economic, as well as in military matters change continuously, with the result that each people's political and administrative arrangements also need appropriate modifications.

These modifications may take place gradually, in which case the new elements who infiltrate the ruling class will not effect a radical change in its attitude and structure. If, on the contrary, the changes in the composition of the ruling class take place in a tumultuous and rapid fashion, the replacement of the old minority by the new elements may be almost completed in the course of one or two generations. In the first case, the prevailing influence is, as we called it elsewhere, the aristocratic tendency; in the second it is the one which we called the democratic.

It is rather difficult if not impossible to nullify completely either one of these two tendencies. The absolute predominance of the aristocratic tendency would presuppose that the ideas and conditions of human association never change; experience shows the absurdity of that assumption. On the other hand, the democratic tendency could absolutely triumph only on condition that the sons would not inherit the means, contacts, and advantages in training which enabled their progenitors to capture all the choice positions.

The private ownership of land and capital has been regarded as the major cause responsible for the hereditary nature of political control. Now I shall not deny the modicum of truth contained in that assertion. But we have already seen, to our satisfaction, that the state control of the means of production would leave the administrators of the state—who are sure to be a minority—in a position where they should be able to combine all economic and political power in their hands and to appropriate the largest share in such a manner as would advance the career of their own sons and protégés.

In the remote past, rapid and almost complete renewals of the ruling class took place not infrequently in the wake of an irruption of barbaric tribes which had not yet found a fixed habitat. They established themselves in the conquered country and supplanted there the previous rulers. Very often the success of the invaders was due to the discord and the decadence of the old dominant minority, and almost always to the apathy, sometimes to the connivance, of the lower class in the invaded territory.

These political cataclysms were not at all rare events in the oriental empires of antiquity. The Mesopotamian civilization suffered several of them, and the havoc which the Hyksos worked in Egypt is a well-known story. Invasions of the same type were, at various intervals, the ruin of the Chinese and Indian civilizations; the fall of Rome and the invasions of the Arabs and Turks are all part of the same chronicle.

With the progress of civilization, the zone populated by barbarians became more and more restricted, while the densely settled areas of industrious, peaceful agriculturers and artisans increased apace. A much improved technology put into their hands weapons of defense which had not been available against the raiders led by Genghis Khan and Tamerlane. Catastrophes caused by external forces have thus become more and more unlikely, if not utterly impossible.

In our time, the violent convulsions of the social order are the product of internal factors. The ruling class, attacked by a political force from below, disintegrates. Instead of invasions, we have today revolutions. It will suffice to mention here the great French revolution; what took place in Japan between 1853 and 1886 may well be called a revolution too. And there is finally the Russian revolution, the most violent of all. But no matter how violent and whatever the causes of the cataclysms that revolutionize the composition and the structure of the ruling class, almost invariably some elements, more or less numerous, of the old ruling class will enter the ranks of the new.

From an objective study of historical events one may draw this conclusion: The best regimes, that is, those lasting a long time and able to avoid the violent convulsions which have plunged mankind back into barbarism, are the mixed regimes. We call them mixed because in them neither the autocratic nor the liberal principle rules supreme, and the aristocratic tendency is tempered by a gradual but continuous renewal of the ruling class, enabling it thus to absorb the better elements into its ranks. But in order that such a regime may long endure, conditions must exist which not even the wisest legislator can create by fiat. The necessary multiplicity and balance of the ruling forces, if they are to function well, require a highly civilized community. Also, the church ought to be separated from the state; economic decisions must not be monopolized by the political decision-makers; the means of violence must never be controlled by any single faction of the people; last, men of cultural and technical accomplishment ought to be given access to the ruling class.

But more is needed: a great deal of education, which is always a slow process, and long experience in devising the most practical means of domesticating the base instincts which so often are joint to the will to power—instincts which again and again reasserted themselves after a protracted period of political and social peace, just when they seemed to be extinct forever.

PROGRESS AS CREATED BY HISTORICAL THINKING

R. G. COLLINGWOOD

The term 'progress', as used in the nineteenth century when the word was much in people's mouths, covers two things which it is well to distinguish: progress in history, and progress in nature. For progress in nature the word 'evolution' has been so widely used that this may be accepted as its established sense; and in order not to confuse the two things I shall restrict my use of the word 'evolution' to that meaning, and distinguish the other by the name 'historical progress'.

'Evolution' is a term applied to natural processes in so far as these are conceived as bringing into existence new specific forms in nature. This conception of nature as evolution must not be confused with the conception of nature as process. Granted the latter conception, two views of natural process are still possible: that events in nature repeat one another specifically, the specific forms remaining constant through the diversity of their individual instances, so that 'the course of nature is uniform' and 'the future will resemble the past', or that the specific forms themselves undergo change, new forms coming into existence by modification of the old. The second conception is what is meant by evolution.

In one sense, to call a natural process evolutionary is the same thing as calling it progressive. For if any given specific form can come into existence only as a modification of one already established, the establishment of any given form presupposes that of which it is a modification, and so on. If a form *b* is a modification of *a*, and *c* of *b*, and *d* of *c*, the forms *a, b, c, d*, can only come to exist in that order. The order is progressive in the sense that it is a series of terms which can come into existence only in that order. To say this, of course, implies nothing as to why the modifications arise, or whether they are large or small. In this sense of the word 'progress', progressive only means orderly, that is, exhibiting order.

But progress in nature, or evolution, has often been taken to mean more than this: namely the doctrine that each new form is not only a modification of the last but an improvement on it. To speak of improvement is to imply a standard of valuation. This, in the case of breeding new forms of domestic animals or plants, is intelligible enough: the value implied is the new form's utility for human purposes. But no one supposes that natural evolution is designed to produce such utilities; the standard implied, therefore, cannot be that. What is it?

Kant held that there was one form of value, and only one, that was independent of human purposes, namely the moral value of the good will. All other kinds of goodness, he argued, are merely goodness for some postulated purpose, but the goodness of morality does not depend on any postulated purpose, and thus moral goodness, as he put it, is an end in itself. On this view the evolutionary process has been truly progressive, because it has led through a determinate series of forms to the existence of man, a creature capable of moral goodness.

If this view is rejected, it is very doubtful whether any other standard of valuation can be found which would entitle us to call evolution progressive except merely in the sense of being orderly. Not because the idea of value finds no place in our view of nature, for it is difficult to think of any organism except as striving to maintain its own existence, and such effort implies that, at least for itself, its existence is not a mere matter of fact but something of value; but because all values seem merely relative. The archaeopteryx may in fact have been an ancestor of the bird, but what entitles us to call the bird an improvement on the archaeopteryx? A bird is not a better archaeopteryx, but something different that has grown out of it. Each is trying to be itself.

But the view of human nature as the noblest outcome of the evolutionary process did undoubtedly underlie the nineteenth-century conception of historical progress as guaranteed by a law of nature. That conception, in fact, depended on two assumptions or groups of assumptions. First, that man is or contains in himself something of absolute value, so that the process of nature in its evolution has been a progress in so far as it has been an orderly process leading to the existence of man. From this it followed that, since man obviously did not control the process leading to his own existence, there was in nature as such an inherent tendency towards the realization of this absolute value: in other words, 'progress is a law of nature'. Secondly, the assumption that man, as a child of nature, is subject to natural law, and that the laws of historical process are identical with the laws of evolution: that historical process is of the same kind as natural process. It followed that human history was subject to a necessary law of progress, in other words that of the new specific forms of social organization, art and science, and so forth, which it brings into existence each is necessarily an improvement on the last.

The idea of a 'law of progress' may be attacked by denying either of these two assumptions. It may be denied that man has in him anything of absolute value. His rationality, it may be said, only serves to make him the most maleficent and destructive of the animals, and is rather a blunder or a cruel joke of nature than her noblest work; his morality is only (as the modern jargon goes) a rationalization or ideology which he has devised to conceal from himself the crude fact of his bestiality. From this point of view, the natural process that has led to his existence can no longer be regarded as a progress. But further: if the conception of historical process as a mere extension of natural process is denied, as it must be by any sound theory of history, it follows that there is no natural and in that sense necessary law of progress in history. The question whether any particular historical change has been an improvement must consequently be a question to be answered on its merits in each particular case.

The conception of a 'law of progress', by which the course of history is so governed that successive forms of human activity exhibit each an improvement on the last, is thus a mere confusion of thought, bred of an unnatural union between man's belief in his own superiority to nature and his belief that he is nothing more than a part of nature. If either belief is true, the other is false: they cannot be combined to produce logical offspring.

Nor can the question, whether in a given case an historical change has or has not been progressive, be answered until we are sure that such questions have a meaning. Before they are raised, we must ask what is meant by historical progress, now that it has been distinguished from natural progress; and, if anything is meant, whether the meaning is one applicable to the given case we are considering. For it would be hasty to assume that, because the conception of historical progress as dictated by a law of nature is nonsensical, the conception of historical progress itself is therefore nonsensical.

Assuming, then, that the phrase 'historical progress' may still have a meaning, we must ask what it means. The fact that it has suffered confusion through contamination with the idea of evolution does not prove it meaningless; on the contrary, it suggests that it has a certain basis in historical experience.

As a first attempt to define its meaning, we might suggest that historical progress is only another name for human activity itself, as a succession of acts each of which arises out of the last. Every act whose history we may study, of whatever kind it is, has its place in a series of acts where one has created a situation with which the next has to deal. The accomplished act gives rise to a new problem; it is always this new problem, not the old problem over again, which the new act is obliged to solve. If a man has discovered how to get a meal, next time he is hungry he must find out how to get another, and the getting of this other is a new act arising out of the old. His situation is always changing, and the act of thought by which he solves the problems it presents is always changing too.

This is no doubt true, but it is not to our purpose. It is just as true of a dog as of a man, that every meal must be a different meal: just as true, that every time a bee gathering honey visits a flower, it must be a different flower; just as true, that every time a body moving in a straight line or an open curve comes to a part of space, it must be a different part. But these processes are not historical processes, and to quote them as throwing light on the historical process would betray the old fallacy of naturalism. Moreover, the novelty of the new situation and the new act is not a specific novelty, for the new act may be a new act of exactly the same kind (for example, setting the same snare again in the same place); so that we are not even discussing the evolutionary aspect of natural process, which is the point at which that process seems most akin to the historical. The search for a fresh meal takes place even in the most completely static or non-progressive society.

The idea of historical progress, then, if it refers to anything, refers to the coming into existence not merely of new actions or thoughts or situations belonging to the same specific type, but of new specific types. It therefore presupposes such specific novelties, and consists in the conception of these as improvements. Suppose, for example, a man or a community had lived on fish, and, the fish-supply failing, had sought food in a new way, by digging for roots: this would be a change in the specific type of situation and activity, but it would not be regarded as a progress, because the change does not imply that the new type is an improvement on the old. But if a community of fish-eaters had changed their method of catching fish from a less to a more efficient one, by which an average fisherman could catch ten fish on an average day instead of five, this would be called an example of progress.

But from whose point of view is it an improvement? The question must be asked, because what is an improvement from one point of view may be the reverse from another; and if there is a third from which an impartial judgement can be passed on this conflict, the qualifications of this impartial judge must be determined.

Let us first consider the change from the point of view of the persons concerned in it: the older generation still practising the old method while the younger has adopted the new. In such a case the older generation will see no need for the change, knowing as it does that life can be lived on the old method. And it will also think that the old method is better than the new; not out of irrational prejudice, but because the way of life which it knows and values is built round the old method, which is therefore certain to have social and religious associations that express the intimacy of its connexion with this way of life as a whole. A man of the older generation only wants his five fish a day, and he does not want half a day's leisure; what he wants is to live as he has lived. To him, therefore, the change is no progress, but a decadence.

It might seem obvious that by the opposite party, the younger generation, the change is conceived as a progress. It has given up the life of its fathers and chosen a new one for itself: it would not do this (one might suppose) without comparing the two and deciding that the new is better. But this is not necessarily the case. There is no choice except for a person who knows what both the things are between which he is choosing. To choose between two ways of life is impossible unless one knows what they are; and this means not merely looking on one as a spectacle, and practising the other, or practising one and conceiving the other as an unrealized possibility, but knowing both in the only way in which ways of life can be known: by actual experience, or by the sympathetic insight which may take its place for such a purpose. But experience shows that nothing is harder than for a given generation in a changing society, which is living in a new way of its own, to enter sympathetically into the life of the last. It sees that life as a mere incomprehensible spectacle, and seems driven to escape from sympathy with it by a kind of instinctive effort to free itself from parental influences and bring about the change on which it is blindly resolved. There is here no genuine comparison between the two ways of life, and therefore no judgement that one is better than the other, and therefore no conception of the change as a progress.

For this reason, the historical changes in a society's way of life are very rarely conceived as progressive even by the generation that makes them. It makes them in obedience to a blind impulse to destroy what it does not comprehend, as bad, and substitute something else as good. But progress is not the replacement of the bad by the good, but of the good by the better. In order to conceive a change as a progress, then, the person who has made it must think of what he has abolished as good, and good in certain definite ways. This he can only do on condition of his knowing what the old way of life was like, that is, having historical knowledge of his society's past while he is actually living in the present he is creating: for historical knowledge is simply the re-enactment of past experiences in the mind of the present thinker. Only thus can the two ways of life be held together in the same mind for a comparison of their merits, so that a person choosing one and rejecting the other can know what he has gained and what he has lost, and decide that he has chosen the better. In short: the revolutionary can only regard his revolution as a progress in so far as he is also an historian, genuinely re-enacting in his own historical thought the life he nevertheless rejects.

---

2. Equality

Most of us favor human equality—at least in the abstract. **Equality** *has a positive sound, it has motivated some of this century's great revolutions, and it engages the imagination of the Afro-Asian masses who must painfully construct governments among the ashes of colonialism. But by* **equality** *do we mean an equal distribution of talent, equal opportunities to achieve, or equal division of man's rewards and riches? Or does* **equality** *simply bring to mind a moral precept that we consider all others our equals?*

Beyond the important problem of defining equality is the question of its consequences. Alexis de Tocqueville's observations of the American republic in the nineteenth century led him to conclude that parity of opinion and free association among social classes help sustain democracy. But Edward Shils, writing in the aftermath of McCarthyism, views the consequences of equality differently. Shils predicts that in a culture where one man and his opinions are considered as good as another, the passion for equality may lead to the conformist tyranny of the majority. If this is true, we have come a long way from the eighteenth-century view, manifested in the French Revolution, that equality liberates man from the yoke of oppression and special privilege.

Both theorists and practicing politicians have based their ideas on the assumption that all men have a passionate desire for equality; but, as Robert Lane documents, many members of the American working class do not want equality—are indeed afraid of it. Among the American lower-middle working classes interviewed by Lane, the myths of an individualistic system are firmly rooted. Lane's sample accepted the prevailing order because the working class got its share; and they strongly objected to the idea of men being equalized, the lower orders raised, and their own hard-earned status given to others as a right and not as a reward for effort. At least in New Haven (the site of Lane's study), the brotherhood of working men is overshadowed by the symbols and requirements of a competitive industrial system.

THE ADVANTAGES OF EQUALITARIANISM

ALEXIS DE TOCQUEVILLE

Democracy does not attach men strongly to one another, but it places their habitual intercourse on an easier footing.

If two Englishmen chance to meet at the antipodes, where they are surrounded by strangers whose language and manners are almost unknown to them, they will first stare at each other with much curiosity and a kind of secret uneasiness; they will then turn away, or if one accosts the other, they will take care to converse only with a constrained and absent air, upon very unimportant subjects. Yet there is no enmity between these men; they have never seen each other before, and each believes the other to be a respectable person. Why, then, should they stand so cautiously apart? We must go back to England to learn the reason.

When it is birth alone, independent of wealth, that classes men in society, everyone knows exactly what his own position is in the social

Pages 178–180: From *Democracy in America*, Volume II, by Alexis de Tocqueville, translated by Phillips Bradley. Copyright 1945 by Alfred A. Knopf, Inc. Reprinted by permission. Title supplied by the editor.

scale; he does not seek to rise, he does not fear to sink. In a community thus organized men of different castes communicate very little with one another; but if accident brings them together, they are ready to converse without hoping or fearing to lose their own position. Their intercourse is not on a footing of equality, but it is not constrained.

When a moneyed aristocracy succeeds to an aristocracy of birth, the case is altered. The privileges of some are still extremely great, but the possibility of acquiring those privileges is open to all; whence it follows that those who possess them are constantly haunted by the apprehension of losing them or of other men's sharing them; those who do not yet enjoy them long to possess them at any cost or, if they fail, to appear at least to possess them, this being not impossible. As the social importance of men is no longer ostensibly and permanently fixed by blood and is infinitely varied by wealth, ranks still exist, but it is not easy clearly to distinguish at a glance those who respectively belong to them. Secret hostilities then arise in the community; one set of men endeavor by innumerable artifices to penetrate, or to appear to penetrate, among those who are above them; another set are constantly in arms against these usurpers of their rights; or, rather, the same individual does both at once, and while he seeks to raise himself into a higher circle, he is always on the defensive against the intrusion of those below him.

Such is the condition of England at the present time, and I am of the opinion that the peculiarity just adverted to must be attributed principally to this cause. As aristocratic pride is still extremely great among the English, and as the limits of aristocracy are ill-defined, everybody lives in constant dread lest advantage should be taken of his familiarity. Unable to judge at once of the social position of those he meets, an Englishman prudently avoids all contact with them. Men are afraid lest some slight service rendered should draw them into an unsuitable acquaintance; they dread civilities, and they avoid the obtrusive gratitude of a stranger quite as much as his hatred.

Many people attribute these singular antisocial propensities and the reserved and taciturn bearing of the English to purely physical causes. I may admit that there is something of it in their race, but much much more of it is attributable to their social condition, as is proved by the contrast of the Americans.

In America, where the privileges of birth never existed and where riches confer no peculiar rights on their possessors, men unacquainted with one another are very ready to frequent the same places and find neither peril nor advantage in the free interchange of their thoughts. If they meet by accident, they neither seek nor avoid intercourse; their manner is therefore natural, frank, and open; it is easy to see that they hardly expect or learn anything from one another, and that they do not care to display any more than to conceal their position in the world. If their demeanor is often cold and serious, it is never haughty or constrained; and if they do not converse, it is because they are not in a humor to talk, not because they think it their interest to be silent.

In a foreign country two Americans are at once friends simply because they are Americans. They are repulsed by no prejudice; they are attracted by their common country. For two Englishmen the same blood is not enough; they must be brought together by the same rank. The Americans notice this unsociable mood of the English as much as the French do and are not less astonished by it. Yet Americans are connected with England by their origin, their religion, their language, and partially by their customs; they differ only in their social condition. It may therefore be inferred that the reserve of the English proceeds from the constitution of their country much more than from that of its inhabitants.

THE DISADVANTAGES OF EQUALITARIANISM

EDWARD A. SHILS

Populism proclaims that the will of the people as such is supreme over every other standard, over the standards of traditional institutions, over the autonomy of institutions and over the will of other strata. Populism identifies the will of the people with justice and morality.

American populism survives in our minds as a type of progressive rural radicalism. It has left behind memories of great humanitarians like Norris and LaFollette and of idealistic reformers who in a great society sought to give power back to the people—through the referendum, the initiative and the recall, through control of the railroads and the public utilities, etc. But populism has many faces. Nazi dictatorship had markedly populistic features in its practice, in its constant invocation of the will of the people as its justification and the good of the people as its end, and in the "direct" relationship of the people and their leader unmediated by institutions. Bolshevism has a strand of populism in it too, although, like National Socialism and other dictatorships, its practice rejects the will of the people as a guide; nonetheless, in Bolshevism too the praise, however spurious, of the people continues an older tradition of belief in their superior wisdom and virtue. Populism is not confined to the "left" and it is not confined to the lower classes. It can enter into the outlook of governing classes, into the professions, into strata which do not from their own interior life produce a populistic outlook. In the United States, populism lives on in persecutory legislative investigations, in the security-loyalty policy of the federal Government and in the loyalty policies of the lesser bodies. McCarthy is the heir of LaFollette.

Pages 98–104: Reprinted with the permission of The Free Press from *The Torment of Secrecy* by Edward A. Shils. Copyright 1956 by The Free Press, a corporation. Title supplied by the editor.

What was populism if not the distrust of the effete East and its agents in the urban Middle West? Was not populism the forerunner of "grass roots" democracy? Did it not seek to subject the Government to the people's will, to tumble the mighty from their high seats, to turn legislators into registrants of the people's will? Was it not suspicious of the upper classes of the East? Did it not seek a world free from the constricting entanglements of the Old World, with its hierarchical pretenses and its dynastic ambitions? Was not populism "folksy," quick to use Christian names, hail-fellow-well-met, in contrast with the cold, inhuman impersonality of upper-class etiquette? Did not populism speak about the "interests," the "cliques," "caucuses," "lobbies" and "rings" which held the people in chains, depriving them of the fruit of their labors? Did not populism allege to protect the people and their government from conspiracies, from cells of conspirators who, contrary to the people's will and through the complacency or collusion of their rulers, were enabled to gain control of society? Does not populism deny the right of privacy on behalf of publicity and does it not do so to protect the people from conspiratorial secrecy?

Populism is distrustful of the "overeducated." The great state universities which the Middle West has created were intended to provide education and learning which would be different from the arid refinements, useless subtleties, and the leisured snobbery of Harvard, Yale and Princeton. They were intended to reach a different class of students, to provide them with something different from what the universities of the East were doing. They were intended to produce hard-headed, tough-minded citizens, capable of keeping their government in their own hands, and technicians and civil servants of popular government. The higher reaches of pure science and scholarship, in which some of the Middle Western state universities have taken a great place, were not the first responsibilities of those universities.

When populism goes on the warpath, among those they wish to strike are the "overeducated," those who are "too clever," "the highbrows," the "longhairs," the "eggheads," whose education has led them away from the simple wisdom and virtue of the people. Progressive populism did not hesitate to intrude into the internal affairs of its universities, and loyalist populism in its fear of secrecy still does not hesitate to do so. It is not difficult to see in Senator McCarthy's fulminations against Harvard, that "sheltered sanctuary" of the Fifth Amendment of the Constitution of the United States, the "grass roots" prophet assailing the aristocratic battlements of pure learning which have despised the wisdom of the people. From the perpetual harassment of the local schoolteacher in the small town to the enthusiasm of the state legislatures in enquiring into subversion in the educational system, to the grand passions of the Congressional committee investigating subversion and conspiracy in the universities and private foundations, the resentment against the learned person who is not "one of the boys" is at work. Populists, whether they are radical reformers or congressional investigators pursuing weak links in security, are all extremely suspicious and hostile towards the more sophisticated person, who, they think, stands apart and does not share what is on his mind with the likes of them, who thinks he is better than they are, and secretly might be thinking of subverting them. All the recent preoccupation with those who withhold themselves in enclaves differentiated from the rest of the society reveals more than a trace of populistic hostility towards those whose learning has drawn them away from the common life.

Populism, although it is known historically as a primarily Middle Western and Southern phenomenon, is a much more widespread phenomenon. It exists wherever there is an ideology of popular resentment against the order imposed on society by a long-established, differentiated ruling class, which is believed to have a monopoly of power, property, breeding and culture. The Middle West and, to a lesser extent, the South, where the populace was coming into political self-consciousness and the ruling class was not near enough at hand to impose its culture through immediate personal relationships, but powerful enough at a distance to make its political and economic power felt, were the proper birthplaces of American populism. In the South, an older aristocratic ruling class lay in ruins without property or power; its economic and political feebleness and pretensions to breeding and culture were a fertile ground for populistic denunciation of the upper classes. The Middle West, feeling deprived by an Eastern and ethnically alien ruling class, was even more fertile ground. Both regions possessed resentfully aggressive classes who provided the motive force for populism.

Populism, by its tendency as an organized political movement and more so by the permeative tradition which it has injected into an already favorably predisposed egalitarianism, has brought about a peculiar inequality. Originally a protest against the wealthy and great, in their splendor and state, it inclines easily by the radicalism of its emphasis towards an inverted inegalitarianism. Populism is tinged by the belief that the people are not just the equal of their rulers; they are actually better than their rulers and better than the classes—the urban middle classes—associated with the ruling powers.

The mere fact of popular preference is therefore regarded as all-determining. Emanation from the people confers validity on a policy and on the values underlying it. Populism does not deny ethical standards of objective validity, but it discovers them in the preferences of the people. The belief in the intrinsic and immediate validity of the popular will has direct implications for the rule of law. It denies any degree of autonomy to the legislative branch of government, just as it denies autonomy to any institutions. Demanding that all institutions be permeated by the popular will or responsive to it—since the validity of the popular will is self-evident—populism inclines towards a conception of the legislative branch which may be designated as "identity" in contrast with "representation." Legislators are expected to be "identical" with the popular will rather than "representatives" who will interpret it. Populism is impatient of institutional traditions and boundaries; it finds the delimitation of jurisdictions so much "bureaucratic red tape" which strangles the popular will. It is impatient of institutional procedures which impede the direct expression of the popular will and the forceful personalities who assume the responsibility of being vessels of the popular will. Populism is impatient of distinctions and it abhors the division of powers which would restrain and confine the popular will. Populism is blind to the possibility of the impartial and disinterested performance of duty. It hates the civil service, which it regards as an obstacle to substantive justice, but also because it believes that everything is "political." From Andrew Jackson to Mr. Scott McLeod, populists have been convinced that civil servants cannot be trusted to carry out the orders of their political superiors unless they are imbued with the beliefs of their superiors.

Populism seeks substantive justice. It cares not at all for the traditional rules in spheres of life outside its own immediate sphere. It regards the legal system as a snare for the guileless, a system of outdoor relief for lawyers and judges; it regards administration as a morass for the entrapment of the unwary and the virtuous. It regards politicians as artful dodgers, as evaders of responsibility, as twisters with fine words but ready to compromise away the interests of those for whom they stand. It regards the monetary system and the banks as a vast system of traps for depriving the poor of what they are entitled to and for enriching idlers.

Populism—not just populism in the specific historical meaning, although that was an instance of the species—regards parliamentary politicians as very inferior beings with no inherent virtue in themselves or in their institution. Politicians are at best errand boys with little right to judgment on their own behalf if that judgment seems to contradict popular sentiment. The administrative branch is even less exalted—discolored as it is by corruption and indolence at an earlier date and excessive education and looking-down on the ordinary people in latter days. The derogatory attitude towards the politician described above, which originated in quite a different moral climate, articulated perfectly with the populist view. But, even without that reinforcement, populism in all countries—even in countries with memories of aristocratic ruling classes, e.g., Germany—is hostile to the politician.

Populism is not, however, recalcitrant to leadership. Great spellbinders who would bring populists substantive justice are capable of moving them and of bending them to their will. Middle Western populism produced its great men, like LaFollette and Norris—morally serious men whose genuine concern for the poor and whose aversion for great inequality in wealth, power and status, endeared them to their grave and sober German-American and Scandinavian-American constituencies —and like Bryan, the great spellbinder who fought the war of the country against the city, of the plain man against the banker, who stood for simple rectitude and orthodox religion and whose later role in the fundamentalist struggle against secularism was part of the broader pattern of populism. The areas which produced the populism of the end of the nineteenth century and the early twentieth century have continued to produce them. There is a straight line from Ben Tillman to Huey Long and Eugene Talmadge; from Bryan and LaFollette to Gerald L. K. Smith, Father Coughlin and Senator McCarthy, Gerald Nye, William Langer and many others.

Populism acclaims the demagogue who, breaking through the formalistic barriers erected by lawyers, pedants and bureaucrats, renews the righteousness of government and society. Populism is impatient of checks and balances, it is restive under the restraints imposed by the separation of powers. Senator McCarthy's appeal to subordinate employees of the executive branch to bring to him whatever they deem relevant to the security of the country from the Communist conspiracy is characteristically populist in its disregard for the boundaries of institutions and for the niceties of institutional responsibilities. The detailed control of the policy of an executive agency, through the threat and actuality of investigations or through forcing the appointment of particular individuals to key posts, such as the Senate Subcommittee on Government Investigations attempted to exercise over the Voice of America and the United States Information Service, or which the appointment of Mr. McLeod has rendered possible in the State Department, seems right and proper from the populist point of view. The legislator is the agent of the people's will and it is his obligation to make that will prevail everywhere and immediately. There is no division of responsibilities which is legitimate to the populist.

The populistic conception of the politician affects not only the expectations held by the populace regarding the politician's behavior. It also affects the politician's own conception of his obligations.

THE FEAR OF EQUALITY

Robert E. Lane

We move in equalitarian directions; the distribution of income flattens out; the floor beneath the poorest paid and least secure is raised

From *The American Political Science Review*, 1959 (March), *53*: 35–51.

and made more substantial. Since the demise of Newport and Tuxedo Park, the very rich have shunned ostentatious display. The equality of opportunity, the chance to rise in the world is at least as great today as it was thirty years ago. The likelihood of declining status is less. Where does the energy for this movement come from? Who is behind it?

Since 1848, it has been assumed that the drive for a more equalitarian society, its effective social force, would come from the stratum of society with the most to gain, the working classes. This was thought to be the revolutionary force in the world — the demand of workers for a classless society sparked by their hostility to the owning classes. It was to be the elite among the workers, not the *lumpenproletariat*, not the "scum," who were to advance this movement. Just as "liberty" was the central slogan of the bourgeois revolution, so "equality" was the central concept in the working class movement. Hence it was natural to assume that whatever gains have been made in equalizing the income and status of men in our society came about largely from working class pressure.

But on closer investigation the demands for greater liberty or "freedom" turn out to have been of an ambiguous nature. The middle classes sought freedom of speech and action in large part for the economic gains that this would give them, and moralized their action with the theology of freedom. But the freedom that they gained was frightening, for it deprived them of the solidary social relationships and the ideological certainty which often gave order and meaning to their lives. On occasion, then, they sought to "escape from freedom." The older unfree order had a value which the earlier social commentators did not appreciate.

There is a parallel here with the movement toward a more equalitarian society. The upper working class, and the lower middle class, support specific measures embraced in the formula "welfare state," which have equalitarian consequences. But, so I shall argue, many members of the working classes do not want equality. They are afraid of it. In some ways they already seek to escape from it. Equality for the working classes, like freedom for the middle classes, is a worrisome, partially rejected, by-product of the demand for more specific measures. Inequality has values to them which have been overlooked. It is these attitudes on status and equality that I shall explore here.

Extended Interviews with Fifteen Men

This discussion is based upon extended interviews of from ten to fifteen hours each (in from four to seven sessions) with a sample of American urban male voters. The sample is a random selection from the white members on a list of 220 registered voters in a moderate income (not low income) housing development where income is permitted to range between $4,000 and $6,500, according to the number of dependents in the family. Out of fifteen asked to participate, fifteen agreed, for a modest cash consideration. The characteristics of the sample, then, are as follows:

> *They are all men, white, married, fathers, urban, Eastern seaboard.*
>
> *Their incomes range from $2,400 to $6,300 (except for one who had just moved from the project. His income was $10,000 in 1957.)*
>
> *Ten had working class (blue collar) occupations such as painter, plumber, oiler, railroad fireman, policeman, machine operator.*
>
> *Five had white collar occupations such as salesman, bookkeeper, supply clerk.*
>
> *Their ages ranged from 25 to 54; most are in their thirties.*
>
> *Twelve are Catholic, two are Protestants, one is Jewish.*
>
> *All are native born; their nationality backgrounds are: six Italian, five Irish, one Polish, one Swedish, one Russian, one Yankee. Most are second or third generation Americans.*
>
> *All were employed at the time of the interviews.*
>
> *Their educational distribution was: three had only grammar school education; eight had some high school; two finished high school; one had some college; one completed graduate training.*

The interviews with these men were taped, with the permission of the interviewees, and transcribed. They were conducted by means of a schedule of questions and topics followed by conversational improvised probes to discover the underlying meanings of the answers given. The kinds of questions employed to uncover the material to be reported are illustrated by the following: "What do you think the phrase 'All men are created equal' means?" "How would you feel if everyone received the same income no matter what his job?" "Sometimes one hears the term 'social class'—as in working class or middle class. What do you think this term 'social class' means?" "What class do you belong to?" "How do you feel about it?" There were also a number of questions dealing with status, private utopias, feelings of privilege or lack of privilege, and other topics, throughout the interview schedule which sometimes elicited responses bearing on the question of social and economic equality.

How to Account for One's Own Status?

It is my thesis that attitudes toward equality rest in the first instance upon one's attitude toward one's own status. Like a large number of social beliefs, attitudes toward equality take their direction from beliefs about the self, the status of the self, one's self-esteem or lack thereof. It is necessary, therefore, first to explore how people see themselves in American hierarchical society.

The American culture and the democratic dogma have given to the American public the notion that "all men are created equal." Even more insistently, the American culture tells its members: "achieve," "compete," "be better, smarter, quicker, richer than your fellow men"; in short, "be unequal." The men I interviewed had received these inequalitarian messages, some eagerly, some with foreboding. Having heard them, they must account for their status, higher than some, lower than others. They must ask themselves, for example, "Why didn't I rise out of the working class, or out of the 'housing project class,' or out of the underpaid office help class?" And, on the other hand, "Why am I better off than my parents? or than the fellows down the road in the low rental project? or the fellows on relief?" Men confronted with these questions adopt a variety of interesting answers.

Is It Up to Me?

The problem of accounting for status is personally important for these men only if they think that their decisions, effort, and energy make a difference in their position in life. Most of my subjects accepted the view that America opens up opportunity to all people; if not in equal proportions, then at least enough so that a person must assume responsibility for his own status. Thus O'Hara, a maintenance oiler in a factory, in a typical response, comments that the rich man's son and the poor man's son "have equal opportunity to be President . . . if they've got the education and the know how." But, he goes on to say, "some of them have a little more help than others." This is the constant theme: "all men can better themselves," the circumstances of American life do not imprison men in their class or station—if there is such a prison, the iron bars are within each man.

There were a few, of course, who stressed the differences of opportunity at birth, the mockery of the phrase "all men are created equal." Here, as only rarely in the interviews, a head of steam builds up which might feed radical social movements—but this is true for only a few of the sample. Three or four angry young or middle aged men deny the Jeffersonian phrase. Rapuano, an auto parts supply man, says:

> *How could you say we were born equal when, for instance, when I was born, I was born in a family that were pretty poor. You get another baby born in a family that has millions.*

And Kuchinsky, a house painter, says:

> *Are we created equal? I don't believe we are, because everybody's got much more than one another and it's not right, I think. Of course,*

> *ah, we have no choice. I mean we can't do nothing about it. So we're not as equal as the next party, that's for sure.*

And Ferrera, a salesman, says:

> *All men created equal? Ah, very hypocritical, cause all men are not created equal—and—I don't know—you really pick some beauties don't you? . . . The birth of an individual in a [social] class sort of disputes this.*

To these men, then, subordination and life position is attributable not so much to the efforts of the individual, something for which he must assume responsibility, as to the circumstances of birth, over which he has no control. Yet for each of those men the channels of advancement were seen as only partly blocked. Rapuano, for example, says elsewhere that income is generally proportionate to ability. Like the theme of "moral equality," the theme of differential life chances from birth is easily available. What is surprising is not that it is used at all, but rather that it is used so infrequently.

Reducing the Importance of the Struggle

When something is painful to examine, people look away, or, if they look at it, they see only the parts they want to see. They deny that it is an important something. So is it often with a person's class status when the reference is upward, when people must account not for the strength of their position, but for its weakness. How do they do this?

In the first place they may *insulate themselves*, limit their outlook and range of comparisons. Ferrera, an insurance salesman, who says, "It's pretty hard for me to think there is anyone in the upper class and I'm not in the upper class," slides into a prepared position of insulated defense:

> *I think a lot of people place a lot of stress on the importance of social classes [but] I feel that I have a job to do, I have my own little unit to take care of. If I can do it to the best ability that is instilled in me at birth or progress through the years, I feel that I rightly deserve the highest classification you can get. I don't particularly like the headings, "upper, middle, working, and lower."*

It is a resentful narrowing of focus in this case: two years at an inferior college may have led to ambitions which life then failed to fulfill. Contrast this to Woodside, a policeman with a Middlewestern rural background, who accepts the "categories" of social class rather willingly. He says, after dealing with the moral and intangible aspects of equality:

> [*"Are there any people whom you regard as not equal to you?"*]
> *Well, that is a tough question. Well, in fairness, I'd say all people
> are equal to one another in his own category. When I say category,
> I mean you couldn't exactly expect a person that had very little knowl-
> edge to be, we'll say, should have a position where a person with a lot
> more education had it.*

Equality must be treated within classes, not between them, to be meaningful—and in this way the problem of placing oneself becomes tolerable, or sometimes rather gratifying.

A second device for reducing the importance of class position is to
deny its importance. This is not to deny the importance of getting ahead,
but to limit this to the problem of job classification, or occupational
choice—nothing so damaging to the self-esteem as an ordering of persons on a class scale. Rapuano, resisting the class concept, says:

> *I don't think it [social class] is important. I mean whenever I went
> and asked for a job, the boss never asked me what class I was in. They
> just wanted to know if I knew my business. Oh yes, and I don't think
> in politics it makes any difference.*

Others maintain that for other countries social class is important, but
not for Americans. There are rich and poor, perhaps, but not status,
class, or deference levels to be accounted for.

A third device for reducing the significance of the struggle for
status and "success" is *resignation*, a reluctant acceptance of one's fate.
When some men assume this posture of resignation one senses a pose;
their secret hopes and ambitions will not down. For others it rings true.
When Dempsey, a factory operative, speaks of his situation at the age
of 54, one believes him:

> *It's hard, very hard. We seem to be struggling along now, as it is,
> right here, to try and get above our level, to get out of the rut, as you
> might say, that we're probably in right now. . . . [But] After you get
> to a certain age, there, you stop—and you say, "Well, I can't go any
> further." I think I've gotten to that point now.*

But when Sokolsky reports that he is contented with his station in life,
it does not seem authentic:

> *Being in the average group [He wouldn't assign himself a class status]
> doesn't bother me. I know I make a living—as long as I make a living,
> and I'm happy and I have what I want—try to give my family what
> they want. It doesn't bother me—no. I'm satisfied.*

But then he adds: "I hope to God my children will do better than their
father did."

Contrast these views with those of Johnson, a plumber, who says, "I feel someday I'll be better off. I feel that way because I believe I have it within me to do it"; and with Flynn, a white collar worker, who answers:

> *No, I'm nowhere near satisfied. It seems to me every time I start to move up a little bit, all the levels move up one step ahead of me. I can't ever get out of this area. I have a certain desire and willingness to do something extra.*

The Working Class Gets Its Share

When comparing their status with those lower on the scale, however each man may define it, it is easy to point with pride to achievement, material well-being, standing in the community. But satisfaction with one's self and one's friends depends on seeing some advantage in one's situation *vis-a-vis* those who live and work on a higher status level. At first, this seems to be a difficult task, but in many simple ways it can be easily done. Our sample, for example, found ways of ascribing greater happiness, power, and even income to the working class than would be found in the upper class.

The equality of happiness is a fruitful vein. Lower income and status is more tolerable when one can believe that the rich are not receiving a happiness income commensurate with their money income. "Are the rich happier than people who are just average?" O'Hara does not think so:

> *I think lots of times they're never happy, because one thing is, the majority of them that are rich have got more worries. You see a lot more of them sick than you do, I think, the average. I think a lot of your mental strain is a lot greater in the higher class — in the rich class — than in the other.*

And Johnson, a maintenance plumber, says:

> *Well, even though this rich man can go places and do things that others can't afford, there's only certain things in life that I think make people happy. For instance, having children, and having a place to live — no matter where it is, it's your home . . . the majority of these big men — I don't think they devote as much time and get a thrill out of the little things in life that the average guy gets, which I think is a lot of thrills.*

Indeed, hardly a man thought the rich were happier. And yet, O'Hara says, on another occasion, "What is the most important thing that money can buy? Happiness, when you come down to it." Perhaps he means that money buys happiness for the average man, but not for the rich. But more likely he means "I can take care of a gnawing and illegitimate envy by appropriating happiness for me and my kind."

Power, like happiness, is awarded to the working (or lower middle) class. The sheer fact of numbers gives a sense of strength and importance. Costa, a factory operative, says, for example, "People like you [the interviewer] are the minority and people like me are the majority, so we get taken care of in the long run." Whether a person sees himself as middle class or working class, he is likely to believe that most people belong to his class. This being true, his class, people like him, become the most important force in electoral decisions. O'Hara puts it this way:

> *The biggest part of the people in this country are working class. And I think they've got the most to do with — they've got a big part to do with running this country — because the lower class, a lot of them don't vote, when you come down to it, they don't have the education to vote, and your upper class isn't that much — isn't as great as the other, so really when you come down to it, it's your working class that's deciding one way or the other.*

Not only do they "have the biggest part to do with running the country," they are crucial for the economy. This is not only as producers — indeed no one mentioned the theme which romantic writers on the laboring man and the immigrant have often employed — "they cleared the land and built the cities." Rather it is because of their power to shatter the economy and their power to survive in a depression that they are important. Kuchinsky explains this as follows:

> *I think the lower class of people are the important people. I think so because of the business end of it. Without us, I don't think the business-man could survive. I mean if we don't work — of course, they have the money, but, ah, a lot of times during the crash which was an awful thing, too, I think a lot of 'em lived so high that they couldn't stand it any more when they went broke, and they committed a lot of suicides there. But we were used to living that way, it didn't bother us.*

Today, as perhaps never before, the working class man can see his status loss compared to white collar workers compensated by income advantages. Thus, De Angelo, a factory operative and shop steward, reports:

> *You got people working in offices, they might consider themselves upper class, y'know, a little better than the working man. But nine times out of ten the working man is making more money than he is.*

And in the same vein, Rapuano says:

> *I certainly would hate like hell to be a white collar worker in the middle class and making the money that the white collar worker does. I would rather be a worker in the lower class, and making their money, see?*

Of course, this assignment of income advantages to the working class hinges upon a narrowing of the range of competition—but this is the range that makes a difference for these men.

Moral Equality

Another device for dealing with subordination in a society where invidious comparison with others is constantly invited represents, in effect, a borrowing from an older classical or religious tradition—an emphasis upon the intangible and immeasurable (and therefore comfortingly vague) spiritual and moral qualities. The only clearly adequate expression of this religious view was given by McNamara, a gentle and compassionate bookkeeper, who said "All men are created equal? That's our belief as Catholics," implying some sort of religious equality, perhaps such an idea as is captured in the phrase "equality of the soul." Woodside, a Protestant policeman, takes, in a way, a secular 18th Century version of this view when he says that men are equal "not financially, not in influence, but equal to one another as to being a person." Being a person, then, is enough to qualify for equal claims of some undefined kind.

But it seems probable that when men assert their own equality in this vague sense, typically phrased in something like O'Hara's terms: "I think I'm just as good as anybody else. I don't think there's any of them that I would say are better," something other than moral or spiritual equality is at issue. These moral qualities are what the educated commentator reads into the statement, but O'Hara means, if I may put words in his mouth, "Don't put on airs around me," "I'm trying to preserve my self-respect in a world that challenges it; I therefore assert my equality with all." "I won't be pushed around." "I know my rights," and, to the interviewer: "Just because you're a professor and I'm an oiler, it doesn't mean you can patronize me." And when Sokolsky, a machine operator and part-time janitor, says, in the interview, "The rich guy—because he's got money he's no better than I am. I mean that's the way I feel," he is not talking about moral or spiritual qualities. He is saying, in effect to his prosperous older brother and his snobbish wife, "Don't look down on me," and to the world at large: "I may be small, but I will protect my self-esteem." These men are posting notices similar to the motto on the early American colonies' flags: "Don't tread on me."

Speaking of moral virtues, we must observe how easy it would have been to take the view that the morality of the middle levels of society was superior because the rich received their wealth illegitimately. None of my clients did this. Nor did they stress the immoral lives of the wealthy classes, as did Merton's sample[1] some thirteen years ago—a commentary, perhaps, upon changing attitudes toward the upper classes taking place over this period. The psychic defenses against subordination available in stressing moral equality or superiority were used—but only rarely.

People Deserve Their Status

If one accepts the view that this is a land of opportunity in which merit will find a way, one is encouraged to accept the status differences of society. But it is more than logic which impels our men to accept these differences. There are satisfactions of identification with the going social order; it is easier to accept differences which one calls "just" than those that appear "unjust"; there are the very substantial self-congratulatory satisfactions of comparison with those lower on the scale. Thus this theme of "just desserts" applies to one's own group, those higher, and those lower.

So Kuchinsky says: "If you're a professor, I think you're entitled to get what you deserve. I'm a painter and I shouldn't be getting what you're getting." Furthermore, confidence in the general equity of the social order suggests that the rewards of one's own life are proportionate to ability, effort, and the wisdom of previous decisions. On ability, Costa, a machine operator, says:

> I believe anybody that has the potential to become a scientific man, or a professor, or a lawyer, or a doctor, should have the opportunity to pursue it, but there's a lot of us that are just made to run a machine in a factory. No matter what opportunities some of us might have had, we would never have reached the point where we could become people of that kind. I mean everybody isn't Joe DiMaggio.

And on the wisdom of earlier decisions, Johnson, a plumber, says:

> I don't consider myself the lower class. In between someplace. But I could have been a lot better off but through my own foolishness, I'm not. [Here he refers back to an earlier account of his life.] What causes poverty? Foolishness. When I came out of the service, my wife had saved a few dollars and I had a few bucks. I wanted to have a good time. I'm throwing money away like water. Believe me, had I

[1] Robert K. Merton, *Mass Persuasion; The Social Psychology of a War Bond Drive* (New York: Harper, 1946).

used my head right, I could have had a house. I don't feel sorry for myself—what happened, happened, you know. Of course you pay for it.

But the most usual mistake or deficiency accounting for the relatively humble position is failure to continue one's education due to lack of family pressure ("they should have made me"), or youthful indiscretion, or the demands of the family for money, or the depression of the thirties.

The Upper Classes Deserve to be Upper

Just as they regard their own status as deserved, so also do they regard the status of the more eminently successful as appropriate to their talents. Rapuano, an auto parts supply man, reports:

Your income—if you're smart, and your ability calls for a certain income, that's what you should earn. If your ability is so low, why hell, then you should earn the low income. ["Do you think income is proportionate to ability now?"] I would say so. Yes.

But there is a suggestion in many of the interviews that even if the income is divorced from talent and effort, in some sense it is appropriate. Consider Sokolsky again, a machine operator and part-time janitor, discussing the tax situation:

Personally, I think taxes are too hard. I mean a man makes, let's say $150,000. Well, my God, he has to give up half of that to the government—which I don't think is right. For instance if a man is fortunate enough to win the Irish Sweepstakes, he gets 150—I think he has about $45,000 left. I don't think that's right.

Even if life is a lottery, the winner should keep his winnings. And De Angelo, a machine operator, comes spontaneously to the same conclusion:

I think everybody needs a little [tax] relief. I mean, I know one thing, if I made a million dollars and the government took nine-tenths of it—boy, I'd cry the blues. I can't see that. If a man is smart enough to make that much, damn it, he's got a right to holler. I'm with the guy all the way.

Because he is "smart enough" to make the money, it is rightfully his. Surely, beyond the grave, there is a spectre haunting Marx.

The concept of "education" is the key to much of the thinking on social class and personal status. In a sense, it is a "natural" because it fits so neatly into the American myth of opportunity and equality, and provides a rationale for success and failure which does minimum damage to the souls of those who did not go to college. Thus in justifying their own positions, sometimes with reference to the interview situation, my clients imply, "If I had gone to college (like you) I would be higher up in this world." Costa, a machine operator, speaks this theme:

> *Now what would be the advantage of you going 20 years to school so you wind up making $10,000 a year, and me going 8 years to school, making $10,000. You would be teaching the young men of tomorrow, the leaders of tomorrow, and I would be running a machine. You would have a lot more responsibility to the country as a whole than I would have. Why shouldn't you be rewarded in proportion.*

McNamara, a mild mannered bookkeeper who went to night school to get his training in accounting and bookkeeping, emphasizes education in response to the question: "Do you think it's easy or hard to get from one class to another?"

> *Well, I think it's hard because . . . not because of the class itself, or what the influence they have on you, but you just seem to reach a certain point, and if you don't have it, you just don't—you don't make the grade. I've found that to be true. I always seem to be one step away from a good spot. And it's no one's fault—it's my fault. I just don't have the education—just don't—just don't have what it takes to take that step.*

And Sokolsky, a machine operator and part-time janitor, says, in his justification of income differences:

> *A man that gets out of eighth grade—I don't think he would have the ability to do the job as a man that got out of college.*

But later, he says, of politicians and businessmen:

> *If a man with more education has been in politics, he should get the job, but if there's a man that, let's say, just got out of high school, and he's been around in politics all his life, I think he should have a chance too. It's how good he is. There's some big, business people who just haven't got it. [But] there could be some men with a gift of gab—maybe just out of eighth grade—they could sell anything.*

What is it about education that justifies differences in income? In the above interviews it is clear that education is thought to increase skills which should be suitably rewarded. Furthermore, it appears that the time necessary for educational preparation deserves some reward

—a recurrent theme. With education goes responsibility—and responsibility should be rewarded. But there is also some suggestion in the interview material that the pain and hard (unpleasant) work associated with going to school deserves compensation. People who did not like school themselves may be paying homage to those who could stick it out. It is a question whether O'Hara, a maintenance oiler, implies this when he says:

> *I think a person that is educated deserves more than somebody that isn't. Somebody who really works for his money really deserves it more than somebody that's lazy and just wants to hang around.*

In this and other ways, education serves as a peg on which to hang status; and, like "blood," whether a person got the education or not is not his "fault," or at least it is only the fault of an irresponsible youth, not a grown man.

The Lower Classes Deserve No Better Than They Get

By and large those in the lower orders are those who are paid daily (not weekly) or are on relief; they live in slums or in public housing projects (but not middle income projects); they do not live respectable lives; they have only grammar school education; they may have no regular jobs. Closer to home, those slightly lower in status are people like "The lady next door who has a little less than I have," the man who can't afford to take care of his kids properly in the project, people who spend their money on liquor, the person with less skill in the same line of work.

The rationale for their lower status turns chiefly on two things: their lack of education and therefore failure to know what they want or failure to understand lifesmanship, and their general indifference. It is particularly this "not caring" which seems so salient in the upper working class mind. This is consonant with the general view that success is a triumph of the will and a reflection of ability. Poverty is for lazy people, just as middle status is for struggling people. Thus Ruggiero, an office building maintenance man, accounts for poverty by saying: "There's laziness, you'll always have lazy people." De Angelo, a factory operative, sees it this way:

> *A guy gets married and, you know, he's not educated too well, he doesn't have a good job and he gets a large family and he's in bad shape, y'know what I mean. It's tough; he's got to live in a lousy rent—he can't afford anything better.*

But De Angelo takes away some of this sympathy the next moment when he goes on to say:

> *But then you get a lot of people who don't want to work; you got wel-*
> *fare. People will go on living on that welfare — they're happier than*
> *hell. Why should they work if the city will support them?*

In general, there is little sympathy given to those lower in the scale, little reference to the overpowering forces of circumstance, only rare mention of sickness, death of a breadwinner, senility, factories moving out of town, and so forth. The only major cause of poverty to which no moral blame attaches is depression or "unemployment" — but this is not considered a strikingly important cause in the minds of my clients. They are Christian in the sense that they believe "The poor ye have with you always," but there is no trace of a belief that the poor are in any way "blessed."

What If There Were Greater Equality of Opportunity and Income?

We have examined here the working (and lower middle) class defenses of the present order. They are well organized and solidly built. By and large these people believe that the field is open, merit will tell. They may then deprecate the importance of class, limit their perspectives, accept their situation reluctantly or with satisfaction. They may see the benefits of society flowing to their own class, however they define it. They tend to believe that each person's status is in some way deserved.

How would these lower middle and working class men feel about a change in the social order such that they and their friends might suddenly be equal to others now higher or lower in the social order? Most of them wouldn't like it. They would fear and resent this kind of equality.

Abandonment of a Rationale

Changing ideas is a strain not to be lightly incurred, particularly when these ideas are intimately related to one's self-esteem. The less education one has, the harder it is to change such ideas. Painfully these men have elaborated an explanation for their situation in life; it helps explain things to their wives who take their status from them; it permits their growing children to account for relative social status in school; it offers to each man the satisfactions of social identity and a measure of social worth. Their rationales are endowed with moral qualities; the distribution of values in the society is seen as just and natural. While it gives satisfactions of an obvious kind to those who contemplate those beneath them, it also gives order and a kind of reassurance, oddly enough, to those who glance upwards towards "society" or "the four hundred." This reassurance is not unlike the reassurance provided by the belief in a Just God while injustices rain upon one's head. The feudal serf, the Polish peasant, the Mexican peon believed that theirs was a moral and a "natural order" — so also the American working man.

The Problem of Social Adjustment

Equality would pose problems of social adjustments, of manners, of how to behave. Here is Sokolsky, unprepossessing, uneducated, and nervous, with a more prosperous brother in the same town. "I'm not going to go over there," he says, "because every time I go there I feel uncomfortable." On the question of rising from one social class to another, his views reflect this personal situation:

> *I think it's hard. Let's say — let's take me, for instance. Supposing I came into a lot of money, and I moved into a nice neighborhood — class — maybe I wouldn't know how to act then. I think it's very hard, because people know that you just — word gets around that you . . . never had it before you got it now. Well, maybe they wouldn't like you . . . maybe you don't know how to act.*

The kind of equality with others which would mean a rapid rise in his own status is a matter of concern, mixed, of course, with pleasant anticipation at the thought of "telling off" his brother.

Consider the possibility of social equality including genuine fraternization, without economic equality. Sullivan, a railroad fireman, deals with this in graphic terms:

> *What is the basis of social class? Well, things that people have in common . . . Money is one, for instance, like I wouldn't feel very comfortable going around with a millionaire, we'll say . . . He could do a lot and say a lot — mention places he'd been and so on — I mean I wouldn't be able to keep up with him . . . and he wouldn't have to watch his money, and I'd have to be pinching mine to see if I had enough for another beer, or something.*

And, along the lines of Sokolsky's comments, Sullivan believes that moving upwards in the social scale is easier if one moves to a new place where one has not been known in the old connection. Flynn holds that having the right interests and conversational topics for the new and higher social group will make it possible — but otherwise it could be painful. Kuchinsky, the house painter, says "I suppose it would feel funny to get into a higher class, but I don't believe I would change. I wouldn't just disregard my friends if I came into any money." Clinging to old friends would give some security in that dazzling new world.

De Angelo, a factory operative, also considers the question of whether the higher status people will accept the *arriviste*, but for himself, he dismisses it:

> *I wouldn't worry much about whether they would accept or they wouldn't accept. I would move into another class. I mean—I mean—I don't worry much about that stuff. If people don't want to bother with me, I don't bother with them, that's all.*

These fears, while plausible and all too human on the face of it, emerged unexpectedly from the interview material designed to capture ideas and emotions on other aspects of class status. They highlight a resistance to equalitarian movements that might bring the working class and this rejecting superior class—whether it is imaginary or not—in close association. If these were revolutionaries, one might phrase their anxieties: "Will my victims accept me?" But they are not revolutionaries.

These are problems of rising in status to meet the upper classes face to face. But there is another risk in opening the gates so that those of moderate circumstances can rise to higher status. Equality of opportunity, it appears, is inherently dangerous in this respect: there is the risk that friends, neighbors, or subordinates will surpass one in status. O'Hara has this on his mind. Some of the people who rise in status are nice, but:

> *You get other ones, the minute they get a little, they get big-headed and they think they're better than the other ones—where they're still —to me they're worse than the middle class. I mean, they should get down, because they're just showing their illiteracy—that's all they're doing.*

Sokolsky worries about this possibility, too, having been exposed to the slights of his brother's family. But the worry over being passed by is not important, not salient. It is only rarely mentioned.

Deprivation of a Meritorious Elite

It is comforting to have the "natural leaders" of a society well entrenched in their proper place. If there were equality there would no longer be such an elite to supervise and take care of people—especially "me." Thus Woodside, our policeman, reports:

> *I think anybody that has money—I think their interest is much wider than the regular working man. . . . And therefore I think that the man with the money is a little bit more educated, for the simple reason he has the money, and he has a much wider view of life—because he's in the knowledge of it all the time.*

Here and elsewhere in the interview, one senses that Woodside is glad to have such educated, broad-gauged men in eminent positions. He certainly opposes the notion of equality of income. Something similar creeps into Johnson's discussion of social classes. He feels that the upper classes, who "seem to be very nice people," are "willing to lend a helping hand—to listen to you. I would say they'd help you out more than the middle class [man] would help you out even if he was in a position to help you out." Equality, then, would deprive society, and oneself, of a group of friendly, wise, and helpful people who occupy the social eminences.

The Loss of the Goals of Life

But most important of all, equality, at least equality of income, would deprive people of the goals of life. Every one of the fifteen clients with whom I spent my evenings for seven months believed that equality of income would deprive men of their incentive to work, achieve, and develop their skills. These answers ranged, in their sophistication and approach, across a broad field. The most highly educated man in the sample, Farrel, answers the question "How would you feel if everyone received the same income in our society?" by saying:

> *I think it would be kind of silly . . . Society, by using income as a reward technique, can often insure that the individuals will put forth their best efforts.*

He does not believe, for himself, that status or income are central to motivation—but for others, they are. Woodside, our policeman, whose main concern is not the vistas of wealth and opportunity of the American dream, but rather whether he can get a good pension if he should have to retire early, comes forward as follows:

> *I'd say that [equal income]—that is something that's pretty—I think it would be a dull thing, because life would be accepted—or it would —rather we'd go stale. There would be no initiative to be a little different, or go ahead.*

Like Woodside, Flynn, a white collar worker, responds with a feeling of personal loss—the idea of such an equality of income would make him feel "very mad." Costa, whose ambitions in life are most modest, holds that equality of income "would eliminate the basic thing about the wonderful opportunity you have in this country." Then, for a moment the notion of his income equalling that of the professional man passes pleasantly through his mind: "don't misunderstand me—I like the idea"; then again, "I think it eliminates the main reason why people become engineers and professors and doctors."

Rapuano, whose worries have given him ulcers, projects himself into a situation where everyone receives the same income, in this case a high one:

> *If everyone had the same income of a man that's earning $50,000 a year, and he went to, let's say 10 years of college to do that, why hell, I'd just as soon sit on my ass as go to college and wait till I could earn $50,000 a year, too. Of course, what the hell am I going to do to earn $50,000 a year — now that's another question.*

But however the question is answered, he is clear that guaranteed equal incomes would encourage people to sit around on their anatomy and wait for their pay checks. But he would like to see some levelling, particularly if doctors, whom he hates, were to have their fees and incomes substantially reduced.

That These Sacrifices Shall Not Have Been in Vain

The men I talked to were not at the bottom of the scale; not at all. They were stable breadwinners, churchgoers, voters, family men. They achieved this position in life through hard work and sometimes bitter sacrifices. They are distinguished from the lower classes through their initiative, zeal and responsibility, their willingness and ability to postpone pleasures or to forego them entirely. In their control of impulse and desire they have absorbed the Protestant ethic. At least six of them have two jobs and almost no leisure. In answering questions on "the last time you remember having a specially good time" some of them must go back ten to fifteen years. Nor are their good times remarkable for their spontaneous fun and enjoyment of life. Many of them do not like their jobs, but stick to them because of their family responsibilities — and they do not know what else they would rather do. In short, they have sacrificed their hedonistic inclinations, given up good times, expended their energy and resources in order to achieve and maintain their present tenuous hold on respectability and middle status.

Now in such a situation to suggest that men be equalized and the lower orders raised and one's own hard-earned status given to them as a right and not a reward for effort, seems to them desperately wrong. In the words of my research assistant, David Sears, "Suppose the Marshall Plan had provided a block and tackle for Sisyphus after all these years. How do you think he would have felt?" Sokolsky, Woodside, and Dempsey have rolled the stone to the top of the hill so long, they despise the suggestion that it might have been in vain. Or even worse, that their neighbors at the foot of the hill might have the use of a block and tackle.

The World Would Collapse

As a corollary to the view that life would lose its vigor and its savor with equality of income, there is the image of an equalitarian society as a world running down, a chaotic and disorganized place to live. The professions would be decimated: "People pursue the higher educational levels for a reason—there's a lot of rewards, either financial or social," says Costa. Sullivan says, "Why should people take the headaches of responsible jobs if the pay didn't meet the responsibilities?" For the general society, Flynn, a white collar man, believes that "if there were no monetary incentive involved, I think there'd be a complete loss. It would stop all development—there's no doubt about it." McNamara, a bookkeeper, sees people then reduced to a dead level of worth: with equal income "the efforts would be equal and pretty soon we would be worth the same thing." In two contrasting views, both suggesting economic disorganization, Woodside believes "I think you'd find too many men digging ditches, and no doctors," while Rapuano believes men would fail to dig ditches or sewers "and where the hell would we be when we wanted to go to the toilet?"

Only a few took up the possible inference that this was an attractive, but impractical ideal—and almost none followed up the suggestion that some equalization of income, if not complete equality, would be desirable. The fact of the matter is that these men, by and large, prefer an inequalitarian society, and even prefer a society graced by some men of great wealth. As they look out upon the social scene, they feel that an equalitarian society would present them with too many problems of moral adjustment, inter-personal social adjustment, and motivational adjustment which they fear and dislike. But perhaps, most important, their life goals are structured around achievement and success in monetary terms. If these were taken away, life would be a desert. These men view the possibility of an equalitarian world as a paraphrased version of Swinburne's lines on Jesus Christ, "Thou hast conquered, oh pale equalitarian, and the world has grown gray with thy breath."

Some Theoretical Implications

Like any findings on the nature of men's social attitudes and beliefs, even in such a culture-bound inquiry as this one, the new information implies certain theoretical propositions which may be incorporated into the main body of political theory. Let us consider seven such propositions growing more or less directly out of our findings on the fear of equality:

(1) The greater the emphasis in a society upon the availability of "equal opportunity for all," the greater the need for members of that

society to develop an acceptable rationalization for their own social status.

(2) The greater the strain on a person's self-esteem implied by a relatively low status in an open society, the greater the necessity to explain this status as "natural" and "proper" in the social order. Lower status people generally find it less punishing to think of themselves as correctly placed by a just society than to think of themselves as exploited, or victimized by an unjust society.

(3) The greater the emphasis in a society upon equality of opportunity, the greater the tendency for those of marginal status to denigrate those lower than themselves. This view seems to such people to have the factual or even moral justification that if the lower classes "cared" enough they could be better off. It has a psychological "justification" in that it draws attention to one's own relatively better status and one's own relatively greater initiative and virtue.

(4) People tend to care less about *equality* of opportunity than about the availability of *some* opportunity. Men do not need the same life chances as everybody else, indeed they usually care very little about that. They need only chances (preferably with unknown odds) for a slightly better life than they now have. Thus: Popular satisfaction with one's own status is related less to equality of opportunity than to the breadth of distribution of some opportunity for all, however unequal this distribution may be. A man who can improve his position one rung does not resent the man who starts on a different ladder half way up.

These propositions are conservative in their implications. The psychological roots of this conservatism must be explored elsewhere, as must the many exceptions which may be observed when the fabric of a social order is so torn that the leaders, the rich and powerful, are seen as illegitimate—and hence "appropriately" interpreted as exploiters of the poor. I maintain, however, that these propositions hold generally for the American culture over most of its history—and also, that the propositions hold for most of the world most of the time. This is so even though they fly in the face of much social theory—theory often generalized from more specialized studies of radicalism and revolution. Incidentally, one must observe that it is as important to explain why revolutions and radical social movements do *not* happen as it is to explain why they do.

The more I observed the psychological and physical drain placed upon my sample by the pressures to consume—and therefore to scratch in the corners of the economy for extra income—the more it appeared that competitive consumption was not a stimulus to class conflict, as might have been expected, but was a substitute for or a sublimation of it. Thus we would say:

(5) The more emphasis a society places upon consumption —through advertising, development of new products, and easy install-

ment buying—the more will social dissatisfaction be channeled into intra-class consumption rivalry instead of inter-class resentment and conflict. The Great American Medicine Show creates consumer unrest, working wives, and dual-job-holding, not antagonism toward the "owning classes."

As a corollary of this view: (6) The more emphasis a society places upon consumption, the more will labor unions focus upon the "bread and butter" aspects of unionism, as contrasted to its ideological elements.

We come, finally, to a hypothesis which arises from this inquiry into the fear of equality but goes much beyond the focus of the present study. I mention it here in a speculative frame of mind, undogmatically, and even regretfully:

(7) The ideals of the French Revolution, liberty and equality, have been advanced because of the accidental correspondence between these ideals and needs of the bourgeoisie for freedom of economic action and the demands of the working class, very simply, for "more." Ideas have an autonomy of their own, however, in the sense that once moralized they persist even if the social forces which brought them to the fore decline in strength. They become "myths"—but myths erode without support from some major social stratum. Neither the commercial classes nor the working classes, the historical beneficiaries of these two moralized ideas (ideals or myths), have much affection for the ideals in their universal forms. On the other hand, the professional classes, particularly the lawyers, ministers, and teachers of a society, very often do have such an affection. It is they, in the democratic West, who serve as the "hard core" of democratic defenders, in so far as there is one. It is they, more frequently than others, who are supportive of the generalized application of the ideals of freedom and equality to all men. This is not virtue, but rather a different organization of interests and a different training. Whatever the reason, however, it is not to "The People," not to the business class, not to the working class, that we must look for the consistent and relatively unqualified defense of freedom and equality. The professional class, at least in the American culture, serves as the staunchest defender of democracy's two greatest ideals.

---

3. *Fraternity*

Historians and sociologists have traced the social development of man from communal societies, united by kinship and class ties, to mobile, diffuse societies in which individual merit largely determines personal rank. But even in today's open society, fraternity—the existence of communal ties among men—still ranks close to the quest for equality among extant political myths. What are its consequences?

The following selections focus on three aspects of fraternity. First, the American historian Frederick Jackson Turner analyzes the role of fraternity in building the American West. Second, sociologist David Riesman examines the stultifying limitations of public opinion and the lack of shared, stable norms that would provide a firm anchor for today's "lonely crowd." Finally, Richard Hoggart describes the subtle, defensive uses of fraternity by the English working class.

Consider carefully the sociopolitical contexts in which these fraternal patterns develop. The mutual social and psychological supports of a developing American West helped the frontiersmen cope with an unexplored environment and form patterns of group behavior. The uses of fraternity among the British working class serve to protect ego and kin relations in a stratified class society. In the prototype of a mass society, described by Riesman, the shifting norms of the peer group are a poor substitute for declining class, institutional, and public sources of standards for appropriate behavior.

DEVELOPMENT THROUGH FRATERNITY

FREDERICK JACKSON TURNER

The pioneer life from which Lincoln came differed in important respects from the frontier democracy typified by Andrew Jackson. Jackson's democracy was contentious, individualistic, and it sought the ideal of local self-government and expansion. Lincoln represents rather the pioneer folk who entered the forest of the great Northwest to chop out a home, to build up their fortunes in the midst of a continually ascending industrial movement. In the democracy of the Southwest, industrial development and city life were only minor factors, but to the democracy of the Northwest they were its very life. To widen the area of the clearing, to contend with one another for the mastery of the industrial resources of the rich provinces, to struggle for a place in the ascending movement of society, to transmit to one's offspring the chance for education, for industrial betterment, for the rise in life which

Condensed from Chapter IX from *The Frontier in American History* by Frederick Jackson Turner. Copyright 1920 by Frederick Jackson Turner. Copyright 1948 by Caroline M. S. Turner. Reprinted by permission of Holt, Rinehart and Winston, Inc. Title supplied by the editor.

the hardships of the pioneer existence denied to the pioneer himself, these were some of the ideals of the region to which Lincoln came. The men were commonwealth builders, industry builders. Whereas the type of hero in the Southwest was militant, in the Northwest he was industrial. It was in the midst of these "plain people," as he loved to call them, that Lincoln grew to manhood. As Emerson says: "He is the true history of the American people in his time." The years of his early life were the years when the democracy of the Northwest came into struggle with the institution of slavery which threatened to forbid the expansion of the democratic pioneer life in the West. In President Eliot's essay on "Five American Contributions to Civilization," he instances as one of the supreme tests of American democracy its attitude upon the question of slavery. But if democracy chose wisely and worked effectively toward the solution of this problem, it must be remembered that Western democracy took the lead. The rail-splitter himself became the nation's President in that fierce time of struggle, and armies of the woodsmen and pioneer farmers recruited in the Old Northwest made free the Father of Waters, marched through Georgia, and helped to force the struggle to a conclusion at Appomattox. The free pioneer democracy struck down the slave-holding aristocracy on its march to the West.

The last chapter in the development of Western democracy is the one that deals with its conquest over the vast spaces of the new West. At each new stage of Western development, the people have had to grapple with larger areas, with bigger combinations. The little colony of Massachusetts veterans that settled at Marietta received a land grant as large as the State of Rhode Island. The band of Connecticut pioneers that followed Moses Cleaveland to the Connecticut Reserve occupied a region as large as the parent State. The area which settlers of New England stock occupied on the prairies of northern Illinois surpassed the combined area of Massachusetts, Connecticut, and Rhode Island. Men who had become accustomed to the narrow valleys and the little towns of the East found themselves out on the boundless spaces of the West dealing with units of such magnitude as dwarfed their former experience. The Great Lakes, the Prairies, the Great Plains, the Rocky Mountains, the Mississippi and the Missouri, furnished new standards of measurement for the achievement of this industrial democracy. Individualism began to give way to coöperation and to governmental activity. Even in the earlier days of the democratic conquest of the wilderness, demands had been made upon the government for support in internal improvements, but this new West showed a growing tendency to call to its assistance the powerful arm of national authority. In the period since the Civil War, the vast public domain has been donated to the individual farmer, to States for education, to railroads for the construction of transportation lines.

Moreover, with the advent of democracy in the last fifteen years upon the Great Plains, new physical conditions have presented themselves which have accelerated the social tendency of Western democracy. The pioneer farmer of the days of Lincoln could place his family on a flatboat, strike into the wilderness, cut out his clearing, and with little or no capital go on to the achievement of industrial independence. Even the homesteader on the Western prairies found it possible to work out a similar independent destiny, although the factor of transportation made a serious and increasing impediment to the free working-out of his individual career. But when the arid lands and the mineral resources of the Far West were reached, no conquest was possible by the old individual pioneer methods. Here expensive irrigation works must be constructed, coöperative activity was demanded in utilization of the water supply, capital beyond the reach of the small farmer was required. In a word, the physiographic province itself decreed that the destiny of this new frontier should be social rather than individual.

Magnitude of social achievement is the watchword of the democracy since the Civil War. From petty towns built in the marshes, cities arose whose greatness and industrial power are the wonder of our time. The conditions were ideal for the production of captains of industry. The old democratic admiration for the self-made man, its old deference to the rights of competitive individual development, together with the stupendous natural resources that opened to the conquest of the keenest and the strongest, gave such conditions of mobility as enabled the development of the large corporate industries which in our own decade have marked the West.

. . . There has been a steady development of the industrial ideal, and a steady increase of the social tendency, in this later movement of Western democracy. While the individualism of the frontier, so prominent in the earliest days of the Western advance, has been preserved as an ideal, more and more these individuals struggling each with the other, dealing with vaster and vaster areas, with larger and larger problems, have found it necessary to combine under the leadership of the strongest. This is the explanation of the rise of those preëminent captains of industry whose genius has concentrated capital to control the fundamental resources of the nation. If now . . . we try to pick out from the influences that have gone to the making of Western democracy the factors which constitute the net result of this movement, we shall have to mention at least the following:

Most important of all has been the fact that an area of free land has continually lain on the western border of the settled area of the United States. Whenever social conditions tended to crystallize in the East, whenever capital tended to press upon labor or political restraints to impede the freedom of the mass, there was this gate of escape to the free conditions of the frontier. These free lands promoted individualism, economic equality, freedom to rise, democracy. Men would not accept inferior wages and a permanent position of social subordination when this promised land of freedom and equality was theirs for the taking. Who would rest content under oppressive legislative conditions when with a slight effort he might reach a land wherein to become a co-worker in the building of free cities and free States on the lines of his own ideal? In a word, then, free lands meant free opportunities. Their existence has differentiated the American democracy from the democracies which have preceded it, because ever, as democracy in the East took the form of highly specialized and complicated industrial society, in the West it kept in touch with primitive conditions, and by action and reaction these two forces have shaped our history.

In the next place, these free lands and this treasury of industrial resources have existed over such vast spaces that they have demanded of democracy increasing spaciousness of design and power of execution. Western democracy is contrasted with the democracy of all other times in the largeness of the tasks to which it has set its hand, and in the vast achievements which it has wrought out in the control of nature and of politics. It would be difficult to over-emphasize the importance of this training upon democracy. Never before in the history of the world has a democracy existed on so vast an area and handled things in the gross with such success, with such largeness of design, and such grasp upon the means of execution. In short, democracy has learned in the West of the United States how to deal with the problem of magnitude. The old historic democracies were but little states with primitive economic conditions. . . .

Western democracy has been from the time of its birth idealistic. The very fact of the wilderness appealed to men as a fair, blank page on which to write a new chapter in the story of man's struggle for a higher type of society. The Western wilds, from the Alleghanies to the Pacific, constituted the richest free gift that was ever spread out before civilized man. To the peasant and artisan of the Old World, bound by the chains of social class, as old as custom and as inevitable as fate, the West offered an exit into a free life and greater well-being among the bounties of nature, into the midst of resources that demanded manly exertion, and that gave in return the chance for indefinite ascent in the scale of social advance. "To each she offered gifts after his will." Never again can such an opportunity come to the sons of men. It was unique, and the thing is so near us, so much a part of our lives, that we do not even yet comprehend its full significance. The existence of this land of opportunity has made America the goal of idealists from the days of the Pilgrim Fathers. With all the materialism of the pioneer movements, this idealistic conception of the vacant lands as an opportunity for a new order of things is unmistakably present. . . .

To the old native democratic stock has been added a vast army of recruits from the Old World. There are in the Middle West alone four million persons of German parentage out of a total of seven millions in the country. Over a million persons of Scandinavian parentage live in the same region. The democracy of the newer West is deeply affected by the ideals brought by these immigrants from the Old World. To them America was not simply a new home; it was a land of opportunity, of freedom, of democracy. It meant to them, as to the American pioneer that preceded them, the opportunity to destroy the bonds of social caste that bound them in their older home, to hew out for themselves in a new country a destiny proportioned to the powers that God had given them, a chance to place their families under better conditions and to win a larger life than the life that they had left behind. He who believes that even the hordes of recent immigrants from southern Italy are drawn to these shores by nothing more than a dull and blind materialism has not penetrated into the heart of the problem. The idealism and expectation of these children of the Old World, the hopes which they have formed for a newer and freer life across the seas, are almost pathetic when one considers how far they are from the possibility of fruition. He who would take stock of American democracy must not forget the accumulation of human purposes and ideals which immigration has added to the American populace.

In this connection it must also be remembered that these democratic ideals have existed at each stage of the advance of the frontier, and have left behind them deep and enduring effects on the thinking of the whole country. Long after the frontier period of a particular region of the United States has passed away, the conception of society, the ideals and aspirations which it produced, persist in the minds of the people. So recent has been the transition of the greater portion of the United States from frontier conditions to conditions of settled life, that we are, over the large portion of the United States, hardly a generation removed from the primitive conditions of the West. If, indeed, we ourselves were not pioneers, our fathers were, and the inherited ways of looking at things, the fundamental assumptions of the American people, have all been shaped by this experience of democracy on its westward march. This experience has been wrought into the very warp and woof of American thought. . . .

In enumerating the services of American democracy, President Eliot included the corporation as one of its achievements, declaring that "freedom of incorporation, though no longer exclusively a democratic agency, has given a strong support to democratic institutions." In one sense this is doubtless true, since the corporation has been one of the means by which small properties can be aggregated into an effective working body. Socialistic writers have long been fond of pointing out also that these various concentrations pave the way for and make possible social control. From this point of view it is possible that the masters of industry may prove to be not so much an incipient aristocracy as the pathfinders for democracy in reducing the industrial world to systematic consolidation suited to democratic control. The great geniuses that have built up the modern industrial concentration were trained in the midst of democratic society. They were the product of these democratic conditions. Freedom to rise was the very condition of their existence. Whether they will be followed by successors who will adopt the exploitation of the masses, and who will be capable of retaining under efficient control these vast resources, is one of the questions which we shall have to face.

This, at least, is clear: American democracy is fundamentally the outcome of the experiences of the American people in dealing with the West. Western democracy through the whole of its earlier period tended to the production of a society of which the most distinctive fact was the freedom of the individual to rise under conditions of social mobility, and whose ambition was the liberty and well-being of the masses. This conception has vitalized all American democracy, and has brought it into sharp contrasts with the democracies of history, and with those modern efforts of Europe to create an artificial democratic order by legislation. The problem of the United States is not to create democracy, but to conserve democratic institutions and ideals. In the later period of its development, Western democracy has been gaining experience in the problem of social control. It has steadily enlarged the sphere of its action and the instruments for its perpetuation. By its system of public schools, from the grades to the graduate work of the great universities, the West has created a larger single body of intelligent plain people than can be found elsewhere in the world. Its political tendencies, whether we consider Democracy, Populism, or Republicanism, are distinctly in the direction of greater social control and the conservation of the old democratic ideals.

To these ideals the West adheres with even a passionate determination. If, in working out its mastery of the resources of the interior, it has produced a type of industrial leader so powerful as to be the wonder of the world, nevertheless, it is still to be determined whether these men constitute a menace to democratic institutions, or the most efficient factor for adjusting democratic control to the new conditions.

Whatever shall be the outcome of the rush of this huge industrial modern United States to its place among the nations of the earth, the formation of its Western democracy will always remain one of the wonderful chapters in the history of the human race. Into this vast shaggy continent of ours poured the first feeble tide of European settlement. European men, institutions, and ideas were lodged in the American wilderness, and this great American West took them to her bosom, taught them a new way of looking upon the destiny of the common man, trained them in adaptation to the conditions of the New World, to the creation of new institutions to meet new needs; and ever as society on her eastern border grew to resemble the Old World in its social forms and its industry, ever, as it began to lose faith in the ideals of democracy, she opened new provinces, and dowered new democracies in her most distant domains with her material treasures and with the ennobling influence that the fierce love of freedom, the strength that came from hewing out a home, making a school and a church, and creating a higher future for his family, furnished to the pioneer.

She gave to the world such types as the farmer Thomas Jefferson, with his Declaration of Independence, his statute for religious toleration, and his purchase of Louisiana. She gave us Andrew Jackson, that fierce Tennessee spirit who broke down the traditions of conservative rule, swept away the privacies and privileges of officialdom, and, like a Gothic leader, opened the temple of the nation to the populace. She gave us Abraham Lincoln, whose gaunt frontier form and gnarled, massive hand told of the conflict with the forest, whose grasp of the ax-handle of the pioneer was no firmer than his grasp of the helm of the ship of state as it breasted the seas of civil war. She has furnished to this new democracy her stores of mineral wealth, that dwarf those of the Old World, and her provinces that in themselves are vaster and more productive than most of the nations of Europe. Out of her bounty has come a nation whose industrial competition alarms the Old World, and the masters of whose resources wield wealth and power vaster than the wealth and power of kings. Best of all, the West gave, not only to the American, but to the unhappy and oppressed of all lands, a vision of hope, and assurance that the world held a place where were to be found high faith in man and the will and power to furnish him the opportunity to grow to the full measure of his own capacity. Great and powerful as are the new sons of her loins, the Republic is greater than they. The paths of the pioneer have widened into broad highways. The forest clearing has expanded into affluent commonwealths. Let us see to it that the ideals of the pioneer in his log cabin shall enlarge into the spiritual life of a democracy where civic power shall dominate and utilize individual achievement for the common good.

TRIAL BY OTHER-DIRECTED JURY

David Riesman

The parents in the era dominated by other-direction lose their once undisputed role; the old man is no longer "the governor"—and the in-

From *The Lonely Crowd: A Study of the Changing American Character* (New Haven: Yale University Press, 1950), pp. 90–102. Title supplied by the editor.

staller of governors. Other adult authorities such as the governess and grandmother either almost disappear or, like the teacher, take on the new role of peer-group facilitator and mediator—a role not too different perhaps from that of many clergymen who, in the adult congregation, move from morality to morale.

. . . [M]oreover, the city in which the other-directed child* grows up is large enough and stratified enough—taking into account its ring of suburbs—to create an age- and class-graded group for him. It will be possible to put him into school and playground, and camp in the summer, with other children of virtually the same age and social position. If the adults are the judge, these peers are the jury. And, as in America the judge is hemmed in by rules which give the jury a power it has in no other common-law land, so the American peer-group, too, cannot be matched for power throughout the middle-class world.

The Trial

While the inner-directed parent frequently forced the pace of the child in its home "duties," as, for example, in cleanliness and toilet-training habits, the other-directed parent, more apt to be permissive in such matters, forces the pace, with like impatience, in the child's social life, though often hardly aware of doing so. Parents today are the stage managers for the meetings of three- and four-year-olds, just as, in earlier eras, the adults managed marriages. Hence, while "self-demand" feeding schedules are gaining ground for infants, self-demand is not observed when it comes to socialization outside the home. The daily schedule is an effort, with mother as chauffeur and booking agent, to cultivate all the currently essential talents, especially the gregarious ones. It is inconceivable to some supervising adults that a child might prefer his own company or that of just one other child.

The child is thus confronted by what we have termed his sociometric peers and is not surrounded by those who are his peers in less visible matters, such as temperament and taste. Yet since there are no *visible* differences he is hard put to it to justify, even to be aware of, these *invisible* differences. On the overt level the situation is highly standardized: any given child faces the culture of the fives or the sixes at a particular moment of the fashion cycle in child-training and child-amusement practices. Indeed it is this very standardization which . . . weakens the power of the parents, whose deviation from the standards is felt by them and by the child to demonstrate their inexperience and inadequacy. In this setting the adults are anxious that the child succeed in the peer-group and therefore are concerned with his "adjust-

---

*A person is "other-directed" when he responds to the current expectations and needs of his contemporaries rather than to deep-seated individual expectations and needs.—*Editor's note.*

ment." They, too, tend to ignore and even suppress invisible differences between their child and the children of others. Such differences might cast doubt on their own adjustment, their own correct tuning to the signals concerning child rearing.

The majority of children learn very fast under these conditions; the same adult authorities who patronize children's intellects (and therefore slow them down) are perhaps not sufficiently impressed with how poised in many social situations modern other-directed children are. These children are not shy, either with adults or with the opposite sex whom they have accompanied to proms and parties and seen daily in and out of school. This adaptability, moreover, prepares the child for a type of social mobility somewhat different from the social-climbing experiences of the parvenu in an inner-directed environment. The latter only rarely acquired the intellectual and social graces of his new associates — or he ridiculously accentuated them. He either kept his rough and lowly manners or painfully tried to learn new ones as he moved up; in either case the standard, limited code of conduct expected of him was unequivocal. In contrast with this the other-directed child is able to move among new associates with an almost automatic adjustment to the subtlest insignia of status.

Bearing in mind these positive achievements of other-directed sociability, let us turn our attention from what the peer-group teaches and evokes to what it represses. Today six-year-olds and up have a phrase — "he [or she] thinks he's *big*" (or "he thinks he's *something*") — which symbolizes the role of the peer-group in the creation of other-directed types. The effort is to cut everyone down to size who stands up or stands out in any direction. Beginning with the very young and going on from there, overt vanity is treated as one of the worst offenses, as perhaps dishonesty would have been in an earlier day. Being high-hat is forbidden.

Temper, manifest jealousy, moodiness — these, too, are offenses in the code of the peer-group. All "knobby" or idiosyncratic qualities and vices are more or less eliminated or repressed. And judgments of others by peer-group members are so clearly matters of taste that their expression has to resort to the vaguest phrases, constantly changed: cute, lousy, square, darling, good guy, honey, swell, bitch (without precise meaning), etc. Sociometry reflects this situation when it asks children about such things as whom they like to sit next to or not to sit next to, to have for a friend, a leader, and so on. The judgments can be meaningfully scaled because, and only because, they are all based on uncomplicated continua of *taste*, on which the children are constantly ranking each other.

But to say that judgments of peer-groupers are matters of taste, not of morality or even opportunism, is not to say that any particular child can afford to ignore these judgments. On the contrary he is, as never before, at their mercy. If the peer-group were—and we continue to deal here with the urban middle classes only—a wild, torturing, obviously vicious group, the individual child might still feel moral indignation as a defense against its commands. But like adult authorities in the other-directed socialization process, the peer-group is friendly and tolerant. It stresses fair play. Its conditions for entry seem reasonable and well meaning. But even where this is not so, moral indignation is out of fashion. The child is therefore exposed to trial by jury without any defenses either from the side of its own morality or from the adults. All the morality is the group's. Indeed, even the fact that it is a morality is concealed by the confusing notion that the function of the group is to have fun, to play; the deadly seriousness of the business, which might justify the child in making an issue of it, is therefore hidden.

"The Talk of the Town": The Socialization of Preferences

In the eyes of the jury of peers one may be a good guy one day, a stinker the next. Toleration, let alone leadership, depends on having a highly sensitive response to swings of fashion. This ability is sought in several ways. One way is to surrender any claim to independence of judgment and taste—a kind of plea of nolo contendere. Another is to build a plea for special consideration by acquiring unusual facility in one's duties as a consumer—in performance, that is, of the leisure arts. With good luck one may even become a taste and opinion leader, with great influence over the jury.

Each particular peer-group has its group fandoms and lingoes. Safety consists not in mastering a difficult craft but in mastering a battery of taste preferences and the mode of their expression. The preferences are for articles or "heroes" of consumption and for members of the group itself. The proper mode of expression requires feeling out with skill and sensitivity the probable tastes of the others and then swapping mutual likes and dislikes to maneuver intimacy.

Now some of this is familiar even in the period depending on innerdirection; it is important, therefore, to realize the degree to which training in consumer taste has replaced training in etiquette. Formal etiquette may be thought of as a means of handling relations with people with whom one does not seek intimacy. It is particularly useful when adults and young, men and women, upper classes and lower classes, are sharply separated and when a code is necessary to mediate exchanges across these lines. Thus etiquette can be at the same time a means of approaching people and of staying clear of them. For some, etiquette may be a matter of little emotional weight—an easy behavioral cloak; for others the ordering of human relations through etiquette can become highly charged emotionally—an evidence of characterological compulsiveness. But in either case etiquette is concerned not with encounters between individuals as such but with encounters between them as representatives of their carefully graded social roles.

In comparison with this, training in consumer taste, which tends to replace etiquette among the other-directed, is useful not so much across age and social class lines as within the jury room of one's age and class peers. As in some groups—children as well as adults—discussion turns to the marginal differentiation between Cadillacs and Lincolns, so in other groups discussion centers on Fords and Chevrolets. What matters in either case is an ability at continual testing out of others' tastes, often a far more intrusive process than the exchange of courtesies and pleasantries required by etiquette. Not, of course, that the child always gets close to the "others" with whom he is exchanging consumption preferences—these exchanges are often mere gossip about goods. Yet a certain emotional energy, even excitement, permeates the transaction. For one thing, the other-directed person acquires an intense interest in the ephemeral tastes of the "others"—an interest inconceivable to the tradition-directed or inner-directed child whose tastes have undergone a less differentiated socialization. For another thing, the other-directed child is concerned with learning from these interchanges whether his radar equipment is in proper order.

It has always been true in social classes dominated by fashion that to escape being left behind by a swing of fashion requires the ability to adopt new fashions rapidly; to escape the danger of a conviction for being different from the "others" requires that one can be different—in look and talk and manner—from *oneself* as one was yesterday. Here, also, it is necessary to see precisely what has changed. In general the processes of fashion are expanded in class terms and speeded in time terms. In the leisure economy of incipient population decline the distributive machinery of society improves, in terms of both income distribution and goods distribution. It becomes possible to accelerate swings of fashion as well as to differentiate goods by very minute gradients. For, in its late stages, mass production and mass distribution permit and require a vast increase not only in quantity but in qualitative differences among products—not only as a consequence of monopolistic efforts at marginal differentiation but also because the machinery and organization are present for rapidly designing, producing, and distributing a wide variety of goods.

This means that the consumer trainee has a lot more to learn than in the early days of industrialization. To take one example, the foreigner who visits America is likely to think that salesgirls, society ladies, and movie actresses all dress alike, as compared with the clear status differences of Europe. But the American knows—has to know if he is to get along in life and love—that this is simply an error: that one must look for small qualitative differences that signify style and status, to observe for instance the strained casualness sometimes found in upper-class dress as against the strained formality of working-class dress. In the days of etiquette the differences were far more sharp.

One must listen to quite young children discussing television models, automobile styling, or the merits of various streamliners to see how gifted they are as consumers long before they have a decisive say themselves—though their influence in family councils must not be underestimated. Children join in this exchange of verdicts even if their parents cannot afford the gadgets under discussion; indeed, the economy would slow down if only those were trained as consumers who at any given moment had the wherewithal.

The wider ambit of taste socialization today is shown in still another decisive change from the era depending on inner-direction. Then, by the rules of etiquette and class, certain spheres of life were regarded as private: it was a breach of etiquette to intrude or permit intrusion on them. Today, however, one must be prepared to open up on cross-examination almost any sphere in which the peer-group may become interested. It may become fashionable, as some articles in the "Profile of Youth" series in the *Ladies' Home Journal* have shown, for young girls to discuss their rivals' necking techniques with their particular partner. While the game of post office is old, the breakdown of privacy for reasonably serious love-making is new. Dating at twelve and thirteen, the child is early made aware of the fact that his taste in emotions as well as in consumer goods must be socialized and available for small talk. Whereas etiquette built barriers between people, socialized exchange of consumer taste requires that privacy either be given up, or be kept, like a liberal theologian's God, in some interstices of one's nature. Before the peer-group jury there is no privilege against self-incrimination.

The same forces that consolidate the socialization of tastes also make for more socialized standards of performance. The other-directed child, learning to play the piano, is in daily competition with studio stars. He cannot remember a period when either his peers or their adult guides were not engaged in comparing his performance with these models. Whatever he attempts—an artistic accomplishment, a manner of speaking, a sleight-of-hand trick—the peer-group is on hand to identify it in some way and to pass judgment on it with the connoisseurship typical of the mass-media audience. Soon enough this process becomes internalized, and the child feels himself in competition with Eddie Duchin or Horowitz even if no one else is around. Hence it is difficult for the other-directed child to cultivate a highly personalized gift: the standards are too high, and there is little private time for maturation.

The newer pattern of popularity depends less on ability to play an instrument than on ability to express the proper musical preferences. In the fall of 1947 I conducted some interviews among teenagers in Chicago concerning their tastes in popular music and also consulted professional musicians, juke-box listings, and other sources to round out my impressions. My interest was principally in seeing how these young people used their musical interests in the process of peer-group adjustment. Like the "trading cards" which symbolize competitive consumption for the eight- to eleven-year-olds, the collection of records seemed to be one way of establishing one's relatedness to the group, just as the ability to hum current tunes was part of the popularity kit. The requirements were stiffer among girls than boys, though the latter were not exempt. Tunes meant people: roads to people, remembrances of them. At the same time the teen-agers showed great anxiety about having the "right" preferences. When I had the occasion to interview a group its individual members looked around to see what the others thought before committing themselves—at least as to specific songs or records, if not as to a general type of music, such as symphonic or hillbilly, where they might be certain as to their group's reactions. Readers who have not themselves observed the extent of this fear of nonconformity may be inclined to dismiss it by remarking that young people have always been conformists in their groups. True; yet it seems to me that the point is one of degree and that the need for musical conformity is today much more specialized and demanding than it was in an earlier era, when some children could be, or were forced by their parents to be, musical, and others could leave music alone.

Even among those interviewed who took piano lessons musical interest as such seemed virtually nonexistent. One boy of fourteen did appear to have genuine musical interests, playing "classics" on the piano. His mother told the interviewer, however, that she was not letting him practice too much lest he get out of step with the other boys, and was insisting that he excel in sports. "I hope to keep him a normal boy," she said. These research experiences seem to hint that preferences in the consumption field are not viewed as a development of the human ability to relate oneself discriminatingly to cultural objects. For the objects are hardly given meaning in private and personal values when they are so heavily used as counters in a preferential method of relating oneself to others. The cultural objects, whatever their nature, are mementos that somehow remain unhumanized by the force of a genuinely fetishistic attachment.

Moving somewhere beyond mere taste-exchanging are those opinion leaders who try to influence verdicts as well as to repeat them—a dangerous game indeed. The risks are minimized, however, by playing within the limits imposed by marginal differentiation. Thus my interviews showed that each age group within a limited region and class had its own musical taste; the younger ones, for instance, liked "sweet" stuff that was "corn" to those slightly older. Within this general trend a girl might decide that she could not *stand* Vaughn Monroe or that Perry Como was tops. If she expressed herself so forcibly in detail, the chances were that she was, or wanted to be, an opinion leader. For many of the young people did not express any strong likes or specific dislikes —though they might share a strong revulsion against a whole taste range, like hot jazz or hillbilly. These latter were the opinion followers, scarcely capable even of marginal differentiation.

The other-directed person's tremendous outpouring of energy is channeled into the ever expanding frontiers of consumption, as the inner-directed person's energy was channeled relentlessly into production. Inner-directed patterns often discouraged consumption for adults as well as children. But at other times, and especially in the higher social strata less affected by Puritan asceticism, the inner-directed person consumed—with time out, so to speak, for saving and for good behavior —as relentlessly as he (or his progenitors) produced. Most clearly in the case of upper-class conspicuous consumption, he lusted for possessions and display, once the old tradition-directed restraints had worn away. He pursued clear acquisition and consumption goals with a fierce individualism. To be sure, his goals were socially determined, but less by a contemporary union of consumers than by inherited patterns of desire, hardly less stable than the desire for money itself. Goals such as fine houses, fine horses, fine women, fine objets d'art—these could be investments because their value scarcely changed in the scale of consumption preference.

These relatively stable and individualistic pursuits are today being replaced by the fluctuating tastes which the other-directed person accepts from his peer-group. Moreover, many of the desires that drove men to work and to madness in societies depending on inner-direction are now satisfied relatively easily; they are incorporated into the standard of living taken for granted by millions. But the craving remains. It is a craving for the satisfactions others appear to attain, an *objectless craving*. The consumer today has most of his potential individuality trained out of him by his membership in the consumers' union. He is kept within his consumption limits not by goal-directed but by other-directed guidance, kept from splurging too much by fear of others' envy, and from consuming too little by his own envy of the others.

Today there is no fast line that separates these consumption patterns of the adult world from those of the child, except the consumption objects themselves. The child may consume comics or toys while the adult consumes editorials and cars; more and more both consume in the same way. In the consumers' union of the peer-group the child's discipline as a consumer begins today very early in life—and lasts late. The inner-directed child was supposed to be job-minded even if the job itself was not clear in his mind. Today the future occupation of all moppets is to be skilled consumers.

This is visible early in children's play-at-consumption, facilitated by a noticeable increase in the range of children's toys. Added to boys' toys, for example production-imitating equipment like trucks and steam shovels or toy soldiers and miniature war matériel, is a whole new range of objects modeled after the service trades: laundry trucks, toy telephones, service stations, and so forth. Added to girls' toys, the doll and her wardrobe, are juvenile make-up outfits and voice recorders.

These props of the child's playtime hours, however, are not so striking as the increasing rationalization of children's preferences in everything they consume. In the period of inner-direction children accepted trade-marked cereals largely because that was what was set for them at table. Today they eat Wheaties, or some other breakfast food, to the tune of some specific reason that all can talk about: "Wheaties makes champions." And comics, children will say if pressed, "relax champions." In this way the other-directed child rapidly learns that there always is and always must be a reason for consuming anything. One "reason" is that the commodity he is consuming is the "best" in its line. As a child develops as a consumer trainee, advertising no longer is given all the credit for answering the question of what is the best in its line. The product approved by most of the others, or by a suitable testimonial from a peer consumer, becomes the "best." The most popular products, by this formula, are the products that happen to be used by the most popular. And to be sure, these pace setters themselves have a "reason," often enough picked out from the mass media, if not from the advertising pages; thus the hunt for the reason goes on in an endless regress. Blake wrote: "The child's toys and the old man's reasons/ Are the fruits of the two seasons." In the consumers' union, toys and reasons become amalgamated and . . . the line between childhood and age tends to become an amorphous one.

These patterns place extra burdens on girls, partly because women are the accepted consumption leaders in our society, partly because women, much more than men, feel pressure to play any role they are accepted in by the men. At every social level boys are permitted a greater amount of aggression than girls; they are also permitted a wider range of preferences and can get by with a good deal of aggressive resistance to the taste-exchanging process.

Finally, the child consumer trainee becomes a consumer tutor in the home circle, "bringing up" mother as well as father. *Life* magazine once ran a leading article on "Teen-age Fun," showing the etiquettes and pastimes prevailing in certain American cities; these pastimes were news even to some recent high-school graduates. Teen-agers must initiate adults rather than vice versa; typical is the case, also cited in *Life*, where teachers at a Denver high school imitated the idiomatic greeting style of the "most popular" boy.

"US" — THE BEST AND THE WORST OF IT

RICHARD HOGGART

In any discussion of working-class attitudes much is said about the group-sense, that feeling of being not so much an individual with 'a way to make' as one of a group whose members are all roughly level and likely to remain so. I avoid the word 'community' at this stage because its overtones seem too simply favourable; they may lead to an under-estimation of the harsher tensions and sanctions of working-class groups.

Certainly working-class people have a strong sense of being members of a group, and just as certainly that sense involves the assumption that it is important to be friendly, co-operative, neighbourly. 'We are all in the same boat'; 'it is no use fighting one another'; but 'in unity is strength'. One's mind goes back to the movements of the last century, to the hundreds of 'Friendly' societies, to the mottoes of the unions: the Amalgamated Society of Engineers, with 'Be United and Industrious'; the Provisional Committee of the National Union of Gas Workers and General Labourers choosing, in the late 'nineties, 'Love, Unity and Fidelity'. And the 'Love' in the last recalls the strength which this sense of unity acquired from a Christian background.

The friendly group tradition seems to me to have its strength initially from the ever-present evidence, in the close, huddled, intimate conditions of life, that we are, in fact, all in the same position. You are bound to be close to people with whom, for example, you share a lavatory in a common yard. That 'luv' which is still the most common form of address, and not only to people in their own class, by tram and bus conductors and by shop-keepers, is used automatically, but still indicates something. To call anyone 'neighbourly' or 'right sociable' is to offer a high compliment; a club may be praised because it is a 'real sociable place'; the most important recommendation for lodgings or seaside 'digs' is that they are 'sociable', and this outweighs overcrowding; and a church is just as likely to be weighed in the same scales. 'Ar' Elsie got married at All Saints',' they will say, of the church they chose from several nearby, not one of which can claim them as parishioners — 'it's a nice friendly church.' The story of a Christmas party at the local will end, 'It was a luvly night. Everybody got real friendly.' Good neighbourliness consists not just in 'doing fair by each other', but in being 'obliging' or 'always ready to oblige'. If the neighbours in a new area seem to lack the right kind of neighbourliness, the newcomer will insist that she 'just can't settle'.

The sense of a group warmth exercises a powerful hold, and continues to be missed when individuals have moved, financially and

From *The Uses of Literacy* by Richard Hoggart. Oxford University Press, Inc., 1957. Reprinted by permission of Oxford University Press, Inc., and Chatto & Windus, Ltd.

probably geographically, out of the working-classes. I have noticed that self-made men now living in villas — grocers who have done well and own a small chain of local shops; jobbing builders who have advanced so far as to be putting up fields of private 'semis' — like to join the crowd at football matches. They drive up in a car now and wear shaggily prosperous Harris tweed, but many of them still go on the terraces rather than in the stands. I imagine they enjoy recapturing something of the mateyness of the ranks, much as a commissioned Q.M. will usually be found in the non-commissioned bar at a unit dance.

This is not a very self-conscious sense of community; it is worlds away from the 'fellowship in service' of some of the socially purposive movements. It does not draw its main strength from — indeed, it precedes, and is more elementary than — the belief in the need to improve each other's lot jointly which gave rise to such organisations as the Co-operative movement. It arises chiefly from a knowledge, born of living close together, that one is inescapably part of a group, from the warmth and security that knowledge can give, from the lack of change in the group and from the frequent need to 'turn to a neighbour' since services cannot often be bought. It starts from the feeling that life is hard, and that 'our sort' will usually get 'the dirty end of the stick'. In most people it does not develop into a conscious sense of being part of 'the working-class movement': the 'Co-ops' are today less typical of the outlook of the majority in the working-classes than the small privately-owned corner-shops serving a couple of streets. The attitude finds expression in a great number of formal phrases — 'Y've got to share and share alike'; 'y've got to 'elp one another out'; 'y've got to 'elp lame dogs'; 'we must all pull together'; 'it's sink or swim together'. But for the most part these are actually spoken only on special occasions, at singsongs and festivals.

The solidarity is helped by the lack of scope for the growth of ambition. After the age of eleven, when the scholarship boys and girls go off to the grammar-school, the rest look increasingly outward to the real life which will begin at fifteen, to the life with the group of older men and women which, for the first few years after school, forms the most powerfully educative force they know. Once at work there is for most no sense of a career, of the possibilities of promotion. Jobs are spread around horizontally, not vertically; life is not seen as a climb, nor work as the main interest in it. There is still a respect for the good craftsman. But the man on the next bench is not regarded as an actual or potential competitor. It is not difficult to understand, therefore, the strong emotional hold of the 'go slow — don't put the other man out of a job' attitude. Working-class people number several vices among their occupational attitudes, but not those of the 'go-getter' or the 'livewire', nor those of 'the successful smilers the city can use'; 'keen types' are mistrusted.

Whatever one does, horizons are likely to be limited; in any case, working-class people add quickly, money doesn't seem to make people happier, nor does power. The 'real' things are the human and companionable things—home and family affection, friendship and being able to 'enjoy y'self': 'money's not the real thing', they say; and 'Life isn't worth living if y'sweating for extra money all t' time.' Working-class songs often ask for love, friends, a good home; they always insist that money does not matter.

There are exceptions: those who still hold to the line Matthew Arnold satirised—'Ever remember, my dear Dan, that you should look forward to being one day manager of that concern.' Among some of the more avidly respectable this shows in the way boys are urged to 'get on', to pass that scholarship, to be careful of their 'penmanship' since gentlemen in offices like 'a neat hand'. And there are sharp-eyed little men whom the rest regard with charity as wrong-headed, who 'never let a penny go'. They take on extra work at nights and weekends and are always anxious to make an extra bob-or-two at the hour when others are having a good time. These people are not usually moving upward or out of their class; they are running agitatedly round inside it, amassing the unconsidered trifles which are always about.

The attitude to bachelors probably shows as well as anything the tolerance which is extended to established exceptions within the group. The occasional bachelor in any neighbourhood is likely to be living at home with a widowed mother or in the family of a married sister. Such a bachelor can usually be found on most nights in a fixed corner of the local pub or club, since he is likely to be quiet and regular in his habits. Perhaps a certain kind of shyness has helped to make him a bachelor; he is in some ways a lone bird, but he cannot be called lonely. He is respected in the neighbourhood. He is not thought of as a man-on-the-loose and therefore as a potential Don Juan. He probably figures, rather, as a harmless uncle of indeterminate age, one who is 'always very polite' and 'quiet-spoken' and is said to be good to his mother or sister. There is sometimes a touch of amusement in this attitude, as though behind it is a feeling that old So-and-so has been a little scared of the physical relations with a woman which marriage entails. But this is not normally an expression of scorn; nor is such a bachelor likely to be regarded as selfish or queer or antisocial. Some men, it is felt, are born bachelors; they are therefore a real part of the neighbourhood.

That minority who become conscious of their class-limitations and take up some educational activity—so as to 'work for their class' or 'improve themselves'—tend to be ambiguously regarded. The respect for the 'scholar' (like the doctor and the parson) to some extent remains. I remember sitting, not long after I had won a scholarship, next to a middle-aged bachelor miner in a working-men's club. Whenever he paid for his rum-and-hot-milk he passed me a half-crown from the

change. I tried to refuse: 'Tek it, lad, and use it for thee education,'
he said. 'Ah'm like all miners. Ah only waste t'bluddy stuff.' On the
other hand, there is often a mistrust of 'book-learning'. What good does
it do you? Are you any better off (i.e. happier) as a clerk? or as a teacher?
Parents who refuse, as a few still do, to allow their children to take up
scholarships are not always thinking of the fact that they would have to
be fed and clothed for much longer; at the back is this vaguely formulated but strong doubt of the value of education. That doubt acquires
some of its force from the group-sense itself: for the group seeks to
conserve, and may impede an inclination in any of its members to make
a change, to leave the group, to be different.

The group, I suggested, works against the idea of change. It does more
than this: it imposes on its members an extensive and sometimes harsh
pressure to conform. Those who become different, through education
and in one or two other ways, may often be allowed for, and I do not
want to suggest a strong automatic hostility to any departure at all from
the group or its attitudes. Indeed, one of the marked qualities of working-class groups is a wide tolerance in some things; but it is a tolerance
which works freely only if the chief class assumptions are shared.

    The group is close: it is likely to regard someone originally from
a town forty miles away as 'not one of us' for years; and I have seen it
unconsciously and insensitively cruel for a long time—and kind, too,
in many things—towards a foreign wife. The group watches, often
with a low unallowingness, an unimaginative cruelty which can make for
much unhappiness. 'Ah wunder what she meant by that?'; 'Ooh, don't
things get about!'; 'It doesn't do to let others know too much' are common phrases. Wondering what the neighbours will say is as common
here as elsewhere; perhaps more common, in its own way. Working-
class people watch and are watched in a manner which, because horizons are limited, will often result in a mistaken, and lowering, interpretation of what the neighbours do. A working-class woman may be
known to act as a 'sitter-in' at the place where she cleans all day; but if
she is brought home at the end of the evening she is likely to ask to
be left a couple of streets away. What would the neighbours say if they
saw her coming home with a man?

    The group does not like to be shocked or attacked from within.
There may be little of the competitive urge to keep up with the Joneses,
but just as powerful can be the pressure to keep down with the Atkinses.
Hence the frequent use, long before advertisers made so much of its
value, of the appeal to the ordinary and the unextreme, 'any decent
man would . . .', 'it's not natural', 'I like 'im; 'e's always the same'.
If you want to be one of the group you must not try to 'alter people's
ways', and you will be disliked if you imply a criticism of their ways by

acting differently yourself; if you infringe the taboos you will run into disfavour:

> *There's such a thing as mass thought, you know. If you think the same as the man next to you, you're all right. But if you don't, if you're seen bringing in a book [i.e. into work] or anything like that, you're not. It's very difficult to stand up to ridicule.*

All classes require conformity to some degree; it needs to be stressed here because there is a tendency to stress upper- and middle-class conformity and to regard the working-classes as more free from it.

Acting beyond the ideas of the group, 'acting posh', 'giving y'self airs', 'getting above y'self', 'being lah-de-dah', 'thinking y'self too good for other people', 'being stuck-up', 'turning y'nose up at other people', 'acting like Lady Muck'—all these are much disliked and not very sensitively discriminated. The genuine 'toff' might be found amusing, as he was fifty years ago, and the 'real gentleman' (who will talk to you 'just like I'm talking to you now') is still likely to be admired, even though he is obviously one of 'Them'. Neither inspires a feeling as strong as that aroused by the person who is putting on 'posh' airs because he thinks they are better than working-class airs. 'Ay, and what do you dislike most, then?' asks Wilfred Pickles. 'Stuck-up fowk.' Roars of applause. 'Jolly good! and will you just tell me what you like most?' 'Good neighbourly fowk.' Increased applause. '. . . and very right too. Give her the money.'

Whatever their origins, Gracie Fields and Wilfred Pickles hardly qualify as members of the working-classes now. But both are still warmly 'alright' because they remain of them in spirit and have conquered the 'moneyed classes' with their working-class wit and attitudes. 'They love Wilfred Pickles down South,' working-class people will say, meaning that people not of their class love him: there is some pride that their values, those of the unpolished and 'straight', are appreciated by other classes. Their 'comics' have stormed the posh citadels; 'good luck to 'em!'

We frequently hear that the English working-classes are gentle, gentler than those of almost any other country, gentler today than their own parents and grandparents. Undoubtedly there has been a decrease in the amount of sheer brutality in the towns during the last fifty years, a decline in the rough and savage stuff which sometimes made the streets at night and particularly at weekends places to avoid. The hooliganism and rowdyism which caused the police to work in pairs in several areas of many towns have almost gone. We no longer hear, except very occasionally, of bare-fist fights on bits of waste-ground, of broken-bottle fights inside bars, of regular assaults by gangs on girls at fairgrounds, of so much animal drunkenness.

It would be a deluding and foolish archaism which regretted the loss of all this, which assumed that its decline meant the loss of some gusto among the working-classes, that the gentleness is merely a passivity. But that same generation which was often coarse and savage could also be gentle: I think again of my grandmother, who saw brutalities which would shock a woman of almost any class today and was herself often harshly crude. But she, in common with many of her generation, had in some things an admirable gentleness and fineness of discrimination. Perhaps the gentleness we notice is not so much a new feature as an old strain which is more evident, has been allowed more room to operate today. It must have taken generations to develop, is the product of centuries in which people got along pretty well together, were not persistently harassed by the more violent evidences of the powers above them, and felt—however severe their troubles—that law was fairly generally applicable and authority not hopelessly corrupt. I have not forgotten the experiences of the 'Hungry Forties' of the last century; but I think also of the Russian serfs and of the Italian attitude towards civil servants even today. All this has no doubt bred a reasonableness, a remarkably quiet assumption that violence is the last ditch.

If I draw further attention, then, to the strain of coarseness and insensitivity running through working-class life, I do so not to infer that other classes have not their own forms, nor to deny all that is usually said about gentleness, but to restore a balance which we have been inclined to lose during the last twenty years. The evidence must be chosen with unusual care, must not include habits which simply seem coarse by the usage of other classes. Thus, working-class speech and manners in conversation are more abrupt, less provided with emollient phrases than those of other groups: their arguments are often conducted in so rude a way that a stranger might well think that after this, at the worst, fighting would follow, and at the best a permanent ending of relations. I find that even now, if I am not to be misunderstood, I have to modify a habit of carrying on discussion in an 'unlubricated' way, in short sharp jabs that are meant to go home—and yet not meant really to hurt. Neither the phrasing nor the rhythms of working-class speech have the easing and modified quality which, in varying degrees, is characteristic of other classes. The pattern of their speech follows more closely the pattern of emotions they are feeling at the time, whether it be exasperation, as in the rows, or gaiety, as in that occasional shrieking of working-class housewives out for a day at the sea which dismays some who sit in the front gardens of private hotels. There is, of course, a 'calling a spade a spade' arrogance which makes a few working-class people overdo the rougher elements in their speech when with others from a different class.

But working-class life, whatever changes there may have been, is still closer to the ground than that of most other people. [There is] the prevalent grime, the closeness and the difficulties of home life, . . . ; we have to remember as well that the physical conditions of the working-lives of men, and of some women, are often noisy, dirty and smelly. We all know this in our heads, but realise it freshly only if we have to pass through some of those deep caverns in Leeds where the engines clang and hammer ceaselessly and the sparks fly out of huge doorways and men can be seen, black to the shoulders, heaving and straining at hot pieces of metal: or through the huge area in Hull which has a permanent pall of cooking fish-meal over it, seeping through the packed houses. The heavy, rough and beast-of-burden work is still there to be done and working-class people do it. These are not conditions which produce measured tones or the more padded conversational allowances.

Thus the rows which are so much a part of the life of any working-class neighbourhood, and of many working-class families, can be easily misinterpreted. They are understandably a part of the neighbourhood's life: in narrow, terraced streets, with thin party-walls, they could hardly be kept private anyhow, unless they were conducted in very subdued voices. They certainly are not quietly conducted, and so they become one of the interests of the neighbourhood. Children, hearing that 'Old So-and so's up t'street are 'aving a right row', will gather in a group as near as they can. And if a row goes on too long or too noisily for the patience of a neighbour, he can always hammer on the party-wall or rattle a poker on the fire-back.

It would be wrong to assume from this that working-class people are congenitally quarrelsome and continually rowing. Some rows are nasty and distressing, and some families are known to be 'always 'aving rows', and these will probably not be regarded as the most respectable. Many families — perhaps most — will have an occasional row. All this will not be automatically regarded as bringing disrepute to the neighbourhood. It is accepted that disputes — perhaps about the amount of money spent on drinking, perhaps among womenfolk about the sharing of household duties, perhaps about 'another woman' — will arise from time to time, and that they will erupt into vivid, quick, noisy war. In my experience, rows about drinking are the most common, and those about the 'other woman' (or man) the least common.

If I may digress for a moment on this latter aspect: these affairs, as I knew them, seemed generally to concern a man in his late thirties or early forties, a man who was slightly more dapper than his acquaintances, though in the same sort of work. His wife would have lost her physical appeal, so he sought interest elsewhere. Yet the woman he 'took up with' was likely enough to be married herself and of roughly the same age as his own wife — and to a stranger no more attractive physically. The two would probably become drinking companions in a known place. The wife would soon learn what was going on and fierce rows would blow up (on more than one occasion I remember a much more serious development—an early-morning 'bashing' of the man by the injured husband on a piece of waste-ground). The oddest feature of all was that sometimes the two women became friendly, and settled into a relationship which the connections of the husband with each of the women not only did not preclude but seemed to nourish.

Most of the rows I experienced were not thought of as shocking occurrences. Rows of that kind took place in the truly slummy areas, with drunken fights between the menfolk or, worse, between men and women or, worst of all, between women alone. Such events would really shock an ordinary working-class neighbourhood.

I remember too that in our neighbourhood we accepted suicides as a moderately common occurrence. Every so often one heard that So-and-so had 'done 'erself in', or 'done away with 'imself' or 'put 'er 'ead in the gas-oven', since the gas-oven was the most convenient means of self-destruction. I do not know whether suicide took place more often in the sort of groups I am speaking of than in middle-class groups. It did not happen monthly or even every season, and not all attempts suc-ceeded; but it happened sufficiently often to be part of the pattern of life. Among the working-classes it could not be concealed, of course, any more than a row could; everyone quickly knew about it. The fact I want to stress is that suicide was not felt to be simply a personal matter or one confined to the family concerned, but that it was felt to be bound up with the conditions of the common life. Sometimes the cause was that a girl had 'got 'erself into trouble' and for one reason or another could not go through with it: just as often it was that, for those who put their heads on a pillow inside the oven-door, life had become unendurable; they were ill and treatment seemed to be doing no good; they were out of work; or, whatever they did, the debts piled up. This was not long ago. The fact that suicide could be accepted—pitifully but with little suggestion of blame—as a part of the order of existence shows how hard and elemental that life could be.

Does this altogether explain, for example, the way many working-class men speak when no women are present? In part, perhaps; but one has to be careful of special pleading here. George Orwell, noting that working-class men use four-letter words for natural functions freely, says they are obscene but not immoral. But there are degrees and kinds of obscenity, and this sort of conversation is often obscene and nothing else, obscene for the sake of obscenity in a dull, repetitive and brute way. And there are kinds of immorality; such men may use short and direct words about sex which at first are a relief after the allusion of cabaret shows and the literature of sexual sophistication. But they use those words so indiscriminately and talk so preponderantly about sex as often to reveal a calloused sensibility. Listen to them speaking of their sexual adventures and plans; you are likely to feel smothered by the boring animality, the mongrel-dogs-rutting-in-alleyways quality. It is a quality which owes as much to an insensitivity in relations as to a freedom from hypocrisy. To each class its own forms of cruelty and dirt; that of working-class people is sometimes of a gratuitously debasing coarseness.

---

4. Freedom

There is no more glorious and stirring goal in the history of man than the quest for political freedom.

Historically, to obtain freedom has meant to throw off the yoke of tyranny, to liberate the human spirit from repressive economic and social controls. But when the old constraints have been removed, freedom may bring problems. In the first selection that follows, Robert Heilbroner describes the impact of modern technological and political change on developing societies; he discusses their "leap into freedom," which unsettles them and creates anxieties about their future. Psychoanalyst Erich Fromm then asserts that Western man has experienced the same anxieties; and, Fromm maintains, increasing individual choices and political opportunities cause some men to seek escape from the "burdens" of freedom.

How can we educate man to enjoy making decisions in a complex political system? Psychiatrist Robert Lindner pursues but one aspect of this ancient problem. Accepting Freud's thesis that the development of civilization occurs at the cost of human development, Lindner outlines some prescriptions for human rebellion that are designed to break the social chains man has forged for himself and thus liberate his capacity to use the technocracy he has created through self-sacrifice and repression.

THE DESIRE FOR FREEDOM

ROBERT L. HEILBRONER

. . . The revolutionary concept of a meaningful future—of social progress—has finally penetrated to those vast areas of the world which

Pages 79–92: *The Future As History* by Robert L. Heilbroner. Copyright © 1959, 1960 by Robert L. Heilbroner. Reprinted by permission of Harper & Row, Publishers and the William Morris Agency. Title supplied by the editor.

until just recently existed silently and inertly alongside the ferment of the West. And with this change in attitude toward the future, there are being brought about not only the most rapid readjustments in world events, but—with the rising up of the new continents—the very inception of historic change on a truly world scale.

The Terrible Ascent

In its ultimate implications this is perhaps the most important revolution which mankind has ever experienced. Its eventual beneficiaries number more than a billion and a half human beings who are today the *misérables* of the earth.

Yet if their awakening from an agelong slumber marks the turning of a new page for humanity, it is also the commencement of a chapter of tragedy and sorrow. For the metamorphosis from poverty into decency will be a struggle of Herculean proportions and Sisyphian discouragement. Far from leading in a gradual progression toward enlightenment and well-being, it is almost certain to result at first in increased misery, violence, and unrest.

Typically a country which is now entering the mainstream of world history displays a schizophrenic attitude toward the world. In part it nurses its bitter memories of the past; in part it reaches for the future with a naïve enthusiasm. Hopefully and under good leadership, the latter attitude may come to predominate. But corresponding to this energizing shift of mind cannot come a commensurate mobilization of resources. What hinders the advance to the new future is not, so to speak, the lack of an automobile. It is not even the lack of shoes. It is the lack of a road.

Merely to highlight this terrible absence of the wherewithal for advance, let us contrast that most basic resource—power—in India and the United States. In India, in 1953, man and beast produced 65 per cent of all the nation's economic energy, and of the remaining 35 per cent of inanimately produced power almost three-quarters was secured by the burning of dung.[1] In the United States human and animal power together accounted for but one per cent of the nation's economic energy, and the use of primitive animal fuels was zero. As a consequence, India's total electric power supply was only about one-fiftieth of America's, and, on a per-capita basis, less than half of that. The total amount of electric power generated by India would not suffice to light up New York City.

To this typical and crippling lack of power—a lack which can be duplicated in industrial requirements of every description—must be added the further handicap of an absence of the institutions needed for its repair. Nothing like a "capital market" to mobilize savings exists

[1]Wit and Clubok, "Atomic Power Development in India," *Social Research,* Autumn 1958, p. 290.

in most underdeveloped nations. Chronic shortages of foreign ex-change restrict their import programs to a minimum. And perhaps most crippling of all is a lack of adequate *human* resources: workmen who can read and who understand the rhythms of industrial produc-tion, businessmen whose attitude toward business is to produce rather than to gouge, specialists of every variety, government officials who can transcend a tradition of bureaucratic indifference and petty graft. In a word, such societies tend to lack an "economic" population. They are made up of peasants rather than farmers, laborers rather than workers, peddlers and speculators rather than managers, sinecurists rather than government administrators. To be sure, this condition of economic backwardness varies considerably from, say, Mexico, to colonial Africa. But in general outline these maladies of underdevelopment are visible and vitiating in all.

Under these conditions there is only one way in which a massive and rapid economic advance can be begun, much less carried through. It must be done from the top. When men do not know what to do, when by habit they do the wrong things, when they do not understand the signals of the market place, or when this market place does not yet exist, then men must be told what to do. Every emergent nation, in beating its way to progress, must adopt a greater or lesser degree of centralized control over its economy, and the lower down on the scale is its starting point, the greater does that degree of control tend to be.

Thus we find a degree of collectivism vigorously espoused by nearly every underdeveloped nation—sometimes, as in Pakistan or Egypt, of a nationalist military complexion; sometimes, as with India, Indone-sia, Ghana, of socialist leanings. No doubt the ideological preferences of their leaders play a role in this general collectivist orientation. Their bitter past experience with *laissez faire*, their disbelief in the willingness of the capitalist West, even now, to mount a really major effort of eco-nomic assistance, their susceptibility to Marxian optimism—all these factors play their roles. Yet at bottom the appeal of collectivism is not intellectual or emotional. It is functional.

For even if the backward nations wished to develop under the aegis of capitalism, capitalism is not so easily achieved. It rests on inner motivations, inner disciplines, on learned habits of economic "ration-ality" which cannot be inculcated into a peasant population overnight. In England it took generations before the uprooted yeomanry stopped burning down the factories they despised. In Prussia, Frederick the Great used to complain that his merchants were so timid and unventure-some that he had to drag them to their profits "by their noses and ears." Thus capitalism must grow up slowly, out of the experience of genera-tions—and it is even doubtful in today's world if it would grow at all. Certainly it cannot be imposed, full-blown. But collectivism can. Peas-ants, moneylenders, petty bureaucrats can be told—ordered—to do what must be done. As a means of beginning the huge transformation of a society, an economic authoritarian command has every advantage over the incentives of enterprise.

Hence the very least that one can expect of the new economies is a powerful and prominent degree of central direction and control within a "free enterprise" milieu. But the logic of events does not stop with this arrangement. On the contrary, in the setting of underdevelopment, powerful forces are likely to press "mixed economies" in the direction of political and economic extremes.

For the enthusiasm of the initial awakening of a people soon outruns the reality of its sluggish progress. No matter how heroic the efforts of its regime, no underdeveloped nation can hope to make headway quickly. Indeed the fearsome possibility is that at first its condition may deteriorate. The early stages of the new industrialization will only add to the social dislocation which began under colonialism. The initial heavy investments will weigh upon rather than uplift the general population. Not least, the pressures of population growth, which are the main enemy of progress in nearly every underdeveloped land, will grow worse as broad health and sanitation measures take effect.

Thus the road to progress may well be more terrible than the roadless and mindless existence of the past. Nevertheless, once the great march has begun, it is no longer possible to turn back. The changes in the balance of the old static society cannot be undone. There is no choice but to tread the road to its conclusion — however long and agonizing the journey may be. . . .

Thus economic development, in its agonizing slow pace, will not give rise to a glad acquiescence in the future and a sense of relief that progress is now on the march. On the contrary, every step forward is apt to worsen the mood of disaffection, to stir the fires of impatience. Economic development in its early stages is not a process of alleviating discontent. Initially it is the cause of deepening it.

The "Leap into Freedom"

Needless to say, all this lends a dark color to the outlook for a mild economic transition. High hopes, once aroused, are not so easily retired, and a government which does not satisfy the aspirations on which it rides into power will soon give way to another which will promise to do more.

This leads to two likely prospects. The first is the rise of authoritarian regimes in the underdeveloped nations. For the capacity for action of parliamentary governments is apt to prove inadequate to the heroic demands of rapid development. Parliamentary governments, even in those rare cases where they do not merely represent the privileged classes of peasant nations, naturally act to *slow down* the pace of social change by seeking to accommodate minority interests—a function which may be highly desirable once a level of tolerable social satisfaction has been reached, but hardly one which is apt to commend itself to a newly aroused and highly dissatisfied people.

Even in Western governments, built upon fairly stable social foundations, we have seen how vulnerable and weak are parliamentary regimes in times of stress, unless they produce their own "strong men" —as witness the cases of pre-Mussolini Italy and pre-Hitler Germany, of republican Spain and postwar France. Among the underdeveloped nations, bereft of any tradition of democratic compromise and cohesion, this tendency is a thousandfold multiplied. Thus we find the emergence of the soldier-ruler: in Pakistan, in Egypt, in China, in Burma, in Taiwan, in the succession of Latin-American junta governments. And while this array clearly reveals that not every authoritarian government is itself an agency for economic transformation, it stands to reason that, with the added stresses and strains of rapid development, the "attractions" of authority are made all the greater.

But the second prospect is even more sobering. It is the likelihood that the predominant authoritarianism will veer increasingly to the extreme Left.

For in their situations of genuine frustration, one lesson will not be lost upon the underdeveloped nations. This is the fact that two peasant countries in the twentieth century have succeeded in making the convulsive total social effort which alone seems capable of breaking through the thousand barriers of scarcity, ineptitude, indifference, inertia. These are the Soviet Union and now, even more impressively, China. It might be objected that the underdeveloped nations could also fasten their gaze on other nations, such as Western Germany or Japan, which have also recently shown startling rates of growth. But these are nations with their initial industrial "transformations" behind them. They began where the underdeveloped regions now seek to arrive. Russia to a considerable degree and China even more unmistakably began at scratch.

We are only beginning to appreciate the magnitude of the Chinese effort. Until recently we have been so repelled by the severity of the Chinese communist methods, with their Spartan communes, that we have overlooked what is the most significant fact about these methods. This is the attainment of what seems to be by far the largest rate of economic growth ever achieved by any peasant nation. According to the best estimates we now have (which discount China's own extravagant claims), China's per-capita output has been growing since 1952 at a rate of over 6 per cent a year.[2] This is a pace of advance which is

[2] A. Doak Barnett, *Communist Economic Strategy: The Rise of Mainland China* (National Planning Association, 1959), table 2. See also William V. Hollister, *Chinese Gross National Product and Social Accounts, 1950–1957* (Illinois, 1958); and Wilfred Malenbaum, "India and China: Contrasts in Development Performance," *American Economic Review,* June 1959.

between *double* and *triple* the rate of growth thus far achieved by India under non-collectivist conditions.

Meanwhile an equally startling performance has been evinced by the Soviet Union. Until the present decade of world history, the generally accepted paragon of economic progress was the United States. This is no longer true. Mr. Allen W. Dulles, comparing our performance with the Soviets has noted:

> *Whereas Soviet gross national product was about 35 percent of that of the United States in 1950 . . . by 1962 it may be about 50 percent of our own. This means that the Soviet economy has been growing and is expected to grow through 1962 at a rate roughly twice that of the economy of the United States.*[3]

To be sure, what strikes us in considering both instances of economic growth is the immense human price which has been paid for material progress. Russia's social agonies of development—the use of forced labor, the mass executions, the bludgeoning of the peasant into collectives and the Stakhanovist methods of securing industrial discipline—all these are well known. In the case of China, the human cost is even more nakedly revealed in the use of human labor as "capital." Essentially China has achieved its startling increases in output—in the case of food, a tripling of crops since 1949; in the case of steel, a sevenfold increase in the same period—by massively applying organized human effort in the same fashion and with the same huge end results as the Pharaohs used in constructing the pyramids. . . .

There is no blinking the arduousness of this choice. Even existence at the very margin of life can be worsened by the extreme efforts of an all-out development drive, for people at the margin of existence can be driven over that margin into premature death. But this hideous price must be weighed against a continuation of the present state of affairs. In this truly anguishing choice, our own preferences for gradualism may well reflect nothing but our inability to appreciate the intolerable condition of life as it now exists in much of the world. Looking at the alternatives from below rather than from above, it is understandable that it may not be the *price* but the *promise* of rapid advance which exerts the more powerful sway. As the late John Foster Dulles has written: "We can talk eloquently about liberty and freedom, and about human rights and individual freedoms, and about the dignity and worth of the human personality, but most of our vocabulary derives from a period when our own society was individualistic. Consequently it has little meaning to those who live under conditions where individualism means early death."[4]

[3]*New York Times*, April 29, 1958.
[4]John Foster Dulles, *War or Peace* (New York, 1950), p. 257.

It would be both foolish and dangerous to maintain that all under-developed countries "must" sooner or later succumb to a rigorous communist collectivism in order to effect a major economic advance. Between one backward nation and another there are vast differences in needs, resolves, resources. One cannot easily generalize over a spectrum that includes such different cases as Brazil and Burma, Libya and Turkey. In many of the backward nations the critical determining factor may be the "historic force" of a commanding, but democratic and gradualist figure, such as a Nehru or a Muñoz Marin. . . .

But it is not enough to come to a halt with this prospect for communism's expansion among the backward nations. In terms of anticipating the trends of world history, what is even more important for us to realize is that individual economic improvement, even at best, is not likely to come fast enough to satisfy the aspirations of the people. For in every underdeveloped nation, economic growth—with the exception of an increase in foodstuffs—is, at first, essentially a process of accumulating capital goods under forced draft, of alleviating as quickly as possible the crippling capital scarcity of the past. This necessarily means that the pace of *tangible* advance in the living standards of the masses is very slow, and nearly as imperceptible in communist nations with huge growth rates as in "mixed-economy" nations with smaller rates. Dams, reservoirs, roads, education, steel mills—all the basic necessities for advance—cannot be consumed, do not replace ragged clothes and hovels.

In this situation even the most sincerely motivated and efficient government is apt to find itself with an impatient and dissatisfied populace. Thus despite—or worse, because of—their all-out economic and social effort, fast-growing but still impoverished economies are likely to be impelled to seek incentives other than the self-sustaining impetus of economic improvement. These incentives may take the form of sheer compulsion, as has been the case in the communist states. But there is as well another means of mobilizing the stamina and morale needed to sustain the great ascent. This is the conscious direction of aspirations *away* from material ends, toward glory, conquest, or faith. In a word, it is the employment of a fierce and often bellicose nationalism as a compensation for the inevitable disappointments of the early stages of economic growth.

We have seen the development of such a nationalism in virtually every nation which has begun the steep economic climb. In China as well as in Russia there has been recourse not only to a deliberately stimulated patriotism, but to the encouragement of smoldering grudges against colonialism and capitalism. In dictatorships of a more rightist leaning, such as Egypt, nationalistic incentives and diversions of a still cruder nature have been used: the reawakening of ancient loyalties and racialisms, the fanning of atavistic military and religious ambitions, the appeal, as in the days of heroic history, to the memories of the past.

It is probable that a degree of inflamed nationalism is an inseparable concomitant of forced economic development. The unfortunate result is that an era which could be a prelude to building for a great future runs the grave risk of becoming instead a period of heightened tensions and increased chances for the destruction even of present frail standards. The spread of high aspirations to the peoples whose conditions are now the least human on earth is a great and irreversible drama of our times, but during our lifetimes the drama promises to be as tragic as it may ultimately be ennobling.

THE BURDENS OF FREEDOM

Erich Fromm

Man first emerged from the animal world as a freak of nature. Having lost most of the instinctive equipment which regulates the animal's activities, he was more helpless, less well equipped for the fight for survival, than most animals. Yet he had developed a capacity for thought, imagination and self-awareness, which was the basis for transforming nature and himself. For many thousands of generations man lived by food gathering and hunting. He was still tied to nature, and afraid of being cast out from her. He identified himself with animals and worshiped these representatives of nature as his gods. After a long period of slow development, man began to cultivate the soil, to create a new social and religious order based on agriculture and animal husbandry. During this period he worshiped goddesses as the bearers of natural fertility, experienced himself as the child dependent on the fertility of the earth, on the life-giving breast of Mother. At a time some four thousand years ago, a decisive turn in man's history took place. He took a new step in the long-drawn-out process of his emergence from nature. He severed the ties with nature and with Mother, and set himself a new goal, that of being fully born, of being fully awake, of being fully human; of being free. Reason and conscience became the principles which were to guide him; his aim was a society bound by the bonds of brotherly love, justice and truth, a new and truly human home to take the place of the irretrievably lost home in nature. . . .

Yet today, when man seems to have reached the beginning of a new, richer, happier human era, his existence and that of the generations to follow is more threatened than ever. How is this possible?

Condensed from Chapter 9 from *The Sane Society* by Erich Fromm. Copyright © 1955 by Erich Fromm. Reprinted with permission of Holt, Rinehart and Winston, Inc., and Routledge & Kegan Paul, Ltd. Title supplied by the editor.

Man had won his freedom from clerical and secular authorities, he stood alone with his reason and his conscience as his only judges, but he was afraid of the newly won freedom; he had achieved "freedom from"—without yet having achieved "freedom to"—to be himself, to be productive, to be fully awake. Thus he tried to escape from freedom. His very achievement, the mastery over nature, opened up the avenues for his escape. . . .

The new era started with the idea of individual initiative. Indeed, the discoverers of new worlds and sea lanes in the sixteenth and seventeenth centuries, the pioneers of science, and the founders of new philosophies, the statesmen and philosophers of the great English, French and American revolutions, and eventually, the industrial pioneers, and even the robber barons showed marvelous individual initiative. But with the bureaucratization and managerialization of Capitalism, it is exactly the individual initiative that is disappearing. Bureaucracy has little initiative, that is its nature; nor have automatons. The cry for individual initiative as an argument for Capitalism is at best a nostalgic yearning, and at worst a deceitful slogan used against those plans for reform which are based on the idea of truly human individual initiative. Modern society has started out with the vision of creating a culture which would fulfil man's needs; it has as its ideal the harmony between the individual and social needs, the end of the conflict between human nature and the social order. One believed one would arrive at this goal in two ways; by the increased productive technique which permitted feeding everybody satisfactorily, and by a rational, objective picture of man and of his real needs. Putting it differently, the aim of the efforts of modern man was to create a sane society. More specifically, this meant a society whose members have developed their reason to that point of objectivity which permits them to see themselves, others, nature, in their true reality, and not distorted by infantile omniscience or paranoid hate. It meant a society whose members have developed to a point of independence when they know the difference between good and evil, where they make their own choices, where they have convictions rather than opinions, faith rather than superstitions or nebulous hopes. It meant a society whose members have developed the capacity to love their children, their neighbors, all men, themselves, all of nature; who can feel one with all, yet retain their sense of individuality and integrity; who transcend nature by creating, not by destroying.

So far, we have failed. We have not bridged the gap between a minority which realized these goals and tried to live according to them, and the majority whose mentality is far back, in the Stone Age, in totemism, in idol worship, in feudalism. Will the majority be converted to sanity—or will it use the greatest discoveries of human reason for its own purposes of unreason and insanity? Will we be able to create a vision of the good, sane life, which will stir the life forces of those afraid of marching forward? This time, mankind is at one crossroad where the wrong step could be the last step.

In the middle of the twentieth century, two great social colossi have developed which, being afraid of each other, seek security in ever-increasing military rearmament. The United States and her allies are wealthier; their standard of living is higher, their interest in comfort and pleasure is greater than that of their rivals, the Soviet Union and her satellites, and China. Both rivals claim that their system promises final salvation for man, guarantees the paradise of the future. Both claim that the opponent represents the exact opposite to himself, and that his system must be eradicated — in the short or long run — if mankind is to be saved. Both rivals speak in terms of nineteenth-century ideals. The West in the name of the ideas of the French Revolution, of liberty, reason, individualism. The East in the name of the socialist ideas of solidarity, equality. They both succeed in capturing the imagination and the fanatical allegiance of hundreds of millions of people.

There is today a decisive difference between the two systems. In the Western world there is freedom to express ideas critical of the existing system. In the Soviet world criticism and expression of different ideas is suppressed by brutal force. Hence, the Western world carries within itself the possibility for peaceful progressive transformation, while in the Soviet world such possibilities are almost non-existent; in the Western world the life of the individual is free from the terror of imprisonment, torture or death, which confront any member of the Soviet society who has not become a well-functioning automaton. Indeed, life in the Western world has been, and is even now sometimes as rich and joyous as it has ever been anywhere in human history; life in the Soviet system can never by joyous, as indeed it can never be where the executioner watches behind the door.

But without ignoring the tremendous differences between free Capitalism and authoritarian Communism today, it is short-sighted not to see the similarities, especially as they will develop in the future. Both systems are based on industrialization, their goal is ever-increasing economic efficiency and wealth. They are societies run by a managerial class, and by professional politicians. They both are thoroughly materialistic in their outlook, regardless of Christian ideology in the West and secular messianism in the East. They organize man in a centralized system, in large factories, political mass parties. Everybody is a cog in the machine, and has to function smoothly. In the West, this is achieved by a method of psychological conditioning, mass suggestion, monetary rewards. In the East by all this, plus the use of terror. It is to be assumed that the more the Soviet system develops economically, the less severely will it have to exploit the majority of the population, hence the more can terror be replaced by methods of psychological manipulation. The West develops rapidly in the direction of Huxley's *Brave New World*, the East *is* today Orwell's "1984." But both systems tend to converge.

What, then, are the prospects for the future? The first, and perhaps most likely possibility, is that of atomic war. The most likely outcome of such a war is the destruction of industrial civilization, and the regression of the world to a primitive agrarian level. Or, if the destruction should not prove to be as thorough as many specialists in the field believe, the result will be the necessity for the victor to organize and dominate the whole world. This could only happen in a centralized state based on force—and it would make little difference whether Moscow or Washington were the seat of government. But, unfortunately, even the avoidance of war alone does not promise a bright future. In the development of both Capitalism and of Communism as we can visualize them in the next fifty or a hundred years, the process of automatization and alienation will proceed. Both systems are developing into managerial societies, their inhabitants well fed, well clad, having their wishes satisfied, and not having wishes which cannot be satisfied; automatons, who follow without force, who are guided without leaders, who make machines which act like men and produce men who act like machines; men, whose reason deteriorates while their intelligence rises, thus creating the dangerous situation of equipping man with the greatest material power without the wisdom to use it.

This alienation and automatization leads to an ever-increasing insanity. Life has no meaning, there is no joy, no faith, no reality. Everybody is "happy"—except that he does not feel, does not reason, does not love.

In the nineteenth century the problem was that *God is dead*; in the twentieth century the problem is that *man is dead*. In the nineteenth century inhumanity meant cruelty; in the twentieth century it means schizoid self-alienation. The danger of the past was that men became slaves. The danger of the future is that men may become robots. True enough, robots do not rebel. But given man's nature, robots cannot live and remain sane, they become "Golems," they will destroy their world and themselves because they cannot stand any longer the boredom of a meaningless life.

Our dangers are war and robotism. What is the alternative? To get out of the rut in which we are moving, and to take the next step in the birth and self-realization of humanity. The first condition is the abolishment of the war threat hanging over all of us now and paralyzing faith and initiative. We must take the responsibility for the life of all men, and develop on an international scale what all great countries have developed internally, a relative sharing of wealth and a new and more just division of economic resources. This must lead eventually to forms of international economic co-operation and planning, to forms of world government and to complete disarmament. We must retain the industrial method. But we must decentralize work and state so as to give it *human proportions*, and permit centralization only to an optimal point which is necessary because of the requirements of industry. In the economic sphere we need co-management of all who work in an enterprise, to permit their active and responsible participation. The new forms for such participation can be found. In the political sphere, return to the town meetings, by creating thousands of small face-to-face groups, which are well informed, which discuss, and whose decisions are integrated in a new "lower house." A cultural renaissance must combine work education for the young, adult education and a new system of popular art and secular ritual throughout the whole nation.

Our only alternative to the danger of robotism is humanistic communitarianism. The problem is not primarily the legal problem of property ownership, nor that of sharing *profits*; it is that of sharing *work*, sharing *experience*. Changes in ownership must be made to the extent to which they are necessary to create a community of work, and to prevent the profit motive from directing production into socially harmful directions. Income must be equalized to the extent of giving everybody the material basis for a dignified life, and thus preventing the economic differences from creating a fundamentally different experience of life for various social classes. Man must be restituted to his supreme place in society, never being a means, never a thing to be used by others or by himself. Man's use by man must end, and economy must become the servant for the development of man. Capital must serve labor, things must serve life. Instead of the exploitative and hoarding orientation, dominant in the nineteenth century, and the receptive and marketing orientation dominant today, the *productive orientation* must be the end which all social arrangements serve.

No change must be brought about by force, it must be a simultaneous one in the economic, political and cultural spheres. Changes restricted to *one* sphere are destructive of every change. Just as primitive man was helpless before natural forces, modern man is helpless before the social and economic forces created by himself. He worships the works of his own hands, bowing to the new idols, yet swearing by the name of the God who commanded him to destroy all idols. Man can protect himself from the consequences of his own madness only by creating a sane society which conforms with the needs of man, needs which are rooted in the very conditions of his existence. A society in which man relates to man lovingly, in which he is rooted in bonds of brotherliness and solidarity, rather than in the ties of blood and soil; a society which gives him the possibility of transcending nature by creating rather than by destroying, in which everyone gains a sense of self by experiencing himself as the subject of his powers rather than by conformity, in which a system of orientation and devotion exists without man's needing to distort reality and to worship idols.

Building such a society means taking the next step; it means the end of "humanoid" history, the phase in which man had not become fully human. It does not mean the "end of days," the "completion," the state of perfect harmony in which no conflicts or problems confront men. On the contrary, it is man's fate that his existence is beset by contradictions, which he has to solve without ever solving them. When he has overcome the primitive state of human sacrifice, be it in the ritualistic form of the Aztecs or in the secular form of war, when he has been able to regulate his relationship with nature reasonably instead of blindly, when things have truly become his servants rather than his idols, he will be confronted with the truly human conflicts and problems; he will have to be adventuresome, courageous, imaginative, capable of suffering and of joy, but his powers will be in the service of life, and not in the service of death. The new phase of human history, if it comes to pass, will be a new beginning, not an end.

Man today is confronted with the most fundamental choice; not that between Capitalism or Communism, but that between *robotism* (of both the capitalist and the communist variety), or Humanistic Communitarian Socialism. Most facts seem to indicate that he is choosing robotism, and that means, in the long run, insanity and destruction. But all these facts are not strong enough to destroy faith in man's reason, good will and sanity. As long as we can think of other alternatives, we are not lost; as long as we can consult together and plan together, we can hope. But, indeed, the shadows are lengthening; the voices of insanity are becoming louder. We are in reach of achieving a state of humanity which corresponds to the vision of our great teachers; yet we are in danger of the destruction of all civilization, or of robotization. A small tribe was told thousands of years ago: "I put before you life and death, blessing and curse — and you chose life." This is our choice too.

THE REVOLUTIONIST'S HANDBOOK

ROBERT LINDNER

The happy capacity to utilize the rebellious urge in a positive, progressive, life-affirming manner entails the individualization of the person. Because currently the term "individualism" has acquired a sociopolitical significance, and large segments of society regard it with abhorrence, it seems necessary to recover the word for psychology by redefining it.

Individualization is a biological fact, provided for by the mechanics
of evolution.[1] Among all orders and species that live there can be remarked great or small differences as between their units. If the differences observed are not—and in many cases they are not—of a physical
nature, then they are noticeable in the sphere of performance; and if
not even here, then certainly in the qualitative nature of psychic characteristics which any given viable unit possesses. For man, especially,
is it true that a differential flexibility in relation to the environment
is a particularly variable factor. This flexibility is, however, more than
a matter of endowment, more than a matter of the physical arrangement
of his organs and parts and how he employs them. Beyond these, variability in flexibility is provided for endlessly by the character of intimate
relationships existing prior to the birth of each person, and by relational
circumstances determining the psychic atmosphere or climate or environment in which his development takes place. It is a fact, then, that
not all cats are gray in the dark, and that the keynote of life is its heterogeneity.

Heterogeneity in living matter of the human order has been used
as a knife that cuts both ways. Some have employed it to argue for a
rabid kind of individualism in the social life and arrangements of men,
rationalizing from it to a jungle-type law that would excuse each of us
from responsibility to the other. In a contrary manner, still others have
deplored biologically given diversification, regarded it as something
evil, and promoted the idea that it has somehow to be bred or beaten
out of the race so that an ideal (ideal to them, that is) society can the
more readily be achieved. There is, however, a third and more valid
position, one which applauds dissimilarity among men out of the conviction, substantiated by research, that only through the orchestra-
tion of human diversity can harmonious social living be brought
about and each person retain yet offer his unique contribution to the
whole. This is the position maintained today among biologists who are
not mentally strap-hung by blind faith in social or political systems which
seek justification from specially selected or purposefully distorted
scientific findings.

Individualization, then, is a good thing, a thing to be desired, and
a primary technique for achieving men's goal of an evolutionary break-
through. But such is the condition of the world and of society that individualization is discouraged and even punished. This seems to be
because the true individual represents a threat to the herd and is, as
well, an object of its envy. Authority demands that he be suppressed in
the interest of establishing its dominion. The mass resents the rare
spirit who crashes through the gray wall and emerges into the light of
disparateness. It therefore has to see to his suppression by punishing

[1]Leo Loeb, *The Biological Basis for Individuality* (Springfield, Illinois: Charles Thomas, 1944); also
E. W. Sinnott, "The Biological Basis of Democracy," *Yale Review*, 1945, *35*: 61–73.

him for his uniqueness and, in this manner, holding the rebellious inclinations of its members in check. In consequence of all this, the rebellious individualist lives constantly with anxiety. Only occasionally can he give expression to his individuality and, when he does, he usually —and with good cause—fears the results. For these reasons, he is quite likely to give but partial and unworthy expression to his distinction from the group.

True individualization demands the exploitation of those unique attributes—in any and all of the spheres of activity and thought—of a person. It is powered by the canalized rebellious instinct and has at least two motivations. One of these is the urgent need to express the individualistic qualities of the person. Of these the world can never have too much nor, in the giving, are the person's resources depleted. The second of the motivations is unequivocally an altruistic one, aimed at change and alteration of the society for the betterment of all concerned.

Unless these two motivations exist together, it is senseless to speak of individualization in its psychological meaning. Lacking the first, we get an artificial rebellion wherein the altruism has to be suspected of originating not from pure intellectual-emotional recognition of the necessity for change, but in a defense against personal sadism. Lacking the second, we come up with the eccentric, the pseudo rebel, who pretends rebellion by small, chiefly irritating departures from the group. In this category are included the purposeless (because merely self-satisfying) defiances of custom and mores—erratic dress, flaunting of fashion, departure from the accepted in manners, rootless infringement of custom. But when both motivations appear, we are justified in regarding the protest as genuine, the activity as positively rebellious, and the person a real rebel. Finally, the result of rebellious expression based upon the fulfillment of such motivational conditions is generally good in the special ethical sense employed herein.

It is at this juncture . . . that the question of freedom arises. Actually, what does "free" mean? Wherein does freedom apply to rebellion?

We owe to Freud the profoundest statements yet made about the nature of man, but ever since he provided us with a description of man's nature psychology has been held poised on the horns of a dilemma. Because implicit in the Freudian view is a tragic and apparently insoluble tension between man and society, it has seemed quite impossible to reconcile the nature of man with the nature of the societies he builds. To almost every thinker who has considered the problem, it has appeared that so long as men erect groups they cannot be free; that is, that a condition of social living must be a surrender of freedom or, at the very least, a sacrifice to some degree of "naturalness" and "spontaneity." And since a quality of humanness is, without doubt, an instinct or penchant or necessity to erect societies, if "naturalness" and "spontaneity" are also innate qualities of humanness, we have the stuff of which endless tragedy is made.

Many psychoanalysts have attempted to resolve the dilemma outlined above. Freud himself was most pessimistic about it. "The desire for a powerful and uninhibited ego may seem to us intelligible," he wrote, "but, as is shown by the times we live in, it is in the profoundest sense antagonistic to civilization." Nevertheless, his pessimism did not prevent him from developing a systematic psychology the applicatory art of which is designed specifically for the achievement by an individual of "freedom" and the alteration of what is most repressive in society. Nor has such pessimism affected those who followed Freud. Jung, for example, has only applause for the one who has cast off the chains of convention and worked out, with or without psychiatric aid, an "original" standpoint, so becoming "exceptional," "free," and closer to his (Jung's) ideal of "archaic man." More recently, Fromm has recommended that man be "himself," "for himself," and exercise his "freedom to." But through them all—through Jung, Fromm, Horney, and all the rest—seems to run an image of a "natural," "spontaneous," "archaic," or primordial creature whose recovery (or, better, rediscovery) is important for social well-being, and whose attributes personify "freedom." . . .

The increasing use of intelligence in the guidance of affairs must also be taken into consideration here. While it is a fact that man's intellectual capacity has not altered significantly from that of his early prehistoric ancestors—the tools discovered together with the oldest human remains indicate a brain capacity only slightly if at all inferior to that of modern man—the employment of intelligence as a governor in the affairs and relations of men has taken great forward strides. With this has come the ability to foresee outcomes of action and to predict, to some degree, the course of events, thus making unlimited "naturalness" and "spontaneity" unfeasible.

Finally, it must be taken into account that survival is impossible in a state of isolation, as Ashley Montagu has so well demonstrated in a recent work that assembles evidence from numerous scientific sources.[2] Congregate life is a condition of life, and all forms practice it to some extent instinctually, although in a vagrant few the evidence for social cooperativeness remains slight. We may speak, therefore, of a social instinct, an urge for forms to collect in aggregates, as a perimeter for individual "naturalness."

It follows from the foregoing that absolute freedom is impossible even if it were—as it is not—desirable; and that when we talk of freedom we necessarily employ the term in a relative sense. As a word it must be used descriptively to cover instances of activity which are always

[2]Ashley Montagu, *On Being Human* (New York: Henry Schuman, 1951).

and everywhere relative to situations that present themselves to the individual, to circumstances, and to surrounding conditions. But this does not mean that man cannot be free. It means, rather, that freedom has its limits and boundaries, limits and boundaries set by necessity, circumscribed by instinct, and defined by the predictive intelligence. And it is to these limits that the truly rebellious person can go in his behavior and thought . . . Which means, in its turn, that an appreciation for necessity, and a capacity to realize it, has somehow to be acquired by those who strive to become positively rebellious. In the few who are naturally rebellious this ability for defining the limits of freedom exists; in those whom we would rear to be rebellious it must be implanted somehow; and in those whom we would alter toward positive rebellion it must be encouraged.

Fortunately, a mechanism for measuring limits and sounding necessity is a part of human equipment and a feature of the psychic life of every man. Freud referred to it as "reality testing," defining thereby the innate disposition of all life to make estimates, based on experiment, of what is and is not real, and specifically in man to test and check continuously both for actuality and for the extent of his operations within this actuality. In all but the truly rebellious, however, the function of reality testing is impaired. Among the adjusted mass there is imposed between the person and actuality the impenetrable aura given off by the authoritarian superego, which distorts the reality beyond into the hallucinatory shape of that superego. Among the psychopathic, such has been the character of their development that a confused coextension of the self with reality is mistakenly made. Among the neurotic there has been bred an immense fear of reality and a reaction of systematic avoidance of it, which, in its turn, mangles what is actual to the point where the distortion and not reality becomes the stimulus to their thought and behavior. . . .

It is one of the major attractive contentions of psychoanalysts that their particular mode of therapy promotes "freedom." . . . Professor Louis Schneider, an exceptionally astute and psychologically informed sociologist, has lately pointed out the disparity between clinical and social approaches to the problem and warned against the typical error of psychiatric writers in projecting clinical concepts and descriptions onto the social structure, indicting their tendency to prescribe for society on the basis of data obtained in the clinic. What he has to say is particularly pertinent to our discussion and we can profit by the following liberal quotation:[3]

> *Upon completion of a highly successful psychoanalytical therapy a person who has greatly suffered from, say, "rigidity," who sharply*

[3]L. Schneider, "Some Psychiatric Views on 'Freedom' and the Theory of Social Systems," *Psychiatry*, 1949 (August), *12*: 256 f.

manifests "discrepancy between potentialities and accomplishments," and so on, manages to obtain considerable "flexibility," to realize his potentialities, to develop considerable self-confidence, to function harmoniously, without serious or incapacitating self-conflicts. It is certainly then justifiable to say that he is in some sense "free" whereas previously he was not. But in just what sense? He is free from certain devastating conflicts, he is "happier," he can expend energy on "externals," that was before expended in fruitless "internal" self-engagements. But is he perfectly "free" to act like a Roman centurion or a Trobriand Islander? Would he even want to? He still exists necessarily, as a being, relative to time, place, the hopes and expectations of relatives and friends—many of which he probably wants to fulfill—and even the circumstances of his upbringing. Whereas previously he was a "neurotic" restaurateur on a main avenue in a big city he is now perhaps a "free" or non-"neurotic" restaurateur on a main avenue in a big city. It is impossible to be "free" in any absolute sense even if one grants that the restaurateur might become a playwright or indeed a psychiatrist. He would always have to be somebody or something in particular, and thereby he would have a specific self and specific roles. Is freedom originality? Then it is always a specific kind of originality. It is not possible to be "original" in abstracto. The very pre-condition of "freedom"—originality and so on—is a set of limitations. To emerge into human-ness and in fact to envisage the problems of "freedom" man must be a particular, and particularly, specifically socialized being.

It appears, then, that the various prescriptions of many psychologists for freedom—either "freedom from" or "freedom to"—are but airy verbalizings, insubstantial although eloquent products of wishful good intentions. Most of them tacitly hypothecate a model who never was or could be—the "'good,' 'natural' man" (who resides somewhere beneath the veneered surface of civilized man) "from whose 'spontaneous' interactions with others a 'good society' will emerge"; most of them unjustifiably transpose from clinic to society (the less astute ones in the opposite direction); most of them erroneously assume the feasibility—and the more absurd ones even the desirability—of absolute freedom. Patently, therapies operating under such illusions and pointed toward such nonexistent goals must fail.

But, we may now ask, are there forms of therapy which do not offer such vain promises, therapies which lead to real if not absolute freedom? . . . At the moment we can say only that treatment which points toward the evocation of rebellion and does not thwart this most basic instinct of man yields an individual who is free to the outer edges of freedom. And his is a true freedom, functioning from a base line of immediate recognition of necessity as a limiting factor and operating without constraint according to the actualities founded upon necessity. This, he understands, provides the protestant urge with an extensive field of operations, making for the widest possible unencumbered exercise of individuality. For the true insight and grasp of what is actual liberates him, its possessor, from every illusory, distorting, interfering, and obscuring element that passes between the ego and the world. And this, he knows, is freedom.

Part II

Political Ideology: Motive, Weapon, Rationalization

Ideology is more a rubric than a precise term with universal meaning. In its most general sense it implies the relationship of ideas and beliefs to political systems and public policies. On another level it implies a belief system linking thought with the social and emotional life of the thinker—and connecting both with the real world of political developments. In popular political discourse and in formal political theories ideologies are used to answer certain recurring questions: How is power to be exercised? Who rules in the political system? What is the "just," "legitimate," "right" policy?

In the twentieth century several coherent belief systems have been politically active. To be sure, there are vast differences between historical Marxism and the political uses of Marxism by the Soviet Union and China. But Marxism's emphasis on the superstructure of industrial society, and the role of the capitalistic and working classes within that structure, provides a focus for political discourse today. Despite the fact that many social scientists point out the irrelevance of Victorian Marxism to the modern world, their intellectual debt to Marx is revealed in the frequency with which concepts of "social class," "political economy," and "historical change" must deal with his work.

It would be difficult to overestimate the impact of Socialism, a second belief system, on Western intellectual thought and the modern welfare state. And Liberalism, with its emphasis on rationality, pluralistic powers, and individual efforts, has also been fundamental to extant political thought. The influence of a social contract between the government and the citizen, a balanced polity of separate political institutions, and a strong and independent middle class, for instance, can be found in the civics textbooks introducing American schoolchildren to the foundations of our stable political system.

Marxism, Socialism, and Liberalism all have their roots in the eighteenth-century Enlightenment, a period full of buoyant faith in human reason. The totalitarian nightmares of the twentieth century, however, have led to the collapse and transformation of these "rational" ideologies. We are painfully aware of the extent to which individuals and nations pervert belief systems for irrational and destructive purposes. Perhaps the concept of the "authoritarian personality," formulated by social scientists who fled from Nazi Germany, and the reality of an Eichmann trial reveal how far we have fallen from the ideal of the rational philosophers. That ideologies removed from their historic context by state propaganda agencies and commercial public opinion industries have become trite is evidenced in the daily rhetoric of demagogues and the subtle manipulations of policy-makers.

As a result of this end to ideological innocence there has been increasing study of the seduction of political ideas and the mobilization of the emotional furor such ideas produce. Indeed, whether ideology is any longer relevant to political policy has become an issue of debate. The transformation of nineteenth-century capitalism, the pressures of new economic and social forces, and the changing intellectual issues may account for this development. Nevertheless, the central concern of this debate is the role of reason in discussing and participating in public events. This question—the intrinsic role of reason in human freedom and the relationship of knowledge and power it suggests—demands serious research and reflection.

---

5. Classical Ideologies

Once upon a time, patterns of ideas deduced from clear major premises influenced political behavior and justified public policies. Thomism, Marxism, Democratic Socialism, and nineteenth-century Manchester Liberalism are cases in point. Nowadays, however, we are less certain about the autonomy of political ideas and the extent to which their rational content influences men. The rea-

*sons for this change, as suggested in the introduction to Part II,
are rooted in the structural changes of postwar society and the
irrationality obvious in responses to political events and personalities.*

*In reviewing the development of French Socialism, André
Philip notes changes in the economic and social prerequisites
of socialist policies. The affluence of the skilled worker and the
more pervasive incorporation of the working people into the
French political system have helped reduce the conflict and the
schism that have marked the history of republican France.
Yet these same changes lead Philip to reject the notion that the
working class can remain the major agency for constructive
political reform.*

*Samuel Huntington attempts to define Conservatism, a
second classical ideology. No longer, he claims, can conservatism be employed to defend the interests of a particular social
stratum (e.g., an aristocracy) or a particular political system
(e.g., an absolute monarchy). The essence of conservatism today
is the defense of established and legitimate institutions and
beliefs. According to this definition, both entrenched socialists
and American liberals defending themselves against McCarthyism can fall within the class of "conservative" political men
enunciating "conservative" doctrines. Note the vagueness of
the political ideology articulated in this selection, a vagueness
that is itself evidence of the declining concern about classical
political ideologies in modern society.*

*There is much more historical specificity in Louis Hartz'
influential analysis of the antecedents of American Liberalism.
He documents, and most persuasively, that decentralized political and economic institutions, fostered by the absence of an
established Church and a ruling class, blended effectively with
the theories of limited government and social contract propounded by the seventeenth-century political theorist John
Locke to provide a foundation for the American Republic.*

SOCIALISM AND SOCIAL CLASSES

ANDRÉ PHILIP

Our concern is not to undertake a theoretical analysis of socialism in the
abstract but rather to understand what socialism should be for us, at

From *Dissent*, 1958, Winter: 20–21, 24–27, 29, 31.

this time, in our Western civilization. Hence I raise the question: Is socialism primarily the expression of clearly defined interests of a specific social class? Or is it the manifestation of a desire for justice and liberty, assuming different forms throughout history but seeking through this diversity of forms a constant moral ideal?

Socialism and Social Classes

I should like to review the fundamental ideas of Marx, which may be condensed in the following statements:

1. History is motored by the class struggle.
2. Class structure is dependent on the organization of the owner-ship of the means of production.
3. Political power is essentially a reflection of productive power.
4. The working class continuously increases its numbers, little by little absorbing the old middle classes as these are destroyed by tech-nological progress.
5. Furthermore, the pauperization of the masses and social inequal-ity are continuously increasing, so that the struggle between the capi-talist class and the proletariat becomes increasingly bitter and leads inevitably to revolution.

According to this theory, the achievement of socialism seems to be a development which, without appealing to justice, results simply from the inexorable laws of history. The workers will move toward socialism because they can't help doing so; in defending their immedi-ate interests, they will gradually become aware of the necessity for the revolution. This will be achieved by their vanguard, who, during a tran-sitional period, will set up a "dictatorship of the proletariat."

These Marxist formulations, I would contend, no longer conform to the realities of advanced industrial societies. The fact is that we must take account of a growing process of social differentiation which charac-terizes our society and of its inevitable psychological and political con-sequences. . . .

The Progressive Differentiation of the Working Class

a. Modern industry needs a certain number of skilled workers, who, depending on the country and the industry, represent a quarter to a third of all wage earners.

First, there are the old craftsmen in the preindustrial sense of the term. In machine-tool shops, for example, such workers construct new machines or new devices for old machines in accordance with engineers' designs.

Here we see a professional aristocracy which, having been reduced in numbers and influence by the industrial advances of the nineteenth century, is today being reconsolidated. Indeed, with the progress of automation, we can foresee the day when work which today is semi-automatic will become totally mechanized; then skilled workers will again become the core of a working class whose function will be to oversee, adapt, and repair automatically operating machines.

Though in France these skilled workers do not at the present time command a very high wage, they continue to enjoy a prestige which other workers do not. The skilled worker is often proud of his professional qualifications. He has an inner wish to take the initiative, to master the machine rather than be mastered. He is interested in his work and management must respect his independence. Often there is less difference between a skilled worker of this kind and a technical manager than between a skilled worker and one who merely performs a routine specialized operation.

It is this intermediary status that helps explain the skilled worker's ambivalent attitude. He is one of an elite which in the past was in the vanguard of social and political battles. Today it is again he whom we find in all countries at the top of trade-union organizations. But at the same time he is becoming more and more conservative in defense of his own interests against the unskilled workers. In the colonies especially he easily becomes a petty bourgeois who defends his privileges against the native laboring masses.

Here then is a worker who is alert, organized, and responsible but has at the same time a tendency to establish himself in the existing system to the extent that this system is really receptive to his initiative and offers him a chance to rise on the social scale.

b. But the majority of workers are still semi-skilled or unskilled laborers who are actually the product of the nineteenth-century industrial revolution.

To the extent that he works on a piece-rate basis, the semi-skilled worker has improved his living standard considerably. But his road is blocked; he sees no way to advance within the plant hierarchy. At the same time he is completely without security, for with any fluctuation in production he may be laid off. And as for his work itself, it is almost without interest. The factory is simply the place where, without making any sense out of it, he passively carries out tasks and orders so that he can make a living.

This situation can lead the specialized worker to one of two attitudes:

1. He may have an escape fantasy whereby he invests in a political myth his hopes and profound desire for change. But he carries over into his political life his factory-learned reflexes, his habit of not thinking, of merely submitting to orders. His class consciousness is simply a

directed resentment; it is not a considered expression of working-class life but an evasion of the reality to which he must submit. The man who at the factory fears the boss, will away from work fear the party. These are the workers who, with a docile violence, rally to Communism or fascism, according to the times. In fact they are not able to believe in democracy while in their everyday lives they experience a reality which is the exact opposite of democracy.

2. But often such a worker commits his dream of escape to some non-political sphere. This is so especially when he has been betrayed politically and has lost the hope of a complete change in his working conditions. So he devotes himself to the highest possible output in order to raise his standard of living and thus ape the petty bourgeois life which he sees all about him.

While the skilled worker strives to provide himself with a comfortable home and a little garden, the unskilled makes do with a motorbike, movies, football, dancing, and betting. Observations made recently both in Austria and in Great Britain demonstrate a growing trend toward the disintegration of this part of the working class and toward the development of attitudes which are a-collective, if not a-social. The individual is beginning to emerge from the masses; but disoriented and disillusioned, he craves little more than the most mediocre pleasures. In short, we find here a dispensable, dissociated man who has not yet succeeded in making new social ties. This man is likely to be neither a responsible trade unionist nor a political militant; he leaves activism to others, himself only following and allowing himself from one moment to the next to be seduced by the extreme right or the extreme left.

c. But one group that is becoming more and more important is that of the white-collar workers and office holders, that is, the salaried middle class, which now includes more than a third of all workers and which seems to be constantly increasing. At the bottom levels, the living standard of this group is generally no higher than that of the working class. But members of this group are distinguished from workers strictly defined by the fact that they manipulate not machines but human relations and that, in addition, they participate in the power of the managers.

An office worker's budget is about the same as a worker's, but its composition is more nearly like that found in the higher social classes. This worker in effect continually skirts the edges of the bourgeois world; he prepares the materials for executive decisions and puts them into effect.

Because of the diversity of its elements, it is hard to define the character of this group. Frequently a good deal of its work is monotonous and uninteresting, comparable in this to the work of unskilled workers. (Perhaps here the progress of automation will lead to concentrating responsible judgment in a minority and pushing the majority into the position of the worker who executes one simple operation and submits to an increasing insecurity in his job.) The psychological attitude of this group is analogous to that of the barely skilled worker: disgust with work that is devoid of interest, passivity, malaise, and self-expression by escape fantasies. One small step up the salary scale, however, and a strong similarity with the middle class can be found: a wish to move closer to the executive layer, which is at once admired and envied, a longing for independence, and a resistance to proletarianization, here with a rightist orientation. But once we go up the social ladder another step and reach the more satisfied white-collar worker, we find a group that is more likely to be attracted by democratic socialism.

In our analysis of a series of sociological groups we find that each has peculiar characteristics while at the same time embodying contradictory elements. Still, two phenomena characterize our epoch: *mobility* between groups and the progressive *institutionalization* of the conflicts bred among them.

1. Clearly there is an intergroup mobility which will go on increasing with industrial advances.

This evolution is far less advanced in the European countries than in the United States, for in Europe the educational system still operates as a social barrier, setting classes against one another. Despite the accomplishments that have been made in assuring free primary education, the lower social strata are kept in an inferior position because they have not had sufficient opportunity for intellectual development. Class differences also continue to be expressed in external signs. Only a minority of the people own cars; most workers have to be satisfied with bicycles; living quarters impose a serious barrier between classes. Nevertheless, at the present time class mobility appears to be increasing, even sometimes disquietingly so: the elite worker who succeeds in getting a higher salary and acquiring professional competence usually tries, not to move up to the top factory jobs, but to leave the factory and become a craftsman, tradesman, or a miniature industrialist.

2. Social conflicts are officially recognized and institutionalized. The existence of trade unions, which organize not only specialized workers but also professionals, white-collar workers and civil servants, has given these diverse groups the possibility of expressing themselves freely. The general acceptance of collective bargaining tends to regulate conflicts in accordance with commonly agreed-upon rules.

The Consequences

The result of these [changes] is that in the world of today we no longer find the simple class differentiation that Marx observed, but rather a host of groups, each with its private interests and each in opposition to its neighboring group. In the Marxist system, the division into two classes whose antagonism would increase to the ultimate point of revolution made it possible to offer to one of these classes, the workers, a total vision of the world and a myth of social transformation which renewed their hopes and aroused them to revolt. Today we no longer have a generalized conception of the oneness of civilization capable of orienting and inspiring men. There are only battling groups, each defending its private, often variable, interests, with no common standard that would allow us to judge them and order them by relative importance. . . .

In conclusion it very much appears that the world of today does not correspond at all to the analysis Marx made in the mid-nineteenth century and that working-class unity is at this moment no more than a romantic illusion. Instead of two polarized classes we find a multitude of groups which have divergent interests and have thus lost a consensus of social value. An ideology capable of defining socialism cannot emerge automatically from any of these groups. Undoubtedly an economic interpretation of history can demonstrate the *conditions* for the realization of a political ideal, the obstacles that stand in the way of its achievement, and the lines of force that might favor it. But analysis of a social situation cannot, by itself, lead to the elaboration of a doctrine, or even to the definition of a principle of action. *A fact cannot be turned into a value.* It is not in defense of this or that interest group that a man can be termed political. Socialism is not the automatic expression of the interests of one group, whatever the group; *it is a political choice in the name of a universal moral ideal which must be found elsewhere than in analysis of the social fact.*

CONSERVATISM AS AN IDEOLOGY

SAMUEL P. HUNTINGTON

Theories of Conservatism

First, the *aristocratic* theory defines conservatism as the ideology of a single specific and unique historical movement: the reaction of the feudal-aristocratic-agrarian classes to the French Revolution, liberalism, and the rise of the bourgeoisie at the end of the eighteenth century and during the first half of the nineteenth century. In Mannheim's words, modern conservatism is "a function of *one particular* historical and sociological situation."[1] Liberalism is the ideology of the bourgeoisie, social-

From *The American Political Science Review*, 1957 (June), *51*: 454–460, 473.

[1]Karl Mannheim, "Conservative Thought," in Paul Kecskemeti (ed.), *Essays on Sociological and Social Psychology* (New York, 1953), pp. 98–99. . . .

ism and Marxism the ideologies of the proletariat, and conservatism the ideology of the aristocracy. Conservatism thus becomes indissolubly associated with feudalism, status, the *ancien régime,* landed interests, medievalism, and nobility; it becomes irreconcilably opposed to the middle class, labor, commercialism, industrialism, democracy, liberalism, and individualism. This concept of conservatism is popular among critics of the "New Conservatism." For, as Louis Hartz has brilliantly demonstrated [see pages 105–109], the United States lacks a feudal tradition. Hence, the efforts of intellectuals and publicists to propagate conservative ideas in middle-class America must be doomed to failure.

Second, the *autonomous* definition of conservatism holds that conservatism is not necessarily connected with the interests of any particular group, nor, indeed, is its appearance dependent upon any specific historical configuration of social forces. Conservatism is an autonomous system of ideas which are generally valid. It is defined in terms of universal values such as justice, order, balance, moderation. Whether or not a particular individual holds these values high depends not on his social affiliations but upon his personal capacity to see their inherent truth and desirability. Conservatism, in this sense, is, as Russell Kirk says, simply a matter of "will and intelligence"; the principles of conservatism "are not confined to the interests of a single class"; conservatives may be drawn from "all classes and occupations. . . ."[2] This theory of conservatism is obviously popular among the "New Conservatives." It implies not only that conservatism is relevant and desirable in contemporary America, but that it is the preferable political philosophy under any historical circumstances.

Third, the *situational* definition views conservatism as the ideology arising out of a distinct but recurring type of historical situation in which a fundamental challenge is directed at established institutions and in which the supporters of those institutions employ the conservative ideology in their defense. Thus, conservatism is that system of ideas employed to justify any established social order, no matter where or when it exists, against any fundamental challenge to its nature or being, no matter from what quarter. The essence of conservatism is the passionate affirmation of the value of existing institutions. This does not mean that conservatism opposes all change. Indeed, in order to preserve the fundamental elements of society, it may be necessary to acquiesce in change on secondary issues. No person can espouse the conservative ideology, however, unless he is fundamentally happy with the established order and committed to its defense against any serious challenge. Conservatism in this sense is possible in the United States today only if there is a basic challenge to existing American institutions which impels their defenders to articulate conservative values. . . .

[2]Russell Kirk, *A Program for Conservatives* (Chicago, 1954), pp. 22, 38–39; Peter Viereck, *Conservatism Revisited* (New York, 1949), p. 9.

Ideational and Institutional Ideologies:
The Absence of a Conservative Ideal

Among writers espousing all three definitions of conservatism substantial agreement exists that at least the following are major components of the conservative creed—the essential elements of Burke's
theory.

(1) Man is basically a religious animal, and religion is the foundation of civil society. A divine sanction infuses the legitimate, existing,
social order.

(2) Society is the natural, organic product of slow historical growth.
Existing institutions embody the wisdom of previous generations. Right
is a function of time. "Prescription," in the words of Burke, "is the
most solid of all titles. . . ."

(3) Man is a creature of instinct and emotion as well as reason.
Prudence, prejudice, experience, and habit are better guides than reason, logic, abstractions, and metaphysics. Truth exists not in universal
propositions but in concrete experiences.

(4) The community is superior to the individual. The rights of
men derive from their duties. Evil is rooted in human nature, not in
any particular social institutions.

(5) Except in an ultimate moral sense, men are unequal. Social
organization is complex and always includes a variety of classes, orders,
and groups. Differentiation, hierarchy, and leadership are the inevitable characteristics of any civil society.

(6) A presumption exists "in favour of any settled scheme of government against any untried project. . . ." Man's hopes are high, but
his vision is short. Efforts to remedy existing evils usually result in even
greater ones.

Assuming these propositions to be a fair summary of representative conservative ideas, what do they suggest as to the relative merit
of the aristocratic, autonomous, and situational theories? . . .

The autonomous definition fails because the appearance of conservatism in history is not a matter of random chance. The aristocratic
definition restricts conservatism to too small a segment of the social
process. The autonomous definition frees it too completely from any
connection with the social process. The characteristic elements of conservative thought—the "divine tactic" in history; prescription and tradition; the dislike of abstraction and metaphysics; the distrust of individual human reason; the organic conception of society; the stress
on the evil in man; the acceptance of social differentiation—all serve
the overriding purpose of justifying the established order. The essence
of conservatism is the rationalization of existing institutions in terms of
history, God, nature, and man. . . .

The conservative ideology is the product of intense ideological and social conflict. It appears only when the challengers to the established institutions reject the fundamentals of the ideational theory in terms of which those institutions have been molded and created. If the challengers do not question the basic values of the prevailing philosophy, the controversy between those for and against institutional change is carried on with reference to the commonly accepted ideational philosophy. Each group attempts to show that its policies are more in accord with the common ideals than those of the other group. After the Civil War in America, for instance, the conflict between American Whig and American Democrat was fought, as Hartz has pointed out, within a shared framework of Lockean values. Consensus precluded conservatism.

When the challengers fundamentally disagree with the ideology of the existing society, however, and affirm a basically different set of values, the common framework of discussion is destroyed. The rejection of the prevailing ideology by the challengers compels it to be abandoned by the defenders also. No ideational theory can be used to defend established institutions satisfactorily, even when those institutions in general reflect the values of that ideology. The perfect nature of the ideology's ideal and the imperfect nature and inevitable mutation of the institutions create a gap between the two. The ideal becomes a standard by which to criticize the institutions, much to the embarrassment of those who believe in the ideal and yet still wish to defend the institutions. Eventually the defenders are faced with an unavoidable choice: either they must abandon their ideology in order to defend their institutions and substitute a conservative philosophy for their old ideational theory, or they must adhere to their ideational theory at the risk of further contributing to the downfall of those institutions which largely embody their ideals. The defense of any set of institutions against a fundamental challenge, consequently, must be phrased in terms of the conservative logic, sanctity, and necessity of the institutions *qua* institutions irrespective of the degree to which they correspond to the prescriptions of this or that ideational philosophy.

The challenging social force must present a clear and present danger to the institutions. The mere articulation of a dissident ideology does not produce conservatism until that ideology is embraced by significant social groups. The *philosophes* of the mid-eighteenth century generated no conservative ideology; the events of 1789 and the subsequent years did. Conservatism, in Mannheim's words, "first becomes conscious and reflective when other ways of life and thought appear on the scene, against which it is compelled to take up arms in the ideological struggle."[3] If the defenders of the established order are successful, in due course they gradually cease to articulate their conserv-

---

[3]Mannheim, *op. cit.*, p. 115.

ative ideology and substitute for it a new version of their old ideational theory. If their defense is unsuccessful, they abandon either their old ideational premises or their new conservative ideology. If they are inclined to be congenital conservatives, they will accept the new order as the inevitable work of destiny. Burke, Bonald, and de Maistre, for instance, all in part believed that the triumph of the French Revolution might be decreed by Providence and that once this became obvious, it would "not be resolute and firm, but perverse and obstinate" to oppose it.

On the other hand, the unsuccessful conservative who remains attached to the ideals of his old ideational philosophy becomes a reactionary, *i.e.*, a critic of existing society who wishes to recreate in the future an ideal which he assumes to have existed in the past. He is a radical. No valid distinction exists between "change backward" and "change forward." Change is change; history neither retreats nor repeats; and all change is away from the status quo. As time passes, the ideal of the reactionary becomes less and less related to any actual society of the past. The past is romanticized, and, in the end, the reactionary comes to support a return to an idealized "Golden Age" which never in fact existed. He becomes indistinguishable from other radicals, and he normally displays all the distinctive characteristics of the radical psychology.

The nature of conservatism as an institutional ideology precludes any permanent and inherent affiliation or opposition between it and any particular ideational ideology. No necessary dichotomy exists, therefore, between conservatism and liberalism. The assumption that such an opposition does exist derives, of course, from the aristocratic theory of conservatism and reflects an overconcern with a single phase of western history at the end of the 18th and the beginning of the 19th centuries. The effort to erect this ephemeral relationship into a continuing phenomenon of political history only serves to obscure the fact that in the proper historical circumstances conservatism may well be necessary for the defense of liberal institutions. The true enemy of the conservative is not the liberal but the extreme radical no matter what ideational theory he may espouse. Different radicals advance different panaceas, but they all have the same psychology which conservative thinkers have not been slow to identify. Hooker's sixteenth-century Puritan, Metternich's "presumptuous man," Burke's "metaphysical scribbler," Hawthorne's Hollingsworth, Cortés' "self-worshipping man," Hoffer's twentieth century "true believer," are all one and the same. . . .

Conservatism is not, as the aristocratic interpretation argues, the monopoly of one particular class in history. Nor is it, as the autonomous school contends, appropriate in every age and place. It is, instead, relevant in a particular type of historical situation. That is the situation in which American liberalism finds itself today. Until the challenge of communism and the Soviet Union is eliminated or neutralized, a major aim of American liberals must be to preserve what they have created. This is a limited goal but a necessary one. Conservatism does not ask ultimate questions and hence does not give final answers. But it does remind men of the institutional prerequisites of social order. And when these prerequisites are threatened, conservatism is not only appropriate, it is essential. In preserving the achievements of American liberalism, American liberals have no recourse but to turn to conservatism. For them especially, conservative ideology has a place in America today.

LIBERALISM AS FOUNDATION

Louis Hartz

One of the central characteristics of a nonfeudal society is that it lacks a genuine revolutionary tradition, the tradition which in Europe has been linked with the Puritan and French revolutions: that it is "born free," as Tocqueville said. And this being the case, it lacks also a tradition of reaction: lacking Robespierre it lacks Maistre, lacking Sydney it lacks Charles II.* Its liberalism is what Santayana called, referring to American democracy, a "natural" phenomenon. But the matter is curiously broader than this, for a society which begins with Locke, and thus transforms him, stays with Locke, by virtue of an absolute and irrational attachment it develops for him, and becomes as indifferent to the challenge of socialism in the later era as it was unfamiliar with the heritage of feudalism in the earlier one. It has within it, as it were, a kind of self-completing mechanism, which insures the universality of the liberal idea. Here . . . is one of the places where Marx went wrong in his historical analysis, attributing as he did the emergence of the socialist ideology to the objective movement of economic forces.

*Maximilien de Robespierre: Jacobin leader of the French Revolution who was an admirer of Rousseau, a critic of the monarchy, and a devoted republican. In the name of "democracy" Robespierre helped instigate the Reign of Terror.

Joseph de Maistre: conservative eighteenth-century Frenchman who reacted against the decline of the aristocracy and the waning power of the monarchy. In his writings Maistre proposed a world in which the Pope would rule as an absolute authority.

Algernon Sydney: seventeenth-century British political theorist who advocated republicanism to the extreme that the Parliament and the people could create kings. Sydney served on Oliver Cromwell's council for a time after the Civil War in England, yet he believed that the power of Parliament was delegated and therefore somewhat limited.

Charles II: English king who regained the throne in the Restoration and ruled in constant struggle with Parliament over religious toleration and taxation. Finally Charles dissolved Parliament and until his death ruled as an absolute monarch. His reign, however, was marked by the growing strength of Parliament and the formation of the Whig and Tory parties. — *Editor's note.*

Actually socialism is largely an ideological phenomenon, arising out of the principles of class and the revolutionary liberal revolt against them which the old European order inspired. It is not accidental that America which has uniquely lacked a feudal tradition has uniquely lacked also a socialist tradition. The hidden origin of socialist thought everywhere in the West is to be found in the feudal ethos. The *ancien régime* inspires Rousseau; both inspire Marx.

Which brings us to the substantive quality of the natural liberal mind. And this poses no easy problem. For when the words of Locke are used and a prior Filmer* is absent, how are we to delineate the significance of the latter fact? In politics men who make speeches do not go out of their way to explain how differently they would speak if the enemies they had were larger in size or different in character. On the contrary whatever enemies they fight they paint in satanic terms, so that a problem sufficiently difficult to begin with in a liberal society becomes complicated further by the inevitable perspectives of political battle. Take the American Revolution. With John Adams identifying the Stamp Act with the worst of the historic European oppressions, how can we distinguish the man from Lilburne or the philosophers of the French Enlightenment? And yet if we study the American liberal language in terms of intensity and emphasis, if we look for silent omissions as well as explicit inclusions, we begin to see a pattern emerging that smacks distinctively of the New World. It has a quiet, matter of fact quality, it does not understand the meaning of sovereign power, the bourgeois class passion is scarcely present, the sense of the past is altered, and there is about it all, as compared with the European pattern, a vast and almost charming innocence of mind. Twain's "Innocents Abroad" is a pretty relevant concept, for the psyche that springs from social war and social revolution is given to far suspicions and sidelong glances that the American liberal cannot easily understand. Possibly this is what people mean when they say that European thought is "deeper" than American, though anyone who tries to grapple with America in Western terms will wonder whether the term "depth" is the proper one to use. There can be an appalling complexity to innocence, especially if your point of departure is guilt.

Now if the *ancien régime* is not present to begin with, one thing follows automatically: it does not return in a blaze of glory. It does not flower in the nineteenth century in a Disraeli or a Ballanche, however different from each other these men may be. I do not mean to imply that no trace of the feudal urge, no shadow whatsoever of Sir Walter Scott, has been found on the hills and plains of the New World.

*Sir Robert Filmer: seventeenth-century English royalist who defended the divine rights of the British monarchy and criticized the social contract theory propounded by Thomas Hobbes. Filmer's *Patriarcha* (1680) is perhaps best known as the object of republican criticism from Algernon Sydney and John Locke.—*Editor's note.*

One can get into a lot of useless argument if he affirms the liberalness of a liberal society in absolute mathematical fashion. The top strata of the American community, from the time of Peggy Hutchinson to the time of Margaret Kennedy, have yearned for the aristocratic ethos. But instead of exemplifying the typical Western situation, these yearnings represent an inversion of it. America has presented the world with the peculiar phenomenon, not of a frustrated middle class, but of a "frustrated aristocracy"—of men, Aristotelian-like, trying to break out of the egalitarian confines of middle class life but suffering guilt and failure in the process. The South before the Civil War is the case par excellence of this, though New England of course exemplifies it also. Driven away from Jefferson by abolitionism, the Fitzhughs of the ante-bellum era actually dared to ape the doctrinal patterns of the Western reaction, of Disraeli and Bonald. But when Jefferson is traditional, European traditionalism is a curious thing indeed. The Southerners were thrown into fantastic contradictions by their iconoclastic conservatism, by what I have called the "Reactionary Enlightenment," and after the Civil War for good historical reasons they fell quickly into oblivion. The South, as John Crowe Ransom has said, has been the part of America closest to Old World Europe, but it has never really been Europe. It has been an alien child in a liberal family, tortured and confused, driven to a fantasy life which, instead of disproving the power of Locke in America, portrays more poignantly than anything else the tyranny he has had. . . .

Surely, then, it is a remarkable force: this fixed, dogmatic liberalism of a liberal way of life. It is the secret root from which have sprung many of the most puzzling of American cultural phenomena. Take the unusual power of the Supreme Court and the cult of constitution worship on which it rests. Federal factors apart, judicial review as it has worked in America would be inconceivable without the national acceptance of the Lockian creed, ultimately enshrined in the Constitution, since the removal of high policy to the realm of adjudication implies a prior recognition of the principles to be legally interpreted. At the very moment that Senator Benton was hailing the rise of America's constitutional fetishism, in France Royer-Collard and the Doctrinaires* were desperately trying to build precisely the same atmosphere around the Restoration Charter of 1814, but being a patchwork of Maistre and Rousseau, that constitutional document exploded in their faces in the July Revolution. *Inter arma leges silent.* If in England a marvelous

---

*Thomas Hart Benton: American politician who, as Senator from Missouri, became an ardent supporter of Andrew Jackson and advocated gradual abolition of slavery, a position which cost him his Senate seat.

Pierre Paul Royer-Collard: French statesman and philosopher who believed in a constitutional monarchy. Royer-Collard became a leader of the Doctrinaires, a moderate group that urged compromise in the unsettled period after the defeat of Napoleon and loyalty to the Charter of 1814 as a basis for stability.—*Editor's note.*

organic cohesion has held together the feudal, liberal, and socialist ideas, it would still be unthinkable there that the largest issues of public policy should be put before nine Talmudic judges examining a single text. But this is merely another way of saying that law has flourished on the corpse of philosophy in America, for the settlement of the ultimate moral question is the end of speculation upon it. Pragmatism, interestingly enough America's great contribution to the philosophic tradition, does not alter this, since it feeds itself on the Lockian settlement. It is only when you take your ethics for granted that all problems emerge as problems of technique. Not that this is a bar in America to institutional innovations of highly non-Lockian kind. Indeed, as the New Deal shows, when you simply "solve problems" on the basis of a submerged and absolute liberal faith, you can depart from Locke with a kind of inventive freedom that European Liberal reformers and even European socialists, dominated by ideological systems, cannot duplicate. But the main point remains: if Fitzhugh and De Leon* were crucified by the American general will, John Marshall and John Dewey flourished in consequence of their crucifixion. The moral unanimity of a liberal society reaches out in many directions.

At bottom it is riddled with paradox. Here is a Lockian doctrine which in the West as a whole is the symbol of rationalism, yet in America the devotion to it has been so irrational that it has not even been recognized for what it is: liberalism. There has never been a "liberal movement" or a real "liberal party" in America: we have only had the American Way of Life, a nationalist articulation of Locke which usually does not know that Locke himself is involved; and we did not even get that until after the Civil War when the Whigs of the nation, deserting the Hamiltonian tradition, saw the capital that could be made out of it. This is why even critics who have noticed America's moral unity have usually missed its substance. Ironically, "liberalism" is a stranger in the land of its greatest realization and fulfillment. But this is not all. Here is a doctrine which everywhere in the West has been a glorious symbol of individual liberty, yet in America its compulsive power has been so great that it has posed a threat to liberty itself. Actually Locke has a hidden conformitarian germ to begin with, since natural law tells equal people equal things, but when this germ is fed by the explosive power of modern nationalism, it mushrooms into something pretty remarkable. One can reasonably wonder about the liberty one finds in [Edmund] Burke. . . .

The decisive domestic issue of our time may well lie in the counter

*George Fitzhugh: nineteenth-century American author and editor who was an aggressive defender of slavery. Fitzhugh's *The Failure of Free Society* (1854) is a polemic stressing the virtues of the Southern slave economy and social order over the capitalism of the North.

Daniel De Leon: American socialist leader and a Marxian revolutionist who was active in the nineteenth-century labor movements. De Leon helped start the Industrial Workers of the World (1905), but he and his Socialist Labor group were soon eliminated. — *Editor's note.*

resources a liberal society can muster against this deep and unwritten tyrannical compulsion it contains. They exist. Given the individualist nature of the Lockian doctrine, there is always a logical impulse within it to transcend the very conformitarian spirit it breeds in a Lockian society: witness the spirit of Holmes and Hand. Given the fact . . . that "Americanism" oddly disadvantages the Progressive despite the fact that he shares it to the full, there is always a strategic impulse within him to transcend it: witness the spirit of Brandeis, Roosevelt, and Stevenson. In some sense the tragedy of these movements has lain in the imperfect knowledge they have had of the enemy they face, above all in their failure to see their own unwitting contribution to his strength. The record of Brandeis was good on civil liberties, but anyone who studies his Progressive thought will see that he was, for good or bad, on that score a vital part of the compulsive "Americanism" which bred the hysteria he fought. The Progressive tradition, if it is to transcend the national general will, has got to realize, as it has not yet done, how deeply its own Jacksonian heroes have been rooted in it. . . .

. . . [O]ne cannot say of the liberal society analysis that by concentrating on national unities it rules out the meaning of domestic conflict. Actually it discovers that meaning, which is obscured by the very Progressive analysis that presumably concentrates on conflict. You do not get closer to the significance of an earthquake by ignoring the terrain on which it takes place. On the contrary, that is one of the best ways of making sure that you will miss its significance. The argument over whether we should "stress" solidarity or conflict in American politics misleads us by advancing a false set of alternatives.

---

6. Authoritarianism

Out of the probings into man's political irrationality has come a corpus of literature devoted to the psychological uses of ideology — the ways in which men employ belief systems to satisfy their personal cravings. That some men seek to dominate others and that other men wish to be dominated is not a new finding of political psychology, but never before have totalitarian and authoritarian behavior been so urgently examined.

In a brilliant excursion into intellectual history, Irving Howe and Lewis Coser identify some of the ideological components of a totalitarian system. Their discussion is followed by two

*empirical examinations of the recent American political move-
ment known as McCarthyism. One dimension of an authoritarian syndrome is intolerance of both ambiguity and political
dissent. Martin Trow describes this characteristic among small
businessmen seemingly displaced by the demands of large-scale
social organizations. The essay by Seymour Lipset attributes
the characteristic of identification with rigid, hierarchical
power to Senator McCarthy's followers. (It should be noted,
of course, that this psychological dimension is only part of
the explanation for McCarthy's appeal.) Lipset's careful use
of survey evidence also dispels a general notion that all forms
of intolerance are linked; specifically, Lipset points out that
intolerance of ethnic minorities, such as Jews, was not necessarily related to a pro-McCarthy position.*

TOTALITARIANISM AS IDEOLOGY

IRVING HOWE AND LEWIS COSER

A political party, wrote Edmund Burke at the dawn of the nation-
state, "is a body of men united, for promoting by their joint endeavors
the national interest, upon some particular principle in which they are
all agreed."[1]

This description no longer holds fully for any political party, but
least of all for Stalinism. And not merely because the Communist
parties have no genuine stake in the national interest, but more important, because they are not united upon "some particular principle."
The totalitarian party is "unprincipled" in the root sense of the term.
All parties may violate their principles, yet the act of violation implies
a certain recognition of norms. By contrast, the totalitarian party cannot, in any precise sense, be said to violate its principles: it can be described by its structure, its characteristics, its power goals, but not by
any stable ideology or group of ideas. *The movement exists far less for the
ideology than the ideology for the movement.*

Though the ideological spokesman of Stalinism advanced claims
in regard to its ultimate ends that might seem similar to those of classical socialist thought, such pronouncements were manipulative, hortatory, and self-deceptive—generally a mixture of the three. For these

Pages 542–548 from: *The American Communist Party: A Critical History*. Reprinted by permission of the
Beacon Press, copyright © 1957 by Irving Howe and Lewis Coser. Title supplied by the editor.
[1]Edmund Burke, *Thoughts on the Cause of the Present Discontents* (Cambridge, England, 1930), p. 96.

statements of ultimate ends had no controlling or restraining influence on the actual behavior of the Stalinist movement; the claim it made to the heritage of socialism could not in itself lead to a softening of the cruelties in the Siberian labor camps, though a shrewd political expediency might. In the life of the totalitarian movement, the instrumental swallows up the ideological.

Or almost. For if the above is a usable description of the objective workings of the Stalinist movement, it is not sufficient for grasping the subjective processes of Stalinist thought. Many individual Stalinists were obviously entangled with ideology as no one else in our time has been. They felt that their version of "Marxism" provided them with omniscient knowledge of the course of History—knowledge so complete as to constitute a *possession* of History; that it made possible a finished program and a final answer; and that the decisions of the party were the means for realizing the decrees of History. Yet it is no contradiction to say that in a movement for which ideology had become a device there were many people whose submission to ideology was total, fanatical, and ruthless. On the contrary: the existence of such people was a precondition for such a movement.

Beliefs concerning the nature of History are here important insofar as they support the Stalinist myth, yet they cannot in themselves serve as guides to political or moral courses of action. History as such cannot provide values, though it may help and permit valuation. Moral and political principles, however, are based on choices among opposing possibilities; hence, an acceptance of or identification with the supposed decrees of History, simply because they are supposed decrees of History, is an amoral act, leading more often than not to colorblindness in the choice of values. It is here, in its reliance upon History, that Stalinism came closest to being an ideology. If, however, we mean by a genuine ideology a pattern of ideal norms that guide policy, something very different controlled the Stalinist movement. In the Communist parties ideologies were conceived as instruments of power, manipulable according to the needs of a given moment and very seldom serving as either check or standard for behavior.

Further qualifications are necessary, however, for in the relation between the Stalinist movement and the tradition of Marxism we face a highly complex and perhaps unprecedented problem. Stalinism, it is true, manipulated and exploited Marxist concepts and terms—but to say this is not yet fully to describe the relationship. Recognizing how deeply the Marxist mode of thought has seeped into the modern mind, the Stalinist movement stressed its claim to being the true receptacle of Marxism with a vigor second only to its claim to socialism and the tradition of the October Revolution. Particularly insofar as they were uncritically or even enthusiastically honored by most of its opponents, these claims constituted a major source of Stalinist power and prestige.

Yet it would clearly have been impossible for the Stalinist movement to keep reiterating these claims without, in some way, coming to give them a certain credence itself.

Stalinism grew out of, even as it destroyed, a movement that had been deeply attached to the letter of Marxism. The older leaders of the Stalinist movement, who had once known what it meant to live in a non-totalitarian atmosphere, were trained in a school of exegetics that sharpened wits through prolonged polemics over the meaning of Marxist doctrine. In the world of their youth, a ready capacity to cite Marxist classics, and to cite them with some relevance, could bring prestige and political preferment. But the new Stalinist functionaries, those who were themselves products of Stalinism and had never lived in any other milieu, showed very little interest in Marxist or any other form of speculative thought. They no longer needed to engage in debates with brilliant opposition leaders, as Stalin had once done.

Priding themselves on being practical men, they attached very little prestige to intellectual work and betrayed no desire to emulate Stalin's pretensions as a political theoretician. They looked upon Marxism as a vocabulary useful in controlling followers abroad, a group of symbols that helped cement social loyalty at home, and a body of dogmatics to be guarded by professional scholiasts, who in turn were themselves to be guarded. As Stalinism grew older, its relationship to Marxist doctrine became more manipulative, though seldom to the point of being entirely free of self-deception.

Fascinated as they now were by the mechanics of power, the Stalinist leaders, if they read Marxist works at all, were likely to turn to those dealing with political strategy and tactics rather than those concerned with ultimate goals or values. Lenin's *What Is to Be Done?* or *Left Wing Communism* might still be read by them with a certain interest, for while the topics of these pamphlets were not immediately relevant to the problems of Stalinism, they could be regarded as manuals of political warfare rich in suggestion to political strategists of almost any kind. By contrast, Marx's philosophical and economic studies were likely to be neglected by most Stalinist leaders—even though the need to validate their claim to the Marxist heritage, as well as to give themselves satisfactions akin to those felt by patrons of scholarship, prompted the Communist parties to publish these works.

Like one of the dark heretical cults of the Middle Ages which celebrated the devil through the ritual and imagery of Christ, Stalinism missed no occasion for proclaiming its Marxist orthodoxy. It defiled the intentions of Marx, his ethical passion and humanistic prophecy, but it clothed a rejection of his vision in the very language through which he had expressed it. Not for the first time in history, the vocabulary of a great thinker was turned against him, to corrupt his ideas and mock his values. Unlike other totalitarian and quasi-totalitarian movements, Stalinism was unable or unwilling to develop its own vocabulary, being an ideologically "dependent" system, an aftermath rather than a beginning.

But it would be an error to suppose that this dependence on the trappings of Marx's system was a mere useless survival. For many Stalinists it provided an indispensable means of reassurance: as long as the old words remained it was easier to evade the fact that new ideas had taken over. For the party, it facilitated the strategy of political access. The Stalinist claim to the Marxist tradition enabled it to compete for the allegiance of European workers who had been brought up in the Socialist movements, particularly those who were taught to suspect the Social Democratic parties as reformist. To have surrendered the signs and symbols it had appropriated from Marxism would have meant to face the enormously difficult task of trying to establish itself in the labor movement through a new vocabulary and what it would have had to acknowledge as a new set of ideas. Strategically, it proved far more advantageous to appear as the defender of orthodox Marxism even while ruthlessly emasculating it. The humanist elements in Marxism were discarded, the passion for man that animates Marx's writing was eliminated, and instead those aspects of Marx's thought were emphasized which might be said to be most tainted by the Hegelian *hubris* of claiming to know what the future *must* be.

So understood, Marxism could provide a feeling of having reached a "total view" which permits one to identify with History and act in accordance with its inner rhythm. The "essence" of History having been grasped, it then became possible to proclaim the primacy of *praxis*. From that point on, since there need be no further desire to question the underlying principle of social existence, strategy and tactics became all-important. The uncritical acceptance of a metaphysical assumption proved in practice to be a shield against any further assaults by metaphysical doubt or contemplative temptations. It was through works that the faith was to be manifested and tested. Theory, even while ritually celebrated, became an object of contempt.

This mixture of knowingness and a pragmatic rejection of abstract thought—a remarkable reflection, by the way, of the profoundly ambiguous feeling of the modern world toward the intellectual vocation—provided the Stalinist leaders and intellectuals with a sense of certainty in a time of doubt. And for the intellectuals it offered the sanction of doing, or seeming to do, something "real."

The elements in Marxism that have proved most attractive to the Stalinists were those most intimately tied to nineteenth-century progressivism, a mode of thought still powerful in the life of the European "left." Appearing before the world as fellow progressives—*fellow progressives in a hurry*—the Stalinists were able to utilize many aspects of the liberal tradition and to claim that far from being enemies of Western humanism—as, by contrast, many Nazi ideologues openly declared themselves—they were actually its true heirs.

Precisely to the extent that the left tradition in the West did adhere indiscriminately to a simple optimistic theory of progress, it became most vulnerable to Stalinist infiltration. For if all change tends to be impelled by the logic of History in a progressive direction, those who seemed to stand for the most change would also seem to be the greatest progressives. Put so crudely, the "progressivist" ideology comes close to intellectual caricature; but so, often enough, does political life itself. No Stalinoid intellectual in Paris would have been so unsophisticated as to accept the formula as we have reduced it here, but in the subtle writings of many a Stalinoid intellectual in Paris there was buried exactly this deification of "progress."

And precisely to the extent that modern progressivism committed itself to what might be called technological optimism—the notion that the growth of a society's productive forces automatically renders it "progressive"—did it, in turn, become most vulnerable to Stalinist influence. For the technological optimist, Dnieperstroy is an irrefutable argument.

Ideology in the Stalinist movement was both exalted and degraded as in no other movement, exalted in that it was constantly put to work and accorded formal honor, degraded in that it was never allowed any status in its own right but came to be regarded as a weapon in the struggle for power.

This relationship between Stalinism and its ideology followed from a fundamental attitude of totalitarian movements toward social and personal reality. The most terrifying assumption of the totalitarian mind is that, given the control of terror, anything is possible. In Orwell's *1984* and Milosz's *The Captive Mind* this idea is reiterated again and again, out of a despairing conviction that almost anyone can say the words but almost no one can apprehend their full significance. Given modern technology, total state control, the means of terror, and a rationalized contempt for moral values, you can do anything with men, anything with their minds, anything with words, anything with the past.

Reality is not something one recognizes or experiences; reality is something one manufactures, sometimes in anticipation, sometimes in retrospect. One day Beria is a hero of the Soviet Union, the next day a villain—which is neither so bad nor unusual. What is new is that by the third day *he does not exist*. His past has been destroyed, his name removed from the records. Many political movements have claimed to control the present, and others the future; totalitarianism was the first, however, which systematically proceeded to remake the past.

To do this, it was necessary to regard words and ideas as instrumentalities that could be put to any use. Nothing in thought or language need impose any limit. As Milosz wrote: *"What is not expressed does not exist.* Therefore if one forbids men to explore the depths of human nature, one destroys in them the urge to make such explorations; and the depths in themselves slowly become unreal."[2] And Orwell, in describing the totalitarian attitude to thought and language, pushed everything to an extreme which helped make the reality all the clearer:

> *To know and not to know, to be conscious of complete truthfulness while telling carefully constructed lies, to hold simultaneously two opinions which cancelled out, knowing them to be contradictory and believing in both of them, to use logic, to repudiate morality while laying claim to it, to believe that democracy was impossible and that the Party was the guardian of democracy, to forget whatever it was necessary to forget, then to draw it back into memory again at the moment when it was needed, and then promptly to forget it again, and above all, to apply the same process to the process itself—this was the ultimate subtlety: consciously to induce unconsciousness, and then, once again, to become unconscious of the act of hypnosis you had just performed. Even to understand the word "doublethink" involved the use of doublethink.*[3]

SMALL BUSINESSMEN, POLITICAL TOLERANCE, AND SUPPORT FOR McCARTHY

MARTIN TROW

In the past few years social scientists have responded to the threat symbolized by but by no means confined to Joseph McCarthy and have made efforts to explain the variety of illiberal and repressive movements that flourished during much of the first decade following World War II. Such social scientists as Parsons, Reisman, Shils, Hofstadter, and Lipset have written books or essays on the men, sentiments, and movements that came to be known as the "radical right." These writings, and especially the essays that were collected in the volume *The New American Right*,[1] show an impressively high measure of agreement on the nature of the social forces underlying such diverse popular movements as McCarthyism, the movement for the Bricker amendment, and the many organized actions against "subversion" in schools, libraries, the mass media, and elsewhere. In addition to the generally high measure of agreement (or at least convergence) in these essays, they are also, taken together, both highly persuasive and based on almost no empirical evidence at all, at least so far as their efforts to explain the popular support of these movements are concerned.

---

[2]Czeslaw Milosz, *The Captive Mind* (New York, 1953), p. 215.

[3]George Orwell, *1984* (New York, 1949), p. 36.

Reprinted from "Small Businessmen, Political Tolerance, and Support for McCarthy" by Martin Trow from *American Journal of Sociology*, 1958, Volume 64, by permission of The University of Chicago Press. Copyright 1958 by The University of Chicago.

[1]Daniel Bell (ed.), *The New American Right* (New York: Criterion Books, 1955).

The essayists in *The New American Right* treated McCarthyism as one manifestation of the new "radical right," largely assumed its close connection with political intolerance, and discussed the nature and sources of both as part of their interpretation of the larger phenomenon. And they saw the rise of this "radical right" as largely a consequence (or manifestation) of the increasing importance during the postwar years of "status politics" — the projection of people's status anxieties and frustrations onto the political arena — and the correlative decline in the relative importance of class or "interest" politics. Moreover, say the writers, the "status politics" which underlies the rise of the "radical right" tends to flourish in prosperous times, as "interest politics" is associated with depression and economic discontent. And the essayists deal with the "radical right's" mass support chiefly by speculating on the likely locations in our society of pockets of acute status anxieties or concerns. They do this job so thoroughly that they have left little room for surprise regarding the social composition of McCarthy's popular support. The essays show, and quite persuasively, how and why McCarthy got disproportionate support almost everywhere: among old Americans and among new Americans; among the upwardly mobile, the downwardly mobile, and the low status non-mobile; among Catholics, Yankee Protestants, and rural fundamentalists; among workers, small businessmen, the new middle class, and the "new rich," etc. This kind of analysis, which explains every possible or supposed appearance of the phenomenon, is, of course, in part a function of the paucity of data on the issue. But, while such an analysis precludes surprises, it also explains a good deal too much. Unless we can account for the actual distribution of support for a given issue or for a leader or spokesman of this political tendency, without finessing the crucial questions of "more or less," then our analysis loses much of its power and cogency.

A study done in Bennington, Vermont, during 1954 provided data for an intensive analysis of some of the social and social-psychological characteristics of McCarthy supporters in the general population. And though the movement and its leader are no longer part of the American political scene, the Bennington study indicates that the social forces that made for support of McCarthy did not die with his power or his person but remain available to other illiberal and repressive men and movements of the radical right. If that is so, then the study of McCarthy's popular support not merely is of interest to the antiquarian but may shed light on one aspect of the continuing vulnerability of a mass democratic society to radical, right-wing movements. . . .

McCarthy's Support and Political Tolerance

The widespread assumption that support for McCarthy was almost always associated with political intolerance seems to gain empirical support when we observe that support for McCarthy and political intolerance were both strongly related to the amount of formal education completed. There is nothing very startling about this: we hardly need an extensive study to know that McCarthy gained much of his popular support from poorly educated, lower-class people who are, as many studies tell us, also least likely to be tolerant of unpopular political minorities and views.

But the matter becomes not quite so routine when we examine the relationship between support for McCarthy and political tolerance holding formal education constant. When we do this, the relationship between intolerance and support for McCarthy almost or wholly disappears. On every educational level McCarthy's supporters were about as likely as his opponents to have been tolerant toward the exercise of free speech by political dissidents. In other words, while support of McCarthy and political intolerance were both related to formal education, they were very little related to each other.

The implications of this finding are many. In its simplest terms it means that, whatever the character and content of the *public* fight between McCarthy and his more prominent opponents, the sources of his support and popularity in the population at large appear to have had little relation to how strongly people support the principles of free speech.

The division over McCarthy in the population at large, at least in Bennington, was not a division between the supporters of and encroachers upon civil liberties. To see it that way is to overlook the very genuine elements of "radicalism" — of anticonservatism — in the McCarthy appeal. On the one hand, many of those who disapproved of McCarthy and his methods did so not out of any particular concern for the preservation of civil liberties or freedom of speech for unpopular minorities but rather out of a feeling that what is done to suppress "subversion" be done in conservative ways through regular legislative or judicial or administrative procedures. But these men, as their responses to our questions show, were often no more concerned with the preservation of freedom of speech than McCarthy himself and much less so than many of his followers. For many of these latter, the majority of them lower class, with little formal schooling, McCarthy's appeal was not that of a man *repressing* free speech but of a man *exercising* it, in what appeared to be bold and fearless ways. Moreover, much of his boldness, violence, and aggression was directed precisely against the conservative authorities and institutions — the "big shots," the "stuffed shirts," the "bureaucrats" — against whom many of his supporters felt anger and resentment. The men who opposed McCarthy, by and large, were solid, better educated, middle-class citizens who identified with the authorities and institutions which were McCarthy's chief targets of attack by the summer of 1954. Many an executive or engineer who watched McCarthy alternately patronize and bully Army Secretary Stevens felt, and not without reason, that he himself and men like him were also under attack.

Our finding that McCarthy's support and political intolerance were not strongly related to each other does not rest solely or even primarily on the one tabulation which shows that the apparent relationship disappears when education is held constant. That finding did indeed stimulate further inquiry in that same direction, but, as evidence accumulated, it became apparent in many other ways that the social forces underlying McCarthy's popular support were simply not the same as those making for political intolerance. And, like most empirical findings, this one posed a question: If support for McCarthy were not simply an expression of political intolerance, what were its social sources, and how did they differ from the social sources of political intolerance?

. . . In précis, we found that political tolerance is a norm or cluster of norms, very strongly related to cultural sophistication, or "cosmopolitanism," and thus to the level of formal education achieved — *and to very little else*. By contrast, popular support for McCarthy can best be understood as the channeling of certain dissatisfactions with aspects of the social, economic, and political orders. There are two elements present in that formulation: the presence of considerable discontent and dissatisfaction and the ways and directions in which those dissatisfactions are channeled. We found the highest levels of support for McCarthy in social classes and categories which, on one hand, show considerable hostility toward important elements in the social structure and, on the other hand, do not have their hostilities and discontents channeled into and through existing political and economic institutions. By contrast, neither the *level* of discontent nor the *channeling* of discontent appeared to have appreciable bearing on the levels of political tolerance characteristic of these same classes and social categories.

McCarthy's Support, Political Tolerance, and Occupation

Part of the evidence on which these general propositions are based bears on the relation of economic class and occupation to the sentiments in question. When we divide our sample into the two broad categories of "manual" and "non-manual" workers, the latter including both salaried and self-employed white-collar people, we find little or no difference between them in their support of McCarthy, holding formal education constant. Even when we divide the "non-manual" category into "lower-" and "upper-middle-class" categories, on the basis of income, we still find no appreciable differences in attitudes toward McCarthy within educational categories. But when we distinguish *within* the middle class between salaried and self-employed men, we found marked differences in their respective levels of support for McCarthy.

In every educational category the small businessmen showed a distinctly higher proportion of McCarthy supporters than did the salaried men of similar education, and, among those who had not been to college, the small businessmen were even more pro-McCarthy than the manual workers. And the differences were substantial. For example, among the men who did not finish high school, two-thirds of the small businessmen supported McCarthy, as compared with only half the workers who did and only a little more than a third of the salaried employees who did. Among the men who had been to college the differences by occupational group are smaller but still substantial: where one in three of these better-educated small businessmen supported McCarthy, only a little over one in five of the salaried employees with this education did.

There are a number of possible interpretations of this finding, some of which were investigated and rejected in light of the Bennington data. The interpretation that gained strongest support from the data can be summarized in the hypothesis that small businessmen in our society disproportionately tend to develop a generalized hostility toward a complex of symbols and processes bound up with industrial capitalism: the steady growth and concentration of government, labor organizations, and business enterprises; the correlative trend toward greater rationalization of production and distribution; and the men, institutions, and ideas that symbolize these secular trends of modern society. These trends and their symbols were, we believe, McCarthy's most persuasive targets. Quite apart from the questions of Communists in government, and blunders or worse in foreign policy, the congruence between McCarthy's attacks on and small businessmen's hostility to the dominant characteristics and tendencies of modern society account, we believe, for much of the disproportionate support McCarthy gained from small businessmen.

This hypothesis can be explored further by looking at the connections between support for McCarthy and attitudes toward the most characteristic economic institutions of our society, that is, large corporations and trade unions. A simple but serviceable typology emerges from responses to questions asking how the respondent feels about big companies and trade unions and permits us to distinguish empirically four important and easily recognizeable patterns of orientations toward the dominant economic institutions in the population at large. The group which expressed approval of labor unions but suspicion of the power of big companies, (I), is closest to the familiar "labor-liberals," who in this country gave their support to the labor-oriented, administrative liberalism of the New Deal and its descendants. The pro-big business, antiunion group, (IV), resemble the equally familiar "right-wing conservatives." The orientation I have called "moderate conservatism," (III), is held by people who are reconciled to the continued

existence both of big companies and of trade unions; this is the dominant political orientation of both major parties today.

To the student of right-wing radicalism the most interesting of
these four orientations is that which expresses hostility toward both
big business and trade unions (II). At the risk of some distortion, I
have called this orientation "nineteenth-century liberalism." In the
middle of the twentieth century the important thing about this orientation is not its intellectual content but rather its emotional tone, its
diffused anger, and its generalized suspicion toward modern tendencies
of all kinds. Among our respondents, this nineteenth-century liberalism appears both as a wistful nostalgia for a golden age of small farmers
and businessmen and also as an expression of a strong resentment and
hatred toward a world which makes no sense in terms of older ideas
and which is conducted in apparent violation of old truths and values
of economic and political life.

. . . [W]e find that there were scarcely any differences among
holders of three of the four orientations in their proportions of Mc-
Carthy supporters.

But among the poorly educated, as among the better educated,
the nineteenth-century liberals gave McCarthy distinctly higher proportions of support than any of the other three orientations we examined. Among the men who had less than four years of high school,
the difference between the nineteenth-century liberals and all the
others in the proportions supporting McCarthy is the difference between two-thirds and a half. Among the better educated, the difference is between a half as compared with a third of all others who gave
McCarthy their support.

There are two findings here which are perhaps of equal interest
to the student of right-wing radicalism. The first—that there was little
difference in the support McCarthy gained among labor-liberals,
moderate conservatives, and right-wing conservatives—contradicts the
widespread liberal assumption that McCarthy got much of his mass
support from the traditional right-wing conservatives. The other
finding, with which we are chiefly concerned here, is that men holding
the nineteenth-century liberal orientation toward big business and trade
unions showed a markedly greater vulnerability to McCarthy's appeal.
These men, as I have noted, are often angrily confused and deeply
resentful of a world that continually offends their deepest values. But
as important is the fact that this particular well of resentment and indignation has no effective and institutionalized channels of expression.
Right-wing conservatives have substantial power in the business community and the Republican party; labor-liberals are a strong force in the
trade unions, some big-city machines, and are well represented in the
Democratic party; and the moderate conservatives have everything else.
It is precisely the political orientation which has no institutionalized

place on the political scene, little representation or leadership in the major parties, which sought that voice and place through McCarthy. And he expressed for them their fear and mistrust of bigness and of the slick and subversive ideas that come out of the cities and the big institutions to erode old ways and faiths.

It should come as no surprise to find that the small businessmen in our sample were distinctly more likely than manual workers or salaried employees to hold nineteenth-century liberal views regarding trade unions and large corporations. Where small businessmen comprised only one-fifth of the men in these occupational categories in our sample, they contributed a third of the nineteenth-century liberals. Moreover, the small businessmen who *held* these views gave McCarthy a very high measure of support. The very highest proportion of McCarthy supporters among these categories was found among the poorly educated small businessmen holding these nineteenth-century liberal attitudes; almost three out of four of these men were McCarthy supporters. Here is evidence that a generalized fear of the dominant currents and institutions of modern society was an important source of McCarthy's mass appeal, not *only* among small businessmen, but perhaps especially among a group like small businessmen whose economic and status security is continually threatened by those currents and institutions.

One can hardly consider the connection between economic class and right-wing radicalism in America without thinking of the analysis of the Nazi party's mass support before Hitler took power, an analysis developed by such men as Erich Fromm, Sigmund Neumann, Karl Mannheim, Emil Lederer, and Alfred Meusal. The comparison suggests itself despite, or perhaps even because of, the very great differences in the historical backgrounds and in the social, political, and economic contexts of right-wing radical movements in Europe and the United States. All the observers of naziism are agreed that lower-middle-class tradesmen, shopkeepers, and artisans gave the Nazis a disproportionately large measure of their support before the Nazis took power. And they did so, these observers agree, because of their deep-seated fear of radical proletarianism, on one hand, and of the rapid rationalization of production and distribution—that is to say, the large corporation and the department store—on the other. (These fears involved their concern with *both* material and status security.) To the small German proprietor, Hitler promised to crush radical proletarianism and control big business.

Nothing could seem further from the social scene that these writers were speaking of—societies undergoing almost continuous crisis, experiencing intense class conflicts and increasingly wide desperation and despair—than the general climate in a relatively prosperous, small New England town in 1954. The chief characteristic of Bennington's social and political climate was an absence of intense class conflict or conflict of any kind; rather there was a very considerable amount of tolerance, good humor, and the appearance of widespread optimism about the future. Similarly, nothing could seem more inappropriate to the political orientations of Benningtonians than the apocalyptic analysis applied to pre-Hitler Europe. What is perhaps surprising is that in this climate of optimism, good humor, and low-temperature politics, small businessmen in Bennington were apparently responding to the pressures of industrial capitalism in ways not wholly unlike their beleaguered cousins in the Middle Europe of twenty-five years ago, though at much lower levels of intensity.

McCarthy's Support and Salaried Employees

But this comparison of the social sources of Hitler's popular support with McCarthy's shows one very striking anomaly. Students of naziism usually speak of the disproportionate support the Nazis got from the German lower middle class, in which they lump small tradesmen, artisans, and businessmen together with lower white-collar salaried employees. The evidence would seem to justify their approach: Hans Gerth's study of the membership of the Nazi party in 1933 shows that both small proprietors and salaried employees were disproportionately represented in the membership of the Nazi party and to about the same degree, both groups supplying about twice the proportion of Nazi party members as compared with their representation in the population at large.[2] And the students of naziism explain Hitler's support among the salaried white-collar workers in much the same way they explain the support the Nazis got from the small proprietors: largely in terms of their status anxieties—anxieties arising especially out of the discrepancy between their precarious and deteriorating economic positions and their status claims and aspirations.

By contrast, in Bennington the salaried employees not only were not as pro-McCarthy as the small businessmen but were strikingly low in the support they gave him, as indicated above. This was true not only of the better-educated managers, executives, technicians, and salaried professionals who might be expected to identify with McCarthy's high-status targets. It was also true of the less-well-educated and low-income white-collar men. Less than 30 per cent of the very large group of salaried employees gave McCarthy their approval and support, as compared with over half of all the small businessmen and merchants.

How can we account for the fact that, while the analysis of the anxieties and politics of small businessmen in pre-Hitler Germany is not irrelevant to our understanding of the political orientations of small businessmen in Bennington in 1954, the behaviors of the salaried em-

[2]Hans Gerth, "The Nazi Party: Its Leadership and Composition," *American Journal of Sociology*, 1940 (January), 45: 517–541, especially Table 1.

ployees in the two situations were almost diametrically opposite? The
answer seems to lie in the general orientation of the two classes to
modern industrial society. Salaried employees, whether in Germany
or the United States, or in the new countries of the Near and Far East,
are in general *not* alienated from the dominant trends and institutions
of modern society; these trends and developments of concentration,
specialization, rationalization, and bureaucratization have created the
class of salaried employees and are its natural habitat. But, while accepting the general shape and direction of modern society, the salaried
employees in Europe responded violently to short-run crises in capitalist society—to inflation, depression, mass unemployment, and their
consequent insecurities of livelihood and social status. In this light it
is not surprising that the general orientation of white-collar people in
a booming and expanding economy such as the United States has had
since World War II should be moderate, conservative, and generally
complacent about the political economy and its direction. And this because of, not despite, the fact that the tendencies toward concentration
and centralization are great and swift-moving. In pre-Hitler Germany
the same classes turned to Hitler in great numbers as the large organizations which structured their lives and careers proved increasingly
incapable of providing the material and status security they demanded.
Their response was not against large organization but against the collapse of bureaucratic society and toward a man and a party which
promised to revive and extend it.

By contrast, small businessmen react not so much to short-run crises
in the economy as to its long-range tendencies and direction of development—against the society itself rather than merely to failures of
its economy. The tendencies which small businessmen fear—of concentration and centralization—proceed without interruption in depression,
war, and prosperity and irrespective of the party in power; thus they are
always disaffected, though probably the acute pinch they feel in de-
pressions makes their anxieties and angers sharper and more pointed.
In this light, the small businessmen in prosperous Bennington of 1954
were not so fundamentally different in their response to the social and
economic pressures of modern society from the equivalent strata in
pre-Hitler Germany, or from their opposite members in the France
of Poujade.

Occupation and Political Tolerance

It remains to be said, and with some emphasis, that the disproportionate
support small businessmen gave to McCarthy is *not* evidence that they
constitute a pool of repressive and illiberal sentiments of all kinds.
On the contrary, we can see that, despite their vulnerability to a right-
wing demagogue like McCarthy, small businessmen are no more politically intolerant than are salaried employees or manual workers of

similar education. Here again we find that occupation and economic class, and all the varied discontents that flow from membership in different class and occupational groups, seem to have little bearing on political tolerance, certainly as compared with the bearing of formal education and cultural sophistication. By contrast with support of McCarthy, tolerance of dissidence appears to be almost wholly a function of the degree to which men have learned and internalized the rules of the democratic political game: in the United States this, in turn, is closely related to general political awareness and sophistication, acquired in part through formal education and through exposure to the serious political media which support those norms, rather than through economic or occupational experience. Where political tolerance for the most part is a norm held and enforced in the sub-cultures of sophisticated men, most of whom have been to college, popular support for McCarthy, by contrast, seemed to have been largely the channeled expression of various kinds of socially engendered discontents.

The "Radical Right" and Popular Sentiments

Our findings clearly indicate that students of public opinion on political issues might well be wary of such concepts as the "radical right" and its "pseudo-conservative" members, with all the assumptions regarding a coherent if latent structure of attitudes in the general population that those terms imply. Supporters of the "radical right" have been seen not only as having supported McCarthy but also as hostile to the New Deal, organized labor, the graduated income tax, and the United Nations, as authoritarian in character, intolerant of political non-conformists, and prejudiced against racial and religious groups. Whatever may be said or learned regarding the leaders and activists of right-wing radical movements, it is not likely that these characteristics and sentiments will be found in close association in the population at large. In this respect "radical rightism" may be like "liberalism," whose articulate representatives are usually civil libertarians, internationalists, in favor of organized labor and social welfare programs, whereas in the population at large these supposed components of "liberalism" do not tend to be found together. . . .

THE SUPPORTS OF McCARTHYISM

SEYMOUR M. LIPSET

Efforts to account for adherence to extremist political ideologies, and to McCarthyism in particular, have suggested that such groups cannot

From *The Radical Right,* edited by Daniel Bell (Great Meadows, New Jersey: S. G. Phillips, Inc., 1963), pp. 411–420. Title supplied by the editor.

be explained solely or even primarily by an analysis of the values and interests of their supporters. Rather, it has been argued that the support for extremist ideologies and conspiracy theories of politics is also related to personality structure—i.e., that certain types of people find such politics congruent with their psychological needs. These hypotheses have often been linked to the findings in *The Authoritarian Personality*,[1] which suggested there is a definite personality type that is oriented toward strong leadership, is intolerant, dislikes ambiguity, and so forth.

. . . One of the earliest analyses of McCarthy support, Harold Hodges' study of a Wisconsin town, reported that "the statistically typical McCarthy supporter . . . is more conformistic, agreeing that there are too many 'oddballs' around, that the 'good' American doesn't stand out among his fellow Americans, and that children should not develop hobbies which are rare or unusual. . . . He expresses a more misanthropic social outlook, concurring with the statement that 'people are out to cheat you' and that there is 'wickedness, cheating and corruption all about us.'"[2] The Sokol community survey . . . also reported a strong relationship between personality traits and support of McCarthy. Those who were more intolerant of ambiguity were also more pro-McCarthy. This relationship held even when examined within the categories of education and religious affiliation, two variables that have been shown to affect such attitudes.[3] To test these hypotheses on a broader scale, data taken from a national survey made by the National Opinion Research Center (N.O.R.C.) in 1953, which contained items taken from the original Authoritarian Personality scale, have been reanalyzed here.

Propensity to agree with items designed to measure authoritarian predispositions correlated highly with attitudes toward McCarthy within educational, occupational, or religious groupings. For example, within the three educational categories of college, high school, and grammar school, those high on the Authoritarian Personality scale were much more likely to have approved of the McCarthy committee in June, 1953, than those with low scores. Seemingly, reactions to the Senator were not only a function of social position, perception of self-interest, or party identification, but were also affected by that component of "character" that the Authoritarian Personality scale measures.

[1]T. W. Adorno, Else Frenkel-Brunswik, Daniel Levinson, and R. Nevitt Sanford, *The Authoritarian Personality* (New York: Harper & Brothers, 1950).

[2]Harold M. Hodges, "A Sociological Analysis of McCarthy Supporters" (unpublished paper, San Jose State College), pp. 2–3.

[3]See H. H. Hyman and Paul Sheatsley, "'The Authoritarian Personality—A Methodological Critique," in R. Christie and M. Jahoda (eds.), *Studies in the Scope and Method of "The Authoritarian Personality"* (Glencoe, Illinois: The Free Press, 1954), pp. 94–96.

It is significant to note that the largest differences in response to McCarthy occurred within the category of the college-educated. Those among them who were low on the Authoritarian Personality scale were least likely to approve of the Senator, but the college-educated who were high on the measure of authoritarianism gave more support to the Mc-Carthy committee than any segment of those who had not gone beyond grade school. Since various studies have indicated that propensity to give an authoritarian response is inversely related to education, this finding suggests that the Authoritarian Personality ·scale serves best as a predictor of attitude predispositions among the well educated. Among the less educated, a high authoritarianism score reflects in some part attitudes common to the group, which are also subject to modification by more education. If someone is well educated and still gives authoritarian responses, then the chances are that he really has a basic tendency to react in an authoritarian fashion. However, . . . there is a relationship between propensity to give "authoritarian" responses and support of McCarthy within the three education groups.

Although McCarthy never attacked minority ethnic groups and seemed to have consciously tried to avoid linking Jews to Communism, many of his critics have felt certain that McCarthyism appealed to re-ligious and racial bigots. Liberals have generally believed that anti-Semitism and rightist politics are associated, and have therefore as-sumed that, while any given form of right-wing extremism may not be overtly anti-Semitic, such movements attract anti-Semites. With respect to McCarthyism, there has been the further assumption that those who believed in Jews as a hidden source of social ills would also be disposed to believe in a hidden domestic Communist conspiracy that had in-filtrated the government. The evidence available from the various stud-ies bearing on this issue, however, does not bear out these assumptions.

The I.N.R.A. pre-election study in 1954 asked respondents whether they would be more or less likely to vote for a Congressional candidate if they knew he was Jewish. About 3 per cent said they would be more likely to vote for a Jewish candidate; 17 per cent gave an anti-Semitic response, saying that they would be more likely to oppose a Jewish candidate; while the remaining four-fifths of the sample said knowledge of Jewish background would not affect their vote decision. Comparing the relationship between sentiments toward Jewish Congressional candidates and attitudes to candidates who were pro- or anti-McCarthy produced the startling result that the small group of philo-Semites —those who were favorable to Jewish candidates—were much more likely to be pro-McCarthy than those who were against Jewish Congres-sional candidates. The latter were also much more likely to be anti-McCarthy than those who said their vote would not be influenced by the candidate's being Jewish.

This result is so surprising as to suggest the existence of an intervening factor associated with one or the other attitude so as to produce a spurious result. To check on such a possibility, the relationship between McCarthyism and anti-Semitism was analyzed within education groups, religious groups, and party-identification groups. The finding, however, still occurred in all. Among the college-educated, as among the high-school- or grammar-school-educated, the same pattern held up—the small per cent of those who were philo-Jewish were more pro-Mc-Carthy. Catholics were less anti-Semitic than Protestants, but within both religious groups McCarthy support and anti-Semitism were inversely related. The relationship was also sustained within the three political categories of Democrats, Republicans, and Independents.

If we assume that there is some reliability in this result, that it truly measured popular attitudes at the time, it is conceivable that the result is a product of McCarthy's association with various minority ethnics including Jews. The I.N.R.A. study was made after McCarthy's association with Roy Cohn and David Schein, two men publicly identified as Jews, had become a matter of public discussion and controversy. This identification may have led many rank-and-file supporters of the Senator to perceive Jews as being on their side. All this is highly speculative, but the fact remains that the I.N.R.A. results do produce a result that reverses any assumptions about a positive relationship between McCarthyism and anti-Semitism.

The finding that McCarthy supporters were not prone to accept anti-Semitic beliefs is reinforced by a report of a November, 1954, N.O.R.C. study based on a national sample of 1200 Christian respondents. This survey found no relationship between attitudes toward McCarthy and willingness to accept Jews as next-door neighbors. When educational differences were controlled, no consistent linkage between the two attitudes could be observed. (However, since writing this article, my own further analysis of the data of this study has indicated that there is a slight relationship between rejecting Jews as neighbors and being pro-McCarthy in the total sample.)

The lack of a positive relationship between McCarthyism and anti-Semitism may reflect a more general absence of any relationship between ethnic prejudice and McCarthy support. A 1954 Gallup survey inquired, "Would you object to having your children attend a school where the majority of pupils are Negro?" Over half of the sample (about 55 per cent indicated they would object. When the sample was divided between followers and opponents of McCarthy within educational categories, there was no consistent relationship between the willingness to send one's children to a predominantly Negro school and attitudes toward McCarthy. The followers of the Senator were no more and no less liberal on this issue than his opponents.

But if these surveys challenge the liberal intellectuals' belief that McCarthyites were generally intolerant people, there is some evidence to suggest that at least one type of anti-Semitism may have contributed to a small part of McCarthy's support. Data from the 1953 N.O.R.C. survey suggest that those individuals who believed that Jews were disproportionately apt to be Communists were somewhat more likely to approve of the McCarthy committee than those who did not mention Jews. This survey, taken early in the Senator's career as chairman of the Senate investigating committee on government operations, found that a majority (60 per cent) approved of his committee. Of the 8 per cent in the sample who mentioned Jews as being disproportionately Communist, 69 per cent approved of the committee, while among respondents who did not list Jews, 59 per cent reacted favorably to McCarthy. While these results differ from those found in the other surveys, further specification of the relationship within social categories reduces their significance as indicators of greater anti-Semitic sentiments among McCarthyites. When elementary-school-, high-school-, and college-educated respondents are examined separately, the relationship holds among those who did not go beyond elementary school. Of this low-educated group, those who were pro-McCarthy more often mentioned Jews as being Communist than did those who were anti-McCarthy. Within the category of the high-school-educated, there was no relationship between propensity to identify Jews with Communists and attitudes toward the McCarthy committee, while among the college-educated the relationship was *reversed*. In this stratum, presumably the best informed of the three, the anti-McCarthy group more often saw Jews as disproportionately Communist.

The four surveys are not, of course, directly comparable, for many reasons. Cohn and Schein were not an issue when the 1953 N.O.R.C. interviews were taken but had become a major source of controversy by the time of the 1954 studies, at which period McCarthy had lost considerable support. More important perhaps is the fact that the studies were asking very different questions. The 1954 surveys were touching on general attitudes toward Jews, while the 1953 poll was tapping the reactions of the very small group who see Jews as more Communistically inclined than non-Jews. Most of the respondents felt that "only a few" Jews are Communists. In fact, studies of the social base of American Communism indicate that while the overwhelming majority of Jews have opposed Communism, Jews have contributed disproportionately to the support of the American Communist Party. Those, therefore, who mention Jews as Communists may be reflecting greater knowledge and concern about Communism rather than anti-Semitism as such.

Analysis of other data in the 1953 N.O.R.C. survey tends to sustain the interpretation that the fact that McCarthy supporters were more likely to mention Jews as disproportionately Communist reflects concern with the Communist issue rather than anti-Semitism. Respondents were asked whether they had heard any criticism of Jews in the last six months. About one-fifth, 21 per cent, reported that they had heard such criticism. Those whose acquaintances included critics of Jews were proportionately *less* favorable to McCarthy than those who did not report hearing anti-Semitic remarks. The respondents mentioned the specific types of attacks they heard. These break down into a variety of criticisms of Jews as having too much political or economic power, being unscrupulous in business, being socially clannish, *and* those involving charges that Jews are more likely than others to be Communists, or spies and traitors. Most of the anti-Jewish criticisms reported, however, did not concern Communism or spying. Individuals who mentioned hearing anti-Semitic comments not involving Communism were most likely of all to be anti-McCarthy, while the small group that mentioned having heard that Jews were Communists tended to show a larger than average support for the Wisconsin Senator. These results suggest that "normal anti-Semitic" stereotypes—that is, those concerning presumed negative Jewish economic or social traits—were more common in the social environment of people who were against the Senator than of those who were for him.

Given the limitations of the measures of anti-Semitism and the varying results in the three surveys, it is impossible to draw any conclusions about a relationship between anti-Semitism and propensity to support or oppose McCarthy. The available evidence clearly does not sustain the thesis that McCarthy received disproportionate support from anti-Semites. . . .

. . . McCarthy's support was differentially based on the lower strata of manual workers, the less educated, and, within the middle class, farmers and self-employed businessmen. From a political standpoint, he recruited more heavily from the conservative groups, from Republicans, backers of right-wing policies on domestic issues, isolationists, and those most concerned with the need for a "tough" anti-Russian policy. In terms of religious and ethnic characteristics, he was disproportionately backed by his Catholic co-religionists, by members of lower-status Protestant denominations, and by those of recent immigrant stock, particularly Irish and German Catholics.

The evidence does not bear out any assumptions about a link between ethnic prejudice, particularly anti-Semitism, and McCarthyism. It does, however, argue for the thesis that McCarthy drew disproportionate support from those whose personality traits or social background led them to give "authoritarian" responses to items from the Authoritarian Personality scale—that is, persons who were generally intolerant of ambiguity, approved of strong leadership, and favored harsh punishment for violations of social norms.

7. The End of Ideology?

Recently some intellectuals have declared that ideology itself is no longer relevant to a discussion of political man. In the first selection that follows, Seymour Lipset undertakes to relate a pattern of personal social and economic values to the structure of political beliefs. In doing so, he points out that various patterns of values — not just one — can be related to a stable democratic political system.

The other selections constitute a debate between two American intellectuals about the role of ideology in political life today. In the exchange between Daniel Bell and Henry David Aiken — an exchange that might helpfully be read in conjunction with the concluding chapter of Bell's **The End of Ideology** *(1961) — note how often a fundamental difference in the concept of ideology and its political uses is expressed by the participants. To Aiken the argument against ideology implies a rejection of the political relevance of knowledge, while to Bell it removes the temptation to interject one's personal feelings into what should be a rational analysis. To Aiken the end-of-ideology argument applies only to a specific genre, namely Marxism; to Bell the argument applies to all political beliefs that become a kind of "secular religion." To Aiken the rejection of ideology involves the dismissal of political ideas that reach toward an ideal politics; to Bell the rejection of ideology permits rational rather than emotional analysis of those politics of the modern world. For the student this debate raises the questions of whether one is to debate issues or policies, whether the intellectual is to be a critic of policies or a participant in policy-making, and whether there is a need for pragmatic political discourse or the more elevating and polemic style of ideological rhetoric.*

BEYOND POLITICAL IDEAS

SEYMOUR M. LIPSET

Though the United States and Great Britain are both urbanized, industrialized, and stable politically, they are integrated around different

Reprinted from *The First New Nation* © 1963 by Seymour Martin Lipset, Basic Books, Inc., Publishers, pages 213–224. Title supplied by the editor.

values and class relations. Tocqueville's *Democracy in America* and Bagehot's *The English Constitution* accurately specified these different organizing principles. According to Tocqueville, American democratic society was equalitarian and competitive (achievement oriented); according to Bagehot, Britain was deferential (elitist) and ascriptive. As both Tocqueville and Bagehot indicated, a society in which the historic ties of traditional legitimacy had been forcibly broken could sustain a stable democratic polity only if it emphasized equality and if it contained strong, independent, and competitive institutions. Conversely, if the privileged classes persisted and continued to expect ascriptive (aristocratic) and elitist rights, a society could have a stable democratic system only if the lower classes accepted the status system. Suffice it to say now that a stable democracy can result from different combinations of pattern variables.

The United States, more than any other modern non-Communist industrial nation, emphasizes achievement, equalitarianism, universalism, and specificity. These four tend to be mutually supportive. This does not mean that other stable combinations are not possible or that the "American" combination does not exhibit tensions. From the perspective of the polity, however, this combination of variables does encourage stable democracy. The upper classes can accept improvements in the status and power of the lower strata *without feeling morally offended.* Since all men and groups are expected to try to improve their position *vis á vis* others, success by a previously deprived group is not resented as deeply as in countries whose values stress the moral worth of ascription. Similarly, the emphasis on equalitarianism, universalism, and specificity means that men can expect — and within limits do receive — fair treatment according to the merits of the case or their ability. Lower-class individuals and groups which desire to change their social position *need not be revolutionary*; consequently their political goals and methods are relatively moderate. There is little class consciousness on their part, since this consciousness is in part an adaptation to the behavior of the upper class in those societies characterized by ascription, elitism, particularism, and diffuseness. The latter values imply that men will be treated by others and will treat each other diffusely in terms of class status. American values support interaction with an individual in terms of his role as worker in one situation, as suburban dweller in another, as a member of the American Legion in a third, and so forth. . . .

Britain has come to accept the values of achievement in its economic and educational system, and to some extent in its political system, but retains a substantial degree of elitism (the assumption that those who hold high position be given generalized deference) and ascription (that those born to high place should retain it). Tocqueville described the British class system as an "open aristocracy," which can be entered by achievement but which confers on new entrants many of the diffuse perquisites of rank enjoyed by those whose membership stems from their social background. Thus Britain differs from the United States in having, in terms of pattern variables, a strong emphasis on ascriptive, elitist, particularistic, and diffuse values.

In the nineteenth century the British business classes challenged the traditional pre-industrial value integration. But the British upper class (in contrast to most Continental aristocracies) did not strongly resist the claims of the new business classes, and later those of the workers, to take part in politics. . . . [W]hen pressure for political participation developed within these classes in Britain, it was members of already enfranchised classes who took the leadership in reform movements. If communication between the different strata in Britain had been blocked by jealously guarded privileges — as it had been in France — conflicts over the suffrage might have become more divisive. As Robert Michels once pointed out, the presence of upper-class leaders in a working-class party serves to reduce conservatives' hostility toward it. To the extent that the social system permits a "left" party to recruit leaders from the existing elite, it is easier for this party to become an accepted part of the polity. It is worth noting that, unlike the British Labour Party, the German socialists have recruited few, if any, leaders from the old upper classes.

Thus the *economy* and *polity* in Britain have been characterized by achievement, elitism, universalism, and diffuseness. The *social class* system, however, retains many elements of ascription, elitism, particularism, and diffuseness. The traditional upper classes and their institutions — the public schools, the ancient universities, and the titled aristocracy — remain at the summit of the social structure. At the same time, achievers in job and school are not barred from securing diffuse elite status, and the lower classes feel that the political institutions operate for their benefit. Like the liberal bourgeoisie before them, the British workers have never seriously developed the objective of eliminating the old privileged classes, either socially or economically. Having been allowed into the political club almost as soon as British labor developed organizations of its own, working-class leaders have supported the rules of the parliamentary game. Unlike many early Continental socialist parties, they were willing, while a small minority party, to cooperate with one of the older parties. And currently they remain the only socialist party whose policies "sustain" the legitimacy of aristocracy; their leaders, like other members of the Establishment, willingly accept aristocratic titles and other honors from the Crown.

The deference shown to the system by the leaders and the rank and file of the labor movement is not simply a reaction to the strength of the status system. The British upper class has long shown a high level of sophistication in handling the admission of new strata to the "club."

Thus in 1923, as Labour was about to form its first government, the *Sunday Times* printed a manifesto by Richard Haldane (Viscount of Cloan) urging that the two old parties give Labour a fair chance at government:

> *We have to recognize that a great change is in progress. Labour has attained to commanding power and to a new status. There is no need for alarm. All may go well if as a nation we keep in mind the necessity of the satisfaction of two new demands — that for recognition of the title to equality, and for more knowledge and its systematic application to industry and to the rest of life. . . . The result of the General Election may prove a blessing to us if it has awakened us to our neglect of something momentous which has been slowly emerging for years past. . . . Three quarters of a century since, the old Whigs, wise in their limited way, refused to meet the Chartist movement merely with a blank refusal. Thereby they earned our gratitude. For while most of the nations of Europe were plunged into revolution as a result of turning deaf ears to their violent progressives, we were saved, and remained in comparative quiet. . . . We had spoken with the enemy in the gate, and he had turned out to be of the same flesh and blood as ourselves. . . .*[1]

Edward Shils, in *The Torment of Secrecy*, seeks to account for the great emphasis on publicity concerning political matters in the United States, e.g., congressional investigations, as contrasted with the stress on privacy and secrecy in Britain. His explanation hinges on the fact that Britain is still a deferential society as compared with the United States:

> *The United States has been committed to the principle of publicity since its origin. The atmosphere of distrust of aristocracy and of pretensions to aristocracy in which the American Republic spent its formative years has persisted in many forms. Repugnance for governmental secretiveness was an offspring of the distrust of aristocracy.*
>
> *In the United States, the political elite could never claim the immunities and privileges of the rulers of an aristocratic society. . . .*
>
> *American culture is a populistic culture. As such, it seeks publicity as a good in itself. Extremely suspicious of anything which smacks of "holding back," it appreciates publicity, not merely as a curb on the arrogance of rulers but as a condition in which the members of society are brought into a maximum of contact with each other.*
>
> *. . . Great Britain is a modern, large-scale society with a politicized population, a tradition of institutionalized pluralism, a system of representative institutions and great freedom of enquiry, discussion,*

[1]Quoted in Kingsley Martin, *The Crown and the Establishment* (London: Hutchinson, 1962), p. 88.

> *and reporting. . . . British political life is strikingly quiet and con-*
> *fined. Modern publicity is hemmed about by a generally well-respected*
> *privacy. . . .*
>
> *Although democratic and pluralistic, British society is not popu-*
> *list. Great Britain is a hierarchical country. Even when it is distrusted,*
> *the Government, instead of being looked down upon, as it often is*
> *in the United States, is, as such, the object of deference because the*
> *Government is still diffused with the symbolism of a monarchical and*
> *aristocratic society. The British Government, of course, is no longer*
> *aristocratic . . . [But it] enjoys the deference which is aroused in the*
> *breast of Englishmen by the symbols of hierarchy which find their*
> *highest expression in the Monarchy. . . .*
>
> *The acceptance of hierarchy in British society permits the Gov-*
> *ernment to retain its secrets, with little challenge or resentment.*
> *. . . The deferential attitude of the working and middle classes is*
> *matched by the uncommunicativeness of the upper-middle classes*
> *and of those who govern. . . . The traditional sense of the privacy*
> *of executive deliberations characteristic of the ruling classes of Great*
> *Britain has imposed itself on the rest of the society and has established*
> *a barrier beyond which publicity may not justifiably penetrate.*[2]

The protection from populist criticism which an elitist system gives
to all who possess the diffuse status of "leaders" extends not only to
the political and intellectual elites but to school teachers and the school
system as well. A study of the comparative position of teachers in England and America points this out well:

> *Conservative, Labour, and Liberal parties alike have consistently*
> *held to the view that the content of education and methods of in-*
> *struction are not matters for popular debate and decision, but should*
> *be left in the hands of teachers themselves and of other professional*
> *educators. This being so, individuals or groups seeking to "use" the*
> *schools for their own purposes are confronted, not by the hastily*
> *constructed defenses of the teacher or of a single school or school*
> *board, as in America, but by the massive disregard of experienced poli-*
> *ticians and administrators. This willing delegation of educational issues*
> *to educators is possible because the latter form a coherent and pre-*
> *dictable element in the authority structure that moulds society. . . .*
>
> *The relation between the school and the family also differs in the*
> *two countries. In America, for the most part, the parents hand over*
> *their child to the school system, but maintain a continuous scrutiny*
> *over progress. In England, "interference" by the parents in the*
> *school is resisted both by teachers and by educational administrators.*

[2]Edward A. Shils, *The Torment of Secrecy* (Glencoe, Illinois: The Free Press, 1956), pp. 37–51. . . .

> *Parents' associations and parent-teacher associations are becoming increasingly common, but they limit their activities to social functions and to meetings at which school policy is explained but not debated.*[3]

Ralph Turner also shows how variations in the basic values of the two societies impinge on their educational systems. American education reflects the norms of *contest mobility*, "a system in which elite status is the prize in an open contest and is taken by the aspirants' own efforts. . . . Since the 'prize' of successful upward mobility is not in the hands of the established elite to give out, the latter are not in a position to determine who shall attain it and who shall not." Conversely, British education reflects the norms of *sponsored mobility*, in which "elite status is *given* on the basis of some criterion of supposed merit and cannot be *taken* by any amount of effort or strategy. Upward mobility is like entry into a private club, where each candidate must be 'sponsored' by one or more of the members."

The American system, with its emphasis on the common school and opportunities for further education at every level, encourages all to advance themselves through their own efforts. "Every individual is encouraged to think of himself as competing for an elite position, so that in preparation he cultivates loyalty to the system and conventional attitudes."[4] Conversely, the British system has always selected the minority who will go ahead in the educational system at a relatively early age. Those not selected, the large bulk of the population, are taught to "regard themselves as relatively incompetent to manage society. . . . The earlier that selection of the elite recruits can be made, the sooner the masses can be taught to accept their inferiority and to make 'realistic' rather than phantasy plans."[5] Those selected for the elite, on the other hand, are removed from competition and admitted to a school, either public or grammar, in which there is great emphasis on absorbing the elite's aesthetic culture, manners, and sense of paternalism toward the non-elite. Unlike the situation in America, where in the absence of a sense of a special elite culture the masses retain their right and ability to determine taste, English society operates on the assumption that only the elite may determine what is high or low quality.

In his discussion of the sources of stability of English democracy, Harry Eckstein observes that authority patterns vary among the classes —authoritarian relations increase as one moves down the social ladder. Within the British elite, he suggests, social relations

[3]George Baron and Asher Tropp, "Teachers in England and America," in A. H. Halsey, Jean Floud, and C. A. Anderson (eds.), *Education, Economy, and Society* (New York: The Free Press, 1961), p. 548.

[4]Ralph Turner, "Modes of Social Ascent Through Education: Sponsored and Contest Mobility," in A. H. Halsey, Jean Floud, and C. A. Anderson (eds.), *Education, Economy, and Society* (New York: The Free Press, 1961), pp. 122, 125. . . .

[5]*Ibid.*, p. 126. . . .

tend to be quite surprisingly democratic, or at least consultative and comradely; here . . . we might note the ubiquity of committees at every conceivable level in the higher civil service, the unusual use of staff committees in the military services, and the easy relations among officers of all ranks in military regiments, especially in elitist regiments like the Guards . . . , while behavior among pupils [in upper-class public schools] is modeled to a remarkable extent on the political system.

[Conversely, where hierarchical relations are involved, as] between members of the Administrative Class [of the Civil Service] and their underlings, officers and their men, managers and their help, relations are highly non-consultative and certainly not comradely. . . .[6]

The United States and Great Britain differ, of course, not only in these patterns, but in the extent to which the same value orientations dominate the key status, economic, and political subsystems of the society. Presumably, Eckstein would relate the stability of American populist democracy to the fact that there are egalitarian social relations within all levels. American society has more homogeneity of values than the British. On the other hand, the particular distribution of different value orientations in Britain would also seem to be congruent with the stability of an industrialized democracy, since it legitimates open participation by all groups in the economy and polity, while the diffuse elitism rewards all with a claim to high position.

THE REVOLT AGAINST IDEOLOGY

HENRY DAVID AIKEN

Can it any longer be doubted that, on all sides of the Iron Curtain, the age of Leviathan is upon us? And for serious men does there remain any significant form of activity that is politically indifferent? We still profess loyalty to the ideal of "free inquiry," but the fact is that, directly or indirectly, governments supply the major resources, and politics most of the incentives, for our scientific research. And if some fortunate scientists of eminence are still encouraged to do "pure" or "basic" research, according to their interest, the primary reason is not that such studies exemplify one of man's essential intrinsic goods, but that the state cannot survive without them. Indeed, our universities and governments, along with our great industrial complexes, look increasingly like

[6]Harry Eckstein, *A Theory of Stable Democracy* (Princeton, N.J.: Monograph No. 10. Center for International Studies, Princeton University, 1961), pp. 15–16.

the interlocking arms of a great, if also headless, political establishment. Free enterprise (who doubts it?) is everywhere a dead issue save in the mythology of fundamentalist Republicanism, and whether our political leaders favor state capitalism or corporate socialism, the welfare state is accepted by all as an irremovable reality. Politics provide the primary themes of our literature, and when the critics charge a novelist or poet with "retreating from life," what they mean by "life" does not need to be construed. "Aesthetics" signifies merely enfeeblement and irrelevance; the "pure" artist, like the pure scientist, is a dying species, and none will mourn him save perhaps a few old "new critics" who, be it added, well understood the political meaning of their own dandified aestheticism. Our most exigent moral perplexities are overwhelmingly political, and our gods, such as they are, seem wholly preoccupied with affairs of state.

I must admit, however, that there still exists one quiet place where a man may go if he is nauseated by problems of politics and hence of power, and one course of study which he may still pursue without fear of political encroachment: he may go, that is, to the graduate school of any great university and take up the subject known there as "philosophy." Among the intellectuals, to my knowledge, we philosophers alone are politically inert. The meaning of the concept of political obligation fascinates some few of my colleagues, but I have rarely heard them, in congress assembled, discuss their political obligations. And if any were asked to offer their opinions concerning the ends, or limits, of government they would probably either decline to answer or regard the question as philosophically improper.

In order to prove the rule, there remain a few notorious exceptions such as Bertrand Russell, Jean-Paul Sartre, and Professor Sidney Hook. But we have Russell's own word for it that his politics, like his ethics, and his philosophy have nothing in common except that both were hatched under the same head of hair, and both Sartre and Hook are frequently dismissed by their more academic colleagues as publicists who have deserted philosophy for careers as ideologists and politicians. Recalling the greatest names in the history of philosophy from Socrates to Aquinas and from Hobbes to Mill, one may wonder momentarily how such a state of affairs could have come to pass. But when one remembers what men have done, and in many parts of the world are still prepared to do, in the name of a political philosophy, the answer seems evident: from a "pragmatic" point of view, political philosophy is a monster, and wherever it has been taken seriously, the consequence, almost invariably, has been revolution, war, and eventually, the police state. Russell himself once wrote an essay entitled, "The Harm that Good Men Do." Many would regard this as an appropriate subtitle for any honest and realistic history of political philosophy. With Socrates, political philosophy became a gadfly; in Plato, a monstrous dream; in Rousseau, Fichte, Hegel, Marx, and the rest, it has become a scourge and an obscenity. . . .

Just what is wrong with political philosophy as a genre nonetheless remains obscure. Of course many political philosophies from Plato to Aquinas, and from Hobbes and Rousseau to Hegel and Marx, have been tied to the kites of theological or metaphysical systems. And for some, no doubt, this fact suffices to put them beyond the pale. But roundhouse objections to "metaphysics" are less fashionable than they were some years ago. In fact, under pressure from the philosophers of ordinary language, philosophical analysts are increasingly reluctant to proscribe as meaningless any established form of discourse on principle, as the positivists used to do with the propositions, not only of metaphysics and theology, but also of ethics. In this respect, recent analytical philosophy has steadily moved in the direction of pragmatism, or, I had better say, the direction in which pragmatism has tended to move since the days of William James. Any form of utterance, so it is now argued, is to be interpreted and judged only in the light of its own characteristic "practical bearings." Thus, for example, if political philosophers in their own terms are given to general moral evaluations of political activities and institutions, the question is only whether such appraisals, all things considered, are acceptable as value judgments: that is to say, do they express commitments to which, on sober second thought and in view of the historical record, we should be ready to give our own conscientious assent? Do the lines of social action which they commend appear on the whole to be worth the trouble it would take to realize them? Above all, would we in conscience be able to give our blessings to the sort of "representative man" who might emerge if such lines of action were resolutely pursued?

Questions of this sort, which I take more seriously, have produced another round of objections which, although they do not rule out political philosophy on supposedly semantical or logical grounds, do nonetheless seem to condemn it virtually as a genre. These objections are all the more telling and all the more significant since they come from a quarter in which there has been no general animus against metaphysics and no self-denying ordinance which would exclude from the purview of philosophy any problem that is not purely a conceptual problem about the "logic" of expressions. . . .

Marxism and Ideology: The First Revolt

. . . And if the professional philosophers now decline to do political philosophy, it may be argued that this is owing to their own disillusionment with the achievements of their predecessors rather than to any inherent fault in political philosophy as a genre. It remains to ask whether there may be, after all, some deep-lying confusion of mind, some pervasive logical fault or category mistake, which really does afflict political philosophy as a form of discourse.

As a way of confronting this question, it may prove useful to examine certain aspects of the widespread attack against the modern offspring of and successor to political philosophy, namely, ideology. Most of the "anti-ideologists," as I shall call them, share certain attitudes in common with the existentialists; indeed, it is my impression that some of them owe more to the latter, and particularly to Camus, than they have as yet acknowledged. They owe something also to the pragmatists; in fact, most American anti-ideologists fancy their own point of view as essentially "pragmatic." But (generally speaking) they go beyond the existentialists and the pragmatists in contending that ideological thinking is the function of certain features of the social situation in which intellectuals as a group find themselves in an era of exact science, advanced technology, and the welfare state. In predicting the end of ideology, they thus imply that the social and intellectual conditions which have been conducive to ideological thinking are now disappearing. Their own role, in effect, is to make certain that the prediction will come true.

Now the primary target of our contemporary Western anti-ideologists is, of course, Marxism. And in prophesying the end of ideology, it is the end of Marxism of which they mainly dream. It is worth remembering, therefore, that: (a) Marx was the first great critic of political philosophy; and (b) he was also the first great prophet of the end of the ideological age.

According to Marx, ideology always involves a conception of reality which systematically "inverts" the whole relation of thought to being.[1] As a form of thought, therefore, ideology is inherently confused; it stands to science, in Marx's words, as an inverted image in a "camera obscura" stands to a veridical perception. This inversion, of which Hegel's "objective" idealism is a prime philosophical example, results directly or indirectly from that process of "alienation" whereby human artifacts, including "ideas," are invested with a power and a reality that are supposedly independent both of their producers and of the material conditions and operations involved in their production. Such an investment, which philosophers call "reification," is also necessarily accompanied by "mystification," i.e., by an obscuring of the interests and relationships that actually determine social behavior. For example, in imputing an independent reality and power to their reified ideas

---

[1]In this section I have been aided by Stanley W. Moore's *The Critique of Capitalist Democracy, An Introduction to the Theory of the State in Marx, Engels, and Lenin* (New York: Paine-Whitman Publishers, 1957). Moore's fourth chapter, "Ideology and Alienation," pp. 114–137, is highly compressed and schematic, but I know of no other discussion of the subject which, within its limits, is so clear and so accurate. I have also benefited from Norman Birnbaum's *The Sociological Study of Ideology (1940–1960)*, *Current Sociology*, Vol. IX, No. 2, 1960 (Oxford: Basil Blackwell). Birnbaum's essay, which he subtitles "A Trend Report," is a masterly survey of current literature on the subject of ideology, including Marxist ideological theory. It also contains an invaluable critical bibliography.

and principles, their rights and duties, their ends and "reasons," men thereby conceal from themselves the fact that it is they, the creators of such entities, whose underlying actions and whose work alone give them whatever significance they may have.

Except for genuinely empirical science, the whole cultural "superstructure" of hitherto existing societies is permeated by the same process of alienation and ideological inversion. For this reason it would be a radical mistake to conceive of ideology as limited to political philosophy; on the contrary, ideology also includes, among other things, religion, ethics, art, metaphysics, and the "dismal science" of economics. Properly understood, political philosophies are merely special applications of far-flung ideological patterns that invest them with their own magical "authority" and "justification." Furthermore, since alienation is a social process, ideologies, whether as wholes or as parts, are to be understood as expressions, not of the interests of isolated individuals, but of the conflicting concerns—or better, tendencies—of social classes. It is thus only by relating political ideologies to their objective social conditions and causes that we can begin to interpret their true objective meaning (i.e., what they signify or portend within the order of nature), and hence, by stages, to correct the inverted images of reality which they present to the ideologists themselves. One of the primary functions of Marxism, in fact, is precisely to provide the intellectual, including the social-theoretical, tools for such interpretations and corrections, and thus for the first time to enable us, in principle, to demythologize ideology.

But it is one thing to explain ideology and another to overcome it. Mankind as a whole can permanently overcome ideological thought (and action) not by any process of purely conceptual analysis on the part of individual philosophers, but only by removing the material causes of alienation which, according to Marx, are rooted in the institution of private property. And it is for this reason, and this reason alone, that Marx's historical prophecy of the coming of world socialism amounts at the same time to a prophecy of the end of the ideological ages.

Disillusionment in the West: The Second Revolt Against Ideology

Marx's view of ideology underlies the thinking of most of our own anti-ideologists. However, they go beyond Marx in extending the pejorative associations of the term to the role of ideology in ordering human attitudes. Thus, they not only regard ideological doctrines as wrong-headed; they also object to their employment as vehicles for the formation, guidance, and control of social behavior. But they go Marx one better in another way, for they also regard Marxism itself as a prime example of ideology.

The first non-Marxist writer, so far as I know, explicitly to inquire whether we might be approaching the end of the ideological age was Raymond Aron in his book, *The Opium of the Intellectuals*. The prevailing temper of Aron's book is not unlike that of Camus's *The Rebel*. There are also a number of striking parallels between Aron's point of view and that of Karl Popper, as developed in the latter's *The Open Society and its Enemies*. For example, there is the same constitutional distrust of large-scale social planning, the same insistence upon the impossibility of large-scale historical predictions of social behavior, and the same celebration of the virtues of "the open society." Above all, there is the same castigation of any attempt to determine the drift and meaning of human history as a whole and hence of the attempt to formulate universal and necessary laws of historical development.

"The last great ideology," says Aron, "was born of the combination of three elements: the vision of a future consistent with human aspiration, the link between this future and a particular social class, and trust in human values above and beyond the victory of the working class, thanks to planning and collective ownership." Aron believes that at the present time the hope aroused by that ideology is gone beyond peradventure. One main reason for this disillusionment, so he argues, is that "Confidence in the virtues of a socio-technique has begun to wane." Furthermore, on this side of the Iron Curtain, no one believes any longer in the reality of a social class that will carry us, under the leadership of the socio-economic engineers, to the frontiers of the classless society. Like Camus and Popper, Aron cannot bring himself flatly to renounce the values of the Enlightenment; but in practice he is no more able than they to take them with absolute seriousness as governing ideals for the reconstruction of society in the 20th century. In his own terms, he no longer fully believes in the vision of a future consistent with "human aspirations." And it is this fact perhaps that accounts for the vein of pessimism and the self-division which run through his writing.

In any case, it is plain that for Aron the approaching end of the age of ideology represents also a crisis of faith and of hope for mankind. On the penultimate page of his book, Aron asks, "Does the rejection of fanaticism encourage a reasonable faith, or merely skepticism?" His analogical answer is that "one does not cease to love God when one gives up converting pagans or the Jews and no longer reiterates 'No salvation outside the Church.'" Coming as late as it does in Aron's book, this has something like the effect of an unprepared major cadence at the end of a funeral march. What is its basis? No matter how personal one's religion may be, it is hard to see how it could fail to be attenuated by a radical renunciation of one's belief that it should prevail. If one really gives up trying to convert the "pagans," does this not entail reservations about the value as well as the possibility of converting them? If so, does this not also suggest that one has ceased completely to love God or else that only a gesture toward the love of Him remains? Making due allowance for the analogy, I cannot, as a pragmatist, see how one can be said actively to seek a less cruel lot for humanity if one can trust no technique and no plan for its amelioration. To will the end is to will the means, and to reject the means is, in practice, to renounce the end. Like Peirce in another connection, one is minded to say to the political as well as to the epistemological moralists: "Dismiss make-believe!" This means also, so far as I can see, "Dismiss professions of 'reasonable faith' if you do not believe in the *power* of reason; and do not talk about abolishing 'fanaticism,' unless you believe that there is a way (or 'technique') of abolishing it." Like all anti-ideologists, Aron is opposed to the expectation of "miraculous changes" either from a revolution or an economic plan. Very well. The question is whether he gives us any reason to expect unmiraculous changes from any sort of concerted human action. "If tolerance is born of doubt, let us teach everyone to doubt all the models and utopias, to challenge all the prophets of redemption and the heralds of catastrophe." And, "If they alone can abolish fanaticism, let us pray for the advent of the skeptics." The rhetoric is appealing. But it smacks of ideology, in Aron's own sense. For toleration is also a principle and a method. And it too has its dangers.

These comments are not made in a spirit of mockery. My purpose is rather to make clear what may be implied in the prophecy that we are living at the end of the ideological age, the age, in Mr. Aron's own apt words, in which men still actively search "for a purpose, for communion with the people, for something controlled by *an idea and a will*" (my italics). As he points out, we Westerners have suffered an increasing fragmentation of our universe; our poetry becomes more and more obscure and diffuse, and our poets are isolated from one another as well as from "the big public" which "in their heart of hearts, they long to serve"; our scientists have ideas aplenty but no control over their use or indeed any consistent belief in the possibility of their control; our scholars control limited areas of specialized knowledge, but present-day science "seems to leave . . . [them] as ignorant of the answers to the ultimate questions as a child awakening to consciousness"; and our economists and sociologists, for all their facts and statistics, their jargon and their lore, have not the vaguest notion whether "humanity is progressing toward an atomic holocaust or Utopian peace." This process of fragmentation and dissociation, moreover, is not new; it has been going on at an ever more rapid pace, at least since the Renaissance. But here precisely, as Aron admits, "is where ideology comes in. . . ." For ideology represents the insistent demand for a coherent *way* of individual and social life, an orientation toward the world and toward the human predicament, controlled as he says both by an idea and by a will, or, rather, by a will infused with an idea and an idea animated by will. Ideology, as Aron tacitly acknowledges, is a creature of alienation; but it represents also a passion to reduce alienation, to bring it down to bearable human proportions. It also represents the belief that alienation may be reduced through collective human endeavors. Thus, by his own account, an end to the age of ideology would amount to this extent to a virtual skepticism about the possibility of reducing alienation through corporate planning and action (ideas infused with will). And this means that man has no choice but to live with alienation. Here, however, one faces precisely one of those metaphysical and historical "necessities" against which the anti-ideologists themselves rail when they find them in the writings of other ideologists. Here, too, it seems, we are faced with a "simplified" idea of man's fate which, as in the case of the Stoicism it is plainly a variant of, forms the basis of still another ideology, an idea that in this instance is, if I may say so, fused with inaction.

The Sociological Critique of Ideology

Aron's analysis of ideology, although suggestive, does not take us very far. Let us therefore cross the ocean to the heartland of contemporary anti-ideology. In the United States perhaps the leading anti-ideologist is the sociologist and social critic, Professor Daniel Bell. Bell, who knows his Marx, is also a good strategist. Already in the introduction to his book, *The End of Ideology*, he moves beyond Aron, for, unlike the latter, he proposes to make a positive virtue of alienation. "Alienation," he tells us flatly, "is not nihilism but a positive role, a detachment, which guards one against being submerged in any cause, or accepting any particular embodiment of community as final. Nor is alienation deracination, a denial of one's roots or country." This persuasive definition has its points. It is also an interesting instance of the notion of an idea fused with will which Bell, like Aron, tends to identify with ideology.

As befits a sociologist, Bell is concerned not just with the content of ideas but with their social origins, causes, and roles. Thus, in an attempt to locate the sources of ideological thinking, he begins his analysis with a characterological division of the intelligentsia into two main types: (a) the "scholars"; and (b) the "intellectuals." The scholar, as Bell conceives him, "has a bounded field of knowledge, a tradition, and seeks to find his place in it, adding to the accumulated, tested knowledge of the past as to a mosaic." He is, so to say, a "pro" for whom "the show must go on," however and whatever he himself may feel about it. Accepting the scholarly tradition within which he has found a place, he is able to judge himself, or at least his scholarly performance, by impersonal and objective standards. And if he performs with a modicum of efficiency and does not stray beyond the limits of his scholarly "competence," he is entitled to a modicum of self-respect. Indeed, his self-respect, like his role-governed conception of himself, is a function of his assurance of the respect of his peers and, more indirectly, of the society of which his discipline is an established part.

The intellectual, on the other hand, has no such responsibility or security. Lacking a scholarly discipline, perhaps lacking the talent for achievement within such a discipline, which can hold him continuously responsible to "objective" methods and to "facts" wholly independent of himself, his only recourse is an endless dialectic and critique of general ideas. And because he is without a legitimate social role to play within society, he perforce finds himself alienated from its institutions and is left to manipulate his "ideas" in a mood of unrequited and unfocused resentment. He doesn't so much think with his ideas as feel through them. In the discourses of an intellectual, therefore, the thing to look to is not his argument, which, where it exists, is merely a vehicle for his resentments, but rather to the effect which it is meant to induce. He presents his readers not with information but with a goad and with an outlet for their own repressed emotions of estrangement or violence. He may, in the process, tell them something, but it is doing something to them that is his real, if unavowed, aim. For him, the beginning and end of a process of reflection is not a specific problem about objective processes and events; as Professor Bell charges, he begins always with "*his* experience, *his* perceptions of the world, his privileges and deprivations, and judges the world by these sensibilities." For him, the "world" is not a thing in itself, but rather his will and his idea, and if there is something *there*, in itself, then he acknowledges it only as something which he is up against and which exists only in so far as he is up against it. His business, in Marx's words, is not to understand the world, but to change, or better, to overcome it. And if he can't change it in any other way, he may at least reject it, and thus, by an obvious inversion, still show his superiority to it.

In this way, every statement and every discussion becomes for the intellectual an implicitly political move in an endless game of power. Of course he fancies his own moves really to be in the interest (*n. b.*) of "justice" or "freedom," while those of his "opponents," whether they invoke the names of "legitimacy" or of "law and order," are actually made in the interest of business as usual which it is the function of the established order to protect and to promote. The sad fact remains, however, that the intellectual's power *is* severely limited by the existing system. Hence, in order to maintain the illusion of his freedom or of his power to realize it, he is obliged, as Bell puts it, to embark "upon what William James called 'the faith ladder,' which in its vision of the future cannot distinguish possibilities from probabilities, and converts the latter into certainties."

What is the nature of the conceptual tools with which the "free-floating" and unscholarly intellectual does his work? In order to answer this question, Bell is obliged to move from sociology to logic and semantics. Thus he speaks repeatedly, in terms which I find merely more explicit than Aron's, of ideology as being somehow a "fusion" of thought with emotion or passion which at one and the same time does the trick of "simplify[ing] ideas, establish[ing] a claim to truth, and, in the union of the two, demand[ing] a commitment to action." The result—and it is this which Bell most seriously objects to—is not just a "transformation" of ideas, but also a transformation of people. The typical effect of any ideological argument is, then, a kind of conversion. The road by which the ideologist comes to Damascus doesn't matter; what matters is that he is made to see the light. Says Bell: "Ideology is the conversion of ideas into social levers. Without irony, Max Lerner once entitled a book 'Ideas Are Weapons.' This is the language of ideology. It is the commitment to the consequences of ideas."

Bell is rarely more analytical than this, but toward the end of his study he does say one further thing which is at least symptomatic of the point of view which he represents: "If the end of ideology has any meaning, it[sic]is to ask for the end of rhetoric, and rhetoricians, of 'revolution,' of the day when the young French anarchist Vaillant tossed a bomb into the Chamber of Deputies, and the literary critic Laurent Tailhade declared in his defense: 'What do a few human lives matter; it was a *beau geste.*'" The general idea that concerns us here is not the tacit identification of ideology with revolutionary activity, especially of the more bizarre and feckless sort, but rather its identification with rhetoric.

If by "rhetoric" Bell means the use of language in order to persuade or influence others—and many things he says suggest that this is his meaning—then his vision of the end of ideology as an end to rhetoric is a utopian fantasy. Worse, it is an evil fantasy, for it implies a conception of human relations which would deprive us of the right to address one another except for the purpose of comparing notes about matters of fact. Consider what would happen were such a fantasy to come true. In any ordinary sense, it would mean a virtual end to discourse, to communication, and to argument. For it would mean an end to any speech-act addressed to others with a view to their guidance, their instruction, their edification, or their pleasure, with a view, in short, to changing their minds. Indeed, the image of man implicit in Bell's dream of the end of ideology is precisely one of an academic grind or functionary to which he himself, as a counter-ideologist and counter-rhetorician, is fortunately unable to conform.[2]

The American anti-ideologists, Bell included, regard themselves as pragmatists. However, we should remind ourselves that it is the great pragmatists who have insisted, time out of mind, that ideas have consequences and that, indeed, their operative meaning can only be construed in consequential terms. Rhetoric, from this point of view, is not necessarily a bad or degenerate form of expression; rather it is a dimension of any form of speech which is addressed to others. Furthermore, pragmatism is also a normative theory which asks us to evaluate any form of speech, and hence of rhetoric, in terms of its consequences. The question, therefore, is not whether a discourse persuades or influences other minds and other hearts, but how it does so and with what effect. Not every rhetorician is a demagogue. Plato's Socrates professed to despise the Sophists because they were rhetoricians, and this Socrates, I surmise, is the grandfather of all the countless anti-rhetoricians and anti-ideologists from his day to Bell's. But it should not be forgotten that Socrates himself was a master rhetorician and that his admirers ignore the fact because they believe his cause was just. Moreover, Socrates was not only a lover of truth; he was also, politically, a reactionary whose hatred of the Sophists was directed not only to their rhetoric but also to their liberal, democratic, and plebeian political and social attitudes. In saying this, I do not mean to attack our latter-day anti-ideologists by innuendo. I do mean to say that the plain effect of *their* rhetoric is to reinforce acceptance of our own institutional status quo and to declass those "intellectuals" who seek to modify in any radical way the fundamental structures of "Western" political life.

There remains a secondary sense of the term "rhetoric" which Bell may also have in mind. In this sense, rhetoric means eloquence. So conceived, the demand for an end to rhetoric is tantamount to a request

---

[2]What Bell does not sufficiently emphasize is that the intellectuals' "faith ladders" have indeed converted possibilities into certainties. Otherwise it is hard to see why he and his fellow anti-ideologists make such a hullabaloo about ideology and why they are enthralled with the thought that we have reached the end of the age of ideology. The simple fact is that ever since the French Revolution the intellectuals, with the help of their ideologies, have been moving mountains. And if *their* ideologies are exhausted, as Bell contends, this does not necessarily entail the end of ideology as such. No doubt the old ideologies of the right and the left have lost much of their power to persuade, and no doubt, all over the world, radicalism and intellectualism in our time must inevitably take new forms. But they will persist, by Bell's own analysis, until every intellectual has become a scholar (or worker) and until every scholar becomes a scholar (or worker) merely; that is, until there are no full- or part-time "out-groups" (to employ a fashionable term of sociological analysis) and no general ideas for them to think with. At this point one begins to have visions of an academic utopia within which there are no "free-floating" intellectuals, no alienated, critical minds, such as Professor Bell's, that are not wholly committed to their vocations and that possess an over-plus of energy and passions that is not expended in the conduct of their own "researches." In such a utopia (if I may speak metaphorically) there would be no New York and no Concord, but only a series of semi-urban centers for semi-advanced study for semi-advanced scholars who would sternly deny themselves the use of any concept or the affirmation of any statement whose "practical bearings" cannot be shown to lie wholly within the range of their legitimate scholarly activity or work. Such a utopia, I fancy, would have no place even for counter-ideologists like Professor Bell whose own "restless vanity" (the phrase is his) is evidently not sated by the rewards that accrue from the performance of his scholarly labors.

for plain talk and, so to say, for an age of prose. So far so' good. But there may be more to it than this. Elsewhere Bell harps upon the theme that "Throughout their history, Americans have had an extraordinary talent for compromise in politics and extremism in morality." It is plain that Bell is repelled by "this moralism," though, I gather, not so much because it is hypocritical but rather because, as moral, it is uncompromising. "The saving grace, so to speak, of American politics, was that all sorts of groups were tolerated, and the system of the 'deal' became the pragmatic counterpart of the philosophic principle of toleration. But in matters of manners, morals, and conduct—particularly in the small towns—there has been a ferocity of blue-nosed attitudes unmatched by other countries." And again, "It has been one of the glories of the United States that politics has always been a pragmatic give-and-take rather than a series of wars-to-the-death." Of course this last is *not* true. Among our national "glories" have been a war for independence and a civil war, both of them (among other things) wars of principle. Our periods of "give-and-take" have usually also been periods of drift and complacency which have ended in orgies of political corruption and degradation. In one domain, however, Bell believes that our underlying political "postures" have not been "pragmatic." "One of the unique aspects of American politics is that . . . foreign policy has always been phrased in moralistic terms. Perhaps the very nature of our emergence as an independent country forced us to constantly adopt a moral posture in regard to the rest of the world; perhaps being distant from the real centers of interest conflict allowed us to employ pieties, rather than face realities. But since foreign policy has usually been within the frame of moral rather than pragmatic discourse, the debate in the fifties became centered in moral terms."

These passages are typical. In asking for an end to rhetoric, what Bell appears to be calling for is, among other things, an end to *moral* discourse and a beginning of consistent "pragmatic discourse" in every sphere of political life. What does this mean? So far as I can make out, it means an end to judgment and to principle, to praise and to blame, in the political domain and a beginning of plain, unvarnished "politicking" in the name of our "realistic" national, social, or individual "interests." It means, in effect, that in political discourse two and only *two* forms of expression are to be regarded as legitimate: (a) realistic, verifiable statements of fact; and (b) bald, undisguised expressions of first-personal (singular or plural) interest. On such a view, one would be permitted to say, "I don't like segregation and I will try—without, however, upsetting the apple cart—to do what I can to limit segregationist practices," but not "Segregation is an affront to the humanity of the Negro people," or, "Those who practice segregation are unfair and unjust." What is wrong with moral, as distinct from "pragmatic," discourse? It is not to be doubted that moral discourse is more eloquent and more incitive, and in this sense more rhetorical, than the "pragmatic" forms of speech which Bell prefers. But what is wrong with eloquence *per se*? No doubt it should not be used to cloud an issue, to obscure relevant facts, or to promote unreason. But this is no more a necessary consequence of moral discourse than of any other form of eloquence. Without eloquence, especially in times of crisis, few great political movements would succeed. In fact, eloquence, including the eloquence of moral judgment, is native to the language of politics, and particularly so, as Bell himself admits, in democratic societies where persuasion of the great masses is a condition of success. Thus to put an end to eloquence would be to put an end, not only to "moralism" (which is usually nothing more than the morality of those with whom we disagree) and to "ideology," but also to any form of politics in which great issues are stated or argued in terms of human rights and responsibilities and in which it is essential to gain the approval of the people, or their representatives, before any fundamental change in governmental policy is made. Perhaps a tightly knit, self-interested, and all-powerful elite might get along (among its members) with "pragmatic discourse" alone. But despite Bell, democratic politics does not just mean "bargaining between legitimate groups and the search for consensus." It means also a form of politics in which men are governed by, and hence with reference to, principles and ideals — in a word, to morals and to ideology.

. . . Now political ideology is nothing but political discourse (as distinct from political science) on its most general formative level. It is, that is to say, political discourse insofar as the latter addresses itself, not just to specific, piecemeal reforms, but to the guiding principles, practices, and aspirations by which politically organized societies, absolutely or else in certain typical situations, ought to be governed. This being so, political ideologies inevitably include, among their leading articles, statements of general principle or method and expressions of basic attitude, orientation, and concern which, as they stand, are so highly abstract as to appear to many minds preoccupied with day-to-day problems of "practical politics" virtually meaningless. Such statements are of course habitually formulated in terms like "general welfare," "common good," "justice," "equality," "democracy," "security," and the rest.

But these very terms, so natural or even essential, when one is defining and appraising political practices or systems, also tend through over-use to become mere counters which elicit from us the tired, stock response that leaves us, and hence the practices themselves, unchanged. Or worse, because our responses are dull and routine, and hence *practically* of no political importance, we may conclude that all general philosophical discussions of politics are pointless and that one political ideology is just as good — or bad — as any other. What does matter, so we feel, is not what we say or think about "the system," but only what we do within it. And so, by stages, we are led to the conservative conclusion that political manifestoes, declarations of independence, and constitutions (with their embarrassing ideological preambles) make no difference to society as a going concern. In short, so far as we are concerned, ideology is useless verbiage. On the other side, unfortunately, we discover to our dismay that other peoples, politically and intellectually less "advanced" than ourselves, are enflamed, sometimes to the point of revolution, by ideological discourses, fresher and more affecting, in part because less literal and less abstract, than those to which we are accustomed. And to our contempt for our own ineffectual ideological abstractions we now add a positive hatred (or fear) of an ideological rhetoric which suddenly endows those same abstractions with a new life that disturbs our own.

It should be observed, however, that our very hatred is itself a back-handed tribute to the power of ideology. And if, out of a misplaced loyalty to "reason," we merely limit ourselves to "exposing" it, we stand in danger of losing our world. Most of us, realizing that the world is *never* well lost, find ourselves drawn back inescapably into the ideological struggle which, if we are to win it for ends that are right and just, requires that we produce a counter-rhetoric more imaginative, more distinguished, and more durable than that of our opponents. But if, as literalists of the imagination, we still decline to go the whole hog, resorting now only to formal reaffirmation of the old abstract "principles" which no later than yesterday we professed to find meaningless, who will believe us? Why should they? They have heard the same golden words mouthed a thousand times on the party platforms by hacks who have no notion of their meaning. And, if it comes to that, what *do* they mean?

In science it normally suffices to state a fact, and one man may do this as well and as accurately as another. But in the sphere of conduct much more is involved. For here we have to do with matters of attitude and intention and with problems of authenticity, legitimacy, and authority. Here words must not only predict what will be but determine what shall be; they must not only inform but also prepare and initiate lines of action. And what *is* it that is being determined, prepared, and initiated? This, so I contend, can be fully revealed only through the "poetry" which the ideologist may afford us. . . .

It remains to say a word about "simplism," that final bogey of the anti-ideological mentality. Through rhetoric, according to Bell, ideology infuses ideas with passion, thus, as might be expected, winning friends and influencing people. But the principal underhanded intellectual (or is it, too, rhetorical?) trick of the ideologists is to "simplify ideas." It therefore seems necessary to remind the anti-ideologist that simplification, so far from being a fault peculiar to ideology, is, as William James well knew, a large part of the saving virtue of rationality itself. To oppose simplism on principle, in politics as in every other sphere of activity, is not to make a legitimate demand for recognition of the complexities and diversities of political life, but, in effect, to ask for an abandonment of policy and a fatal acquiescence in the drift of events. For simplification is an essential feature of any rational initiation of action. To refuse to simplify when one confronts a problem is in effect to reject the obligation to reach a solution; it is to make a game of possibilities and hence to move automatically outside the context of agency and choice. Every procedure that helps us to make decisions does so precisely by reducing the range of possibilities which we may reasonably be expected to consider. And every method, in setting a limit to the considerations that ought to be taken into account, thereby secures our deliberations against an endless spread of doubts.

On this score particularly, Professor Bell seems merely disingenuous when he tells us—incidentally letting a fair-sized ideological cat out of his own elastic bag—that although "There is now more than ever some need for utopia, in the sense that men need—as they have always needed—some vision of their potential, some manner of fusing passion with intelligence. . . . The ladder to the City of Heaven can no longer be a 'faith ladder,' but an empirical one; a utopia has to specify *where* one wants to go, *how* to get there, the costs of the enterprise, and some realization of, and justification for the determination of *who* is to pay." There is a rather terrible irony in the fact that Bell, who in other contexts is so prone to rail against those who think in terms of all or none, should find it so hard at this point to think in terms of degree. Were one seriously to try, in detail and at the outset, to meet all his requirements for a "good" utopia, the magnitude and complexity of the task would paralyze thought. The "good" utopian, like the unholy ideologist, must settle for considerably less if he is ever to bring his deliberations to a conclusion. And if he eventually does reach a conclusion, then no matter how long he reflects and however precise his calculations, it will have been conceived in sin. For it will always reflect a radical simplification of the possibilities and the alternatives which a more scrupulous utopian would think it obligatory to consider.

But Bell's advocacy of even his "good" utopias is, at best, half-hearted. For he really has no faith in any long-range scheme aimed at the amelioration of society as a whole. "Ideology," he tells us, "makes it unnecessary for people to confront individual issues on their individual merits." But in one sense this is true of any rule, any procedure, and any plan, including the plans of piecemeal social engineers like Bell and Popper. What would be the point of any such scheme, however limited in its scope, unless it relieved us of the necessity of confronting every blessed individual issue on its (otherwise) individual merits? And if it comes to that, what is an "individual issue," and what is it to confront one on its "individual merits"? Is the issue of desegregation, for example, one such issue or is it many? Indeed, is the issue of desegregating one individual classroom in one individual school in one God-forsaken county of the state of Mississippi an individual issue? And if it is, what, pray, are *its* individual merits? How far do these extend?

One of the overwhelming advantages of a bill of human rights (which is nothing but a schedule of enforced ideological commitments), is that it drastically reduces the number of "issues" over which men in societies must continue to quarrel. In this way it reduces the terrible wear and tear of political life which, even in the best-run societies, is nearly unendurable. Bell and his allies, following Popper (and at a distance Bergson), are admirers of the "open society." But of course a completely open society, if such ever existed, would be not a society, but a chaos. If an "open society" is one in which each individual issue is decided, *ad hoc*, on its own peculiar merits, then who wants an "open society"? And if a "closed society" is one in which, owing to the presence of a prevailing ideology (or constitution), many issues are, in any practical sense, dead issues, why then let us by all means continue to have a closed society. Were we Americans seriously to invoke the principle that individual cases should be settled exclusively on their (otherwise) individual merits, we would have to repudiate our Declaration of Independence and to dismantle our whole constitutional system and the characteristic rule of law which it provides. . . .

Let us no longer mince words. Our own anti-ideological foxes are no more "empirical" and no less rhetorical than their leonine opponents; they are, on broad issues, merely more indecisive and more eclectic. As it stands, their point of view is so lacking both in consistency and in clarity that, as I have discovered at some cost, it is virtually impossible to argue with them without fear of doing them some frightful injustice. Still, out of a sophisticated but paralyzing fear of over-simplification, they have managed to fashion a kind of counter-ideology, or fetish, of complexity, difficulty, and uniqueness. They tell us that "the present belongs to the living" and that we should lift from our shoulders "the heavy hand of the future" as well as "the dead hand of the past." Yet they evidently have not the courage to say that the preamble to the American Constitution, which speaks among other things of securing the "Blessings of Liberty to ourselves *and our Posterity*," is so much wicked ideological flourish and moonshine. Their "pluralism" has become a kind of mania which, when pressed to its own counter-ideological extremes, leads inescapably (as William James long ago perceived) to anarchism and, at last, to nihilism. Were their political and social attitudes generally to prevail in the West—and it is primarily of the West that they speak in talking of the end of ideology—the result would be a pessimistic *carpe diem* philosophy which would render us helpless in the world struggle against the ideology of Communism. At home, in the political parties, in the Congress, and in the courts, it continually weakens what remains of our national commitment to the ideological principles that animate our constitutional system; in the Presidency, it provides merely the covering excuses for a spate of uncorrelated, "piecemeal" moves which, however admirable from a tactical point of view and however skillful as "pragmatic" politics, result in an ever increasing loss of basic political control and social direction. Curiously, the over-all picture is one of Hegelian "gray on gray." The only difference is that unlike our anti-ideologists Hegel knew that gray on gray is the color of barrenness, of late autumn and approaching winter.

IDEOLOGY—A DEBATE

Daniel Bell and Henry David Aiken

DANIEL BELL: Define your terms, the philosophers enjoin us. One of the difficulties with Henry David Aiken's essay, "The Revolt Against Ideology," is the multiplicity of senses in which he uses the word "ideology," as well as the ambiguity of his prescriptions. He begins by citing with approval the Marxian conception that ideologies are "inverted images of reality"—ideas falsely divorced from the material conditions that produce them—and that the function of social analysis is to "demythologize ideology"; and he concludes—no longer mincing words!—by saying that persons like myself, who talk of the "end of ideology," would "render us helpless in the world struggle against the ideology of Communism" and weaken "what remains of our national commitment to the ideological principles that animate our constitutional system."

Now, since I accept a Marxian conception of ideology as the starting point for analysis, and since I call myself a pragmatist (as does Mr. Aiken), I am puzzled by the transitions through which I end up as subversive of my own ideals, if not of my country's. Let me therefore indicate what I mean by the "end of ideology," and later confront Mr. Aiken himself directly.

Reprinted from *Commentary* (October 1964), by permission; copyright © 1964 by the American Jewish Committee.

The Marxian discussion of ideology flows from the concern with alienation. But the context is as broad as the "human condition" itself. The root of it all is in man's unhappy awareness of a divided consciousness, and his yearning or search for an Absolute. In Christian terms, man is separated from God and searches for re-unification through the figure of Christ. For Hegel, religious alienation is but one aspect of a cosmic drama in which everything is rent by duality — spirit and matter, nature and history, God and man — and the "realization," or the "end of philosophy," will occur when all dualities are overcome, when man no longer is both subject and object, or lives between society and State.

Marx's great vision provided a naturalistic foundation for the Hegelian drama. The source of man's duality, he said, lay not in thought but in the division of labor and in the social classes. The "realization" of philosophy, in other words, lay in economics, and the agency of human fulfillment was not the Idea but the Proletariat. The unity of "thought and being," the union of appearance and reality, and the end of all ideology (a phrase, as Lewis Feuer reminds us, that was first used by Engels in his essay on Feuerbach) would come, said Marx, when man finally conquered material necessity and began living in a purposeful, self-directed community.

Marxism itself, however, became an ideology with the assumption, to be found in Marx's later work as well as in the vulgarization of his thought by Engels, that there was a single key to the "realization" of philosophy — the abolition of private property. Abolish private property, and all exploitation would disappear. As Communist apologists later put it, there could be no classes and exploitation in the Soviet Union because there was no private property in Soviet society.

It is necessary to emphasize some distinctions in order to focus the questions that divide us. Originally, "ideology" simply meant sense impressions; in opposition to the rationalists, the ideologues sought to "purify" ideas by accepting only those which come through the senses. For Marx, "ideology" referred to beliefs which masked private interests; thus, such doctrines as natural rights, with their claim to a universal transcendental validity, were really constructed to justify the needs of the bourgeoisie. Among the specific examples of ideology that Marx gives (in the essays on *The Jewish Question*) are the guarantees of property rights and civil rights in the various state constitutions of the United States. In the 20th century, "ideology" acquired a broader and more impassioned meaning. As the political struggles of the age took on the intensity of the earlier religious wars, the word came to denote in politics what the terms "creed" or "faith" had meant in religion.

During its crusading Bolshevik phase, Marxism became a *total* ideology. As I used the term: "A *total* ideology is an all-inclusive system of comprehensive reality, it is a set of beliefs, infused with passion, and seeks to transform the whole of a way of life. This commitment to ideology—the yearning for a 'cause' or the satisfaction of deep moral feel-ings—is *not* necessarily the reflection of interests in the shape of ideas. Ideology . . . in the sense used here is a secular religion."

Those of us who speak of the "end of ideology" mainly mean to reject this mode of commitment, which had such a disastrous effect on the thought and politics of the radical and utopian movements of the past two generations. As developed by such writers as Raymond Aron, Ed-ward Shils, C. A. R. Crosland, and S. M. Lipset, the theme of the "end of ideology" has become a call for an end to apocalyptic beliefs that refuse to specify the costs and consequences of the changes they envision. The "end-of-ideology" school (if a school it is) is skeptical of rationalistic schemes that assume they can blueprint the entire life of a society; it argues that the existing political tags "conservative" and "liberal" have lost their intellectual clarity; it is critical of existing in-stitutions, but it does not accept the assumption that social change is *necessarily* an improvement. In short, it is pragmatic in the triple sense in which Dewey used the term: it defines the consequence of an action as a constitutive element of the truth of a proposition; it assumes the inextricable relation of ends and means; and it believes that values, like any empirical proposition, can be tested on the basis of their claims.

Now the curious thing is that none of this history—either of the term "ideology" or of the background of radicalism—is reflected in Mr. Aiken's discussion of ideology. He does not say whether these judg-ments on the past were wrong or right. He treats the word "ideology" only as a formal problem for analysis. The reason, perhaps, is that he is out to make a case—a lawyer's case, not a philosopher's case—and he goes at it in the best lawyer's manner.

The central point in his discussion of my own contribution to the theme is his analysis of the word "rhetoric." I wrote: "If the 'end of ideology' has any meaning, it is to ask for the end of rhetoric, and rhetoricians, of 'revolution,' of the day when the young French anarchist Vaillant tossed a bomb into the Chamber of Deputies and the literary critic Laurent Tailhade declared in his defense: 'What do a few human lives matter; it was a *beau geste!*' "

After quoting this passage, Mr. Aiken comments: "If by 'rhetoric' Bell means the use of language in order to persuade or influence others —and many things suggest that this is his meaning—then his vision of the end of ideology as an end to rhetoric is a utopian fantasy. Worse, it is an evil fantasy, for it implies a conception of human relations which would deprive us of the right to address one another except for the pur-poses of comparing notes about matters of fact."

I submit that the two paragraphs have nothing to do with each other. I was calling attention to the *distortion* of the discourse of persuasion—after all, what is a bomb?—rather than its classical use. The "end of rhetoric," in the context I gave it, plainly means an end to a way of thinking and acting which substitutes the worship of the Word —the verbal fetish of Revolution—for a moral analysis of consequences. If the fetishism of commodities is the "secret" of capitalism, is not the fetishism of rhetoric—the reliance on political slogans—the "secret" of radicalism?[1]

Next: I wrote that American life has suffered from an excess of "moralism." My examples were the small-town fundamentalist restrictions on personal conduct; McCarthyism—an extension of such moralizing in politics; and the formulation of foreign policy from one administration to the next in moralistic terms. (And, one can now say, the political rhetoric of Barry Goldwater.)

Writes Mr. Aiken: "In asking for an end to rhetoric, what Bell appears to be calling for is, among other things, an end to *moral* discourse and a beginning of consistent 'pragmatic discourse' in every sphere of political life. What does this mean? So far as I can make out, it means *an end to judgment and to principle* [my italics], to praise and to blame, in the political domain and a beginning of plain, unvarnished 'politicking' in the name of our 'realistic' national, social, or individual 'interests.'"

Again I call foul, this time at the shift from *moralistic* to *moral.* Moralizing, or being moralistic, is a distortion of the moral mode. It is the "ideological" use of morality for the sake of a hidden purpose.

As it happens, I do believe in "pragmatic discourse"; but is pragmatic discourse without principle? Isn't Locke's *Letter on Toleration* a form of pragmatic discourse? Isn't Kant's distinction between public and private—one the realm of agreed-upon procedure, the other the realm of conscience—a pragmatic one in its context? Pragmatic discourse in politics emphasizes the search for a reasoned consensus, rather than treating political issues as a war-to-the-death. It involves an "ethic of responsibility," but as Richard McKeon has pointed out, "responsibility is determined by the reciprocities in the actions of men." Where there is no reciprocity, conflict may—and at times should —develop. Between a racist and myself there is no reciprocity; between a Nazi and myself there is no reciprocity; between a Communist and myself there is no reciprocity. But where there is, or can be, an acceptance of the rules of the game—of the process of open discourse and reciprocity—there *should be* social compromise. Is this not judgment —and principle?

---

[1]Even sillier is Mr. Aiken's next comment. "There remains a second sense of the term 'rhetoric' which Bell *may also have in mind.* [Italics mine.] In this sense, rhetoric means eloquence. So conceived, the demand for an end to rhetoric is tantamount to a request for plain talk, and so to say, for the age of prose." Now really!

What is the lawyer's case that Mr. Aiken is seeking to make? On the one hand, it is a cumbersome theoretical formulation; on the other, a simplified political point.

Mr. Aiken writes: "Now political ideology is nothing but political discourse . . . on its most general formative level. It is, that is to say, political discourse insofar as the latter addresses itself, not just to specific, piecemeal reforms, but to the guiding principles, practices, and aspirations by which politically organized societies, absolutely or else in certain typical situations, ought to be governed. . . . Here words must not only predict what will be but determine what shall be; they must not only inform but also prepare and initiate lines of action. And what *is* it that is being determined, prepared, and initiated? This, so I contend, can be fully revealed only through the 'poetry' which the ideologist may afford us."

Here Mr. Aiken completely muddies the waters. For he has simply taken an old-fashioned definition of *political philosophy* and arbitrarily called it—despite the tortuous history of the word—*political ideology.* In fact a number of writers today—usually conservative ones who ask for a return to first principles—have decried the absence of political philosophy in the schools, charging modern political theory with "scientism." By calling for political ideology, Mr. Aiken has given us a stylish way of posing the problem. But otherwise the only gain is in confusion.

His political barb is more pointed: "I do not mean to attack our latter-day anti-ideologists by innuendo. I do mean to say that the plain effect of *their* rhetoric is to reinforce acceptance of our institutional status quo and to declass those 'intellectuals' who seek to modify in any radical way the fundamental structures of 'Western' political life."

If you set up a straw man, it will burn brightly when you put a match to it. As in so much of Mr. Aiken's essay, there is a fine resonance but an astonishing lack of specificity in these statements. I don't know what Mr. Aiken regards as the "fundamental structures of 'Western' political life." To my mind, the fundamental structure is the democratic process, and this I do not want to change. To speak further for myself, since the question of political identification is at issue, I am a democratic socialist, and have been for almost all of my politically conscious years. As such, I wish to see a change in the fundamental structures of our economic life. I deplore the social and economic power of the corporation. I detest the cult of efficiency which sacrifices the worker to the norms of productivity. I favor national planning in the economy. I want to see more public enterprise. And I want to introduce other criteria than those of the market or the private profit motive as means of allocating resources in the society. I have guiding general principles, rooted in conceptions about the nature of work and community, which shape these views. But I also have a test which guides the introduction of these changes; and I think the differences between Mr. Aiken and me on this question are the nub of the issue.

I wrote: "There is now more than ever some need for utopia, in the sense that men need — as they have always needed — some vision of their potential, some manner of fusing passion with intelligence. . . . The ladder to the City of Heaven can no longer be a 'faith ladder,' but an empirical one; a utopia has to specify *where* one wants to go, *how* to get there, the costs of the enterprise, and some realization of, and justification for, the determination of *who* is to pay."

To this, Mr. Aiken retorts: "Were one seriously to try, in detail and at the outset, to meet all his requirements for a 'good' utopia, the magnitude and complexity of the task would paralyze thought."

I find it hard to understand these remarks. The context of my discussion was quite clear. I pointed out that Lenin instigated the Russian Revolution with no idea at all of the meaning of planning or socialization (other than the simple-minded notion, expressed in *State and Revolution*, that the entire economy would be run like a single enterprise), and that the lives of millions of people were thus committed on the basis of an abstract promise. Or, to take another example: when Stalin decided in 1929 on the ruthless collectivization of agriculture in line with the ideological premise that individual peasant property should be eliminated, was not the question of costs and consequences relevant? Or again, to bring the issue closer to home: if an urban renewal program bulldozes a neighborhood in response to the liberals' ideological image of "slum clearance," should one not apply tests of the consequence of this action for community life?

Does Mr. Aiken want to build a bridge to the future without any tests of costs and consequences? His fear is that such a demand would inhibit all change. But why? Is it really so difficult? Have we no resources at all in sociological and economic knowledge to assess the social costs of change? Surely we know enough by now about the effects of social change — the devastation in the depressed areas, the school dropouts, the manifold impact of automation — to understand what our *failure* to plan has cost.

But all this is bootless, for I am asking Mr. Aiken to be concrete, and he is relentlessly abstract. Yet if the debate is to have any meaning, if Mr. Aiken wants to be radical, let him state in detail what he wants to be radical about. Then we can argue whether it is desirable or not, and what criteria we should use. But is it not the mark of the ideologue that he is usually so general and vague?

From past experience as well as from this exchange, I feel that what is really involved here is not a conflict of intellectual positions but a conflict of contrasting temperaments. Once upon a time there was a primary and meaningful tension between the orthodox and the antinomians. The orthodox, whether priests, clerks, or scholars, believed in a ritual or a tradition, a set of "right" beliefs, which were enforced in varying degrees on the society. The antinomians—gnostics, vagabonds, bohemians, rebels—resisted institutional authority, were defiant of tradition, law, and system, and sought to guide their lives by esoteric standards of conduct.

Such divisions used to be clear. But the history of the past several hundred years has been the absorption, or containment, of heresy. . . .

The shock of change, though, is real enough: the realization that escapes no one is that the egalitarian and socially mobile society which the "free-floating intellectuals" associated with the Marxist tradition have been calling for during the last hundred years has finally emerged in the form of our cumbersome, bureaucratic mass society, and has in turn engulfed the heretics. With this realization begins the process of disengagement. But it is not generally a process of responsible social thought and self-scrutiny, not an attempt to find out what kind of institutional structures in a large-scale society will best accommodate the older visions of community and individual freedom and self-determination. One simply labels oneself a radical, calls for (but rarely produces) utopian thought, and argues that the great need is to be "critical." Such disengagement is, quite simply, an escape from intellectual responsibility. Mr. Aiken's essay, with its abstract talk of moral discourse, provides a lovely cover for such an escape.

But if the old division of political temperaments into orthodox and antinomian has apparently broken down, there is still perhaps some usefulness in a three-part classification: the ideologues, the moralists, and the skeptics.

Ideologies, as organized systems of belief with ready formulas for the manipulation of the masses, are, in effect, new orthodoxies. The yearning for an ideology, the hunger for a cause, the craving for belief often mask the conformist's desire for power or the rebel's unconscious need to submit to authority. Such a reductive analysis, of course, risks the traducing of individuals who may be genuinely motivated to serve mankind selflessly or to search for new means of implementing their ideals. However, the judgment itself is not of persons but of the nature of ideologies, and of the way in which the "functional necessities" of organizing and implementing ideologies traduce all idealism.

To go back to Marx's original sense of the term, an ideology is an illusion, a false consciousness. Or, as Philip Rieff has recently remarked, "only an illusory history, or an illusory religion, or an illusory politics, could lead humans to the therapy of commitment." The yearning for a cause, for some transcendent purpose, is, of course, one of the deepest impulses of the sentient human being. The danger, always, is that this impulse will be manipulated in ways that betray its idealism. Such seductions are rarely overt or crude. It is usually the apocalyptic element, the call for a last act of violence in order to end violence, of a final deed of murder to eliminate murder, which is the agency of the ideologue's betrayal. In the dialectic of betrayal, means become ends and justifications of themselves.

Then there are those often lonely protestants who have stood outside the corridors of ideology or the pathways of power, and have spoken as moralists. In the tradition of prophecy, the moralists, on the basis of conscience, call injustice to account. In his tone and in his wrath, Mr. Aiken strikes me as a quondam moralist—which makes me all the more puzzled by his present effort to patch shreds of ideology into an intellectual argument. He does so, as I have pointed out, only be tearing the word "ideology" from its historical and sociological context, and by arbitrarily identifying it with political philosophy and moral discourse.

But why not speak directly in the language of morals and ethics? I can account for this failure only by the fact that the religious tradition —which has been the foundation of prophecy—has itself been undermined, and that the moralist has consequently lost much of his basis of judgment. Jeremiah and Deutero-Isaiah could call for a return to tradition, a departure from the merely ritualistic observance of the law; but what can Mr. Aiken ask us to return to? The modern moralist can become either an existentialist or an ideologue, and the option now seems to be running in the latter direction. . . .

Where the theme of the "end of ideology" is currently most relevant is in Eastern Europe, among the intellectuals who have experienced at first hand the deadening effects of an official ideology, and among the young generation for whom ideology is simply flatulent rhetoric. (It is curious that Mr. Aiken seems to assume that ideology is always nascent and passionate, and neglects its more pervasive role as a coercive, official force.) In a recent issue of *Survey*, a Czech writer describes the calloused attitude to politics of those who have grown up in an ideological regime: "A strange, frightening breed, this new generation, these men and women born during the last war or even later, who never knew any other social order and who are the products of our society. Purposeful, tough, smart, resourceful in handling their own affairs, down-to-earth, uncommunicative outside their own group, full of obvious pity for their fathers and their ridiculous manoeuvers, full of energy to get the best out of life now and for themselves.

"To them, ideology and politics and, indeed, any form of public activity are a lot of bunk, just hollow words with little relation to reality.

Not that they are anti-Communists, a meaningless term in their ears: they just could not care less. They were born into socialism and they live in socialism and what they see around *is* socialism. Pretty dull and shabby, and certainly nothing much to write home about. . . .

"If there is still to come the final ignominy of a burial·of Marxism-Leninism as we understand it today, it will be effortlessly carried out by these generations already born into socialism. And so it should be! For I believe that these young people, these young socialists will at last realize, because of what we did, that there is no socialism without freedom and that life is far more important than ideology."

The intention, then, of the "revolt against ideology" is not to make one insensitive to injustice or to the need for a transcendent moral vision. It is, rather, to make one wary of the easy solution and to deny that any embodiment of community is final. I once wrote that one of the tragedies of Marxism was that Marx, having provided a naturalistic explanation of the meaning of alienation, then narrowed the concept by locating its source entirely in the rule of private property. As we know now, to our sorrow, there are other, more debasing forms of degradation and dehumanization — the systems of totalitarianism — than economic exploitation.

However, the thinking connected with the "end of ideology" is not directed against Marxism or any other radical creed; nor does it involve a quarrel with utopianism and its visions. What it does is give us a perspective on modern history which emphasizes that the achievement of freedom and the defense of the individual constitute a permanent revolution; and it tells us that this revolution resists any final definition. It is for the sake of individual freedom that the claims of doubt must always take precedence over the claims of faith, and that the commitment to action must proceed from the ethic of responsibility.

HENRY DAVID AIKEN: On the whole Mr. Bell's reply confirms my earlier impression of the essential intellectual and spiritual confusion of the anti-ideology movement, the poverty of its ideas, and its total lack of a coherent, substantive social and political philosophy that goes a step beyond reaffirmation of shibboleths about which both of our major political parties (at least until Goldwater's ascendancy) have been in all-too-complete agreement for a generation.

There is, to be sure, one small part that doesn't quite jibe with this impression, but it is so curiously, almost touchingly, inconsistent with the remainder that I can only wonder about the degree of Mr. Bell's self-awareness in mentioning it. Specifically, he says that he has been a "democratic socialist for almost all of [his] . . . politically conscious years." Can he be serious? In other writings, including *The End of Ideology*, he has opted emphatically and without qualification for "the mixed economy"—which, of course, no socialist could accept save as a temporary stop-gap.

Socialism, I take it, is above all the position that at least the control and operation of the means of production, distribution, and exchange should be in the hands of society as a whole rather than of private individuals, groups, or corporations. Actively to take steps to bring about socialism in the United States would at once involve Mr. Bell (or anyone else) in a very sharp and deep disensus, both politically and ideologically, with the great majority of the American people, including virtually the whole industrial-business-governmental-scholarly establishment. In this country the existing democracy, or republic, is for practical purposes incompatible with socialism. And just for that reason, as S. M. Lipset, Mr. Bell's ally, has pointed out, socialism is here politically and ideologically a dead issue. Mr. Bell knows this. He must realize therefore that being a socialist in America is, for most men, rather like being a Christian: it is entirely safe to be one because socialism, for all but a revolutionary few, is outside the bounds of political possibility. In short, Mr. Bell's "socialism," the wishful and wistful sincerity of which we need not question, is, in Marx's sense, entirely utopian, and hence practically and functionally meaningless. Mr. Bell often has written perceptively and relevantly about sources of alienation among American workers. But what has he to offer, as a *socialist*, toward its drastic alleviation? I submit: nothing, or next to nothing. Here is precisely the sort of ideological schizophrenia which, in part, my essay was designed to expose.

But let me at once remove a possible source of misconception. Mr. Bell has spoken for himself; as for me, I am not a Marxist, vestigial, revisionist, or otherwise. My fundamental intellectual and moral antecedents are British, American, and Jewish. And although I mean always to speak of Marx *and* Engels with respect, I find it hard to understand how Mr. Bell could have gained the impression that my "citing" [*sic*] of the Marxist conception of ideology as "inverted images of reality" was meant to be approving.

However this may be, let me say for the record that I consider the Marxist (and hence Bellean) theory of ideology itself as at once vague, confused, programmatic, and useful nowadays only for purposes of popular polemicizing. On this score, Lenin's theory of ideology is surprisingly better, since it freely acknowledges Marxism to be an ideology, and since it perceives that, in general, ideology can be properly conceived, not in aprioristic, metaphysically pejorative terms, but functionally and dynamically as a form of thought which, for better or for worse, is meant to focus, guide, and energize the minds (and bodies) of men in society. As Lenin saw, it is the role, not the content, which determines whether a theory or doctrine is working ideologically. Thus, in the context of social action, scientific theories, philosophical doctrines, religious creeds, and even sociological statistics, may all serve an ideological role, just as well, or better, than ideas that are, or are supposed to be, "inverted images of reality." And let me add, finally, lest again I be misunderstood, that I am not remotely a Leninist either —although, in justice, I am bound to say that, after Marx himself, Lenin remains the most interesting and suggestive among Marxist thinkers. Lenin is, above all, an institutionalist in his approach to the problems and tasks of socialism, which is precisely what Bell is not. Alas, it was my reading of Lenin that, ironically, convinced me that world socialism is probably a utopian dream.

Mr. Bell's own variations on a theme by Marx are, from my point of view, conceptually and historically regressive, polemically misleading, and ultimately (when taken seriously) debilitating so far as the causes of the alienated, the disenfranchised, and the disinherited are concerned. Moreover, they leave our "confrontation," as Mr. Bell calls it, quite unaffected—except insofar as they inadvertently help to show (what I myself earlier pointed out) that the anti-ideologists, and especially Mr. Bell, are in effect merely quasi-Marxian conservatives who have done little or nothing to advance the master's theory of ideology, but on the contrary have merely applied his ideas rather mechanically and obviously to Communism itself in defense of the primary political and social status quo in the "free world." My contention was—and is —that the anti-ideologists leave us at once morally, intellectually, and, if I may say so, metaphysically helpless in "our" confrontation not only with the Communist world, but also with the great "neutralist" movements that are emerging all over the globe, and especially in the ex-colonial areas where neither socialism nor (political) democracy appears to stand a chance of realization. Now is a time, if there ever was one, for creative and constructive social and political thought. In such a situation what are the anti-ideologists doing, really, but warning us against the dangers of the faith ladder? Well, maybe we just do need a bit of faith in the future of humanity.

Mr. Bell says that pragmatism, at least in Dewey's version, defines "the consequences of an action as a constitutive element of the truth of a proposition." This, I would say, is rather the way Dewey must look under water. I myself think that Dewey's doctrine of the continuum of means and ends is a notable contribution to moral philosophy. But Mr. Bell makes no genuine use of it; he merely *says* he does. Marx, I may add, was implicitly employing this methodological principle in his own attacks upon utopianism, and especially utopian socialism. Mr. Bell and his "socialist" friends do not employ it; quite the contrary, theirs is a merely ideal, sentimental socialism, untouched by the slightest hesitation about what socialist aspirations can mean in a historical context in which no determinate program exists for realizing it. As for the thesis that "values, like any empirical proposition [*sic*], can be tested on the basis of their claims," it is one of the weirdest attempts at redaction of the Dewey-Hook theory regarding the empirical, or even scientific, verifiability of value judgments that I have yet seen.[2]

Mr. Bell claims that I treat the word "ideology" only as a formal problem for analysis, and that the reason for this is that I am out to make a lawyer's rather than a philosopher's case. How odd. Well, I did mean to make a case, the best I knew how to make. And it is all the same to me how Mr. Bell chooses to classify it, so long as it is, as he allows, "the best" of its kind. As a means to a moral and ideological end, I was and am interested in the "formal" problem which the word "ideology" presents to the logical analyst, although Mr. Bell at the outset appears to deny this when he complains that I do not "define" ideology. It was not my purpose to define it, but to study and to characterize what other people, including Mr. Bell, seem to think about it. I tried to determine what Mr. Bell might be taken to mean and then to show that, once *his* rhetoric was stripped to its fighting weight, even his notions of ideology did not commit him, or us, to an across-the-board attack upon ideology as such. Again, I suggested that all ideologies should be judged, not *en bloc*, but in the light of their own respective practices and envisageable consequences. And it was precisely in these terms that I attempted to appraise the merits of Mr. Bell's own anti-ideological ideology. He doesn't reply to my specific contentions — including in particular the charge that the anti-ideological school has fallen into a weary, disillusioned *carpe diem* philosophy which may be suitable for self-centered valetudinarians but is certainly unsuitable for determined, untired, radical liberals who believe that the free world has a real future if it moves boldly and creatively and immediately on its own terrible problems of poverty, inequality, prejudice, and fear. In short, my aim has been to employ the study of a word in use, in order to expose, and if possible transcend, a point of view which in the past I myself have found all too tempting.

[2]Anyone interested in why I consider this theory indefensible can find the reason in my essays on Hook and Dewey, [in] *Commentary*, February and October, 1962. An earlier, more detailed version of the same position may be found in my book, *Reason and Conduct*.

Eventually, Mr. Bell gets around to quoting a passage from my essay in which, after the preparation I thought I needed, I state what in my judgment a political ideology, if not a total ideology, really comes to. By extrapolation it would be easy to derive from this my views about "total ideology," were these not already available in my little book, *The Age of Ideology.* So the charge that I don't provide a "definition" of political ideology (at the outset?) strikes me as somewhat perverse. As for the point that the "definition" of political ideology which I offer is merely a misleading definition of political philosophy, let me reply that if Mr. Bell can bring himself to take another look at my essay, he will find that I myself actually lead off by asking why so many people declare political philosophy to be dead. I turn later to a consideration of ideology precisely in order to find an answer to that question. And in fact I was led in the first instance into a discussion of the end-of-ideology school through an attempt to discover what, at bottom, people now object to in political philosophy. If my "definition" of political ideology turns out to be nothing but a "stylish" redaction of "the old-fashioned definition of political philosophy," so be it. For then in re-furbishing ideology, I shall have done, as I meant to do, two jobs at once.

On this score, there remains only to be added that in my opinion the ideologists often have treated the problems of political philosophy more imaginatively and in greater depth than their more classical predecessors. And the reason for this is that they nearly always see the necessity of viewing a political philosophy (or ideology) not only in the perspective of a system of moral principles, but also within the context of a philosophy of history, a metaphysical *Weltanschauung,* and, if one can be found, a theology. It is this context, largely lacking except in negative terms in the works of the anti-ideologists, which gives depth and range and power to a political ideology. And, indeed, if one knows where to look for it, the greatest classical political philosophies, such as Plato's and Aquinas's, have always provided it.

Mr. Bell's cry of "foul" in response to my charge, or informed guess, that the anti-ideologists are not only anti-moralistic but also anti-moralists who really mean to go altogether beyond "good and evil," is premature. My advice to him here is to re-read, not my words, but his own. In the passage about total ideology which he quotes from his own book, there is this sentence: "This commitment to ideology—the yearning for a cause, the satisfaction of deep *moral* feelings—is not . . . " etc. (my italics). Here, plainly, is not the obvious pejorative adjective "moralistic" but the now pejorated adjective "moral" itself. There are other analogous passages in Mr. Bell's writings, as well as a good many that might be quoted to advantage from the writings of his allies. I stand my ground: Mr. Bell's attack is not directed merely against "moralism"—which, of course, is nothing but the other chap's morals — but against morality as a form of discourse, a form of policy, a way of deciding what is to be done (and said).

Mr. Bell asks me, as I hoped he might, to be concrete. Very well (although it should be emphasized that there is nothing wrong with being abstract when the problems at issue are abstract and general, as they are to a degree in the present context). I believe in the necessity of constant, incessant pressure from the Left upon the Establishment and the status quo in order to rectify grave social wrongs: injustices, inequalities, and other miseries that are removable through collective social action. I believe, furthermore, in a never-ending "resistance" and spiritual rebelliousness. In our time, I think that the first order of business is a continuing, stop-at-nothing effort to obtain, not merely a nuclear test ban, but a progressive, ultimately total, dismantling of our entire machinery for nuclear warfare, lest some benighted Goldwater, unacquainted with the theory of games, should not merely threaten to use it, but use it. I believe in the necessity of a foreign policy for America which is predicated on the principle that any sort of brinksmanship, in whatever cause, is deeply immoral, a test not of courage but of inhumanity or madness or both. I seek, further, an approach to the problems of "underdeveloped" regions and nations which is radically non-military and which is completely indifferent to questions of ideology, race, color, or previous condition of servitude. I want us to pursue a realistic policy in regard to China, one which recognizes that China is a permanent, or semi-permanent, political and social reality which cannot be dealt with by the methods employed by the American government during the past decade. Whether we "like" the Chinese government is quite irrelevant. It belongs in the UN if Spain and Russia and Egypt belong. But this is merely emblematic. It is the "either-or" mentality exemplified by the anti-ideologists in their thinking about the confrontation between the Communist worlds and the "free" worlds which seems to me so inhuman, so dangerous, so suicidal.

Domestically, I applaud a hard, tough, *uncompromising* effort to bring the Negro people up to scratch, legally, politically, economically, humanly. People deplore the riots. What they should deplore are the causes of the riots: and what they should do about them is to remove those causes. *This can be done*, particularly if we divert a third or a half of the money and effort spent on building the military establishment, moon shots and all the rest of it, into imaginative public-works projects, educational developments, medical programs, and humanistic social activities in which all classes and colors of Americans participate together. Harlem (and "Harlem" works a bit like "Goldwater," as a type-word) is a national, not a regional, problem, and it can't wait a generation for a solution. There is also the immense aesthetic and even

religious problem of saving America and the world from total permanent disfigurement. Much of New York, for example, is now so hideous
that one wonders how human beings can endure it. But it is a dream city
by comparison with Detroit and Chicago. The countryside is in ruins.
The air stinks. The water, what there is of it, is undrinkable. And so
on. A world as ugly, as fearful, as uncertain of itself as ours needs
sympathy, but it needs continual action — bold, determined, and radical. Nothing else will suffice.

In part the differences between Mr. Bell's party and my own are doctrinal. But there are indeed basic differences of attitude or posture
toward the whole conduct of life of men in societies. This becomes
apparent in our respective conceptions of the democratic process itself.
For Mr. Bell, it seems, democracy virtually means compromise. For me,
compromise is as compromise does: some compromises are desirable;
some necessary; others are dishonorable. Where questions of civil
liberty, economic equality, and social justice are concerned, I consider
compromise with the "interests," with prejudice, with indifference to
be dishonorable, and I do not commend it. All too often, even in a
democracy, compromise suggests, not sweet reasonableness and good
will, but inaction, vacillation, collaboration, timidity. For me democracy
is, minimally, a device for checking the accumulation of political power;
maximally, it is a mode of participation in the communal life and a sharing of fundamental responsibilities toward the common good. What
lies between seems to me, often, less admirable.

More broadly still, for Mr. Bell it appears that problems of politics generally are to be viewed, first, as problems of calculation and,
secondly, as problems of adjustment (or compromise). For me, they
involve much more, as is evident in my views about the role of rhetoric
in political thought and discourse. To my mind, therefore, the end of
ideology is, in a sense, almost tantamount to the end of politics itself.
Beneath all, the anti-ideologists are men of doubt; their temperament,
in the language of William James, is that of the "tough-minded." All
too often, sadly, the same is true of me, but I do not glory in the fact.
Pessimism is a fact of life; optimism, in our time at least, almost a matter of grace. Thought, analysis, inquiry — and the itch of doubt which
animates inquiry — are *of course* indispensable conditions of rational
life. But aspiration, passion, hope, volition, and choice also belong in-
alienably to the life of the mind and the spirit. Without them, in the heat
of the day, we languish, we perish. We must not allow ourselves to be
paralyzed by thought; rather we must *use* it. We must not let it divert
us from the necessity of action. We *dare* not forever stand and wait;
we *dare* not continue to temporize. It is late, and there is a world at
stake.

8. Ideologies for Modernity

It need hardly be said that the intellectual collapse of older political theories and the incorporation of other ideologies into operating political systems have ended the relevance of classical belief systems for public life. Yet, as Eric Hoffer argues, the breakup of the older value systems and social forms itself creates a need to believe in some coherent and reassuring set of political ideas, whatever they may be. The growth of mass political expectations, the bureaucratization of modern life, and the military policy uses of the "pure sciences" are examples of modern ideological developments.

Modern man in a mass society, suggests Hoffer, needs to transfer the emotional force of affirmation from worn-out ideologies to new substitutes. The psychological affinity of totalitarianism, Communism, and statism may be more crucial than the intellectual context of these belief systems. The emergence of mass political desires is a major support for appropriate political beliefs that meet psychological needs or provide explanations of political phenomena which deflect frustration from the rulers to the "real" source of difficulties — e.g., colonists, Jesuits, capitalists, or Jews.

In our organizational society, as Robert Presthus demonstrates, it is a subtle interlacing of status expectations and beliefs about legitimate power that sustains the major institutions and the corporate structure. The learned behavior of appropriate command and deference leads to patterns of role playing that subtly shape an operating political ideology which, although stated otherwise, is often inimical to our public democratic creed.

Members of the "academy," even those who debunk older forms of "unrealistic" and "utopian" ideologies, are not immune to the pressures for some ideological premises. Walter Goldstein and S. M. Miller examine Herman Kahn's military strategy (or "ideology") for impending atomic war and his application of mathematical game theory to public policy. In the name of scientific realism, contend the critics, Kahn has made pseudo-scientific assumptions about human behavior that perceive man as more calculating and "rational" (in weighting his response to the number of atomic megadeaths, for instance) than did the philosophers of the Enlightenment, who were intoxicated with man's quest for pure reason and political knowledge.

THE APPEAL OF MASS MOVEMENTS

Eric Hoffer

The Interchangeability of Mass Movements

When people are ripe for a mass movement, they are usually ripe for any effective movement, and not solely for one with a particular doctrine or program. In pre-Hitlerian Germany it was often a tossup whether a restless youth would join the Communists or the Nazis. In the overcrowded pale of Czarist Russia the simmering Jewish population was ripe both for revolution and Zionism. In the same family, one member would join the revolutionaries and the other the Zionists. Dr. Chaim Weizmann quotes a saying of his mother in those days: "Whatever happens, I shall be well off. If Shemuel [the revolutionary son] is right, we shall all be happy in Russia; and if Chaim [the Zionist] is right, then I shall go to live in Palestine."[1]

This receptivity to all movements does not always cease even after the potential true believer has become the ardent convert of a specific movement. Where mass movements are in violent competition with each other, there are not infrequent instances of converts—even the most zealous—shifting their allegiance from one to the other. A Saul turning into Paul is neither a rarity nor a miracle. In our day, each proselytizing mass movement seems to regard the zealous adherents of its antagonist its own potential converts. Hitler looked on the German Communists as potential National Socialists: "The *petit bourgeois* Social-Democrat and the trade-union boss will never make a National Socialist, but the Communist always will."[2] Captain Röhm boasted that he could turn the reddest Communist into a glowing nationalist in four weeks.[3] On the other hand, Karl Radek looked on the Nazi Brown Shirts (SA) as a reserve for future Communist recruits.[4]

Since all mass movements draw their adherents from the same types of humanity and appeal to the same types of mind, it follows: (a) all mass movements are competitive, and the gain of one in adherents is the loss of all the others; (b) all mass movements are interchangeable. One mass movement readily transforms itself into another. A religious movement may develop into a social revolution or a nationalist movement; a social revolution, into militant nationalism or a religious movement; a nationalist movement, into a social revolution or a religious movement.

Pages 16–20 (Chapter 3), 142–146 (Chapter 14) from *The True Believer* by Eric Hoffer. Copyright 1951 by Eric Hoffer. Reprinted by permission of Harper & Row, Publishers. Title supplied by the editor.
    [1]Chaim Weizmann, *Trial and Error* (New York: Harper & Brothers, 1949), p. 13.
    [2]Hermann Rauschning, *Hitler Speaks* (New York: G. P. Putnam's Sons, 1940), p. 134.
    [3]Konrad Heiden, *Der Fuehrer* (Boston: Houghton Mifflin, 1944), p. 30.
    [4]Fritz August Voigt, *Unto Caesar* (New York: G. P. Putnam's Sons, 1938), p. 283.

It is rare for a mass movement to be wholly of one character. Usually it displays some facets of other types of movement, and sometimes it is two or three movements in one. The exodus of the Hebrews from Egypt was a slave revolt, a religious movement and a nationalist movement. The militant nationalism of the Japanese is essentially religious. The French Revolution was a new religion. It had "its dogma, the sacred principles of the Revolution—*Liberté et sainte égalité*. It had its form of worship, an adaptation of Catholic ceremonial, which was elaborated in connection with civic *fêtes*. It had its saints, the heroes and martyrs of liberty."[5] At the same time, the French Revolution was also a nationalist movement. The legislative assembly decreed in 1792 that altars should be raised everywhere bearing the inscription: "The citizen is born, lives and dies for *la Patrie*."[6]

The religious movements of the Reformation had a revolutionary aspect which expressed itself in peasant uprisings, and were also nationalist movements. Said Luther: "In the eyes of the Italians we Germans are merely low Teutonic swine. They exploit us like charlatans and suck the country to the marrow. Wake up Germany!"[7]

The religious character of the Bolshevik and Nazi revolutions is generally recognized. The hammer and sickle and the swastika are in a class with the cross. The ceremonial of their parades is as the ceremonial of a religious procession. They have articles of faith, saints, martyrs and holy sepulchers. The Bolshevik and Nazi revolutions are also full-blown nationalist movements. The Nazi revolution had been so from the beginning, while the nationalism of the Bolsheviks was a late development.

Zionism is a nationalist movement and a social revolution. To the orthodox Jew it is also a religious movement. Irish nationalism has a deep religious tinge. The present mass movements in Asia are both nationalist and revolutionary.

The problem of stopping a mass movement is often a matter of substituting one movement for another. A social revolution can be stopped by promoting a religious or nationalist movement. Thus in countries where Catholicism has recaptured its mass movement spirit, it counteracts the spread of communism. In Japan it was nationalism that canalized all movements of social protest. In our South, the movement of racial solidarity acts as a preventive of social upheaval. A similar situation may be observed among the French in Canada and the Boers in South Africa.

[5]Carl L. Becker, *The Heavenly City of the Eighteenth-Century Philosophers* (New Haven: Yale University Press, 1932), p. 155.

[6]A. Mathiez, "Les Origins des Cultes Revolutionnaires," p. 31. Quoted by Carlton J. H. Hayes, *Essays on Nationalism* (New York: Macmillan, 1926), p. 103.

[7]Frantz Funck-Brentano, *Luther* (London: Jonathan Cape, 1939), p. 278.

This method of stopping one movement by substituting another for it is not always without danger, and it does not usually come cheap. It is well for those who hug the present and want to preserve it as it is not to play with mass movements. For it always fares ill with the present when a genuine mass movement is on the march. In pre-war Italy and Germany practical businessmen acted in an entirely "logical" manner when they encouraged a Fascist and a Nazi movement in order to stop communism. But in doing so, these practical and logical people promoted their own liquidation.

There are other safer substitutes for a mass movement. In general, any arrangement which either discourages atomistic individualism or facilitates self-forgetting or offers chances for action and new beginnings tends to counteract the rise and spread of mass movements. . . . Here we shall touch upon one curious substitute for mass movements, namely migration.

Emigration offers some of the things the frustrated hope to find when they join a mass movement, namely, change and a chance for a new beginning. The same types who swell the ranks of a rising mass movement are also likely to avail themselves of a chance to emigrate. Thus migration can serve as a substitute for a mass movement. It is plausible, for instance, that had the United States and the British Empire welcomed mass migration from Europe after the First World War, there might have been neither a Fascist nor a Nazi revolution. In this country, free and easy migration over a vast continent contributed to our social stability.

However, because of the quality of their human material, mass migrations are fertile ground for the rise of genuine mass movements. It is sometimes difficult to tell where a mass migration ends and a mass movement begins—and which came first. The migration of the Hebrews from Egypt developed into a religious and nationalist movement. The migrations of the barbarians in the declining days of the Roman Empire were more than mere shifts of population. The indications are that the barbarians were relatively few in number, but, once they invaded a country, they were joined by the oppressed and dissatisfied in all walks of life: "it was a social revolution started and masked by a superficial foreign conquest."[8]

Every mass movement is in a sense a migration—a movement toward a promised land; and, when feasible and expedient, an actual migration takes place. This happened in the case of the Puritans, Anabaptists, Mormons, Dukhobors and Zionists. Migration, in the mass, strengthens the spirit and unity of a movement; and whether in the form

[8]H. G. Wells, *The Outline of History* (New York: Macmillan, 1922), pp. 482–484.

of foreign conquest, crusade, pilgrimage or settlement of new land it is practiced by most active mass movements.

The Fanatics

When the moment is ripe, only the fanatic can hatch a genuine mass movement. Without him the disaffection engendered by militant men of words remains undirected and can vent itself only in pointless and easily suppressed disorders. Without him the initiated reforms, even when drastic, leave the old way of life unchanged, and any change in government usually amounts to no more than a transfer of power from one set of men of action to another. Without him there can perhaps be no new beginning.

When the old order begins to fall apart, many of the vociferous men of words, who prayed so long for the day, are in a funk. The first glimpse of the face of anarchy frightens them out of their wits. They forget all they said about the "poor simple folk" and run for help to strong men of action — princes, generals, administrators, bankers, landowners — who know how to deal with the rabble and how to stem the tide of chaos.

Not so the fanatic. Chaos is his element. When the old order begins to crack, he wades in with all his might and recklessness to blow the whole hated present to high heaven. He glories in the sight of a world coming to a sudden end. To hell with reforms! All that already exists is rubbish, and there is no sense in reforming rubbish. He justifies his will to anarchy with the plausible assertion that there can be no new beginning so long as the old clutters the landscape. He shoves aside the frightened men of words, if they are still around, though he continues to extol their doctrines and mouth their slogans. He alone knows the innermost craving of the masses in action: the craving for communion, for the mustering of the host, for the dissolution of cursed individuality in the majesty and grandeur of a mighty whole. Posterity is king; and woe to those, inside and outside the movement, who hug and hang on to the present.

Whence come the fanatics? Mostly from the ranks of the noncreative men of words. The most significant division between men of words is between those who can find fulfillment in creative work and those who cannot. The creative man of words, no matter how bitterly he may criticize and deride the existing order, is actually attached to the present. His passion is to reform and not to destroy. When the mass movement remains wholly in his keeping, he turns it into a mild affair. The reforms he initiates are of the surface, and life flows on without a sudden break. But such a development is possible only when the anarchic action of the masses does not come into play, either because the old order abdicates without a struggle or because the man of words allies himself with strong men of action the moment chaos threatens to break loose. When the struggle with the old order is bitter and chaotic and victory can be won only by utmost unity and self-sacrifice, the creative man of words is usually shoved aside and the management of affairs falls into the hands of the noncreative men of words — the eternal misfits and the fanatical contemners of the present.

The man who wants to write a great book, paint a great picture, create an architectural masterpiece, become a great scientist, and knows that never in all eternity will he be able to realize this, his innermost desire, can find no peace in a stable social order — old or new. He sees his life as irrevocably spoiled and the world perpetually out of joint. He feels at home only in a state of chaos. Even when he submits to or imposes an iron discipline, he is but submitting to or shaping the indispensable instrument for attaining a state of eternal flux, eternal becoming. Only when engaged in change does he have a sense of freedom and the feeling that he is growing and developing. It is because he can never be reconciled with his self that he fears finality and a fixed order of things. Marat, Robespierre, Lenin, Mussolini and Hitler are outstanding examples of fanatics arising from the ranks of noncreative men of words. Peter Viereck points out that most of the Nazi bigwigs had artistic and literary ambitions which they could not realize. Hitler tried painting and architecture; Goebbels, drama, the novel and poetry; Rosenberg, architecture and philosophy; von Shirach, poetry; Funk, music; Streicher, painting. "Almost all were failures, not only by the usual vulgar criterion of success but by their own artistic criteria." Their artistic and literary ambitions "were originally far deeper than political ambitions: and were integral parts of their personalities."[9]

The creative man of words is ill at ease in the atmosphere of an active movement. He feels that its whirl and passion sap his creative energies. So long as he is conscious of the creative flow within him, he will not find fulfillment in leading millions and in winning victories. The result is that, once the movement starts rolling, he either retires voluntarily or is pushed aside. Moreover, since the genuine man of words can never wholeheartedly and for long suppress his critical faculty, he is inevitably cast in the role of the heretic. Thus unless the creative man of words stifles the newborn movement by allying himself with practical men of action or unless he dies at the right moment, he is likely to end up either a shunned recluse or in exile or facing a firing squad.

[9]Peter Viereck, *Metapolitics* (New York: Alfred A. Knopf, 1941), pp. 156 and 170.

The danger of the fanatic to the development of a movement is that he cannot settle down. Once victory has been won and the new order begins to crystallize, the fanatic becomes an element of strain and disruption. The taste for strong feeling drives him on to search for mysteries yet to be revealed and secret doors yet to be opened. He keeps groping for extremes. Thus on the morrow of victory most mass movements find themselves in the grip of dissension. The ardor which yesterday found an outlet in a life-and-death struggle with external enemies now vents itself in violent disputes and clash of factions. Hatred has become a habit. With no more outside enemies to destroy, the fanatics make enemies of one another. Hitler—himself a fanatic—could diagnose with precision the state of mind of the fanatics who plotted against him within the ranks of the National Socialist party. In his order to the newly appointed chief of the SA after the purge of Röhm in 1934 he speaks of those who will not settle down: ". . . without realizing it, [they] have found in nihilism their ultimate confession of faith . . . their unrest and disquietude can find satisfaction only in some conspiratorial activity of the mind, in perpetually plotting the disintegration of whatever the set-up of the moment happens to be."[10] As was often the case with Hitler, his accusations against antagonists (inside and outside the Reich) were a self-revelation. He, too, particularly in his last days, found in nihilism his "ultimate philosophy and valediction."[11]

If allowed to have their way, the fanatics may split a movement into schism and heresies which threaten its existence. Even when the fanatics do not breed dissension, they can still wreck the movement by driving it to attempt the impossible. Only the entrance of a practical man of action can save the achievements of the movement.

THE INSTITUTIONAL APPARATUS

ROBERT PRESTHUS

Power to initiate, to communicate, to reward, to sanction, to shape public opinion—these are the prerogatives and tactics of oligarchy. As a result, policy and orders flow from the top downward, limiting the rank and file to an essentially negative role. Having neither the power of initiation, which permits the oligarchy to decide what shall be done and when, nor of choosing the avenues of consultation, which can be

[10]Hans Bernd Gisevius, *To the Bitter End.*(Boston: Houghton Mifflin, 1947), pp. 121–122.
[11]H. R. Trevor-Roper, *The Last Days of Hitler* (New York: Macmillan, 1947), p. 4.

Pages 51–58: From *The Organizational Society*, by Robert Presthus. Copyright 1961 by Robert Presthus. Reprinted by permission of Alfred A. Knopf, Inc. Title supplied by the editor.

used to ensure favorable reactions to their policies, nor the control of patronage, which ensures discipline, the majority can only ratify. When such actions sharply violate their expectations, the mass may exercise a veto power, but such contingencies are remote since they occur only if the minority loses the tactical skill that brought it to power in the first place.

In democratic societies the tendency toward oligarchy stands out most sharply in crises, when the use of arbitrary methods for democratic ends becomes acceptable. An obvious example is the way in which military and security imperatives are accepted during wartime. Most of us regard such invasions as a temporary inconvenience, a necessary tribute to national survival. Similarly, during wartime certain groups shelve ideals which previously had seemed irreducible. For example, physical scientists made great contributions during and after World War II through their research on new weapons. It is well known that their professional ethic centers on individual independence, on the free exchange of information, and on a rigorous disavowal of authority as a basis for truth. These values, moreover, are not merely desirable; they are supposedly among the essentials of scientific progress. Yet apparently they could be set aside. We find, for example, that during World War II the 30,000 scientists in the Office of Scientific Research and Development were controlled by about "thirty-five men in senior positions."[1] This minority assigned research, established policy vis-à-vis the military and the public, and generally ran things according to "convenient, authoritarian military liaisons."[2]

Hierarchy and oligarchy seek *rationality*, [a] common structural characteristic of large-scale organization. Rationality may be defined as the capacity for objective, intelligent action. It is usually characterized by a patent behavioral nexus between ends and means. While rationality is always limited by human error, inadequate information, and chance, within these limits the rational person applies intelligence, experience, and technical skills to solve his problems. In an ideal-typical organization rationality is sought by organizing and directing its many parts so that each contributes to the whole product. Specialization, careful recruitment, job analysis, and planning are among the obvious means to this end.

We know that a society tends to produce individuals who possess its dominant characteristics. The rationality of the big organization is similarly instilled in its members. Not only are its structure and procedures designed to enhance predictability, but individuals too become, insofar as possible, animated instruments. Individual discretion is limited by regulations and precedents that cover all anticipated events, and such regulations tend to become ends in themselves. As a result,

---

[1]Vanevar Bush, *Modern Arms and Free Man* (New York: Simon and Schuster, 1949), pp. 6–7.

[2]"The Great Science Debate," *Fortune* (June 1946), p. 236.

individuals try to find written authority for every action and to avoid action when such cannot be found. The very interpretation of rules and the search for authority to act (or not to act) become valued skills. Knowledge of the rules and how they can be bent gives the individual security and a share of organized power. He thus develops a vested interest in preserving the rules against change.

Rationality is also sought through the division of labor and through recruitment on a scientific basis. Job requirements, including both technical skill and emotional qualities, are determined by men selected for their ability to determine such qualifications. Skill and character are matched with such specifications, insuring that placement is as objective as possible. This rational distribution of human effort is reinforced by the fact that organization units are also set up on a specialized basis. Such specialization enables the individual (and the organization) to develop exceptional skill.

Even the specialist's isolation contributes to his skill because he finds satisfaction in the complete mastery of his role. Denied an understanding of the larger scheme, he magnifies the limited insights and satisfactions that are within his grasp. He is, as it were, driven to this end. Objective, impersonal standards become all the more acquisitive because he is often unaware of their implications. He thinks everyone lives that way. One is reminded of the Prussian staff officer who spent a lifetime seeking ways to reduce mobilization time by one half-hour. As Merton and others have shown, certain dysfunctions follow, including a resistance and an inability to change.

Another significant by-product occurs: the decision-making process becomes highly diffused, the product of an organizational mind. *Organized irresponsibility* follows. Decision making in the big organization becomes vague and impersonal, the instrument of an anonymous, fragmented intelligence. Each decision is the result of various technical and personal considerations, the sum of the contributions of everyone involved in the deciding process. This diffusion means that "everyone" (i.e., no one) is responsible. In extreme cases the condition may lead to arbitrary and immoral behavior, particularly when compounded by intense personal identification with the state, the party, the church, or the "organization." In every case, the probabilities that the organization may act unjustly are increased by the weakening of individual responsibility. Only "the system" is responsible.

The modern culmination of this system was seen in the Nazi apparatus. "The crime is handed down from chief to sub-chief until it reaches the slave who receives orders from above without being able to pass them on to anybody. One of the Dachau executioners weeps in prison and says, 'I only obeyed orders. The Führer and the Reichsführer, alone, planned all this and then they ran away. Gluecks received orders from Kaltenbrunner and, finally, I received orders to carry out the shootings. I have been left holding the bag because I was only a little *Hauptscharführer* and because I couldn't hand it on any lower down the line. Now they say that I am the assassin.'"[3] This suggests why the big organization more often causes a crime of logic than one of passion, to use Camus' phrase.

Such procedures and attitudes are often necessary to handle the volume and diversity of activity in big organizations. Methods for handling each type of problem are prescribed, with each specialist contributing to the decision on the basis of his skill and jurisdiction. This overriding technical ethos increases the probability that personal factors will be minimized. Ideally, there is no way that such elements can affect the decision process. The specialist's loyalty is to the work process and to his own technical skill, rather than to any mitigating aspects of a case. As Weber shows, to do otherwise would evoke considerable anxiety, so strong are the demands of precedent and procedure.

The organization, in sum, is rationally planned to achieve its ends. Like the human organism, it has a directing center that transmits cues to the entire organization. Authority, rewards, and sanctions are allocated in ways that ensure that its members work together. . . . [H]ierarchy and oligarchy are perhaps the main instruments for so doing. The first assigns authority, responsibility, status, income, and deference in a descending scale from top to bottom, providing a chain of graded interpersonal relationships that insures the delegation of all sanctioned impulses. Oligarchy makes its contribution by monopolizing power and the distribution of the organization's scarce values. Men work for status, recognition, and security; oligarchy permits the organization's elite to determine the conditions under which such values are allocated.

All this is highly idealized, of course. Informal centers of power compete with the elite for influence in determining how resources are to be distributed. Unanticipated consequences subvert the organization's formal goals. Individuals persist in giving their latent objectives priority over organizational claims. Nevertheless, in organizations with high morale, i.e., those in which the legitimacy of means and ends is widely endorsed, the image is generally accurate. The resulting bond between the elite and the rank and file ensures identification, consensus, and even a sense of real participation among the latter.

We conclude . . . by considering two common assumptions about big organizations: that they are characterized by "*efficiency*" and "*freedom from conflict*." Both assumptions need to be qualified. Despite the fact that organizations exude an aura of "efficiency," being highly organized to achieve their goals by means of the structural characteristics outlined above; and despite the fact that individuals, hired on the basis

[3] Albert Camus, *The Rebel* (New York: Random House, 1959), p. 182.

of training and expertise, pursue their specialties with authority and discretion and in accordance with prescribed rules; and despite the fact that everyone is briskly competent and appears to know exactly what he is doing; the belief in the "efficiency" of bureaucratic organization is almost impossible to sustain. Not only is the very concept of "efficiency" virtually impossible of definition, except in some gross, tautological sense such as "the achievement of organizational goals with the minimum expenditure of resources," but no competent research exists demonstrating the "efficiency" of the bureaucratic model compared with some alternative. While some of its characteristics, such as specialization and oligarchy, probably increase productivity and discipline, it is fair to conclude that a rigorous demonstration of its "efficiency" has not yet been made.

As Karl Mannheim has said, the advantages of modern organizations lie mainly in their tendency to increase group rationality by placing power and authority in relatively few hands.[4] This permits the organization's major policies to be determined with limited conflict and great finality. Once this has been done, the energies of the entire organization can be devoted to the task of carrying them out. Centralized authority and the conclusive resolution of the essential value question, "What is to be done?" is the major operational advantage of the bureaucratic model. But even this impressive advantage leaves unanswered questions about the effect of oligarchic decision making upon morale, and about the caliber of decisions reached without full participation.

A related characteristic often imputed to the bureaucratic model is its "conflict-free" nature. This assumption is rarely analyzed, yet it is directly related to whatever "efficiency" the model achieves. The declining market value of conflict in contemporary society is surely related to the dysfunctions of conflict as a personal bureaucratic skill. If one assumes that centralized authority is required to achieve order and continuity in the organization, it follows that conflict must be muted and confined to the organization's elite. Once decisions are reached at this level, further argument is prohibited. As in the British Cabinet, an administered consensus occurs, ensuring "collective responsibility" and a united front before the organization and the outside world. That executives who disagree strongly with policy decisions must resign if they feel unable to accept the institutional decision suggests the intensity of this demand for consensus. The "conflict-free" assumption also provides psychological gains, reinforcing authority by the implication that the revealed decision is the "one best way," scientifically achieved in line with the experience, inside information, and knowledge possessed by the organization's leaders. Patent conflict, by contrast, suggests that

[4]Karl Mannheim, *Man and Society in an Age of Reconstruction* (New York: Harcourt, Brace, 1941), pp. 244, 293–295.

since equally wise and expert men can disagree on an issue, there is some question about the very existence of objectively superior alternatives, and of the organization's ability to discover them. In this sense, the very premises of organizational logic are challenged by conflict.

The strategic advantages of conflict repression are also apparent in the internecine struggles among competing units of the organization. Here, too, dissent is confined within the unit, enabling the latter to present a united front in its endless competition with other units for a larger share of the organization's resources. Elites have a direct stake in such consensus because any inability to maintain equilibrium and its attending competitive advantages brings disapproval from higher echelons which also desire on their own part to convey upward an image of cohesion within their larger sphere. The weight of such expectations is shown by the fact that the gravest offense in bureaucratic society is to go over the head of one's superior, to reveal conflict to outsiders.

The "conflict-free" assumption is undercut by the inherent tension between authority based upon hierarchy and that based upon the expertise of the many specialists found in the typical big organization. Understandably, each element tends to define its own role as the ultimate basis for authority. Those in hierarchical positions will insist that final authority must reside at the top, because the disparate skills, training, and professional introversion of specialists require some disinterested and superior co-ordinating influence. On the other hand, specialists will rarely grant that those in formal positions of authority fully merit the authority, power, and income which they usually enjoy. While the intensity of this conflict varies, it is in some degree a built-in characteristic of all big organizations. In view of this, it seems that instead of defining the bureaucratic model as "conflict free," we ought to regard it as a system in which conflict is inherent. At the same time, there are no doubt significant operational gains coming from the kind of centralized authority which enables modern organizations to administer consensus through [various] means . . . .

. . . [T]he major structural characteristics of big organizations [include] *size, specialization, hierarchy, status, authority, oligarchy, co-optation, rationality* and *"efficiency."* These characteristics constitute the *bureaucratic model,* an ideal type of all large-scale organizations. Such organizations provide a distinctive work environment for their members. Behavioral expectations are clearly prescribed, and interpersonal relations are structured by nice distinctions among the authority, status, and rank of those concerned. At the same time, conflict is always present. This reflects the tensions between those in hierarchical positions, who monopolize organizational power and rewards, and those in specialist roles. . . .

HERMAN KAHN: IDEOLOGIST OF MILITARY STRATEGY

Walter Goldstein and S. M. Miller

How to govern military technology—which potential weapons should have priority in development, what should be the "mix" of weapons in the military arsenal—and how to relate military strategy to foreign policy have become awesome problems in the nuclear age. Since traditional military analysts are limited by pre-nuclear preconceptions and training, a new secular type has recently emerged to fill the gap: the system analyst. This new breed is composed of younger non-military men with abstract research experience. Adept at mathematical formulations, they particularly lean on the theory of games to structure and compute conflict situations and their impassive outcomes. They are "cool," hard-headed, and unemotional as they contemplate the possibilities of 200 million deaths in wartime. Uncommitted to any narrow military policy, they operate from the premise that any unexamined strategy yearns for an imaginative "scenario."

They wield considerable influence in Washington today. Brilliant, imaginative, and inventive where others are confused or fearful, their logical analyses have appealed to the new enthusiasts in the political and military Establishment. . . .

Among the most distinguished of the "new men," blessed with and prodded by the vision of thermonuclear nightmare, is Herman Kahn. His two recent books, *On Thermonuclear War*, and *Thinking About the Unthinkable*, have bulged with premonitions, conjectures, abstract models and contrived scenarios of nuclear conflict. The sustained and unemotional quality of his work can be taken as representative of his strategic colleagues—Schelling, Morgenstern, Knorr, Kissinger, Wohlstetter, etc. In many ways Kahn's work is more bizarre and sensitive to common-sense objections; but it has been precisely this quality of fantasy-plus-realistic analysis that has confused his critics. Some critics, like James Newman in the *Scientific American*, bore an emotional revulsion against his outlook, while others, like Amitai Etzioni in the *Columbia University Forum*, failed to grapple with Kahn's system in its own terms. This critique attempts to test both the internal consistency of Kahn's analysis and the relevance of his findings to the tensions of the Cold War.

I

Kahn's major assumption is that nuclear war can be less than catastrophic. Contrary to the beliefs of those unilateralists and fatalists who refuse to look at "the facts," Kahn insists that thermonuclear annihi-

From *Dissent*, 1963, Winter: 75–85.

lation can be carefully graduated, and that the threat of annihilation can therefore be viewed as a manipulable instrument of national policy.

The viability of nuclear war is discussed in two basic ways by Kahn. First, he argues that not all nuclear wars would proceed to the stage of full destruction. The "S.U." (that faceless evil he constantly anticipates) may decide to obliterate an American city one day; the U.S.A. may respond with the destruction of Leningrad. Since a "tit-tat-tit" (*sic*) exchange of cities might ensue, a rigid control must be exercised over all the button-pushers involved, lest the war "escalate" toward a limitless catastrophe. The factor of rationality, therefore, will limit the contingent processes of nuclear war, and strategists will be justified in programming such "measured cadences of nuclear reprisal" as feinting bluffs, surprise attacks and "canned" reprisals.

Secondly, Kahn posits the feasibility of nuclear war upon the premise that the levels of destruction could certainly be less than catastrophic. If we examine more closely what is likely to happen, Kahn argues, we can see that not all human life will be snuffed out by such a war if only because any *sane* aggressor would aim at the victim's retaliatory weapons (the "counterforce strategy") and not its cities. The industrial cities and the areas surrounding missile bases are most likely to be hard hit, but the "hinterland," less heavily attacked, would be able to rebuild the economic and military power of the nation. Judging from the post-World War II rebuilding of the Soviet Union, Kahn estimates that the recovery period after a "counterforce" attack would be about ten years. . . .

II

Kahn's basic procedure is to state his assumptions, offer possible alternative assumptions, assign quantitative estimates (even though many of them are just guesses) to various possibilities, trace a series of projected consequences and then launch upon a general *tour d'horizon*. His work is mathematical in orientation and shows a distinct aversion to the more subtle, descriptive modes of strategic writing. Replete with tabular presentations, it is frequently unashamedly slick. In recommending the distribution of radiation counters to reduce the panic after a nuclear holocaust (lest the people confuse the nausea caused by the poisoned water supply with that of radiation poisoning), Kahn displays a human insensitivity that is quite astonishing. The essential point to note is that each of his premises is based not upon empirical evidence but upon abstracted inferences. This allows him to draw a wide (and often contradictory) series of conclusions—ranging from provocative first-strike schemes at one extreme, to careful arms reduction plans at the other. It is the basic lack of strategic coherence that in the long run makes his work both perilous and obfuscating.

The central assumption of Kahn's strategy is that of the feasibility of nuclear war. The two strands of this assumption are, first, that total destruction is unlikely (since it is irrational from the point of view of the enemy) and, second, that recovery from less than total destruction can occur in a relatively short time. Let us examine this latter contention . . . .

Kahn emphasizes that the pattern of Russian and German recovery after World War II can be taken as predictive of post-World War III through VIII reactions. He admits that the destruction of any fairly prolonged nuclear war (a week or a month perhaps) would cause much more damage than that of World War II; and also that the dangers of radiation may lead to much more widespread debilitation than has previously occurred in wartime. He fails to admit, though, that after 1945 a considerable amount of aid came to the most battered areas from the outside, such as the vast American aid that went to West Germany or the transplantation of German capital goods into Eastern Europe. In a post-World War III era, such aid could not be forthcoming and recovery would thus be far slower. If the assumption of limited destructiveness were relaxed, the possibility of recovery would be all but ruled out, since the replacement of, say, 40% of the capital assets of a highly geared economy might well take two generations — even in the conditions of peace time.

In order for "recovery" to take place after a fairly minor destruction, it is unquestionable that severe governmental controls would have to be exerted. Immediately after air raids, martial law would have to be enforced to ensure an equitable sharing of the remaining shelter, clothing, and uncontaminated food and water supplies. Kahn dismisses this problem by saying that the blasted areas of the country should be written off, or that the high American standards of consumer comfort and of local government could be temporarily relaxed. "Objective studies," he claims, indicate that the post-attack environment "would not be so hostile as to preclude, at least in the long run, decent and useful lives for the survivors and their descendants." This belief sustains him as he waves aside the prediction that martial law, aggressive economic planning, the suppression of political unrest and other garrison state measures might prevail even in the nation that "won" a nuclear war. . . .

Kahn is particularly vulnerable in his public opinion analysis. His "sampling" of opinion seems to have been most haphazard. Even assuming, though, that Kahn's unspecified collection of respondents had provided a sensitive profile of U.S. opinion, this does not necessarily mean that his conclusions are valid. Do his poll responses mean that people are willing to go to war with the possibilities of millions of deaths or that they think the willingness to risk destruction will prevent war? The latter possibility — "standing up to the Russians" — seems to be closer to the current modes of American thinking. Any student of public opinion analysis should know how intricate it is to measure and how quickly the changing of world events can produce a disproportionate change in the opinion set of a nation. But even if Kahn's assertion (that most Americans would accept 60 million American deaths as a legitimate sacrifice, to be "better dead than red") is well-founded *now*, would this resolve be maintained after destruction and death had begun? . . .

III

The problem of credibility . . . [is] especially important to Kahn's system.

If a nation is to be deterred by the threat of retaliatory military power from carrying out an aggressive act, two conditions must be met:

(1) The nation utilizing the deterrence strategy must have the second strike (or retaliatory) strength to inflict an "unacceptable" amount of damage upon the first strike aggressor. That is, its second-strike capacity must be sufficiently invulnerable to ensure that a costly reprisal can be imposed upon the enemy.

(2) The potential aggressor must be convinced that its intended victim would unquestionably carry out its threat to retaliate against an "intolerable" aggression. For example, if the Russians were to feel that the U.S. might not carry out the threat to bomb Moscow in case Soviet troops invaded West Berlin, then the whole strategy of deterrence would lose its effective credibility.

This competition to threaten and counter-threaten can quickly deteriorate, especially in an unyielding conflict such as that in Berlin, to a nonsensical game of "chicken." If the two nuclear super-powers were to gamble frequently with such tactics for any length of time, it is unlikely that the world could ever regain either a rational or stable enough equilibrium to resolve its outstanding conflicts. This Kahn disputes. A limited holocaust, in the first rounds of a game of chicken, would be of inestimable benefit as an heuristic device. Either it would emphasize the need for disarmament and world government, or it would insist that counterforce tactical weapons are a dire necessity for an effective foreign policy in an age of nuclear conflict. Significantly, Kahn relies —as he ultimately admits in hoping that an accidental war will never begin—upon "faith" in the sanity of men: surely they will realize when the first tactical gambit occurs, that the retaliation to it should be similarly limited and not total!

The deterrence strategists suggest a list of offenses which would instantly be punishable by nuclear assault, and they envisage using counterforce missiles as the cutting edge of a new, offensive foreign policy (i.e., one of Controlled Threats and Reprisals). The likelihood of credibility in the threat would depend upon the untrammelled authority of the military decision-makers. An automatic nuclear response can be auto-

matic *only* if the military leaders in the field meet no political interference in making their decisions. If politicians in Washington make the
decision, then automaticity does not occur, not even if "hard talk"
should become the propaganda specialty of the White House. If the
Soviets should ever doubt the willingness of the President and Congress
to abdicate power to the military, they would be entitled to doubt the
credibility of the American response.

The automatic response approach assumes that events are clear-cut
and easily readable. Does the Soviet stopping of Western trucks on the
autobahn to Berlin or the American pressure upon Laos suggest that
"massive retaliation" is in the offing? Moreover, is there in reality such
an obvious set of national interests, unchanging over a period of time,
that a list of unacceptable transgressions can be compiled? Another disturbing feature is that it would probably be a difficult *political* problem
to remove a nuclear assault-rating once it had been attached, even if
the attachment had been made to a prestigious but intrinsically worthless and indefensible bastion such as the Off-shore Islands. Would
the Soviets understand and respect our touchiness about prestige
prizes? . . .

IV

Kahn and his colleagues have been obliged to posit an ahistorical
level of total rationality and predictability in the affairs of the nuclear
super-powers. Each side is expected to behave as if the fanatical hostility
of the Cold War had dissolved and as if operational concessions can
quickly be negotiated to obviate an exchange of cities. Can one have
the confidence in the rationality assumption that Kahn and the game
theoreticians have placed upon it? Can we be sure that a losing nation
in a nuclear war would not go all out in a Doomsday-type maneuver
and destroy its enemy, itself and the planet? Irrational, yes; impossible,
no, as Kahn himself recognizes. The likelihood of a *limited* nuclear war
and of a partial survival must therefore be doubted as strongly as the
capacity of a country to act with flawless intelligence and predictability,
or its capacity to withstand and recover from a nuclear assault. Bernard
Brodie faces this problem of irrationality squarely, in his *Strategy in
the Missile Age*, while Kahn simply insists upon his subjective credo
that button-pushers, even in the most tense and ambiguous of crises,
would not enact their own "self-fulfilling prophecy:" i.e., by pushing all
the available buttons in a spasm of panic. . . .

V

In his efforts to scrutinize military policy Kahn recognizes that accidental war is an urgent and worrying possibility. The technology of
Deterrence contains a structural defect which can be minimized but not

eliminated, for accidental war presents a series of forbidding probabilities that cannot be easily ignored.

In listing some of the sources of system accidents Kahn makes a
genuine contribution by analyzing the instability of sensitive, quick-
acting systems. With his general belief that most dangers can be overcome if intelligence is applied—"bright makes right"—Kahn launches
into a discussion of fail-safe procedures. The greatest reliance is placed
upon improved communications between opponents so that a victim
could be notified of an accidental triggering of first strike weapons before he is able to take retaliatory action. Since it would be easy to fool
the victim by assuring it that the missile flying towards it has been set
off accidentally, or that it is a dud, confidence in the enemy's truthfulness would have to be total. Unfortunately, it is the very lack of such
confidence that frequently impedes conciliatory behavior at times of
great crisis, as was seen in 1870 and in 1914, when the actual *casus belli*
was withdrawn but the wars began all the same. Arms races engender
distrust, and even Kahn concedes that our fear of fear, itself, is worse
than our fear of the Soviet Union. . . .

The more diversified the military establishment and the more sensitive the weapons in the thermonuclear arsenals, the greater will be
the dangers of accidental war. Kahn argues that hardened bases can reduce the dangers since immediate retaliation against the enemy would
not be necessary (i.e., as a form of counterforce insurance). It is all the
more pity, therefore, that he rejects the proposals of those minimum or
finite deterrence advocates—the "non-provocative" and moderate men
in the profession—who urge that shelters, first-strike bases and other
"tactical" instruments should never be built. The virtue of the "moderate" case is that—assuming disarmament negotiations have failed—the
minimum force needed to deter war is simply a second strike force. If
reasonably invulnerable, these missiles could be assured of wreaking an
unacceptable amount of damage upon the aggressor's urban "hostages."
Since Kahn himself admits that no nation has ever lost—or ever would
dare to lose—20 per cent of its population, this "non-offensive" deterrent should be far more effective and "safe."

Despite Kahn's concern for the problem of accidental war (including the ubiquitous threat of escalation from limited to extensive war),
he has swept the dangers under his system net. Kahn has succumbed
to the favorite *deus ex machina* of so many social scientists—the improved quality of communications. This assumes, however, that each
side can predict the opponent's movements with understanding and
confidence and that it will not seek for hidden motives in the enemy's
stratagems. This assumption has already been severely questioned, and
the doubts remaining can only be reinforced by the number of Intelligence failures that have marred strategic planning during previous
wars and crises.

VI

While analyzing Kahn's work within his own frame of reference, we have ignored the relevance of external criteria. Kahn's perspectives appear to be even more limited when we contrast them to the torturous and confusing reality of the struggle to co-exist. They demonstrate that the weakest element in his analysis is unquestionably the political one.

Kahn's analysis is limited to two nations, unfriendly to each other. This is the essential nature of the argument of strategic analysts who see international relations as a two-country problem, involving the U.S.A. and the U.S.S.R. (This mode of analysis may spring from the fact that the theory of games originated as a two-person, zero-sum framework in which the winner takes all.) What happens when nuclear weapons are more widely distributed (the *nth*-country problem)? Would the military strength of one nation be sufficient to deter several potential aggressors? Would not symmetry be constantly endangered, particularly if political alliances were shifting, as well they might be? Would behaviors and reactions be as predictable and rational as required by Deterrence theory? Conceivably, they might be in the long-run, but it is getting us over the next ten years that is the crucial issue.

The chief difficulty with Kahn's book is that it is a study of war and its prevention that ignores politics and oversimplifies the complex realities of political conflict. This is particularly noticeable in the *nth*-country problem for Kahn does not worry unduly over allies, their reactions to policies, the need for compromise among them, their national interests, and the weaknesses of their collective decision-making. His worst failure is the implicit conception that the problems of national security can be neatly dichotomized. On the one side there are the mechanical and essentially pessimistic formulae of the nuclear strategists, who daily await the onset of conflict; on the other there are the optimistic schemes of political compromise and adjustment that determine the success or failure of our foreign policy.

It can quickly be seen, for example, that the difficulties of the U.S. foreign policy — particularly in relation to those emerging nations that are undergoing a rapid social and economic change — presently stem from non-military causes. Even if there were no Soviet threat, U.S. policy would have to face a series of challenging crises in these volatile countries. Similarly, it should be seen that nuclear threats often provide merely the shadow of crisis and not the root cause itself. Given the Soviet challenge, the rigid and unimaginative lines that the U.S. has been pursuing has led to recurring hot, tepid, and cold wars. (This does not assume that Soviet policy has been flexible and imaginative.) Should this dogmatism continue, either or both powers will be isolated from the tide of social and economic revolution that is sweeping through the hungry, tropical areas of the world. An isolation of this kind might leave the fearful, nuclear owners in an unenviable position: their foreign policies would be reduced to a "nuclear nullity"—as Liddell Hart has put it—because of their armed and oversensitive mistrust, and they would be forced to act as conservative advocates of a *status quo* because of their fear of radical change.

Nor would the righting of military inequality reduce political crises. The military superiority of the U.S. which prevailed until the U.S.S.R. manufactured its first A-bomb did not reduce conflict nor deeply inhibit the U.S.S.R.'s effort to achieve what it considered to be its indispensable buffer zones in Eastern Europe (or even in Korea). Gross military imbalance may always tempt action but only if the political bases for action exist. Even where imbalances do threaten to produce a decisive superiority of one side, inequities in striking power are not necessarily self-propelling stimuli towards political and military action. However infinite the deterrent value of nuclear arms, there is always a sound reason for a country equipped with a superior arsenal to desist from striking, or for an inferior power to make limited encroachments outside its zone of influence.

In freeing military "hardware" and its disposition from foreign policy, Kahn has isolated moral questions from political considerations and military decisions. The decisions for war and calculated destruction are made by people and not by military necessity. In reifying military tactics and strategy, Kahn has obscured the concrete aims of peoples and governments and has reversed Clausewitz' dictum by making politics the servant of war.

. . . [I]t is Kahn's "realism" which is his pride and strong point, and also the target of his unrelenting enquiries. As is common with the new breed of anti-sentimental strategic "scientists," the result is a realism that starts with abstract assumptions, blots out much of the world's political experience and ends with big conclusions. C. Wright Mills has aptly characterized this Euclidean system-building as "crackpot realism." The strong light that system analysts have shed on current military operations should not obscure the fact that their vision is based upon such questionable premises as the total rationality of conflict, the extension of communications, and the perfectibility of nuclear gadgets. . . .

Part III

Political Resources: The Open Society and Its Friends

Much of political history has been concerned with revolt, instability, and the rise and fall of mass movements. The selections that follow point out the interplay between rulers and ruled, powerful and powerless, which bolsters a critical, open society. The United States is an example of a liberal, pluralistic nation in which neither information nor power is monopolized by a single entity and in which the participation of citizens in the deliberations of government is visible. In other nations, too, the public can no longer be ignored by majesterial fiat, military force, or a secure ruling class. The expansion of nationalistic self-determination, the extension of universal suffrage, and the decline of old powers and their authoritative edicts are evident throughout the world.

Part III concentrates on three areas of concern to those who study the open society: the relationship of political leaders to followers and the characteristics of both; the social processes that sustain democracy; and the psychological conditions that successfully cultivate reason in human affairs.

Among the critical issues raised by these selections are the following: What kinds of training and socialization are most productive for political leaders in a free society? How do these leaders cultivate and sustain publics capable of rational reflection and critical evaluation? What are the limits of tolerance and controversy and how are these developed, especially by political institutions that have a vested and legitimate interest in securing support for their own favored policies and power arrangements? What are the patterns of influence and zones of agreement between leaders and followers in a political party, a governmental agency, and a community facing a policy decision? Finally, what political and social arrangements bolster self-confidence and the tolerance of cultural and political diversity?

---

9. The Revolt of the Masses

The twentieth century has been termed "the era of mass participation" and "the hallmark of political irrationality." The Spanish critic José Ortega y Gasset has linked these two characteristics in his inquiry into the alienation of man from himself and his society. Next, Stein Rokkan's cogent historical perspective on popular voting underscores the anonymity of the secret ballot and its role in the extension of political participation. Within the "American Hybrid," as Robert Dahl calls our political system, governmental decisions are made through an endless process of bargaining and appeasement of the demands of small groups. Neither a coherent elite nor an agitated mass, led by aspiring rulers of a counterelite, dominates the regime.

In contrast to extended suffrage, plural power centers, and other devices to represent public opinion in limited government, political mass participation can have three unfortunate consequences: (1) disruption of the regime by transient popular pressures unchecked by legitimate and established representative institutions; (2) the atomization of existing publics, agencies, and classes either by or for the benefit of a ruling stratum that uses popular rhetoric to insure its dominance;[1] (3) the loss of qualitative standards or norms following the atomization of existing structures.[2]

In evaluating the likelihood of such consequences here, the student should ask himself the following questions: Precisely what political processes or developments are coming under control of the "mass"? What specific changes in political relations between the rulers and the ruled occur in the development of a "mass society"? What evidence is there to relate mass

---

[1]C. Wright Mills, in *The Power Elite* (New York: Oxford University Press, 1956) deals cogently with this subject.

[2]See Walter Lippmann, *The Public Philosophy* (Boston: Little, Brown, 1955).

tendencies causally with political diseases such as anomie or alienation that are usually attributed to a mass society? Do the same carefully defined and historically specific trends toward mass participation necessarily produce comparable political consequences in different societies at the same time? At different times? In ancient and in modern societies?

THE RISE OF MASS SOCIETY
JOSÉ ORTEGA Y GASSET

The Coming of the Masses

There is one fact which, whether for good or ill, is of utmost importance in the public life of Europe at the present moment. This fact is the accession of the masses to complete social power. As the masses, by definition, neither should nor can direct their own personal existence, and still less rule society in general, this fact means that actually Europe is suffering from the greatest crisis that can afflict peoples, nations, and civilisation. Such a crisis has occurred more than once in history. Its characteristics and its consequences are well known. So also is its name. It is called the rebellion of the masses. In order to understand this formidable fact, it is important from the start to avoid giving to the words "rebellion," "masses," and "social power" a meaning exclusively or primarily political. Public life is not solely political, but equally, and even primarily, intellectual, moral, economic, religious; it comprises all our collective habits, including our fashions both of dress and of amusement.

Perhaps the best line of approach to this historical phenomenon may be found by turning our attention to a visual experience, stressing one aspect of our epoch which is plain to our very eyes. This fact is quite simple to enunciate, though not so to analyse. I shall call it the fact of agglomeration, of "plenitude." Towns are full of people, houses full of tenants, hotels full of guests, trains full of travellers, cafés full of customers, parks full of promenaders, consulting-rooms of famous doctors full of patients, theatres full of spectators, and beaches full of bathers. What previously was, in general, no problem, now begins to be an everyday one, namely, to find room. . . .

Strictly speaking, the mass, as a psychological fact, can be defined without waiting for individuals to appear in mass formation. In the presence of one individual we can decide whether he is "mass" or not. The mass is all that which sets no value on itself—good or ill—based on specific grounds, but which feels itself "just like everybody," and nevertheless is not concerned about it; is, in fact, quite happy to feel itself as one with everybody else. Imagine a humble-minded man who, having tried to estimate his own worth on specific grounds—asking himself if he has any talent for this or that, if he excels in any direction—realises that he possesses no quality of excellence. Such a man will feel that he is mediocre and commonplace, ill-gifted, but will not feel himself "mass."

When one speaks of "select minorities" it is usual for the evil-minded to twist the sense of this expression, pretending to be unaware that the select man is not the petulant person who thinks himself superior to the rest, but the man who demands more of himself than the rest, even though he may not fulfil in his person those higher exigencies. For there is no doubt that the most radical division that it is possible to make of humanity is that which splits it into two classes of creatures: those who make great demands on themselves, piling up difficulties and duties; and those who demand nothing special of themselves, but for whom to live is to be every moment what they already are, without imposing on themselves any effort towards perfection; mere buoys that float on the waves. This reminds me that orthodox Buddhism is composed of two distinct religions: one, more rigorous and difficult, the other easier and more trivial: the Mahayana—"great vehicle" or "great path"—and the Hinayana—"lesser vehicle" or "lesser path." The decisive matter is whether we attach our life to one or the other vehicle, to a maximum or a minimum of demands upon ourselves.

The division of society into masses and select minorities is, then, not a division into social classes, but into classes of men, and cannot coincide with the hierarchic separation of "upper" and "lower" classes. It is, of course, plain that in these "upper" classes, when and as long as they really are so, there is much more likelihood of finding men who adopt the "great vehicle," whereas the "lower" classes normally comprise individuals of minus quality. But, strictly speaking, within both these social classes, there are to be found mass and genuine minority. . . . [A] characteristic of our times is the predominance, even in groups traditionally selective, of the mass and the vulgar. Thus, in the intellectual life, which of its essence requires and presupposes qualification, one can note the progressive triumph of the pseudo-intellectual, unqualified, unqualifiable, and, by their very mental texture, disqualified. Similarly, in the surviving groups of the "nobility," male and female. On the other hand, it is not rare to find today amongst working men, who before might be taken as the best example of what we are calling "mass," nobly disciplined minds.

There exist, then, in society, operations, activities, and functions of the most diverse order, which are of their very nature special, and which consequently cannot be properly carried out without special gifts. For example: certain pleasures of an artistic and refined character, or again the functions of government and of political judgment in public affairs. Previously these special activities were exercised by qualified minorities, or at least by those who claimed such qualification. The mass asserted no right to intervene in them; they realised that if they wished to intervene they would necessarily have to acquire those special qualities and cease being mere mass. They recognised their place in a healthy dynamic social system. . . .

No one, I believe, will regret that people are today enjoying themselves in greater measure and numbers than before, since they have now both the desire and the means of satisfying it. The evil lies in the fact that this decision taken by the masses to assume the activities proper to the minorities is not, and cannot be, manifested solely in the domain of pleasure, but that it is a general feature of our time. Thus . . . I believe that the political innovations of recent times signify nothing less than the political domination of the masses. The old democracy was tempered by a generous dose of liberalism and of enthusiasm for law. By serving these principles the individual bound himself to maintain a severe discipline over himself. Under the shelter of liberal principles and the rule of law, minorities could live and act. Democracy and law — life in common under the law — were synonymous. Today we are witnessing the triumphs of a hyperdemocracy in which the mass acts directly, outside the law, imposing its aspirations and its desires by means of material pressure. It is a false interpretation of the new situation to say that the mass has grown tired of politics and handed over the exercise of it to specialised persons. Quite the contrary. That was what happened previously; that was democracy. The mass took it for granted that after all, in spite of their defects and weaknesses, the minorities understood a little more of public problems than it did itself. Now, on the other hand, the mass believes that it has the right to impose and to give force of law to notions born in the café. I doubt whether there have been other periods of history in which the multitude has come to govern more directly than in our own. That is why I speak of hyperdemocracy.

The same thing is happening in other orders, particularly in the intellectual. I may be mistaken, but the present-day writer, when he takes his pen in hand to treat a subject which he has studied deeply, has to bear in mind that the average reader, who has never concerned himself with this subject, if he reads does so with the view, not of learning something from the writer, but rather, of pronouncing judgment on him when he is not in agreement with the commonplaces that the said reader carries in his head. If the individuals who make up the mass believed themselves specially qualified, it would be a case merely of personal error, not a sociological subversion. *The characteristic of the hour is that the commonplace mind, knowing itself to be commonplace, has the assurance to proclaim the rights of the commonplace and to impose them wherever it will.* As they say in the United States: "to be different is to be indecent." The mass crushes beneath it everything that is different, everything that is excellent, individual, qualified, and select. Anybody who is not like everybody, who does not think like everybody, runs the risk of being eliminated. And it is clear, of course, that this "everybody" is not "everybody." "Everybody" was normally the complex unity of the mass and the divergent, specialised minorities. Nowadays, "everybody" is the mass alone. Here we have the formidable fact of our times, described without any concealment of the brutality of its features.

The Rise of the Historic Level

Such, then, is the formidable fact of our times. . . . It is, furthermore, entirely new in the history of our modern civilisation. Never, in the course of its development, has anything similar happened. If we wish to find its like we shall have to take a leap outside our modern history and immerse ourselves in a world, a vital element, entirely different from our own; we shall have to penetrate the ancient world till we reach the hour of its decline. The history of the Roman Empire is also the history of the uprising of the Empire of the Masses, who absorb and annul the directing minorities and put themselves in their place. Then, also, is produced the phenomenon of agglomeration, of "the full." For that reason, as Spengler has very well observed, it was necessary, just as in our day, to construct enormous buildings. The epoch of the masses is the epoch of the colossal. We are living, then, under the brutal empire of the masses. Just so; I have now twice called this empire "brutal," and have thus paid my tribute to the god of the commonplace. Now, ticket in hand, I can cheerfully enter into my subject, see the show from inside. Or perhaps it was thought that I was going to be satisfied with that description, possibly exact, but quite external; the mere features, the aspect under which this tremendous fact presents itself when looked at from the view-point of the past? If I were to leave the matter here and strangle off my present essay without more ado, the reader would be left thinking, and quite justly, that this fabulous uprising of the masses above the surface of history inspired me merely with a few petulant, disdainful words, a certain amount of hatred and a certain amount of disgust. This all the more in my case, when it is well known that I uphold a radically aristocratic interpretation of history. Radically, because I have never said that human society *ought* to be aristocratic, but a great deal more than that. What I have said, and still believe with ever-increasing conviction, is that human society *is* always, whether it will or no, aristocratic by its very essence, to the extreme that it is a society in the measure that it is aristocratic, and ceases to be such when it ceases to be aristocratic. Of course I am speaking now of society and not of the State. No one can imagine that, in the face of this fabulous seething of the masses, it is the aristocratic attitude to be satisfied with making a supercilious grimace, like a fine gentleman of Versailles. Versailles—the Versailles of the grimaces—does not represent aristocracy; quite the contrary, it is the death and dissolution of a magnificent aristocracy. For this reason, the only element of aristocracy left in such beings was the dignified grace with which their necks received the attentions of the guillotine; they accepted it as the tumour accepts the lancet. No; for anyone who has a sense of the real mission of aristocracies, the spectacle of the mass incites and enflames him, as the sight of virgin marble does the sculptor. Social aristocracy has no resemblance whatever to that tiny group which claims for itself alone the name of society, which calls itself "Society"; people who live by inviting or not inviting one another. Since everything in the world has its virtue and its mission, so within the vast world this small "smart world" has its own, but it is a very subordinate mission, not to be compared with the herculean task of genuine aristocracies. I should have no objection to discussing the meaning that lies in this smart world, to all appearance so meaningless, but our subject is now one of greater proportions. Of course, this self-same "distinguished society" goes with the times. Much food for thought was given me by a certain *jeune fille en fleur,* full of youth and modernity, a star of the first magnitude in the firmament of "smart" Madrid, when she said to me: "I can't stand a dance to which less than eight hundred people have been invited." Behind this phrase I perceived that the style of the masses is triumphant over the whole area of modern life, and imposes itself even in those sheltered corners which seemed reserved for the "happy few."

I reject equally, then, the interpretation of our times which does not lay clear the positive meaning hidden under the actual rule of the masses and that which accepts it blissfully, without a shudder of horror. Every destiny is dramatic, tragic in its deepest meaning. Whoever has not felt the danger of our times palpitating under his hand, has not really penetrated to the vitals of destiny, he has merely pricked its surface. The element of terror in the destiny of our time is furnished by the overwhelming and violent moral upheaval of the masses; imposing, invincible, and treacherous, as is destiny in every case. Whither is it leading us? Is it an absolute evil or a possible good? There it is, colossal, astride our times like a giant, a cosmic note of interrogation, always of uncertain shape, with something in it of the guillotine or the gallows, but also with something that strives to round itself into a triumphal arch.

The fact that we must submit to examination may be formulated under two headings: first, the masses are today exercising functions in social life which coincide with those which hitherto seemed reserved to minorities; and secondly, these masses have at the same time shown themselves indocile to the minorities—they do not obey them, follow them, or respect them; on the contrary, they push them aside and supplant them.

Let us analyse what comes under the first heading. By it I mean that the masses enjoy the pleasures and use the instruments invented by the select groups, and hitherto exclusively at the service of the latter. They feel appetites and needs which were previously looked upon as refinements, inasmuch as they were the patrimony of the few. Take a trivial example: in 1820 there cannot have been ten bathrooms in private houses in Paris (see the *Memoirs of the Comtesse de Boigne*). But furthermore, the masses today are acquainted with, and use with relative skill, many of the technical accomplishments previously confined to specialised individuals. And this refers not only to the technique of material objects, but more important, to that of laws and society. In the [Eighteenth] Century, certain minority groups discovered that every human being, by the mere fact of birth, and without requiring any special qualification whatsoever, possessed certain fundamental political rights, the so-called rights of the man and the citizen; and further that, strictly speaking, these rights, common to all, are the only ones that exist.

Every other right attached to special gifts was condemned as being a privilege. This was at first a mere theory, the idea of a few men; then those few began to put the idea into practice, to impose it and insist upon it. Nevertheless, during the whole of the [Eighteenth] Century, the mass, while gradually becoming enthusiastic for those rights as an ideal, did not feel them as rights, did not exercise them or attempt to make them prevail, but, in fact, under democratic legislation, continued to feel itself just as under the old regime. The "people" —as it was then called—the "people" had learned that it was sovereign, but did not believe it. Today the ideal has been changed into a reality; not only in legislation, which is the mere framework of public life, but in the heart of every individual, whatever his ideas may be, and even if he be a reactionary in his ideas, *that is to say, even when he attacks and castigates institutions by which those rights are sanctioned.* To my mind, anyone who does not realise this curious moral situation of the masses can understand nothing of what is today beginning to happen in the world. The sovereignty of the unqualified individual, of the human being as such, generically, has now passed from being a juridical idea or ideal to be a psychological state inherent in the average man. And note this, that when what was before an ideal becomes a component part of reality, it inevitably ceases to be an ideal. The prestige and the magic that are attributes of the ideal are volatilised. The levelling demands of a generous democratic inspiration have been changed from aspirations and ideals into appetites and unconscious assumptions.

Now, the meaning of this proclamation of the rights of man was none other than to lift human souls from their interior servitude and to implant within them a certain consciousness of mastery and dignity. Was it not this that it was hoped to do, namely, that the average man should feel himself master, lord, and ruler of himself and of his life? Well, that is now accomplished. Why, then, these complaints of the liberals, the democrats, the progressives of thirty years ago? Or is it that, like children, they want something, but not the consequences of that something? You want the ordinary man to be master. Well, do not be surprised if he acts for himself, if he demands all forms of enjoyment, if he firmly asserts his will, if he refuses all kinds of service, if he ceases to be docile to anyone, if he considers his own person and his own leisure, if he is careful as to dress: these are some of the attributes permanently attached to the consciousness of mastership. Today we find them taking up their abode in the ordinary man, in the mass.

The situation, then, is this: the life of the ordinary man is today made up of the same "vital repertory" which before characterised only the superior minorities. Now the average man represents the field over which the history of each period acts; he is to history what sea-level is to geography. If, therefore, today the mean-level lies at a point previously only reached by aristocracies, the signification of this is simply that the level of history has suddenly risen—after long subterraneous preparations, it is true—but now quite plainly to the eyes, suddenly, at a bound, in one generation. Human life taken as a whole has mounted higher. The soldier of today, we might say, has a good deal of the officer; the human army is now made up of officers. Enough to watch the energy, the determination, the ease with which each individual moves through life today, snatches at the passing pleasure, imposes his personal will.

Everything that is good and bad in the present and in the immediate future has its cause and root in the general rise of the historic level. But here an observation that had not previously occurred to us presents itself. This fact, that the ordinary level of life today is that of the former minorities, is a new fact in Europe, but in America the natural, the "constitutional" fact. To realise my point, let the reader consider the matter of consciousness of equality before the law. That psychological state of feeling lord and master of oneself and equal to anybody else, which in Europe only outstanding groups succeeded in acquiring, was in America since the [Eighteenth] Century (and therefore, practically speaking, always) the natural state of things. And a further coincidence, still more curious, is this: when this psychological condition of the ordinary man appeared in Europe, when the level of his existence rose, the tone and manners of European life in all orders suddenly took on a new appearance which caused many people to say: "Europe is becoming Americanised." Those who spoke in this way gave no further attention to the matter; they thought it was a question of a slight change of custom, a fashion, and, deceived by the look of things, attributed it to some influence or other of America on Europe. This, to my mind, is simply to trivialise a question which is much more subtle and pregnant with surprises. Gallantry here makes an attempt to suborn me into telling our brothers beyond the sea that, in fact, Europe has become Americanised, and that this is due to an influence of America on Europe. But no; truth comes into conflict with gallantry, and it must prevail. Europe has not been Americanised; it has received no great influence from America. Possibly both these things are beginning to happen just now; but they did not occur in the recent past of which the present is the flowering. There is floating around a bewildering mass of false ideas which blind the vision of both parties, Americans and Europeans. The triumph of the masses and the consequent magnificent uprising of the vital level have come about in Europe for internal reasons, after two centuries of education of the multitude towards progress and a parallel economic improvement in society. But it so happens that the result coincides with the most marked aspect of American life; and on account of this coincidence of the moral situation of the ordinary man in Europe and in America, it has come about that for the first time the European understands American life which was to him before an enigma and a mystery. There is no question, then, of an influence, which indeed would be a little strange, would be, in fact, a "refluence," but of something which is still less suspected, namely, of a levelling. It has always been obscurely seen by Europeans that the general level of life in America was higher than in the Old World. It was the intuition, strongly felt, if unanalysed, of this fact which gave rise to the idea, always accepted, never challenged, that the future lies with America. It will be understood that such an idea, widespread and deep-rooted, did not float down on the wind, as it is said that orchids grow rootless in the air. The basis of it was the realisation of a higher level of average existence in America, in contrast with a lower level in the select minorities there as compared with those of Europe. But history, like agriculture, draws its nourishment from the valleys and not from the heights, from the average social level and not from men of eminence.

We are living in a levelling period; there is a levelling of fortunes, of culture among the various social classes, of the sexes. Well, in the same way there is a levelling of continents, and as the European was formerly lower from a vital point of view, he has come out the gainer from this levelling. Consequently, from this standpoint, the uprising of the masses implies a fabulous increase of vital possibilities, quite the contrary of what we hear so often about the decadence of Europe. This is a confused and clumsy expression, in which it is not clear what is being referred to, whether it is the European states, or European culture, or what lies underneath all this, and is of infinitely greater importance, the vital activity of Europe.

. . . [A]s regards the vitality, it is well to make clear . . . that we are in the presence of a gross error. Perhaps if I give it another turn, my statement may appear more convincing or less improbable; I say, then, that today the average Italian, Spaniard, or German is less differentiated in vital tone from the North American or the Argentine than he was thirty years ago. And this is a fact that the people of America ought not to forget.

THE COMPARATIVE STUDY OF POLITICAL PARTICIPATION

Stein Rokkan

Students of political behavior have again and again been struck by [the] contrast between the "one citizen, one vote" provisions of political democracy and the persistent inequalities in the actual processes of decision-making. Study after study has underscored the contrast between the high proportions of voters and the very low proportions of politically concerned and alert citizens within the mass electorate; on the one hand a large majority of *only-voters*, of citizens who turn up at their polling stations but show very little articulate concern about the issue of politics, only rudimentary knowledge of the alternatives, and no willingness to take an active part in the conflict between the parties, and on the other hand a small minority of active participants in the political system, of articulate and informed citizens motivated to act and to take a stand.

These inequalities have persisted in all mass democracies; they invariably became even more marked with the extension of the suffrage to women. The improvement of educational standards, the spread of the mass media of communication, and the organizational work of the mass parties may have helped to raise the "political literacy" levels in most systems, but the basic inequalities in participation have remained. The persistence of the inequalities raises a series of questions about the implications of the introduction of universal suffrage for the functioning of modern political systems. So far, such questions of functional relationships have mainly been raised in discussions of evidence from single countries. To gain a comparative perspective on such "macro-macro" consequences we shall clearly have to do much more to collate data from countries differing in their characteristic sequences of development toward full-fledged democracy and differing in the political

From *Essays on the Behavioral Study of Politics*, editor, Austin Ranney. Urbana: The University of Illinois Press, 1962, pp. 71–80, 83–85.

alignments of the masses of citizens enfranchised through these developments. We need *historical* comparisons of the processes of decision-making which led to the expansion of the electorate and the standardization of registration and voting procedures; we need *statistical* comparisons of trends in political reactions of the masses of lower class citizens and of women after their entry into the electorate; and we need *institutional and structural* comparisons of the different ways in which the pressures of the mass electorate, the parties, and the elective bodies are dovetailed into a broader system of decision-making among interest organizations and private and public corporate units.

These are the three sets of problems I consider crucial in any systematic study of the structural contexts of political participation: (1) the series of decisions which *set the formal conditions* for the political mobilization of the masses of inarticulate subjects within each territory, (2) the actual *rates of mobilization* to political activity and the conditions making for higher or lower rates, (3) the conditions for given types of tie-ins between party-political activities and participation in *other policy-influencing groups, collectivities, and organizations.* . . .

The Institutional Settings and the Structural Restraints

Discussing the progress of democracy in the United States, Alexis de Tocqueville pointed to an "invariable rule in the history of society" —once the first step had been taken to reduce the qualifications for the vote, it would be impossible to halt the movement at any point short of universal suffrage.[1] It is extraordinary to see how Tocqueville's projections turned out to fit the actual developments toward full-fledged formal democracy in nation-state after nation-state. The decisions to extend the vote were not uniformly a response to pressures from below; they were as often the results of contests for influence at the top and of deliberate moves to broaden the bases for an integrated national power structure. The French Revolution had sown its plebiscitarian seeds, and the success of Napoleon III had a distinct impact on political minds in western Europe. By a much-debated historical coincidence, the two great Conservative leaders, Disraeli and Bismarck, proceeded in 1867 within months of each other to extend the suffrage further than their Liberal antagonists had wanted. In both cases these "leaps in the dark" were motivated by a profound belief that the entry of the working classes into the electorate would strengthen the unity and stability of the nation-state. Disraeli expressed great faith in the working class and saw a major source of strength for the Conservative party in these new entrants into the electorate. In the words of a *Times* obituary sixteen years later, Disraeli discerned the Conservative working man "in the inarticulate

---

[1]Alexis de Tocqueville, *De la Démocratie en Amérique* (Paris: Gosselin, 1835), Vol. 1, chapter 4.

mass of the English populace" just as "the sculptor perceived the angel in a block of marble."[2] Bismarck also saw a major ally against the Liberals in the working class and was clearly very much influenced in his decision by his secret conversations with Ferdinand Lassalle — the Junker and the Socialist found a common ground in their belief in the integrating and centralizing impact of the introduction of universal manhood suffrage. The motive for extending the suffrage to the workers was patently not to create a channel for the articulation of the interests of the economically dependent strata; the objective was to strengthen the policies of centralization by enlisting the support of the least articulate classes in German society. Bismarck even toyed with the possibility of introducing a system for ensuring numerical support through the tacit acquiescence of the inarticulate masses; the votes of those who did not turn out were to be counted in favor of the governmental candidates. Lassalle developed the idea (he called it his *Zauberrezepte*) of ensuring results in the same direction by a system of obligatory voting. This idea was not taken up in the debate over the constitution of the North German Federation but was later to become a standard strategy in efforts to ensure an equilibrium of power in mass suffrage systems.

At the heart of the bitter debates over the extension of the suffrage were conflicting expectations concerning the repercussions of the entry of the "politically illiterate" into the arena: conflicting views of the allegiances and probable reactions of these masses once they were enfranchised and conflicting evaluations of the possibilities of controlling and channeling these new forces. Liberals tended to express fear of an irresponsible and disruptive radicalization of politics; Conservative and Christian party leaders were more likely to see in the enfranchisement of the lower classes and of all women a major strategic move in the stabilization of the national system against the attacks from the Socialist Left. An extraordinary variety of institutional compromises were tried out in response to these conflicting pressures. The history of these innovations is not of merely antiquarian interest; these developments set the stage for the organization of mass politics in each country and the particular solutions reached at each stage helped to determine the conditions for the integration of the lower classes into the national community. . . .

It would be difficult to devise an electoral measure more calculated to alienate the lower classes from the national political system than the one promulgated in Prussia in 1849: all adult men were given the vote, but the workers and the lower middle class were given only a token chance to influence the elections because of the three-class division of the electorate. What is even more remarkable about the Prussian case is that it was possible to maintain for more than two generations a system

[2]The London *Times*, April 18, 1883, quoted in R.T. McKinzie, *British Political Parties* (London: Macmillan and Co., 1955), p. 147. . . .

of universal manhood suffrage with oral voting at public sessions. Of other countries only Denmark kept up provisions for public voting for any length of time after the introduction of near-universal manhood suffrage. In France the provisions for secrecy were largely nominal far into the era of the Third Republic; mayors and other officials had little difficulty in controlling the votes of the less articulate. In most other countries of western Europe provisions for the secrecy of the vote either preceded or were developed *pari passu* with the extension of the suffrage.

The extraordinary contrast between the electoral systems of Prussia and the Reich from 1870 to 1918 has given rise to a great deal of discussion among historians and political theorists. In Prussia there was a system of extremely unequal, open, and indirect elections; in the Reich, a system of equal, secret, and direct voting, which was for a Diet without decisive influence in the affairs of the nation. There is a wealth of evidence to show that this constellation of institutions was highly disfunctional; the extension of the suffrage appeared to encourage the participation of the lower classes, but the contrast between the two systems of elections made for widespread resentment and helped to isolate the workers in permanent opposition to the regime.

Ernst Fraenkel has recently suggested that the introduction of secret voting in the Reich contributed decisively to the isolation of the urban working class in *eine soziale Ghettopartei*.[3] What he has in mind is that the deep resentments caused by the Prussian system of unequal and open voting could find secret and safe expression in votes for the Reichstag without any pressure on the ordinary voter to articulate his feelings openly in his community. In the deeply divided German society, the introduction of secret voting in fact tended to keep the newly enfranchised citizens in isolation outside the national political system and clearly did not contribute to the integration of the polity.

Interestingly enough, the evidence for the developments in other countries, particularly in Britain, suggest the opposite. The Ballot Act was passed five years after the decisive extension of the suffrage in 1867 and coincided with the great efforts of the Conservative party to organize clubs of workingmen for political action. The Ballot Act drastically reduced the opportunities for local influence on the worker vote through bribery and chicanery but at the same time made it possible for the "deferent working man" to vote with his superiors without making this an issue in his day-to-day life with his fellow workers. The decisive difference between the developments in Britain and in Germany after the extension of the suffrage in 1867 was no doubt due to the action of the parties; in Britain both the Conservatives and the Liberals developed mass organizations aimed at the new entrants into the

[3]Ernst Fraenkel, "Parlament und öffentliche Meinung," in *Zur Geschichte und Problematik der Demokratie: Festgabe für H. Herzfeld* (Berlin: Duncker & Humblot, 1958), p. 178.

electorate; in Germany the parties on the right remained *Honoratioren-parteien* and left it to the Social Democrats to develop a network of political, social, and cultural organizations for the workers which kept them clearly apart from the rest of the body politic. The introduction of secret voting in both countries accentuated these differences in development.

This contrast raises a series of intriguing questions about the functions for political systems of the introduction of institutions for the safeguarding of the privacy of the voting act. It is remarkable how little attention has been given in the literature to the effects of these profound changes in electoral prodedures. What can be said at this stage will of necessity be based on speculation and only scattered and unsystematic evidence.

Tocqueville would clearly have seen in the provisions for secrecy a further extension of the tendency for the centralizing nation-state to enter into direct communication with each individual subject and to undermine all intermediary powers. The essential effect of the secrecy institution is to accentuate the equality of each voter by isolating him from the hierarchical influences in the local community. Through the secrecy provisions the power of the local aristocracy, the notables, and the clergy is further reduced and, to follow the Tocqueville model, the tendencies toward centralization correspondingly strengthened.

In sociological terms we might say that in the situation of secret voting the individual adult is cut off from all his roles in the subordinate systems of the household, the neighborhood, the work organization, the church, and the civil association and set to act exclusively in the abstract role as a citizen of the over-all political system; there will be no feedback from what he does in this anonymous role to what he does in the other roles and therefore no need for him to take responsibility for the act of voting in his everyday interaction in his regular environment.

The obvious manifest reasons for introducing the secrecy provisions were the numerous public scandals over attempts at intimidation and bribery. The primary motive for the introduction of the ballot system was to make it possible to escape sanctions from superiors; this was the essence of the Chartists' early demands and has also been a basic concern of working-class movements.

What has been less emphasized in histories of electoral institutions is that the provisions for secrecy could cut the voter off from his peers as well as his superiors. It is often overlooked that there are two distinct elements in the secrecy provisions: the first is to make it *possible* for the voter to keep his decision private and avoid sanctions from those he *does not* want to know; the second is to make it *impossible* for the voter to prove how he voted to those he *does* want to know. The very rigorous rules set up in country after country for the invalidation of all irregularly marked ballots was directed to the second point; they were devised to ensure that the citizen could no longer treat his vote as a commodity for sale. He might well be bribed, but the price per vote would clearly decrease as soon as it proved impossible to check whether it was actually delivered. The salient point here is that by ensuring the complete anonymity of the ballots it became possible not only to reduce bribery of the economically dependent by their superiors but also to reduce the pressures towards conformity and solidarity within the working class.

The secrecy provisions clearly constituted an important mechanism of escape for the politically inarticulate entrants to the electorate. The actual political effects of making the vote private varied enormously, however, with the organizational environments of these citizens. In Germany the Social Democratic party was able, at least in the major cities, to create a highly homogeneous working-class environment through the development of a wide variety of secondary organizations; it became what Sigmund Neumann has called *eine integral Partei*, a party that could claim the allegiance of its voters in all their social roles and therefore could isolate them from disturbing cross-pressures. In this case the introduction of secret voting for the Reichstag contributed further to the isolation of this subsystem since it reduced to a minimum the need for community interaction about political differences. In Britain the mass-directed efforts of the Conservative and the Liberal parties subjected the new entrants into the electorate to conflicting pressures; in this situation the institution of secrecy became an important device for the stabilization of the system since it allowed legitimate withdrawal from open political strife, not just by abstaining from the vote, but also by keeping preferences private and without consequence in everyday life. With increasing social mobility and the cross-cutting influences brought about by expanding associations in the community and the nation, more and more workers must have come under conflicting political pressures and must have felt the need for such provisions for the privatization of the act of voting.

What is crucial here is that this need for privatization tends to be much more marked among the politically inarticulate than among those who for one reason or another have become motivated to concern themselves with public issues. Under regulations for secret voting there is an important *asymmetry* in the system-voter relationship; the system is pledged to the safeguarding of the secrecy of the vote, but the worker is under no legal obligations to keep his preferences private, however little he can do to provide direct proof of his actual behavior at the poll. The institution of secret voting in this way places every citizen before another set of alternative decisions: should he keep his vote completely to himself, as is his right, or should he make his preference known to others within his primary groups only, to those within the organizations and associations he is part of, or to the general public?

This, in fact, brings about a stratification of the electorate on a "privacy-publicity" dimension: from those who never reveal their vote to anyone to those who publicly take their stand on the alternatives set and openly proclaim how they will or have voted. The active and militant in the political parties clearly cannot make much use of the secrecy provisions which may be important for them in the choice of particular candidates. However, it is part of their community role to commit themselves publicly between the major alternatives.

The Political Mobilization of the Inarticulate Strata

The effects of the secrecy provisions on the behavior of the masses of workers and later of women enfranchised through the final universalization of the suffrage have never been systematically studied. The marked contrasts in the turnout proportions between parallel elections in Prussia and in the Reich have frequently been documented, but no detailed ecological comparisons of results in open elections and results in secret elections have, as far as I have been able to ascertain, ever been attempted. Erik Högh has under way a fascinating analysis of the electoral registers for a sample of Danish constituencies from the period of open elections: here it will be of the greatest interest to analyze the extent of participation and the political preferences of the various categories of manual workers. . . .

However limited the possibilities of historical comparisons, cross-national analyses of survey data are clearly essential in any attempt to reach some understanding of the implications of mass suffrage for the functioning of Western-type political systems. Comparisons of the extent and scope of participation within the lower socio-economic strata can help us to gain insight into the functional importance of the right to vote: What does the suffrage mean for citizens in these strata? Is voting a peripheral activity of little consequence, or does it fit in with a wider range of participant activities in the community, in associations, in politics? Sample surveys can give us data on these wider contexts of participation, and comparisons of such data across communities and across national systems can give us clues to an understanding of the importance of the structural settings and the alternatives in the system for the recruitment of active participants from the lower strata within each society.

Our recent attempt at comparing data on participation from two systems differing as much from each other as Norway and the United States[4] points to a possible line of research in this direction. Our principal concern here was with the extent of political participation within the lower strata of two electorates: the workers as con-

[4]Stein Rokkan and Angus Campbell, "Citizen Participation in Political Life: Norway and the United States of America," *International Social Science Journal*, 1960, *12*: 71–72.

trasted with the salaried employees, the professional people and the businessmen; the primary-educated as contrasted with the secondary-educated and the college-educated. We found for both countries the usual differences in turnout between the strata, and we found consistent differences in the same direction for the extent of attention to the mass media during the campaign. We dealt with replications of "micro-micro" breakdowns. What changed the character of the analysis was the finding that there were no such uniform differences between the strata for organizational activity in politics. Using a simple index of participation based on party membership, attendance at meetings, and electoral work, we found no consistent differences between strata in the Norwegian sample but a marked and consistent one in the United States. We interpreted this to reflect the contrast between the two regimes in the alternatives set for the citizens, both as voters and potential recruits to party activity: in Norway a markedly class-distinct, "status-polarized" party system, in the United States much less correspondence between the lines of socio-economic cleavage and the lines of political conflict. To explore this further we proceeded to a third-order "macro-micro-micro" comparison. We placed the parties in the two systems in order of rank according to the proportions of manual workers among their voters, and we found that the class character of the parties made a decisive difference in the recruitment of active participants in political work. In the Norwegian Labour party we found manual workers more likely to be active than middle class voters. In the more heterogeneous Democratic party in the United States we found a tendency in the opposite direction: the level of participation was slightly lower for workers than for middle class voters. The most marked status differentials in participation were found within the parties with the lowest proportions of working-class voters—the opposition parties in Norway and the Republican parties in the United States. This, of course, cannot be taken to be conclusive evidence; the differences were found within nation-wide cross-sections and will need to be tested by categories of communities. However, the findings do suggest important hypotheses for continued comparative research: they accentuate the importance of assembling data on the character of the political choices confronting the worker, on the opportunities open to him for experience and training in organizational skills, and on the channels of recruitment from class-distinct associations such as unions to membership and activity in political parties.

Perhaps the most important set of factors to be taken into account in any cooperative study of participation bears on the organizational bases for the recruitment of active supporters in party-political work: How open, direct, and stable are the channels of recruitment from the given economic, cultural, or religious organization to the given party? What are the alternative "policy pay-offs" of other affiliations, other modes of influence, or for the given organization? What are the alternative prospects of achievement and advancement for the active participants in the given organization?

Questions along these lines may be raised for any association or organization and for any party. They are of particular importance in comparative studies of the socio-economic bases for party conflict. In pushing further our tentative comparisons between Norway and the United States, these are exactly the questions we shall want to explore in detail: the character of the tie-ins between the different labor unions and the parties, the distinctiveness of the union votes, the extent of recruitment from union activity to political activity, and the relationships between union activity and participation in other organizations and associations in the community and the nation.[5]

POLITICAL OPPORTUNITIES IN THE AMERICAN HYBRID

Robert A. Dahl

I [have] defined the "normal" American political process as one in which there is a high probability that an active and legitimate group in the population can make itself heard effectively at some crucial stage in the process of decision. To be "heard" covers a wide range of activities, and I do not intend to define the word rigorously. Clearly, it does not mean that every group has equal control over the outcome.

In American politics, as in all other societies, control over decisions is unevenly distributed; neither individuals nor groups are political equals. When I say that a group is heard "effectively" I mean more than the simple fact that it makes a noise; I mean that one or more officials are not only ready to listen to the noise, but expect to suffer in some significant way if they do not placate the group, its leaders, or its most vociferous members. To satisfy the group may require one or more of a great variety of actions by the responsive leader: pressure for substantive policies, appointments, graft, respect, expression of the appropriate emotions, or the right combination of reciprocal noises.

Thus the making of governmental decisions is not a majestic march of great majorities united upon certain matters of basic policy. It is the steady appeasement of relatively small groups. Even when these groups add up to a numerical majority at election time it is usually not useful to construe that majority as more than an arithmetic expression. For to an extent that would have pleased Madison enormously, the numerical majority is incapable of undertaking any co-ordinated action.

[5]A report of a comparison of union-party tie-ins is in progress [in 1962].

It is the various components of the numerical majority that have the means for action.

As this is familiar ground, let me summarize briefly and dogmatically some well-known aspects of the constitutional rules: the groups they benefit, those they handicap, and the net result. When we examine Congress we find that certain groups are overrepresented, in the sense that they have more representatives (or more representatives at key places) and therefore more control over the outcome of Congressional decisions than they would have if the rules were designed to maximize formal political equality. Equal representation in the Senate has led to overrepresentation of the less densely populated states. In practice this means that farmers and certain other groups—metal mining interests, for example—are overrepresented. State legislatures overrepresent agricultural and small-town areas and hence do not redistrict House seats in accordance with population changes; even the House significantly underrepresents urban populations. The operation of the seniority principle and the power of the committee chairman has led the voters in one-party or modified one-party states to be significantly overrepresented. According to one recent estimate, there are twenty-two such states. Geographically these include the solid South, the border states, upper New England, four midwestern states, Oregon, and Pennsylvania. Of these only Pennsylvania is highly urban and industrial. Because of the operation of the single-member district system in the House, on the average, a net shift of 1 per cent of the electorate from one party to the other will result in a net gain of about 2.5 per cent of the House seats for the benefited party; and because of the operation of the two-member district in the Senate, a shift of 1 per cent will result in a net gain for the benefited party of about 3 per cent of the Senate seats. Hence when large heterogeneous groups, like the farmers, shift their party support the legislative effects are likely to be considerably exaggerated.

All those politicians and officials concerned with the election or re-election of a President, and hence with the vagaries of the electoral college, must necessarily be responsive to a somewhat different set of groups. Again, the general picture is so well known that I need only enumerate a few points. In general the presidential politicians must be responsive to populous states with large electoral votes; to states that are marginal between the parties, i.e., to the two-party states; to the "key" states, i.e., those both marginal and populous; to key groups in the key states—ethnic, religious, occupational; to relatively large nationwide groups; and to heavily populated urban and industrial areas. A careful examination of these will show, I think, that they are different from, and often have goals that run counter to, the groups that predominate in Congress.

The bureaucracies are much more complex. In varying degrees they must be responsive to both presidential and Congressional politicians. But the presidential and Congressional politicians to whom they must respond are themselves rather a narrow and specialized group. In Congress, typically, it is the chairmen of the House and Senate Appropriations Committess, of the relevant subcommittees, and of the relevant substantive committees. Among presidential politicians, administrators must usually be responsive to the Budget Bureau, to the departmental secretary, and, of course, to the President himself. They must also be responsive to their own specialized clienteles. The most effective clientele obviously is one like the farmers, that is also well represented in Congress and even in the executive branch; sometimes bureaucracy and clientele become so intertwined that one cannot easily determine who is responsive to whom.

This is the normal system. I have not attempted to determine in these pages whether it is a desirable system of government nor shall I try to do so now. For appraisal of its merits and defects would require a subtle and extended discussion lying beyond [these] bounds . . . .

This much may be said of the system. If it is not the very pinnacle of human achievement, a model for the rest of the world to copy or to modify at its peril, as our nationalistic and politically illiterate glorifiers so tiresomely insist, neither, I think, is it so obviously a defective system as some of its critics suggest.

To be sure, reformers with a tidy sense of order dislike it. Foreign observers, even sympathetic ones, are often astonished and confounded by it. Many Americans are frequently dismayed by its paradoxes; indeed, few Americans who look upon our political process attentively can fail, at times, to feel deep frustration and angry resentment with a system that on the surface has so little order and so much chaos.

For it is a markedly decentralized system. Decisions are made by endless bargaining; perhaps in no other national political system in the world is bargaining so basic a component of the political process. In an age when the efficiencies of hierarchy have been re-emphasized on every continent, no doubt the normal American political system is something of an anomaly, if not, indeed, at times an anachronism. For as a means to highly integrated, consistent decisions in some important areas—foreign policy, for example—it often appears to operate in a creaking fashion verging on total collapse.

Yet we should not be too quick in our appraisal, for where its vices stand out, its virtues are concealed to the hasty eye. Luckily the normal system has the virtues of its vices. With all its defects, it does nonetheless provide a high probability that any active and legitimate group will make itself heard effectively at some stage in the process of decision. This is no mean thing in a political system.

It is not a static system. The normal American system has evolved, and by evolving it has survived. It has evolved and survived from aristocracy to mass democracy, through slavery, civil war, the tentative uneasy reconciliation of North and South, the repression of Negroes and their halting liberation; through two great wars of world-wide scope, mobilization, far-flung military enterprise, and return to hazardous peace; through numerous periods of economic instability and one prolonged depression with mass unemployment, farm "holidays," veterans' marches, tear gas, and even bullets; through two periods of postwar cynicism, demagogic excesses, invasions of traditional liberties, and the groping, awkward, often savage, attempt to cope with problems of subversion, fear, and civil tension.

Probably this strange hybrid, the normal American political system, is not for export to others. But so long as the social prerequisites of democracy are substantially intact in this country, it appears to be a relatively efficient system for reinforcing agreement, encouraging moderation, and maintaining social peace in a restless and immoderate people operating a gigantic, powerful, diversified, and incredibly complex society.

This is no negligible contribution, then, that Americans have made to the arts of government—and to that branch, which of all the arts of politics is the most difficult, the art of democratic government.

---

10. The Democratic Political Man

The personal qualities of political leaders and their relations with their followers or constituents have concerned public men since the days of Aristotle and Cicero. In the first selection that follows, Stimson Bullitt, writing partly from his own political experience, enumerates the "virtues, skills, and attitudes" that he believes the superior politician must have in the twentieth century.

The articulation of exact relationships between political leaders and their followers remains an intellectual challenge. In the conclusion of his important book on public opinion in American politics, the late V. O. Key, Jr., accepting the challenge, writes lucidly about the role of political activists (i.e., persons highly active and influential in politics) in the formation of mass public opinion.

Finally, in a provocative discussion of the nature of American political parties, Herbert McClosky and his associates report on a nationwide study of party leaders and their rank-and-file supporters, undertaken to determine, among other things, their outlooks on key national issues. The study gives persuasive evidence that ideological and political differences between the Republican and Democratic parties are more evident among party leaders than among rank-and-file members.

THE DEMOCRATIC POLITICAL CLASS— AN ARSENAL OF CIVIC ASSETS

STIMSON BULLITT

Here is a catalogue of those virtues, skills, and attitudes which an American politician needs in the second half of the twentieth century in order better to lead a government of free men. The possessor of all these assets is the answer to a good citizen's prayer and would fit the terms of a convention nominating speech. . . .

Some knowledge of history is needed for a politician to understand government, and a sense of history is essential for him to avoid living only in the present and therefore assuming either that his own epoch is eternal or that it is easy to transform. Without a sense of history he lacks the standard of judgment which can protect him from measures which are excessively radical (Does he know how many ideal commonwealths have been brought to pass by slaughter of leaders or enactment of a new code of laws?) or reactionary (Will he be like the trembling purchasers of full-page ads proclaiming that forty days remained in which to save their country's way of life?).

Toward the same end of perspective, he needs an inner life with a system of principles for his direction. This is both important and rare. The intensity of contemporary stresses makes some sensitive and thoughtful persons crack up or turn inward, leaving the field to nimble men who are directed by ambition and the pleasure of their peers rather than by any more permanent rules. They are undented by the forces to which they yield, unaware of the strains and indifferent to the public good. To be wiser and more effective, a politician has to take pains to be a whole man. To keep an outlook of freedom and wide horizons, he must do three things: At intervals, he must take time for reflection under conditions of peace and leisure; he must have a few friends who care neither about politics nor about his personal success; and he must practice some diversion remote from his work. Unless he exists as a distinct person he cannot be much use to others or much pleasure to himself. . . .

In the course of a political career several returns to private life will disorder a politician's routine but at the same time offer him a chance to give better service when he is in office. The result is to follow two careers, practiced in alternation, one public and one private. The advantage of these sojourns, which do not have to be in obscurity but should be free from pressure, is the chance to acquire a better comprehension of the present by giving attention to the past and future. A politician is better able to understand and contend with the present if he does not live in it continually. In office, a politician's reading time is short, and almost all his study is consumed by periodicals and technical reports because he must concentrate on immediate problems. Life is too short to allow him at the same time to bolt each day's raw facts and to digest information and conclusions about long periods. The exceptions, such as Churchill and Theodore Roosevelt, are too few to matter. A philosopher politician is a personality of which I cannot conceive and for which I therefore cannot hope. But a politician enabled by periods of tranquillity to improve his sense of the past and future and his own identity is both possible and to be desired.

A sense of history, an inner life, and periods free from responsibility for daily decisions, all tend to give a politician a sounder judgment in his decisions, and they tend to make his policies moderate and more definite and realistic in direction. A person who remains in the commotion of dealing with daily problems cannot be committed to anything but action for its own sake or a temporary survival on other people's terms. One can be aloof without ever being committed, but one cannot become committed to any significant end without from time to time being aloof.

Shaw said that democracy is a device which insures that people are governed no better than they deserve. Whether they are is no business of a politician. He has no right to say to people, as though he were a fireman standing with his hose and looking at a burning house outside the city limits, "Everything I give you beyond this point is beyond my duty and puts you in debt to me." A deserving constituency should get a politician whose ego is in close balance, with that self-esteem which a man must have to act with his full force, yet without the notion that he is at the center of the universe, a notion which distorts a man's judgment and morals by fixing his eyes on himself. He has a will to win, but curbs his thirst for glory and crusading spirit to permit the detachment necessary to act in a way that is wise and good. Justice Holmes wrote: "A man is bound to be parochial in his practice — to give his life, and if

necessary his death, for the place where he has his roots. But his thinking should be cosmopolitan and detached. He should be able to criticize what he reveres and loves." This politician does not enter a suicide
pact with a lost cause, but will submit to humble compromise to trade
a halfway measure for half a loaf. His attitude contrasts with the adolescent martyrdom of one who suffers total defeat by inflexible devotion to his plan because he puts his pride or self-pity above his conception of the public interest, while pretending to put principle first,
pretending he would rather be right than useful, though in political
terms he is not even right.

This imagined superior politician's own mind directs his acts, yet
like most men he is a political animal, not a member of a more solitary
species, like the great cats. The public opinion polls are not his compass
needle. His constituents influence but do not own him. He does not
think he is the Great White Father Figure leading the scorned masses
beside the still waters of social security. He may prefer three cheers to
three meals, but he is immune to that pernicious disease which attacks
an otherwise able leader whose outlook is immature and woolly: first
worshiping the cheering crowd; then, as he sees himself reflected in
their eyes, coming to believe himself the proper object of their worship.
As a free man he does his duty as his brother's keeper by enabling his
fellows to be free.

A politician should be able to reach a decision and stick to it long
enough for the people whom he affects to act on it. The process of compromise is a constructive element of democratic government only if
a politician interrupts it at recurring intervals and steers a straight line
which enables other people to take directed action. Otherwise they cannot know where they stand or what is practical or safe to do. Whether his
problem is a budget, a foreign aid plan, or a zoning code, a politician
should know when to halt deliberation and fix his course. Only if others
can count on him to hold fast once in a while can they proceed in reference to him, get up speed, and make some distance before his course
is changed again. That part of government touched by a politician stag-
nates if he never ceases to alter his position according to the moment-
by-moment resolution of forces upon each other and upon him. . . .

A politician gives better service if his loyalties are divided and if they
are graded in order of their importance to the public interest. If he has
no loyalties he is useless. If his loyalties are in the wrong order he is less
useful than he could be. If his loyalty is attached to a single object he
is likely to do harm. His first preference should be to his principles and
to all the people to whom his unit of government is responsible. This

group should rank above his constituency if the two are not identical, that is, if his constituency is a part of the whole, as is the case for most legislators except city councilmen elected at large. If he loves his policies as himself he may ignore their defects and continue to cling to them after they have become obsolete. On the other hand, the public interest suffers if his friends come first. But for his decisions to be untouched by friendship impairs his service. The supporters of such a politician may be fewer in number, and therefore as a unit less effective in his cause, than the group surrounding a politician who cares enough about his friends to stand by them to some extent. At the same time this smaller group of supporters is composed of a larger than normal proportion of fanatic types who adhere to him, not from affection but from devotion to his policies and devotion to him for his attachment to his policies. Their backing and counsel tend to warp his judgment.

As a support or substitute for character in politicians, a moderate ambition has value which a voter should not scorn. It makes a man assume some virtues which he lacks. An ambitious politician knows that his practice of them does more to advance or support his success than mere verbal tributes to good. He knows that honesty is a good policy. The wish for future trust and recognition restrains him from selfish excesses and spurs him to work. Unless he has superior strength of character, a politician without hope of some reward beyond that which inheres in virtue is likely to be dangerous or useless. As a marriage can be held together by character in the absence of love, so by moderate ambition in the place of character the commonwealth can be assisted, if not sustained.

A politician ought to be a teacher. Powers of advocacy are not enough because they cause only a superficial persuasion, not enduring understanding. By eloquence, you can carry people away against their better judgment some of the time. By teaching, you make them harder to fool. If you are a better man than your opponents, you need not worry. Mr. Truman's conduct of the Presidency suffered from his lack of teaching skill. Some of his best proposals failed because he was unable to convince the American people of their worth.

Some politicians ignore their teaching function and do not try to exercise it, but, regardless of intention or awareness, all teach by character and conduct, if not interpretation of ideas. A politician can teach even better than schoolteachers those things which are within his experience. As broker between government and people, he explains public problems to citizens. Their comprehension may enable them better to form the basic policy which is passed back to him to be translated into legislation or administration. His teaching assists his constituents, his country, and himself. If people understand what he is about, they may be more willing to support him. This is particularly important where he acts for the welfare of a unit broader than his constituency or a special interest group within it. People may know what they like, but a politician can help them learn their long-range wants. . . .

Imagination is an important quality in a politician. In public affairs, all things under the sun have been tied together in a web of cause and effect. Not long ago, if a politician could understand what was before his eyes and within his experience, he could handle his job. It stood within these horizons. Now his mind must see the sparrow fall in a far-off land and know its effect on his constituents.

In one type of public man vision is short, although his sight is clear in the cozy, brightly lit cell of his philosophy. He sees government in terms of administrative competence and the balance sheet. Another type sees it in terms of each man's dignity, singularity, and capacity to exceed himself. One bases policy on hopes, the other on regrets. As a symbol of political outlook a rainbow is better than a ledger. Politics needs both.

A politician need not be an original thinker, but a new idea should not make him flinch. In proposals for action, his thought need be only just far enough ahead of his time to be within the understanding of his constituents, yet beyond their natural vision. Any more is a dangerous adornment of little use to him, while to fall short keeps him from being a leader, although he may be a success. If he should come to believe the wisdom of some advanced idea for action he should keep it to himself until the time comes, if ever, when he may advocate it without making many of his listeners angry, bewildered, or afraid. He ought to propose an attainable end, one to which the voters probably can be persuaded to go, not one to which they would move their affairs if only they could be induced to agree with him. When Solon was asked if he had left the Athenians the best laws that could be given, he replied, "The best they could receive."

A free government requires that some of its politicians be willing to try new ideas. A disadvantage of intellectually mature politicians is that many of them are indifferent to new ideas for action, even though unafraid of them. A mature politician's freedom from illusions about the nature of the world is often coupled with a reluctance to experiment because he doubts whether a proposed change of course will work or do good. Among mature politicians this common distaste for trying new ideas is partly inherent in maturity and partly the result of the fact that to obtain mature politicians people tend to elect old ones;

age and maturity combined accentuate the preference for habitual patterns. Like the golden mean, the ideal of philosopher kings has limits. Old, mature men who have lost passion, vigor, and illusions, tend to be not only temperate and sensible but also bound by a taste for the tried and, so far, true. . . .

A useful end for him to urge is a tentative ideal pattern for society. This is not to propose a single step ahead of the existing path of progress, it is not to recommend another car in each garage or nonstop flights to Tahiti but a whole new framework for a way of life. Only by this means can people be enabled to evaluate their present way and, if they find it wanting, to decide on the best alternative target. For a long time, political talkers have been chewing a stale cud. In America politicians now are needed who will spell out brighter, better worlds and show us roads for their approach.

But regardless of the end proposed, whether a far-off comprehensive scheme or the location of a bridge, the politician should take a stand, not confine himself to fearless endorsements of completed public works or praise of great dead men, or pronouncements like the Aztec lords' annual vow to keep the sun on its course. Otherwise, he is worth little to his constituents, and politics is not worth its cost to him.

In personal terms the price of political success is so high, and knowledge is so uncertain about its causes, that you might as well enjoy yourself by taking sides. It is not necessary that your convictions be strong. Nor do your stands have to be consistent, either in sequence on one subject or on several subjects at once. And of course you need not take a stand on every issue. But you must stand up for something in order to exist separate from the abstraction of mankind, and to be a man. Of the Spartan kings at Thermopylae, Demaratus lived longer, but most people ever since would rather have been Leonidas.

At the proper time and place, a politician has the duty to discuss with his constituents every item of policy in his program. But although he should propose utopian public ends, he is wise to say nothing of the lifetime goals he has set for himself. It is presumptuous to think anyone is much interested in them, and they may prove embarrassing. He has to take more pains to keep the remnants of his privacy than one whose daily life is less exposed. He need not affect beliefs he lacks, like Henry of Navarre who decided Paris was worth a mass, but taste and discretion bid him to contain those almost inexpressible thoughts. His ultimate, unattainable ends, if he has any, are properly revealed by his conduct. . . .

Unless a politician's courage is exercised as an act of responsibility, it is at most an indirect assistance to the cause of freedom or the commonwealth. The public good need not be a motive. Nor does it matter whether the nature of his action is combative zest, the nerve to confront a danger in order to escape it, or willingness to risk a loss for chance of gain. But the public good is not served unless his intent is the defense of a principle, a policy, or at least a portion of the public. Bravery for one's family is a private virtue. If his aim is merely to win elections, a politician's willingness to stand up to angry crowds is gambler's nerve which proves his ambition rather than his public spirit.

Of all brave efforts which contribute to the general good, the ones of highest value are those efforts which a politician makes when he declares the truth, and next most valuable are those he makes when he fulfills his word. Veracity most helps the cause of freedom at those times when veracity depends on courage. And courage as an element of probity inspires less folly than courage does in other forms. Even where the public welfare is a politician's conscious aim in exposing himself to harm, the public does not gain by it when his action is misled by narcissistic motives supplemental to the motive of the common good. The memory of Marcus Curtius was honored for his having caused improvement of his city's central square, whose beauty and convenience were impaired by a gulf, which closed as soon as he had galloped into it on his horse. But evidence of the price which divine forces had set for their performance of this piece of public work was thin enough to suggest that substantial elements of his decision were excessive pride and a pleasure in self-display.

Yet for a politician the problem is not solved by any kind of bravery alone. To serve the public interest, or the cause of freedom, virtue cannot be coupled with continual defeat. Popular admiration for success encourages belief in the morals practiced by winners; people often despise the high principles for which a loser stood. If he makes a gallant losing fight, the crowd will cheer him when he leaves the ring, but next week it will go to watch the other fellow fight. Many candidates are pragmatists about the ethics of what it takes to win, yet primitives in their assumption, with inconclusive proof, of a causal connection between methods and elections. If a man has been elected after dodging issues or defaming his opponent, he and others will perform the beastly ritual again.

A politician's basic task is to draw the line between the public interest and his own survival. It can be claimed that this continual decision is not moral but strategic, that it is a matter of judgment alone because except in office politicians cannot do much public good. This would be so if man were just a scale. But his judgment is distorted by his hunger for success. Idealism and good sense may cause him to identify his country's fortune with his own, but then, deluded by conceit, he sees their major causal sequence in reverse. He must have courage to speak about the important things with more honesty than his judgment suggests. Discretion is not worth as much as valor. As he follows the line between truth and success he needs courage to favor the former.

Furthermore, an aspiring mankind should have men and women willing to risk their rank to save their honor. To be a politician of a democratic nation, one no longer needs to risk his property or life. The public interest is served by the effects and example of politicians who would rather be right, whose "nerve of failure" sustains them on their own way, undaunted by the chances of rejection or defeat. Even if he loses more often than others, a politician who peddles the truth is his constituents' gain. And he strengthens their stomach for truth by often repeating the dose.

PUBLIC OPINION AND DEMOCRATIC POLITICS

V. O. KEY, JR.

The exploration of public attitudes is a pursuit of endless fascination —and frustration. Depiction of the distribution of opinions within the public, identification of the qualities of opinion, isolation of the odd and of the obvious correlates of opinion, and ascertainment of the modes of opinion formation are pursuits that excite human curiosity. Yet these endeavors are bootless unless the findings about the preferences, aspirations, and prejudices of the public can be connected with the workings of the governmental system. The nature of that connection [can be] suggested by the examination of the channels by which governments become aware of public sentiment and the institutions through which opinion finds more or less formal expression.

When all these linkages are treated, the place of public opinion in government has still not been adequately portrayed. The problem of opinion and government needs to be viewed in an even broader context. Consideration of the role of public opinion drives the observer to the more fundamental question of how it is that democratic governments manage to operate at all. Despite endless speculation on that problem, perplexities still exist about what critical circumstances, beliefs, outlooks, faiths, and conditions are conducive to the maintenance of regimes under which public opinion is controlling, at least in principle, and is, in fact, highly influential.

. . . In an earlier day public opinion seemed to be pictured as a mysterious vapor that emanated from the undifferentiated citizenry and in

Pages 535–543: From *Public Opinion and American Democracy* by V. O. Key, Jr. Copyright 1961 by V. O. Key, Jr. Reprinted by permission of Alfred A. Knopf, Inc.

some way or another enveloped the apparatus of government to bring it into conformity with the public will. These weird conceptions . . . passed out of style as the technique of the sample survey permitted the determination, with some accuracy, of the distribution of opinions within the population. Vast areas of ignorance remain in our information about people's opinions and aspirations; nevertheless, a far more revealing map of the gross topography of public opinion can now be drawn than could have been a quarter of a century ago.

Despite their power as instruments for the observation of mass opinion, sampling procedures do not bring within their range elements of the political system basic for the understanding of the role of mass opinion within the system. Repeatedly, as we have sought to explain particular distributions, movements, and qualities of mass opinion, we have had to go beyond the survey data and make assumptions and estimates about the role and behavior of that thin stratum of persons referred to variously as the political elite, the political activists, the leadership echelons, or the influentials. In the normal operation of surveys designed to obtain tests of mass sentiment, so few persons from this activist stratum fall into the sample that they cannot well be differentiated, even in a static description, from those persons less involved politically. The data tell us almost nothing about the dynamic relations between the upper layer of activists and mass opinion. The missing piece of our puzzle is this elite element of the opinion system. That these political influentials both affect mass opinion and are conditioned in their behavior by it is obvious. Yet systematic knowledge of the composition, distribution in the social structure, and patterns of behavior of this sector of the political system remains far from satisfactory.

The longer one frets with the puzzle of how democratic regimes manage to function, the more plausible it appears that a substantial part of the explanation is to be found in the motives that actuate the leadership echelon, the values that it holds, in the rules of the political game to which it adheres, in the expectations which it entertains about its own status in society, and perhaps in some of the objective circumstances, both material and institutional, in which it functions. Focus of attention on this sector of the opinion system contrasts with the more usual quest for the qualities of the people that may be thought to make democratic practices feasible. That focus does not deny the importance of mass attitudes. It rather emphasizes that the pieces of the puzzle are different in form and function, and that for the existence of a democratic opinion-oriented system each piece must possess the characteristics necessary for it to fit together with the others in a working whole. The superimposition over a people habituated to tyranny of a leadership imbued with democratic ideals probably would not create a viable democratic order.

Values and Motives of the Activist Subculture

The traits and characteristics of political activists assume importance in the light of a theory about why the leadership and governing levels in any society behave as they do. That theory amounts to the proposition that these political actors constitute in effect a subculture with its own peculiar set of norms of behavior, motives, and approved standards. Processes of indoctrination internalize such norms among those who are born to or climb to positions of power and leadership; they serve as standards of action, which are reinforced by a social discipline among the political activists. In some regimes the standards of the ruling groups prescribe practices of firmness toward the governed who are regarded as menials with no rights; they deserve no more than the rough and arbitrary treatment they receive. The rules of the game may prescribe that the proper practice for rulers is to maximize their own advantage as well as the correlative deprivations of the ruled. The ignorant, the poor, and the incompetent may be seen as entitled to what they get, which is very little. Or the rules of the game of a regime may mitigate the harshness of these outlooks by a compassionate attitude toward the wretched masses who cannot help themselves. Hence, we may have little fathers of the people. The point is that the politically active classes may develop characteristic norms and practices that tend to guide their behavior. In a loose sense these may be the norms of a subculture, that of the specialists in politics and government. Beliefs generally accepted among these persons tend to establish habits and patterns of behavior with considerable power of self-maintenance or persistence through time.

While the ruling classes of a democratic order are in a way invisible because of the vagueness of the lines defining the influentials and the relative ease of entry to their ranks, it is plain that the modal norms and standards of a democratic elite have their peculiarities. Not all persons in leadership echelons have precisely the same basic beliefs; some may even regard the people as a beast. Yet a fairly high concentration prevails around the modal beliefs, even though the definition of those beliefs must be imprecise. Fundamental is a regard for public opinion, a belief that in some way or another it should prevail. Even those who cynically humbug the people make a great show of deference to the populace. The basic doctrine goes further to include a sense of trusteeship for the people generally and an adherence to the basic doctrine that collective efforts should be dedicated to the promotion of mass gains rather than of narrow class advantage; elite elements tethered to narrow group interest have no slack for maneuver to accommodate themselves to mass aspirations. Ultimate expression of these faiths comes in the willingness to abide by the outcome of popular elections. The growth of leadership structures with beliefs including these broad articles of faith is probably accomplished only over a considerable period of time, and then only under auspicious circumstances.

If an elite is not to monopolize power and thereby to bring an end to democratic practices, its rules of the game must include restraints in the exploitation of public opinion. Dimly perceptible are rules of etiquette that limit the kinds of appeals to public opinion that may be properly made. If it is assumed that the public is manipulable at the hands of unscrupulous leadership (as it is under some conditions), the maintenance of a democratic order requires the inculcation in leadership elements of a taboo against appeals that would endanger the existence of democratic practices. Inflammation of the sentiments of a sector of the public disposed to exert the tyranny of an intolerant majority (or minority) would be a means of destruction of a democratic order. Or by the exploitation of latent differences and conflicts within the citizenry it may at times be possible to paralyze a regime as intense hatreds among classes of people come to dominate public affairs. Or by encouraging unrealistic expectations among the people a clique of politicians may rise to power, a position to be kept by repression as disillusionment sets in. In an experienced democracy such tactics may be "unfair" competition among members of the politically active class. In short, certain restraints on political competition help keep competition within tolerable limits. The observation of a few American political campaigns might lead one to the conclusion that there are no restraints on politicians as they attempt to humbug the people. Even so, admonitions ever recur against arousing class against class, against stirring the animosities of religious groups, and against demagoguery in its more extreme forms. American politicians manifest considerable restraint in this regard when they are tested against the standards of behavior of politicians of most of those regimes that have failed in the attempt to establish or maintain democratic practices.

The norms of the practice of politics in an order that has regard for public opinion include broad rules of etiquette governing relations among the activists, as well as rules governing the relations of activists with the public. Those rules, in their fundamental effect, assure the existence of a minority among the political activists; if those who control government can suppress opposition activists, an instrument essential for the formation and expression of public opinion is destroyed. A body of customs that amounts to a policy of "live and let live" must prevail. In constitutional democracies some of these rules are crystallized into fundamental law in guarantees such as those of freedom of speech, freedom of press, and the right to appeal to the electorate for power. Relevant also are procedures for the protection of property rights; a political opposition may be destroyed by expropriation as well as by execution. While such rules extend in their application to the entire population, one of their major functions is to prevent politicians from putting each other into jail or from destroying each other in the ordinary course of their competitive endeavors. All these elements of the rules of the game gain strength, not from their statement in the statutes and codes, but from their incorporation into the norms that guide the behavior of the political activists.

Form and Structure

Certain broad structural or organizational characteristics may need to be maintained among the activists of a democratic order if they are to perform their functions in the system. Fundamental is the absence of sufficient cohesion among the activists to unite them into a single group dedicated to the management of public affairs and public opinion. Solidification of the elite by definition forecloses opportunity for public choice among alternative governing groups and also destroys the mechanism for the unfettered expression of public opinion or of the opinions of the many subpublics. Maintenance of division and competition among political activists requires the kinds of etiquette that have been mentioned to govern their relations among themselves. Those rules, though, do not create the cleavages among the activists. Competitive segments of the leadership echelons normally have their roots in interests or opinion blocs within society. A degree of social diversity thus may be, if not a prerequisite, at least helpful in the construction of a leadership appropriate for a democratic regime. A series of independent social bases provide the foundations for a political elite difficult to bring to the state of unification that either prevents the rise of democratic processes or converts them into sham rituals.

At a more earthy level, maintenance of a multiplicity of centers of leadership and political activism requires arrangements by which men may gain a livelihood despite the fact that they are out of power. Consider the consequences for the structure of opinion leadership of a socio-economic system in which those skilled in the arts of governance have open to them no way of obtaining a livelihood save by the exercise of those skills. In the United States the high incidence of lawyers among the politically influential provides a base of economic independence; the defeated politician can always find a few clients. Extensive reliance on part-time, amateur politicians in representative bodies and in many governing commissions has assured an economic cushion for many political activists. The custom of making many such offices economically unattractive has, in effect, required that they be filled by persons with an economic base independent of the public treasury. Opinion leaders and managers often find economic independence in posts with business associations and other voluntary societies. Communications enterprises, important in the operation of democracies, gain independence from government by their commerical position.

The structure of government itself, through its many independent units and agencies, assures havens of some security for spokesmen for a variety of viewpoints. All this may boil down to the contention that development and maintenance of the type of leadership essential for the operation of a democratic political order is facilitated by the existence of a social system of some complexity with many centers that have some autonomy and economic independence. Perhaps a safer formulation would be that societies that do not meet these requisites may encounter difficult problems in the support of a fractionalized stratum of political activists; they need to construct functional equivalents of the means we have been describing to assure the maintenance of competing centers of leadership.

When viewed from another angle, these comments about the utility of independent foundations for competing sectors of the political elite relate to the more general proposition that regimes deferential to public opinion may best flourish when the deprivations contingent upon the loss of an election are limited. The structure of government itself may also contribute to that loss limitation. In federal regimes and in regimes with extensive devolution to elective local governmental authorities the prospect of loss of a national election may be faced with some equanimity, for the national minority may retain its position in many subordinate units of the nation and remain in a measure undisturbed by the alternations of control within the nation as a whole. The same function of loss limitation may be served by constitutional and customary expectations that limit the permissible range of governmental action.

Another characteristic may be mentioned as one that, if not a prerequisite to government by public opinion, may profoundly affect the nature of a democratic order. This is the distribution through the social structure of those persons highly active in politics. . . . [I]n the United States the political activists—if we define the term broadly—are scattered through the socio-economic hierarchy. The upper-income and occupational groups, to be sure, contribute disproportionately; nevertheless, individuals of high political participation are sprinkled throughout the lesser occupational strata. Contrast the circumstances when the highly active political stratum coincides with the high socio-economic stratum. Conceivably the winning of consent and the creation of a sense of political participation and of sharing in public affairs may be far simpler when political activists of some degree are spread through all social strata. The alternative circumstance may induce an insensitivity to mass opinion, a special reliance on mass communications, and a sharpened sense of cleavage and separatism within the political order. The contention made here amounts to more than the axiom that democracies can exist only in societies that possess a well-developed middle class. In a modern industrial society with universal suffrage the chances are that a considerable sprinkling of political activists needs to exist in groups below the "middle class," however that term of vague referent may be defined. The correct general proposition may be that the operation of democratic processes may be facilitated by the distribution of persons participating in the order through all strata of the electorate. When the belief that democracy depended upon the middle class flourished, a comparatively narrow suffrage prevailed.

Allied with these questions is the matter of access to the wider circles of political leadership and of the recruitment and indoctrination of these political activists. Relative ease of access to the arena of active politics may be a preventive of the rise of intransigent blocs of opinion managed by those denied participation in the regularized processes of politics. In a sense, ease of access is a necessary consequence of the existence of a somewhat fragmented stratum of political activists. Systems built on rigid class lines or on the dominance of clusters of families may be especially prone to the exclusion of those not to the proper status born—or married. Yet ease of access does not alone suffice. It must be accompanied by means, either deliberate or informal, for the indoctrination of those admitted in the special mores and customs of the activist elements of the polity. Otherwise, ease of access may only facilitate the depredations of those alienated from the values of the political order. By their nature democratic political systems have large opportunity—if there is the necessary will—to extend widely opportunities for political participation in lesser capacities and thereby to sift out those capable of achieving access to the more restricted circles of influentials. Whether the builders of political orders ever set about deliberately and systematically to tackle such problems of recruitment and indoctrination may be doubtful. Those problems may be solved, when they are solved, by the unconscious and unwilled processes of evolutionary adaptation of social systems.

This discussion in terms of leadership echelons, political activists, or elites falls painfully on the ears of democratic romantics. The mystique of democracy has in it no place for ruling classes. As perhaps with all powerful systems of faith, it is vague on the operating details. Yet by their nature governing systems, be they democratic or not, involve a division of social labor. Once that axiom is accepted, the comprehension of democratic practices requires a search for the peculiar characteristics of the political influentials in such an order, for the special conditions under which they work, and for the means by which the people keep them in check. The vagueness of the mystique of democracy is matched by the intricacy of its operating practices. If it is true that those who rule tend sooner or later to prove themselves enemies of the rights of man—and there is something to be said for the validity of this proposition—then any system that restrains that tendency however slightly can excite only awe.

ISSUE CONFLICT AND CONSENSUS AMONG PARTY LEADERS AND FOLLOWERS[1]

HERBERT McCLOSKY, PAUL J. HOFFMANN, AND ROSEMARY O'HARA

American political parties are often regarded as "brokerage" organizations, weak in principle, devoid of ideology, and inclined to differ
chiefly over unimportant questions. In contrast to the "ideological"
parties of Europe—which supposedly appeal to their followers through
sharply defined, coherent, and logically related doctrines—the American parties are thought to fit their convictions to the changing demands
of the political contest.[2] According to this view, each set of American
party leaders is satisfied to play Tweedledee to the other's Tweedledum.

Pressures Toward Uniformity and Cleavage

Although these "conclusions" are mainly derived from *a priori* analysis
or from casual observations of "anecdotal" data (little systematic effort
having been made so far to verify or refute them), they are often taken
as confirmed—largely, one imagines, because they are compatible with
certain conspicuous features of American politics. Among these features
is the entrenchment of a two-party system which, by affording both
parties a genuine opportunity to win elections, tempts them to appeal
to as many diverse elements in the electorate as are needed to put
together a majority.[3] Since both parties want to attract support from the
centrist and moderate segments of the electorate, their views on basic
issues will, it is thought, tend to converge. Like giant business enterprises competing for the same market, they will be led to offer commodities that are in many respects identical.[4] It is one thing for a small
party in a multi-party system to preserve its ideological purity, quite
another for a mass party in a two-party system to do so. The one has
little hope of becoming a majority, and can most easily survive by remaining identified with the narrow audience from which it draws its
chief supporters; the other can succeed only by accommodating the con-

[1]This article is the first of a series reporting the findings of a national field study of political belief
and affiliation among American party leaders and followers. The study was carried out through the
Laboratory for Research in Social Relations at the University of Minnesota under grants made to the
senior author by the Committee on Political Behavior of the Social Science Research Council, and
supplementary grants from the Graduate School Research Fund. The manuscript was prepared at
the Survey Research Center, University of California, Berkeley, under a Fellowship in Legal and
Political Philosophy awarded to the senior author by the Rockefeller Foundation.

[2]Maurice Duverger, *Political Parties, Their Organization and Activity in the Modern State* (New York, 1955),
p. 102.

[3]The analysis of these and related tendencies associated with the American party system is ably set
forth in Pendleton Herring, *The Politics of Democracy* (New York, 1940), p. 102 and *passim*. Also, James
M. Burns, *Congress on Trial: The Legislative Process and the Administrative State* (New York, 1949), p. 34.

[4]See especially E. E. Schattschneider, *Party Government* (New York, 1942), p. 92 and *passim*; and V. O.
Key, *Politics, Parties, and Pressure Groups*, 4th ed. (New York, 1958), ch. 8; Howard R. Penniman, *Sait's
American Parties and Elections*, 5th ed. (New York, 1952), p. 162.

flicting claims of many diverse groups—only, in short, by blunting ideological distinctions.[5]

Constraints against enlarging intellectual differences also spring from the loosely confederated nature of the American party system, and from each national party's need to adjust its policies to the competing interests of the locality, the state, and the nation.[6] Many party units are more concerned with local than with national elections, and prefer not to be handicapped by clear-cut national programs. Every ambitious politician, moreover, hopes to achieve a *modus vivendi* tailored to the particular and often idiosyncratic complex of forces prevailing in his constituency, an objective rarely compatible with doctrinal purity.[7] Often, too, local politics are largely nonpartisan or are partisan in ways that scarcely affect the great national issues around which ideologies might be expected to form.[8] The development and enforcement of a sharply delineated ideology is also hindered by the absence in either party of a firmly established, authoritative, and continuing organizational center empowered to decide questions of doctrine and discipline.[9] Party affiliation is loosely defined, responsibility is weak or non-existent, and organs for indoctrinating or communicating with party members are at best rudimentary.

Cultural and historical differences may also contribute to the weaker ideological emphasis among American, as compared with European, parties. Many of the great historical cleavages that have divided European nations for centuries—monarchism vs. republicanism; clericalism vs. anti-clericalism; democracy vs. autocracy, etc.—have never taken root in this country. Apart from the slavery (and subsequently the race) issue, the United States has not experienced the intense class or caste conflict often found abroad, and contests of the capitalism vs. socialism variety have never achieved an important role in American politics. In addition, never having known a titled nobility, we have largely been freed from the conflicts found elsewhere between the classes of inherited and acquired privilege.

Consider, too, the progress made in the United States toward neutralizing the forces which ordinarily lead to sharp social, and hence intellectual and political, differentiation. The class and status structure of American society has attained a rate of mobility equalling or exceeding that of any other long established society. Popular education, and other facilities for the creation of common attitudes, have been developed on a scale unequalled elsewhere. Improvements in

---

[5]William Goodman, *The Two-Party System in the United States* (New Jersey, 1956), p. 43.
[6]Duverger, *op. cit.*, pp. 187, 418.
[7]Pendleton Herring, *op. cit.*, p. 133
[8]*American State Legislatures*, ed. Belle Zeller (New York, 1954); but see also Malcolm E. Jewell, "Party Voting in American State Legislatures," *American Political Science Review*, Vol. 49 (September, 1955), pp. 773–791.
[9]Report of the Committee on Political Parties, American Political Science Association, *Toward a More Responsible Two-Party System* (New York, 1950), *passim*.

transportation and communication, and rapid shifts in population and industry have weakened even sectionalism as a source of political cleavage. Rural-urban differences continue to exist, of course, but they too have been diminishing in force and have become less salient for American politics than the differences prevailing, for example, between a French peasant proprietor and a Parisian *boulevardier*.[10] In short, a great many Americans have been subjected in their public lives to identical stimuli—a condition unlikely to generate strong, competing ideologies.

The research reported here was designed not to refute these observations but to test the accuracy of the claim that they are sufficient to prevent differences in outlook from taking root in the American party system. We believed that the homogenizing tendencies referred to are strongly offset by contrary influences, and that voters are preponderantly led to support the party whose opinions they share. We further thought that the competition for office, though giving rise to similarities between the parties, also impels them to diverge from each other in order to sharpen their respective appeals. For this and other reasons, we expected to find that the leaders of the two parties, instead of ignoring differences alleged to exist within the electorate, would differ on issues more sharply than their followers would. We believed further that even in a brokerage system the parties would serve as independent reference groups, developing norms, values, and self-images to which their supporters could readily respond.[11] Their influence, we felt, would frequently exceed that of ethnic, occupational, residential and other reference groups. In sum, we proceeded on the belief that the parties are not simply spokesmen for other interest groups, but are in their own right agencies for formulating, transmitting, and anchoring political opinions, that they attract adherents who in general share those opinions, and that through a feedback process of mutual reinforcement between the organization and its typical supporters, the parties develop integrated and stable political tendencies. Other hypotheses will be specified as we present and analyze our findings.

Procedures

The questions considered in this paper were part of a large field study made in 1957–1958 on the nature, sources, and correlates of political affiliation, activity, and belief in the American party system (hereafter referred to as the PAB study). Pilot studies on Minnesota samples had

[10]Data bearing on these generalizations will be presented in companion articles which specifically deal with sectional and rural-urban influences on issue outlook.

[11]*Cf.* James W. Prothro, Ernest Q. Campbell, and Charles M. Grigg, "Two Party Voting in the South: Class vs. Party Identification," *American Political Science Review*, Vol. 52 (March, 1958), pp. 131–139. Also, Peter H. Odegard and E. Allen Helms, *American Politics: A Study in Political Dynamics* (New York, 1947 ed.), pp. 809–821.

led us to suspect that many "settled" notions about party affiliation and belief in America would not stand up under careful empirical scrutiny; further, we felt that little progress would be made in the exploration of this subject until a comprehensive portrait of party membership in America had been drawn. Accordingly, a nationwide study was launched to acquire a detailed description of party leaders and supporters, gathering data on their backgrounds, political experiences, personality characteristics, values, motivations, social and political attitudes, outlooks on key issues, and related matters.

For our samples of party "leaders" we turned to the Democratic and Republican national conventions, largely because they are the leading and most representative of the party organs, their delegates coming from every part of the United States and from every level of party and government activity. Our samples ranged from governors, senators, and national committeemen at the one end to precinct workers and local officials at the other. In the absence of comprehensive information about the characteristics of the party élites in America, no one can say how closely the convention delegates mirror the total party leadership. We felt it fair to assume, nevertheless, that the delegates represented as faithful a cross section of American party leadership as could be had without an extraordinary expenditure of money and labor. Using convention delegates as our universe of leaders also held some obvious advantages for research, since the composition of this universe (by name, address, party, state, sex, place of residence, and party or public office) can usually be ascertained from the convention calls. Of the 6,848 delegates and alternates available to be sampled, 3,193 actually participated; 3,020 (1,788 Democrats and 1,232 Republicans) completed and returned questionnaires that were usable in all respects.[12] The proportion of returns was roughly equivalent for both sets of party leaders.

The rank and file sample, which we wanted both for its intrinsic value and for its utility as a control group, was obtained by special arrangement with the American Institute of Public Opinion. In January 1958, Gallup interviewers personally distributed our questionnaire to 2,917 adult voters in two successive national cross-section surveys. Some 1,610 questionnaires were filled out and returned, of which 1,484 were completely usable. This sample closely matched the national population on such characteristics as sex, age, region, size of city, and party affiliation, and, though it somewhat oversampled the upper educational levels, we considered it sufficiently large and representative for most of our purposes. Of the 1,484 respondents, 821 were Democratic supporters (629 "pure" Democrats, plus 192 whom we classified

---

[12]This gratifyingly large number of returns of so lengthy and detailed a questionnaire was attained through a number of follow-up mailings and special letters. These and other procedures designed to check the adequacy of the sample will be fully described in the volume containing the report of the overall study. The difference in the number of returns from the two parties was largely a result of the greater number of Democratic delegates to begin with.

as "independent" Democrats) and 623 were Republican supporters (479 "pure" Republicans, plus 144 "independent" Republicans). Forty respondents could not be identified as adherents of either party.

The lengthy questionnaire developed for the study was designed to be self-administered. It contained, in addition to questions on the respondents' personal backgrounds, a number of queries on their political history and experience, their attitudes toward the party system and toward such related matters as party organization, discipline and responsibility, their self-images with regard to social class and liberalism-conservatism, their reference group identifications, and their views on party leadership and ideology. The largest part of the questionnaire consisted of 390 scale items, randomly arranged, which when sorted and scored fell into 47 scales for measuring the personality, attitude, and value characteristics of each of the respondents. We had validated and used all but three of these scales in earlier studies.

The questions most relevant for the present article were those which asked each respondent to express his attitudes toward twenty-four important national issues, and to state whether he believed support for each issue should be "increased," "decreased," or "remain as is." The list of issues and the responses of each sample will be found in Tables 2-a through 2-e, where for convenience of analysis, the issues have been grouped under five broad headings: Public Ownership, Government Regulation of the Economy, Equalitarianism and Human Welfare, Tax Policy and Foreign Policy.

In tabulating the results, we first scored each individual on each issue and then computed aggregate scores for all the members of a given sample. To begin with, percentages were used to show the proportion who favored increasing, decreasing, or retaining the existing level of support on each issue. But as it was clumsy to handle three figures for each issue, we constructed a single index or "ratio of support" which would simultaneously take account of all three scores. The index was built by assigning a weight of 1.0 to each "increase" response in the sample, of 0 to each "decrease" response, and of .50 to each "remain as is" (or "same") response. Thus the ratio-of-support score shown for any given sample is in effect a mean score with a possible range of 0 to 1.0, in which support for an issue increases as the scores approach 1.0 and decreases as they approach 0. In general, the scores can be taken to approximate the following over-all positions: .0 to .25 — strongly wish to reduce support; .26 to .45 — wish to reduce support; .46 to .55 — satisfied with the *status quo*; .56 to .75 — wish to increase support; and .76 to 1.00 — strongly wish to increase support. Note that the differences in degree suggested by these categories refer not to the *strength of feeling* exhibited by individuals toward an issue but rather to the *numbers of people* in a sample who hold points of view favoring or opposing that issue.

Because they include "same" and "no code" as well as "increase" and "decrease" responses, our ratios of support sometimes flatten the differences between groups. Had we employed only the percentage scores for the "increase" or "decrease" responses, the differences between samples would in many instances have seemed larger. Nevertheless, the ratio of support offers so many advantages that we have employed it as our principal measure. For one thing, as the equivalent of a mean score, it takes into account all scores, omitting no respondent from the tabulation. For the same reason it enables us to assess the amount of dispersion or homogeneity exhibited by any sample and makes it easy to calculate significances of difference.[13] Reliance upon a single, uniform statistic also allows us to make ready comparisons not only *between* but *within* samples, and to determine quickly how large the differences actually are. By observing whether a ratio of support is above or below .50 we can see at once whether a particular group predominantly favors or opposes the issue in question, and how strongly it does so. The use of ratio scores also makes it possible to compare issues as well as groups, e.g., to see whether one issue is more preferred than another.

For further information on the meaning of the issue responses, we also compared samples on a number of related scales and items. Tabulating and statistical operations were carried out to control for demographic influences like education, occupation, age, and sectionalism; to ascertain homogeneity of opinion within the several samples; to rank the issues according to the magnitude of the differences between samples; to compare members' positions on issues against official platform statements; and to determine whether leaders and followers are able to name the issues which actually divide the parties. Some of the findings yielded by these operations will be considered here, while others, for reasons of space, will have to be reserved for future publications.

A word of caution before we turn to the findings. The respondents were offered only the twenty-four issues that impressed us in February, 1957, as most significant and enduring. However, they may not all be as salient today as they seemed at that time. Nor, within the limitations of a single questionnaire, could we explore every issue that informed observers might have considered important. Some presumably vital issues such as states rights, political centralization, and expansion of government functions could not be stated explicitly enough

---

[13]The measure of dispersion used for this purpose was the standard deviation, which was computed by using the scores of 0, .50 and 1.00 as intervals in the calculations. To avoid having to calculate separate significances of difference for each of the comparisons we wanted to observe, we simply made the assumption—erring on the side of caution—that the maximum variance of .50 had occurred in each instance. The magnitude of the significance of difference is, in other words, often greater than we have reported. The significance test used in this procedure was the critical ratio. Unless otherwise indicated, all the differences reported are statistically significant at or beyond the .01 level.

within our format to be tested properly. These are issues that are so generalized as to encompass many other specific issues, and so highly charged as to awaken a profusion of symbolic and emotive associations.

The *form* of our issue questions may also be open to criticism, for space limitations prevented our subjects from indicating how strongly they felt and how much they knew about each of the issues. This deficiency, however, may be less important than it appears, since for the groups we most wanted to compare (e.g., Democratic vs. Republican leaders), the degree of political knowledge and intensity is likely to be rather similar. The difficulty is greater when comparing leaders with followers, but is somewhat offset by controlling for education and socio-economic status. Although some subtleties of interpretation are bound to be lost because these variables have been omitted, we are satisfied that our issue questions in their present form furnish a useful measure for assessing *group* (as distinguished from *individual*) opinion.

Finally, one may wonder about the value of opinions stated on a questionnaire compared with the worth of views formally expressed by an organization or implicit in the actions of its leaders. Advantages can be cited on both sides. The beliefs expressed in official party statements or in legislative roll calls, it might be claimed, represent the *operating* beliefs of the organization by virtue of having been tested in the marketplace or in the competition of legislative struggle. Positions taken on issues on which a party stakes its future may be more valid evidence of what the party truly believes than are the opinions expressed by in-

Table 1

AVERAGE DIFFERENCES IN THE RATIO-OF-SUPPORT SCORES AMONG
PARTY LEADERS AND FOLLOWERS FOR FIVE CATEGORIES OF ISSUES

Category of Issues	Democratic Leaders vs. Republican Leaders	Democratic Followers vs. Republican Followers	Democratic Leaders vs. Democratic Followers	Republican Leaders vs. Republican Followers	Democratic Leaders vs. Republican Followers	Republican Leaders vs. Democratic Followers
a. Public Ownership of Resources	.28	.04	.06	.18	.10	.22
b. Government Regulation of the Economy	.22	.06	.08	.10	.12	.16
c. Equalitarianism, Human Welfare	.22	.05	.08	.21	.06	.25
d. Tax Policy	.20	.06	.06	.20	.04	.26
e. Foreign Policy	.15	.02	.05	.08	.07	.10
Average Differences in Ratio Scores for all Categories	.21	.04	.07	.15	.08	.20

Sample Sizes: Democratic Leaders, 1,788; Republican Leaders, 1,232; Democratic Followers, 821; Republican Followers, 623.

dividual members under conditions of maximum safety. On the other hand, the responses to the issue and attitude questions in the PAB study represent the anonymous, private opinions of party leaders and followers, uncomplicated by any need to make political capital, to proselytize, to conciliate critics, or to find grounds for embarrassing the opposition at the next election. Hence they may for some purposes represent the most accurate possible reflection of the "actual" state of party opinion. The controversy over the value of the two approaches is to some extent spurious, however, for they offer different perspectives on the same thing. In addition, considerable correspondence exists between the party positions evident in congressional roll calls and the privately expressed opinions of the party leaders in our study.[14]

Findings: Comparisons Between Leaders

No more conclusive findings emerge from our study of party issues than those growing out of the comparisons between the two sets of party leaders. Despite the brokerage tendency of the American parties, their active members are obviously separated by large and important differences. The differences, moreover, conform with the popular image in which the Democratic party is seen as the more "progressive" or "radical," the Republican as the more "moderate" or "conservative" of the two.[15] In addition, the disagreements are remarkably consistent, a function not of chance but of systematic points of view, whereby the responses to any one of the issues could reasonably have been predicted from knowledge of the responses to the other issues.

Examination of Tables 2-a-e shows that the leaders differ significantly on 23 of the 24 issues listed and that they were separated on 15 of these issues by .18 or more ratio points—in short, by differences that are in absolute magnitude very large. The two samples are furthest apart in their attitudes toward public ownership and are especially divided on the question of government ownership of natural resources, the Democrats strongly favoring it, the Republicans just as strongly wanting it cut back. The difference of .39 in the ratio scores is the largest for any of the issues tested. In percentages, the differences are 58 per cent (D) vs. 13 per cent (R) in favor of increasing support, and 19 per cent (D) vs. 52 per cent (R) in favor of decreasing support. Both parties preponderantly support public control and development of atomic energy, but the Democrats do so more uniformly.

---

[14]See, for example, the congressional roll-call results reported by Julius Turner, *Party and Constituency: Pressures on Congress*, The Johns Hopkins University Studies in Historical and Political Science Series, LXIX, #1 (1951). The complexities affecting the determination of party votes in Congress are thoroughly explored in David B. Truman, *The Congressional Party: A Case Study* (New York, 1959).

[15]Conservatism is here used not in the classical but in the more popular sense, in which it refers to negative attitudes toward government ownership, intervention, and regulation of the economy; resistance to measures for promoting equalitarianism and social welfare through government action; identification with property, wealth, and business enterprise; etc.

Table 2-A

COMPARISON OF PARTY LEADERS AND FOLLOWERS ON "PUBLIC
OWNERSHIP" ISSUES, BY PERCENTAGES AND RATIOS OF SUPPORT

Issues	Leaders		Followers	
	Dem. N = 1,788	*Repub.* N = 1,232	*Dem.* N = 821	*Repub.* N = 623
		(%s down)		
Public Ownership of Natural Resources				
% favoring: Increase	57.5	12.9	35.3	31.1
Decrease	18.6	51.9	15.0	19.9
Same, n.c.*	23.8	35.2	49.7	49.0
Support Ratio	.69	.30	.60	.56
Public Control of Atomic Energy				
% favoring: Increase	73.2	45.0	64.2	59.4
Decrease	7.2	15.3	7.1	10.0
Same, n.c.	19.6	39.7	28.7	30.6
Support Ratio	.83	.65	.79	.75
Mean Support Ratios for the Public Ownership Category	.76	.48	.70	.66

*n.c. = no code.

V. O. Key, among others, has observed that the Republican party
is especially responsive to the "financial and manufacturing community,"[16] reflecting the view that government should intervene as little
as possible to burden or restrain prevailing business interests. The
validity of this observation is evident throughout all our data, and is
most clearly seen in the responses to the issues listed under Government
Regulation of the Economy, Equalitarianism and Human Welfare,
Tax Policy. Democratic leaders are far more eager than Republican
leaders to strengthen enforcement of anti-monopoly laws and to increase regulation of public utilities and business. Indeed, the solidarity
of Republican opposition to the regulation of business is rather overwhelming: 84 per cent want to decrease such regulation and fewer than
.01 per cent say they want to increase it. Although the Democrats, on
balance, also feel that government controls on business should not be
expanded further, the differences between the two samples on this issue
are nevertheless substantial.

The two sets of leaders are also far apart on the farm issue, the
Democrats preferring slightly to increase farm supports, the Republicans wanting strongly to reduce them. The Republican ratio score of

[16]Key, *op. cit.*, p. 239.

Table 2-B

COMPARISON OF PARTY LEADERS AND FOLLOWERS
ON "GOVERNMENT REGULATION OF THE ECONOMY" ISSUES,
BY PERCENTAGES AND RATIOS OF SUPPORT

Issues	Leaders		Followers	
	Dem. $N = 1,788$	Repub. $N = 1,232$	Dem. $N = 821$	Repub. $N = 623$
		(%s down)		
Level of Farm Price Supports				
% favoring: Increase	43.4	6.7	39.0	23.0
Decrease	28.1	67.4	27.6	40.3
Same, n.c.	28.5	25.8	33.4	36.7
Support Ratio	.58	.20	.56	.41
Government Regulation of Business				
% favoring: Increase	20.2	0.6	18.6	7.4
Decrease	38.5	84.1	33.4	46.2
Same, n.c.	41.3	15.3	48.0	46.4
Support Ratio	.41	.08	.43	.31
Regulation of Public Utilities				
% favoring: Increase	59.0	17.9	39.3	26.0
Decrease	6.4	17.6	11.1	12.0
Same, n.c.	34.6	64.5	49.6	62.0
Support Ratio	.76	.50	.64	.57
Enforcement of Anti-Monopoly Laws				
% favoring: Increase	78.0	44.9	53.2	51.0
Decrease	2.9	9.0	7.9	6.6
Same, n.c.	19.1	46.1	38.9	42.4
Support Ratio	.88	.68	.73	.72
Regulation of Trade Unions				
% favoring: Increase	59.3	86.4	46.6	57.8
Decrease	12.4	4.5	8.9	10.6
Same, n.c.	28.3	9.2	44.5	31.6
Support Ratio	.73	.91	.69	.74
Level of Tariffs				
% favoring: Increase	13.0	19.2	16.6	15.2
Decrease	43.0	26.3	25.3	21.3
Same, n.c.	43.9	54.5	58.1	63.4
Support Ratio	.35	.46	.46	.47
Restrictions on Credit				
% favoring: Increase	24.8	20.6	26.1	25.7
Decrease	39.3	20.6	22.2	23.8
Same, n.c.	35.9	58.8	51.8	50.5
Support Ratio	.43	.50	.52	.51
Mean Support Ratios for "Government Regulation of the Economy" Category	.59	.48	.58	.53

.20 on this issue is among the lowest in the entire set of scores. The magnitude of these scores somewhat surprised us, for while opposition to agricultural subsidies is consistent with Republican dislike for state intervention, we had expected the leaders to conform more closely to the familiar image of the Republican as the more "rural" of the two parties.[17] It appears, however, that the party's connection with business is far more compelling than its association with agriculture. The Republican desire to reduce government expenditures and to promote independence from "government handouts" prevails on the farm question as it does on other issues, while the Democratic preference for a more regulated economy in which government intervenes to reduce economic risk and to stabilize prosperity is equally evident on the other side. Party attitudes on this issue appear to be determined as much by ideological tendencies as by deliberate calculation of the political advantages to be gained by favoring or opposing subsidies to farmers. Comparison of our findings with Turner's earlier data on farm votes in Congress[18] suggests, in addition, that the sharp party difference on the farm issue is neither a recent development nor a mere product of the personal philosophy of the present Secretary of Agriculture [Ezra Taft Benson].

Having implied that agricultural policies partly result from principle, we must note that on three other issues in this category (trade unions, credit, and tariffs), principle seems to be overweighed by old-fashioned economic considerations. In spite of their distaste for government interference in economic affairs, the Republicans almost unanimously favor greater regulation of trade unions and they are more strongly disposed than the Democrats toward government intervention to restrict credit and to raise tariffs. Of course, party cleavages over the credit and tariff issues have a long history,[19] which may by now have endowed them with ideological force beyond immediate economic considerations.[20] The preponderant Democratic preference for greater regulation of trade unions is doubtless a response to recent "exposures" of corrupt labor practices, though it may also signify that the party's perspective toward the trade unions is shifting somewhat.

The closer Republican identification with business, free enterprise, and economic conservatism in general, and the friendlier Democratic attitude toward labor and toward government regulation of the econ-

[17]The friendlier attitude toward farmers among Democratic leaders than Republican leaders is borne out in the responses to several other questions used in the study. For example, the Republican leaders list farmers as having "too much power" far more frequently than do the Democratic leaders. Equally, the Democrats are significantly more inclined to regard farmers as having "too little power."
[18]Turner, *op. cit.*, p. 64.
[19]See John B. Johnson, Jr., *The Extent and Consistency of Party Voting in the United States Senate*, Ph.D. thesis, University of Chicago, 1943. By applying the Rice Index-of-Likeness to Senate votes, Johnson finds the tariff to have been the most partisan issue before the Congress in the years 1880–1940.
[20]Corinne Silverman, "The Legislator's View of the Legislative Process," *Public Opinion Quarterly*, Vol. 18 (1954–1955), p. 180.

omy, are easily observed in the data from other parts of our question-naire. Republican leaders score very much higher than Democratic leaders on, for example, such scales as economic conservatism, inde-pendence of government, and business attitudes. On a question asking

Table 2-C

COMPARISON OF PARTY LEADERS AND FOLLOWERS
ON "EQUALITARIAN AND HUMAN WELFARE" ISSUES,
BY PERCENTAGES AND RATIOS OF SUPPORT

Issues	Leaders		Followers	
	Dem. $N = 1,788$	*Repub.* $N = 1,232$	*Dem.* $N = 821$	*Repub.* $N = 623$
	(%s down)			
Federal Aid to Education				
% favoring: Increase	66.2	22.3	74.9	64.8
Decrease	13.4	43.2	5.6	8.3
Same, n.c.	20.4	34.5	19.5	26.8
Support Ratio	.76	.40	.85	.78
Slum Clearance and Public Housing				
% favoring: Increase	78.4	40.1	79.5	72.5
Decrease	5.6	21.6	5.8	7.9
Same, n.c.	16.0	38.3	14.6	19.6
Support Ratio	.86	.59	.87	.82
Social Security Benefits				
% favoring: Increase	60.0	22.5	69.4	57.0
Decrease	3.9	13.1	3.0	3.8
Same, n.c.	36.1	64.4	27.5	39.2
Support Ratio	.78	.55	.83	.77
Minimum Wages				
% favoring: Increase	50.0	15.5	59.0	43.5
Decrease	4.7	12.5	2.9	5.0
Same, n.c.	45.2	72.0	38.1	51.5
Support Ratio	.73	.52	.78	.69
Enforcement of Integration				
% favoring: Increase	43.8	25.5	41.9	40.8
Decrease	26.6	31.7	27.4	23.6
Same, n.c.	29.5	42.8	30.7	35.6
Support Ratio	.59	.47	.57	.59
Immigration into United States				
% favoring: Increase	36.1	18.4	10.4	8.0
Decrease	27.0	29.9	52.0	44.6
Same, n.c.	36.9	51.7	37.6	47.4
Support Ratio	.54	.44	.29	.32
Mean Support Ratios for "Equalitarian and Human Welfare" Category	.71	.50	.70	.66

respondents to indicate the groups from which they would be most and least likely to take advice, 41 per cent of the Democratic leaders but only 3.8 per cent of the Republican leaders list trade unions as groups from which they would seek advice. Trade unions are scored in the "least likely" category by 25 per cent of the Democrats and 63 per cent of the Republicans. Similarly, more than 94 per cent of the Republican leaders, but 56 per cent of the Democratic leaders, name trade unions as groups that have "too much power." These differences, it should be noted, cannot be accounted for by reference to the greater number of trade union members among the Democratic party leadership, for in the 1956 conventions only 14 per cent of the Democrats belonged to trade unions, and while an even smaller percentage (4 per cent) of the Republicans were trade unionists, this disparity is hardly great enough to explain the large differences in outlook. The key to the explanation has to be sought in the symbolic and reference group identifications of the two parties, and in their underlying values.

Nowhere do we see this more clearly than in the responses to the Equalitarian and Human Welfare issues. The mean difference in the ratio scores for the category as a whole is .22, a very large difference and one that results from differences in the expected direction on all six issues that make up the category. On four of these issues—federal aid to education, slum clearance and public housing, social security, and minimum wages—the leaders of the two parties are widely separated, the differences in their ratio scores ranging from .36 to .21. The percentages showing the proportions who favor increased support for these issues are even more striking. In every instance the Democratic percentages are considerably higher: 66 vs. 22 per cent (education); 78 vs. 40 per cent (slum clearance and housing); 60 vs. 23 per cent (social security); and 50 vs. 16 per cent (minimum wages). The Democratic leaders also are better disposed than the Republican leaders toward immigration: twice as many of them (36 per cent vs. 18 per cent) favor a change in policy to permit more immigrants to enter. The overall inclination of both party élites, however, is to accept the present levels of immigration, the Democratic ratio score falling slightly above, and the Republican slightly below, the midpoint.

More surprising are the differences on the segregation issue, for, despite strong southern influence, the Democratic leaders express significantly more support for enforcing integration than the Republicans do. Moreover, the difference between the two parties rises from .12 for the national samples as a whole to a difference of .18 when the southern leaders are excluded. In his study of Congress, Turner found that the Republicans gave more support to Negro rights than the Democrats did.[21] The reversal of this finding in our data does not

[21]Turner, *op. cit.*, p. 54.

necessarily mean that a change has occurred since Turner made his study, but only that the votes of the congressional parties do not always reflect the private feelings of the national party leadership. Then, too, southern influence is disproportionately stronger in the Democratic congressional party than in the national Democratic organization as a whole, and disproportionately weaker in the Republican congressional party than in the Republican organization as a whole.

Examination of the actual magnitude of the ratio scores in this category reveals that the Republicans want not so much to abrogate existing social welfare or equalitarian measures as to keep them from being broadened. The Democrats, by comparison, are shown to be the party of social equality and reform, more willing than their opponents to employ legislation for the benefit of the underprivileged. Support for these inferences and for the greater liberalism of the Democrats can be found elsewhere in our data as well. Analysis of the scale results show Republican leaders scoring higher than Democratic leaders on such measures as chauvinism, élitism, conservatism, and right-wing values, and lower on tolerance, procedural rights, and faith in democracy. No differences worth noting, however, were found for ethnocentrism, faith in freedom, or the California F scale. The Democrats had a slightly higher average score on the left-wing scale, but the number of leaders in either party who scored high on this measure was fairly small.

The self-images and reference group identifications of the two parties also should be noted in this connection. For example, many more Democratic than Republican leaders call themselves liberal and state that they would be most likely to take advice from liberal reform organizations, the Farmers' Union, and (as we have seen) from the trade unions; only a small number consider themselves conservative or would seek advice from conservative reform organizations, the National Association of Manufacturers, or the Farm Bureau Federation. The Republicans have in almost all instances the reverse identifications: only a handful regard themselves as liberal or would seek counsel from liberal organizations, while more than 42 per cent call themselves conservative and would look to the NAM or to conservative reform organizations for advice. Almost two-thirds of the Republicans (compared with 29 per cent of the Democrats) regard the Chamber of Commerce as an important source of advice. Businessmen are listed as having "too much power" by 42 per cent of the Democrats but by only 9 per cent of the Republicans. The Democrats are also significantly more inclined than the Republicans to consider Catholics, Jews, and the foreign born as having "too little power." While self-descriptions and reference group identifications often correspond poorly with actual beliefs—among the general population they scarcely correspond at all, in fact—we are dealing, in the case of the leaders, with a politically

Table 2-D

COMPARISON OF PARTY LEADERS AND FOLLOWERS ON "TAX POLICY"
ISSUES, BY PERCENTAGES AND RATIOS OF SUPPORT

Issues	Leaders		Followers	
	Dem. N = 1,788	Repub. N = 1,232	Dem. N = 821	Repub. N = 623
		(%s down)		
Corporate Income Tax				
% favoring: Increase	32.3	4.0	32.0	23.3
Decrease	23.3	61.5	20.5	25.7
Same, n.c.	44.4	34.5	47.5	51.0
Support Ratio	.54	.21	.56	.49
Tax on Large Incomes				
% favoring: Increase	27.0	5.4	46.6	34.7
Decrease	23.1	56.9	13.8	21.7
Same, n.c.	49.9	37.7	39.6	43.6
Support Ratio	.52	.24	.66	.56
Tax on Business				
% favoring: Increase	12.6	1.0	24.6	15.9
Decrease	38.3	71.1	24.1	32.6
Same, n.c.	49.1	27.8	51.3	51.5
Support Ratio	.37	.15	.50	.42
Tax on Middle Incomes				
% favoring: Increase	2.7	0.8	4.5	3.0
Decrease	50.2	63.9	49.3	44.3
Same, n.c.	47.1	35.3	46.2	52.6
Support Ratio	.26	.18	.28	.29
Tax on Small Incomes				
% favoring: Increase	1.4	2.9	1.6	2.1
Decrease	79.2	65.0	77.5	69.6
Same, n.c.	19.4	32.1	20.9	28.3
Support Ratio	.11	.19	.12	.16
Mean Support Ratios for "Tax Policy" Category	.36	.19	.42	.38

informed and highly articulate set of people who have little difficulty
connecting the beliefs they hold and the groups that promote or obstruct those beliefs.

Our fourth category, Tax Policy, divides the parties almost as
severely as do the other categories. The mean difference for the category as a whole is .20, and it would doubtless have been larger but for
the universal unpopularity of proposals to increase taxes on small
and middle income groups. Table 2-d shows that the differences between the parties on the tax issues follow the patterns' previously
observed and that tax policy is for the Democrats a device for redis-

tributing income and promoting social equality. Neither party, however, is keen about raising taxes for *any* group: even the Democrats have little enthusiasm for new taxes on upper income groups or on business and corporate enterprises. The Republican leaders are overwhelmingly opposed to increased taxes for *any* group, rich *or* poor. This can be seen in their low ratio scores on the tax issues, which range from only .15 to .24. But while they are far more eager than the Democratic leaders to cut taxes on corporate and private wealth, they are less willing to reduce taxes on the lower income groups. These differences, it

Table 2-E

COMPARISON OF PARTY LEADERS AND FOLLOWERS ON "FOREIGN POLICY" ISSUES, BY PERCENTAGES AND RATIOS OF SUPPORT

Issues	Leaders		Followers	
	Dem. N = 1,788	*Repub.* N = 1,232 (*%s down*)	*Dem.* N = 821	*Repub.* N = 623
Reliance on the United Nations				
% favoring: Increase	48.9	24.4	34.7	33.4
Decrease	17.6	34.8	17.3	19.3
Same, n.c.	33.5	40.7	48.0	47.3
Support Ratio	.66	.45	.59	.57
American Participation in Military Alliances				
% favoring: Increase	41.5	22.7	39.1	32.3
Decrease	17.6	25.7	14.0	15.4
Same, n.c.	40.9	51.6	46.9	52.3
Support Ratio	.62	.48	.62	.58
Foreign Aid				
% favoring: Increase	17.8	7.6	10.1	10.1
Decrease	51.0	61.7	58.6	57.3
Same, n.c.	31.1	30.7	31.3	32.6
Support Ratio	.33	.23	.26	.26
Defense Spending*				
% favoring: Increase	20.7	13.6	50.5	45.7
Decrease	34.4	33.6	16.4	15.4
Same, n.c.	44.8	52.8	33.0	38.8
Support Ratio	.43	.40	.67	.65
Mean Support Ratios for "Foreign Policy" Category (excl. Defense Spending)	.54	.39	.49	.47

*See footnote 23.

should be remarked, are not primarily a function of differences in the income of the two samples. Although there are more people with high incomes among the Republican leaders, the disproportion between the two samples is not nearly great enough to account for the dissimilarities in their tax views.

Of the five categories considered, Foreign Policy shows the smallest average difference, but even on these issues the divergence between Democratic and Republican leader attitudes is significant. Except for defense spending the Democrats turn out to be more internationalist than the Republicans, as evidenced in their greater commitment to the United Nations and to American participation in international military alliances like NATO. Twice as many Democrats as Republicans want the United States to rely more heavily upon such organizations, while many more Republicans want to reduce our international involvements. Both parties are predominantly in favor of cutting back foreign aid — a somewhat surprising finding in light of Democratic public pronouncements on this subject — but more Republicans feel strongly on the subject. Our data thus furnish little support for the claim that the parties hold the same views on foreign policy or that their seeming differences are merely a response to the demands of political competition.[22]

Nevertheless, it would be incorrect to conclude that one party believes in internationalism and the other in isolationism. The differences are far too small to warrant any such inference. Traces of isolationism, to be sure, remain stronger in the Republican party than in the Democratic party — an observation buttressed by the finding that twice as many Republicans as Democrats score high on the isolationism scale. The pattern of Republican responses on both the issue and scale items signifies, however, that the leaders of that party generally accept the degree of "internationalism" now in effect, but shrink from extending it further. Consider too, the similarities in the leaders' scores on defense spending, for despite their greater leaning toward isolationism, the Republicans are no more inclined than the Democrats to leave the country defenseless.[23]

[22]*Cf.* Turner, *op. cit.*, p. 56, in which he found differences on foreign policy difficult to assess in Congress, partly because of its tie with the executive branch; see also, George Belknap and Angus Campbell, "Political Party Identification and Attitudes Toward Foreign Policy," *Public Opinion Quarterly*, Vol. 15 (Winter, 1951–1952), pp. 608–619.

[23]The issue of defense spending has been kept separate from the other foreign policy issues because the magnitude of the scores for some of the leaders and all of the followers were obviously inflated by the launching of Sputnik I in November, 1957. The Sputnik incident occurred between the first and second wave of the leader survey and produced an increase in the number favoring defense spending of 40 per cent for the Democrats and 33 per cent for the Republicans. While this is a fascinating testimonial to the influence sometimes exercised by events on public opinion, its effect in this case was to distort scores in such a way as to make the leader and follower samples non-comparable. With proper caution, however, comparisons can be made between the Democratic and Republican leaders since both samples were affected in roughly the same way by Sputnik. For a similar reason we can also compare the Democratic followers with the Republican followers. Comparisons between leaders and followers on this issue cannot, however, be justified from our data.

Table 3

RANK ORDER OF DIFFERENCES IN THE SUPPORT-RATIO SCORES
OF PARTY LEADERS AND FOLLOWERS*

Democratic vs. *Republican* *Leaders*	*Diff. between ratio scores****	*Democratic* vs. *Republican* *Followers*	*Diff. between ratio scores*
Issues		*Issues*	
1. Natural Resources	+.39	Farm Supports	+.14
2. Farm Supports	+.38	Gov't. Reg. of Business	+.12
3. Fed. Aid. to Edu.	+.37	Taxes-Large Income	+.10
4. Taxes-Corp.	+.33	Minimum Wages	+.09
5. Reg.-Business	+.33	Taxes-Business	+.09
6. Taxes-Large Inc.	+.28	Reg. Pub. Util.	+.07
7. Pub. Housing	+.27	Taxes-Corp.	+.07
8. Reg. Pub. Util.	+.26	Social Security	+.07
9. Social Security	+.23	Fed. Aid to Edu.	+.06
10. Taxes-Business	+.22	Reg. Trade Unions	−.05
11. Minimum Wages	+.21	Natural Resources	+.05
12. Reliance on U.N.	+.21	Public Housing	+.05
13. Anti-Monopoly	+.20	Taxes-Small Income	−.04
14. Atomic Energy Control	+.18	American Participation, NATO	+.04
15. Reg. Trade Unions	−.18	Atomic Energy Control	+.04
16. American Participation, NATO	+.13	Immigration	−.03
17. Enforce Integration	+.12	Defense Spending	+.02
18. Tariffs	−.11	Taxes-Middle Income	−.02
19. Foreign Aid	+.10	Reliance on U.N.	+.02
20. Increase Immigration	+.10	Tariffs	−.01
21. Taxes-Small Income	−.08	Enforce Integration	−.01
22. Taxes-Middle Income	+.08	Restriction Credit	+.01
23. Restriction Credit	−.07	Foreign Aid	−.01
24. Defense Spending	+.03	Anti-Monopoly	.00

In treating issues in the Elmira election study of 1948, Berelson, Lazarsfeld, and McPhee[24] found it helpful to distinguish between "style" and "position" issues. "Style" issues principally yield symbolic, psychological, or subjective gratifications, and have relatively intangible consequences; "position" issues reflect direct, personal and material interests, and have more objective consequences. According to the Elmira report, "position" issues (or what politicians might call "bread and butter" issues) divide voters more sharply than style issues. Most

[24]Bernard R. Berelson, Paul F. Lazarsfeld, and William N. McPhee, *Voting* (Chicago, 1954), ch. 9.

N's. Democratic Leaders: 1,788; Republican Leaders: 1,232; Democratic Followers: 821; Republican Followers: 623.
*The plus sign means that the first group listed in the heading is more favorable to the issue named than the second group; the minus sign means that the second group is the more favorable.
***Leaders and Followers cannot be compared on defense spending, for reasons given in footnote to Table 2-E.

Democratic Leaders vs. Followers	Diff. between ratio scores	Republican Leaders vs. Followers	Diff. between ratio scores
Issues		*Issues*	
Immigration	+.25	Fed. Aid to Edu.	−.39
Anti-Monopoly	+.15	Taxes-Large Income	−.32
Taxes-Large Income	−.15	Taxes-Corp.	−.28
Taxes-Business	−.13	Taxes-Business	−.27
Reg. Pub. Util.	+.12	Natural Resources	−.25
Tariffs	−.11	Pub. Housing	−.23
Restrict. Credit	−.09	Reg. Business	−.22
Natural Resources	+.09	Social Security	−.22
Fed. Aid to Edu.	−.08	Farm Supports	−.22
Foreign Aid	+.08	Minimum Wages	−.18
Reliance on U.N.	+.07	Reg. Trade Unions	+.17
Minimum Wages	−.05	Immigration	+.13
Social Security	−.05	Reliance on U.N.	−.12
Reg. Trade Unions	+.05	Enforce Integration	−.12
Atomic Energy Control	+.04	Taxes-Middle Income	−.11
Farm Supports	+.02	Atomic Energy Control	−.10
Reg. Business	−.02	American Participation, NATO	−.10
Enforce Integration	+.01	Reg. Public Utilities	−.07
Taxes-Middle Income	−.01	Anti-Monopoly	−.04
Taxes-Corporation	−.01	Foreign Aid	−.03
Taxes-Small Income	−.01	Taxes-Small Income	+.03
American Participation, NATO	−.01	Restriction Credit	−.01
Public Housing	.00	Tariffs	−.01
Defense Spending	**	Defense Spending	**

of the issues tested in the present study would have to be classified as
"position" issues, but five of them—United Nations, international alliances, foreign aid, immigration, and segregation—could be classified
as style issues. Four others—natural resources, atomic energy, education, and slum clearance—contain both symbolic and material elements
and can best be described as "mixed."

Although the classification is crude, the findings it yields are
generally consistent with the claims of the Elmira study. On the fourteen position issues—taxes, trade unions, tariffs, minimum wages, farm
prices, social security, credit restrictions, and the regulation of business, public utilities and monopolies—Democratic and Republican
leaders show an average ratio score difference of .21. On the style
issues the two parties differ by .13—a significantly smaller difference.

**Size of difference required for differences to be significant at .01 level: Democratic Leaders vs.
Republican—.048; Democratic Followers vs. Republican Followers—.068; Democratic Leaders vs. Democratic Followers—.054; Republican Leaders vs. Republican Followers—.063.

Largest of all, however, are the differences for the "mixed" issues, which average more than .30. This result should occasion little surprise, for when ideology and interest are *both* at work, partisanship is likely to be intensified. Several considerations could account for the superiority of position over style issues as causes of political cleavage: they are "bread and butter" issues, and are thus more often subject to pressure by organized interest groups; they have immediate and tangible consequences, which may lead politicians to pay greater attention to them than they do to issues whose payoff is more uncertain; and, finally, they are not so likely to be part of the common core of values upon which the community structure rests.

Comparison of the magnitude of the differences between groups can be seen in Table 3, where we have ranked the issues, high to low, according to the size of the difference between the groups being compared. By presenting a rank-order of differences for the two leader groups, for the two follower groups, and for the leaders and followers of each party, this table makes it possible to observe not only which issues most and least divide the several party groups, but whether they divide the leaders and followers in the same way.

Notice that the issues commonly thought to be most divisive do not always evoke the greatest cleavage between the parties. Immigration, tariffs, civil rights, monopoly control, and credit regulation fall toward the lower end of the rank order, while farm supports, federal aid to education, slum clearance, social security, minimum wages, public housing, and issues dealing with the regulation and taxation of business fall toward the upper end. Though by no means uniformly, the older, more traditional issues appear to have been superseded as sources of controversy by issues that have come into prominence chiefly during the New Deal and Fair Deal.

Comparisons Between Followers

So far we have addressed ourselves to the differences between Democratic and Republican *leaders*. In each of the tables presented, however, data are included from which the two sets of party *followers* may also be compared.

The observation most clearly warranted from these data is that the rank and file members of the two parties are far less divided than their leaders. Not only do they diverge significantly on fewer issues—seven as compared with 23 for the leader samples—but the magnitudes of the differences in their ratio scores are substantially smaller for every one of the 24 issues. No difference is larger than .14, and on the majority of the issues the disparity is smaller than .05. Insofar as they differ at all, however, the followers tend to divide in a pattern similar to that shown by the leaders, the correlation between their rank orders being .72. All the issues on which the followers significantly disagree are of the "bread and butter" variety, the more symbolic issues being so remotely experienced and so vaguely grasped that rank and file voters are often unable to identify them with either party. Policies affecting farm prices, business regulation, taxes, or minimum wages, by contrast, are quickly felt by the groups to whom they are addressed and are therefore more capable of arousing partisan identifications. It should also be noted that while the average differences are small for all five categories, they are smallest of all for foreign policy—the most removed and least well understood group of issues in the entire array.[25]

Democratic and Republican followers were also compared on a number of scales and reference group questions. The results, while generally consistent with the differences between the leaders, show the followers to be far more united than their leaders on these measures as well. Even on business attitudes, independence of government, and economic conservatism, the differences are small and barely significant. No differences were found on such scales as tolerance, faith in democracy, procedural rights, conservatism-liberalism (classical), the California F scale and isolationism. The average Democrat is slightly more willing than the average Republican to label himself a liberal or to seek advice from liberal organizations; the contrary is true when it comes to adopting conservative identifications. Only in the differential trust they express toward business and labor are the two sets of followers widely separated.

These findings give little support to the claim that the "natural divisions" of the electorate are being smothered by party leaders.[26] Not only do the leaders disagree more sharply than their respective followers, but the level of consensus among the electorate (with or without regard to party) is fairly high. Inspection of the "increase" and "decrease" percentage scores (Tables 2-a-e) shows that substantial differences of opinion exist among the electorate on only five of the 24 issues (credit restrictions, farm supports, segregation, and corporate and business taxes). Of course, voters may divide more sharply on issues at election time, since campaigns intensify party feeling and may also

---

[25]For comparative data on party affiliation and issue outlooks among rank and file voters, see Angus Campbell, Phillip E. Converse, Warren E. Miller, and Donald E. Stokes, *The American Voter* (in press), especially chs. 8 and 9 dealing with issues and ideology. The text of this important report on the 1956 election study carried out by the Michigan Survey Research Center unfortunately reached us too late to be used to full advantage in the present analysis. The findings of the Michigan and the PAB studies, relative to the role of issues and ideology among the general population, corroborate and supplement each other to a very great degree.

[26]Cf. Stephen K. Bailey, *The Condition of Our National Parties* (monograph), Fund for the Republic, 1959.

intensify opinions on issues. Available data from election studies allow no unequivocal conclusion on this point,[27] but even the party-linked differences found among voters during elections may largely be echoes of the opinions announced by the candidates — transient sentiments developed for the occasion and quickly forgotten.

Leader Conflict and Follower Consensus: Explanations

Considering the nature of the differences between the leader and follower samples, the interesting question is not why the parties fail to represent the "natural division" in the electorate (for that question rests on an unwarranted assumption) but why the party élites disagree at all, and why they divide so much more sharply than their followers?

Despite the great pressures toward uniformity we have noted in American society, many forces also divide the population culturally, economically, and politically. The United States is, after all, a miscellany of ethnic and religious strains set down in a geographically large and diverse country. Many of these groups brought old conflicts and ideologies with them, and some have tried to act out in the new world the hopes and frustrations nurtured in the old. Then, too, despite rapid social mobility, social classes have by no means been eliminated. No special political insight is needed to perceive that the two parties characteristically draw from different strata of the society the Republicans from the managerial, proprietary, and to some extent professional classes, the Democrats from labor, minorities, low income groups, and a large proportion of the intellectuals.[28] Partly because the leaders of the two parties tend to overrespond to the modal values of the groups with which they are principally identified, they gradually grow further apart on the key questions which separate their respective supporters.[29] The Republican emphasis on business ideology is both a cause and a consequence of its managerial and proprietary support; the greater Democratic emphasis on social justice, and on economic and social levelling, is both the occasion and the product of the support the party enjoys among intellectuals and the lower strata. These inter-relationships are strengthened, moreover, by the tendency for a party's

[27]The data reported by the Elmira study of 1948 show the supporters of the two parties to be largely in agreement on issues. See Berelson, *et al.*, *Voting*, pp. 186, 190, 194, 211. The findings of the 1956 Michigan Survey suggest strongly that most voters, even at election time, do not know much about issues and are unable to link the parties with particular issues. Campbell and his associates conclude, for example, that "many people fail to appreciate that an issue exists; others are insufficiently involved to pay attention to recognized issues; and still others fail to make connections between issue positions and party policy." *The American Voter*, ch. 8.

[28]For an analysis of the connection between intellectuals and liberal politics, see Seymour M. Lipset, *Political Man* (New York, 1960), ch. 10; also Paul F. Lazarsfeld and Wagner Thielens, Jr., *The Academic Mind* (Glencoe, 1958), chs. 1 and 2.

[29]Samuel P. Huntington, "A Revised Theory of American Party Politics," *American Political Science Review*, Vol. 44 (1950), p. 676.

dominant supporters to gain a disproportionate number of positions in its leadership ranks.[30]

The differences which typically separate Democratic from Republican leaders seem also to reflect a deep-seated ideological cleavage often found among Western parties. One side of this cleavage is marked by a strong belief in the power of collective action to promote social justice, equality, humanitarianism, and economic planning, while preserving freedom; the other is distinguished by faith in the wisdom of the natural competitive process and in the supreme virtue of individualism, "character," self-reliance, frugality, and independence from government. To this cleavage is added another frequent source of political division, namely, a difference in attitude toward change between "radicals" and "moderates," between those who prefer to move quickly or slowly, to reform or to conserve. These differences in social philosophy and posture do not always coincide with the divisions in the social structure, and their elements do not, in all contexts, combine in the same way. But, however crudely, the American parties do tend to embody these competing points of view and to serve as reference groups for those who hold them.

Party cleavage in America was no doubt intensified by the advent of the New Deal, and by its immense electoral and intellectual success. Not only did it weld into a firm alliance the diverse forces that were to be crucial to all subsequent Democratic majorities, but it also made explicit the doctrines of the "welfare state" with which the party was henceforth to be inseparably identified. Because of the novelty of its program and its apparently radical threat to the familiar patterns of American political and economic life, it probably deepened the fervor of its Republican adversaries and drove into the opposition the staunchest defenders of business ideology. The conflict was further sharpened by the decline of left-wing politics after the war, and by the transfer of loyalties of former and potential radicals to the Democratic party. Once launched, the cleavage has been sustained by the tendency for each party to attract into its active ranks a disproportionate number of voters who recognize and share its point of view.

Why, however, are the leaders so much more sharply divided than their followers? The reasons are not hard to understand and are consistent with several of the hypotheses that underlay the present study.

(1) Consider, to begin with, that the leaders come from the more articulate segments of society and, on the average, are politically more aware than their followers and far better informed about issues.[31] For them, political issues and opinions are the everyday currency of party competition, not esoteric matters that surpass understanding. With

---

[30]PAB data supporting this generalization will be presented in a future publication.

[31]For the effects of education on issue familiarity, see Campbell *et al., The American Voter*, ch. 8.

their greater awareness and responsibility, and their greater need to defend their party's stands, they have more interest in developing a consistent set of attitudes—perhaps even an ideology. The followers of each party, often ignorant of the issues and their consequences, find it difficult to distinguish their beliefs from those of the opposition and have little reason to be concerned with the consistency of their attitudes. Furthermore, the American parties make only a feeble effort to educate the rank and file politically, and since no central source exists for the authoritative pronouncement of party policy,[32] the followers often do not know what their leaders believe or on what issues the parties chiefly divide. In short, if we mean by ideology a coherent body of informed social doctrine, it is possessed mainly by the articulate leadership, rarely by the masses.

(2) Differences in the degree of partisan involvement parallel the differences in knowledge and have similar consequences. The leaders, of course, have more party spirit than the followers and, as the election studies make plain, the stronger the partisanship, the larger the differences on issues. The leaders are more highly motivated not only to belong to a party appropriate to their beliefs, but to accept its doctrines and to learn how it differs from the opposition party. Since politics is more salient for leaders than for followers, they develop a greater stake in the outcome of the political contest and are more eager to discover the intellectual grounds by which they hope to make victory possible. Through a process of circular reinforcement, those for whom politics is most important are likely to become the most zealous participants, succeeding to the posts that deal in the formation of opinion. Ideology serves the instrumental purpose, in addition, of justifying the heavy investment that party leaders make in political activity. While politics offers many rewards, it also makes great demands on the time, money, and energies of its practitioners—sacrifices which they can more easily justify if they believe they are serving worthwhile social goals. The followers, in contrast, are intellectually far less involved, have less personal stake in the outcome of the competition, have little need to be concerned with the "correctness" of their views on public questions, and have even less reason to learn in precisely what ways their opinions differ from their opponents'. Hence, the party élites recruit members from a population stratified in some measure by ideology, while the rank and file renews itself by more random recruitment and is thus more likely to mirror the opinions of a cross section of the population.

(3) Part of the explanation for the greater consensus among followers than leaders resides in the nature and size of the two types of groups. Whereas the leader groups are comparatively small and selec-

---

[32]E. E. Schattschneider, *op. cit.*; *Toward A More Responsible Two-Party System, passim.*

tive, each of the follower groups number in the millions and, by their very size and unwieldiness, are predisposed to duplicate the characteristics of the population as a whole. Even if the Republicans draw disproportionately from the business-managerial classes and the Democrats from the trade union movement, neither interest group has enough influence to shape distinctively the aggregate opinions of so large a mass of supporters. Size also affects the nature and frequency of interaction within the two types of groups. Because they comprise a smaller, more selectively chosen, organized, and articulate élite, the leaders are apt to associate with people of their own political persuasion more frequently and consistently than the followers do. They are not only less cross-pressured than the rank and file but they are also subjected to strong party group efforts to induce them to conform. Because their political values are continually renewed through frequent communication with people of like opinions, and because they acquire intense reference group identifications, they develop an extraordinary ability to resist the force of the opposition's arguments. While the followers, too, are thrown together and shielded to some extent, they are likely to mingle more freely with people of hostile political persuasions, to receive fewer partisan communications, and to hold views that are only intermittently and inconsistently reinforced. Since, by comparison with the leaders, they possess little interest in or information about politics, they can more easily embrace "deviant" attitudes without discomfort and without challenge from their associates. Nor are they likely to be strongly rewarded for troubling to have "correct" opinions. The followers, in short, are less often and less effectively indoctrinated than their leaders. The group processes described here would function even more powerfully in small, sectarian, tightly organized parties of the European type, but they are also present in the American party system, where they yield similar though less potent consequences.

(4) Political competition itself operates to divide the leaders more than the followers. If the parties are impelled to present a common face to the electorate, they are also strongly influenced to distinguish themselves from each other.[33] For one thing, they have a more heightened sense of the "national interest" than the followers do, even if they do not all conceive it in the same way. For another, they hope to improve their chances at the polls by offering the electorate a recognizable and attractive commodity. In addition, they seek emotional gratification in the heightened sense of brotherhood brought on by the struggle against an "outgroup" whose claim to office seems always, somehow, to border upon usurpation. As with many ingroup-outgroup distinctions, the participants search for moral grounds to justify their

[33]See E. E. Schattschneider, *Party Government*, p. 192.

antagonisms toward each other, and ideologies help to furnish such grounds. Among the followers, on the other hand, these needs exist, if at all, in much weaker form.

Leaders Versus Followers

In comparing each party élite with its own followers we were mainly interested in seeing how closely each body of supporters shared the point of view of its leaders, in order to test the hypothesis that party affiliation, even for the rank and file, is a function of ideological agreement. In predicting that the parties would tend to attract supporters who share their beliefs, we expected, of course, to find exceptions. We knew that many voters pay little attention to the ideological aspects of politics and that, in Gabriel Almond's phrase, a party's more "esoteric doctrines" are not always known to its followers.[34] Nevertheless we were not prepared for the findings turned up by this phase of the inquiry, for the differences between leaders and followers—among the Republicans at least—are beyond anything we had expected. Indeed, the conclusion is inescapable that the views of the Republican rank and file are, on the whole, much closer to those of the Democratic leaders than to those of the Republican leaders. Although conflicts in outlook also exist between Democratic leaders and followers, they are less frequent or severe.

If we turn once again to the table of rank order differences, we see that the Democratic followers differ significantly from their leaders on twelve of the 23 issues, and that the average difference in the ratio scores of the two samples is .07. Democratic leaders and Republican followers differ significantly on only eleven of the 23 issues, with an average difference between them of only .08. Notice, by contrast, that Republican leaders and followers diverge significantly on 18 of the 23 issues, and show an average difference of .16. To complete the comparison, the Republican leaders and Democratic followers were in disagreement on 19 of the 23 issues, their average difference being .20. As these comparisons make plain, there is substantial consensus on national issues between Democratic leaders and Democratic and Republican followers, while the Republican leaders are separated not only from the Democrats but from their own rank and file members as well.

Examination of the Democratic scores shows the leaders to be slightly more "progressive" than their followers on most of the issues on which differences appear. The leaders are, for example, more favorable to public ownership of natural resources, to regulation of monopolies and public utilities, to a reduction of tariffs, and to a liberalized

---

[34]Gabriel Almond, *The Appeals of Communism* (Princeton, 1954), pp. 5–6, and ch. 3.

credit policy. They are more internationalist on the foreign aid and United Nations issues and substantially more sympathetic to the maintenance and expansion of immigration. The results showing the relative radicalism of the two samples are not unequivocal, however, for on several issues—federal aid to education, minimum wages, and taxes on business enterprise and large incomes—the followers take the more radical view. Nor are the differences significant on such issues as atomic energy, slum clearance, segregation, farm price supports, government control of business and trade unions, and taxes on middle and small income groups. In general, the followers turn out more radical chiefly on a few of the bread and butter issues—a reflection, no doubt, of their lower socio-economic status. When we control for occupation, the differences between Democratic leaders and followers on these issues largely disappear.

Consideration of the scores of Republican leaders and followers shows not only that they are widely separated in their outlooks but also that the leaders are uniformly more conservative than their followers. Only on the immigration issue is this trend reversed. The followers hold the more "radical" ideas on the two public ownership issues, on five of the six equalitarian and human welfare issues, on four of the seven regulation-of-the-economy issues, and on four of the five tax policy issues. They are also more willing to place greater reliance upon the U.N. and upon international military alliances. Observe that the largest differences occur on those issues which have most sharply separated New Deal-Fair Deal spokesmen from the hard core of the Republican opposition—federal aid to education, redistribution of wealth through taxes on business, corporations and the wealthy, public ownership of natural resources, public housing, regulation of business, social security, farm price supports, minimum wages, and trade union regulations.

In short, whereas Republican leaders hold to the tenets of business ideology and remain faithful to the spirit and intellectual mood of leaders like Robert A. Taft, the rank and file Republican supporters have embraced, along with their Democratic brethren, the regulatory and social reform measures of the Roosevelt and Truman administrations. This inference receives further support from the scores on our Party Ideology scale where, on a variety of attitudes and values which characteristically distinguish the leaders of the two parties, the Republican followers fall closer to the Democratic than to the Republican side of the continuum. Thus, in addition to being the preferred party of the more numerous classes, the Democrats also enjoy the advantage over their opponents of holding views that are more widely shared throughout the country.

Assuming the findings are valid, we were obviously wrong to expect that party differentiation among followers would depend heavily upon ideological considerations.[35] Evidently, party attachment is so much a function of other factors (e.g., class and primary group memberships, religious affiliation, place of residence, mass media, etc.) that many voters can maintain their party loyalties comfortably even while holding views that contradict the beliefs of their own leaders.

Still, we are not entitled to conclude that issue outlook has no effect on the party affiliation of ordinary members. It is conceivable, for example, that the Republican party has come to be the minority party partly because the opinions of its spokesmen are uncongenial to a majority of the voters. We have no way of knowing from our data — collected at only a single point in time — how many "normally" Republican voters, if any, have defected to the Democrats or fled into independency because they disapprove of Republican beliefs. At the present stage of the analysis, we have no grounds for going beyond the proposition that political affiliation without conformity on issues is possible on a wide scale. In future analyses we shall attempt to learn more about the nature of the relationship between belief and party affiliation by stratifying voters according to the frequency with which they conform to the beliefs of their party leaders. We hope, in this way, to discover whether those who conform least are also less firm in their party loyalties.

The Homogeneity of Support for Leaders and Followers

So far we have only considered conflict and agreement *between* groups. We should now turn to the question of consensus *within* groups. To what extent is each of our samples united on fundamental issues?

In order to assess homogeneity of opinion within party groups, standard deviation scores were computed on each issue for each of the four samples. The higher the standard deviation, of course, the greater the disagreement. The range of possible sigma scores is from 0 (signifying that every member of the sample has selected the same response) to .500 (signifying that all responses are equally divided between the "increase" and "decrease" alternatives). If we assume that the three alternative responses had been randomly (and therefore equally) selected, the standard deviations for the four samples would fall by chance alone around .410. Scores at or above this level may be taken to denote extreme dispersion among the members of a sample while scores in the neighborhood of .300 or below suggest that unanimity within the sample is fairly high. By these somewhat arbitrary criteria we can observe immediately (Table 4) that consensus within groups is

---

[35]See the discussion bearing on this conclusion in Campbell *et al., op. cit.,* chs. 8 and 9. Also, Avery Leiserson, *Parties and Politics: An Institutional and Behavioral Approach* (New York, 1958), pp. 162–166.

Table 4

CONSENSUS WITHIN PARTY GROUPS: RANK ORDER OF HOMOGENEITY OF SUPPORT ON TWENTY-FOUR ISSUES

Average Rank Order*	Issue	Democratic Leaders		Republican Leaders		Democratic Followers		Republican Followers	
		Rank Order	Sigma	Rank Order	Sigma	Rank Order	Sigma	Rank Order	Sigma
1	Tax on Small Incomes	1	.220	6	.270	1	.224	1	.250
2	Tax on Middle Incomes	3	.276	4	.248	6	.292	2	.278
3	Social Security Benefits	5	.282	8	.296	2	.266	3	.286
4	Minimum Wages	6	.292	5	.268	4	.276	4	.294
5	Enforcement of Anti-Monopoly	2	.246	13	.321	8	.324	7	.314
6	Regulation of Public Utilities	8	.307	10	.300	10	.336	5.5	.310
7	Slum Clearance	4	.276	23	.386	3	.274	5.5	.310
8	Regulation of Trade Unions	12	.356	3	.240	9	.331	15	.345
9	Government Regulation of Business	17	.376	1	.192	20	.363	8	.315
10	Tax on Business	9	.338	2	.236	19	.362	16	.348
11	Level of Tariffs	10	.350	16	.344	11	.338	9	.316
12	Public Control of Atomic Energy	7	.302	20	.362	7	.312	13	.340
13	Federal Aid to Education	13	.360	24	.394	5	.283	11	.322
14	Foreign Aid	19	.383	12	.317	12.5	.340	12	.340
15	Tax on Large Incomes	11	.356	9	.298	17	.358	22	.379
16	American Participation in Military Alliances, NATO	14	.370	18	.351	14	.350	14	.344
17	Immigration into U.S.	21	.399	17	.345	12.5	.340	10	.318
18	Corporate Income Tax	16	.375	7	.284	21	.371	17	.361
19	Restrictions on Credit	22	.400	14	.324	16	.358	18	.362
20	Defense Spending	15	.371	15	.334	22	.380	21	.366
21	Public Ownership of Natural Resources	20	.393	19	.354	15	.352	19	.362
22	Reliance on U.N.	18	.380	22	.384	18	.359	20	.365
23	Level of Farm Supports	24	.421	11	.306	23	.414	23	.397
24	Enforce Integration	23	.416	21	.382	24	.418	24	.399

*The range of sigma scores is from .192 to .421, out of a possible range of .000 (most united) to .500 (least united). Hence, the lower the rank order the greater the unity on the issue named.

greater on most issues than we would expect by chance alone, but that it is extremely high in only a few instances. Although the Republican leaders appear on the average to be the most united and the Democratic leaders the least united of the four groups, the difference between their homogeneity scores (.340 vs. .310) is too small to be taken as conclusive. The grounds are somewhat better for rejecting the belief that leaders are more homogeneous in their outlooks than their followers, since the hypothesis holds only for one party and not for the other.

While generalizations about the relative unity of the four samples seem risky, we can speak more confidently about the rank order of agreement *within* samples. In Table 4 we have ranked the issues according to the degree of consensus exhibited toward them by the members of each of the four party groups. There we see that the leaders of the Republican party are most united on the issues that stem from its connections with business — government regulation of business, taxes (especially on business), regulation of trade unions, and minimum wages. The Democratic leaders are most united on those issues which bear upon the support the party receives from the lower and middle income groups — taxes on small and middle incomes, anti-monopoly, slum clearance, social security, and minimum wages. The Republican leaders divide most severely on federal aid to education, slum clearance, U.N. support, segregation, and public control of atomic energy and natural resources; the Democratic leaders are most divided on farm prices, segregation, credit restrictions, immigration, and the natural resources issue. Among the followers the patterns of unity and division are very similar, as attested by the high correlation of .83 between the rank orders of their homogeneity scores. Both Republican and Democratic followers exhibit great cohesion, for example, on taxes on small and middle incomes, social security, slum clearance, and minimum wages. Both divide rather sharply on segregation, farm price supports, defense spending, U.N. support, and taxes on large incomes. The two sets of followers, in short, are alike not only in their opinions on issues but in the degree of unanimity they exhibit toward them.

Inspection of the homogeneity data furnishes additional evidence on the between-group comparisons made earlier. Whereas Democratic and Republican followers divide on issues in approximately the same way, the two sets of leaders differ from each other in this respect also (the correlation between their rank orders on homogeneity is only .28). Democratic leaders and followers tend to unite or divide on the same issues for the most part (*r* equals .77), but Republican leaders and followers are not parallel in this respect either (*r* equals .30). The pattern of homogeneity and dispersion among Republican followers is, in fact, much closer to that of the Democratic leaders (*r* equals .75).

In computing scores for homogeneity we were in part concerned to test the belief that political parties develop greatest internal solidarity on those questions which most separate them from their opponents. According to this hypothesis, external controversy has the effect of uniting the members further by confronting them with a common danger. Whether or not this hypothesis would be borne out in a study of small, sectarian parties we cannot say, but it receives no support from the present study of the American mass parties. Comparisons of the rank order data in Tables 3 and 4 show that there is no consistent connection between interparty conflict and intra-party cohesion. The correlations between the rank orders of difference and the rank orders of homogeneity are in every case insignificant.[36]

Summary and Conclusions

The research described in this paper — an outgrowth of a nationwide inquiry into the nature and sources of political affiliation, activity, and belief — was principally designed to test a number of hypotheses about the relation of ideology to party membership. Responses from large samples of Democratic and Republican leaders and followers were compared on twenty-four key issues and on a number of attitude questions and scales. Statistical operations were carried out to assess conflict and consensus among party groups and to estimate the size and significance of differences. From the data yielded by this inquiry, the following inferences seem most warranted:

1. Although it has received wide currency, especially among Europeans, the belief that the two American parties are identical in principle and doctrine has little foundation in fact. Examination of the opinions of Democratic and Republican leaders shows them to be distinct communities of co-believers who diverge sharply on many important issues. Their disagreements, furthermore, conform to an image familiar to many observers and are generally consistent with differences turned up by studies of Congressional roll calls. The unpopularity of many of the positions held by Republican leaders suggests also that the parties submit to the demands of their constituents less slavishly than is commonly supposed.

2. Republican and Democratic leaders stand furthest apart on the issues that grow out of their group identification and support — out of the managerial, proprietary, and high-status connections of the one, and the labor, minority, low-status, and intellectual connections of the other. The opinions of each party élite are linked less by chance than by membership in a common ideological domain. Democratic leaders typically display the stronger urge to elevate the lowborn, the uneducated, the deprived minorities, and the poor in general; they are also

---

[36]For an interesting set of comparative data on the relation of internal party cohesion to issue outlook, see Morris Davis and Sidney Verba, "Party Affiliation and International Opinions in Britain and France, 1947–1956," *Public Opinion Quarterly*, Winter 1960–1961.

more disposed to employ the nation's collective power to advance humanitarian and social welfare goals (e.g., social security, immigration, racial integration, a higher minimum wage, and public education). They are more critical of wealth and big business and more eager to bring them under regulations. Theirs is the greater faith in the wisdom of using legislation for redistributing the national product and for furnishing social services on a wide scale. Of the two groups of leaders, the Democrats are the more "progressively" oriented toward social reform and experimentation. The Republican leaders, while not uniformly differentiated from their opponents, subscribe in greater measure to the symbols and practices of individualism, *laissez-faire*, and national independence. They prefer to overcome humanity's misfortunes by relying upon personal effort, private incentives, frugality, hard work, responsibility, self-denial (for both men and government), and the strengthening rather than the diminution of the economic and status distinctions that are the "natural" rewards of the differences in human character and fortunes. Were it not for the hackneyed nature of the designation and the danger of forcing traits into a mold they fit only imperfectly, we might be tempted to describe the Republicans as the chief upholders of what Max Weber has called the "Protestant Ethic."[37] Not that the Democrats are insensible to the "virtues" of the Protestant-capitalistic ethos, but they embrace them less firmly or uniformly. The differences between the two élites have probably been intensified by the rise of the New Deal and by the shift of former radicals into the Democratic party following the decline of socialist and other left-wing movements during and after the war.

3. Whereas the leaders of the two parties diverge strongly, their followers differ only moderately in their attitudes toward issues. The hypothesis that party beliefs unite adherents and bring them into the party ranks may hold for the more active members of a mass party but not for its rank and file supporters. Republican followers, in fact, disagree far more with their own leaders than with the leaders of the Democratic party. Little support was found for the belief that deep cleavages exist among the electorate but are ignored by the leaders. One might, indeed, more accurately assert the contrary, to wit: that the natural cleavages between the leaders are largely ignored by the voters. However, we cannot presently conclude that ideology exerts no influence over the habits of party support, for the followers do differ significantly and in the predicted directions on some issues. Furthermore, we do not know how many followers may previously have been led by doctrinal considerations to shift their party allegiances.

4. Except for their desire to ingratiate themselves with as many

---

[37]Max Weber, *Protestant Ethic and the Spirit of Capitalism* (London, 1948), ch. V.

voters as possible, the leaders of the two parties have more reason than their followers to hold sharply opposing views on the important political questions of the day. Compared with the great mass of supporters, they are articulate, informed, highly partisan, and involved; they comprise a smaller and more tightly knit group which is closer to the wellsprings of party opinion, more accessible for indoctrination, more easily rewarded or punished for conformity or deviation, and far more affected, politically and psychologically, by engagement in the party struggle for office. If the leaders of the two parties are not always candid about their disagreements, the reason may well be that they sense the great measure of consensus to be found among the electorate.

5. Finding that party leaders hold contrary beliefs does not prove that they *act* upon those beliefs or that the two parties are, in practice, governed by different outlooks. In a subsequent paper we shall consider these questions more directly by comparing platform and other official party pronouncements with the private opinions revealed in this study. Until further inquiries are conducted, however, it seems reasonable to assume that the views held privately by party leaders can never be entirely suppressed but are bound to crop out in hundreds of large and small ways—in campaign speeches, discussions at party meetings, private communications to friends and sympathizers, statements to the press by party officials and candidates, legislative debates, and public discussions on innumerable national, state, and local questions. If, in other words, the opinions of party leaders are as we have described them, there is every chance that they are expressed and acted upon to some extent. Whether this makes our parties "ideological" depends, of course, on how narrowly we define that term. Some may prefer to reserve that designation for parties that are more obviously preoccupied with doctrine, more intent upon the achievement of a systematic political program, and more willing to enforce a common set of beliefs upon their members and spokesmen.

6. The parties are internally united on some issues, divided on others. In general, Republican leaders achieve greatest homogeneity on issues that grow out of their party's identification with business, Democratic leaders on issues that reflect their connection with liberal and lower-income groups. We find no support for the hypothesis that the parties achieve greatest internal consensus on the issues which principally divide them from their opponents.

In a sequel to this paper we shall offer data on the demographic correlates of issue support, which show that most of the differences presented here exist independently of factors like education, occupation, age, religion, and sectionalism. Controlling for these influences furnishes much additional information and many new insights but does not upset our present conclusions in any important respect. Thus, the parties must be considered not merely as spokesmen for other interest groups but as reference groups in their own right, helping to formulate, to sustain, and to speak for a recognizable point of view.

---

11. Social Authority and Affluence

Neither formal constitutions nor established political institutions alone can sustain an open, free political system like that of the United States. The economic and social requisites of democratic systems are also an issue of major concern to statesmen and political scientists. In the first selection that follows, Seymour Lipset presents a new analysis of an old proposition: that the possibility of democracy in any country is related to the state of economic development. Next, Andrew Hacker contends that unquestioning acceptance of a small ruling social class was, for a century and a half, a basic requisite for liberal democracy in the United States.

Although the citizen's view of political leaders as benevolent is in itself no guarantee of democratic politics, critical and favorable views of political authority each play their roles in sustaining a political system. Fred Greenstein's empirical study, reported here, illustrates one method by which a political scientist seeks to explore this important aspect of political socialization.

SOME SOCIAL REQUISITES OF DEMOCRACY: ECONOMIC DEVELOPMENT AND POLITICAL LEGITIMACY

Seymour M. Lipset

The conditions associated with the existence and stability of democratic society have been a leading concern of political philosophy. In this paper the problem is attacked from a sociological and behavioral standpoint, by presenting a number of hypotheses concerning some social

From *The American Political Science Review*, 1959 (March), 53: 69, 73–85, 103.

requisites for democracy, and by discussing some of the data available to test these hypotheses. In its concern with conditions — values, social institutions, historical events — external to the political system itself which sustain different general types of political systems, the paper moves outside the generally recognized province of political sociology. This growing field has dealt largely with the internal analysis of organizations with political goals, or with the determinants of action *within* various political institutions, such as parties, government agencies, or the electoral process. It has in the main left to the political philosopher the larger concern with the relations of the total political system to society as a whole.

Introduction

. . . Comparative generalizations dealing with complex social systems must necessarily deal rather summarily with particular historical features of any one society within the scope of the investigation. In order to test these generalizations bearing on the differences between countries which rank high or low in possession of the attributes associated with democracy, it is necessary to establish some empirical measures of the type of political system. Individual deviations from a particular aspect of democracy are not too important, as long as the definitions unambiguously cover the great majority of nations which are located as democratic or undemocratic. The precise dividing line between "more democratic" and "less democratic" is also not a basic problem, since presumably democracy is *not* a quality of a social system which either does or does not exist, but is rather a complex of characteristics which may be ranked in many different ways. For this reason it was decided to divide the countries under consideration into two groups, rather than to attempt to rank them from highest to lowest. Ranking *individual* countries from the most to the least democratic is much more difficult than splitting the countries into two classes, "more" or "less" democratic, although even here borderline cases such as Mexico pose problems.

Efforts to classify all countries raise a number of problems. Most countries which lack an enduring tradition of political democracy lie in the traditionally underdeveloped sections of the world. It is possible that Max Weber was right when he suggested that modern democracy in its clearest forms can only occur under the unique conditions of capitalist industrialization.[1] Some of the complications introduced by the sharp variations in political practices in different parts of the earth can be reduced by dealing with differences among countries within political culture areas. The two best areas for such internal comparison

[1] See Max Weber, "Zur Lage der burgerlichen Demokratie in Russland," *Archiv für Sozialwissenschaft und Sozialpolitik*, 1906, 22: 346 ff.

are Latin America as one, and Europe and the English-speaking countries as the other. More limited comparisons may be made among the Asian states, and among the Arab countries.

The main criteria used in this paper to locate European democracies are the uninterrupted continuation of political democracy since World War I, *and* the absence over the past 25 years of a major political movement opposed to the democratic "rules of the game."[2] The somewhat less stringent criterion employed for Latin America is whether a given country has had a history of more or less free elections for most of the post-World War I period. Where in Europe we look for stable democracies, in South America we look for countries which have not had fairly constant dictatorial rule. No detailed analysis of the political history of either Europe or Latin America has been made with an eye toward more specific criteria of differentiation; at this point in the examination of the requisites of democracy, election results are sufficient to locate the European countries, and the judgments of experts and impressionistic assessments based on fairly well-known facts of political history will suffice for Latin America.

Economic Development and Democracy

Perhaps the most widespread generalization linking political systems to other aspects of society has been that democracy is related to the state of economic development. Concretely, this means that the more well-to-do a nation, the greater the chances that it will sustain democracy. From Aristotle down to the present, men have argued that only in a wealthy society in which relatively few citizens lived in real poverty could a situation exist in which the mass of the population could intelligently participate in politics and could develop the self-restraint necessary to avoid succumbing to the appeals of irresponsible demagogues. A society divided between a large impoverished mass and a small favored elite would result either in oligarchy (dictatorial rule of the small upper stratum) or in tyranny (popularly based dictatorship). And these two political forms can be given modern labels: tyranny's modern face is Communism or Peronism; oligarchy appears today in the form of traditionalist dictatorships such as we find in parts of Latin America, Thailand, Spain or Portugal.

As a means of concretely testing this hypothesis, various indices of economic development—wealth, industrialization, urbanization and education—have been defined, and averages (means) have been computed for the countries which have been classified as more or less

---

[2] The latter requirement means that no totalitarian movement, either Fascist or Communist, received 20 per cent of the vote during this time. Actually, all the European nations falling on the democratic side of the continuum had totalitarian movements which secured less than seven per cent of the vote.

democratic in the Anglo-Saxon world and Europe and Latin America.

In each case, the average wealth, degree of industrialization and urbanization, and level of education is much higher for the more democratic countries, as the data presented in Table 1 indicate. If we had combined Latin America and Europe in one table, the differences would have been greater.

The main indices of *wealth* used here are per capita income, number of persons per motor vehicle and per physician, and the number of radios, telephones, and newspapers per thousand persons. The differences are striking on every score, as Table 1 indicates in detail. In the more democratic European countries, there are 17 persons per motor vehicle compared to 143 for the less democratic countries. In the less dictatorial Latin American countries there are 99 persons per motor vehicle, as against 274 for the more dictatorial ones. Income differences for the groups are also sharp, dropping from an average per capita income of $695 for the more democratic countries of Europe to $308 for the less democratic ones; the corresponding difference for Latin America is from $171 to $119. The ranges are equally consistent, with the lowest per capita income in each group falling in the "less democratic" category, and the highest in the "more democratic" one.

Industrialization — indices of wealth are clearly related to this, of course — is measured by the percentage of employed males in agriculture, and the per capita commercially produced "energy" being used in the country, measured in terms of tons of coal per person per year. Both of these indices show equally consistent results. The average percentage of employed males working in agriculture and related occupations was 21 in the "more democratic" European countries, and 41 in the "less democratic," 52 in the "less dictatorial" Latin American countries, and 67 in the "more dictatorial." The differences in per capita energy employed in the country are equally large.

The degree of *urbanization* is also related to the existence of democracy. Three different indices of urbanization are available from data compiled by International Urban Research (Berkeley, California), the percentage of the population in places of 20,000 and over, the percentage in communities of 100,000 and over, and also the percentage residing in standard metropolitan areas. On all three of these indices of urbanization, the more democratic countries score higher than the less democratic, for both of the political culture areas under investigation.

Many have suggested that the better educated the population of a country, the better the chances for democracy, and the comparative data available support this proposition. The "more democratic" countries of Europe are almost entirely literate: the lowest has a rate of 96 per cent, while the "less democratic" nations have an average literacy rate of 85 per cent. In Latin America, the difference is between an

Table 1

A COMPARISON OF EUROPEAN, ENGLISH-SPEAKING AND LATIN AMERICAN
COUNTRIES, DIVIDED INTO TWO GROUPS, "MORE DEMOCRATIC" AND
"LESS DEMOCRATIC," BY INDICES OF WEALTH, INDUSTRIALIZATION,
EDUCATION, AND URBANIZATION[1]

A. Indices of Wealth

Means	Per Capita Income[2] in $	Thousands of Persons Per Doctor[3]	Persons Per Motor Vehicle[4]	Telephones Per 1,000 Persons[5]	Radios Per 1,000 Persons[6]	Newspaper Copies Per 1,000 Persons[7]
European and English-speaking Stable Democracies	695	.86	17	205	350	341
European and English-speaking Unstable Democracies and Dictatorships	308	1.4	143	58	160	167
Latin American Democracies and Unstable Dictatorships	171	2.1	99	25	85	102
Latin American Stable Dictatorships	119	4.4	274	10	43	43
Ranges						
European Stable Democracies	420–1,453	.7– 1.2	3–62	43–400	160–995	242–570
European Dictatorships	128– 482	.6– 4	10–538	7–196	42–307	46–390
Latin American Democracies	112– 346	.8– 3.3	31–174	12– 58	38–148	51–233
Latin American Stable Dictatorships	40– 331	1.0–10.8	38–428	1– 24	4–154	4–111

B. Indices of Industrialization

Means	Percentage of Males in Agriculture[8]	Per Capita Energy Consumed[9]
European Stable Democracies	21	3.6
European Dictatorships	41	1.4
Latin American Democracies	52	.6
Latin American Stable Dictatorships	67	.25
Ranges		
European Stable Democracies	6–46	1.4 –7.8
European Dictatorships	16–60	.27–3.2
Latin American Democracies	30–63	.30–0.9
Latin American Stable Dictatorships	46–87	.02–1.27

[1] A large part of this table has been compiled from data furnished by International Urban Research. University of California, Berkeley, California.

[2] United Nations, Statistical Office, *National and Per Capita Income in Seventy Countries*, 1949, Statistical Papers, Series E, No. 1, New York, 1950, pp. 14–16.

[3] United Nations, *A Preliminary Report on the World Social Situation, 1952*, Table 11, pp. 46–8.

[4] United Nations, *Statistical Yearbook, 1956*, Table 139, pp. 333–338.

[5] *Ibid.*, Table 149, p. 387.

C. Indices of Education

Means	Percentage Literate[10]	Primary Education Enrollment Per 1,000 Persons[11]	Post-Primary Enrollment Per 1,000 Persons[12]	Higher Education Enrollment Per 1,000 Persons[13]
European Stable Democracies	96	134	44	4.2
European Dictatorships	85	121	22	3.5
Latin American Democracies	74	101	13	2.0
Latin American Dictatorships	46	72	8	1.3
Ranges				
European Stable Democracies	95–100	96–179	19–83	1.7–17.83
European Dictatorships	55– 98	61–165	8–37	1.6– 6.1
Latin American Democracies	48– 87	75–137	7–27	.7– 4.6
Latin American Dictatorships	11– 76	11–149	3–24	.2– 3.1

D. Indices of Urbanization

Means	Per Cent in Cities over 20,000[14]	Per Cent in Cities over 100,000[15]	Per Cent in Metropolitan Areas[16]
European Stable Democracies	43	28	38
European Dictatorships	24	16	23
Latin American Democracies	28	22	26
Latin American Stable Dictatorships	17	.12	15
Ranges			
European Stable Democracies	28–54	17–51	22–56
European Dictatorships	12–44	6–33	7–49
Latin American Democracies	11–48	13–37	17–44
Latin American Stable Dictatorships	5–36	4–22	7–26

[6]*Ibid.*, Table 189, p. 641. The population bases for these figures are for different years than those used in reporting the numbers of telephones and radios, but for purposes of group comparisons, the differences are not important.

[7]United Nations, *A Preliminary Report . . . , op. cit.*, Appendix B, pp. 86–89.

[8]United Nations, *Demographic Yearbook, 1956*, Table 12, pp. 350–370.

[9]United Nations, *Statistical Yearbook, 1956, op. cit.*, Table 127, pp. 308–310. Figures refer to commercially produced energy, in equivalent numbers of metric tons of coal.

[10]United Nations, *A Preliminary Report . . . , op. cit.*, Appendix A, pp. 79–86. A number of countries are listed as more than 95 per cent literate.

[11]*Ibid.*, pp. 86–100. Figures refer to persons enrolled at the earlier year of the primary range, per 1,000 total population, for years ranging from 1946 to 1950. The first primary year varies from five to eight in various countries. The less developed countries have more persons in that age range per 1,000 population than the more developed countries, but this biases the figures presented in the direction of increasing the percentage of the total population in school for the less developed countries, although fewer of the children in that age group attend school. The bias from this source thus reinforces the positive relationship between education and democracy.

[12]*Ibid.*, pp. 86–100.

[13]UNESCO, *World Survey of Education*, Paris, 1955. Figures are the enrollment in higher education per 1,000 population. The years to which the figures apply vary between 1949 and 1952, and the definition of higher education varies for different countries.

[14]Obtained from International Urban Research, University of California, Berkeley, California.

[15]*Ibid.*

[16]*Ibid.*

average rate of 74 per cent for the "less dictatorial" countries and 46 per cent for the "more dictatorial." The educational enrollment per thousand total population at three different levels, primary, post-primary, and higher educational, is equally consistently related to the degree of democracy. The tremendous disparity is shown by the extreme cases of Haiti and the United States. Haiti has fewer children (11 per thousand) attending school in the primary grades than the United States has attending colleges (almost 18 per thousand).

The relationship between education and democracy is worth more extensive treatment since an entire philosophy of democratic government has seen in increased education the spread of the basic requirement of democracy. As Bryce wrote with special reference to Latin America, "education, if it does not make men good citizens, makes it at least easier for them to become so."[3] Education presumably broadens men's outlooks, enables them to understand the need for norms of tolerance, restrains them from adhering to extremist and monistic doctrines, and increases their capacity to make rational electoral choices.

The evidence bearing on the contribution of education to democracy is even more direct and strong in connection with individual behavior *within* countries, than it is in cross-national correlations. Data gathered by public opinion research agencies which have questioned people in different countries with regard to their belief in various democratic norms of tolerance for opposition, to their attitudes toward ethnic or racial minorities, and with regard to their belief in multi-party as against one-party systems have found that *the most important single factor differentiating those giving democratic responses from others has been education*. The higher one's education, the more likely one is to believe in democratic values and support democratic practices. All the relevant studies indicate that education is far more significant than income or occupation.

These findings should lead us to anticipate a far higher correlation between national levels of education and political practice than in fact we do find. Germany and France have been among the best educated nations of Europe, but this by itself clearly did not stabilize their democracies. It may be, however, that education has served to inhibit other anti-democratic forces. Post-Nazi data from Germany indicate clearly that higher education is linked to rejection of strong-man and one-party government.

If we cannot say that a "high" level of education is a sufficient condition for democracy, the available evidence does suggest that it comes close to being a necessary condition in the modern world. Thus if we

---

[3]Quoted in Arthur P. Whitaker, "The Pathology of Democracy in Latin America: A Historian's Point of View," *American Political Science Review*, 1950, *44*: 112; see also Karl Mannheim, *Freedom, Power, and Democratic Planning* (New York: 1950).

turn to Latin America, where widespread illiteracy still exists in many countries, we find that of all the nations in which more than half the population is illiterate, only one, Brazil, can be included in the "more democratic" group.

There is some evidence from other economically impoverished culture areas that literacy is related to democracy. The one member of the Arab League which has maintained democratic institutions since World War II, Lebanon, is by far the best educated (over 80 per cent literacy) of the Arab countries. In the rest of Asia east of the Arab world, only two states, the Philippines and Japan, have maintained democratic regimes without the presence of large anti-democratic parties since 1945. And these two countries, although lower than any European state in per capita income, are among the world's leaders in educational attainment. The Philippines actually ranks second to the United States in its proportion of people attending high school and university, while Japan has a higher level of educational attainment than any European state.

Although the various indices have been presented separately, it seems clear that the factors of industrialization, urbanization, wealth, and education, are so closely interrelated as to form one common factor. And the factors subsumed under economic development carry with it the political correlate of democracy.

Before moving to a discussion of the inner connections between the development complex and democracy, mention may be made of a study of the Middle East, which, in its essential conclusions, substantiates these empirical relationships for another culture area. A survey of six Middle Eastern countries (Turkey, Lebanon, Egypt, Syria, Jordan, and Iran), conducted by the Columbia University Bureau of Applied Social Research in 1950–1951, found high associations between urbanization, literacy, voting rates, media consumption and production, and education.[4] Simple and multiple correlations between the four basic variables were computed for all countries for which United Nations statistics were available, in this case 54. The multiple correlations, regarding each as the dependent variable in turn, are as follows:[5]

Dependent Variable	Multiple Correlation Coefficient
Urbanization	.61
Literacy	.91
Media Participation	.84
Political Participation	.82

[4]The study is reported in Daniel Lerner, *The Passing of Traditional Society* (Glencoe, Illinois: The Free Press, 1958). These correlations are derived from census data; the main sections of the survey dealt with reactions to and opinions about the mass media, with inferences as to the personality types appropriate to modern and traditional society.

[5]*Ibid.*, p. 63. The index of political participation was the per cent voting in the last five elections. . . .

In the middle East, Turkey and Lebanon score higher on most of these indices than do the other four countries analyzed, and Lerner points out that the "great post-war events in Egypt, Syria, Jordan and Iran have been the violent struggles for the control of power — struggles notably absent in Turkey and Lebanon, where the control of power has been decided by elections."[6]

One of Lerner's contributions is to point to the consequences, for overall stability, of disproportionate development in one direction or another, and the need for coordinated changes in all of these variables. Thus, he compares urbanization and literacy in Egypt and Turkey, and concludes that although Egypt is far more urbanized than Turkey, it is not really "modernized," and does not even have an adequate base for modernization, because literacy has not kept abreast. In Turkey, all of the several indices of modernization have kept pace with each other, with rising voting participation (36 per cent in 1950), rising literacy, urbanization, etc. In Egypt, by contrast, the cities are full of "homeless illiterates," who provide a ready audience for political mobilization in support of extremist ideologies. On Lerner's scale, following the assumption of the functional interdependence of "modernization" factors, Egypt should be twice as literate as Turkey, since it is twice as urbanized. The fact that it is only half as literate explains, for Lerner, the "imbalances" which "tend to become circular and to accelerate social disorganization," political as well as economic.[7]

Lerner introduces one important theoretical addition, the suggestion that these key variables in the modernization process may be viewed as historical phases, with democracy a part of later developments, the "crowning institution of the participant society," one of his terms for a modern industrial society. His view on the relations between these variables, seen as stages, is worth quoting at some length:

> *The secular evolution of a participant society appears to involve a regular sequence of three phases. Urbanization comes first, for cities alone have developed the complex of skills and resources which characterize the modern industrial economy. Within this urban matrix develop both of the attributes which distinguish the next two phases — literacy and media growth. There is a close reciprocal relationship between these, for the literate develop the media which in turn spread literacy. But, literacy performs the key function in the second phase. The capacity to read, at first acquired by relatively few people, equips them to perform the varied tasks required in the modernizing society. Not until the third phase, when the elaborate technology of industrial development is fairly well advanced, does a society begin to produce newspapers, radio networks, and motion pictures on a massive scale.*

[6]*Ibid.*, pp. 84–85.
[7]*Ibid.*, pp. 87–89. . . .

> *This in turn, accelerates the spread of literacy. Out of this interaction*
> *develop those institutions of participation (e.g., voting) which we find*
> *in all advanced modern societies.*[8]

Lerner's thesis concerning the functional interdependence of these elements of modernization is by no means established by his data, but the material presented in this paper offers an opportunity for research along these lines. Deviant cases, such as Egypt, where "lagging" literacy is associated with serious strains and potential upheaval, may also be found in Europe and in Latin America, and their analysis, a task not attempted here, will clarify further the basic dynamics of modernization, and the problem of social stability in the midst of institutional change. . . .

Increased wealth is not only related causally to the development of democracy by changing the social conditions of the workers, but it also affects the political role of the middle class through changing the shape of the stratification structure so that it shifts from an elongated pyramid, with a large lower-class base, to a diamond with a growing middle class. A large middle class plays a mitigating role in moderating conflict since it is able to reward moderate and democratic parties and penalize extremist groups.

National income is also related to the political values and style of the upper class. The poorer a country, and the lower the absolute standard of living of the lower classes, the greater the pressure on the upper strata to treat the lower classes as beyond the pale of human society, as vulgar, as innately inferior, as a lower caste. The sharp difference in the style of living between those at the top and those at the bottom makes this psychologically necessary. Consequently, the upper strata also tend to regard political rights for the lower strata, particularly the right to share in power, as essentially absurd and immoral. The upper strata not only resist democracy themselves, but their often arrogant political behavior serves to intensify extremist reactions on the part of the lower classes.

The general income level of a nation will also affect its receptivity to democratic political tolerance norms. The values which imply that it does not matter greatly which side rules, that error can be tolerated even in the governing party can best develop where (a) the government has little power to affect the crucial life chances of most powerful groups, or (b) there is enough wealth in the country so that it actually does not make too much difference if some redistribution does take place. If loss of office is seen as meaning serious loss for major power groups, then they will be readier to resort to more drastic measures in seeking to retain or secure office. The wealth level will also affect the extent to which given countries can develop "universalistic" norms among its

[8]*Ibid.*, p. 60. . . .

civil servants and politicians (selection based on competence; perform-ance without favoritism). The poorer the country, the greater the em-phasis which is placed on nepotism, *i.e.*, support of kin and friends. The weakness of the universalistic norms reduces the opportunity to develop efficient bureaucracy, a condition for a modern democratic state.

Less directly linked but seemingly still associated with greater wealth is the presence of intermediary organizations and institutions which can act as sources of countervailing power, and recruiters of partici-pants in the political process in the manner discussed by Tocqueville and other exponents of what has come to be known as the theory of the "mass society." They have argued that a society without a multitude of organizations relatively independent of the central state power has a high dictatorial as well as a revolutionary potential. Such organizations serve a number of functions necessary to democracy: they are a source of countervailing power, inhibiting the state or any single major source of private power from dominating all political resources; they are a source of new opinions; they can be the means of communicating ideas, particularly opposition ideas, to a large section of the citizenry; they serve to train men in the skills of politics; and they help increase the level of interest and participation in politics. Although there are no reliable data which bear on the relationship between national pat-terns of voluntary organizations and national political systems, evi-dence from studies of individual behavior within a number of differ-ent countries demonstrates that, independently of other factors, men who belong to associations are more likely to hold democratic opin-ions on questions concerning tolerance and party systems, and are more likely to participate in the political process — to be active or to vote. Since we also know that, within countries, the more well-to-do and the better educated one is, the more likely he is to belong to voluntary or-ganizations, it seems likely that the propensity to form such groups is a function of level of income and opportunities for leisure within given nations.

It is obvious that democracy and the conditions related to stable democracy discussed here are essentially located in the countries of northwest Europe and their English-speaking offspring in America and Australasia. It has been argued by Max Weber among others that the factors making for democracy in this area are a historically unique con-catenation of elements, part of the complex which also produced capi-talism in this area. The basic argument runs that capitalist economic development (facilitated and most developed in Protestant areas) created the burgher class whose existence was both a catalyst and a necessary condition for democracy. The emphasis within Protestantism on individual responsibility furthered the emergence of democratic values. The greater initial strength of the middle classes in these coun-tries resulted in an alignment between burghers and throne, an alignment which preserved the monarchy, and thus facilitated the legitimation of democracy among the conservative strata. Thus we have an interrelated cluster of economic development, Protestantism, monarchy, gradual political change, legitimacy and democracy. Men may argue as to whether any aspect of this cluster is primary, but the cluster of factors and forces hangs together. . . .

The data available are . . . of a sufficiently consistent character to support strongly the conclusion that a more systematic and up-to-date version of Aristotle's hypothesis concerning the relationship of political forms to social structure is valid. Unfortunately . . . this conclusion does not justify the optimistic liberal's hope that an increase in wealth, in the size of the middle class, in education, and other related factors will necessarily mean the spread of democracy or the stabilizing of democracy. As Max Weber, in discussing the chances for democracy in Russia in the early 20th century pointed out: "The spread of Western cultural and capitalist economy did not, *ipso facto*, guarantee that Russia would also acquire the liberties which had accompanied their emergence in European history. . . . European liberty had been born in unique, perhaps unrepeatable, circumstances at a time when the intellectual and material conditions for it were exceptionally propitious."[9]

These suggestions that the peculiar concatenation of factors which gave rise to western democracy in the nineteenth century may be unique are not meant to be unduly pessimistic. Political democracy exists and has existed in a variety of circumstances, even if it is most commonly sustained by a limited cluster of conditions. To understand more fully the various conditions under which it has existed may make possible the development of democracy elsewhere. Democracy is not achieved by acts of will alone; but men's wills, through action, can shape institutions and events in directions that reduce or increase the chance for the development and survival of democracy. To aid men's actions in furthering democracy was in some measure Tocqueville's purpose in studying the operation of American democracy, and it remains perhaps the most important substantive intellectual task which students of politics can still set before themselves.

LIBERAL DEMOCRACY AND SOCIAL CONTROL

ANDREW HACKER

Liberal democrats, like all those who elect to paddle in the placid waters of liberalism, show a charming imperviousness to the existence of power.

[9]Richard Pipes, "Max Weber and Russia," *World Politics*, 1955, 7: 383.

From *The American Political Science Review*, 1957 (December), *51*: 1009–1014, 1017–1021, 1024–1026.

It is the ingenuousness which permitted the ideology of individualism to flourish for well over a century in the Western world. But all chickens — political as well as others — eventually come home to roost; and the failure to imbibe the home truths set down by such ungentlemanly characters as Thrasymachus, Machiavelli, and Pareto now accounts for the dilemmas, reconsiderations, and tortured defenses of liberal democracy which we see abounding on all sides.

Liberal democracy — that uneasy compromise which was never a compromise at all — is, from the moral standpoint, the worthiest of political creeds.[1] It can arouse the enthusiasm of the humane, the heretical, and the responsible: in short, of all men of good will. But the tenets of liberal democracy can only be a guide for governors and governed in a community if there exists a halcyon situation in which the traditional status system is placidly taken for granted by all in the community. Only in this way can attention be focussed on the preservation of liberties and the encouragement of individual development. For social arrangements set the stage for the allocation of power, interests, and status. As long as these arrangements are not questioned in their fundamentals, then the conditions for promoting the liberal democratic ethic are possible of attainment. It goes without saying that any community must maintain a consensus if it is to survive. The question to be explored continually, then, is what propositions must be agreed upon. The startling fact of our time is that there are fundamental propositions about the allocation of power which were sublimely taken for granted heretofore and which are now being called to the bar to defend themselves. That they have no ultimate defense is the tragedy of liberal democracy in the modern world.

Liberal democracy in America never had a politics. It was essentially an upper-middle-class and upper-class creed. Unable, through ignorance — or unwilling, because of sensibility — to make explicit its class basis, its proponents persuaded themselves that the ideology was accepted on its merits. In point of fact, it was the class and not the ideology which was accepted. Liberal democracy, the creed of that class, was the received ideology simply because the men who promulgated it were the men who had deference automatically and unquestioningly accorded to them. The liberal democratic tradition in America has had an infinitely smaller constituency than we prefer to believe. The man in the street accepted political, economic, and social

---

[1]"Liberal democracy," for present purposes, must be defined briefly and arbitrarily. It describes both an ideology and an institutional system; and its appeal is to those who claim to be fearful alike of the consequences of elite rule and of direct democracy. Both ideology and institutions, therefore, postulate a dynamic equilibrium between two values: (1) majority rule and human equality, i.e., that each shall count for one in political arrangements and that self-government, with the majority decision prevailing, is the best government; and (2) individual rights and constitutional guarantees, i.e., that there shall be an optimum area in which neither government nor society shall interfere with the individual in his pursuit of activities he thinks good. Both of these values, Liberal Democrats postulate, are crucial: neither must be allowed to overwhelm the other. . . .

arrangements the basis for which he did not in the least perceive or comprehend. If he occasionally rebelled at them, it was not for the purpose of furthering individual liberty in the liberal democratic sense; it was rather status or interest revolt in the name of popular or direct democracy. For if liberal democracy never had a politics it never had to have one either. The classes, which supplied the personnel for the positions of power and prestige, had the built-in means of control which exist in any stratified society. In short, the basis of power of liberal democracy has traditionally been deference to a ruling class.

The Class Basis of Liberal Democracy

Whether we like to admit it or not, a society which encourages the full flowering of individual liberty is, and can only be, a stratified society. Such encouragement requires a strong measure of tolerance on the part of those with power. The man in the street, as John Stuart Mill never ceased repeating, is fearful of the unusual and the idiosyncratic. It is only a secure class which can afford to set down the conditions which allow for nonconformist behavior. This means that social controls must exist which, on one side of the coin, will allow a ruling class to exercise the significant power without having to worry about the emotional insecurities of the mass of men; and, on the other, will divert the mass of men from questioning the fact that a small class has arrogated to itself the privilege of deciding what forms of behavior are to be tolerated.

For almost a century and a half, America had just such an unquestioned class. It ruled the country without having to worry about public opinion or popular emotion. And the social control which permitted this class to hold informal sway was the very traditional one of deference. Deference here is not to be thought of as an Old World retainer tugging at his forelock as the lord of the manor drives by. It means more simply that the bulk of the community defers to a small section and does not think to question that this class will hold the important positions and make the vital decisions. America has had such a class, and to it has been delegated national power in its economic, political, and social aspects. These "old" Americans possess, for the most part, some common characteristics. First of all, they are "WASPs"—in the cocktail party jargon of the sociologists. That is, they are white, they are Anglo-Saxon in origin, and they are Protestant (and disproportionately Episcopalian). To their Waspishness should be added the tendency to be located on the Eastern seaboard or around San Francisco, to be prep school and Ivy League educated, and to be possessed of inherited wealth. Talcott Parsons has generalized about such a group:

> There is a continuing tendency for earlier economic developments to leave a 'precipitate' of upper groups, the positions of whose mem-

> *bers are founded in the achievements of their ancestors, in this case*
> *relatively recent ones. By historical necessity these groups are strong-*
> *est in the older parts of the country. Hence the cities of the Eastern*
> *seaboard have tended to develop groups that are the closest approach*
> *we have — though still very different from their European equivalent*
> *— to an aristocracy. They have generally originated in business in-*
> *terests, but have taken on a form somewhat similar to the mercantile*
> *aristocracies of some earlier European societies, such as the Han-*
> *seatic cities.*[2]

There is no point in belaboring the definitional question of whether or not this group or groups constitutes a "class." What is being said is simply that it was these people who, without serious question on any-one's part, entered, *au naturel*, the positions of power in the political and economic worlds. They provided the presidential candidates, the diplomatic personnel, the cabinet officers, the judges and influential lawyers, and the heads of the important banks, investment houses, commercial interests, and the boards of directors of many of the great corporations. They also, of course, dominated the churches and the institutions of higher learning. In short, it was this group which exer-cised national power. Of course, immigrants gained access to seats of municipal power quite soon; and on the frontiers of the economy trails were blazed by men who, if of old American stock, did not spring from the ruling class. But the power of the city politician was localized, and the Robber Baron was too busy on the industrial front to worry much about national politics and social arrangements. At all events, we must not overestimate the national power of the city boss or the entrepreneur, despite their flamboyant behavior and the publicity which attended it. In reality, it was members of the traditional ruling group who made the decisions which set the tone and atmosphere in which American politics was to be conducted. It is, of course, true that this pool of the privileged was not a caste. Failure to possess any one of the requisites mentioned above did not debar a potential entrant. Certainly, inherited wealth did not have to go back further than one generation. Analogy with the European aristocracies is, as Parsons points out, misleading. A better comparison would be with what has been referred to in con-temporary Britain as "The Establishment." The basis of this group is partly family, education, and social standing; but it is also to be defined in terms of a set of position-holders, or role-players. As long as people from a narrow and specified background have virtually automatic access to the seats of power, then we are speaking of a "ruling class." When recruitment for these positions is based primarily on talent, the power inherent in the roles does not necessarily diminish, but it would

[2]"Social Strains in America," in Daniel Bell (ed.), *The New American Right* (New York, 1955), p. 125.

be more proper to refer to an "elite." However, one of the "talents" demanded for ascendency may often be possession of the manners and attitudes acquired only through the breeding and education gained by virtue of membership in the dominant class.

At all events, nothing is lost if we refer to an old ruling class in American life. This group did not possess the corporate self-awareness of the British aristocracy. Furthermore, it would be idle to accuse its members of any conspiratorial designs. If there were common objectives and common outlooks among this ruling class, it was simply because those who belonged to it were pretty much the same kind of people. Through constant contacts in clubs, churches, boards of directors, governmental bodies, and in each other's homes, they informed one another of what was going on. But again it must be stressed that such transmission, consultation, and concert can hardly be construed as "a plot against the people." Rather it was a spontaneous—and oftentimes childlike—effort to perform the tasks and duties they sincerely believed to be theirs by right.

The spontaneous character of this activity ought to be apparent if we consider it in its ideological aspect. The promotion of liberal democracy was one of the chief endeavors of the old ruling class. This was not for the sake of that ideology's own intrinsic beauty, nor was it for the purpose of giving the mass of the community an opportunity to develop their potentialities. Rather, the idea of a limited government was for their own class benefit. The reasons for this, on the economic side, are quite clear. But in the process, this class came to defend the Bill of Rights, the common law, and the whole idea of decency, civility, and fair play—in short, the framework of liberal democracy. The judges and lawyers who came from this class were willing to interpret the Constitution in such a way that dissenters would be allowed free rein to express their thoughts. This tolerance, however, came not from any abstract love for civil liberties. It is simply that the ruling class itself counted *among its own members* individuals who possessed radical views and who tended to display idiosyncratic behavior. In order to protect its own kind, it was prepared to give strength to the law by ensuring that the Bill of Rights was a living doctrine. Tolerance, therefore, was an internalized class tolerance. The Harvard atheist of good family, the transcendental rebel with manners and breeding, the Utopian socialist who paid heed to the rules of gentlemanly intercourse—these were, after all, "our kind of people" and had to be safeguarded from the coercive power both of the state and of society in general.

The whole rationale of the liberal democratic scheme—incorporating the ideas of individual liberty and limited government—was that it could work as long as it had only to protect a particular section of the community. It takes power to guarantee freedom. And the power of the ruling class was exercised only to carve out an area of freedom for its own members. On the one hand, it shaped the law so that property rights and freedom of expression would be sanctioned; on the other, it kept the emotions of the majority at bay. It is vital to take note of this because there are many who believe that the protection of the Bill of Rights ought to be extended to cover *all* men and not simply a privileged few. In abstract terms this, of course, is a worthy belief. But what must be confronted is the question of *who*, if there is no established ruling class, is to defend the liberties of the larger constituency of citizens which has developed. It must not be thought that their fellow-citizens, or the state, or even the courts are in a position to protect *any* dissident whatsoever. Certainly, in the past, the nonconformist, if he was simply an average citizen, was not so protected. This privilege was reserved for a few.

For the Constitutional gentlemen who acted as the guardians of the common law and the Bill of Rights were traditionally in a position where they could well form a bulwark around those in need of such a hedge. If the Overseers of Harvard College or the Justices of the Supreme Court wished to condone an unpopular act, the deference they commanded stood between them and the breath of popular criticism. And even if at times, the deference showed a tendency to wear thin, the established position of these lawyers, judges, educators, and business-men in the social and economic structure gave them the ability to ignore the clamorings of the ordinary man. The ruling class, then, combined civility and power. Educated in a humane tradition, conscious of the value of free expression, and willing to protect their own sort, they shaped the instruments of law and social institutions so that at least the civil liberties of a few were protected. The man on the street might well wonder at the wisdom of tolerating such behavior. But he did not consider it his province to question his exclusion from participating in making these mysterious judgments.

Furthermore, it must be stressed that the ruling class was quite conscious of the limitations on its power. It made no effort to educate the population to the *merits* of liberal democracy. Nor did it seek to protect those outside its own membership. The civil liberties of the trade union organizer in Colorado, of the Negro in Alabama, of the disabled factory worker in Pennsylvania or of the nonconformist professor of economics in a small Midwestern college—these persons were not considered proper materials for defense. Had the ruling class sought, say, to put its power behind the radicals of the I.W.W. it would have so endangered its foundation of deference that the existence of the class itself would come into question. Courts, universities, boards of directors all drew a firm line as to who would merit their help. This could not be otherwise. The dynamics of American growth let the ruling class know in no uncertain terms that its power had perceptible limitations.

It is proper, therefore, when speaking of the defense of liberal democracy to ask just *who* the defenders are. In the first century of our Republic's existence, one could readily point to these guardians: the old ruling class. Through the deference accorded to them and by virtue of their established economic power, they were able to carry the shield for those they chose to protect. The existence of these people cannot be taken for granted. Liberal democracy would have had no meaning without their intervention and interpretation. And if this class was needed to give meaning to the idea of freedom, then one has to ask how long liberal democracy can last without the presence of its protectors.

The New Men

. . . New men, of both immigrant and old stock, are being admitted [to positions of power and responsibility] with greater frequency. Our society and our economy are more complex, more competitive, and more sophisticated. To stand the pace brought on by the complexity of the tasks we must perform, fewer and fewer organizations can afford to keep on those of mediocre competence. In fields ranging from medicine to advertising, from accounting to personnel, from educational administration to the ministry, from the foreign service to journalism—in all of these, skills are required. Even old family firms and partnerships must let in new men (hopefully a son-in-law, but usually not). For without these hands, the ship will surely founder in highly competitive waters. The new men are energetic. They have to be, and they have had to be. But the expenditure of this energy is at a price. The psychic cost is high. For the man who has had to run, to push, and to fight develops an outlook towards himself and towards society quite at variance from that of the man who has easily had power and responsibility thrust upon him.

The *ancien regime* was a leisure class. To be sure, many of its members toiled mightily in the vineyard. But their upbringing and even their adult years were devoid of the pressures imposed on the new men of today. That leisure enabled them to study—not necessarily in a formal, but often in a disciplined, way—the responsibilities and obligations which were to be theirs. The lawyer had, of course, to serve his client. But he was able to serve the common law and the Constitution at the same time. The educational administrator took seriously the claims of "useless" scholarship as well as those of useful preparation for life. In short, men of leisure were able to regard their power as an instrument for transmitting traditional values as well as an instrument for performing particular tasks at hand. These values were sustained by a class which could ignore the demands of career-building and organizational competition. For it is plain enough that there is all too frequently a conflict between, let us say, defending the Bill of Rights and earning a dollar or winning a vote. Simple exhortation is not enough to lead a man to strike a blow for the one at the risk of losing the other. He must first be sure that he is in a position to make a short-run sacrifice for the long-term good.

The new men are not cushioned either by status or by private incomes. If we ask the newly arrived man—who, let it be said, is never completely sure that he has arrived—to take a stand on fundamental liberties, we are asking too much of him. One may, with good reason, demand that a Senator from an old Cincinnati family or a Boston lawyer of wealth and standing stake a claim in defense of the First Amendment. But to ask this of a bright young politician from California or an engineer who has risen through the ranks of an automobile company is asking the impossible. The distinction is not one of character or personality. What distinguishes a Taft from a Nixon is what separates the old from the new men. As Shils points out, the new

> *American elites in business, politics, publicity and learning tend to come great geographical distances from the places of their birth to the places where they work and achieve. The great size of the country makes the loss of local ties in the leadership of the country a common phenomenon. Moreover, the cultures, the professional and social milieu into which the newly ascended leaders come, do not ordinarily possess powerful traditions which impose themselves firmly on most newcomers. There is no aristocratic or gentry pattern of life to which newcomers can clearly aspire and which they can definitely assimilate.*[3]

The new men have neither family nor wealth nor geographical ties to support them. They have only their talent. And the talent must be a "marketable" one: it must accommodate itself to the demands of customers, voters, and colleagues. The *ancien regime* did not have to worry about the market. Either the customer-voter would docilely take what was offered; or, if he had the presumption to refuse the offering, he could be ignored with impunity.

The objective needs of the man in the street have not changed over the years. It is doubtful if he is more tolerant of the unusual or unknown than was his grandfather. What has changed is the fact that more and more of our men of power *must* be directed in their actions by these popular demands, whims, and caprices. We are entering a more perfect democracy in that the customer-voter is now, more than ever before, "always right." The new lawyer, for instance, is not so secure that he can ignore the wishes of his clients. Neither is the new broker or corporation president or university professor. And the stark fact

[3]Edward Shils, *The Torment of Secrecy* (Glencoe, Illinois: The Free Press, 1956), p. 79. . . .

is that a larger and larger proportion of market demands, be they economic or social or political, are in conflict with the traditional values of liberal democracy. The law has ceased to be a profession and has become an arm of our corporate economy. The chief reason for this transformation is to be found in the new lawyers, who know full well that they have no personal choice other than to serve their clients. The modern university cannot be expected to hold up the flag of liberal education against the cries of students—and their future employers —for vocational or pre-professional training. The few institutions which hold out for the traditional values can do so because they are so prestigious and so financially cushioned that they can ignore market demands. But to think that the small New England college will set the future standard for the new campuses of state universities being created in the middle and far west is wishful thinking. While many professors at such campuses might like to follow such a lead, their institution cannot afford to. More and more they will be forced to imitate, and with success, the pattern set by a Michigan State University. What the defenders of liberal education fail to concern themselves with are the structural conditions under which such education—and institutions imparting such education—can flourish. The first condition is internal strength: and power to do the right is hardly bestowed by exhortation. For strength is the strength to ignore the market. Is there not a high positive correlation between size of endowment and whether or not a private institution kept on a professor who pleaded the Fifth Amendment? Today neither the institutions, nor the professors, nor the students, are in a position to tell the consuming public to go to the devil.

America, then, is more democratic than ever before. Careers are open to the talents, and not by virtue of an Horatio Alger-like break. But the new men of power have, in their climb, had no time to develop a sense of responsibility toward what have been our traditional standards—our liberal democratic values. Furthermore, these new men are always personally insecure. They cannot rely on traditional patterns of deference to maintain their power. For they have no family ties or inherited wealth to bolster their careers. But what is more crucial is that deference to the old ruling class has all but ceased to exist in the popular mind. Indeed, just as the new men show small respect for the family connections of those they have joined, so this attitude is spreading throughout society. Despite the fact that we live in a period of prosperity, there is a slackening indulgence of the old rich. Those who are admired are those on their way up. Talent—especially talent in "human relations"—is what is held up as the noteworthy achievement.

But if the new men are admired, they are admired only for the duration of the popular appeal which they evoke for their personal performances. As individuals, the new men cannot be said to command deference in the traditional sense of that word. This means . . . that they must seek other forms of control. The members of the *ancien regime*, who were habitually deferred to simply because of their class connection, never had to concern themselves with control. They ruled; they were obeyed. Their interest was in administration and the pursuit of the right as they saw it. The new men, on the other hand, have been given the instrument of power without a built-in form of control. It is not guaranteed to them that habitual deference will be accorded by those over whom they must exercise power. This potentially anarchic situation necessitates the calling forth of a set of political arrangements far different from those found in traditional societies. The theories of John Locke and John Stuart Mill are not of much use here. What must be called forth is the Machiavellian prescription, as old as Thrasymachus and as new as the latest public relations handbook. For the new men are only able to rule because of what they *do*—not because of what they *are*. The new men are not anything as individuals. All they possess is their wits. For this reason they must think constantly of ways in which to achieve not the deference of the man in the street, for that is impossible to acquire in our age, but simply his obedience. . . .

Conclusion

The new engineers are the focus of power in the emerging American society. They are the ones who have replaced the old ruling class. They are not a class in the old sense, although they are developing into an "Establishment" along a number of significant lines. The new men stand, furthermore, in stark contrast to the tens of thousands of well-rounded, well-adjusted people in middle-management. We know a little about how they differ from their immediate subordinates in terms of personality characteristics. We know a little about how they, rather than others, are recruited for the top echelons. But by and large we must rest content with saying that, as in all ages, they take the leading positions because they are best able to deal with the particular problems at hand. Foxes rather than lions, to use Pareto's distinction, they can meet the imperatives of a time which calls for the sophisticated manipulation of men's attitudes and sensibilities. This minority is the key to American politics and society. Its members are not so much typical as prototypical of the new men who are found not only in industry, but in politics and the military. They are aware of the need for, and familiar with the ways to achieve, control. Controllers rather than controlled, they find their own satisfactions in their careers and in providing the happiness of others. Unlike David Riesman's egoistic "saving remnant," this group does not flee from responsibility. It dimly understands that its role is the important one. The new men must forfeit their own happiness and serve the happiness of a public which cannot and will not plan its own existence. The new men work overtime at their job; they develop ulcers and nervous tensions; they neglect their families, outside interests, and the pursuit of culture. But they do their task with imagination and vigor. It is no understatement to say that they are carrying the rest of us on their backs.

The new men are our new rulers. They are intelligent, but not cultured. They are tolerant in informal social relations, but they have no compassion for those who are subject to political injustice. The American tradition, for them, probably began in 1945. Values are judged not by their place in the prescriptive scheme of things, but by their current utility. For the new men it would be suicide to regard individuals as ends in themselves: they must always be viewed as resources to be managed. Liberty deals not with freedom of expression or with protection from tyranny by the state: rather it is the complex of conditions under which organizational ends can be pursued and organizational order maintained. And truth becomes an image of the world which ordinary men are capable of comprehending without too much strain on their imaginations.

These definitions obviously appear anomalous. But this is simply because the words are the vocabulary of liberal democracy and their content is not. With the rise of the new men the conditions necessary for liberal democracy have seen their day. This means that we must turn to a new set of prescriptions. The focus must be on control and the controllers. The "Legend of the Grand Inquisitor"—*with* its stress on responsibility—has more meaning in prescriptive terms than the legend of the town meeting. The controllers are not men without souls. They are not philistines by nature. And there is good reason to believe that, in time, they can be civilized. But at this point they are simply busy. And if, in their furious activity, they are unknowingly breaking the idols of liberal democracy, we ought to think twice before we complain. For the new men are the products of equality of opportunity. If we *really* believe that careers ought to be open to the talents, regardless of background or adherence to traditional values, then we must accept the new ascendency with a good grace.

THE BENEVOLENT LEADER:
CHILDREN'S IMAGES OF POLITICAL AUTHORITY

FRED I. GREENSTEIN

Society's training of the young, including formal and informal citizenship instruction, character training, and the processes which lead to the

From *The American Political Science Review*, 1960 (December), *54*: 934–943. An expanded version of the same discussion appears in Fred I. Greenstein, *Children and Politics* (New Haven: Yale University Press, 1965), Chapter 3.

development of different personality types, has been seen as an important determinant of adult political behavior by theorists since Plato. In addition, much of our traditional folklore, not to mention much twentieth century literature on personality development, national character, authoritarianism, and electoral preference, points to the utility of examining the individual's early years as one means of illuminating his mature actions.

The present paper considers one aspect of the child's political development — the genesis of his attitudes toward political leaders and the possible ways that this developmental process may affect his adult responses to the formal wielders of power. Citizens' orientations to political authority have a complex and imperfectly understood, but obviously important, bearing on the equilibrium of a body politic.

Two classes of data will be considered: survey literature giving some indication of how adults respond to political leaders, and results of a study of 659 New Haven public and private school children of widely varying socio-economic status, ranging from fourth- through eighth-graders (about nine to thirteen years of age). Paper-and-pencil questionnaires were administered to this sample between January and March of 1958. Findings from these sources are supplemented by a smaller collection of prolonged interviews with individual children and many informal encounters with groups of school children and teachers over a period of about two years.

Adult Orientations to Political Leaders: Ambivalence

Adult orientations to political leaders display a curious inconsistency, which must be noted to give meaning to my New Haven pre-adult findings. To begin with, political roles, such as Senator, Mayor, Governor, and Judge, are in general highly esteemed by adults in the United States. Over the years, the many studies of occupational prestige have shown that people rank these roles well above all but an occasional civilian role (such as physician) in terms of importance and status. On the other hand, responses are much more variable when people are asked to rate individual public officials. The best barometer of this variation is probably the American Institute of Public Opinion's monthly estimates of presidential popularity. For over two decades, national cross-sections have been asked questions such as the following:

> Do you approve or disapprove of the way President X has been handling his job?

During his first term in office, favorable responses to President Truman ranged from 87 percent to 32 percent. Roosevelt and Eisenhower also fluctuated in popularity, although not as sharply.

Perhaps as a function of this blend of respect for high political roles and more qualified opinions toward the men who fill these positions, the mere fact of incumbency seems to have a positive effect on a leader's popularity. Thus it has been found that shortly after a president is elected people who were hitherto opposed to him upgrade their evaluations. This probably is a specific case of what has more generally been called the *fait accompli* effect. For example, support for a law increases after it has been passed and, conversely, people are less likely to back policy proposals if they are told that it will be necessary to change a law, or amend the constitution, to achieve this goal.

But this is not the whole story. As is well known, distinctly anti-"politician" and anti-"politics" views are widespread in the population. The survey literature abounds with evidence that substantial groups of people agree that "It is almost impossible for a man to stay honest if he goes into politics," that it is at best dubious for a young man to make politics his career, and so forth. Unsympathetic images of politics and the politician also are revealed by a great many adults in responses to various questions about the individual's political efficacy, as measured for example by willingness to agree with the statement "I don't think public officials care much what people like me think."

The seeming inconsistency between this set of attitudes and responses to individual political leaders and roles has led one recent commentator to write of "the ambivalent social status of the American politician."[1]

Children's Orientations to Political Leaders: Unqualified Sympathy

Possibly the most striking outcome of the New Haven study was the finding that the prevailing adult skepticism and distrust of politics and the politician simply did not seem to be present in the grade school sample. In spite of a variety of attempts to evoke such responses during my preliminary interviewing and pretesting, there was no evidence even of a frame of reference which would make it possible to use questionnaire items tapping the dimension of political cynicism. Moreover, although the final New Haven questionnaires contained a number of items which might have evoked spontaneous references to the malignancy of politicians, only one or two of the 659 children made statements which could be construed in this way.

Let us now note some more specific findings.

(1) Children are like adults in their ranking of high political roles. Members of the New Haven sample were asked to tell which of a number of adult roles are "most important." Choices offered included the President and Mayor, authority figures of the immediate environment such as school principals and teachers, as well as physicians, clergymen, police chiefs, and judges. At every age level, there were

[1]William C. Mitchell, in the *Western Political Quarterly*, 1959, *12*: 683–698.

more references to the President and Mayor than to any of the other roles. . . .

The younger New Haven children were almost devoid of political knowledge. All but a handful of them knew the names of the President and Mayor, but few knew much more than this. Within the brief age span of this sample, the level of political information increases considerably . . . . But the structure of cognitive information is erected on a foundation of feelings, assessments, and opinions; and the development of critical faculties waits on a later stage. Estimates of the importance of political leaders, incidentally, follow the same developmental course as another adult orientation — party identification. New Haven children described themselves as Republicans or Democrats long before they were able to make any meaningful statements about the parties, or even to link the party labels with the names of conspicuous leaders such as the President and Mayor.

(2) Another point at which the New Haven children's orientations can be compared, at least tentatively, with adult responses, is in their ratings of individual political leaders. Following the various information items which called, for example, for descriptions of the duties of the Mayor, Governor, and President, the children were asked to evaluate these leaders on a four-point scale ranging from "very good" to "bad."

Here children's responses did not merely reflect what might be expected from comparable adult samples. Their modal assessment of each of the three incumbents was in the highest possible category — "very good." Judging from the way national cross-sections of adults responded to the opportunity to rate President Eisenhower during the (shortly post-sputnik) months of this survey, children's views of political leaders are substantially more favorable than those of their elders. [We contrasted] the New Haven responses with the American Institute of Public Opinion's February 1958 report of the President's popularity. Needless to say, this juxtaposition of New Haven findings with national survey data must be treated as suggestive rather than conclusive. However, differences between these groups in evaluation of the President are considerable. Adults seemed to be about five times more willing to criticize the chief executive.

New Haven responses to items dealing with political efficacy also suggest that children are far more positive in their political orientations than adults. Less than two percent of the children said that they would not vote when they reached twenty-one. And over two-thirds agreed that "it makes much difference who wins an election," in contrast to the markedly smaller proportions of adult samples making such statements.

(3) I have already noted that various items in the New Haven questionnaire might have stimulated spontaneous references to graft, cor-

ruption, political immorality, and so forth, if these images were important in children's perception of politics, and that such references were not made. However, a totally different set of orientations did emerge spontaneously in response to several of the open-ended items.

These were the six items asking for descriptions of the duties of local, state, and federal executives and legislative bodies. The items were quite unstructured, simply asking, "What sorts of things does the Mayor (etc.) do?" As might be expected, most of the children who were able to respond made rather straightforward factual assertions — "The Mayor runs the city"; "Congress makes laws"; etc. What was surprising, however, was that a conspicuous minority of the children volunteered affective or affectively-toned responses — especially in descriptions of the Mayor and President. As noted above, only one or two of these statements were unsympathetic. Several classes of response are worth examining in more detail.

A. *Services to children.* About ten percent of the respondents eschewed reference to more widely recognized duties of the mayor and mentioned child-related portions of his role. For example:

> [*The Mayor*] *makes parks and swings. (Fifth grade girl)*
> [*The Mayor*] *repairs the parks, roads, schools, and takes the snow off the roads when it snows. (Fifth grade boy)*

It is a reasonable assumption that when a child's first image of a political leader is in terms of pork-barrel indulgences to the child, his image is a favorable one.

B. *General benevolence.* More generally, children tended to describe political leaders as "helping," "taking care of," and "protecting" people. Benevolent perceptions of this sort were especially evident in descriptions of the President and Mayor, but also occasionally were apparent in descriptions of the Governor and of legislative bodies. For example:

> [*The President*] *deals with foreign countries and takes care of the U.S. (Eighth grade boy)*
> [*The Mayor*] *helps people to live in safety. . . .*
> *The President is doing a very good job of making people be safe. (Fourth grade girl)*
> [*The President*] *gives us freedom. (Eighth grade girl)*
> [*The Board of Aldermen*] *gives us needs so we could live well. (Fourth grade girl)*

In a few cases children went so far as to perceive political authority as a direct source of economic support:

> *The Mayor pays working people like banks. (Fifth grade boy)*
> *[The Mayor] sees that schools have what they need and stores and other places too. (Fifth grade girl)*
> *[The Mayor] helps everyone to have nice homes and jobs. (Fourth grade boy)*

C. *Normative role.* In addition, some children characterized political leaders in positive normative terms—either as people who "do good things," or as people who are specialists in making moral judgments:

> *[The President does] good work. (Sixth grade boy)*
> *[The Mayor] sends men to build parks for us and make our city be a good one. (Fourth grade girl)*
> *[The President] makes peace with every country but bad. (Fifth grade boy)*
> *[The Mayor] talks business to all the people and says what's wrong or bad. (Fourth grade girl)*
> *I think that he [the President] has the right to stop bad things before they start. (Fifth grade girl)*

The frequency of "child-related" references to the Mayor, and of generally "benevolent" and "normative" references to the Mayor and President [was calculated]. Statements of this sort were made by some children at every age level, but benevolent imagery declines with age. Although the total of these classes of images rarely exceeds 15 percent . . . , what is remarkable is that any images of this sort are expressed in answer to such bland, unstructured stimulus questions. Moreover, there were additional descriptions of political leaders with favorable connotations which do not fit as readily into a few simple categories. For example, some children placed emphasis on the wisdom, capability, and solicitousness of public officials:

> *[The President] is in charge of the United States and has many wise men to tell him what is best. (Sixth grade boy)*
> *[The President] worries about all the problems of all the 48 states. Takes care of threatening wars by holding peace conferences. (Seventh grade boy)*
> *[The Mayor] has to keep track of everything that happens in New Haven. (Sixth grade boy)*

The spontaneous appearance of these images suggests that appropriately structured questions would show the imagery of benevolence to be considerably more common among grade school children than [our data] indicates.

The New Haven findings may be summarized as follows: children are at least as likely as adults to perceive high political roles as being important; they seem to be more sympathetic to individual political leaders (and, in general, to politics) than are adults; in at least some cases their actual images of political leaders are qualitatively different from the images one would expect adults to hold, especially in the emphasis on benignancy; and, most important, the widespread adult political cynicism and distrust does not seem to have developed by eighth grade (age 13). Each of these observations rests on a limited sample of respondents, and several are based on fortuitous findings, or comparisons which can only be made tentatively. They are internally consistent and seem to be convincing, but further verification (using more varied and refined techniques) clearly is necessary. However, in this discussion which follows I shall for the moment assume their validity and consider their potential significance.

The Child's View of Political Authority: Its Significance

Two questions are raised by the foregoing data: (1) Why is the child's early view of political authority so strikingly favorable? (2) What, if any, effect does this aspect of an individual's development have on his adult political behavior?

Fully convincing answers to these questions, particularly the second, are not available. This is so not only because the New Haven data are limited, but also because the existing body of generalizations linking childhood experience to adult behavior is quite rudimentary. Speculative answers, however, are a necessary first step to designing research which will extend our understanding of the dynamics of citizens' orientations toward political leaders.

(1) Although many lasting political orientations are acquired before adolescence—for instance, attitudes about the importance of major governmental roles and identifications with parties—early political learning seems to be quite casual. Young children, including the nine- and ten-year-olds who make up the youngest groups in this sample, have few interests beyond the environment of their immediate circle. And in New Haven there seemed to be little formal adult effort to shape the political information and attitudes of grade school children. Social studies curriculum guides, for example, do not suggest teaching until the sixth grade the subject matter which once was known as civics. Only in eighth grade is there mandatory provision for such training.

Nevertheless, political learning progresses during the preadolescent years. This learning has many sources. The most important of them—at least as a determinant of attitudes—undoubtedly is the family. Here (though I have no data based on direct observation) much of the learning probably is inadvertent and incidental to normal family activities. Similarly, inadvertent learning surely takes place in the schools, even in the absence of formal requirements for civic instruction, if only through politically related experiences such as patriotic observances. Among other sources of political learning, the mass media seem to be extremely important, especially during election campaigns.

One antecedent of the highly idealized childhood political images may be whatever political communications are intentionally transmitted to children by their agents of socialization. Even parents and teachers who are personally vehement in their castigation of "politicians" may soften or sugar-coat the political explanations they pass on to children. However, it is likely that the socializing agents pass on something considerably more important than specific political attitudes—namely, general orientations toward the adult world. The child, through the entirety of his experiences with adults, acquires a frame of reference within which to place an especially important class of adult—the political leaders. This seems to be the best way to explain the remarkable lack of political cynicism among children. Children certainly cannot be completely insulated from adult attitudes of distrust toward politics. Rather, it may be hypothesized that, having learned to see adults as many times life size, children simply misperceive and otherwise screen out the discordant negative elements in the adult political environment.

Psychoanalytic theory suggests an integral connection between the feelings one develops toward figures in the primary environment (such as parents) and one's later responses to individuals in the secondary environment (such as politicians). The latter relationships become invested with deep personal feelings, sometimes in the form of direct reflections of primary group relationships, sometimes in the form of compensating reactions to them. This notion is now quite familiar and in fact has been thoroughly vulgarized in the form of popular journalistic references to political "father figures." Vulgarizations notwithstanding, it may have considerable empirical substance. At any rate, a degree of clinical evidence supporting the hypothesis has accumulated. That young children's descriptions of political leaders reflect imagery of benevolence, protectiveness, exceptional sagacity, etc., also is consistent with this hypothesis, although this is scarcely "proof" that an unconscious linking of primary and secondary figures has taken place.

As we have seen, the child's glowing political imagery shows signs of attrition (mainly in the use of "benevolent" language), during the five-year span of this sample. But the greatest change away from political euphoria probably is during adolescence. Disillusionment, following increased realistic political understanding, might produce such changes. Another likely cause would be the adolescent's need to assume adult mannerisms, including in some cases an inside dopester's appraisal of politics. Adolescence is, at any rate, a time for felling idols and perceiving the commanding figures of one's adult environment in a more fallible light.

(2) How does knowledge that the political learning sequence is from childhood idealism to adult realism and cynicism add to our understanding of citizens' responses to political authority? To answer this some further remarks on adult orientations to political leaders are necessary.

The cynical imagery of Americans seems to be less functionally relevant to their political behavior than the positive side of their responses—their respect for high political leaders and their frequent willingness to hold individual leaders in great esteem. This is evident not merely from such relatively narrow mechanisms as the *fait accompli* effect and the general willingness to accept the verdict of elections. The oft-proclaimed stability of the American political system—in spite of a remarkably heterogeneous population—suggests more broadly that powerful psychological mechanisms encouraging political obedience are present in the citizenry. These mechanisms may be as important as many of the more familiar historical, political, economic, and social factors which are drawn on to explain the complex phenomenon of political stability.

Psychologists of various schools, ranging from psychoanalysis to learning theory, have argued that "learning which takes place early in life should have especially great influence on lasting personality characteristics."[2] It also may be that political and social orientations which are acquired early will be particularly influential in adult behavior. As we have seen, the more negative attitudes toward political leaders are chronologically late arrivals, whereas the firm impression that leaders are important people emerges early and almost unconsciously—years before the child has more than a smattering of factual political information. Thus when the adult is in conflict between his two inconsistent assessments of political leaders, the longest held of these would be most likely to influence his response. In this respect it is worth noting that party identification, which also is acquired before the age of political reasoning, is a more important determinant of adult electoral choice than other motivating variables.

The uniquely positive conceptions and misconceptions of leaders displayed by New Haven respondents, statements such as "The Mayor pays working people like banks," certainly are not important in the conscious political imagery of adults. But even here the fact that they once existed may be of some importance in understanding adult political behavior. If the psychoanalytic hypotheses linking political imagery to the primary group relationships which are vital in molding the personality are valid, it could follow that some early political images exercise an unconscious effect on adult choices. To the degree that responses to political authority are deeply rooted in the personality additional

[2]Irvin L. Child, "Socialization," in Gardner Lindzey, *Handbook of Social Psychology* (Cambridge, 1954), p. 678.

predictions might be made. For example, clinical experience suggests that in times of personal or community crisis individuals might tend to resume their earlier ways of viewing authority.

Research Prospects

So far I have attempted to relate two aspects of the way orientations toward political leaders develop, to the likelihood that these orientations will be influential in adult life. I have suggested that if the orientation is learned early, or if it becomes tied to intimate primary group experiences, it should have an especially strong effect on later behavior. To this a single more specific hypothesis about the possibility of regression has been added. Further theorizing and research is necessary to generate more in the way of specific, testable hypotheses. At present the general theories of development which have been spun out by Freud, Piaget, Sullivan, and Erikson, for example, have received only limited empirical verification and are poorly correlated with the empirical norms of development reported by child psychologists and the little which is known about the genesis of political and social orientations.

Theory building and hypothesis elaboration might best proceed in the context of concrete research, since little is known in detail at present about how political behavior develops. The following are some of the *desiderata* of such research:

A. We need to know more about children's political images. The data presented in this paper are no more than a first approximation of how children perceive political authority. Do they differentiate between a wider range of political roles than those presented in the New Haven questionnaire? How do their responses vary over time and space? How prevalent are responses of the sort which arose spontaneously in the present study—imagery of benevolence, for example? New instruments will have to be developed to explore these responses in further detail.

B. We need information on the types of independent variables which are related to differences in childhood political response. Do images of political leaders vary with the child's personality type? Do they vary with his family structure? In view of the continuing interest of social scientists in a number of disciplines in relationships between personality, culture, and social organization, there should be increasing possibilities for interdisciplinary collaboration.

Broader sampling of demographic groups will furnish insight into additional independent variables. Here the speculations about the political stability of nations earlier in this paper suggest that cross-cultural investigation may be promising. Recent studies of children's responses to (non-political) authority figures by Gladys and Harold Anderson show substantial national differences in such perspectives as the expectation of punishment for a misdemeanor.[3]

C. Most important (and most difficult), we need ways of determining in some more precise manner than has been possible here what effects early orientations have on later political behavior. Here progress will be slowest, but by the same token validated propositions will be most rewarding. To a considerable extent advances will be dependent upon accomplishments in basic socialization research. This is an area of investigation in which experiments are not normally possible and knowledge accumulates somewhat uncertainly on the basis of correlational studies. Again, collaboration with ongoing research in other disciplines is both desirable and possible. For example, there have been many longitudinal projects which followed the same samples of children over varying periods of time. Other procedures short of the longitudinal study also exist for studying socialization.

As inevitably slow as the early stages of such research may be, the long run possibilities are exciting. For, as John Dollard has commented, if "the life of the individual is a single connected whole," it will be necessary, in order to enrich our understanding of adult political existence, "to peer down the long avenue of the individual life to see how the present-day event matured."[4]

---

12. Psychological Selfhood and Tolerance

Beyond political systems, beyond the social arrangements that add to or detract from man's humanity or inhumanity to man, the development of the "self" and the human personality is crucially related to politics. For example, the "enhanced self" described by Christian Bay in the first selection is a bulwark against the enticements of demagogues, manipulations by government agencies, and the abandonment of human reason as a tool of political analysis. The self-respecting individual with a strong ego recognizes and tolerates the difference between realistic political perceptions and utopian ideals.

The contemporary political world is ambiguous and contradictory. A second psychological support for reason and freedom is the ability to tolerate this ambiguity and the avoidance of mental rigidity that leads to prejudice and other kinds of

[3]A bibliography of portions of this study which have been published is contained in Harold H. Anderson *et al.*, "Image of the Teacher by Adolescent Children in Four Countries: Germany, England, Mexico, United States," *Journal of Social Psychology*, 1959, *50*: 47–55. . . .
[4]John Dollard, *Criteria for the Life History* (New Haven, 1935), p. 27.

distorted thinking. In the ingenious series of experiments reported here, Milton Rokeach shows that ethnocentric attitudes toward racial and religious groups are related to the personality structure of the individual and, in particular, to the way he goes about solving various intellectual problems.

While there is often just cause for the attribution of responsibility in all political systems, a set response of stereotyped blame accompanies the immature ego and the intolerant self. By projection, displacement, and hasty moralistic judgments an individual or group may unjustly place blame on a set of "industrial villains" or even an entire nation. In his selection included here, Robert Lane reports the responses of a group of typical Americans and concludes, encouragingly, that most of them do not hastily condemn their public officials. The sample that Lane interviewed seemed to recognize that politicans are more often in error than evil; on the basis of this sample it might be said that people seek to understand rather than to blame. In contrast, the intolerant, constricted self thrives on moral indignation and personal attributions of good and evil; such a "disposition toward indignation on the part of a broad public," concludes Lane, "is a disservice to democracy."

THE ENHANCED SELF AND THE STRONG EGO

CHRISTIAN BAY

The Self and the Ego

The self is a crucial conception in a theory of psychological freedom. My first and very rough definition of "freedom" has equated this concept with "self-expression." Idealist philosophers and neo-Freudian psychologists alike have stressed the futility of formal freedom (or, in my language, social freedom) if people pay for it with loss of purpose or anxiety neurosis. Unless people have the psychological capacity for self-expression, a free society can become a menace that they will want to escape. . . .

The self is the individual's awareness of acceptable aspects of his personality; it is part of the individual's consciousness. Let me choose this preliminary definition . . . : *The self is the image of one's own qualities, or evaluated characteristics.*

Pages 169–182: Reprinted from *The Structure of Freedom* by Christian Bay with the permission of the publishers, Stanford University Press. © 1958 by the Board of Trustees of the Leland Stanford Junior University. Title supplied by the editor.

But man's total personality can be compared to an iceberg, in the sense that only a small part of it is visible, even to himself. In other respects it may be compared to a battleground, if we follow Freud's dramatic descriptions of the everlasting and ruthless contest between the id, the superego, and the ego. There is something to be said for the criticism that Freud tended to reify these concepts, in discussing them as if they referred to real layers in the unconscious. "It appears more convenient to distinguish different functions of the mind than to divide it into air-tight compartments," says Franz Alexander,[1] and I agree, even if the reference to "air-tight compartments" is rather exaggerated and certainly does not represent Freud's view. . . .

The ego function is analogous to that of the driver in an automobile or, in Freud's words, the rider on a horse. "The horse provides the locomotive energy, and the rider has the prerogative of determining the goal and of guiding the movement of his powerful mount toward it."[2] The analogy to the superego is brought in if we picture our horseman on a crowded street; and the drama of the conflict is portrayed if we assume that the horse after a long stay in the stable is aching to run at a high speed.

The ego, then, is the mediator between organism and environment; it has or is the decision-making function. It organizes motives and behavior. For the ego, it may be said that the individual organism, too, is part of the environment, and that the task is to decide on and execute a synthesis between the two kinds of demands, the individual's original wishes and the socially derived motives. Alexander suggests that there are three ego functions: "external and internal perception, integration, and executive action."[3] These correspond to the basic functions of the administrator of a social organization; in Lasswell's and McDougal's terms, these are the intelligence function, the recommending function (approximately), and the applying function. "The ego is that part of the organism which assumes the task of harmoniously gratifying our needs and desires," says Alexander, and he proposes that "a healthy ego can best be compared to a democratic state which recognizes private needs of all kinds, gives them a hearing, and meets the conflicting interests by mediation and compromise."[4]

Two points need stressing before I consider the important concept of the ego properly introduced. The government of the democratic state is not necessarily wise and neither necessarily is the ego, even a healthy ego. Its foresight may be poor, and certainly it is as a rule much inferior to the hindsight of the conscious self. Also, the ego may be

---

[1]Franz Alexander, *Fundamentals of Psychoanalysis* (New York: W. W. Norton, 1948), p. 83.

[2]Sigmund Freud, *New Introductory Lectures on Psychoanalysis*, trans. W. T. H. Sprott (London: Hogarth Press, 1933), p. 108.

[3]Alexander, *op. cit.*, p. 87.

[4]*Ibid.*, p. 194. When speaking of the ego as a "part of the organism," incidentally, Alexander comes close to opening himself to the same kind of criticism to which he has subjected Freud . . . .

"unjust," if we continue the analogy with the democratic state. Some egos tend to favor the demands of the id, others those of the super-ego, while again others tend to be inconsistent. I still speak of a healthy ego, so long as it is not (a) incapable of solving the conflict, (b) able to solve it only precariously, with a high degree of ambivalence, or (c) completely dominated by the id or the superego. . . .

The second important point is that the ego is to a large extent composed of unconscious and preconscious functions. This is well brought out in a discussion by Solomon Asch of the relationship between the ego "and its conscious representative, the self. . . . The self, being a phenomenal representation, does not include all that belongs to the ego and at times apprehends the ego wrongly. The ego is prior to the self and far wider than it. The self is not the mirror image of the ego; there is between them the same kind of relation as between the physical object and its psychological representation. There can be grave differences between the person as he is, as science would describe him, and as he would view himself."[5]

Types of Identification and the Role of Self-Esteem

As a preliminary approximation, the "self" has been defined as the image of one's own qualities, or evaluated characteristics. For reasons of linguistic convenience I shall at times speak of "self-image" or "self-awareness" as synonymous with "self."

In terms of the internal dynamics of the individual personality, the boundaries of the self are drawn by the process of repression or dissociation. The self is the individual's awareness of acceptable characteristics of his own personality. . . . [M]any events and insights are so anxiety-provoking that they become barred from consciousness. Psychotherapy consists partly in trying to reduce the anxiety evoked by such events and insights and partly in trying to increase the individual's capacity to tolerate or face the anxiety that remains, so as to reduce the amount of repression. One task of the therapist, in other words, is to extend the patient's self: he learns to register and be aware of a higher proportion of his painful or humiliating experiences and the unflattering self-insights they may occasion. . . .

There are, it seems to me, two main lines of approach in trying to carve out a useful identification concept. One alternative is the operational approach, which can be taken only at the price of some degree of behavioristic superficiality. The other alternative is the dynamic or depth approach, which makes a number of unproved theoretical as-

[5]Solomon E. Asch, *Social Psychology* (New York: Prentice-Hall, 1952), pp. 276, 278.

sumptions necessary. This dilemma is, of course, only one aspect of the general issue between empiricism and the depth approach in psychology. . . .

Instead of defining "identification" operationally in terms of vicarious satisfactions in the success of other people, I wish to try a preliminary depth definition in terms of expansion of or abandonment of the self. *A person identifies with someone or something to the extent that he incorporates this object into his own self or incorporates his self into this object.* This is a preliminary and perhaps somewhat cryptic formulation, which will be improved upon as I proceed. The first real difficulty, it would seem, is how to conceptualize this incorporation process. One plausible and helpful distinction has been suggested by Freud: "Identification is a very important kind of relationship with another person, probably the most primitive, and is not to be confused with object-choice. One can express the difference between them in this way: when a boy identifies himself with his father, he wants to *be like* his father; when he makes him the object of his choice, he wants to *have* him, to possess him; in the first case the ego is altered on the model of his father, in the second case that is not necessary."[6]

In the conceptual scheme of [William] James, a man's bank account is as much part of his self as is his wife. It would seem an important improvement, however, to try to distinguish as sharply as we can between property attitudes and identification attitudes, as Freud does. The former type of attitude involves acquisition, while the latter involves giving something or even sacrificing. Acquiring things, or controlling people, requires no restructuring of the ego, as Freud observes. Neither deeply affects the underlying currents of id and superego, on which the self is floating. Identification with other people, on the other hand, means that images of these people's needs and norms are incorporated in the ego ideal or the superego (or at times take over the superego functions), necessitating a new balance to be established by the ego.

Not all identification attitudes are equally important, however, and at some point on a scale of diminishing importance it is convenient to speak of a mere "favorable attitude" instead of "identification." An individual has many "social selves," as James observed, but not all of them should be considered components of the *self*, as I prefer to use the latter term. A man may be a son, a husband, a father, a teacher, a member of a political party, a member of an orchestra, a friend of Mr. B, an acquaintance of Mr. C, and a great admirer of President Eisenhower. In each of these capacities different attitudes give rise to different demands and expectations on the total self. Which of these attitudes should

[6]Freud, *op. cit.*, pp. 90–91.

be deemed important enough to be considered identifications? Or, to ask the same question in a different way, which of these roles in an individual's life are constituents of his self and which of them are only to be considered external orientations?

The answer is not purely a question of verbal preferences. It must be psychologically plausible, and it should preferably be in terms that lend themselves to empirically meaningful interpretations (it is too much to hope for empirically concise terms at this point). The closest I have been able to get toward an answer satisfying these two criteria is to conceive of the individual's *self-esteem* as a kind of seismograph for determining the relative importance of the various roles and attachments in his life.

Thus, the self has preliminarily been defined as the image of one's own qualities. This image consists primarily of an appraisal of one's own record and competence in all one's important roles or social relationships. What I am saying now is that each role is important to the extent that the individual's self-esteem is enhanced when he feels he is performing the role well or diminished when he feels he is doing poorly in it. When the self-esteem is affected, the role is either part of the self or the self has gone into the role. Or, in identification terms, A's attitude toward B becomes an identification to the extent that A's self-esteem hinges on his constant readiness to exert himself in favor of B's needs and demands.

"Self-esteem" must not be confused with a simple calculation of how one's self adds up, if all "good" qualities are summed up and all "bad" qualities subtracted. A person's self-esteem is in a psychological sense prior to the self-image; it is a concept referring to the person's fundamental feeling of his own worth. It is the fundament on which the self-image is built. If this fundament is firm, the self is capable of facing many unflattering truths. If the fundament is shaky, the self is likely to compensate by refusing to acknowledge weaknesses or other undesirable qualities.

A person's self-esteem may be considered the cathexis of the self or the love of the self. It is developed, as are other aspects of the self, from "reflected appraisals." But the relative importance of the most intimate relationships is probably much greater in the development of self-esteem than in the formation of the more cognitive aspects of the self or self-image. The child who is deeply reassured of the love of his parents, the adult who is securely enjoying the devotion of his spouse or of intimate friends — such people are likely to have a high self-esteem, no matter what many other people may think of them.

And conversely, it may be assumed that persons with a high self-esteem to this extent are able to give their full love to other people.

Sullivan observes: "As one respects oneself so one can respect others. That is one of the peculiarities of human personality that can always be depended on. If there is a valid and real attitude toward the self, that attitude will manifest as valid and real toward others. It is not as ye judge so shall ye be judged, but as you judge yourself so shall you judge others; strange but true so far as I know, and with no exception."[7] Similarly, as you love and esteem yourself (or yourself in the role of pursuing your ego ideal), so you are able to love and esteem other people.

The concept of self-esteem . . . helps me make a crucial distinction between two types of identification: the identifications accompanied by high self-esteem and those accompanied by low self-esteem.

The process of identification serves to extend the self only in so far as the individual has a securely positive self-esteem. Only to that extent does the welfare of certain other people genuinely concern the individual, in the sense that his own well-being is felt to depend immediately on theirs. Only a person enjoying the basic security of a high self-esteem has the surplus from which he can draw a real concern for other people, a concern that equals but never overshadows his concern for his own dignity or maintained self-esteem.

The individual low in self-esteem will have a different type of incentive to identify with other people. He is in a sense fleeing from his self, in search of a new and more satisfactory identity. Let us take Eric Hoffer's "true believer" as our prototype. He is constantly prepared to sacrifice himself for some cause, because his self apart from that cause is worthless. Only a "self-extinguishing" identification with a movement gives him a sense of purpose and personal worth.

The point that belongs in this context is by now clear: *depending primarily on the degree of self-esteem, the process of identification may either enlarge or diminish the individual self.*

By now I am equipped for a second attempt toward defining the identification process. It is convenient to define two analytical types of identification, while assuming that the complexities of life invariably exhibit composite patterns, with elements of both types in different proportions. One type confines the self; the other enlarges it.

Self-sacrificing identification takes place to the extent that an individual comes to consider the general needs of other persons more important than his own. His own needs are substituted by the perceived needs of others, and beyond biological essentials he is concerned with only vicarious satisfactions.

Self-expansive identification takes place to the extent that an individual comes to consider the general needs of other persons *his own.*

[7]Harry S. Sullivan, *Conceptions of Modern Psychiatry* (New York: W. W. Norton, 1953), p. 15.

His individual self incorporates the perceived needs of those persons as equivalent with his own.

Identification, generically considered, takes place to the extent that the individual comes to consider the general needs of one or more other persons either his own or more important than those perceived as his own. One may ask: in the latter case, how can any needs be more important to me than my own? Must we not say that all needs that are important to me are my own, and more so the more important they are? The answer is that the self-sacrificer does make the distinction; he is *in general* motivated to belittle needs he considers "his own," in comparison to the needs he attributes to certain other persons or groups. If he does not make a distinction between "his own" needs and the needs of his objects of identification—it is for most self-sacrificers, probably, quite a sharp dichotomy—then it is a self-expanding and not a self-sacrificing kind of identification. Essentially the same distinction was made by Erich Fromm twenty years ago:

> *Psychologically rather different realities are hiding under Freud's description of "identification," and a less formalistic conceptual scheme would have to differentiate between at least three main types of identification: an acquiring type, i.e., an identification in which I take the other person into my own and by this acquisition strengthen my own ego; an impoverishing type, in which I project myself into some other person and become a part of him, and, lastly, a (conscious or unconscious) feeling of identity, with the conviction that I and the other person are alike and exchangeable.*[8]

It seems to me that the last type is subsumable under the first of the three, since this kind of identification may be seen as an expansion of the self.

There are those who wish to reserve the term "identification" for the self-sacrificing type only, in order to avoid a confusion between two very different psychological processes. Nevitt Sanford argues that there has been a tendency among psychoanalysts to use the term in a loose and shallow manner in deference to common sense usage and in an effort to show that Freudian concepts are adequate also for describing much surface behavior. In harmony with one psychoanalytic usage, Sanford considers identification a *mechanism of defense*. Properly speaking, in his terms, an analyst who is functioning well does not identify with his patient, even if he to some extent must put himself emotionally in the patient's place and be fond of him, though without for a moment losing his task-orientation. "When a patient may properly be said to identify with the analyst, on the other hand, we deal with a process that

---

[8]Erich Fromm, "Sozialpsychologischer Teil," in Max Horkheimer (ed.), *Studien über Autorität und Familie* (Paris: Felix Alcan, 1936), p. 83. (Translated by Bay.)

is unconscious and unrealistic, with a patient who is unsure of himself and, at the moment at least, unconcerned about other people; in desperation he adopts a piece of poor economy as a means of escape from a critical situation."[9] I do not wish to dispute the merits of a narrow identification concept in psychoanalytic theory and therapy, but in a general behavioral theory I wish to make the best of both worlds by using a broad concept close to common usage and at the same time keeping in mind that self-sacrificing identifications as a rule may be considered defense mechanisms set in motion by deficiencies in the ego.

O. H. Mowrer uses the term broadly and makes a distinction between developmental and defensive identification. Sanford, incidentally, objects that both of these processes are developmental and neither is identification. Developmental identification, in Mowrer's terms, is the process whereby the infant becomes stimulated to try to do what his mother does, thus making him learn "to talk, to walk, and to perform other rudimentary *ego functions.*" Defensive identification, on the other hand, is what happens when the child internalizes the parental norms to the point of punishing himself for impulses of which the parents would disapprove. This is the beginning of his conscience or superego.[10]

In my terms, both of Mowrer's types of identification should be considered self-expansive, as a rule, since he incorporates the needs and wishes of other people into his self. However, if the ego development is neglected, and life becomes a tug of war between "bad" impulses and parental superego, then a self-sacrificing type of identification with parents may ensue. The child's attitude to one or both parents may in this case become not unlike the patient's attitude to the analyst after transference; his identification with and complete dependency on his parents become a defense mechanism. He wishes to sacrifice everything for the welfare and glory of his parents, for he is, in the extreme case, totally without ego control and thus without the minimum independence required as a basis for self-esteem.

Among adults extreme cases of self-expansive identification are found in some good marriages and in some friendship relations. It is a matter of unconditional solidarity without any loss of personal identity and integrity. Extreme cases of self-sacrificing identification are found in the sado-masochistic or "symbiotic" marriage situation described by Fromm,[11] in some mothers who "live for their children only," and in Hoffer's "true believer." These identifications are clingings to some substitute for a worthwhile self.

---

[9]Nevitt Sanford, "The Dynamics of Identification," *Psychological Review,* 1955, *62* (2): 108, 106–118. . . .

[10]O. H. Mowrer, *Psychotherapy: Theory and Research* (New York: Ronald Press, 1953), pp. 71–72.

[11]Erich Fromm, *Escape from Freedom* (New York: Rinehart, 1941), p. 159: "Symbiosis, in this psychological sense, means the union of one individual self with another self (or any other power outside of the own self) in such a way as to make each lose the integrity of the own self and to make them completely dependent on each other."

To what extent is man's self-esteem stable, and to what extent does it fluctuate? This is in part a problem of psychological freedom. It may be assumed that the self-esteem tends to be stable to the extent that the general pattern of personality integration has achieved stability. In other words, when basic needs and overt behavior are in fundamental harmony, there would appear to be no internally derived threat to the self-esteem.

Partly, it is also a problem of interpersonal relations. Sudden drops (or increases) in important other people's affection and deference certainly can affect the self-esteem. But the better it has been anchored in a well-integrated personality, the less can it be threatened by a change in other people's behavior.

A low degree of psychological freedom produces two types of instability of self-esteem. The individual may become very easily affected by day-to-day appraisals of other people, so that he may bristle with self-esteem one day and feel terribly inferior the next day. Often, however, a defense mechanism intervenes to remove the strain that extreme fluctuations of this kind would induce and *ambivalence* toward the self is introduced. This is the second type of instability.

In the ambivalence situation, an apparently good self-esteem is achieved by way of removing unflattering insights about oneself from consciousness. But the anxiety is still there, and in turn it stimulates further self-distortions or delusions and further insecurity.

It is time now to turn to the problem of mental health and neurosis in relation to psychological freedom. The crucial problem of understanding the conditions for stability in man's self-esteem cannot be answered without a discussion of neurotic processes. Also, it is important for the clarification of my psychological freedom concept to explain how it differs from concepts such as "maturity" and "mental health."

Mental Health, Maturity, and Psychological Freedom

. . . There are two opposite poles in the ways "maturity" has been defined. One extreme has been to equate maturity with maximal social adjustment, while the other extreme has tended to equate it with maximal individuality and independence vis-à-vis institutions. A caricature of the former approach is attributed to Harry Stack Sullivan, who had a wry sense of humor: "And now, when you have ceased to care for adventure, when you have forgotten romance, when the only things worthwhile to you are prestige and income, then you have grown up, then you have become an adult."[12]

---

[12]Quoted in Thurman W. Arnold, *The Folklore of Capitalism* (Garden City, N.Y.: Blue Ribbon Books, 1937), p. 163.

This caricature is not very far-fetched, however. It is widely observed and agreed that some trends in contemporary education, social work, and psychotherapy are oriented toward helping individuals adjust to their milieus at almost any price, even at the price of suppressing all individuality in the process. Admittedly, it is most important to help individuals get along with their fellows, especially if they have no practical choice between different kinds of milieus. But to make social adjustment the only goal, and to equate it with "maturity," as is often done, would seem to stimulate both individual and, in the long run, social stagnation.

For an opposite type of maturity concept, with no reference to the demands of the social environments, take the following: "We can characterize the mature personality as one who has succeeded in integrating a relatively steady internal environment that is capable of remaining comparatively independent of the immediately present external environment."[13] This is a good definition, both in being cognitively meaningful and in making capacity for independence the criterion, not the capacity for slavish adaptation. But this definition, it seems to me, may be more fruitfully related to "psychological freedom," as the discussion in the remainder of this section will indicate. . . .

"Mental health" and "neurosis" are a different pair of terms, which can be given fairly clear and convenient cognitive meanings. And the most useful employment of these terms, it seems to me, is in relation to the individual's ability to tolerate a realistic self, meaning a realistic image of his own qualities and experiences.

It should be pointed out that "neurosis" as usually conceived is not the logical opposite of mental health. As Abraham H. Maslow says, "It would now be universally agreed upon that the classical neurosis as a whole as well as single neurotic symptoms are characteristically coping mechanisms. If a neurotic symptom does have a function, does do a job for the person, then we must assume that the person is better off for having this symptom."[14] It is the psychosis rather than the neurosis that comes close to being a logical opposite of good mental health. A psychosis has been defined as "a relatively severe mental disease, i.e., one in which there is a loss or disorder in mental processes."[15]

The neurotic individual is struggling to regain his mental health. The psychotic has practically given up the struggle and has little or no help to offer the psychiatrist in his own cure. The mentally healthy person may have avoided the struggle. It is not to be taken for granted, however, that the avoidance of this kind of struggle is always desirable.

---

[13]Harold D. Lasswell and Myres S. McDougal, "Law, Science, and Policy," Working Paper, 1954, Part II.

[14]Abraham H. Maslow, "The Expressive Component of Behavior," in Howard Brand (ed.), *The Study of Personality: A Book of Readings* (New York: John Wiley, 1954), p. 371.

[15]Quoted from Horace B. English, *A Student's Dictionary of Psychological Terms*, 4th ed., in Gardner Murphy, *Personality: A Biosocial Approach to Origins and Structure* (New York: Harper, 1947), p. 995. . . .

Before I elaborate on this last point, let me say that the psychotics do not present any theoretical problems in the study of pyschological freedom, in that they are, as long as the psychosis lasts, completely the victims of their condition. They have barred themselves from insight into important aspects of reality, including some of their own important wishes and needs. The neurotic, too, is deficient in self-insight, but in one sense that is true of all people. "Know thyself" is, strictly speaking, an ideal that can never be attained in full. But while the completely nonneurotic person, if there is such a being, has no internal barriers against self-exploration, the neurotic is able to pry into certain areas of himself only, while other areas are bolted with various "defense mechanisms" . . . .

It is possible to avoid anxiety, and it is possible to avoid neurosis by not looking down "into the abyss," as Kierkegaard said. An example is the case of Phyllis reported by Rollo May, who avoided facing the problems of life by accepting a life in bondage under her strong-willed mother.[16] As this case illustrates, the avoidance of neurosis is not always a desirable goal, if one cares for the growth of freedom. Avoidance of insight and responsibility may prevent the growth of anxiety and neurosis, but at the price of preventing the growth of individuality as well.

The scope of this dilemma becomes a huge one, however, when we consider the impact of society on the individual. Social institutions require conformity to certain kinds of behavior patterns and strongly encourage conformity to the corresponding thought and evaluation patterns as well. Resistance to social pressures easily gives rise to anxieties about one's own values and about oneself, especially if resistance is followed by a measure of social rejection. The safe course of conduct in order to reduce this kind of anxiety is to become a strict conformist —again at the price of giving up the chance of developing individual potentialities. Erich Fromm has described the mechanisms leading to "automaton conformity," and David Riesman has pointed out how the "other-directed" character is heavily predisposed for just this kind of anxiety reduction.

Fromm raises the further question, however, of whether societies may not differ greatly in the extent to which their institutions tend to do violence to individual growth potentials. He poses the problem of how to conceive of a society whose institutional patterns are compatible with meaningful and heterogeneous individual lives: "The sane society is that which corresponds to the needs of man; not necessarily to what he *feels* to be his needs—because even the most pathological aims can be felt subjectively as that which the person wants most—but to what his needs are objectively, as they can be ascertained by the study of man."[17]

---

[16]Rollo May, *The Meaning of Anxiety* (New York: Ronald Press, 1950), pp. 305–309.

[17]Erich Fromm, "The Psychology of Normalcy," *Dissent*, 1954, *1*: 43. In *The Sane Society*, Fromm makes an extensive inquiry into this problem. Cf. also his *Escape from Freedom*, p. 138.

After describing the modern "automaton conformist," Fromm concludes that "he suffers from a defect of spontaneity and individuality that may seem incurable." But he gets along, as do millions of his fellows: "For most of them, the culture provides patterns which enable them *to live with a defect without becoming ill*. It is as if each culture provided the remedy against the outbreak of manifest neurotic symptoms which would result from the defect produced by it."[18]

The background of these considerations causes me to endorse Fromm's "defense of the neurotic," if one may call it that: "The neurotic person can be characterized as somebody who was not ready to surrender completely in the battle for his self . . . from the standpoint of human values, he is less crippled than the kind of normal person who has lost his individuality altogether."[19] Among others who have stressed this point, that the neurotic may be "right" and society "wrong," the most forceful writers have been Robert Lindner and Lawrence K. Frank.[20]

THE OPEN MIND

MILTON ROKEACH

The present investigation is concerned with an analysis of the thinking processes of individuals known to be ethnocentric in their attitudes toward racial and religious outgroups. As has been shown by [several writers] ethnocentrism is dynamically related to the personality structure of the individual. The rather dramatic personality differences found between prejudiced and unprejudiced individuals, both on overt and covert levels, as reported by these writers, strongly suggest that similar differences would also be found between such individuals in the manner in which they go about solving various intellectual problems.

The basic assumption of the present investigation is that one of the characteristics of ethnocentric thinking is a rigidity and inflexibility of the thinking process. It is not necessary to go far beyond common experience to convince ourselves that there is probably nothing more resistant to change than stereotypic attitudes toward outgroups. The main problem which suggested itself for study was whether this type of rigid thinking process operates only in the solution of social problems

---

[18]Erich Fromm, *The Sane Society* (New York: Rinehart, 1955), p. 16. On "automaton conformity," see also *Escape from Freedom*, pp. 185–206.

[19]Fromm, *Escape from Freedom*, p. 139.

[20]See Lawrence K. Frank, *Society As the Patient: Essays on Culture and Personality* (New Brunswick, N.J.: Rutgers University Press, 1950) and Robert M. Lindner, *Prescription for Rebellion* (New York: Rinehart, 1952). . . .

From "Generalized Mental Rigidity As a Factor in Ethnocentrism" in *Journal of Abnormal and Social Psychology*, 1948 (July), *43*: 259–263, 268–274, 276–277. Title supplied by the editor.

or whether it is equally characteristic of the ethnocentric individual in his approach to all kinds of problems.

The main hypothesis, then, can be stated as follows: The rigidity inherent in the ethnocentric person's solution of social problems is not an isolated phenomenon within the personality but is rather an aspect of a general rigidity factor which will also manifest itself in the solution of any problem, be it social or non-social in nature.

We are not alone in hypothesizing the existence of such a general rigidity factor. Gardner Murphy, in his Foreword to Hartley's *Problems in Prejudice*, hints at the existence of such a factor when he says ". . . it is of importance to note the very broad base of *generality* — general rigidity and intolerance — which serves as primary source of the specific phenomena in the prejudice area."[1]

A second hypothesis, closely related to the first, is that the mode of thought of the ethnocentric person in solving problems is more concrete in nature, whereas the mode of thought of the non-ethnocentric person in solving problems is more abstract in nature. Studies in rigidity in feebleminded subjects, in brain-injured and spastic subjects, and in schizophrenia all indicate that concreteness of thinking is usually to be found in rigid persons. If, then, it should turn out that prejudiced people were generally more rigid than non-prejudiced people, greater concreteness of thinking should also be expected in those who are prejudiced.

Rigidity has been variously defined as fixation of response, lack of variability, perseveration, Einstellung, and degree of impermeability of boundaries. It is not considered to be within the scope of this paper to evaluate the ways in which rigidity has been used by various writers. . . . Rigidity in the present report will be defined as the inability to change one's set when the objective conditions demand it, as the inability to restructure a field in which there are alternative solutions to a problem in order to solve that problem more efficiently. . . .

A further comment about the main hypothesis to be tested is now in order. The main hypothesis is really composed of two different but related hypotheses: (1) That individuals who are rigid in solving specific social problems (as measured by an attitude scale) also show up as rigid in solving non-social problems. (2) That there is a general rigidity factor. The primary concern of the present investigation is to gather and present evidence bearing on (1) above. Such evidence will, no doubt, also have relevancy with respect to (2) above, but this is not our primary interest here. Rather, the existence of such a rigidity factor can be accepted on the basis of other evidence already available. Several studies on perseveration have been published, mainly by British psychologists under the leadership of Spearman, which indicate the

[1]E. Hartley, *Problems in Prejudice* (New York: King's Crown, 1946), p. viii.

existence of a perseveration factor. The general procedure in such studies was to devise a battery of tests, each purported to measure perseveration. A factor analysis of such tests has usually indicated the existence of a group factor. Thus, Spearman, in summarizing several such studies, writes: ". . . the evidence for some group factor or factors pervading these tests of perseveration leaves nothing to be desired."[2] And from Rogers: ". . . perseveration has been indicated as a general functional unity, subject to isolation by psychometric procedures."[3]

The Measurement of Ethnocentrism

The California Ethnocentrism Scale, composed of ten items, was used to obtain a measure of the extent of a subject's ethnocentrism. The subject indicated on a six-point scale the degree of his agreement or disagreement with items about zootsuiters, Negroes, Jews, and foreigners. For a definition of the concept of ethnocentrism, the nature of the scale used and the statistical characteristics of the scale the reader is referred to [the work of] Levinson and Sanford[4] and Frenkel-Brunswik, Levinson, and Sanford.[5] In the experiments to be reported the subjects were divided into two groups, those "High" in prejudice and those "Low" in prejudice. Whether a subject was "High" or "Low" was determined by whether he obtained a score falling above or below the median of all subjects participating in a given experiment.

An Experiment with Arithmetic Problems

The Einstellung Experiment as a Test for Rigidity. The technique used is a modification of a technique used by Luchins[6] for the investigation of the Einstellung-effect. Subjects are asked to solve problems in which required quantities of water are to be obtained by manipulating three jars of given capacities. To establish a set, several problems are presented solvable only by one relatively complicated method. Then follow several critical problems solvable both by the complicated method and by a more simple, direct method. . . . The solution of such a problem by the complicated method may be taken as an indication of rigidity.

The Subjects. The subjects were sophomore students taking courses in elementary psychology at the University of California. Since the ethnocentrism scale used asked questions about various minority groups, and since it is a well-established fact that minority members

[2]C. E. Spearman, *Abilities of Man: Their Nature and Measurements* (New York: Macmillan, 1927), p. 296.

[3]Kenneth H. Rogers, "Perseveration," *Journal of Mental Science*, 1935, *81*: 142.

[4]D. J. Levinson and R. N. Sanford, "A Scale for the Measurement of Anti-Semitism," *Journal of Social Psychology*, 1944, *17*: 339–370.

[5]E. Frenkel-Brunswik, D. J. Levinson, and R. N. Sanford, "The Anti-Democratic Personality," in T. M. Newcomb and E. Hartley (eds., *Readings in Social Psychology* (New York: Holt, 1947).

[6]A. S. Luchins, "Mechanization in Problem-Solving: The Effect of Einstellung," *Psychological Monographs*, 1942, *54*, No. 6.

respond favorably to items about their own groups, it was necessary to exclude from consideration all subjects who were thought to belong to minority groups. Those excluded were Negroes, Jews, Chinese, Japanese, Mexicans, and all subjects born outside the continental United States. Information about race and religion was obtained from the face sheet of the Ethnocentrism Scale, and only this information served as a basis for the rejection of a subject from further statistical consideration. On the whole, then, it may be said that the subjects were white, native-born Americans with the possible exception of a few minority members who "slipped through." The average age of these subjects is greater than is usual for college students because of the fact that it included many veterans of World War II.

Procedure. The experiment was administered anonymously to groups of from 35 to 48 subjects at a time. After the instructions for the arithmetic rigidity experiment were read orally, the experimenter placed each problem on the blackboard . . . . There was a 2½-minute time limit per problem. The subjects indicated their solutions to each of the arithmetic problems on a new separate page of a blue examination booklet. At the end of this part of the session the subjects were given copies of the California Ethnocentrism Scale to fill out. Each subject's blue examination booklet and ethnocentrism questionnaire were matched by means of assigned identification numbers.

Design of Rigidity Experiment. . . . [T]he first problem presented is an explanatory problem involving two jars, the purpose being to familiarize the subject with the nature of the problems to follow. The second problem is a *control critical* problem solvable both by the rigid and simple methods. Such a control problem was inserted at the beginning of the experiment for two reasons: First, to demonstrate that when no set has yet been experimentally established most subjects will solve such critical problems by the simple method. Secondly, by eliminating from further statistical consideration those subjects who solve this control problem by the complicated method, the subjects who remain are all equated in that they all demonstrate their ability to solve a critical problem by the simple method.

Problem 3 is a three-jar example. Problems 4 and 5 are test problems solvable only by the set method. These are followed by five critical problems solvable both by the complicated and simple methods. According to the main hypothesis those high on ethnocentrism should continue to use the rigid method of solution in solving each of these five critical problems, while those low in ethnocentrism should more frequently change over to the simple method of solution.

The second hypothesis, namely, that those high in ethnocentrism are more concrete in their mode of thought than those low in ethnocentrism, was tested in two ways:

1. Use of scratch paper. The subjects were instructed to solve each problem on a new right-hand page of the blue examination booklet and, if they wished, to use the left-hand page for scratch work. For each problem, it was possible to determine whether or not scratch paper was used. Evidence of erasures and "piece-meal" solutions were also regarded as scratch-paper solutions. It seemed reasonable to suppose that the use of scratch paper might mean that the subject did not really perceive the problem as a whole but rather saw the problem as being composed of several parts which, when manipulated in a stereotyped temporal and positional fashion, would automatically and mechanically lead to the "correct" solution. It was as if the individual had to use a "crutch" in order to subtract one- or two-digit numbers from each other. It was as if the subject was asked to add 10 and 4 and, instead of giving the solution immediately, had to avail himself of an electric calculator, punch in the number 10, then punch in the number 4, and then read off the sum from the dial or printed tape.

2. Verbalization of response. A second measure of concreteness of mode of thought was to determine whether the subjects indicated their solutions to a given problem verbally or arithmetically. In the instructions the subjects were given a choice of indicating their solutions to each problem arithmetically (e.g., $61 - 31 - 4 - 4 = 22$) or verbally (e.g., "Fill the 61-quart jar, pour off 31 quarts, leaving 30 quarts in the 61-quart jar. Then pour off 4 quarts twice leaving 22 quarts in the big jar"). For each problem the mean number of words used by the two groups was determined. It was reasoned that the use of arithmetical symbols in indicating a solution was a more abstract as well as a more concise and efficient way of writing down the solution than the use of words. . . .

Experiments with Maps

Insofar as possible, an attempt was made to construct the pattern of the new experiment parallel to that of the arithmetic experiment. The subject is presented with five simple maps in booklet form (5″ x 5″), all *identical* except for street names. . . . The subject is allowed to study each map for 15 seconds. After each map is presented the subject turns to the next page where he is asked to "describe in your own words the *shortest* way to go from _____ and _____ Streets, to _____ and _____ Streets."

On all problems the starting point is the southwest corner and the goal is the northeast corner. Each of these maps contains a diagonal pathway which is of no help in reaching the goal. Then follow five critical map problems, *identical* with the previous maps except that the diagonal pathways are usable as short-cuts in reaching the goal. . . .

The Main Experiment

Design of the Map Experiment.   A description of the design of the map experiment follows:
   1. Two explanatory problems.
   2. No control problem was used because preliminary experiments showed that the use of a control problem greatly prevented the later establishment of a set. Instead, a control *group* was used.
   3. Five problems designed to establish a set where the diagonal pathway cannot be used.
   4. Five critical problems, solvable by using or not using diagonal short-cuts.
   5. Opportunity to use scratch paper.
   6. Opportunity for verbalization.
   7. Fifteen seconds to study each map but no time limit to write down the solution.
   Procedure.   The experiment was administered in small groups. The subjects were handed booklets in which the maps and questions relating to each map were mimeographed. The instructions were given orally. Since the session lasted for almost one hour it was not possible to give the California Ethnocentrism Scale during the same period. Instead this was given one week later.
   Subjects.   As in the arithmetic experiments, the subjects were white, native-born with the main minority subjects excluded. The subjects were all taking the first semester course in elementary psychology at the University of California.
   Results. The main experiment was administered to a total of 55 subjects. Of these, 8 were eliminated because of errors in the reproduction of the direction of the diagonal pathway on one or more of the set problems. One was eliminated because of failure to solve two set problems. There then remained 46 subjects, all of whom were equated in that no memory errors were made. These were classified into 23 Highs and 23 Lows on the basis of their scoring above or below the median of this particular group on the California Ethnocentrism Scale.
   . . . [D]ifferences in the expected direction were obtained on rigidity of solutions and on verbalization. The use of scratch paper did not differentiate the two groups and the data, therefore, are not presented. Considering rigidity of solutions, on each critical problem there are more Highs than Lows who persist in using the longer route in spite of the presence of a diagonal short-cut. On the first critical problem (Problem 8), for example, 10 out of 23 Highs (43 per cent), as against only 4 out of 23 Lows (17 per cent), failed to use the diagonal short-cut. Problems 8 and 12 reach the 10-per-cent level of significance but not the 5-per-cent level (chi square=3.68 and 3.06, respectively).

A comparison of the verbalization scores shows that on every problem the mean number of words used is greater for the Highs than for the Lows. The differences for Problems 3, 4, 6, and 7 are significant at the 5-per-cent level using Fisher's t-test (t=2.26, 2.10, 2.42, and 2.03, respectively).

The results found with the map technique, although based on a small number of cases, may be interpreted as confirmation of the hypotheses relating ethnocentrism to a general rigidity factor and to modes of thought associated with rigidity.

In the experiment with the maps, however, it is not known whether the Einstellung-effect is due to the preceding set problems or not. It was anticipated that if the critical problems were presented without the preceding set problems 100 per cent of the subjects would see the diagonal pathway and use it in their solution of the problem. To determine this experimentally a control group was used.

A Control Map Experiment

The control group was composed of 12 subjects. The procedure was identical with that of the main experiment except that the preceding five set map problems were omitted. The subjects solved only the five critical map problems in which the diagonal short-cut may or may not be used. . . .

. . . For problem 8, the first critical problem, 11 out of 12 subjects in the control group (92 per cent), as against 14 out of 46 subjects in the experimental group (30 per cent), solved this problem without using the diagonal short-cut. The differences for Problems 8, 11, and 12 are significant at the 1-per-cent level (chi square=14.4, 8.3, and 7.8, respectively), and for Problem 10 the difference is significant at the 5-per-cent level (chi square =4.6).

It must be admitted frankly that the results obtained for the control group were both surprising and unexpected. Apparently, the spatial technique used is of such a nature that the subjects in the experimental group, instead of becoming more blinded and automatized, became more wary as they went from one problem to the next. Such a suspicious attitude might make for more caution and an increasing awareness of the existence and meaning of the diagonal pathway.

In view of the outcome of the control experiment it is necessary to re-examine the interpretation that a critical map problem solved the long way is an indication of rigidity. The concept of rigidity cannot be applicable to the results found with the map technique unless it can be shown that a set was established. The five preliminary problems solvable by the long method produced no set effect and, if anything, hindered the establishment of a set. It can be shown, however, that the nature of the instructions at the beginning of the experiment was such that it produced the desired set even without the aid of the preliminary map problems. In the instructions nothing was said about the pathway, and the example problem (Problem 1), in which the pathway was present but not usable, was demonstrated by the experimenter. This was done deliberately in order to induce the set that subsequent problems are similar to the explanatory problem. Consider also the existence of two equally long alternative solutions to the goal in the example problem. One involved going one block east and two blocks north; the second involved going two blocks north and one block east. The experimenter, having a choice as to which of these two solutions to demonstrate, gave the solution "one block east, then two blocks north." This, too, was done deliberately in order to establish a set to go east first. It was reasoned that if the subject could be induced to establish such a set he would not be in a position later to utilize the diagonal short-cut *which could be entered only by going north first.*

That the set to go east first was successfully established in most subjects is evidenced by the results found for the first five *preliminary* problems in the main experiment (N=46). The percentages of the subjects using such a solution on each of these five problems are 72, 72, 72, 70, and 63, respectively. Since the alternative solution (go north, then east) is equally good it may be assumed that, by chance, 50 per cent of the subjects would choose each alternative. For the first four out of the five preliminary problems the results significantly deviate at the 1-per-cent level from such a chance distribution (chi square=8.70, 8.70, 8.70, and 7.04, respectively). These results would be difficult to explain on grounds other than that they are due to a set established by the instructions.

A similar analysis of the results of the control experiment shows the same thing. Of the 12 subjects participating in this experiment the numbers solving the five critical problems by going the long way are 11, 6, 6, 7, and 6, respectively. The percentages of these subjects using the "go east, then north" solution for each of the five critical problems are 64, 67, 67, 86, and 67, respectively. This again is to be compared with a theoretical expectancy of 50 per cent.

The above considerations should make it clear that the five problems solvable only by the long method were really intended as additional means to aid in the establishment of a set to go the long way. It was not anticipated that the desired set could be produced by one method alone. What the surprising and unexpected results of the control experiment really seem to show is (1) that a set was established by means of the instructions alone and (2) that the preliminary problems not only failed to add anything but, indeed, weakened the set so established.

Since it has been argued that a set was established in the control experiment as well as in the main experiment, it should be expected that an analysis of the relationship between rigidity and ethnocentrism should confirm the results found in the main experiment. . . .

Subjects 1 and 2 scored highest on ethnocentrism and solved all five critical problems rigidly. There were four subjects in all who solved all five problems rigidly. All of these subjects obtained ethnocentrism scores at or above the median score for the whole group.

With the small number of cases at hand there can be no question but that the relationship is not statistically significant. Nevertheless, [the] data again lend support to the rigidity-ethnocentrism hypothesis. . . .

Summary

The present study was designed to investigate differences in thinking between individuals scoring high and low in ethnocentrism. The main hypothesis was that the rigidity inherent in the ethnocentric person's solution of social problems is not an isolated phenomenon but is rather an aspect of a general rigidity factor which will manifest itself in solving any problem, social or non-social in nature. A second hypothesis was that the mode of thought of the ethnocentric person in solving problems is more concrete than that of the non-ethnocentric person, whereas the mode of thought of the non-ethnocentric person is more abstract in nature.

High-prejudiced and low-prejudiced adults were selected by means of the California Ethnocentrism Scale. High-prejudiced and low-prejudiced children were selected by means of the California Attitude Scale I. Subjects were classified as "High" or "Low" depending on whether they obtained scores falling above or below the median.

In a series of experiments with an arithmetical technique, rigidity was measured by having subjects solve problems in which required quantities of water were obtained by manipulating three jars of given capacities. A set was established by presenting problems solvable by only one complicated method. Then followed critical problems solvable both by a complicated and by a simple method. The results obtained within each experiment . . . confirm the main hypothesis.

A measure of concreteness of thinking was obtained by giving subjects an opportunity to use scratch paper as an aid in solving problems and to indicate their solution either in sentence form or in arithmetical form. The data clearly indicate that those high in ethnocentrism are more concrete in their mode of thought than are those low in ethnocentrism.

In a parallel experiment the hypotheses were tested by a spatial technique. To establish a set, five simple maps, all identical except for street names, were presented for fifteen seconds each. The subjects then described how to go from the southwest to the northeast corner.

Then followed five critical problems identical with the previous problems except that diagonal short-cuts were possible. Again, concrete thinking was measured by verbalization and by the use of scratch paper. Both the main experiment and a control experiment, in which the five problems designed to establish a set were omitted, showed that prejudiced subjects were more rigid than non-prejudiced subjects. The use of scratch paper did not differentiate the two groups, but the results on verbalization confirmed the results in the arithmetic experiments. On all ten problems, in describing how to reach the destination, those high in ethnocentrism used more words than did those low in ethnocentrism.

THE SUBSTITUTION OF ERROR FOR EVIL

Robert E. Lane

In Salem, Massachusetts, in the late seventeenth century, in Torquemada's Spain, among the Dobu of New Guinea, if something went wrong, the first question was, "Who did it?" or "Who is to blame?" Partly this is the product of a metaphysics that makes room for magic and sorcery; partly it arises from a projection of some guilty feelings within the individuals of the time and place; partly it is merely the effort to assign responsibility and hence develop control of a situation. It seems to be a rare question in Eastport. At least, it is less frequent among these men of modest education than might have been supposed.

In the matter of desegregation, the attempt to *understand* the Southern white as well as the Negro by those who believed in desegregation was very strong. Similarly, the easiest and primitively most appealing rationalization of our dropping the bomb on Hiroshima is the old one: "They started it," or "They brought it on themselves," or "They are to blame for their own destruction." Surely a blame-oriented culture would have said this. Instead, overwhelmingly the men used a functional argument—the bomb saved lives. Nor is the situation different in the moral discourse on corruption. There was little effort to blame the low moral standard on the bad men in office; instead there was an accounting of the causes, the temptation, the opportunities, the fallibility of mankind.

But the evidence is stronger than this; indeed, it came first to light in the routine questioning on "who is to blame" or "who is at fault" for the development of the "major problems" facing America, Eastport, and Eastern State as these emerged in the discussion. We shall let O'Hara speak on this. He is a man for whom assertion, conflict,

From *Political Ideology* (New York: The Free Press, 1962), pp. 327–330, 333–338, 343–345. Title supplied by the editor.

authority hold no terror; he is not afraid of criticism or reprisals. He works on the maintenance crew in a large factory and is explaining his situation in the recession: "I know up in the shop right now, they cut the help on the maintenance; . . . they're going to have trouble because you can't get the machinery fixed now, and I thought that—when I got pushed back, here about a month and a half ago, I had to go on nights steady. Of course, then they started rotating since then; but I had to go on 11 to 7, after about eleven years, because they laid off. And your maintenance force up there right now is smaller than it's ever been, and you've got twice as much work as they ever had; . . . they're cutting so darn low they're cutting their own throats." Here we are sure to be close to an issue that is pivotal in a man's life; he is speaking rapidly, leaning forward, emphasizing his words. He goes over it several times, explaining how the machines are "down" because of maintenance problems, and then he continues: "Of course, *you can't blame the company for all of it*. Unions are all right too, if they're run right." In the course of his discussion he comes to the government's responsibility for the decline in defense contracts; he understands the government's position on inflation, discounts it, but allows it some merit. He does not blame the government. O'Hara is a strong Democrat—I asked him later who is to blame for the problem of the defense lag he has outlined. He says: "Well, they [both parties] all holler that they want to cut down armament and everything," and seems about to evade the question, but goes on to say, "The Republicans are in power, so who do you blame?" It is not merely a rhetorical question, for he believes both parties are responsible. The emotion that went into describing the situation dwindles to a thin trickle when it comes time to assign blame for the recession. I asked him whether he has in mind any particular man. "No, I wouldn't say definitely who's who. . . ."

Sullivan, a truck driver, is similar in many ways; he illustrates another facet of this high blame threshold. Of all the "problems," the spy and subversive problem is usually most likely to evoke charges and countercharges of laxity, disloyalty, softness toward Communism. "Things that have bothered me?" asked Sullivan in response to a general question, and he proceeds in a contemplative fashion, "How easy it seemed to be for [pause] a foreign country, mainly Russia, to just walk off with atomic secrets, missiles, and so on—just walk off with them." I asked him, "Are you thinking of any particular case now, or what?" This was his chance. He says: "No, not one in particular—any one of them—[pause] Goldenberg, Greenglass—[pause] it just seemed to be that—[pause] I think it was just too easy. But it couldn't have been them alone. There must have been someone higher up that was making it easy for them." I am ready now for a blast at subversion in the "highest places," and, because he has stopped talking, try to prod him along. "Have you any idea who it might be, or where?" Sullivan pauses thoughtfully, "No," he says, "it probably isn't one person or one de-partment—[pause] the government on the whole, there, was—like I say—the program was probably rigid enough on security, but not on individuals." This comment, by a former pugilist and Marine, is cryptic enough in one sense, but for our purposes it is admirably clear: the problem lies with the system of screening civil servants; this, rather than placing the blame on certain weak, soft, disloyal men in govern-ment.

Often it is hard to distinguish between an analytical attribution of cause, an assignment of responsibility, and a fixing of blame. But in instance after instance, it appeared that the least fruitful questions were ones of "Whose fault was it?" "Who is to blame?" and within the body of the free-flowing discussion the level of indignation about the failures of men and groups to perform as the Eastportians thought they should was at a very low level indeed.

It has been said of the American nativist agitator in the midst of his tales of woe that if you asked him "What?" he will answer "Who?" We are here recounting this story in reverse. Often asked "Who is to blame?" the men of Eastport, to a surprising degree, answered in terms of "what." Queried on the missile lag, their most frequent answer was an anonymous American failure to support science and education; on the decline of business in downtown Eastport, they said the fault was the growth of the suburbs; only in the Little Rock crisis of desegregation (1957) did many men find a person to blame, in this case Governor Faubus. . . .

Moral Conflict in Public Affairs

What we have said about the unmoralistic American may suggest an anesthetized moral nerve. That is not the case. Without talking much about the good and the bad, the Eastport men yet deal sensitively with public issues that present them with moral conflict. Briefly we may look at three such issues: desegregation, the atomic bombing of Hiroshima, and corruption in government.

Johnson, an electric-utility mechanic, wrestles with his conscience on the desegregation problem . . . . He says: "I mean like I have five children and there's five colored kids running around—they have as much right in this world as my children have. . . . But," he con-tinues, "it just isn't right for a colored boy to be dancing with a white girl." Flynn, a railroad supply clerk who is an officer of the Hilltop Com-munity Council, was faced with the problem of what to do about teen-age dances at Hilltop. At first he opposed it; then, when he saw how much the teen-agers wanted it, he supported it, worrying all the time whether or not he was doing the right thing. Costa has a brother-in-law from North Carolina who, as he says, "can't stand the sight of colored people," and Costa himself feels that the Supreme Court desegregation decision was a mistake; things are going too fast in the South for the Southern whites to assimilate. But it is a moral problem for him — he seems free of conventional prejudice as he says: "The nicest people I know are colored people. I would go in their houses; I would eat with them; I would drink with them — that's the way I feel. I work with them."

The dropping of the atomic bomb on Hiroshima presents a moral dilemma of another order, more distant from their lives, more likely to be rationalized in terms of national defense and patriotic sentiment. Perhaps it is the case, as has been suggested, that moral superiority lies with those who condemn the American use of the bomb. If that is true, only two of the men earn these moral credits. But another estimate of moral strength may be made on the basis of the nature of the arguments employed, the effort to assess human costs involved either way (dropping or not dropping the bomb), the sensitivity to suffering and pain, the awareness of the calculations and responsibilities of those who had to decide. Looked at in this way, those who argue against dropping the bomb lose standing: their principal motive seems to be fear that the Japanese will some day retaliate against us. The ten who unequivocally justified our bombing did so largely on the ground that it was less costly in human lives than an invasion, and often they pointed out that it saved Japanese lives as well as American lives. Moreover the discussion was especially sensitive to the suffering involved: "I know it killed an awful lot of people — thousands of people, if I remember right, and people are dying from it today"; "I can't see [people] crippled or, uh, hurt that way"; "I think a lot of 'em [people in government] were well educated here and I think they could have found another solution for that"; "It meant saving a lot more than probably would have been maimed and injured, if they'd gone on fighting any other way."

But it was the arguments that they did not use that revealed their sensitivity to moral questions. Consider the possibilities for relying on the law of retaliation, an eye for an eye and a tooth for a tooth. This was not beyond them — "They didn't worry much about us when the time came for an attack on Pearl Harbor"; "The Japs had done everything inhuman to our men" — but it was rare. The symmetry of Pearl Harbor and Hiroshima was ignored. Nor did they ever, not even once, rely on General Sherman's "War is hell," which with a shrug of the shoulders might have dismissed moral questions as irrelevant to war. In short, they did not evade the need for a judgment, for a moral response.

Almost exactly fifty years ago, Bryce was able to say: "No impression regarding American politics is more generally diffused in Europe than that contained in the question which the traveller who has returned from the United States becomes so weary of being asked,

'Isn't everybody corrupt there?'"[1] Even though today the decline of the bosses and corruption is a familiar theme in American discourse, Eastport, like Europe and the rest of America, is aware of a substantial amount of corruption in government, and sees clearly the discrepancy between the official code and the informal code of behavior. Their reaction is, generally speaking, a tolerant one, certainly not indignant, not moralistic, possibly insufficiently censorious. It is marked by the belief that *the system encourages corruption*, that somehow it is "natural" to politics: "It's true that corruption and politics seem to go hand in hand" (Flynn); "I guess it'll always be in the peoples' minds that a politician is receiving money other than his pay" (Ruggiero). This is true, not because bad people go into politics but because ordinary people do. "If I went out to make an extra dollar [in this way], they'd probably talk about me too" (Dempsey); "We are all subject [to temptation]" (Woodside). And since this is the case, and they are merely people like us, they surely won't do any harm to the country: "In fact you can't blame them. Look, they're out to make money, as long as they figure, as long as they're not hurting anybody" (Sokolsky); "If they can get it, good luck to them. . . . I don't think they take bribes so much" (Dempsey); "I don't believe they're going to do anything to hurt the country" (Johnson). It is as though politics involved a set of fees and payments that, although disapproved of, were still accepted as a cost of doing business; not a high cost, and not one that interfered with the main business, which is the provision of services to the electorate, but still an underhanded business arrangement that exposed the "firm" to considerable criticism. Under these circumstances Eastport is *understanding* and somewhat sympathetic to men who are tempted and who follow the less honorable, but frequently applied, immoral rules. These men reserve their moral indignation for the transgressions of movie stars.

In these three situations there is a conflict between moral claims: the rights of the Negro versus the rights of white Southerners or white Northerners at Hilltop, the humanity of withholding the bomb versus the humanity of an expeditious ending of the war, the violation of honesty and approved practice in corruption versus the conventional "claims" of men to payment for services. In most of these situations there is some advantage to the men themselves in one solution compared to another: they would like to be relieved of "the Negro" problem by having it swept from sight; they had a stake in an earlier end of the war that they did not have in saving Japanese lives; they gain a little something from their own political ties, which become valuable only through informal and slightly disreputable claims for favors. How, then, shall we characterize their major responses to these moral conflicts?

[1]James Bryce, *The American Commonwealth* (New York: Macmillan, 1910), II, p. 156.

In the first place there are several things that they are not. There is little *denial*; they do not maintain that the Negro problem is unimportant, that the Japanese were not "really" badly hurt, that corruption is negligible. With respect to corruption, Bryce felt that under the circumstances a frank admission, which he also observed, was better than "covering things up as the English do."[2] *Hypocrisy*, a form of deceitful denial, was not a feature of this discourse.

Nor is cynicism a feature, in the sense of a belief that the moral code is just for show, that Negroes and whites are out to get what advantage each can of the other, that war has no room for moral considerations, that all men are corrupt and it is only the opportunities that vary, and that, anyway, "Justice is the will of the stronger." Of course, there is a broad conviction that men pursue self-interest, but not to the exclusion of other considerations. It is the difference between a belief in human frailty and a belief in human wickedness.

Bryce says that Americans respond to the question of corruption with a kind of fatalism;[3] Lerner refers to the "despair of ever getting any reform accomplished."[4] There is something to this. A few say, with respect to race prejudice, "You can't change human nature"; germane to the question of atomic bombing, most men believe that "there will always be wars"; on corruption in politics, McNamara speaks for many when he says, "I think it [corruption] goes along with politics like errors go along with baseball." But it is also true that Farrel, a social worker, speaks for many more when he says of corruption, "It's just a question of how you can keep it down to a minimum." And only a few men disapproved of governmental action to help the Negroes, while, those who thought there "will always be wars" believed that continued negotiation, the use of the United Nations, and some limited foreign aid might reduce the probability of imminent war. Fatalism about moral delinquency or an unsatisfactory outcome is not characteristic; rather the view is melioristic; things can be made better.

If the moral conflicts are marked by absence of denial, hypocrisy, cynicism, fatalism, what positive qualities do they have? Of course, they have the opposite of these—a certain candor, a certain hopefulness, some sense that evils can be brought increasingly under control. But beyond that, I think, there is a remarkable attempt to *understand* the situation, a willingness to see both sides of the conflict before judging. The pleasures of denunciation were postponed, not forever, but for long enough to grasp what it was the "other side" might claim. Moreover, I do not think these men have, in a marked sense, turned their consciences over to someone else. For example, it is sometimes said that Hitler's hold on the German people was made greater by their willing-

[2]*Ibid.*, p. 245.
[3]*Ibid.*, pp. 347 ff.
[4]Max Lerner, *America As a Civilization* (New York: Simon and Schuster, 1957), p. 385.

ness to vest in him the definition of right and wrong. Or, in our own experience, David Riesman suggests that the American's sensitivity to group opinion has resulted in his abdicating responsibility for his decisions on right and wrong.[5] Of course, all morality is anchored in convention and group opinion, but the clues to an abnormally atrophied *individual* conscience are not marked in the conversation of the men of Eastport. They do not, for example, support their moral judgments on segregation, Hiroshima, corruption, or other matters such as delinquency, foreign policy, subversion, with such comments as "All of the fellows say . . . ," "Around here we think . . . ," "He's got a bad reputation," "I was just talking to _____ the other day, and he said . . . ." They do not preface their judgments with a glance at me, a hesitation, and, "Maybe you won't agree with this, but . . ."—or with an apologetic gesture of diffidence, or waiver of some kind. Dempsey declines comment here and there ("That, I couldn't say"), but it is the product of a limited mentality, not an other-directed conscience. Costa is deferential; he would prefer to rely on another. Most men do not try to find out how I feel, do not publicly ground their views in the opinions of others, and do not embrace a group and speak for them; they are the custodians of their own consciences, at least in the limited sense described. . . .

Low-Tension Morality and Low-Tension Politics

The introduction to the Declaration of Independence states that "the Laws of Nature and of Nature's God entitle" the people of the United States to revolt and establish a separate nation. Communism has intellectual roots both in an interpretation of history and in a moral doctrine of equality. The arguments that justified the French Revolution to its followers were stated as universal rights—"The Rights of Man." In the Granger Movement, the Populist Movements, the Nonpartisan League, the Progressive movements of 1912, 1924, and 1948, the language of politics was moral language; men sought to protect their rights and to redress wrongs done to them and others. Those who defend the *status quo* make other moral appeals; they call on tradition, a divine order, contractual arrangements implying individual and group integrity as moral sanction for the going order. The language of politics is moral language; it is moralized language. Without this, it must speak only in terms of self- and group-interest and as such loses its power to move men to sacrifice, to forego immediate personal gains for long-term group gains, to subordinate themselves to leadership and discipline. Although the play of "interests" is always significant, no movement, party, or issue endures without a moral justification.

[5]David Riesman, *The Lonely Crowd* (New Haven: Yale University Press, 1950).

Placing this consideration next to the discussion of the unmoralistic tendencies of the American common man at this stage in history —and, according to Tocqueville, in earlier stages, as well—we perceive one reason for the low political tension and the rather low level of political participation in the United States. Politics has not been moralized; the parties have not been invested with strong moral feeling; the issues are not seen as moral issues; the political leaders have not been made moral heroes and villains. This has the effect of reducing the stakes in elections and making the commitment to one political group a rather loose affair that can be dissolved as the situation may require. It permits ticket splitting, switching, and a rapid adjustment when the opposition party wins.

More than that, it deprives politics of the explicit ideological character that is so apparent in other parts of the world. This is so because a forensic ideology cannot survive without a strong moral component in which there are specified evils, villains, exploiters, usurpers, devils on the one hand, and somewhat vaguer restitutions, reforms, heroes, and salvation on the other. This morality, rather than logic, is what holds an ideology together, and without it the whole thing tends to disintegrate into a series of piecemeal and pragmatic adjustments to changing circumstances and demands. Pragmatism too has its moral foundation, but since it is so often inarticulate the morality of pragmatism will not serve as the cement for an ideological structure.

A tendency to moralize is, very often, a tendency to rationalize, that is, to convert real interests and operational motives into principles that embody the moral themes conventionally thought to be sacred in a given society. When this occurs, the grounds on which an opinion is held, the circumstances that would have to be affected before the opinion is "vulnerable," are concealed and protected, and discourse is less likely to be persuasive. Since government by discussion, at every level, is frustrated by this tendency to rationalization, it is dangerous and dysfunctional in the extreme. In this sense chronic moralization, a disposition toward indignation on the part of a broad public, is a disservice to democracy, just as are themes of cynical demoralization in a culture.

The unmoralistic nature of the common men of Eastport, their lack of a sense of sin and evil in the world and in themselves, their belief in a self-adjusting moral order, their tendency to seek to understand rather than to blame, all hold perils for the social order. Perhaps they protect the *status quo* a little too carefully; perhaps they imply too sanguine a view of the outcome of inaction; perhaps they lead not only to a pacific politics but also to a stagnant politics. But when they are supported by a personal moral code that guides men's lives in humane and decent ways, the lack of moralism is, on balance, an advantage in a functioning, changing, democratic society.

Part IV

Political Institutions: Modern and Comparative

Much of political science is directly or indirectly concerned with the institutional structure in which power is utilized, policy suggestions are originated, and the legality of decisions is tested. Part IV begins with informed evaluations of the three familiar, visible branches of American government—the Presidency, the Congress, and the Supreme Court. We then consider the emergence of new political strata which, until recently, had little overt impact on the American polity. In the twentieth-century world of science and technology, men of specialized knowledge play increasingly important roles in the determination of public policy. Scientists and other intellectuals advise or rationalize, create plans for economic development or instruments of destruction. The relations between men of specialized knowledge and men of overt political power are crucial for economic and social progress throughout the world.

We learn in rudimentary ways by comparing phenomena. In grand political theories, the relationships among processes and among nations guide our inquiries. What do we mean by comparative politics, and what kinds of inquiries do we wish to make about the structure and functions of national governments? To answer these questions, sections 15 and 16 join a theoretical discussion of comparative politics with specific empirical inquiry that transcends the boundaries of any one political system. Blending these two endeavors is a fruitful way to pursue meaningful comparative political inquiry.

13. The Three Branches of Government

At one time knowledge about and interest in the American polity were limited chiefly to the structure and functions of political institutions. Although the readings in this book clearly illustrate that this is no longer the case, a study of political institutions would not be complete without some literature on the three branches of government in the United States.

James Burns' study of a master political broker, President Franklin Delano Roosevelt, is useful not only as a yardstick for measuring the political leadership of other Chief Executives but also as the raw material for tracing the situational factors that influence the performance of the world's most important political role. In the second selection, an internal social profile of the United States Senate is cogently presented by an adaptation from Donald Matthews' exhaustive research. Finally, the work of the United States Supreme Court and its expanding influence on policy are introduced by portions of a monumental judicial and political decision—the historical judgment that segregation in public educational facilities is unconstitutional.

THE EXERCISE OF PRESIDENTIAL LEADERSHIP

JAMES MACGREGOR BURNS

The Broker State at Work

If the New Deal had circus-like qualities during the first years, the center ring was occupied by the National Recovery Administration, and the ringmaster presented a fresh new visage on the American scene. General Hugh S. Johnson looked like the old cavalry man that he was; he had a hard, leathery face, squint eyes, and a rough bark of a voice, but underneath, curious qualities crowded one another: he was a sentimentalist, an old hand with businessmen and business ways, a West Pointer, and as mercurial and picturesque as a sideshow barker. Although Johnson's long-time boss Bernard Baruch rated him as only a "good No. 2 man," the general impressed the President enough

Pages 191–202: Abridged from *Roosevelt: The Lion and the Fox*, © 1956 by James MacGregor Burns. Reprinted by permission of Harcourt, Brace & World, Inc. and Martin Secher & Warburg Limited. Title supplied by the editor.

to win the job of running the biggest experiment in peacetime governmental control of the economy that America had ever seen.

Johnson's main task was to induce businessmen to draw up codes of fair competition, which on the President's approval had the full force of law. Administered under the general's supervision by a code authority in each industry, the codes were supposed to stop wasteful competition, to bring about more orderly pricing and selling policies, and to establish higher wages, shorter hours, and better working conditions for workers. Antitrust policies would be softened so that businessmen could co-operate in setting up the codes. Johnson had expected to administer the vast public works section of the bill too, but at the last minute Roosevelt put this under [Harold] Ickes. So furious was the general that he threatened to quit the whole business then and there; the President asked Miss Perkins to "stick with Hugh and keep him sweet," which she did by driving him for hours around Washington until he mastered himself and promised to go on with his part of the job.

And a job it was. Within weeks the NRA burst on the American people like a national call to arms. The NRA eagle was suddenly in every shop window, on magazine covers, in the movies, on girls in chorus lines. Rushing from city to city in an army plane, issuing pronunciamentos at every stop, Johnson orated, politicked, wisecracked, coaxed businessmen into signing codes drawn up by industry representatives hurriedly collected in Washington. The general became the symbol of recovery; for hours he reviewed a climactic parade up Fifth Avenue, trying desperately to greet the endless river of humanity without appearing to give the despised Mussolini salute. Not since 1917 had the whole nation savored such a throbbing sense of unity, of marching together. . . .

The NRA was essentially an expression of the broker state—that is, of the government acting for, and mediating among, the major interest groups. The NRA was the institutional expression of Roosevelt's plan for a partnership of all groups, achieved through friendly co-operation between the government and group leaders. But who were the leaders? It was not surprising that in the haste and confusion Johnson dealt with the business and labor leaders closest at hand, those who were most vocal, best organized, most experienced in dealing with politicians and bureaucrats. Who could speak for that amorphous group, the consumers? A Consumers' Advisory Board was set up but was eased to one side; a member quit indignantly within a few weeks of its establishment.

By the end of 1933 the NRA eagle was fluttering through heavy weather. "N.R.A. is the worst law ever passed," some disillusioned Cleveland grocers wired the President. "N.R.A. means National Run Around," read a labor placard hoisted by a Baltimore picket line.

Protests rose in Congress. William Connery, chairman of the House Labor Committee, asked Roosevelt to tell Johnson to work with "true representatives" of labor. Roosevelt answered patiently that as one "a great deal older than you" he advised the Congressman not to over-state his case. "Most of us who consider ourselves liberals have the same ultimate objective in view. . . ." But the President could not ignore the protests. In March 1934, he appointed a review board under the old reformer and defense attorney Clarence Darrow, which soon was re-porting that the codes had allowed the more powerful interests to seize control or extend their control of industries. Roosevelt trimmed NRA's powers, limited its jurisdiction, eased Johnson out, and put a more domesticated chief, Donald Richberg, in his place. But by the time the Supreme Court administered the *coup de grâce* shortly before NRA's second birthday, it was near administrative and political collapse.

If NRA was the mainspring of the New Deal in shop and factory, the Agricultural Adjustment Act was its counterpart on the farm. The object of the measure was to restore farm prices to parity—to the relationship, that is, they bore to nonagricultural prices in the years 1909 to 1914. To reach this goal, processing taxes were to be levied equal to the difference between the actual prices and parity. The money raised was to finance restriction of production either by renting land and keep-ing it out of production or by paying benefits to farmers in return for their agreement to reduce production—"to kill every third pig or plow every third row under," as the newspapers were soon putting it. But like the NRA, Triple-A was soon revealing the insuperable problems of Roosevelt's middle way.

The act bore telltale marks of its birth pangs. It was drawn up by spokesmen from the larger farm organizations and the farm journals, under the direction of Henry Wallace. The viewpoint of the larger commercial farmers, organized in the American Farm Bureau Federa-tion and the National Grange, had the most weight in the early, vital policy-making process, while the Farmers Union, generally embracing the smaller farmers on more marginal land, and inheriting the old Populist tradition, was scarcely represented. Millions of farmers be-longed to no organization at all; they could not afford the dues, they lacked the time, they could not travel fifty miles to meetings. And no real organization even existed for countless farm laborers on vast Middle Western farms, southern sharecroppers, illiterate farm hands, and migratory workers following the crops in battered Model-T Fords. Dirt farmers, rough in speech and countenance, returned from Wash-ington deriding the men in neckties and white shirts they had seen testi-fying for the AAA bill. . . .

Roosevelt knew that the acid test of the New Deal was recovery. Dur-ing 1933 and 1934 he watched the ups and downs of the nation's

economic temperature like a doctor following the condition of a fever-
ish patient.

He was delighted when employment rose sharply the first four
months after he took office. He proudly showed reporters a chart from
which farm prices had dropped clear off the bottom of the sheet—the
line had now reappeared and was headed up. But in July came a stock
market crash and, even worse, a drop in production. The President
dismissed the crash as due to gamblers: "everybody got to speculating
and things went too fast; that got a perfectly natural corrective," he
told reporters. Anyway, he said, employment looked good. By fall of
1933 he was worried about employment too: "There aren't nearly
enough people back at work," but he thought things were improving.
He wrote Garner about this time that business was "not nearly as badly
off as the New York crowd is howling about, but unemployment is
still serious."

It was all so strange. Things seemed better—the NRA was going
strong; the breath of recovery filled the air—yet the prosaic gauges
of recovery—wages, prices, spending, employment—were moving up
erratically and unpredictably where they were moving up at all. The
situation looked so serious that in September 1933 the President instructed Secretary of War Dern to make ready army rolling kitchens
for feeding the needy where local relief was inadequate. By the end of
1933 the alarmed and disconcerted President was looking for scape-
goats. Prices had dropped, he said, because some people had not approved of NRA codes and because "some of our foreign friends" were
deliberately trying to increase the exchange value of the dollar.
Curiously, the President was almost embracing the idea of foreign
causes of depression—an idea he had lambasted when Hoover used it
in 1932.

Casting about for a solution, Roosevelt took up a notion that
George F. Warren, a Cornell professor, had been pressing for some
time. Drawn from the old quantity theory of money, the idea was that
an increase in the value of gold would be the decisive factor in restoring higher prices. In October 1933 the President decided on this approach. In what has been called probably the "boldest attempt ever
made to give the widest public a brief instruction in complicated economic doctrine and maneuver," Roosevelt told the people in a fireside
chat about his plan to buy gold. "This is a policy and not an expedient,"
he said defensively. But while a government market for gold became a
lasting policy, the Warren theory proved an abortive one; raising the
price of gold did not boost commodity prices.

"Our troubles will not be over tomorrow, but we are on our way
and we are headed in the right direction," the President said in his
radio talk. During 1934 employment did improve somewhat. The cause
lay largely in programs that Roosevelt viewed as essentially humanitarian rather than recovery-producing.

The first of these programs was run by [Harry] Hopkins, more driving and sharp-tongued than ever. Told by Roosevelt to get help to the people fast, he had sat down at his desk while it was waiting in a hallway to be moved into his office, and in a few hours authorized millions of dollars of relief. Spurring and goading his subordinates, infuriating state politicians while playing his own brand of New Deal politics, ignoring bureaucratic protocol, Hopkins spent several hundred millions through the states during the early months of the New Deal and almost a billion on "quicky" projects through the Civil Works Administration in late 1933 and the first half of 1934. . . .

Other agencies added to this outpouring of money. The Reconstruction Finance Corporation, continued from the Hoover days, was lending more money than ever. The TVA, beginning its vast development program in the Tennessee Valley, was converting an area that had been a drain on the economy into a source of economic stimulation. The AAA put into farmers' hands money that quickly found its way to Sears, Roebuck and the local hardware store, and thence to manufacturers, banks, workers.

Roosevelt used all these instruments; he put full reliance on no single one of them. As leader of all the people, as broker among major organized interests, he would take the middle way. He adopted spending policies, but only as a temporary measure until the budget was balanced. He favored tariff reduction, but not where it hurt major American interests. He wanted a "reflationary" price rise, but not an "inflationary" one. He was favorable to organized labor, but only to the point consistent with a partnership of industry, labor, and farmers with government.

Nowhere was the President's role as buffer among major interests, as conciliator of rival viewpoints, more sharply revealed than in a statement he made to a press conference in December 1933: "[Lewis] Douglas' job is to prevent the Government from spending just as hard as he possibly can. That is his job. Somewhere between his efforts to spend nothing . . . and the point of view of the people who want to spend ten billions additional on public works, we will get somewhere, and we are trying to work out a program."

The Politics of Broker Leadership

Every politician tries to win elections by simple "followership"—that is, by gauging carefully group attitudes, opinion trends, party activities, and then taking that position that will reap the most votes on Election Day. A leader, by contrast, actively shapes his political context; he seeks to change the constellation of political forces about him in a direction closer to his own conception of the political good.

The genius of great party leaders lies in their power to forge a majority combination of voters around burning issues of government, and through their personal qualities of leadership to put this combination behind some philosophy of government and program of action. Jefferson, for example, built a national following out of Southern planters, Western grain growers, Northern laborers, frontiersmen, debtors, and other sectional and group elements, and this following, roughly organized in the Republican party, put him into the White House. Jackson, too, was a broker of sections and groups, as all national leaders must be, but he was also a majority leader equipped with definite notions about government and able to win popularity with the great mass of people. Jefferson and Jackson as presidents acted for great popular majorities, and they stand in history for a conception of government by a majority working through a broadly based political party.

Roosevelt during 1933-34 was no Jefferson, no Jackson. He did not conceive of himself as the leader of a majority on the left, as a party leader building a new alignment of political power. His job, as he saw it, was to patch up an ailing economic system, to rescue human lives, to bring about generally agreed-on reforms, and above all to promote economic recovery. These goals—especially the last—could be achieved by coaxing and conciliating leaders of major interests into a great national partnership.

Viewed as a matter of political leadership, Roosevelt's Grand Experiment took the form of what can be called broker leadership. During his first two years in office he seemed to conceive of his presidential role as one of dealing with and mediating among the leaders of organized groups, especially labor, farmers, and businessmen. If the economics of the broker state meant improvisation, a host of energetic and ill-assorted government programs, and economic betterment without real recovery, the politics of broker leadership brought short-term political gains at the expense, perhaps, of long-term strategic advance.

Roosevelt was no theorist. It is doubtful that he chose this course as a result of a well-defined political philosophy. It simply emerged, shaped only roughly by his underlying concept of the public good, from the day-to-day projects and improvisations of his regime. It probably never occurred to him that the NRA, with its functional representation of business and labor groups, and the AAA, dominated by the big farm groups, showed some likeness to the corporate state fashioned by Benito Mussolini, with its syndicates of workers and employers. But George Peek, AAA chief, saw that the power of special interest groups could not be separated from the state, even in a democracy. "The truth is," he said bluntly, "that no democratic government can be very different from the country it governs. If some groups are dominant in the country, they will be dominant in any plan the government undertakes."

Such an approach had profound implications for Roosevelt's political leadership. It meant that he took the more passive method of responding to major political and economic pressures, rather than the more positive one of deliberately building up some voting alignment on the left or right that would recast the basic pattern of political power. It meant that he ignored the possibilities for the future of a voting alignment of great strength—one composed of less privileged farm groups, masses of unorganized or ill-organized industrial workers, consumers, Negroes, and other minority groups. It is significant that the President allowed consumers short shrift in NRA and AAA, that he failed to put pressure behind the food and drug bill that [Rexford] Tugwell had drawn up for the protection of consumers, that he allowed postponement of unemployment and old-age pension measures, that he showed little interest at first in [Robert] Wagner's efforts to strengthen labor's right to organize, that he was hazy and cool on the subject of a pending antilynching bill.

From the standpoint of immediate political gains, however, Roosevelt's way was most effective. The congressional elections of 1934 were coming up. In an "off" election year, with no presidential contest to give a national orientation to the thousands of state and local contests across the nation, American elections tend to break up into forty-eight different arenas, and each of these arenas in turn presents a jumble of guerrilla contests revolving around personalities, patronage, local issues, and hardy election perennials such as corruption and crime. Parties and programs tend to be lost in the dust of battle as candidates and their personal factions struggle for votes.

Speaking for "all the people," unhampered by rigid party control or obligations to a set program, the President was able to adjust his tactics to the needs of each state. He was all the more effective because of his pretense that he was taking no part in state or local campaigns, even in state Democratic politics. Actually, he stuck a finger into a number of crucial contests. Nothing better illustrated his opportunism and flexibility than his handling of the Pennsylvania situation.

Pennsylvania in the early 1930's presented the materials for major political realignment. Governor of the state in 1934 was Gifford Pinchot, the onetime chief forester who had been ousted by Taft in a *cause célèbre*, and later a Bull Mooser with Theodore Roosevelt. Pinchot had long led the progressive elements in the Republican party against such regulars as the oldtime bosses Pew and Grundy. Coming up for re-election to the United States Senate in 1934 was David Reed, a Republican regular. The Pennsylvania Democrats, who had lost part of their liberal potential to the Republican progressives and had not won a Senate seat in sixty years, nominated two able, colorless, organization Democrats, Joseph F. Guffey for Senator and George Earle for governor.

Roosevelt and Pinchot were old friends. They had both fought the Old Guard in their parties, Pinchot far more bellicosely and openly than the other. Although a Republican, Pinchot was vigorously supporting Roosevelt in 1934, and some kind of political tie-in seemed desirable. Early in 1934 the President suggested to Pinchot that he run for thé Senate and indicated that Democratic support might be forthcoming. It soon became clear, however, that the Pennsylvania Democrats would not nominate the governor, for they expected to win with a man of their own. So Pinchot had to run in the Republican primaries, denouncing Old Guard Republican Reed as a mouthpiece of the Mellons and praising Roosevelt. But Roosevelt kept hands off; he would not even allow Ickes to speak for Pinchot in the primary, and Reed won. The governor—and his wife, who was indefatigably ambitious for her husband—thereupon tried to work out a new Progressive Republican-Democratic ticket on which Pinchot would run for Senator and Earle for governor. The Pennsylvania Democracy was not interested, and Roosevelt would not help. In the end Pinchot came out for his archenemy, Reed.

It was a bitter Pinchot who wrote Roosevelt shortly before the election. He wanted to continue to support Roosevelt, Pinchot said, but he could not support Guffey and Earle. "The nomination by the Democrats of two utterly unfit men for the highest offices of this Commonwealth, and my opposition to them, will not make me your enemy unless you so elect. . . . The last word is yours."

Roosevelt's reply was a bit lofty—and revealing. He could not understand why Pinchot would support a reactionary like Reed.

"Also, my dear Gifford, I know you won't mind my telling you that I think you and I have always worked for principles in government above anything else—i.e., the purposes and objectives. You and I also know from long public experience that time and again we cannot get just the men we would select to help us attain these principles and objectives. I am not speaking of Pennsylvania but I do know in New York that I have had to work through many people whom I did not like or even trust—but I have worked with them and through them, in order to obtain the ultimate goal."

That being the case, he concluded, in Pinchot's place he would have kept his hands out of the fight. After this exchange, the breach between the two men was complete, and a Progressive Republican-Democratic coalition was never achieved.

In other states too, the President followed tactics of expediency. California posed a special problem. In that turbulent state Upton Sinclair, the old muckraker and long-time Socialist, had won the Democratic nomination for governor with the backing of hundreds of thousands of supporters of his End Poverty in California plan to enable California's jobless to produce for their needs in state-operated factories and farms. Sinclair's thumping primary victory over the old-time McAdoo-George Creel faction late in August 1934 put the White House in a dither. Should Farley issue the usual routine congratulations to Democratic primary winners? What position should the President take? When Sinclair forced the issue by asking to see the President, Roosevelt decided to deal with the situation personally.

Arriving in Hyde Park, Sinclair found Roosevelt at his most charming. The President told stories with gusto, listened sympathetically while Sinclair described his plan, and then intimated that he would himself come out for "production for use" in a few weeks. He even told the improbable story that his mother had read Sinclair's *The Jungle* to him at breakfast and spoiled his appetite. Striking a liberal posture, he told the Californian, "I cannot go any faster than the people will let me."

Roosevelt thoroughly charmed Sinclair, but if he thought he had weakened the old radical's determination to wage an all-out campaign for EPIC, he mistook his man. By October California was witnessing the most bitter campaign in its history, and regular Democrats like Creel were deserting Sinclair in droves. Faced with this thorny situation, Roosevelt kept hands off. The President's instructions on Sinclair's candidacy, Early told Eleanor Roosevelt, were "(1) Say nothing and (2) Do nothing."

Other administration officials did not follow this injunction. Comptroller of the Currency J. F. T. O'Connor returned to his native state to size up the situation and to try to induce Sinclair to withdraw in favor of the nominee of the Commonwealth and Progressive parties. Failing in this, O'Connor talked with Governor Frank F. Merriam, the Republican candidate for re-election. Whether or not an out-and-out deal was made, the upshot was that Merriam put out some pro-Roosevelt statements, the President never spoke out for either Sinclair or "production for use," and the Republican trounced the Democrat at the polls.

Wisconsin presented another ticklish situation. For some time Roosevelt had maintained close political relations with Senator Robert La Follette, Jr., and other Progressive Republicans. In spring 1934 the La Follette Progressives broke away from the Republican party and established the Progressive party. La Follette had supported Roosevelt measures in the Senate, and the President hoped that he would be re-elected. Wisconsin Democrats felt differently. They had plans of their own, and hoped to exploit the split between Progressives and regular Republicans. To complicate matters further, Progressives in 1932 had combined with Democrats to elect A. G. Schmedeman the first Democratic governor in half a century. But now, in 1934, the Progressives

had a gubernatorial candidate of their own in Philip F. La Follette, and
Schmedeman was running for re-election.

Worried Democrats in Wisconsin urged Roosevelt not to endorse
Bob La Follette. Aroused Progressives demanded recognition for the
"best New Dealer in the Senate." What would Roosevelt do? "My own
personal hope is that they will find some way of sending Bob La Follette
back here," Roosevelt told reporters off the record. "But I cannot
compel the Democracy of Wisconsin to go ahead and nominate him."
Lacking presidential direction, the Wisconsin Democracy put up a
regular Democrat against Senator La Follette.

Faced with this predicament, Roosevelt decided to take a biparti-
san stand. Speaking at Green Bay, Wisconsin, early in August, he
patted both Senator La Follette and Governor Schmedeman on the back
and praised them for their co-operation. Election time brought happy
results for Roosevelt, but not for the Wisconsin Democrats. Both
La Follette brothers won over their Democratic foes, and the local
Democracy continued as a weak opposition party lacking New Deal
support either in Washington or at home.

Minnesota combined still different hues in the splotchy pigmenta-
tion of state-by-state politics. Here, too, a New Dealish third party
—the Farmer Labor party—was involved, and here, too, the Democrats
were shot through with factionalism and dominated by patronage boss-
lets; but in Minnesota, one Democratic faction had been virtually an
adjunct of the Farmer-Laborites. Who wore the Roosevelt mantle in
Minnesota? By 1934 regular Democrats suspected that Roosevelt would
recognize the Farmer-Laborite governor, Floyd B. Olson, and the
Farmer-Laborite Senator, Henrik Shipstead, both candidates for re-
election against regular Democrats.

They suspected correctly. Roosevelt wrote in longhand to Farley:
"In Minnesota *hands off*—don't encourage opposition to Shipstead
or Oleson [sic]." Roosevelt himself was "in a quandary" about Minnesota, he told reporters. In the end both Farmer-Laborites won hand-
somely.

In New Mexico, a childhood friend of Roosevelt, Senator Bron-
son Cutting, was running for re-election as a progressive Republican.
The President and Cutting had had a falling out over the bonus bill,
and administration patronage had gone largely to the Democratic
organization. Cutting and his Democratic opponent, Dennis Chavez,
fought a close race that went into the Senate as a disputed contest;
flying back to New Mexico for some election affidavits, Cutting was
killed in a plane crash. Roosevelt said later that he had told Cutting
that he was willing to give Chavez a job to drop the fight, but Cutting
had turned down the offer. Roosevelt had taken no further action except to tell reporters that Cutting was a "very old boyfriend of mine"
but Chavez was a pretty good congressman.

"I am trying to get across the idea that if we have the right kind of people," Roosevelt had said to his press conference, "the party label does not mean so very much." Of course, he added amid a burst of laughter, that had to be kept off the record.

PROFILE OF THE SENATE

Donald R. Matthews

Originally, a Senate was an assembly of old men. The description is less apt but not too inappropriate when applied to the upper house of the American Congress today. . . . A smaller proportion of the senators are in their thirties than is true for the population, and about the same proportion of senators as ordinary citizens are over sixty-five. It is the late forties and fifties that are "overrepresented" in the "most exclusive gentlemen's club in Washington."

And the Senate is indeed a gentlemen's organization: of the 180 persons who served in the United States Senate between January, 1947, and January, 1957, only three were women. . . .

America was a rural country when most of the postwar senators were born. It is not surprising, then, that a majority of them were born in rural areas. . . . [T]he most consistently overrepresented birthplaces ranged in size from 2,500 to 5,000 inhabitants. These small towns produced twice as many Democrats and four times as many Republicans as one might expect on the basis of chance. Towns with populations of from 5,000 to 50,000 in 1900 reared from one and a half to two times as many senators as might be anticipated, while rural areas and the larger cities produced considerably fewer senators than chance would predict. . . .

Class Origins

Despite a widespread preference not to talk about such matters, few observant Americans would deny that individuals in the United States are ranked or "stratified" on generally accepted scales of social inferiority and superiority. Moreover, most would agree that individuals sharing roughly equal positions in this system of invidious distinctions tend to group into "classes."

. . . [T]he senators were sons, with only a handful of exceptions, of men possessing upper- and middle-class occupations. The children of low-salaried workers, wage earners, servants, and farm laborers, which

From *U.S. Senators and Their World* by Donald R. Matthews (Chapel Hill, North Carolina: University of North Carolina Press, 1960), pp. 13–46. Title supplied by the editor.

together comprised 66 per cent of the gainfully employed in 1900, contributed only 7 per cent of the postwar senators. Only two of the 180 men, Senators Wagner and O'Daniel, were the sons of unskilled, urban wage earners. . . . Among the sons of farmers, some were born in relative poverty, yet it is virtually impossible to ascertain this in specific cases. It is still possible to conclude that very few senators were born in working-class and lower-class families. Moreover, the differences in occupational-class origins of Democrats and Republicans are small. Fifty-eight per cent of each party were the sons of either professionals, proprietors, or officials; the remainder, sons of farmers, low-salaried workers, or wage earners.

Within these necessarily broad categories, important differences exist in the occupational origins of the members of the two parties. The Democrats were more often the sons of lawyers, doctors, professors, and journalists than were the Republicans; the GOP senators were more often the sons of ministers. Among the sons of proprietors and officials, the Democrats mostly came from families headed by merchants, insurance and real estate agents, construction contractors, and bankers. All the sons of manufacturing executives and publishers were Republicans. Finally, among the group of senators born to industrial wage earners, the Republicans tended to be sons of men with quasi-middle-class occupations — printers, carpenters, barbers, and painters — while the Democratic sons of industrial wage earners were born to fathers of somewhat lower status.

Race, Nationality, Creed

America is a land of many peoples — white, black, yellow, red, and all shades between. We are all immigrants and sons of immigrants, but we came to America from different lands and at different times, bringing different religious faiths. The American attitude toward this diversity has varied at different times in our history. At first, people — any people — were needed to work the land and build the factories, but about the time our story begins, this attitude changed to a less welcoming one. The "melting pot" ideology was still lauded in Fourth of July oratory. And, officially, Americans still believed in the words at the base of the Statue of Liberty, "Give me your tired, your poor, your huddled masses yearning to be free. . . ." But the facts of everyday living were different, very different.

As a result, the happy diversity of the American people is dimly reflected in the racial, national, and religious backgrounds of the senators. One out of every ten Americans is a Negro. Negroes may have been amply represented in the Senate in other ways but not, during the period following World War II, by a member of their own race. Immigrants and second-generation whites suffer from a milder discrimination. A substantially smaller proportion of senators than of the white population were first- or second-generation Americans. Moreover, this preference for Anglo-Saxon origins is clearly demonstrated by the fact that all three immigrants who served in the postwar Senate came from Great Britain, Canada, and Germany. Furthermore, virtually all the second-generation Americans in the Senate were from Northwestern and Central Europe, while the many new Americans from other parts of the world were almost unrepresented in the chamber.

This preference for senators with "Yankee" backgrounds — or, failing that, for those with origins that approach as closely as possible the Anglo-Saxon ideal — is also reflected in the religious affiliations of the senators. Protestants are substantially overrepresented, Roman Catholics and Jews underrepresented in the Senate. The same preference for those with high-prestige religious affiliations is found among the Protestants. There are about three times the number of Episcopalians and twice the number of Presbyterians among the Protestant senators as would be found in a randomly selected group of Protestants. The Methodists and Congregationalists have about their fair share of the Senate seats, while the Baptists and Lutherans are considerably underrepresented. . . .

Education

It would be a mistake to assume that senators are "born," not "made." In the race for senatorial office most of the senators began with a considerable headstart. Yet American society is a *relatively* open and competitive society, both in fact and in ideology, and the senators had to display considerable ability, ambition, and achievement to get where they are.

Senators are among the most educated — in the formal sense of the word — of all occupational groups in the United States. Almost 85 per cent of them attended college, a level of education achieved by only 14 per cent of the adult population in 1950. The educational gap between the people and the members of the Senate is actually much wider than these figures indicate: 45 per cent of the senators attended both undergraduate college and law school, and 8 per cent of them performed some other form of postgraduate work.

This high level of education can be accounted for, in part, by the senators' relatively high class origins. Numerous studies show that while the American educational system is one of the most equalitarian in the world, substantial differences in educational opportunities exist between social classes. Financial pressure, lack of motivation for academic success, the unconscious preference of middle-class teachers for middle-class children, and so on, place the child from working- or lower-class families at a distinct disadvantage even when his intelligence is the same as that of the middle-class child. This is far from a total explanation of the superior educational attainments of the senators, for, regardless of their class origins, more senators attended college than the other members of the white adult population. Thus the high educational level of senators is not just the result of their greater opportunities but also reflects exceptional academic interest, ability, and achievement.

There are interesting party-line differences in educational levels, too. The Democrats are more educated than the Republicans. Again, this is not the result of different class origins, for, when the level of education of Democratic and Republican senators with roughly the same class origins are compared, the Democrats come out well ahead, especially among the senators with the lower-class origins. This evidence of the Democrats' greater concern with, or ability for, formal study is supported by several other pieces of evidence. Seventy-two per cent of the Democrats, but only 65 per cent of the Republicans, who entered undergraduate colleges graduated. Of those who did graduate, 24 per cent of the Democrats, but only 14 per cent of the Republicans, were elected to Phi Beta Kappa, the national scholastic honorary society.

What kinds of schools did the senators attend? As undergraduates, the senators studied in 104 different educational institutions. State universities were the most popular type of undergraduate institution — about half of the senators attending undergraduate school went to a state university at one time or another — but a very large share of all college graduates in the United States attended these uniquely American institutions. What type of college graduated the largest share of senators, taking into account the size of its alumni body? . . . Harvard, Yale, Princeton, and the smaller but well-known Eastern colleges graduated more than their share of the senators. The other Ivy League universities and the Big Ten universities can claim only one-third the number of senators among their alumni one would expect on the basis of chance. The less well-known colleges and universities graduated just about their proportional share of future senators. . . .

Almost half the law schools attended by the senators were high-entrance requirement schools (at a time when only one-fifth of all American law schools belonged to that category) and another 30 per cent attended the second-ranking type. [There was also a] considerably greater percentage of Republicans than Democrats attending the first-ranking schools. This may be explained in part by the fact that the best law schools were located in the strongly Republican areas of New England and the Middle West. The Democratic South simply had fewer first-rate law schools for her young men to attend.

Occupation

As might be expected from a group of highly educated men, most of the senators started work near the top of America's occupational hierarchy. Eighty-eight—almost exactly one-half—of the senators began working as lawyers, thirteen as teachers, twelve as journalists, six as professors, six as merchants, five as executives in manufacturing concerns. On the other hand, a few of the senators began work in less desirable jobs. Eight senators, for example, started out as farmers, another eight as clerks, four as salesmen, two as common laborers, three as printers, one each as an electrician, machinist, pipefitter, factory worker, and farm laborer. When all the senators' first occupations are lumped into occupational classes, it is clear that the "log-cabin-to-Capitol-Hill" myth of American politics needs considerable revision. Eighty-one per cent of the senators *started work* in the two highest classes. . . .

The second most striking feature of the occupational histories of the senators is the number of them who at one time or another were lawyers. The legal profession comprises about 0.1 per cent of the American labor force, and yet about half of the senators were lawyers. No other occupational group even approaches the lawyers' record. . . .

So far nothing has been said about the occupational differences between Democrats and Republicans. . . . Half again as many Democrats as Republicans, for example, are lawyers. Republican businessmen outnumber their Democratic counterparts by more than two to one. . . .

At first blush, these occupational differences seem easily explicable in terms of the different policies and electoral followings of the parties. The Republican party is, on the whole, more friendly with, and sensitive to the needs of, the American business community: hence a far larger proportion of its senators are former businessmen. The Democratic party (outside the South) draws a disproportionate share of its support from the lower reaches of the economic hierarchy and from members of minority groups. Leadership selection in such a party is more difficult than in the Republican case. Fewer Democratic voters have the status, education, skills, or opportunity to be active office seekers. By necessity the "underdog" must turn to men and women of relatively high status for political leadership. Yet the upper reaches of American society are mostly Republican. The politically oriented professional man—especially the lawyer—seems to fill this need for "underdog" political leaders. . . . [T]he indications are that this "underdog effect" accounts for a large number of Northern Democratic lawyers.

This [effect], by itself, does not account for the fact that there are more lawyer-senators in the Democratic than in the Republican party.

For the South—where the Democrats claim the allegiance of almost all the electorate and are hardly an "underdog" party—sends a larger proportion of lawyers to the upper house of Congress than does the North. How can this be explained?

Perhaps differences in political opportunities in Northern and Southern states has something to do with it. In the predominantly one-party South the inevitable risks of a political career are considerably lessened and politicians may, therefore, spend a larger share of their lives in public office than in the more competitive North and West. This may place a premium on following the occupation most compatible with sustained political endeavor—law. Seventy per cent of the Democrats from one-party states were lawyers, and only 62 per cent of those from states which lean Democratic and 65 per cent of those from two-party states followed the law as their principal occupation. None of the three Democrats elected from states leaning Republican were lawyers. While the differences are small they are generally in the right direction: where a career in politics is most possible the number of lawyers is highest; where political possibilities are least promising the number of lawyers is smallest.

Another possible key to the large numbers of lawyers from the South is the rural nature of that region. A business class and business values have been largely absent from the region until recent years. While farming has been a major industry, farmers are a relatively unproductive source of political leadership. Perhaps the region's attachment to lawyer-senators is merely a reflection of the dearth of other leaders in a rural world. Once again, there seems to be an element of truth in these speculations. On the whole, the lawyers in the Senate most often come from the very rural and very urban states. But the Southern states send far more lawyers to the Senate than do agrarian states in the North and West. Thus the South's preference for lawyers, while partly a reflection of its one-party system and rural economy, seems to be the result of other factors as well. . . .

Are Democratic and Republican businessmen much the same, or are they different kinds of businessmen? . . . The Democratic businessmen are mostly merchants, contractors, oil and gas producers, and insurance and real estate men. The Republicans tend to be publishers and manufacturing executives. These industry differences between the businessmen in the Senate seem to reflect, to some extent at least, differences in the party preference of different segments of the business community. Publishing and manufacturing are heavily Republican in their sympathies; finance and insurance less clearly so. Oil and gas producers, perhaps because of their concentration in the Southern states, have been a major source of campaign funds for the Democratic party. Contractors, who normally do a large share of their business with the government, may prefer the Democrats' free-spending policies to

Republican "economy." Retail merchants, dependent as they are on mass demand, are also likely to be sympathetic to the party which promises to pump spending power out to the masses of the people. Even if these differences between Democratic and Republican businessmen do not reflect significant party cleavages within the business world, they are big enough and consistent enough to indicate that, in the Senate, Democratic and Republican businessmen tend to be different.

Associational Life

"In no country in the world," De Tocqueville wrote in 1835, "has the principle of association been more successfully used, or more unsparingly applied to a multitude of different objects than in America."[1] This oft-quoted observation is, if anything, more true today than when it was written. As a result, most Americans have spent a significant part of their lives in joining, participating in, and governing voluntary associations.

The senators are no exception; they are extremely active in the nation's private groups. The average senator claims membership in about ten voluntary associations. By way of contrast, Warner and Lunt found that the average "Yankee City" resident belonged to two voluntary associations; in midwestern "Jonesville," Warner found that the average person belonged to only 1.3 associations.[2] Moreover, the senators' joining activities are not typically confined to one or a few types of associations. The most popular associations are lodges, followed closely by college fraternities, professional associations, veterans' and patriotic groups, and social clubs. The variety of associations to which the senators belong is so vast that probably most Americans share a common membership in some sort of private group with at least one senator.

There are a number of reasons for the senators' hyperactivity in the associational life of the country. First of all, this participation seems, in part, to be a reflection of the senators' class position. Numerous studies have shown that the higher an individual's social status, the larger number of associations he is likely to join. . . .

A second, and by no means mutually exclusive, interpretation of the senators' heavy participation in voluntary associations is political. It may be that persons who are extremely active in associations possess the type of personality to which the political career appeals. One must like people to be a politician (or at least appear to), and a record as a

---

[1] A. de Tocqueville, *Democracy in America*, trans., H. Reeve (2 vols.; New York: Alfred A. Knopf, 1946), I, 191.

[2] W. L. Warner and P. S. Lunt, *The Social Life of a Modern Community* (New Haven: Yale University Press, 1941), p. 303; W. L. Warner and Associates, *Democracy in Jonesville* (New York: Harper & Brothers, 1949), p. 131.

"joiner" may indicate the possession of this attitude, as well as the ability to get along with others. It is a well-known fact that persons already in politics consciously seek out associations to join as an aid to electoral success. In politics, the more "brothers" you have, the better.

THE COURT AS POLITICAL INNOVATOR

DECISIONS FROM BROWN V. BOARD OF EDUCATION
AND COMPANION CASES

Brown v. Board of Education · 1954

Mr. Chief Justice Warren delivered the opinion of the Court.

These cases come to us from the States of Kansas, South Carolina, Virginia, and Delaware. They are premised on different facts and different local conditions, but a common legal question justifies their consideration together in this consolidated opinion.

In each of the cases, minors of the Negro race, through their legal representatives, seek the aid of the courts in obtaining admission to the public schools of their community on a nonsegregated basis. In each instance, they had been denied admission to schools attended by white children under laws requiring or permitting segregation according to race. This segregation was alleged to deprive the plaintiffs of the equal protection of the laws under the Fourteenth Amendment. In each of the cases other than the Delaware case, a three-judge federal district court denied relief to the plaintiffs on the so-called "separate but equal" doctrine announced by this Court in *Plessy* v. *Ferguson.* Under that doctrine, equality of treatment is accorded when the races are provided substantially equal facilities, even though these facilities be separate. In the Delaware case, the Supreme Court of Delaware adhered to that doctrine, but ordered that the plaintiffs be admitted to the white schools because of their superiority to the Negro schools.

The plaintiffs contend that segregated public schools are not "equal" and cannot be made "equal," and that hence they are deprived of the equal protection of the laws. Because of the obvious importance of the question presented, the Court took jurisdiction. Argument was heard in the 1952 Term, and reargument was heard this Term on certain questions propounded by the Court.

Reargument was largely devoted to the circumstances surrounding

Decisions from Brown v. Board of Education (1954), *United States Reports,* Vol. 347, pp. 483 ff; Bolling v. Sharpe, *United States Reports,* Vol. 347, pp. 497 ff; and Brown v. Board of Education (1955), *United States Reports,* Vol. 349, pp. 294 ff. Title supplied by the editor.

the adoption of the Fourteenth Amendment in 1868. It covered exhaustively consideration of the Amendment in Congress, ratification by the states, then existing practices in racial segregation, and the views of proponents and opponents of the Amendment. This discussion and our own investigation convince us that, although these sources cast some light, it is not enough to resolve the problem with which we are faced. At best, they are inconclusive. The most avid proponents of the post-War Amendments undoubtedly intended them to remove all legal distinctions among "all persons born or naturalized in the United States." Their opponents, just as certainly, were antagonistic to both the letter and the spirit of the Amendments and wished them to have the most limited effect. What others in Congress and the state legislatures had in mind cannot be determined with any degree of certainty.

An additional reason for the inconclusive nature of the Amendment's history, with respect to segregated schools, is the status of public education at that time. In the South, the movement toward free common schools, supported by general taxation, had not yet taken hold. Education of white children was largely in the hands of private groups. Education of Negroes was almost nonexistent, and practically all of the race were illiterate. In fact, any education of Negroes was forbidden by law in some states. Today, in contrast, many Negroes have achieved outstanding success in the arts and sciences as well as in the business and professional world. It is true that public school education at the time of the Amendment had advanced further in the North, but the effect of the Amendment on Northern States was generally ignored in the congressional debates. Even in the North, the conditions of public education did not approximate those existing today. The curriculum was usually rudimentary; ungraded schools were common in rural areas; the school term was but three months a year in many states; and compulsory school attendance was virtually unknown. As a consequence, it is not surprising that there should be so little in the history of the Fourteenth Amendment relating to its intended effect on public education.

In the first cases in this Court construing the Fourteenth Amendment, decided shortly after its adoption, the Court interpreted it as proscribing all state-imposed discriminations against the Negro race. The doctrine of "separate but equal" did not make its appearance in this Court until 1896 in the case of *Plessy* v. *Ferguson* involving not education but transportation. American courts have since labored with the doctrine for over half a century. In this Court, there have been six cases involving the "separate but equal" doctrine in the field of public education. In *Cumming* v. *County Board of Education* and *Gong Lum* v. *Rice* the validity of the doctrine itself was not challenged. In more recent cases, all on the graduate school level, inequality was found in that specific benefits enjoyed by white students were denied to Negro students of the same educational qualifications. In none of these cases was it necessary to re-examine the doctrine to grant relief to the Negro plaintiff. And in *Sweatt* v. *Painter* the Court expressly reserved decision on the question whether *Plessy* v. *Ferguson* should be held inapplicable to public education.

In the instant cases, that question is directly presented. Here, unlike *Sweatt* v. *Painter*, there are findings below that the Negro and white schools involved have been equalized, or are being equalized, with respect to buildings, curricula, qualifications and salaries of teachers, and other "tangible" factors. Our decision, therefore, cannot turn on merely a comparison of these tangible factors in the Negro and white schools involved in each of the cases. We must look instead to the effect of segregation itself on public education.

In approaching this problem, we cannot turn the clock back to 1868 when the Amendment was adopted, or even to 1896 when *Plessy* v. *Ferguson* was written. We must consider public education in the light of its full development and its present place in American life throughout the Nation. Only in this way can it be determined if segregation in public schools deprives these plaintiffs of the equal protection of the laws.

Today, education is perhaps the most important function of state and local governments. Compulsory school attendance laws and the great expenditures for education both demonstrate our recognition of the importance of education to our democratic society. It is required in the performance of our most basic public responsibilities, even service in the armed forces. It is the very foundation of good citizenship. Today it is a principal instrument in awakening the child to cultural values, in preparing him for later professional training, and in helping him to adjust normally to his environment. In these days, it is doubtful that any child may reasonably be expected to succeed in life if he is denied the opportunity of an education. Such an opportunity, where the state has undertaken to provide it, is a right which must be made available to all on equal terms.

We come then to the question presented: Does segregation of children in public schools solely on the basis of race, even though the physical facilities and other "tangible" factors may be equal, deprive the children of the minority group of equal educational opportunities? We believe that it does.

In *Sweatt* v. *Painter* in finding that a segregated law school for Negroes could not provide them equal educational opportunities, this Court relied in large part on "those qualities which are incapable of objective measurement but which make for greatness in a law school." In *McLaurin* v. *Oklahoma State Regents* the Court, in requiring that a Negro admitted to a white graduate school be treated like all other students, again resorted to intangible considerations: ". . . his ability to study, to engage in discussions and exchange views with other students, and, in general, to learn his profession." Such considerations apply with added force to children in grade and high schools. To separate them from others of similar age and qualifications solely because of their race generates a feeling of inferiority as to their status in the community that may affect their hearts and minds in a way unlikely ever to be undone. The effect of this separation on their educational opportunities was well stated by a finding in the Kansas case by a court which nevertheless felt compelled to rule against the Negro plaintiffs:

> *Segregation of white and colored children in public schools has a detrimental effect upon the colored children. The impact is greater when it has the sanction of the law; for the policy of separating the races is usually interpreted as denoting the inferiority of the negro group. A sense of inferiority affects the motivation of a child to learn. Segregation with the sanction of law, therefore, has a tendency to [retard] the educational and mental development of negro children and to deprive them of some of the benefits they would receive in a racial[ly] integrated school system.*

Whatever may have been the extent of psychological knowledge at the time of *Plessy* v. *Ferguson*, this finding is amply supported by modern authority. Any language in *Plessy* v. *Ferguson* contrary to this finding is rejected.

We conclude that in the field of public education the doctrine of "separate but equal" has no place. Separate educational facilities are inherently unequal. Therefore, we hold that the plaintiffs and others similarly situated for whom the actions have been brought are, by reason of the segregation complained of, deprived of the equal protection of the laws guaranteed by the Fourteenth Amendment. This disposition makes unnecessary any discussion whether such segregation also violates the Due Process Clause of the Fourteenth Amendment.

Because these are class actions, because of the wide applicability of this decision, and because of the great variety of local conditions, the formulation of decrees in these cases presents problems of considerable complexity. On reargument, the consideration of appropriate relief was necessarily subordinated to the primary question — the constitutionality of segregation in public education. We have now announced that such segregation is a denial of the equal protection of the laws. In order that we may have the full assistance of the parties in formulating decrees, the cases will be restored to the docket, and the parties are requested to present further argument on Questions 4 and 5 previously propounded by the Court for the reargument this Term. . . .

Bolling v. Sharpe · 1954

Mr. Chief Justice Warren delivered the opinion of the Court.

This case challenges the validity of segregation in the public schools of the District of Columbia. The petitioners, minors of the Negro race, allege that such segregation deprives them of due process of law under the Fifth Amendment. They were refused admission to a public school attended by white children solely because of their race. They sought the aid of the District Court for the District of Columbia in obtaining admission. That court dismissed their complaint. The Court granted a writ of certiorari before judgment in the Court of Appeals because of the importance of the constitutional question presented.

We have this day held that the Equal Protection Clause of the Fourteenth Amendment prohibits the states from maintaining racially segregated public schools. The legal problem in the District of Columbia is somewhat different, however. The Fifth Amendment, which is applicable in the District of Columbia, does not contain an equal protection clause as does the Fourteenth Amendment which applies only to the states. But the concepts of equal protection and due process, both stemming from our American ideal of fairness, are not mutually exclusive. The "equal protection of the laws" is a more explicit safeguard of prohibited unfairness than "due process of law," and, therefore, we do not imply that the two are always interchangeable phrases. But, as this Court has recognized, discrimination may be so unjustifiable as to be violative of due process.

Classifications based solely upon race must be scrutinized with particular care, since they are contrary to our traditions and hence constitutionally suspect. As long ago as 1896, this Court declared the principle "that the Constitution of the United States, in its present form, forbids, so far as civil and political rights are concerned, discrimination by the General Government, or by the States, against any citizen because of his race." And in *Buchanan* v. *Warley* the Court held that a statute which limited the right of a property owner to convey his property to a person of another race was, as an unreasonable discrimination, a denial of due process of law.

Although the Court has not assumed to define "liberty" with any great precision, that term is not confined to mere freedom from bodily restraint. Liberty under law extends to the full range of conduct which the individual is free to pursue, and it cannot be restricted except for a proper governmental objective. Segregation in public education is not reasonably related to any proper governmental objective, and thus it imposes on Negro children of the District of Columbia a burden that constitutes an arbitrary deprivation of their liberty in violation of the Due Process Clause.

In view of our decision that the Constitution prohibits the states from maintaining racially segregated public schools, it would be unthinkable that the same Constitution would impose a lesser duty on the Federal Government. We hold that racial segregation in the public schools of the District of Columbia is a denial of the due process of law guaranteed by the Fifth Amendment to the Constitution.

For the reasons set out in *Brown* v. *Board of Education*, this case will be restored to the docket for reargument on Questions 4 and 5 previously propounded by the Court.

Brown v. Board of Education · 1955

Mr. Chief Justice Warren delivered the opinion of the Court.

These cases were decided on May 17, 1954. The opinions of that date, declaring the fundamental principle that racial discrimination in public education is unconstitutional, are incorporated herein by reference. All provisions of federal, state, or local law requiring or permitting such discrimination must yield to this principle. There remains for consideration the manner in which relief is to be accorded.

Because these cases arose under different local conditions and their disposition will involve a variety of local problems, we requested further argument on the question of relief. In view of the nationwide importance of the decision, we invited the Attorney General of the United States and the Attorneys General of all states requiring or permitting racial discrimination in public education to present their views on that question. The parties, the United States, and the States of Florida, North Carolina, Arkansas, Oklahoma, Maryland, and Texas filed briefs and participated in the oral argument.

These presentations were informative and helpful to the Court in its consideration of the complexities arising from the transition to a system of public education freed of racial discrimination. The presentations also demonstrated that substantial steps to eliminate racial discrimination in public schools have already been taken, not only in some of the communities in which these cases arose, but in some of the states appearing as *amici curiae*, and in other states as well. Substantial progress has been made in the District of Columbia and in the communities in Kansas and Delaware involved in this litigation. The defendants in the cases coming to us from South Carolina and Virginia are awaiting the decision of this Court concerning relief.

Full implementation of these constitutional principles may require solution of varied local school problems. School authorities have the primary responsibility for elucidating, assessing, and solving these problems; courts will have to consider whether the action of school authorities constitutes good faith implementation of the governing constitutional principles. Because of their proximity to local conditions and the possible need for further hearings, the courts which originally heard these cases can best perform this judicial appraisal. Accordingly, we believe it appropriate to remand the cases to those courts.

In fashioning and effectuating the decrees, the courts will be guided by equitable principles. Traditionally, equity has been characterized by a practical flexibility in shaping its remedies and by a facility for adjusting and reconciling public and private needs. These cases call for the exercise of these traditional attributes of equity power. At stake is the personal interest of the plaintiffs in admission to public schools as soon as practicable on a nondiscriminatory basis. To effectuate this interest may call for elimination of a variety of obstacles in making the transition to school systems operated in accordance with the constitutional principles set forth in our May 17, 1954, decision. Courts of equity may properly take into account the public interest in the elimination of such obstacles in a systematic and effective manner. But it should go without saying that the vitality of these constitutional principles cannot be allowed to yield simply because of disagreement with them.

While giving weight to these public and private considerations, the courts will require that the defendants make a prompt and reasonable start toward full compliance with our May 17, 1954 ruling. Once such a start has been made, the courts may find that additional time is necessary to carry out the ruling in an effective manner. The burden rests upon the defendants to establish that such time is necessary in the public interest and is consistent with good faith compliance at the earliest practicable date. To that end, the courts may consider problems related to administration, arising from the physical condition of the school plant, the school transportation system, personnel, revision of school districts and attendance areas into compact units to achieve a system of determining admission to the public schools on a nonracial basis, and revision of local laws and regulations which may be necessary in solving the foregoing problems. They will also consider the adequacy of any plans the defendants may propose to meet these problems and to effectuate a transition to a racially nondiscriminatory school system. During this period of transition, the courts will retain jurisdiction of these cases.

The judgments . . . , except that in the Delaware case, are accordingly reversed and the cases are remanded to the District Courts to take such proceedings and enter such orders and decrees consistent with this opinion as are necessary and proper to admit to public schools on a racially nondiscriminatory basis with all deliberate speed the parties to these cases. The judgment in the Delaware case — ordering the immediate admission of the plaintiffs to schools previously attended only by white children — is affirmed on the basis of the principles stated in our May 17, 1954, opinion, but the case is remanded to the Supreme Court of Delaware for such further proceedings as that Court may deem necessary in light of this opinion.

14. The New Men of Power

It is often said that the priest was the archetype of the medieval order, the warrior of much of mankind's history, and the self-made business-man of industrial capitalism in the West. In the twentieth century, bureaucrats, scientists, and intellectuals have come to play increasingly important roles in public affairs, applying specialized knowledge and theories of power to public policy. While inquiring how these "new men" have influenced the use of political power, it is also well to ask how the modern political states have influenced the use of knowledge.

The study of large-scale public and private organizations consumes much energy among scholars and among those who forage within these organizations for status, money, and power. No study of that functional, rational ordering of men and re-sources we loosely call bureaucracy can omit the contributions of the German scholar Max Weber. Drawn primarily on the Prussian experience, influenced by the breakup of old social forms rooted in land and an aristocratic heritage, Weber's historical account of bureaucratic growth must be considered by all who deal with its institutional adaptations and political consequences.

Understanding of the "unattached intellectual" and the "bureaucratic intellectual," two types discussed by Robert Merton, contributes to knowledge about the role of intellectuals in the formulation and criticism of public policies. W. R. Schilling's assessment of one kind of critical intellectual, the scientist, completes the selections about new men of power. Schilling discusses the problems in policy-making posed by the entry of scientists into the policy process and suggests the proper course of action for the nonscientific policy-maker when he receives conflicting scientific advice.

BUREAUCRACY: THE NEW FORCE

Max Weber

The Leveling of Social Differences

Bureaucratic organization has usually come into power on the basis of a leveling of economic and social differences. This leveling has been

Pages 224–235: From *Max Weber: Essays in Sociology*, edited and translated by H. H. Gerth and C. Wright Mills. Copyright 1946 by Oxford University Press, Inc. Reprinted by permission. Title sup-plied by the editor.

at least relative, and has concerned the significance of social and economic differences for the assumption of administrative functions.

Bureaucracy inevitably accompanies modern *mass democracy* in contrast to the democratic self-government of small homogeneous units. This results from the characteristic principle of bureaucracy: the abstract regularity of the execution of authority, which is a result of the demand for 'equality before the law' in the personal and functional sense—hence, of the horror of 'privilege,' and the principled rejection of doing business 'from case to case.' Such regularity also follows from the social preconditions of the origin of bureaucracies. The non-bureaucratic administration of any large social structure rests in some way upon the fact that existing social, material, or honorific preferences and ranks are connected with administrative functions and duties. This usually means that a direct or indirect economic exploitation or a 'social' exploitation of position, which every sort of administrative activity gives to its bearers, is equivalent to the assumption of administrative functions.

Bureaucratization and democratization within the administration of the state therefore signify and increase the cash expenditures of the public treasury. And this is the case in spite of the fact that bureaucratic administration is usually more 'economical' in character than other forms of administration. Until recent times—at least from the point of view of the treasury—the cheapest way of satisfying the need for administration was to leave almost the entire local administration and lower judicature to the landlords of Eastern Prussia. The same fact applies to the administration of sheriffs in England. Mass democracy makes a clean sweep of the feudal, patrimonial, and—at least in intent—the plutocratic privileges in administration. Unavoidably it puts paid professional labor in place of the historically inherited avocational administration by notables.

This not only applies to structures of the state. For it is no accident that in their own organizations, the democratic mass parties have completely broken with traditional notable rule based upon personal relationships and personal esteem. Yet such personal structures frequently continue among the old conservative as well as the old liberal parties. Democratic mass parties are bureaucratically organized under the leadership of party officials, professional party and trade union secretaries, et cetera. In Germany, for instance, this has happened in the Social Democratic party and in the agrarian mass-movement; and in England, for the first time, in the caucus democracy of Gladstone-Chamberlain, which was originally organized in Birmingham and since the 1870's has spread. In the United States, both parties since Jackson's administration have developed bureaucratically. In France, however, attempts to organize disciplined political parties on the basis of an election system that would compel bureaucratic organization have repeatedly failed. The resistance of local circles of notables against the ultimately unavoidable bureaucratization of the parties, which would encompass the entire country and break their influence, could not be overcome. Every advance of the simple election techniques, for instance the system of proportional elections, which calculates with figures, means a strict and inter-local bureaucratic organization of the parties and therewith an increasing domination of party bureaucracy and discipline, as well as the elimination of the local circles of notables — at least this holds for great states.

The progress of bureaucratization in the state administration itself is a parallel phenomenon of democracy, as is quite obvious in France, North America, and now in England. Of course one must always remember that the term 'democratization' can be misleading. The *demos* itself, in the sense of an inarticulate mass, never 'governs' larger associations; rather, it is governed, and its existence only changes the way in which the executive leaders are selected and the measure of influence which the *demos*, or better, which social circles from its midst are able to exert upon the content and the direction of administrative activities by supplementing what is called 'public opinion.' 'Democratization,' in the sense here intended, does not necessarily mean an increasingly active share of the governed in the authority of the social structure. This may be a result of democratization, but it is not necessarily the case.

We must expressly recall at this point that the political concept of democracy, deduced from the 'equal rights' of the governed, includes these postulates: (1) prevention of the development of a closed status group of officials in the interest of a universal accessibility of office, and (2) minimization of the authority of officialdom in the interest of expanding the sphere of influence of 'public opinion' as far as practicable. Hence, wherever possible, political democracy strives to shorten the term of office by election and recall and by not binding the candidate to a special expertness. Thereby democracy inevitably comes into conflict with the bureaucratic tendencies which, by its fight against notable rule, democracy has produced. The generally loose term 'democratization' cannot be used here, in so far as it is understood to mean the minimization of the civil servants' ruling power in favor of the greatest possible 'direct' rule of the *demos*, which in practice means the respective party leaders of the *demos*. The most decisive thing here — indeed it is rather exclusively so — is the *leveling of the governed* in opposition to the ruling and bureaucratically articulated group, which in its turn may occupy a quite autocratic position, both in fact and in form. . . .

It is obvious that almost always economic conditions of some sort play their part in . . . 'democratizing' developments. Very frequently we meet with the influence of an economically determined origin of new classes, whether plutocratic, petty bourgeois, or proletarian in character. Such classes may call on the aid of, or they may only call to life or recall to life, a political power, no matter whether it is of legitimate or of Caesarist stamp. They may do so in order to attain economic or social advantages by political assistance. On the other hand, there are equally possible and historically documented cases in which initiative came 'from on high' and was of a purely political nature and drew advantages from political constellations, especially in foreign affairs. Such leadership exploited economic and social antagonisms as well as class interests merely as a means for their own purpose of gaining purely political power. For this reason, political authority has thrown the antagonistic classes out of their almost always unstable equilibrium and called their latent interest conflicts into battle. It seems hardly possible to give a general statement of this.

The extent and direction of the course along which economic influences have moved, as well as the nature in which political power relations exert influence, vary widely. In Hellenic Antiquity, the transition to disciplined combat by Hoplites, and in Athens, the increasing importance of the navy laid the foundation for the conquest of political power by the strata on whose shoulders the military burden rested. In Rome, however, the same development shook the rule of the office nobility only temporarily and seemingly. Although the modern mass army has everywhere been a means of breaking the power of notables, by itself it has in no way served as a leverage for active, but rather for merely passive, democratization. One contributing factor, however, has been the fact that the ancient citizen army rested economically upon self-equipment, whereas the modern army rests upon the bureaucratic procurement of requirements.

The advance of the bureaucratic structure rests upon 'technical' superiority. This fact leads here, as in the whole field of technique, to the following: the advance has been realized most slowly where older structural forms have been technically well developed and functionally adjusted to the requirements at hand. This was the case, for instance, in the administration of notables in England and hence England was the slowest of all countries to succumb to bureaucratization or, indeed, is still only partly in the process of doing so. The same general phenomenon exists when highly developed systems of gaslight or of steam railroads with large and fixed capital offer stronger obstacles to electrification than in completely new areas which are opened up for electrification.

The Permanent Character of the Bureaucratic Machine

Once it is fully established, bureaucracy is among those social structures which are the hardest to destroy. Bureaucracy is *the* means of carrying 'community action' over into rationally ordered 'societal action.' Therefore, as an instrument for 'societalizing' relations of power, bureaucracy has been and is a power instrument of the first order—for the one who controls the bureaucratic apparatus.

Under otherwise equal conditions, a 'societal action,' which is methodically ordered and led, is superior to every resistance of 'mass' or even of 'communal action.' And where the bureaucratization of administration has been completely carried through, a form of power relation is established that is practically unshatterable.

The individual bureaucrat cannot squirm out of the apparatus in which he is harnessed. In contrast to the honorific or avocational 'notable,' the professional bureaucrat is chained to his activity by his entire material and ideal existence. In the great majority of cases, he is only a single cog in an ever-moving mechanism which prescribes to him an essentially fixed route of march. The official is entrusted with specialized tasks and normally the mechanism cannot be put into motion or arrested by him, but only from the very top. The individual bureaucrat is thus forged to the community of all the functionaries who are integrated into the mechanism. They have a common interest in seeing that the mechanism continues its functions and that the societally exercised authority carries on.

The ruled, for their part, cannot dispense with or replace the bureaucratic apparatus of authority once it exists. For this bureaucracy rests upon expert training, a functional specialization of work, and an attitude set for habitual and virtuoso-like mastery of single yet methodically integrated functions. If the official stops working, or if his work is forcefully interrupted, chaos results, and it is difficult to improvise replacements from among the governed who are fit to master such chaos. This holds for public administration as well as for private economic management. More and more the material fate of the masses depends upon the steady and correct functioning of the increasingly bureaucratic organizations of private capitalism. The idea of eliminating these organizations becomes more and more utopian.

The discipline of officialdom refers to the attitude-set of the official for precise obedience within his *habitual* activity, in public as well as in private organizations. This discipline increasingly becomes the basis of all order, however great the practical importance of administration on the basis of the filed documents may be. The naive idea of Bakuninism* of destroying the basis of 'acquired rights' and 'domination' by destroying public documents overlooks the settled orientation of *man* for keeping to the habitual rules and regulations that continue to exist independently of the documents. Every reorganization of beaten or dissolved troops, as well as the restoration of administrative orders destroyed by revolt, panic, or other catastrophes, is realized by appealing to the trained orientation of obedient compliance to such orders. Such compliance has been conditioned into the officials, on the one hand,

---

Bakuninism is an anarchistic philosophy devoted to individual liberation by destruction of oppressive state mechanisms and institutions. The theory was developed by Mikhail Bakunin, a Russian anarchist. — *Editor's note.*

and, on the other hand, into the governed. If such an appeal is successful it brings, as it were, the disturbed mechanism into gear again.

The objective indispensability of the once-existing apparatus, with its peculiar, 'impersonal' character, means that the mechanism — in contrast to feudal orders based upon personal piety — is easily made to work for anybody who knows how to gain control over it. A rationally ordered system of officials continues to function smoothly after the enemy has occupied the area; he merely needs to change the top officials. This body of officials continues to operate because it is to the vital interest of everyone concerned, including above all the enemy. . . .

Economic and Social Consequences of Bureaucracy

It is clear that the bureaucratic organization of a social structure, and especially of a political one, can and regularly does have far-reaching economic consequences. But what sort of consequences? Of course in any individual case it depends upon the distribution of economic and social power, and especially upon the sphere that is occupied by the emerging bureaucratic mechanism. The consequences of bureaucracy depend therefore upon the direction which the powers using the apparatus give to it. And very frequently a crypto-plutocratic distribution of power has been the result.

In England, but especially in the United States, party donors regularly stand behind the bureaucratic party organizations. They have financed these parties and have been able to influence them to a large extent. The breweries in England, the so-called 'heavy industry,' and in Germany the Hansa League with their voting funds are well enough known as political donors to parties. In modern times bureaucratization and social leveling within political, and particularly within state organizations in connection with the destruction of feudal and local privileges, have very frequently benefited the interests of capitalism. Often bureaucratization has been carried out in direct alliance with capitalist interests, for example, the great historical alliance of the power of the absolute prince with capitalist interests. In general, a legal leveling and destruction of firmly established local structures ruled by notables has usually made for a wider range of capitalist activity. Yet one may expect as an effect of bureaucratization, a policy that meets the petty bourgeois interest in a secured traditional 'subsistence,' or even a state socialist policy that strangles opportunities for private profit. This has occurred in several cases of historical and far-reaching importance, specifically during antiquity; it is undoubtedly to be expected as a future development. Perhaps it will occur in Germany.

The very different effects of political organizations which were, at least in principle, quite similar — in Egypt under the Pharaohs and in Hellenic and Roman times — show the very different economic significances of bureaucratization which are possible according to the direction of other factors. The mere fact of bureaucratic organization does not unambiguously tell us about the concrete direction of its economic effects, which are always in some manner present. At least it does not tell us as much as can be told about its relatively leveling effect socially. In this respect, one has to remember that bureaucracy as such is a precision instrument which can put itself at the disposal of quite varied — purely political as well as purely economic, or any other sort — of interests in domination. Therefore, the measure of its parallelism with democratization must not be exaggerated, however typical it may be. Under certain conditions, strata of feudal lords have also put bureaucracy into their service. There is also the possibility — and often it has become a fact, for instance, in the Roman principate and in some forms of absolutist state structures — that a bureaucratization of administration is deliberately connected with the formation of *estates*, or is entangled with them by the force of the existing groupings of social power. The express reservation of offices for certain status groups is very frequent, and actual reservations are even more frequent. The democratization of society in its totality, and in the *modern* sense of the term, whether actual or perhaps merely formal, is an especially favorable basis of bureaucratization, but by no means the only possible one. After all, bureaucracy strives merely to level those powers that stand in its way and in those areas that, in the individual case, it seeks to occupy. We must remember this fact . . . : that 'democracy' as such is opposed to the 'rule' of bureaucracy, in spite and perhaps because of its unavoidable yet unintended promotion of bureaucratization. Under certain conditions, democracy creates obvious ruptures and blockages to bureaucratic organization. Hence, in every individual historical case, one must observe in what special direction bureaucratization has developed.

The Power Position of Bureaucracy

Everywhere the modern state is undergoing bureaucratization. But whether the *power* of bureaucracy within the polity is universally increasing must here remain an open question.

The fact that bureaucratic organization is technically the most highly developed means of power in the hands of the man who controls it does not determine the weight that bureaucracy as such is capable of having in a particular social structure. The ever-increasing 'indispensability' of the officialdom, swollen to millions, is no more decisive for this question than is the view of some representatives of the proletarian movement that the economic indispensability of the proletarians is decisive for the measure of their social and political power position. If 'indispensability' were decisive, then where slave labor prevailed and where freemen usually abhor work as a dishonor, the 'indispensable' slaves ought to have held the positions of power, for they were at least as indispensable as officials and proletarians are today. Whether the power of bureaucracy as such increases cannot be decided *a priori* from such reasons. The drawing in of economic interest groups or other non-official experts, or the drawing in of non-expert lay representatives, the establishment of local, inter-local, or central parliamentary or other representative bodies, or of occupational associations—these *seem* to run directly against the bureaucratic tendency. . . .

Under normal conditions, the power position of a fully developed bureaucracy is always overtowering. The 'political master' finds himself in the position of the 'dilettante' who stands opposite the 'expert,' facing the trained official who stands within the management of administration. This holds whether the 'master' whom the bureaucracy serves is a 'people,' equipped with the weapons of 'legislative initiative,' the 'referendum,' and the right to remove officials, or a parliament, elected on a more aristocratic or more 'democratic' basis and equipped with the right to vote a lack of confidence, or with the actual authority to vote it. It holds whether the master is an aristocratic, collegiate body, legally or actually based on self-recruitment, or whether he is a popularly elected president, a hereditary and 'absolute' or a 'constitutional' monarch.

Every bureaucracy seeks to increase the superiority of the professionally informed by keeping their knowledge and intentions secret. Bureaucratic administration always tends to be an administration of 'secret sessions': in so far as it can, it hides its knowledge and action from criticism. Prussian church authorities now threaten to use disciplinary measures against pastors who make reprimands or other admonitory measures in any way accessible to third parties. They do this because the pastor, in making such criticism available, is 'guilty' of facilitating a possible criticism of the church authorities. The treasury officials of the Persian shah have made a secret doctrine of their budgetary art and even use secret script. The official statistics of Prussia, in general, make public only what cannot do any harm to the intentions of the power-wielding bureaucracy. The tendency toward secrecy in certain administrative fields follows their material nature: everywhere that the power interests of the domination structure toward *the outside* are at stake, whether it is an economic competitor of a private enterprise, or a foreign, potentially hostile polity, we find secrecy. If it is to be successful, the management of diplomacy can only be publicly controlled to a very limited extent. The military administration must insist on the concealment of its most important measures; with the increasing significance of purely technical aspects, this is all the more the case. Political parties do not proceed differently, in spite of all the ostensible publicity of Catholic congresses and party conventions. With the increasing bureaucratization of party organizations, this secrecy will prevail even more. Commercial policy, in Germany for instance, brings about a concealment of production statistics. Every fighting posture of a social structure toward the outside tends to buttress the position of the group in power.

The pure interest of the bureaucracy in power, however, is efficacious far beyond those areas where purely functional interests make for secrecy. The concept of the 'official secret' is the specific invention of bureaucracy, and nothing is so fanatically defended by the bureaucracy as this attitude, which cannot be substantially justified beyond these specifically qualified areas. In facing a parliament, the bureaucracy, out of a sure power instinct, fights every attempt of the parliament to gain knowledge by means of its own experts or from interest groups. The so-called right of parliamentary investigation is one of the means by which parliament seeks such knowledge. Bureaucracy naturally welcomes a poorly informed and hence a powerless parliament—at least in so far as ignorance somehow agrees with the bureaucracy's interests.

The absolute monarch is powerless opposite the superior knowledge of the bureaucratic expert—in a certain sense more powerless than any other political head. All the scornful decrees of Frederick the Great concerning the 'abolition of serfdom' were derailed, as it were, in the course of their realization because the official mechanism simply ignored them as the occasional ideas of a dilettante. When a constitutional king agrees with a socially important part of the governed, he very frequently exerts a greater influence upon the course of administration than does the absolute monarch. The constitutional king can control these experts better because of what is, at least relatively, the public character of criticism, whereas the absolute monarch is dependent for information solely upon the bureaucracy. The Russian czar of the old regime was seldom able to accomplish permanently anything that displeased his bureaucracy and hurt the power interests of the bureaucrats. His ministerial departments, placed directly under him as the autocrat, represented a conglomerate of satrapies,* as was correctly noted by Leroy-Beaulieu. These satrapies constantly fought against one another by all the means of personal intrigue, and, especially, they bombarded one another with voluminous 'memorials,' in the face of which, the monarch, as a dilettante, was helpless.

With the transition to constitutional government, the concentration of the power of the central bureaucracy in one head became unavoidable. Officialdom was placed under a monocratic head, the prime minister, through whose hands everything had to go before it got to the monarch. This put the latter, to a large extent, under the tutelage of the chief of the bureaucracy. Wilhelm II, in his well-known conflict with Bismarck, fought against this principle, but he had to withdraw his attack very soon. Under the rule of expert knowledge, the actual influence of the monarch can attain steadiness only by a continuous com-

*A *satrapy* is a province ruled by a petty prince or a despotic subordinate official.—*Editor's note.*

munication with the bureaucratic chiefs; this intercourse must be methodically planned and directed by the head of the bureaucracy.

At the same time, constitutionalism binds the bureaucracy and the ruler into a community of interests against the desires of party chiefs for power in the parliamentary bodies. And if he cannot find support in parliament the constitutional monarch is powerless against the bureaucracy. The desertion of the 'Great of the Reich,' the Prussian ministers and top officials of the Reich in November 1918, brought a monarch into approximately the same situation as existed in the feudal state in 1056. However, this is an exception, for, on the whole, the power position of a monarch opposite bureaucratic officials is far stronger than it was in any feudal state or in the 'stereotyped' patrimonial state. This is because of the constant presence of aspirants for promotion, with whom the monarch can easily replace inconvenient and independent officials. Other circumstances being equal, only economically independent officials, that is, officials who belong to the propertied strata, can permit themselves to risk the loss of their offices. Today as always, the recruitment of officials from among propertyless strata increases the power of the rulers. Only officials who belong to a socially influential stratum, whom the monarch believes he must take into account as personal supporters, like the so-called *Kanalrebellen* in Prussia, can permanently and completely paralyse the substance of his will.

Only the expert knowledge of private economic interest groups in the field of 'business' is superior to the expert knowledge of the bureaucracy. This is so because the exact knowledge of facts in their field is vital to the economic existence of businessmen. Errors in official statistics do not have direct economic consequences for the guilty official, but errors in the calculation of a capitalist enterprise are paid for by losses, perhaps by its existence. The 'secret,' as a means of power, is, after all, more safely hidden in the books of an enterpriser than it is in the files of public authorities. For this reason alone authorities are held within narrow barriers when they seek to influence economic life in the capitalist epoch. Very frequently the measures of the state in the field of capitalism take unforeseen and unintended courses, or they are made illusory by the superior expert knowledge of interest groups.

THE INTELLECTUAL AND PUBLIC POLICY

ROBERT K. MERTON

Intellectuals' Status and Social Policy

For our purposes, the term "intellectual" need not be defined very precisely. We shall consider persons as intellectuals *in so far as* they

From *Social Theory and Social Structure* (Chapel Hill: The University of North Carolina Press, 1957), pp. 209–211, 214–219, 222–224. Title supplied by the editor.

devote themselves to cultivating and formulating knowledge. They have access to and advance a cultural fund of knowledge which does not derive solely from their direct personal experience.[1] Their activities may be vocational or avocational; this is not decisive. The fact that John Stuart Mill spent many years in the India Office does not rule him out as an intellectual.

It should be noted that "the intellectual" refers to a social role and not to a total person. Although this role overlaps various occupational roles, it need not coincide with these. Thus, we normally include teachers and professors among the intellectuals. As a rough approximation, this may be adequate, but it does not follow that every teacher or professor is an intellectual. He may or may not be, depending on the actual nature of his activities. The limiting case occurs when a teacher *merely* communicates the content of a textbook, without further interpretations or applications. In such cases, the teacher is no more an intellectual than a radio announcer who merely reads a script prepared for him by others. He is then merely a cog in the transmission belt of communicating ideas forged by others.

We shall be concerned with a certain class of intellectuals: those who are specialists in the field of social, economic, and political knowledge. Roughly speaking, this includes social scientists and lawyers. In many respects, their role, particularly with relation to public policy, is sociologically distinct from that of specialists in the physical and biological sciences.

In the first place, there is a considerable degree of *indeterminacy* in the social scientist's findings, in so far as they bear upon projected action. He is confronted with far greater contingencies than, say, the electrical engineer. The latter can predict, for example, how a vacuum tube designed for a particular purpose will work under the very conditions in which it will be used; "pre-testing" in social affairs is only a rough approximation and even so, there is a large measure of contingency in determining the conditions under which the suggested plan will have to operate. The alternatives developed by the social scientist, then, often do not and sometimes cannot have the authority of reliable forecasts adequate for the purpose in hand. Expert knowledge here consists rather in reducing palpable errors of judgment. Such indeterminacy possibly underlies the ambivalence of distrust and hopeful expectation directed toward the social scientist in his capacity as advisor.

Secondly, this element of indeterminacy contributes also toward undermining the relation which exists between experts and clients. In evaluating the expert's competence, the client cannot always rely on results, for the judgment is always comparative. Perhaps the problem could have been solved more effectively by another specialist; perhaps

---

[1]Florian Znaniecki, *The Social Role of the Man of Knowledge* (New York, 1940), pp. 37–38.

it could not. There is a large area of indeterminacy in appraising the expert's performance. And consequently, there is an important fiduciary component in the expert's role. There must be a social organization —e.g., a professional society, a university which affixes a label of competence—which makes it likely that the client's confidence in experts is, *in general,* merited. But the more indefinite the objective standards of appraisal the greater the possibility of interpersonal relations, sentiments, and other nonobjective factors determining the degree of the client's confidence in the expert. Against this background, we can understand one source of discontent among experts who observe a colleague, in terms of technical criteria less competent than themselves, sitting at the right hand of a policy-maker. Indeterminacy of appraisal opens the way for discrepancies between the position of the expert and his competence. It is suggested that such discrepancies are more likely in the case of social scientists who serve as advisors than of technologists operating in fields where the comparative efficiency of their work can be more accurately assessed.

Thirdly, this indeterminacy of appraising achievement in the field of human affairs increases the need for policy-makers to rely on the judgment of experts in recruiting new expert personnel. It is in this way, quite apart from deliberate nepotism, that *cliques* of advisors tend to develop. For those experts who are in an organization are quite likely to call upon other experts *whom they know* and concerning whom they can pass grounded judgment on the basis of this direct familiarity. Networks of personal relations among intellectuals serve often as agencies for establishing self-contained cliques, at least among the more important advisors.

Fourth, the intellectual concerned with human affairs deals with data and problems about which policy-makers are often convinced they have considerable knowledge. It is by no means evident to the policy-maker that the expert has more competence in dealing with these problems than the policy-maker himself. When the social scientist is virtually certain of the validity of his advice, he is, very often, dealing with picayune affairs. When he deals with the larger issues, his relevant knowledge may not be as great as that acquired by the policy-maker through years of firsthand experience. This is, perhaps, a reason for the unenviable plight of the social science intellectual who is consigned to purgatory, never quite clear whether he is destined for heaven or hell. He is on call but is seldom regarded as indispensable. If his advice does not bear out the views of the "men of action," he may be returned to his private purgatory. When there is high indeterminacy in forecasting the consequences of alternative policies, the social scientist's advice can be readily ignored.

Finally, the intellectual dealing with human conduct and culture is concerned with alternatives which have immediate and obvious value-implications. He is peculiarly subject to attack by those whose interests and sentiments are violated by his findings. This aspect of his work coupled with the relatively low order of probability of his predictions concerning the effects of alternative policies renders him especially vulnerable to that rapid turnover of experts which we have come to expect in certain bureaucracies.

For these reasons, and doubtless others, intellectuals concerned with human affairs in general find themselves in a less secure status than the physical and biological scientists who affect public policy.

Bureaucratic Position and Perspectives

. . . In describing the process whereby the intellectual in a bureaucracy is converted into a technician, we proceed on the assumption that perspectives and outlook are largely a product of social position. Intellectuals are oriented toward more or less defined social circles and accommodate their interests, attitudes, and objectives to these circles. The demands and expectations inherent in a social position tend to shape the behavior of the occupants of that position. . . . This view of the formation of role personalities at once directs our attention to differences in the "significant others" for the bureaucratic and unattached intellectual: in short, it requires us to examine the different clientele of the two types of intellectual and the part they play in shaping the intellectual's role.

Remotely or directly, the client of the bureaucratic intellectual is a policy-maker who is concerned with translating certain vague or well-defined purposes into programs of action. The client's demands of the intellectual may vary, but in essentials they can probably all be subsumed under a limited number of types.

The *specificity* of the client's demands upon the bureaucratic intellectual goes far toward determining the nature of the latter's activities. At one extreme, the policy-maker may simply indicate a general area with no indication of the nature of decisions which are contemplated. This is a vaguely defined area in which there will presumably be need for action at some future date (e.g. ethnic relations in Europe or the state of morale in the army). The intellectual is asked to assemble pertinent facts upon the basis of which later decisions may be "intelligently" made. At this point of low specificity of the client's demands, the intellectual has the largest possible scope—at times, an uncomfortably broad scope leading to anxieties as an outcome of imperfect orientation —for defining problems, deciding what are pertinent data and recommending alternative policies. Or a somewhat more definite formulation by the client may be made in the form of indicating a specific area in which policies are to be blocked out and a request made for information bearing on this more clearly defined area (e.g. Serb-Croat relations in Europe or production by small industrial concerns during the war). This delimitation of the field reduces the scope of the intellectual in deciding both the nature of the practical problems and the character of pertinent information. Or the problem may be presented to the intellectual at progressively advanced points in the *continuum of decision*: at the point where alternative policies are being considered or when a specific policy has been adopted and there is need for information on means of implementing this policy through a definite program of action or finally, after a given program has been put into practice and there is a demand for assessing the effectiveness of the program. These intervals in the continuum of decision set different types of problems for the intellectual. In general, there appears to be an inverse relation between the specificity of the problem as defined by the client and scope for initiating policy proposals by the intellectual.

The earlier in the continuum of decision that the bureaucratic intellectual operates, the greater his potential influence in guiding the decision. When the area of inquiry is vaguely indicated by the policy-maker, the intellectual's research can, within limits, focus attention on certain alternative lines of action by ascribing greater weight to certain types of evidence. This seems to have been the case, for example, with Wilson's Fourteen Points which were, in large part, the outgrowth of an appraisal of the total situation by intellectuals "whose brains he borrowed," to use the President's own phrase. In helping to establish such general frameworks of policy, the intellectual can initiate some control from below. In rare situations of this sort, the policy-maker may find himself in the notorious position of the Frenchman in 1848 who, when urged not to join the mob storming the barricades, answered: "I must follow them; I am their leader."

More typically, however, the bureaucratic intellectual finds himself in a position where he is called upon to provide information for alternative or specific policies which have already been formulated by policy-makers. As an expert he is requested to indicate what needs to be taken into account in selecting one or the other of proposed alternatives or in implementing a particular policy. When problems reach the intellectual at this late stage in the continuum of decision, he comes to think largely in instrumental terms and to accept the prevailing definitions of objectives. His perspectives are fixed accordingly. He gets to see only those aspects of the total situation which are directly related to the proposed policy. He may or may not be aware that he is ignoring possible alternatives in his research, by focusing on the consequences or modes of implementing limited alternatives which have been presented to him. He may overlook the fact that a way of seeing also implies a way of not-seeing: that limiting one's purview to alternatives *A* and *B* means ignoring alternatives *C* and *D*.

This problem of relation to the policy-maker takes on an entirely different cast for the unattached intellectual. *His perspectives may be directed by his position within the class structure* but they are somewhat less subject to the immediate control of a *specific* clientele. He characteristically approaches the problem area quite apart from the prior assumptions and interests of a bureaucratic client. He may feel free to consider the consequences of alternative policies which may have been ignored or rejected by the bureaucracy. His limitations are not so much a matter of by-passing alternatives without adequate inquiry. But, not being subjected to the constraints of impending decisions based on his work, the unattached intellectual may dwell in the realm of good intentions and bad programs for action. Even when he formulates both policy and program in realistic terms, it is difficult for his views to *gain access to responsible policy-makers*. So far as affecting public policy is concerned, he who is not in the bureaucracy becomes a small and often a still voice.

From all this arises the dilemma facing the intellectual who is actively concerned with furthering social innovations. Not too inaccurately, this may be expressed in a slogan: he who innovates is not heard; he who is heard does not innovate. If the intellectual is to play an effective role in putting his knowledge to work, it is increasingly necessary that he become a part of a bureaucratic power-structure. This, however, often requires him to abdicate his privilege of exploring policy-possibilities which he regards as significant. If, on the other hand, he remains unattached in order to preserve full opportunity of choice, he characteristically has neither the resources to carry through his investigations on an appropriate scale nor any strong likelihood of having his findings accepted by policy-makers as a basis for action.

Needless to say, full integrity may be found among both the bureaucratic and the unattached intellectuals: the essential differences lie in the relationship to a client and the attendant pressures which play a part in defining the problems which are regarded as significant. Both types of intellectual may have full integrity within the limits of their *definition of problems*. But they have each made an important and, often, a different value decision in accepting or rejecting the definition of a problem. . . . *The crucial point is to recognize the value-implications entailed by the very choice and definition of the problem itself and that the choice will be in part fixed by the intellectual's position within the social structure.* The bureaucratic intellectual who must permit the policy-maker to define the scope of his research problem is implicitly lending his skills and knowledge to the preservation of a particular institutional arrangement. The unattached intellectual may not directly affect the prevailing policy but he does bring forward knowledge which would presumably be of service in modifying the current arrangement. Thus, the intellectual makes his most significant value decision in selecting both his clientele and derivatively, the type of problem with which he shall be concerned.

There is another way in which the orientation of intellectuals entering a bureaucracy tends to change, and this derives from the pressure for action. They tend to become, as the loose phrase has it, "less theoretical and more practical." To what does this refer? The closer to the actual locus of decision, the more necessary it is for broad policy to be translated into programs of action and the larger the number of considerations which must be taken into account, over and above the original formulation of policy. This "taking into account" of additional variables generally means a partial change of the original policy; it means, "compromise with the realities of the case." Thus, the closer to the point of actual decision that the intellectual is located, the more he experiences a pressure to temper the wind to the shorn lamb, that is, to fit his original abstract formulations to the exigencies of the situation. This pressure, operating over a period of time, shapes the general perspectives of the bureaucratic intellectual; he comes increasingly to think in technical and instrumental terms of ways of implementing policies *within a given situation.*

For the unattached intellectual, such shifts in perspective of his bureaucratic colleague often seem a "sell-out." This familiar type of conflict results from the differing positions of the two types of intellectuals within the social structure with, inevitably, some differences in perspective. The unattached intellectual can continue to be adamant in abiding by his formulations, since these are not translated into action, and he often fails to see aspects of the action problem which are constantly borne in on the bureaucratic intellectual. The bureaucratic intellectual, on the other hand, has limited alternatives. (1) He can accommodate his own social values and special knowledge to the values of the policy-makers. (2) He can seek to alter the prevailing policies of the executives in the bureaucratic apparatus. (3) He can respond in terms of a schizoid dissociation between his own values and those of the bureaucracy, by regarding his function as purely technical and without value-implications. The first response involves an incorporation of the bureaucracy's values and sometimes a change in the intellectual's prior outlook. The second, when the isolated intellectual seeks to pit his own grounded views against those of the total apparatus, ordinarily involves ineffectual conflict which is often the prelude to the intellectual's flight from the bureaucracy. The third response which, we suppose, is the most frequent, leads to the "technician role." Since this role is supported by the occupational mores of the intellectual — "As a man of science, I do not indulge in value judgments" — it reduces the conflict otherwise experienced in implementing policies largely at variance with one's own judgments. In short, segmentation of roles permits the intellectual to preserve his sense of personal integrity, although he participates in programs which run counter to his own values.

All this suggests that the unattached and bureaucratic intellectual perform quite different functions with respect to social policy. The unattached intellectual can serve as a gadfly, a critic of established policies by publicly indicating some of their implications and consequences. To a limited degree, then, he may affect the climate of decision. With the growth of mass communication, this function has taken on even greater importance than it had in the past. The bureaucratic intellectual, on the other hand, save in the relatively rare cases where he actually defines policy, is largely limited to developing more effective modes of implementing decisions and of introducing alternative possibilities for action which do not violate the values of the bureaucracy. This suggests that unattached intellectuals may be serving common purposes, even during the war crisis, as effectively as, though differently from, the intellectuals who are devoting "their energies to the war effort" by serving in a public bureaucracy.

But even though the bureaucratic intellectual often accommodates himself to the outlook of policy-makers, he may still project *alternative lines of action which run counter to values and objectives of businessmen in government policy positions*. This clash of values often occurs in the very proposals of policies. . . .

Frustrations of the Intellectual in Bureaucracy

With such patterns of conflict as a background, it is not at all surprising that the intellectual commonly experiences a series of frustrations, once he becomes an integral part of a bureaucracy which is in some measure controlled by those who can neither live with him nor without him. The honeymoon of intellectuals and policy-makers is often nasty, brutish, and short. This has an understandable sociological basis. The intellectual, before he enters upon his bureaucratic post, is wont to consider his intellectual problems in abstraction from the demands of specific other persons. He may feel that a problem is solved on its own merits. Once he finds himself in a bureaucracy, he discovers that the intellectual task itself is closely connected with social relations within the bureaucracy. His selection of problems for study must be guided by what he knows or thinks he knows of his clients or prospective clients; his formulation of the problem, his analyses and reports must be geared to the same relationship to a client. In short, where he had previously experienced a sense of intellectual autonomy —whether real or spurious is for the moment unimportant—he now becomes aware of *visible controls* over the nature and direction of his inquiries. This sense of constraint, particularly when he is by no means clear about the exact wants of the client or if clear, when he disagrees with the nature of these wants, is registered in frustration. The resultant conflicts between the criteria of choosing and analyzing problems as an unattached intellectual and as a bureaucratic intellectual often leads to the flight from bureaucracy and the escape to assumed autonomy.

The high turnover of expert personnel in public bureaucracies is not merely a matter of client dissatisfaction or of criticism by outside groups, such as Congress. It is often the product of the cumulative frustrations experienced by the intellectual who has been previously conditioned to a sense of personal autonomy and cannot abide the visible constraints imposed by a formal organization. Thus, a psychiatrist recently observed a marked rise in the euphoria and optimism of his friends. He was at a loss to explain this, and at first assumed that it was a result of United Nations victories. Only later did he realize that he had encountered a series of friends who had just left Washington bureaucracy for good. They were exhibiting euphoria born of release from frustration.

So, too, Stouffer reports his wartime observation:

> *In the Washington Mêlée one cannot keep the Alpine detachment which is the glory of university research in times of peace. There are many frustrations. . . . All the agencies doing work in sociology or social psychology, such as the Office of War Information, Office of Strategic Services, Military Intelligence and others, have much the same experience.*[2]

It is instructive to examine some of the more familiar types of frustrations which often culminate in disillusionment, for these throw light on the possibilities and limitations of the bureaucratic intellectual in affecting policy. These frustrations can be classified into two main groups: (1) those deriving from conflict of values between the intellectual and the policy-maker, and (2) from the bureaucratic type of organization itself.

1. *Conflicts of values between intellectual and policy-makers:*
   a. Occasionally the bureaucratic intellectual finds himself the target for conflict arising from different universes of discourse of the policy-maker and himself. Research which appears trivial from an immediately practical standpoint may be highly significant for its theoretic implications and may later illumine a series of practical problems. The intellectual is in time compelled to accept new criteria of significance.

[2]Samuel A. Stouffer, "Social Science and the Soldier," in W. F. Ogburn (ed.), *American Society in Wartime* (1943), p. 116.

b. Research findings may be exploited for purposes which run counter to the values of the intellectual; his recommendations for policy based on the weight of the evidence may be ignored and a counter-policy introduced.

c. The intellectual will often not be willing to commit himself on the basis of what seems to him flimsy evidence, whereas the policy-maker must do so because of the urgency for action.

d. Specialists may experience frustrations from being required to work in fields which are outside their sphere of competence, since policy-makers are at times not clear on significant differences between specialists.

2. *Frustrations arising from bureaucratic organization:*

a. Since bureaucracies are organized for action, questions are often asked of intellectuals for which they have no immediate answer. Or, this may invite the "deadline neurosis"; problems may be raised which it is impossible to solve within the allotted time.

The problem of the deadline has perhaps been best described by Robert Louis Stevenson in an entirely different context:

> *This is no cabinet science, in which things are tested to a scruple; we theorize with a pistol to our head; we are confronted with a new set of conditions on which we have not only to pass judgment, but to take action, before the hour is at an end.*

b. Lines of communication between policy-makers and intellectuals may be clogged, leading typically to frustrations.

1) Since policy-makers often do not keep intellectuals informed of impending problems of policy, it is difficult for the latter to determine what are relevant data.

2) Or, there may be the problem of having research findings reach the appropriate policy-maker, who is confronted with a mass of material emanating from different sources.

3) Or, the findings on their way to the policy-maker may be emasculated and distorted by intervening personnel.

4) Or, finally, there is the problem of so formulating the findings that the most significant results will be intelligible to and engage the interest of the policy-maker. The "processing of the material" may require simplification to the point where some of the more complex though significant findings are discarded.

c. Despite all precautions, the intellectual's findings may not be used by those for whom it is intended. This eliminates the very rationale of the intellectual's work and dissipates his interest in his work, leading to the "boondoggling neurosis." (Correlatively, even occasional use of research findings, no matter how limited the context in which these have been put to use, serves to reinvigorate the morale of the intellectual.)

1) The policy-maker will at times reject funded research in the social sciences on the assumption that his first-hand experience has given him a more secure understanding of the situation than the intellectual can possibly attain. This is the more likely to occur if the findings suggest changes in familiar routines and practices, since it is seldom that the intellectual can demonstrate the greater effectiveness of proposed as compared with current arrangements.

This excursion into one phase of the intellectual's role in our society is intended primarily to formulate certain hypotheses. The collection of life-histories, diaries, and journal-books of intellectuals in public bureaucracies, direct participant-observation and historical data can provide a firm and fruitful basis for research in this field.

SCIENTISTS, FOREIGN POLICY, AND POLITICS

WARNER R. SCHILLING

> . . . we must take, so far as we can, a picture of the world into our minds. Is it not a startling circumstance for one thing that the great discoveries of science, that the quiet study of men in laboratories, that the thoughtful developments which have taken place in quiet lecture rooms, have now been turned to the destruction of civilization? . . . The enemy whom we have just overcome had at its seats of learning some of the principal centres of scientific study and discovery, and used them in order to make destruction sudden and complete; and only the watchful, continuous cooperation of men can see to it that science, as well as armed men, is kept within the harness of civilization.[1]

I

These words were spoken in Paris in January 1919 by Woodrow Wilson, addressing the second Plenary Session of the Peace Conference. Wilson believed he had found a watchdog for civilization in the League of Nations. In this he was sadly mistaken. Science and armed men have indeed been harnessed, but in order to promote and maintain the goals of conflicting polities. Whether in the pursuit of these ends the cause of civilization will yet be served remains, we hope, an open question. . . .

From *The American Political Science Review*, 1962 (June), *51*: 287–300.

[1]U.S. Department of State, *Papers Relating to the Foreign Relations of the United States, The Peace Conference*, 13 vols. (Washington, 1942–1947), vol. 3, p. 179.

What has transformed the relationship between science and war has been the fact that in the twentieth century the development of technology has become increasingly dependent upon advances in basic knowledge about the physical world. Moreover, in the technically advanced nations, both the rate of technological innovation and the growth of new scientific knowledge have been increasing exponentially. As crudely measured by the volume of scientific publication, scientific knowledge has been doubling every ten to fifteen years. In a non-Wilsonian world, the consequences of these conditions for national 'security policy have been as necessary as they are obvious. As the United States and the Soviet Union throw one weapons system after another into the effort to maintain at least a balance of terror, neither dares fall behind in either the discovery of new physical relationships or in the application of scientific knowledge to military hardware and political-military strategy. Thus, by the end of the first decade of the Cold War, about 50 per cent of the engineers in the United States and 25 per cent of the scientists were employed by the Federal government, either directly or on contract, and about 65 per cent of the scientific research in universities and 57 per cent of that in private industry was government-financed.[2]

Indicative of the new relationship between science and war, figures and graphs comparing the Great Powers in numbers of scientists and engineers have become as familiar as those in the 1930s which compared the Powers in their output of steel, coal, and oil. Nor is it only in the military field that science and technology have become vital to the course of foreign policy. Science has been harnessed to the advancement of foreign policy goals in such diverse fields as the exploration of space, birth and disease control, weather modification, economic development, and global communications.

Present, prospective, and future developments in science and technology are certain to bring a host of problems and opportunities to those responsible for the conduct of foreign policy. In recognition of this fact, the governments of the major Powers have endeavored to find ways to make themselves more alert to such developments and more active in determining the course of science and technology. The United States and the Soviet Union are the most extensively engaged in this effort, but it should not be forgotten that the nations of Western and Central Europe were among the pioneers in cultivating the relationship between science and government. The three elements that have revolutionized current military technology and strategy (electronics, missiles, and nuclear weapons) had their harbingers in the World War II

---

[2]See Lee A. DuBridge, "The American Scientist: 1955," *Yale Review*, Spring 1955, p. 13, and the *Bulletin of the Atomic Scientists*, March 1957, p. 82, and May-June 1961, p. 254. The figure for private industry is for the year 1959; the others are for the year 1955.

development of British radar, the German V-2, and the American A-bomb, and it is noteworthy that the two European developments were conceived, initiated, and directed by officials and employees of established government organizations. In contrast, the American A-bomb was the result of conceptions and initiatives that came from outside the government—and primarily from exiled Europeans at that.

As an integral part of the efforts of governments to become both more responsive to and responsible for the development of science and technology, scientists have been invited into the highest councils of government, and it is with some of the problems occasioned by the presence of these "new" participants in the making of national policy that the remainder of this article will be concerned. Although some illustrative material will be drawn from the experience of other governments, the paper focuses on problems associated with the participation of scientists in the American policy process. . . .

In their general character, the problems occasioned by the participation of scientists in the determination of high policy are not nearly so novel as is generally supposed. The scientist has been brought into the councils of government because he possesses specialized skills and information believed relevant to the identification and resolution of particular policy problems. His relationship to the policy process is therefore a familiar one, that of an expert. Just as Sputnik I precipitated the establishment of a Special Assistant to the President for Science and Technology, so the earlier problems of fighting World War II and insuring postwar employment had brought the Joint Chiefs of Staff and the Council of Economic Advisers into the Offices of the President.

The central problems in policy-making posed by the entry of scientists into the policy process are thus formally no different from those associated with any other expert involved in the determination of national security policy. In particular, four such problems can be noted. (1) Like all experts, scientists will at times disagree, and the non-scientist (be he politician, administrator, or an expert in some other field) will confront the problem of choosing a course of action in the face of conflicting scientific advice. (2) Like all experts, scientists will at times evince certain predispositions toward the resolution of the policy problems on which their advice is sought, and the non-scientist will confront the problem of identifying the policy predilections peculiar to scientists and being on his guard against them. (3) The non-scientist and scientist will confront one problem in common, and that is how to organize themselves to maximize the contribution that science can make to the government's programs, opportunities, and choices. Finally, (4) the scientist will confront a problem common to all experts who participate in the American policy process, and that is how to engage in politics without debasing the coinage of his own expertise.

II

The difficulties the non-scientist confronts in choosing a course of action in the face of conflicting scientific advice seem inherently no more formidable than those a non-expert would face in deciding what to do in the event of conflicting advice from economists, soldiers, or specialists on Soviet foreign policy. There are at least seven procedures that the non-expert can follow in such circumstances, singly or in combination, and they appear to have about the same promise, for better or for worse, regardless of the kind of experts involved.

The first step the non-scientist can take is to make certain that it is really conflicting *scientific* advice he is receiving. In the fall of 1949 President Truman asked Secretary Acheson to look into the disputes then current within the Atomic Energy Commission and elsewhere about the consequences of undertaking an intensive effort to make an H-bomb. Upon investigation the Secretary of State concluded that the scientists involved were not really very far apart except on the foreign policy issues that were his and Truman's responsibility to decide.[3]

Procedures two and three are simple: the non-scientist may be guided by quantitative or qualitative features of the division (he can side with the majority, or with that side whose past record is the more confidence-inspiring). Failing these, there is, four, the "principle of least harm" and, five, the "principle of minimal choice." In the former, one chooses that course of action which appears to involve the least cost if the technical premise on which it is based proves to be wrong. Thus in World War II, given the American belief that the Germans were hard at work on an A-bomb, it seemed more sensible to spend $2 billion on the assumption that the bomb could be made than to do little or nothing on the assumption that it could not. In the case of the "principle of minimal choice," one chooses that course of action which seems to close off the least number of future alternatives. This was the character of President Truman's first decision on the H-bomb. He decided to go ahead in the effort to explore the feasibility of an H-bomb, but nothing was decided about technical steps of a greater political or military consequence (for example, testing a device if one were fabricated, or preparing to produce the materials that would be required for weapons production in the event of a successful test).[4]

In the case of procedure six the non-scientist can make his choice among conflicting scientists on the basis of whichever technical estimate is most in accord with policy on which he was already intent. (In contrast to the first procedure, where the non-scientist endeavors to factor out of the conflict the policy preferences of the scientists, here he is

---

[3] In this and subsequent undocumented references the present writer has drawn upon personal interviews during 1956–1958 with participants in the H-bomb decision.
[4] . . . On the H-bomb choice, see the present writer's "The H-Bomb Decision: How to Decide Without Actually Choosing," *Political Science Quarterly*, March 1961, pp. 37–38.

factoring into the conflict his own policy preferences.) In the spring of 1942, the British scientists Henry Tizard and F. A. Lindemann (Lord Cherwell) diverged greatly in their estimates of the destruction that could be accomplished by an intensive bombing of the homes of the German working class. There was general agreement among the soldiers and politicians involved that if the lower estimate were correct there were better military uses for the resources the bombing campaign would require, but in the end the campaign was made in the expectation that the higher estimate would prove to be the more accurate (which it did not). This choice was clearly influenced by Churchill's interest in presenting the Russians with a dramatically visible contribution to the war against Germany and by the fact that British air doctrine had long presumed the efficacy of strategic bombing.[5]

In procedure seven the non-scientist is guided by his own sense for the scientific and technical problems involved. In the 1949 H-bomb debate, some of the politicians involved were little deterred by the fact that the scientists were by no means confident that they could make such a weapon and by the possibility that an all-out but failing effort might entail very high costs for the A-bomb program. These politicians were willing to press ahead in part because of their belief that the scientists were not really aware of their own potential. Similarly, when the German soldiers, scientists, and engineers engaged in the development of the V-2 divided on the question of whether it should be launched from mobile or fixed batteries, Hitler's own technical enthusiasm for large, hardened bunkers led him, unwisely as it turned out, to decide on behalf of the latter.[6]

In concluding this survey of the problem of conflicting advice, it should be noted that one of the more likely outcomes is that the actions of the contending scientists may prove much more influential than the procedures followed by the non-scientist. Divided experts will not always be equal in their physical or personal access to the decision-maker, in the persistence with which they state their case, or in the force and clarity of their arguments. Thus, in the H-bomb debate, there were instances where equally qualified scientists differed greatly in the time and energy they spent circulating their views of the technical (and political) prospects, and such differences were by no means without consequence for the judgments of others.

III

The discussion of the policy predispositions displayed by scientists must be entered with considerable caution. The major theoretical premise

---

[5]See C. P. Snow, *Science and Government* (Cambridge, Mass.: Harvard University Press, 1961), pp. 47–51; the review of this book by P. M. S. Blackett in *Scientific American*, April 1961, pp. 192–194; and Winston S. Churchill, *The Second World War: The Hinge of Fate* (Boston: Houghton Mifflin Company, 1950), p. 281. . . .

[6]Maj. Gen. Walter Dornberger, *V-2* (New York: Ballantine Books, 1954), pp. 97, 158–160; and Lt. Gen. James M. Gavin, *War and Peace in the Space Age* (New York: Harper & Brothers, 1958), pp. 76–77.

involved is that all experts will evidence certain predilections with regard to policy and policy-making which are the result of the character
of their expertise: their skills, knowledge, and experience. Since experts differ in the skills, knowledge, and experience they command
(or in the responsibilities with which they are charged), they will differ
in the biases they characteristically exhibit. Thus scientists, soldiers, and
diplomats jointly concerned with a policy problem are likely to approach
the question of how and in what manner it should be resolved with
rather dissimilar predispositions.

These points, however, are easier stated than demonstrated. To
begin with, it should be clear that, insofar as policy is concerned, "the
scientific mind" is as much a chimera as "the military mind." Scientists,
like soldiers and the rest of us, differ greatly in the ideas they have about
the political world and the things that will (or ought to) happen in it,
and their views on foreign policy matters are far more likely to be reflective of these differences than conditioned by their common professional skills and interests. Moreover, even if differences in expertise
or responsibility were the only factors determining the views of policy-
makers (and they certainly are not), one would still have to take account
of the fact that scientists are as varied in their professional skills and
pursuits as soldiers. The perspectives of a theoretical physicist engaged
in basic research are no more to be equated with those of an organic
chemist engaged in applying extant knowledge to the improvement of
an industrial product than is the outlook of a staff officer in Washington
drafting a war plan to be considered identical with that of a general in
charge of a theatre of operations.

In addition to these difficulties, analysis must also contend with the
fact that it is directed toward a moving target. The policy perspectives
that a physicist may have developed as a result of two decades in a university laboratory are unlikely to endure without change after a few
years on a Washington advisory committee. Many American scientists
are well along the same route that transformed the policy perspectives
of large numbers of the American military profession during the war
and immediate postwar years. As a result of new problems and new
responsibilities, these soldiers acquired new skills, knowledge, and experience. In consequence, with regard to their approach to foreign
policy, some are, for all practical purposes, interchangeable between
the Pentagon and the State Department, and one could wish that there
were more diplomats equally well equipped to work on both sides of
the Potomac.

With these reservations in mind, six policy perspectives will be
presented here which seem moderately characteristic of many scientists,
most of them physicists, who have participated in national security policy
in recent times. Most of these predispositions were first evidenced during their work with the military during World War II, and the extent

and manner in which they have been later operative in reference to larger foreign policy issues is not always easy to document, since most of the sources are still classified. Needless to say, in outlining these predispositions, one is presenting a cross between a caricature and a Weberian ideal type, not describing real people. In discussing these predispositions, the present writer does not mean to convey the impression that they are either "good" or "bad" from the point of view of policy or policy-making, or that one or another of these predispositions may not also be evidenced by groups other than scientists. The point to this discussion is that if certain orders of scientists are indeed prone to these or other policy predispositions, the non-scientist will be wise to be alert to them, even if in the event he should conclude that they are all for the good.

Naive Utopianism or Naive Belligerency

C. P. Snow has described the scientist as an impatient optimist in his approach to social wrongs; he is quick to search for something to do and inclined to expect favorable results.[7] Certainly, the scientist's profession inclines him to look at problems in terms of searching for a solution to them. When this perspective is turned to problems of international politics, however, the scientist's approach often appears open to the characterization of "naive utopianism or naive belligerency."[8] His approach to international relations appears simplistic and mechanistic. It is almost as if he conceives of policy being made primarily by forward-looking, solution-oriented, rational-thinking types like himself.

In these perspectives the scientist is likely to find little in common with the diplomat (who is inclined to believe that most of his problems have no solution, and who is in any event too busy with the crises of the day to plan for tomorrow), or with the politician (whose approach to problems is so spasmodic as to seem neither analytical nor rational, and whose policy positions are anyway soon blurred by his efforts to accommodate to the positions of others), or with the professional student of international politics (who, when the opportunity permits, lectures the scientist on the elegant complexity of the political process, but who never seems, to the scientist at least, to have any really good ideas about what to do). It is perhaps these differences in perspective that lead the scientist on occasion to seem "intellectually arrogant"; it is as if he concludes that those who have no promising solutions or are not seeking them cannot be very bright. In his predisposition toward action and solutions, the scientist comes closest to sharing the predilection of the soldier for

[7] C. P. Snow, *The Two Cultures and the Scientific Revolution* (New York: Cambridge University Press, 1959), pp. 9–11.

[8] I am indebted to Hans Speier for the phrasing of this point.

decision, which may be one reason why their partnership has been so spectacularly successful.

The Whole Problem Approach

The first grant made by the United States Government for experimental research was in 1832 to the Franklin Institute. The scientists were asked to investigate the reasons for explosions in steamboat boilers. They reported back not only with a technical explanation but with a draft bill to provide for Federal regulation of steamboats.[9] In this they evidenced the scientist's predilection for the "whole problem approach." The reluctance of scientists to apply their expertise to mere fragments of the total problem, especially under conditions where those who prescribe the fragments do not reveal the whole of which they are a part, was evident in the work of both British and American scientists during World War II. Military officials initially approached the scientists with requests for the development of particular weapons and devices without revealing the military problems or reasoning responsible for their requests. The scientists objected to this procedure, and they were eventually able to persuade the soldiers to inform them of the general military problems involved in order that the scientists might reach their own conclusions about the kinds of weapons and devices the military would need to meet those problems.

In 1952, in connection with an Air Force project on air defense, a group of American scientists were asked to review the prospects for improving the nation's continental air defense. The scientists concluded that some new and promising systems were possible, and they submitted an estimate of what the developments might cost. They also recommended that the money be spent. The Air Force did not approve the recommendation, and as is customary in Washington the disputants on both sides began to search for allies and to leak their cases to the press. Certain Air Force officials, who feared that additional funds for air defense would come at the expense of dollars otherwise available for the Strategic Air Command and who were convinced that this would be militarily undesirable, charged that the scientists by entering into matters of military strategy and budget policy had exceeded both their assignment and their expertise. Commenting on this charge, one of the scientists involved later explained that he would have little interest in working on a study project that did not have the potential for leading into the question of whether the conclusions should be acted upon.[10]

The predisposition to want to be told and to deal with the whole problem no doubt has its base in the professional experience of scien-

[9]Don K. Price, *Government and Science* (New York: New York University Press, 1954), pp. 10–11.

[10]. . . For some of the issues involved in the 1952 air defense study, see U.S. Atomic Energy Commission, *In the Matter of J. Robert Oppenheimer, Transcript of Hearing Before Personnel Security Board* (Washington, 1954), pp. 598–599, 749–750, 763–765, 923–924, 930–931, 935, 938, and also the account in Price, *op. cit.*, pp. 136–138.

tists (and one of the central credos of science) that good ideas on a problem may come from the most unexpected quarters and that the widest possible dissemination of information about a problem will significantly enhance its chances for an early solution. Still, there are problems and problems; some are open to determinate solutions, and others can be resolved only through the exercise of political power. The point about the "whole problem approach," as the air defense example illustrates, is that it not only helps propel the scientists from an advisory to a political role but it serves to make the scientist somewhat blind to the fact that he is so moving. In its most extreme form, the "whole problem approach" coupled with the "intellectual arrogance" perspective can lead to such instances as when, on one high-level advisory committee concerned with several areas of national security policy, a scientist whose formal claim to participation was a knowledge of infra-red ray phenomena was reportedly quite free with his proposals for what political policies should be adopted with regard to the United Nations.

Quantum Jumps versus Improvements

A number of scientists have advanced the proposition that the military tend to be more interested in improving existing weapons than in developing radically new ones, and they have urged that a separate civilian agency be established to undertake such development. Both scientists and soldiers have explained this difference in their approach to military research and development, "quantum jumps versus improvements," with the hypothesis that the soldier's interest in developing entirely new weapons must always be inhibited by his concern for the possibility that war may come in the near future, since in this event his interests are best served by improving existing weapons. It has also been suggested that military leaders, who must be prepared at any time to ask others to take up the weapons at hand and fight with them, cannot afford to let themselves or others become too impressed with the deficiencies of those weapons as compared with others that might have been had.

An explanation less flattering to the military for this difference is the occasional assertion by scientists that theirs is a profession which stimulates original and creative thought, while that of the military tends to develop minds which accept the existing situation without too much question. As indicated in the discussion of the first predilection, this is a judgment which the scientist may extend to the diplomat and the politician as well. The structure of both the domestic and the international political process is normally such as to make "quantum jumps" in policy infeasible. Diplomats and politicians are accustomed to seeing the same old policy problems come around year after year, and they are generally intent on policies which promise only slow and modest change. Scientists, on the other hand, have been demanding and searching for quantum jumps in foreign policy ever since the end of World War II. It is symptomatic that the first proposal developed by the Advisory Committee on Science and Technology to the Democratic National Advisory Council, established in 1959, was for the creation of a new scientific agency, independent of the State and Defense Departments, whose function would be "to face all the problems of disarmament."[11]

Technology for Its Own Sweet Sake

In the summer of 1945, after the A-bomb had been tested but before the first drop on Japan, the Director of the Los Alamos Laboratory, J. Robert Oppenheimer, suggested to his superior, General Leslie Groves, that if some improvements were made in the design of the bomb it would be more effective. Groves decided against the improvements because he did not want to incur any delay in the use of the bomb, which he expected would end the war with Japan. In the summer of 1943, after the Director of the German V-2 project, General Dornberger, had finally secured a first-class priority for the use of the weapon, those responsible for producing it in quantity were increasingly handicapped by the scientists and engineers who kept improving but changing its design. Dornberber was finally obliged to issue a flat order against any further improvements.[12]

There was nothing irresponsible in these scientists' actions. Charged with the technical development of weapons, they would have been remiss in their responsibilities if they had failed to call attention to the prospects for improvement. The point to the examples is that scientists and engineers, in the pursuit of their own responsibilities and interests, may easily lose sight of those of the policy-maker.

The scientists on the General Advisory Committee to the Atomic Energy Commission who recommended against the development of an H-bomb in 1949 did so in part because of their concern for the foreign-policy consequences of introducing a weapon of such destructive power into the world. Oppenheimer, the Chairman of the Committee, later stated that the thermonuclear design developed by Edward Teller in 1951 was "technically so sweet" that, if it had been available in 1949, the Committee would probably not have made the recommendation that it did. Since, with a technically more promising design at hand, one might suppose that the Committee's foreign-policy concerns would have been all the greater, some observers have concluded that in the pursuit

---

[11]See the *Bulletin of the Atomic Scientists*, December 1959, p. 412.
[12]*Oppenheimer Transcript*, p. 33, and Dornberger, *op. cit.*, pp. 134–137.

of his technical interests the scientist can also easily lose sight of his own policy concerns.[13]

Such a judgment ignores the complexity of the Committee's position. For example, one of the reasons why the Committee thought the United States should take the initiative in renouncing the H-bomb was precisely because the device then in view seemed likely to be both difficult to make and of dubious military value. It was thought that for this reason the Russians might be willing to follow the American example and that, if they did not, the United States would not have risked much by the delay. These were considerations which obviously would have been changed if a technically more promising design had been available in 1949.[14] Still, the comments of several scientists close to these events are not without relevance. It is their feeling that there are times when the technician does take over, that when the scientist is faced with an interesting and challenging problem his inclination is to get to work on it, and that under these circumstances he should not be the first person to be expected to keep larger policy considerations in balance.

This predisposition, "technology for its own sweet sake," appears to have its roots in two more of science's central credos: the belief in the value of pursuing knowledge for its own sake, and the belief that the best motivation for the direction of research is the strength and character of individual curiosities. But the direction and strength of scientific interests and curiosities is not necessarily coincident with the requirements of military or foreign policy. One of the most recent examples of the scientist's capacity to get caught up in a challenging problem (assigned, to be sure, by policy-makers) is afforded by the ingenious techniques scientists conceived for evading nuclear-test detection systems and for the design of new systems to meet those evasions. In the light of the later course of negotiations, an American statesman who believed there was considerable foreign-policy gain in a test-ban treaty and who believed that the Russians were at one time seriously interested in such a treaty might well conclude that the formula developed by Watson-Watt, the scientist who fathered radar, with reference to the problem of meeting wartime military requirements was not without its implications for meeting peacetime foreign policy requirements: "Give them the third best to go with; the second comes too late, the best never comes."[15] This observation is not intended as an argument that the interests of the United States would have been better served by a test-ban treaty with a "third best" detection system than by no treaty at all. The point is that the policy-maker must be sensitive to the

[13]*Oppenheimer Transcript*, p. 251. For an extreme judgment, see Robert Jungk, *Brighter than a Thousand Suns* (New York: Harcourt, Brace, 1958), p. 296.

[14]See Oppenheimer's statements in *Oppenheimer Transcript*, pp. 81, 251, 897, and "The H-Bomb Decision: How to Decide Without Actually Choosing," *loc. cit.*, pp. 30–36.

[15]Sir Robert Watson-Watt, *Three Steps to Victory* (London: Odhams, 1957), p. 74.

prospect that, because of the constant advance of technology, his only real choices may be of this order.

The Sense for Paradise Lost

This predisposition is likely to be more characteristic of the scientists who had their graduate training and early professional experience in the years before World War II than of those who have known only war or Cold War conditions. The prewar scientists took it as an article of faith that certain conditions were essential for the progress of science, in particular that scientists be free to select their research problems and that both scientists and scientific information be free to move among as well as within nations. All of these conditions were violated during World War II, and as a result of the Cold War they were never fully re-established. The nuclear physicists had had perhaps the most highly developed sense of international community. They were relatively few in number, had intimate personal relationships at home and abroad, and had been experiencing an exciting exchange of discoveries since Rutherford identified the nucleus in 1911. They also lost the most, for theirs was militarily the most sensitive knowledge, and the pages of the *Bulletin of the Atomic Scientists* offer eloquent testimony to their ideological disturbance.

The result is that the senior scientists tend to be especially sensitive to possibilities which hold some promise for restoring the former order. They may usually be found on the side (or in front) of those urging freer exchange of scientific and military information with allied governments, less secrecy in the circulation of scientific (and sometimes military) information, and more extensive cultural, and especially scientific, exchanges with the Soviet Union. Similarly, the major activities of the Foreign Policy Panel of the President's Science Advisory Committee and of the Office of the Science Adviser to the Secretary of State have been in connection with the Science Attaché program, the facilitation of international scientific programs and conferences, and the exchange of scientists with the Soviet Union.

Science Serves Mankind

For at least 300 years the western scientific tradition has assumed that the unrestricted generation of new knowledge about the world was a social good. Over these years science in its purest form (the discovery of the facts of nature for knowledge's sake alone) became increasingly an autonomous social institution; research scientists were largely disassociated from the practical applications of their discoveries, but they took it for granted that these discoveries would ultimately benefit mankind. The advent of nuclear and bacteriological weapons systems which have the potential of destroying so much of mankind and his works has called this faith sharply into question. It does not take much imagination to wonder if man, in view of his apparent inability to escape from the order of conflicts which have historically resulted in war, would not be better off in a world where the knowledge that has made the new weapons possible did not exist. For some of the senior nuclear physicists this is more than a philosophical question. They are unable to avoid a sense of real personal responsibility; they reason from the premise that they were few, and if they had acted differently weapons development might not have taken the turn it did.

In the immediate postwar years, the apparent contradiction between the good of science and the evil of war was resolved by the expectation that the very destructiveness of the new weapons would lead man to renounce at last the folly of war. The course of foreign policy in later years has weakened these expectations but not destroyed them, as the recent flurry of arms-control proposals premised on the rational self-interest of both sides in avoiding mutual destruction testifies.

The need to preserve their sense of service to mankind led some American scientists to refuse to work on weapons. Similarly, there are reports that several Russian scientists were imprisoned, exiled, or placed under surveillance for refusing to participate in weapons work between 1945 and 1953, and in 1957 a number of Germany's elite physicists announced that they would have no part in nuclear weapons work.[16] Such cases are dramatic, but nowhere have they prevented the development of weapons on which governments were determined. The more consequential resolutions have been those in which scientists have simply identified the good of mankind with the strength of their nation or have endeavored to develop new weapons systems which would be as effective as the old in promoting national policy but which would result in less slaughter if used. This was part of the rationale behind the recommendation made by a group of American scientists in 1951 that the government undertake the development and production of a large number of A-bombs for tactical use in the ground defense of Western Europe. Their hope was that such an innovation would relieve the United States of the burden of having to rely solely on the threat of strategic bombing to contain the Red Army.[17]

The failure of the United States to orbit a satellite before the Soviet Union did was the result of the State Department's insensitivity to the political implications of the event and the decision of the President and the Secretary of Defense not to let a satellite program interfere with military missile programs. A small part of the story, however,

---

[16]See Arnold Kramish, *Atomic Energy in the Soviet Union* (Stanford: Stanford University Press, 1959), p. 105. Kramish states that it is not certain whether the objections of the Russian scientists were technical or political. For the declaration of the German physicists, see the *Bulletin of the Atomic Scientists*, June 1957, p. 228.

[17]*Oppenheimer Transcript*, pp. 584, 594–595, 891–894.

is to be found in the reluctance of some of the American scientists involved in the programming of the International Geophysical Year to see an American IGY satellite propelled by an operational military weapon. Their preference for the less developed but non-military Vanguard over the Army's Redstone appears to have reflected a combination of the "sense for paradise lost" and the "science serves mankind" predispositions, in this case an interest in showing the world the peaceful side of science and in demonstrating that the scientists of the world could cooperate in the interests of knowledge as well as compete in the interests of nations.[18]

IV

· ·

Scientists in Politics

The American political system is not one that insulates its experts from the politics of choice. The scientist involved in high-policy matters is likely to find himself propelled into the political arena, either by a push from behind or by his own interest in seeing that the "right" choices are made. Some of the incentives the scientist may have, to follow up his advice with an effort to see that it is accepted (and to take a hand in a few other matters while he is at it), were outlined and illustrated in the preceding section. It is equally important to recognize that the scientist may find himself on the political firing line, placed there by a politician interested in using the scientist's prestige as an "expert" to disarm the critics of his (the politician's) choices.

Thus, prior to the moratorium on nuclear tests, the Eisenhower administration appeared to be using scientists and their scientific facts on fall-out as a means of justifying and defending a policy that was obviously compounded of a variety of considerations besides that of the radiological hazard. The comparison with Truman's use of the prestige of the Joint Chiefs of Staff to defend his choices in the Korean War comes easily to mind. So, too, do the statements of various Republican leaders that they had lost confidence in the Joint Chiefs and their determination, when they came to power, to get rid of the "Democratic" Chiefs and to appoint Chiefs in sympathy with Republican policies.

The scientist, in short, is not likely to orbit the centers of political power emitting upon request "beeps" of purely technical information. He will inevitably be pulled into the political arena. If his participation there is to be either productive or personally satisfying, both the scientist and the non-scientist need to be highly conscious of the character

---

[18]See Walter Sullivan, *Assault on the Unknown* (New York: McGraw-Hill, 1961), pp. 79–81.

of their activity and the problems involved. The scientist (and many a non-scientist) must learn that the making of foreign policy is not a quest for the "right" answers to the problems of our time. There are only hard choices, the consequences of which will be uncertain and the making of which will often seem interminable in time and irrational in procedure.

The debate and disagreement over these choices will be heated and confused under the best of circumstances, but emotion and misunderstanding can be eased if scientists and non-scientists are both alert to the limits as well as the potential of the scientist's contribution. On the scientist's part, there is the obvious need to exercise the utmost care in making clear to himself and to others the areas where he speaks as a concerned citizen and those where he speaks as a professional expert. More difficult will be the task of learning how and to whom to address himself in each of these capacities when he is dissatisfied with the outcome of a policy decision in which he has participated. There is, as Don Price has pointed out, no clear code in Washington to govern the conduct of dissenting experts, only a "flexible" set of possible relationships with one's immediate superiors and those whose authority competes with or exceeds that of one's superiors. In contrast to the soldier, who can find some although not complete guidance in the doctrine of "civilian control," the very nature of the scientist's intellectual habits and many of his policy predispositions may make especially difficult his task in determining the limits to which he can stretch his dissent.[19]

On their part, the non-scientists need to recognize that scientists can hardly be expected to remain politically indifferent or inactive about the policy issues with which they are involved (especially when no one else in Washington practices such restraint). It was the naivete of this expectation that was so appalling in the conclusion of the Gray Board that Oppenheimer was a security risk because (among other reasons) "he may have departed his role as scientific adviser to exercise highly persuasive influence in matters in which his convictions were not necessarily a reflection of technical judgment, and also not necessarily related to the protection of the strongest offensive military interests of the country."[20] It is unlikely that "civil-scientist" relations will ever get any worse than this. With time and experience one can expect many of these problems to be eased, but it would be unrealistic to expect them to disappear. Military experts have participated in the making of foreign policy far longer than scientists, and the question of how they can best do so is still the subject of more than a little disagreement.

[19]See the discussion in Price, *op. cit.*, pp. 131, 133, 138–142. The point about the scientists' lacking a tradition of "civilian control" was suggested by William T. R. Fox.

[20]U.S. Atomic Energy Commission, *In the Matter of J. Robert Oppenheimer, Texts of Principal Documents and Letters* (Washington, 1954), pp. 19–20. Note the policy disposition in the phrase "strongest offensive military interests." . . .

Policy Processes and Policy

In closing this discussion of scientists and the problems of their organizational and political relationships to others engaged in the determination of foreign policy, it is important to remember that the policy process can bring minds together but it cannot make them think. It is worth
noting that, in the political and administrative structure of the Soviet
Union, no scientist is as institutionally close to the Premier as is the
Special Assistant for Science and Technology to the President of the
United States and that there is no equivalent of the Science Advisory
Office in the Russian Ministry of Foreign Affairs. Yet one would not
say that the foreign policy of the Soviet Union has appeared either ineffectual or insensitive in its response to developments in science and
technology.

The circumstances attendant on the development of radar by the
British from 1935 to 1940 provide a useful insight into both the potential and the limits of effective organization. Essential, obviously,
were the scientific and technical ideas that Watson-Watt and his colleagues had in mind in 1935, ideas which in turn were the result of the
earlier years of research they had been free to conduct in the facilities
of a government laboratory. Certainly, it was important that there were
administrative scientists in the Air Ministry who were so alert to the
military problems of the Air Force that they could see on their own
initiative the need to establish a special scientific committee for the study
of air defense (the Tizard Committee) and who were so alert to the work
of the scientific community that they made their first request for information to Watson-Watt. Of consequence, too, was the fact that the
personal and political relations of the members of the Tizard committee
with the members of the military, administrative, and political hierarchies whose interest and cooperation were vital for the subsequent
progress of the research and development program were relations
characterized by mutual ease, respect, and understanding.

But these conditions would not have led from the formation of the
Tizard Committee in 1935 to a chain of operational radar stations by
1940 and a Fighter Command practiced in their use if it had not been
for the military ideas of members of the Royal Air Force. It was they
who first thought of the formation of a committee to look specifically
into the problem of detection, they who recommended more funds
than those first proposed by the Tizard Committee for the development
of an electromagnetic detection system, and they who were responsible
for the decision to start constructing the stations and training the
personnel while the equipment was still under development.[21] The

[21]For the development of radar, see Watson-Watt, *op. cit.*, pp. 108–109; Snow, *Science and Government*, pp. 24–38, 60–61, 74–75; P. M. S. Blackett, "Tizard and the Science of War," *Nature*, March
5, 1960, pp. 648–649; and Basil Collier, *The Defense of the United Kingdom* (London: H.M.S.O., 1957)
pp. 33, 36–39.

explanation for this interest and support is to be found in their theories about the next World War. They believed the Germans were planning to engage in the strategic bombing of Great Britain, and they wished to be prepared for it.

The point is obvious but important. British scientists and science organization were in the final measure but ready tools. They were good tools, but the use to which they were put was the result of the kind of ideas the military men had about war. The same will hold in the other areas in which science may affect foreign policy. The contributions that science and technology will bring to international politics will largely turn, not so much on the particular arrangements of scientists in the policy-making process, but on the purposes of statesmen and the theories they have about the political world in which they live.

---

15. The Meaning of Comparison in Politics

One consequence of the knowledge explosion of recent decades is the fruition of political studies transcending the boundaries of a single nation-state. Comparative politics is a major concern of political scientists; indeed, some scholars hold that theories and methods of comparison are the heart of political knowledge.

Naturally, in such a period of innovation there is much discussion and some confusion about the exact nature of comparison. How does it differ from simply any study of two national polities? Sigmund Neumann helps answer this question by tracing the historical and intellectual development of comparative politics. His article and the comments contributed by William Livingston and Charles Robson illustrate the need for intensive examination of contemporary comparative models.

COMPARATIVE POLITICS: A HALF-CENTURY APPRAISAL

SIGMUND NEUMANN

In the beginning was Comparison. Or in the words of our centenarian, Woodrow Wilson: "I believe that our own institutions can be understood

From *The Journal of Politics*, 1957 (August), pp. 369–370, 372–380, 382–390.

and appreciated only by those who know somewhat familiarly other systems of government and the main facts of general institutional history. By the use of a thorough comparative and historical method, moreover, a general clarification of views may be obtained. . . . Certainly it does not now have to be argued that the only thorough method of study in politics is the comparative and historical."[1] What has happened to comparative politics since those very early days of our [American Political Science] Association and especially since its official birth in 1903, when the society was founded as "an outgrowth of a movement looking toward a National Conference on Comparative Legislation"?

. . . This tentative appraisal is an attempt to gain some historical perspective for our study of comparative politics, which, to the delight of its lone-wolf oldtimers, suddenly seems to have received a new impetus. Both this reawakened interest and the characteristic stages of the preceding development — with its ups and downs — are not accidental, but a vivid illustration of the unfolding of our discipline within its specific historical and social setting. By its very nature, political science is embedded in time and space. Part and parcel of the social sciences, it shares with them the grandeur and the misery of a critical field. The sciences of man and his decisions ("sciences of ethics" in the meaningful classical terminology) flourish, if they do not actually originate, in times of crisis. As long as society, the state, the world community seem to be in order, one is not concerned about them. It is at the breaking-points of history when man's values are questioned, his institutions shattered, his international bonds cut — it is in the challenge of revolutionary upheaval or in the defense of a threatened system that eminent social scientists come to the fore. . . .

The Stages of Comparative Politics

Rationalist Idealism.   What brought about the first school of political scientists was the deep dissatisfaction among some young academicians who measured the reality of their American community against the ideals of an imagined *polis* and found it wanting. They were not ashamed to be called idealists. It is easy for today's sophisticate to smile at the naiveté of their concepts and convictions, yet their complaints about the disease of "Congressional Government," of "Boss rule," and "the shame of the cities" were real, and so were their models of proper politics. Not that they all agreed on any specific governmental system as the best, but they all shared the deep conviction that such an ideal did exist and could be pragmatically realized in a step-by-step development.

Three fundamental assumptions apparently served as the basis of their conception of comparative politics: the belief in the assured

[1]Woodrow Wilson, *The State. Elements of Historical and Practical Politics* (Boston, 1889), pp. xxxv–xxxvi. . . .

spread of democratic institutions, the essential harmony of interests among peoples, and the basic rationality of men who, by discussion and the interplay of opposing ideas, ultimately, and almost automatically, would reach a common understanding.

Form rather than function, means of communication rather than content-analysis of dynamic forces, were the main concerns of the experts. In comparative politics this meant a primary emphasis on a descriptive study of national institutions, constitutional structures and administrative organizations. This concern reflected not only the natural desire to give the young discipline a definite and concrete framework before it could grapple with the more fluid forces of dispersive dynamics; but such modesty in aim and aspirations was also meant to reject the doubts and accusations of the established older social sciences concerning the "scientific reliability" of politics. It was its essentially political orientation, and therewith its "subjective" ties, which made it suspect in the eyes of the so-called "objective" disciplines. Indeed, the emancipation of political science was to some extent a not-altogether-voluntary declaration of independence; it could have meant expulsion from the temples of the university. And in order to prevent this threatening fate, the young political science desperately tried to keep out of "politics" and to stand so to speak "on neutral ground." Such a position was understandable for the fledgling, whose uneasy flights fluctuated between a childlike dependence on its mother disciplines—philosophy, history, economics and public law—and a fierce fight for emancipation from their tutelage.

The retreat to factual description and expert advice, no doubt, allowed political science to develop pioneering tasks which in a way anticipated certain characteristic contributions of the next phase in its academic process. Yet such deep-seated, defensive dispositions led, especially in later periods, to strange adaptations of a conceptual course which in turn led political science to neglect the essential assignments of its domain. These trying adjustments were aggravated by an additional factor in the American academic picture. Without elaborating here on the complexities of trans-Atlantic acculturation, it is well to remember that the young political science borrowed heavily from continental experiences, as did American universities on the whole. Practically all the founders of the profession had received significant graduate training, if not their higher degrees, in European universities. Germany especially was the academic Mecca of a whole generation of social scientists and through this experience it made a deep impact on the development of higher learning in the United States. What is even more important to recall in this connection is the altogether different intellectual position of the German universities, and of the social sciences in particular, in the Bismarck era. While some of the great German masters —Gneist, Roscher, Schmoller, Treitschke—of those impressionable young Americans wielded considerable influence on the political and social-economic make-up of the new German Empire, their academic role was circumscribed within a limited framework.

The universities, which had once been centers of the fight for freedom, had now been transformed into guardians of training for leadership in important public offices, the judiciary, the bureaucracy, and the teaching profession. To be sure, in performing this crucial function, the academicians could allow themselves the privilege of "freedom of research," especially in the less dangerous fields of philosophy and the arts. Even a professor of economics was permitted to utter some radical thoughts, for the Second Empire was not a totalitarian dictatorship. It did allow for certain aberrations, if only as a safety valve, as long as they did not disturb the political order—and this Hegel's disciples certainly did not do. Enthusiastic academic admirers of the omnipotent state that they were (reassured by the victories of the Iron Chancellor), they glorified the bureaucracy as the unquestioning guarantor of transcendental order against the anarchy of free-floating Western democratic ideas. With the uncomfortable exceptions of a few great liberal non-conformists, such as Theodor Mommsen, they increasingly retreated to the mere recruitment of experts and a conscious separation from policy decisions. This political castration and unassuming ivory-tower isolation was the price they paid for the social prestige they undoubtedly commanded. No wonder that, during the Wilhelminic Empire, a concept of the social sciences developed which sought to rationalize this specific historical plight. It hit most tragically those academic teachers who were born leaders and who in other nations and under different circumstances might well have become the spokesmen of their people. The fateful development of Max Weber serves as a vivid illustration of this crucial estrangement.

Transmitted to an altogether different American atmosphere, such cultural borrowing could easily lead to new tensions between continental systems of rigid abstractions and the concrete world of the pragmatically minded United States. And, strangely, it was often the most abstract theory that made the deepest impression on the master-practitioners of daily life. No doubt, Hegel found disciples, and even Bismarck, admirers among this first generation of American social scientists; some of whom found it difficult to reconcile their admiration with the national fervor after the entry of the United States into World War I. It would not be difficult to show fundamental discrepancies between an inherent inclination toward pragmatic progressive politics and a determined drive for scientific systematics, embraced by the very same people.

What held this pioneer generation together was an unshaken belief in a rational progress which justified the scientific undertaking as a genuine moral crusade and directed the march to man's freedom.

In the search for the proper scientific technique there was undoubtedly much to admire and to adopt in the European universities, especially if their deep-seated societal breaks and persistent presuppositions were obscured by an idealistic perspective. While the stimulus and strength of American political scientists sprang from altogether different sources, a seeming symbiosis of rationalist idealism could thus prevail through the first decades. . . .

Material Positivism. The second phase of American political science research was closely related to the frustrating experiences of the long Armistice between the Great Wars, for they gave rise to a growing disillusionment with the basic tenets of the idealistic school. Instead of the "assured" spread of free institutions, aggressive dictatorships emerged; despite a galaxy of conferences to promote international understanding, the system of collective security collapsed vis-à-vis its first tests; and irrational, integral nationalisms held the perspective of reasonable man and the harmony of interests up to ridicule.

In natural reaction to the sweeping philosophic idealism of the first group of scholars, a new generation turned its interest to the concrete and detailed study of material forces. This positivistic school rejected the naive utopianism of the earlier stage by accepting an equally naive cynicism. Ideologies were presented as subjective sentiments, superfluous and misleading rationalizations of the simple reality of objective power. Obviously such a violent reaction did a great injustice to the actual accomplishments of the early pathfinders of political science. Yet is this not the usual consequence of "scientific progress"? Or, to quote Goethe, "People throw themselves in politics, as they do on the sick-bed, from one side to the other in the belief that they can thus find a better position." In retrospect both periods played their part in the unfolding of political science; and critical though a new team of researchers must be of the position taken by that of its predecessors, one will have to register equally their major contributions to the discipline.

What were the approaches and aims, procedures and postulates of the second stage? First of all it was a sobering phase, suspicious of great panaceas, quick generalizations, broad comparisons and unrecognized deductions; in short, of all speculative theory. Consequently it turned toward detailed, concrete phenomena, toward inductive empiricism, toward measurable and verifiable data in order to make politics at last "scientific."

No doubt, this period of "objective" fact-finding, in its preoccupation with methodological problems, sharpened the tools of our perception and our critical source analysis by introducing and testing elaborate techniques of case studies, survey methods and statistical research. Thus it contributed immeasurably to an exacting delineation of the discipline. Moreover, the material enrichment of comparative-government research during these years of strenuous, painstaking collections gave the field for the first time a substantive foundation from which to operate a rationally controllable body politic and to advance the frontiers of our knowledge. New areas of scholarly inquiry developed, and the machinery of functioning political systems was subjected to intensive analysis. The rise of public administration was probably the most conspicuous corollary to this trend. At times it almost seemed as if the enterprising expansion and proselyting zeal of students of public administration were pre-empting the whole field. In truth, the data brought together consisted mostly of the mere raw material out of which politics is made, and it was not a particularly exciting collection at that. In fact, one might venture to say, with one of comparative government's keenest students, evaluating his own specialty after it had passed this trying period, that it was caught in a "tedious and stagnating routine."[2] . . .

The real problem and peril of this second period only becomes apparent if one probes into the underlying assumptions and expectations of its protagonists; because, proud declarations notwithstanding, this phase had its *raison d'être*, too, and was by no means "free from value judgments." The prevailing philosophy—uncouth and inarticulate to be sure—was that of positivism and, like August Comte's system itself, it was open to "positivist" criticism, so adroitly administered by Vilfredo Pareto, the newly elevated scholarly saint of this very period. This master mind of man's irrationality (seeking out constant and determining "residues" underlying the shifty and "non-logical derivations" of human conduct) indeed appealed to a generation whose belief in progress and rational man had been shaken by the chaos of war and revolution.

This shocking experience, if it was not to lead to the cynic's complete resignation and utter despair (and the American mood was hardly inclined toward such philosophical pessimism), aroused the desire to seek the persistent powers and determining laws which make irresponsible and irascible man operate. In search of this "Open Sesame" of the rationale behind man's irrationalism, twentieth-century scientific inquiry has indeed pushed forward the frontiers of knowledge and has made its pioneers (Freud, Köhler and many others) welcome pathfinders to a new political science. Its novelty was due in no small part to the rich influx in methods and material from neighboring and even distant research disciplines. Yet the pertinent impact of such scientific expansion and crossfield fertilizations was to be felt only later and more fully in its third stage, when a more cautious and confident discipline would weigh, digest and assimilate the findings of other fields.

[2]Karl Löwenstein, "Report on the Research Panel on Comparative Government," *American Political Science Review*, 1944 (June), *38*: 540–548.

Such careful differentiation was certainly not the order of the day in the earlier stages of the explorers' enthusiasm when an uncritical identification with the natural sciences was often proclaimed. Behind such a confession one might even have detected an urge for a simple, over-all formula. And in justice to that past phase, one might remember that it was part and parcel of a cultural crisis—a period which, having lost basic values, was in desperate search for stable concepts, indisputable tenets, absolute standards. Such new signposts the universities' new scientific absolutism was to establish. Whenever its restless youth could not find satisfactory answers, it looked for them outside the lecture halls (and not seldom found them within the university walls). This was the attraction of Marxism that it seemed to give a complete comprehension of past history, a scientific prediction of the inescapable future, and above all a marching order for lost man by giving him a new footing outside himself. For such security he was even ready to surrender his freedom. These were the deeper roots of modern totalitarianism and its fascinating appeal (leaving aside the perplexing question whether the revolution which had found a fatherland had much in common with original Marxism). Only a new image of man and his meaningful place in society could defeat such morbid self-destruction.

Most certainly such a new perspective was not presented by the academic school which won some ardent disciples in the thirties, namely *Geopolitik*. On the contrary, this importation from the continent was the true counterpart to Marxism, and indeed in Europe had widely served as a "Bourgeois Marxism." Now instead of economics it was space that became the absolute and exclusive yardstick. Its attractiveness resided above all in its simultaneous promise of stability and dynamic action, its scientific absoluteness and its presumed concreteness. Geopolitics merged the disturbing complexities of life into one single and seemingly objective factor. In the unending flood of continuous change, space seems to be the invariable, independent of man and events. Rootless man seeks a new hold outside himself. His loud call for action—speedy, glamorous, continuous—in the big world is a desperate move to make him forget the emptiness of his small inner life. The powerful dynamics of the modern world-conqueror is only an expression of man's desire to escape from his despair of real values and from himself. He is at war with the world, because he is not at peace with himself. Yet man cannot escape his responsibility as a man. Nor can a science of society and social order establish itself as a "natural science" without missing its challenge completely.

The very fact that space represented the one stable element, presumably independent of man's decision, by no means made it the most important element in world affairs. But the natural science of politics, with its impressive principles of an everlasting mechanism of power balances, *seemed* to provide a monistic, scientific answer to a world longing for order and stability. When *Geopolitik* became instead the weapon of the unscrupulous Third Reich and an instrument of its unlimited drive for world conquest, it revealed a materialism devoid of any moral evaluation or restraint. The Second World War spelled the end of this cynical power politics and opened the way for a more adequate and exacting approach to a study of the state and society. . . .

Realism with Vision. Politics raised onto this third level must be modest in its claims and steady in its cautious endeavors. It has no blueprints, no great panaceas, no comprehensive concepts to offer, but a continuous adjustment and even improvisation in the light of an ever-changing political scene. Above all, it is impressed by the complexity of politics, the rich texture of the raw material, and the dynamic forces that constitute its full power. In this down-to-earth realism it has taken seriously the warning of the second school, against easy generalizations and untested assumptions. Yet at the same time it has recognized that a mere fact-finding spree may only lead into a no-man's land of mountains of meaningless material, if not directed beforehand by fundamental questions reflecting the researcher's aspirations. For this reason contemporary political scientists have gained a renewed respect for the searching theories and visions of the first generation of political scientists and, as so often is the case, have joined hands with their intellectual grandparents. Woodrow Wilson has been restored to a position commensurate with his contribution and crucial for our time.

What are the chief characteristics of this new phase in the study of politics? They are three-fold: an emphasis on dynamic processes, coupled with a rediscovery of the discipline's forgotten responsibility for policy decisions; a desire for the integration of the social sciences, dictated by a prevailing multi-causal approach to an entangled, intricate reality; and, as a consequence of the radical transformations around us, a new summons to a theoretical reorientation of the whole field. The emergence of these three trends is particularly evident in the field of comparative politics.

Our concern has turned away from a merely formal, legalistic and constitutional approach to a consideration of political dynamics and the processes of decision-making. Only when reaching beyond a mere political morphology of legislative, executive, and judicial forms to the consequential comprehension of the political forces at work — men and movements in governments and parliaments, in political parties and pressure groups, and society's prevailing value structure — can responsible citizens recognize the different nature, purpose, and direction of the political powers in being and in conflict. We want to know where, when, and how politics is made in the constantly changing political scene. Such a new emphasis indicates that the instituted agencies, policies, and procedures must have undergone fundamental changes, too.

It is at such a turning point that comparison gains a new momentum and a deeper meaning. "To know thyself, compare thyself to others." The comparative approach is, above all, an invaluable aid to a people's self-recognition and its sense of responsibility. It is not accidental that the great civilizations, like that of the Renaissance, were developed at the crossroads of history and articulated by the meeting of contrasting systems. This encounter alone made an awakening Western Europe more fully aware of her own character and quality, apart from being naturally and fruitfully influenced by the impact of the strange new forces.

We are again living in such a period of opening frontiers, which will force us to recognize the values and concepts we live by and to test them anew against their challenge from abroad. It is in this crisis of our own society that comparative government becomes significant for the mature citizen. Beyond that, the intensive study of contrasting civilizations provides the necessary background for present-day policy decisions. While our planet is continuously shrinking, bringing the politics of far-distant areas into our compass, thoughtful students of public affairs have often been troubled by our limited "knowledge by experience." Its only substitute seems to be "knowledge by learning," which puts a great responsibility on our generation to make comparative government a live issue—comprehensive and contemporary.

In order to have such contemporary comprehension, comparative politics must widen its area of research far beyond its customary domain. The thoughtful treatise of Dankwart Rustow suggests in this respect a widening of our comparative perspective by a novel "focus on the non-Western world."[3] It rightly questions our whole conceptual framework, which is still narrowly drawn within the patterns of Western experience alone. The altogether different historical setting of political problems and processes among the world's new protagonists necessitates a much more careful comparison of our global complexities. Moreover, this historical shift of power centers is accompanied by a radical upheaval of which the independence movement of formerly colonial peoples is only *one* significant feature. . . .

If one were to look for the historic break-through of the imaginary departmental borderlines which had hitherto been rigidly pa-

[3]Dankwart A. Rustow, "The Comparison of Western and Non-Western Political Systems," (paper read at the American Political Science Association meeting, Washington, D. C., September 8, 1956); see also his *Politics and Westernization in the Near East* (Princeton: Center of International Studies, 1956), and the fundamental reports of the Social Science Research Council's Committee on Comparative Politics, "Comparative Politics of Non-Western Countries" and "A Suggested Research Strategy in Western European Government and Politics," *American Political Science Review*, 1955 (December), *49*: 1022–1049.

trolled against incorrigible inter-departmental snipers and intruders, one might find that the Second World War marked that moment. War emergencies, no doubt, served as a major impetus to persuade difficult people to work together. The Office of Strategic Services and other governmental agencies became graduate schools for inter-departmental training and comprehensive comparisons such as we never attained before or after. Equally, the mushrooming area-study programs, while they naturally constituted a somewhat premature synthesis, did pioneering work in inter-disciplinary cooperation and policy formation, in evaluating research techniques and providing indispensable material stock-taking. Above all, people learned to talk to each other. Such experiences fostered respect for the neighboring fields, an increasing appreciation of their fruitful contributions, and a mounting desire for integration.

It is on the basis of this experience that political science can reassess its sister disciplines and call upon their services without the past trepidations of an immature contender striving for independence and constantly afraid of its former masters and oncoming competitors. The background materials of history and economics, anthropology and linguistics, psychology, psychiatry and sociology, to mention only the main auxiliaries, become a necessity for comparative studies, especially in a depth analysis of the lesser known areas. But the political scientist must also be aware of the fact that these supporting sciences, which emphasize altogether different aspects as their own central concerns, may not always offer the needed material, and that their findings may not always lend themselves to immediate incorporation in his own discipline. In short, he may find himself obliged to search for his own sources of information and his special slant of investigation.

The use of history, for instance, in the study of politics may demand a new perspective of a discipline, which, in its traditional presentation, has often tried to separate itself from policy-making decisions. In fact, the professionals may have forgotten altogether that the historian is "a prophet looking backwards," who, in reviewing past events and rewriting history for his own generation, makes past experience a meaningful part of the present-day challenge. Such novel application of traditional tools, in fact, can restore time-honored though forgotten principles, or open fresh avenues of neglected research. New fruitful concepts may thus evolve in the cross-fertilization of fields. . . .

Not only do concepts change through the ages — and indeed at an accelerated pace in this twentieth century — but also different historical types arise concurrently in our time. The loose application of the same term to the most divergent phenomena and the lack of their clear theoretical differentiation has led to dangerous confusions. Revolutions, like military battles, national and international, have been lost through obsolete strategy. Conceptual clarification thus becomes the indispensable preliminary for politics appropriate to our times. What is needed above all is a new realistic reappraisal of theory's proper place in the social sciences. Neither the beginner's absolute, over-all generalizations nor the complete abandonment of a systematic scheme, such as characterized the despairing second generation of political scientists, could be the answer. It is necessary that our political science concepts be spelled out in time and space, both in their specific historical situation and in their local representation. This puts natural restraints on our theorizing.

The question of a proper approach to a meaningful theory of politics poses a dilemma of an even more fundamental nature. The overwhelming data of our material would fall into a conceivable pattern only if seen through the controlled order of a conceptual framework, which in turn cannot be conceived save in full appreciation of the rich texture of reality. The task of attempting to systematize our knowledge, therefore, is confronted by almost overwhelming difficulties and can proceed only by a simultaneous attack on both theory and practice. Social concepts evolve by stages, remaining necessarily fragmentary and tentative and, at best, present merely a useful working hypothesis for a deeper penetration into an ever-changing reality. Hence a conceptualization of politics must be a constantly renewed effort. . . .

The study of comparative politics necessarily reflects this complexity [of personal, national, and international forces]. Strategically situated at the crossroads of politics, comparative politics must reach out from its national bases into the area of international power politics and at the same time dig down into the personal plight of individuals. Only from such a triple springboard can political science hope to launch a meaningful comparative analysis that will be at the same time comprehensive, circumspect, and contemporary. For that it will need a dynamic discernment of its own, the concerted support of adjoining disciplines, and a fresh theoretical perspective of the social sciences as a whole. The deep dissatisfaction, so widely felt with the teaching and research efforts in our field during the last decade, has centered exactly on these vital points.

It could justly be argued that the traditional scope and method of comparative studies have not really allowed for genuine comparison, that in their formalistic, country-by-country descriptions of isolated aspects of a single culture, students of comparative government have not scientifically tested their inherent democratic bias, have shied away from farther-reaching research hypotheses, have evaded crucial policy issues and thus have missed out on the very contributions which the comparative advance should render to a mature and responsible political science. Such vigorous criticism is indeed a healthy sign that the field is taking a fresh look at itself, and, by measuring its own shortcomings, giving itself a new start.

Even more important and encouraging is the sudden sprouting of numerous productive and stimulating studies in the field, precisely professing these new concerns for dynamic analyses, inter-disciplinary correlation and conceptual differentiation. At this new stage, the discipline demands from its field-workers first of all the opening of virgin territory in the "underdeveloped areas" of Asia, Africa, South America, and a fresh reappraisal of the seemingly familiar landscapes of the Western World. Beyond such necessary groundwork in the by now well-established and defined areas, research must reach out for fruitful inter-regional studies in comparison and contrast. Such far-flung tasks—all too often beyond one man's capacity—necessitate team-work which coordinates and respects the findings of many without hampering individual initiative and enterprise, evaluation and inquisitiveness.

Above all, in such a pioneering phase comparative politics must be cautious in its conceptual framework. Concepts it needs, but they must be now—more than ever—of a dynamic nature, allowing for the fluidity and flexibility of ever-new experiences. There are concepts available which have that quality. It is up to our ingenuity to seek them out. Our definitions of political parties and interest groups, of leaders and followers, of crisis strata and political generations should never petrify the political dynamics, but should present them as what they are: concrete and concise, colorful and consequential. Only such directives will lead to a meaningful confrontation, because, though the comparative approach is as old as political science, the proper use of comparison has hardly been undertaken.

ON PROFESSOR NEUMANN'S COMPARATIVE POLITICS

WILLIAM S. LIVINGSTON

Though he might not accept this phrasing, I should say that Professor Neumann has raised in this paper the two fundamental questions with which comparative government must concern itself in our time —or perhaps in any time. The first is the problem of what we may expect to learn about politics by the comparative method and the second, closely related to the first, is how we may best set about learning it. What distinguishes this paper from many others is the author's ability to view these questions in a rich historical perspective. Indeed his essay is most welcome in these days when political science is worrying the methodological problem like a slavering dog with a juicy new bone. His paper might well be called "The history of efforts by students of comparative government to define for themselves the scope and method

From *The Journal of Politics*, 1957 (August), pp. 479–485.

of their discipline" or perhaps, "Comparative politics: is it a discipline?" It is helpful, and even sobering, to be reminded that these questions are not new, even though our answers to them may differ from those of our predecessors. Dogs have been delighted by bones for a long time and the bones have been pretty much the same even if the newest one does seem to differ somewhat in contour and succulence.

Neumann's historical classification is both interesting and illuminating. I was fascinated by his description of the conditions that helped give form to the early studies of the state in Germany and by his showing how this special character of German political science shaped the work and biases of political study in America when it was formally inaugurated by German-trained American scholars. But the significance of his classification, it seems to me, lies in his portrayal of the evolution of the nature, goals, and techniques of political study in America. He points an unerring finger at the movement from the normative, descriptive effort of the early years into the disillusioned postwar period with its more modest goal of "the concrete and detailed study of material forces." With this I can find no quarrel. And he now suggests that this second period of "material positivism" has given way to greater or at least different ambitions. Perhaps it has. Certainly comparative government is now a-bubble with new ideas, which indeed have led us into such self-consciousness that we are no longer content to study "comparative government" but insist that our province is that of "comparative politics," as witness the title of Professor Neumann's article.

But whether we are now undergoing so profound a transformation as this essay suggests, I am not sure. The difficulty is that any such historical classification must be to a large extent arbitrary, as Professor Neumann would doubtless be the first to agree. Clearly there were empirical, positivistic studies being conducted before the First World War; just as clearly they are still being conducted today. Utopianism and normative analysis did not entirely disappear with the disillusionment of the thirties. And many of these things are still with us today. History, even of "scientific" disciplines, does not fall into such careful patterns, or the work of their practitioners into such neat categories. The article does not, of course, rest on the assumption that they do; Mr. Neumann is pointing to changes in emphases and he has done this with skill and insight. But the most elusive insights and the most difficult analyses are often those concerned with one's own age and it is here that Mr. Neumann leaves the greatest room for suggestion.

Our discipline is nowadays undergoing a searching self-analysis, so ambitious in some quarters that foundation grants have been procured to abet the effort. And the upshot of it is that we are discontented; we are fearful that comparative government has been concerning itself all these years with the wrong things and using the wrong means of accomplishing its purposes. We have seen our colleagues in other social sciences glorying in their new preoccupation with human behavior and their efforts to apply quantitative methods to its explanation. Inevitably our own concern has turned to the fundamental and ever-fascinating question of method and there is now much breast-beating about our deficiencies on this count. Perhaps surprisingly we seem to be fairly well agreed on what these deficiencies are. I should think there would be little challenge to the assertion that comparative government has been too narrowly descriptive, has concentrated too much on form and structure to the exclusion of actual political behavior and the dynamic processes of politics, has made too little use of the techniques and findings of other social sciences, has concerned itself too little with politics in the non-Western world, and has been insufficiently grounded in political theory.

But if these are the errors of the past (or present) we must not assume that merely reversing all these bad habits will provide us with uniformly good ones. Many of these things that we complain of we shall have to keep on doing; otherwise our effort will become as sterile as we say it has been in the past. For example, comparative government will never be able to abandon the attempt to describe institutions, for our descriptions and analyses must serve at least as the raw data of our comparisons; and our descriptions can never be adequate, for as time passes and institutions change, the data that have been collected lose their relevancy. As old institutions are transformed and new ones appear, new analyses and new descriptions must be provided.

Secondly, it would be a mistake to allow the present enthusiasm for the study of processes and behavior to carry us to the point of denying the importance of form and structure. These, too, are part of the stuff of politics and we ignore them at our peril, for it is in relation to them that the dynamics of political life often find their meaning. I should concede (and even insist) that our turning toward behavior will provide a more realistic interpretation of politics and a better framework for comparative study. But we must not recoil so strongly from the felt evils of the past that we throw ourselves too far in the other direction. Perhaps we should acknowledge the possibility that the present emphasis on behavior is gratifying in part because it provides a vantage point for criticizing our predecessors and thus proving our own superiority. Indeed it may be that a few years will bring another disillusionment and we will (without abandoning our interest in behavior) readmit to respectability the ancient studies of public law and constitutional taxonomy.

One reason for this greater emphasis on dynamics and behavior may well derive from the determination to ally ourselves more closely with our sister social sciences, and especially with sociology, psychology, and anthropology, which are the real arenas of the new behaviorism. We are quite properly urged to draw upon them not only for their findings but for their techniques as well. To this one can scarcely object: clearly we must all pursue the truth in common cause. Indeed, I should be the first to proclaim the necessity of recognizing the economic, social, historical, psychological, and cultural determinants of any system of politics. But it seems to me that what is most often meant when our methodologists adjure us to learn from the other social sciences is that we should concentrate upon the use of quantitative techniques for the measurement of political phenomena. Indeed this seems to be a far-reaching concern of political scientists today and here I find myself in an apparent disagreement with Professor Neumann. If I read him correctly, he seems to see a waning of the positivism of his second stage; he finds that our fact finding is now "directed by fundamental questions reflecting the researcher's aspiration." I hope this is so, and I concede his examples, but I still need convincing. It seems to me that in our ardor to be scientific, in our determination to study not forms but behavior, in our commitment to the research techniques of other social sciences, we are still in danger of dwelling so exclusively on quantitative measurement that we stultify our effort to enlarge our horizons and enrich our understanding. I agree most strongly with Professor Neumann's caveat concerning these techniques. If, as some appear to demand, we devote ourselves exclusively to those things that can be measured quantitatively, we risk spending all our efforts on matters that are of less than prime significance—and, what is even more dangerous, we risk assuming that these *are* the matters of prime significance. Obviously where these techniques are appropriate they should be used; accurate measurement is certainly worth more than sloppy guessing. But let us not distort the field of our inquiry by restricting it unnaturally to the things that can be so measured. I do not plead for less than accurate assessment but I should argue strongly that there is still opportunity and need for hypothesis and theory that embrace more than the phenomena appropriate to quantitative measurement; there is still plenty of room for reflective analyses, for insights and interpretations, that do not depend on charts and tables.

The fourth item in our *mea culpa* is the assertion that we have paid too little attention to areas outside the continuum of western culture. Clearly this is so and clearly we are now doing something important about it. A theory of politics that ignores half the globe is manifestly insufficient. And yet a caveat seems appropriate here as well. I hope we shall not turn enthusiastically toward these new areas with the feeling that we have spent enough time on Western politics and that the only real challenge lies beyond these new frontiers. The truth is that the West is by no means exhausted as a field of productive political inquiry and, as a community of scholars, we must not abandon our continuing examination of Western institutions, however laudable and badly needed is the effort to study those of the "non-West." We have not yet been able to formulate an adequate system of generalization about politics in the traditional areas of inquiry; how much more difficult it will be therefore to spread the field of our study over these other tremendously broader and more varied areas which differ in so many fundamental features from the political patterns of the West. More than ever before we shall be confronted with a massive array of variables awaiting analysis and comparison. Certainly we must make the effort but let us not assume that results will come easy. I do not contemplate the early appearance of any general theory or even of any very significant system of generalizations that will serve all areas and all political systems. The differences in the determinants of political behavior and institutions are still far more impressive than the similarities, even in the West. The non-West displays even more variables; confronted by its obvious importance, perhaps we are too ready to assume a homogeneity or a sub-stratum of common (and comparable) elements where none exists. Comparative government must doubtless shift its forces to deal with these new areas and problems, but shifting its forces does nothing to improve its weapons. We shall not improve the prospects of a science of comparative politics by assuming that the non-West possesses a homogeneity that we have never found even in the West. This necessary extension of our frontiers, while greatly increasing our opportunities, also greatly multiplies our problems and all the more urgently demands from us a new conceptualization of our task and a reorientation of our political theory.

Which brings us to what may be the most important part of Professor Neumann's article, namely its demand for a "theoretical reorientation of the whole field." Such a summons must, of course, be addressed to all of political science, but it appears to me that the need is most critical in comparative government. Our need here may be said to lie in two different planes, the one methodological and the other more properly theoretical. By the methodological I mean that research in comparative politics must always be informed by a sound conception of what one is seeking to explain. A lack of such orientation results merely in the massing of random and unrelated data of little use in comparisons and of no use in building a theory. The student must begin with some kind of suppositions or hypotheses about his area of inquiry in order to inform his activity, to guide it meaningfully through the maze of phenomena available for study, and to give form and substance to his conclusions. But in the other, and more important plane, what we shall need is a new effort to contrive or perceive a theory or general explanation of these phenomena, a need that is made critical by the reshaping of the world in our time and by our own new emphases upon behavior and upon the non-West. The old categories of thought, the old classifications of institutions and processes, the old nomenclature impregnated with traditional values—all these must give way to a new kind of comparison, to new labels and categories, to the perception of new relationships, to new explanations; in short, we must look to a conceptual retooling of the discipline. Our world has suddenly grown much larger and we must equip ourselves to deal with it. Theories and explanations that were satisfactory for comparative government are not good enough for comparative politics.

All this makes an ambitious program. It will require the kind of original thought of which most of us are not capable. It behooves us therefore to move somewhat cautiously, taking care to preserve what we know and need while searching for the new. Let us, by all means, lift up our eyes "unto the hills," but let us also keep our feet solidly on the ground. One of the great virtues of Professor Neumann's article is that in it he combines an enthusiastic ambition for his discipline with a cautious judgment of its expectations. It is his own kind of thinking that will lead the way to the new orientation of which he speaks.

ON PROFESSOR NEUMANN'S COMPARATIVE POLITICS

CHARLES B. ROBSON

One has no difficulty in accepting the two major premises of Sigmund Neumann's admirable "tentative appraisal" of the course of political science in the United States in the last half-century. These I take to be (1) that the historical dimension has a peculiar significance for political science, and (2) that the comparative method is essential to any political science worthy of the name. I wish only to bring certain aspects of the historical perspective that Neumann has provided into sharper relief and to emphasize the point that comparison requires criteria for differentiation as well as for the discovery of similarities.

For the purposes of this discussion, I assume that political science concerns itself with those power relationships among men that are involved in the ways in which communities cope with the challenges of community life. The most superficial examination of the circumstances of communities in different times and places indicates that these challenges are not always the same, that the ways of meeting them cannot be reduced in description to a common pattern, and that the components of the power relationships involved vary significantly. This is why any science which essays to comprehend the phenomena of politics systematically must use the method of comparison. This is what Neumann says more impressively in the pungent remarks: "By its very nature, political science is embedded in time and space," and, later, "Social concepts evolve by stages, remaining necessarily frag-

From *The Journal of Politics*, 1957 (August), pp. 485–489.

mentary and tentative and at best present merely a useful working hypothesis for a deeper penetration into an ever-changing reality."

The conceptual tools used by any scientist must be suited to and are, to some degree at least, determined by the phenomena or configurations of phenomena to which he directs his attention. But the phenomena which come under the scientist's observation may be changed in other ways than by shifting the focus of his observation from one temporal or spatial context to another. New instruments and techniques of observation may also bring to his attention data that require radical modifications in his conceptual arsenal. In some of the natural sciences the significance of the historical dimension may be almost exclusively determined by the factor of refinement of instruments for observation and of experimental techniques. For the political scientist, however, the refinements of observation since Aristotle collected the constitutions of the communities of his age and locale have, until recently, not been revolutionary. He has had more and more collections of descriptive detail collected from a wider and wider variety of times and places. Only recently have the techniques of modern anthropology and psychology made it possible for him to penetrate beyond the veil of rational consciousness and given him a radically different kind of data about political behavior.

The assimilation of the data made available by "behavioral science" requires, I suggest, a conceptual adjustment quite distinct from that required by changes in the general environmental situation which the political scientist must take into consideration when he transfers the focus of his observations from Western Europe of the nineteenth century to, let us say, the medieval "city-state" in Italy, or the configurations to be found in China at the period of the Ming dynasty. I believe that the failure to recognize that the conceptual adjustments required by these two quite distinct determinants are different problems and that they must be met by distinctly different responses constitutes the most serious barrier to the development of adequate theory for political science today.

The American political science of the past half century emerged at a time when radical readjustments in theory were demanded with increasing insistence by both types of determinants. The temporal and spatial situations in Western Europe in the period from roughly the seventeenth through the nineteenth centuries elicited the conceptual response associated with the sovereign state and the whole paraphernalia of constitutionalism and the rule of law. It is not without precedent in the history of the discipline that the theory constructed with this conceptual framework was brought to its fullest refinement, in the *Staatslehre* of the German faculties of law, after the realities which it had been reasonably adequate to comprehend had passed away.

Actually, the fledgling science of politics in the United States bore less of the impress of its revered academic relative than might superficially appear to have been the case. Indigenous political science in America had never completely adopted the concept of the sovereign state and its theory of constitutionalism had remained vitally political, resisting all attempts toward sterilization through legalistic or other formalistic conceptualization. Moreover, even those young American scholars who studied in Germany were chiefly impressed by historians and economists who were concerning themselves with the dynamics of change rather than the statics of conservatism. To this John W. Burgess, who more than any other American political scientist strove to integrate the theory of the national sovereign state with American constitutional history and law, may be called to witness. The German preceptors to whom he expressed and demonstrated most indebtedness were Dahlmann, Mommsen, Gneist, Treitschke and, above all, Droysen. The great contribution of German inspiration and training to the development of political science in the United States consisted in the application of the rigorous methods of German historical research to a reinterpretation of the political, economic and social development of the United States. The spirit of this reinterpretation was less that of *Staatslehre* than of the historical schools. This placed the Americans in touch with an earlier and more vital German political science, that represented, for instance, by Dahlmann's *Die Politik auf den Grund und das Mass der Gegebenen Zustaende Zurueckgefuehrt* (1835). This spirit of inquiry had, indeed, been brought to America, along with some other less valuable intellectual luggage, by Francis Lieber, whose *Political Ethics* appeared in the same year as Dahlmann's *Politik*.

The pendulum swing from idealism to positivism which Neumann observes resulted less from an abatement of reformist zeal, it seems to me, than from a preoccupation with internal problems occasioned by the urgency inherent in these problems and the disillusionment caused by the fact that the aftermath of the war had not revealed a world conditioned for the ready reception of the democracy of Wilsonian idealism. The ineptness in foreign languages of two generations of American graduate students contributed its bit to the disillusioned descent into isolationist intellectual attitudes by the elimination of the perspective of comparison from indigenous American political science. In the generations after Burgess, Wilson, the Willoughbys, and Lowell, no native-born American attempted a comprehensive comparative study of political institutions. Had it not been for the fortunate infusion of scholars from abroad, such as Sigmund Neumann and others whose names and works readily come to mind, whom fate condemned to conscious contemplation of contrasting political environments, institutions, and behavior as well as to the acquisition of the linguistic skills to study them, the impulse to develop theory adequate to the comprehension of the manifold significant varieties of political experience might have vanished from the scene of American political science. It was not the fault of these scholars that the textbooks for courses on "Foreign and Comparative Government" had to be filled with dreary descriptions of "new constitutions" and formal accounts of "how this or that country is governed" designed for the maximum possible comprehension of students who lacked the intellectual background necessary for the understanding of political cultures other than their own.

Today the United States of America as a political community finds itself impelled to adjust to a world situation in which it cannot regard its political experience as uniquely significant. It becomes necessary to interpret patterns of political behavior and to anticipate responses in situations to which the generalizations drawn from its traditional interpretations have little relevance. Conversely, the United States must interpret its own institutions and behavior to a world in which the myths and symbols which its people have "lived by" elicit strange and varied responses. Moreover, the conceptual tools which political science in America has fashioned, under the conditioning influences of these myths and symbols, do not supply insights adequate to the demands of these complex tasks.

At this juncture it is not altogether fortunate that American political science finds that new techniques of investigation supply it with the capacity to observe many phenomena hitherto concealed beyond the veil of rational consciousness. It does not yet appear that the insights provided by the use of these newer techniques have offered much aid in the adjustment of the conceptual patterns suitable for ages now past to an "ever changing reality." The inter- and intra-disciplinary controversies which their emergence has engendered have, indeed, tended to overshadow and obscure more fundamental aspects of the challenge of conceptual adjustment to which any possible future political science must respond.

Because they reveal phenomena which lie beyond the veil of rational consciousness, the data accumulated through the use of these techniques seem to require a conceptual framework which transcends the limitations imposed by the thought-patterns of any given culture. Obviously, however, no theory adequate to the exigencies of the day can ignore the variations in culture, for that is precisely what it is required to comprehend. The political scientist must be able to detect the significant distinctive features of the political behavior of men in the primitive Samoan village, in the Greek "polis," in the "sovereign state" system of the Western world in the nineteenth century, and in the various distinct communities in the world today, as well as the features common to them all.

That insights supplied by the techniques of behavioral science will in the long run contribute substantially to a comprehensive political science, we may confidently expect. This happy consummation will, I suggest, be hastened if the conceptual reconstruction required in order to correlate the new data which its techniques of investigation can discover be carefully distinguished from that demanded by other aspects of our historical dilemma.

16. Cross-Cultural Politics

As political problems become more interrelated, as transportation and research facilities expand, cross-cultural or transnational political analysis becomes more commonplace. This topic is introduced by three empirical studies of American and Western European politics. The first two selections, respectively, deal with interest group politics (agriculture in England and the United States) and political mobilization or electoral politicization (in France and the United States). The third is an excerpt from a five-nation study of political culture dealing with the opportunity young people have to participate in discussions and decisions in the family and in the school system. The logic of the last study is that such pre-adult experiences help determine adult political roles and attitudes toward government. Indeed, this study should be related to the material on the politics of education that constitutes Part V of this book.

AGRICULTURAL SUBSIDIES IN ENGLAND AND THE UNITED STATES

J. ROLAND PENNOCK

The view of the British system of government — both formal and informal — that has gained for it the designation "responsible government" may be briefly summarized. The system simplifies the alternatives placed before the electorate. It energizes and activates public

From *The American Political Science Review*, 1962 (September), 56: 621, 624–631.

opinion. Responsibility for public policy is centralized, clearly located, and easily subjected to popular control. Beyond this point the theory, seldom articulated, seems to be that the Government, with the benefit of its synoptic view of the public scene, will seek majority support by acting in the general interest. (In this way, the dubious concept of rule by "a majority" enters into the theory.) Conversely, special interests, particularly those associated with "pressure groups," are less able to secure a definition of the public interest on their own terms. Since pressure groups frequently are interested in legislation requiring the expenditure of public funds, more or less directly for their benefit, this aspect of the British system might be expected to manifest itself especially in connection with such expenditures. The inability of Parliament to vote funds in excess of the budget, and the well known device of Treasury control, as well as the disciplined and programmed nature of political parties, all seem to support this expectation. There are, to be sure, other advantages believed to flow from these features of British government, such as a more rational, coherent, and self-consistent legislative product; but the present article will be confined to the question of vulnerability to demands of special interests for subsidization.

The major objective of this essay is to apply to this problem the findings of a comparative study of the politics of agricultural subsidies and price supports in Britain and America during the postwar period. The general method followed is to combine empirical data from the case study with *a priori* arguments in such a way as to contribute both to the appreciation of the arguments and to their evaluation. . . .

. . . The end result of agricultural politics in the two countries has been to produce heavier subsidization (in one form or another) in Britain than in the United States, instead of the reverse, which orthodox theory would lead us to anticipate. . . . [T]wo out of three possible sets of factors that might lead to this result [are]: the needs or justifications and the organization of interests most directly affected. On balance, it appears doubtful that there is enough here to account for the difference in results, although one can certainly not be dogmatic on the point. At the very least, the substantive comparison suggests the need for examining the matter procedurally — that is, for looking at the processes by which key decisions were made in the two countries and asking whether or not they give support to the standard propositions about the two forms of government.

If the electoral alternatives are kept simple, the man in the voting booth can understand them and wield his power effectively, and anything that strengthens the political effectiveness of the voter-at-large tends to weaken the special interests — so runs the argument. How do the two forms of government stack up in this regard? In one sense there can be no doubt whatever that the British form wins hands down by this test, for at election time there is but one question for the voter to answer — is he for the Government or against it? — with the further possibility that he may have one additional choice if he is against it. There is no question of splitting his ticket. But if we are considering a particular subject, such as agricultural subsidies, the realistic question is whether there is any alternative at all. Since the Second World War there have been five general elections in England. Throughout this period agriculture was the beneficiary of heavy subsidies. At none of these elections was the extent of agricultural subsidy a point at issue between the parties. Yet the policy being pursued did not lack for critics. Such journals as the London *Economist* kept up a continuous drum-fire of criticism of agricultural policy under both Labour and Conservative Governments, alleging that subsidies were too high. An occasional Member of Parliament, like Stanley Evans, lashed out against "featherbedding" the farmers.[1] And the weight of opinion of economists, including agricultural economists, favored the view that the subsidies were at a higher rate than was justifiable. On the other hand, the farmers frequently complained that their profits were not keeping pace with the rising standards of living of other occupational groups. Nonetheless, at no election did the level of subsidies become an issue between the parties. Agricultural policy was greatly debated, but the debates consisted in such matters as rival claims for credit for the benefits the farmers had received, charges that the program was being badly administered, that farmers lacked confidence in the Government (or in the Opposition, as the case might be), and so on. Labour, by promising the reinstitution of bulk purchasing and other devices, tried to hold out the prospect of greater price stability, but was careful not to suggest that average prices would be higher (or lower).

The sensitivity of the parties to the farm vote is nowhere better demonstrated than by the difficulties generally experienced by the Liberal Party in squaring its free-trade, anti-subsidy principles with electoral expediency in the matter of agricultural policy. In 1953 the Party Assembly adopted a resolution calling for the gradual abandonment of guaranteed prices and assured markets for agriculture. Not only did this action call forth heated debate but, after the adoption of the resolution, a prospective Liberal candidate for Parliament announced that "speaking for at least twelve prospective Parliamentary candidates, we do not feel we can fight an election on the present policy, and give notice that we can not do so."[2] Presumably as a conse-

---

[1]Evans, a Labour M.P., was forced to resign as Parliamentary Secretary for the Ministry of Food for persisting in this kind of criticism, including such charges as that the taxpayers had had to pay £12 million during the last year for the production of surplus potatoes. *Parliamentary Debates* (Commons), Vol. 475, col. 1042. The promptness with which the Government called for Evans' resignation and publicly disavowed his views made it clear that they had no intention of being tagged as favoring any diminution of agricultural support.

[2]*Farmer and Stock-Breeder*, Vol. 67, p. 57, April 14–15, 1953. And see *The Times*, April 4, 1953, p. 3, col. a.

quence of this pressure, the resolution adopted in 1954 was much more qualified.[3]

A nice test case is supplied by a by-election held in the Division of South Norfolk in January, 1955. The election was of particular interest because the constituency is marginal as between the major parties and highly agricultural, being in the heart of one of the major farm areas of England. The writer followed the campaign closely, attending several campaign meetings. The constituency was actively cultivated by the candidates and by their supporters ranging all the way up to the Minister of Agriculture himself, Mr. Heathcoat Amory, on the Conservative side, and to Messrs. Hugh Gaitskell and Aneurin Bevan on the Labour side. Both sides insisted that they would maintain subsidies, with no "whittling away," while hinting that their rivals were not altogether reliable in this regard. Neither made any suggestion of increasing the subsidies.

The pattern revealed for this campaign was substantially duplicated in the general elections of 1955 and 1959. In the latter year, for instance, the Conservative election manifesto pledged continuance of the long-term assurances to agriculture, continued support to horticulture by means of tariffs and also by means of new improvement grants to the extent of £7½ million. Labour promised to improve farm security, which, it claimed, had been "whittled away" since 1951, and to give the farmer "protection against unfair foreign competition."[4]

In the United States the picture was quite different. The Agricultural Adjustment Act of 1938, permanent legislation, provided for price supports for "basic" commodities by means of loan and purchase arrangements at rates varying in accordance with a formula relating the percentage of "parity" at which they would be supported to the supply situation. By agreement of both parties the operation of this Act had been suspended during the war and afterwards in favor of provision for a rigid support of basic prices at 90 per cent of parity. This temporary legislation was scheduled to expire on December 31, 1948. By a series of extensions, however, the fixed supports at 90 per cent of parity were not allowed to die until six years later. By stages during this period the Democratic Party became identified with maintenance of the "rigid" support system while the Republicans championed a "flexible" arrangement. An Administration-sponsored bill providing for flexible supports was enacted in 1954 with overwhelming Republican support in both Houses, while the Democrats opposed the flexible principle (with its inevitable lowering of the extent of price support) by more than three-to-one. These positions have been adhered to subsequently and were reflected in the party platforms for presidential elections. In short, the American voter, unlike his British opposite number, had

[3]*Farmers Weekly*, April 30, 1954, p. 42.

[4]D. E. Butler and Richard Rose, *The British General Election of 1959* (London, 1960), pp. 260 and 275.

a significant electoral choice and accompanying possibility of control with regard to agricultural price supports during the 1950s.

Closely connected to the question of choice and control is the matter of energizing public opinion, also a feature included among the reputed attributes of the British system. It is not really a separate point so much as a presumed consequence of clear issues and simple methods of popular control. There can be no doubt that where the parties in Britain are divided on an issue, both the system of parliamentary debates and the election system tend to focus attention upon, and arouse interest in it. But where party competition produces identical positions on a given point, as it tends to do, and as has been the case with the level of agricultural subsidies in Britain, no occasion for public discussion arises. In this country, on the other hand, substantially this issue has played a significant role at each of the last three presidential elections. This is not to argue that there is anything inherent in the American system that accounts for this difference, or that a similar situation would be found if we examined other policy areas. It is merely to point out that the alleged advantage of the British system does not always materialize and that in certain cases the advantage may lie in precisely the opposite direction.

Having said this much, the supposed merit of clear and centralized responsibility in British government has already been dealt with, by implication. The responsibility for the level of agricultural subsidies in Britain is clear; it is pin-pointed. There is only one catch: to oust the Government would not alter the situation, although there is an abundance of opinion in the country at large and among experts to the effect that a change is in order.

Among the *a priori* arguments advanced for the theory that British government is exceptionally well fitted to resist the demands of special interest pressures, perhaps the most frequently cited is the strength of party discipline. Members of Parliament, unlike members of Congress, are not generally susceptible to pressure from constituents to vote this or that benefit for them. With rare exceptions, they will vote as the Whips instruct. Closely related to party discipline is the position of the Government. A single committee, the cabinet, thanks to the combination of the two-party system and strong party discipline, has the power, within limits, not only to formulate the Government's program but also to implement it. Its party members in the House are in the majority and they may be counted upon to support the Government's program. Since the Government will stand or fall, at the next election, on its record as a whole and before the electorate as a whole, so the theory goes, it will be to its interest to resist the pressures of special interests insofar as they appear to distort or run counter to the general interest.

How sound is this reasoning? Of course it is true that M.P.s seldom defy the Whips. But the Whips, as is well known, are two-way lines of communication. Through them the party leaders are kept informed of what the rank-and-file want and what they hear from their constituents and, even more pertinently, of how M.P.s, especially those from marginal districts, assess the impact of particular policies on their chances for reelection. Such information is of interest to party leaders in any democratic country. Even in the United States it is highly relevant to the party's welfare and to the outlook for its general policies. But in the United States a party may lose one House and hold the other or it may lose one or both Houses and hold the Presidency. And under such circumstances it may still see many of its policies effectuated—as was clearly demonstrated under the Eisenhower regime. In Britain, on the other hand, the winner takes all. Under such circumstances it is hardly to be supposed that the news that, say, a score of Members of Parliament might lose their seats at the next election unless something is done for the aged, e.g., or for the farmers, will be without influence on the Government.

In this connection, we may well remind ourselves of Hatschek's law,[5] according to which British political parties start out with well defined sets of principles but progressively lose them and become concerned primarily with obtaining and keeping power. We need only consider the most recent general election campaign to see Hatschek's conclusions substantiated. Each of the major parties seemed to be engaged in trying to prove that, at least in certain important respects, it was not so different from the other as had been thought. The Conservatives proclaimed themselves as the great supporters of the "welfare state," while Labour made light of its attenuated program of nationalization. Such a development undermines the theory that the Government—or for that matter either of the major parties—must have a consistent program. The parties tend to become as free as American parties to bid for the marginal voter, to try to build a majority by seeking the support of various special interest groups—especially those that are particularly aware of their interests and whose votes are believed to be shiftable. Of course, insofar as a bid to one group must obviously be at the expense of other groups or of the whole, some limit is placed to this process. But it is well known that this protective mechanism is very sluggish. Producers tend to be more aware of their interests than consumers or even taxpayers. Moreover, the existence of a large number of traditional or ideological voters strengthens the hand of the special interests by enabling party managers to maneuver without fear of losses from their hard-core supporters. The British situation with respect to special interests may be put in a nutshell. The parties discipline their members, but no one disciplines the parties; and the parties are subject

[5]Julius Hatschek, *Englisches Staatsrecht*, Vol. II (1905), pp. 8 ff. Hatschek's law is described and discussed in Carl J. Friedrich, *Constitutional Government and Democracy*, rev. ed. (Boston, 1950), p. 417.

to the same electoral logic that operates in this country: they must bid for the support of interest groups. Another way to put the matter, using Robert Dahl's expressive phrase, is to say that in Britain, too, what passes for "majority rule" might be more aptly described as "minorities rule."

An examination of British agricultural politics during the postwar period provides numerous examples of the operation of this electoral logic. The case of Stanley Evans, above, is a clear instance of party discipline being used to prevent giving offense to a well-placed pressure group. Although Evans was somewhat of an extremist on this matter, the traditional orientation and class interest of the Labour Party is toward the interests of urban labor. Cheap food, rather than prosperous farmers, would seem to be their natural concern. Moreover, this is the definite and outspoken view of the Cooperative movement, which is affiliated with the Labour Party and sits regularly in its councils. Yet in recent times it has been the prospect of winning a few farm votes from their normal Conservative alignment that has consistently set the course of Labour policy.

How party discipline operates in this kind of situation is well illustrated by a revealing incident that occurred in late 1953 in connection with an Order, laid before Parliament for ratification, increasing the import duties on certain fruits and vegetables. This was an issue calculated to arouse Labour to an anti-farmer stand if anything would, because the cost of the proposed action would be borne directly by consumers. As a matter of fact Labour, then in Opposition, was sharply divided as to what position it should take. Many of its Members, especially those representing the Cooperative movement, were strongly opposed to the tariff increase. Indeed, it appears virtually certain that the Parliamentary Labour Party would have voted to contest the Order had it not been for a strong personal appeal by Tom Williams, Minister of Agriculture in the preceding Labour Government. Although the decision was close, and a number of Labour Members did express themselves vigorously against the Order in the House of Commons, the significant fact is that the Party leadership threw its weight behind the farming interest, and prevailed. Here was party discipline in operation — being used to force a reluctant majority to pursue a policy thought by the leaders to be essential for winning certain marginal districts. (Williams and other Labour leaders had often publicly expressed the view that Labour could not hope to return to power without winning back some of the country areas they had won in 1945 and lost in 1950.)

Compared to this situation, party discipline in the United States is notoriously weak. Orthodox theory holds that weak discipline favors the special interest; but it is not necessarily so. Big city Democrats may refuse to go along with their party's policy of favoring high price supports—and they frequently do; and Republicans from agricultural districts may vote against their party's adherence to "flexible" price supports. Under such circumstances, special interests that are powerful in a minority of legislative districts may find it more difficult to obtain legislative support than under a regime of strong party discipline, operating as described above. On at least two occasions during the Eisenhower administration major price support legislation opposed to the official policy of the Democratic Party (which had a majority in both houses of Congress) and opposed by the House Committee on Agriculture, was yet enacted into law.

The British system is also often thought to be less easily influenced by special interests than the American system because of the subordinated role of committees. Congressional committees have great power and are notoriously likely to be controlled by Congressmen favorably disposed toward the interests whose affairs come under their jurisdiction. It is frequently overlooked, however, that the British system, structurally very different, may lead to functionally similar results. Parliament regularly delegates many important decisions to the Government or to particular Ministries. When legislation takes this form, the Ministries, in certain respects, are cast in the role of Congressional committees: they have great power; their decisions are likely to receive less publicity than those of Parliament, and in any case the process by which they reach their decisions is not one of public debate and ordinarily involves no public scrutiny; they have a tendency—so at least it is alleged in England—to become favorably inclined toward the interests under their wing; and they are readily accessible to those interests.

The case of agriculture illustrates all of these points. The controlling legislation leaves the rate at which agricultural products will be subsidized or supported entirely to Ministerial discretion, operating within the broadest of statutory policy directives. It is true that the Treasury stands always in the immediate background, breathing down the neck of the Ministry, but it must depend largely upon the Ministry's estimate of the needs of the industry. Moreover, all orders made under this provision of law must be made after consultation with representatives of the interests concerned. In practice this means that each year, at what is known as a Price Review, representatives of the Minister of Agriculture sit down with representatives of the National Farmers Union and, in an often prolonged series of meetings, negotiate the guaranteed prices for the following year. Each side is provided with an abundance of data. Certain agreed but rather vague standards guide them. But there is much room for judgment, and hence for haggling; for what are sometimes embittered arguments; and for plain horse-trading. It has been said on good authority that the final decisions are frequently made on the basis of considering the effect in certain marginal constituencies.

The experience of the 1955 Price Review is hardly atypical. It had been the expressed hope of those charged with administering the subsidy policy that Exchequer liability could be progressively decreased at a rate approximating, or at least approaching, the increase in farming efficiency, then estimated at about £25 million *per annum* for products covered by the Review. Applying the principles that had been enunciated to the data as to changed costs and the like, and deducting the presumed efficiency increment, the result would have been no net change in guarantees and subsidies. In fact, however, the Ministry granted a net increase of about £40 million. The reasons advanced for this action were two: (1) that during the previous year crops had been seriously damaged by bad weather; and (2) that the balance of trade situation made it desirable to produce more homegrown feedingstuffs. However, the first of these reasons was not supposed to be relevant, since all figures are based on "normal" weather; and it was not even contended that the second argument was sufficient to justify the increases.

To understand the Price Review of 1955 one must know that a General Election was imminent and that the farmers were known to be disgruntled. The mood of the annual meeting of the National Farmers Union in January was described in the pages of the *Economist* as one of "gloomy resentment."[6] A direct vote of no confidence in the Government's farm policy was narrowly averted; and, as it was, the Union condemned the Government for "gradually undermining" the provisions of the 1947 Act.[7] Off the record, Government officials in a position to know were quite ready to concede (and decry) the effects of the political winds. In Parliament, Labour members, not surprisingly, testified to the same effect. George Brown, Parliamentary Secretary for Agriculture under the Labour Government, declared:

> *The price this year was very nearly not an agreed one. It became an agreed price only because someone politically a little higher than the Minister came along and said, "There will be an election soon, and we must have an agreed price." The Council of the N.F.U. know that. My friends in the industry tell me what is happening.*[8]

And Tom Williams, Labour Minister of Agriculture, asserted that the N.F.U. was on the point of voting its lack of confidence in the Government when the Chancellor of the Exchequer made his peace with them in a speech at the N.F.U.'s annual dinner.[9] Note that it was the Chancellor of the Exchequer who was chosen for this task. Possibly he was

[6]"Resentment on the Farm," *The Economist*, Vol. 174, January 29, 1955, p. 345.
[7]*Ibid.*
[8]*Parliamentary Debates (Commons)*, Vol. 540, col. 1622, May 3, 1955.
[9]*Ibid.*, col. 1532.

chosen (or invited by the N.F.U.) because he was a farmer. But if George Brown was right it appears that this was a clear case of political intervention, perhaps by cabinet action, to urge the Minister of Agriculture to go farther on behalf of the farmers than even he was prepared to do on his own initiative.

.This incident will also serve as a comment on the frequently heard claim that the British Treasury is a powerful roadblock in the way of special interest demands upon public expenditures. Undoubtedly it is, in many situations; but it may also be acutely vulnerable to electoral pressures.

In appraising the argument for, and evidence of British vulnerability to the demands of a special interest group, it should be remembered, too, that British farmers constitute a small part of the population. As a percentage of total production, agricultural production in Britain is less than two-thirds as large as in the United States. In terms of the percentage of the labor force involved, the discrepancy is even greater. Nor is the distribution of farm voters such as to increase their political effectiveness; but rather the contrary.

Touching another of the weaknesses often attributed to the separation of powers, the division of responsibility, we must be careful to examine both sides of the ledger. Divided responsibility does muddy the waters and so complicate the task of a displeased majority wishing to enforce accountability for the act of commission or omission that occasioned its displeasure. This much is true. But how often, on a particular issue, is there a majority? When pressure groups secure special consideration, it is generally the work of an active minority translating its demands into law thanks to the passivity of a large number of legislators. In the American system there are many check-points to the exercise of power; this is the very meaning of the system of checks and balances. If the farm lobby wins at one point its opponents may effectively defend a roadblock at another. This is precisely what often happens. Critics of the system who emphasize vulnerability to pressure groups all too frequently point to examples of success at a particular point in the process without following through to the ultimate result. Moreover, when that ultimate result is to prevent action, it follows from what has just been said that it is by no means necessarily true that a majority will is being frustrated. On the contrary, the necessity of mobilizing more power, or making it effective at another point, tends to mean that there will be more debate, more public discussion, more general education with respect to the matter in question, with the result that other groups than those immediately affected, consumer groups, for instance, are aroused to support their own interests, with the further consequence that when action is taken it will have a wider representative base—and perhaps a very different one—from what would otherwise have been the case. There is every evidence that this is precisely what happened during the long debate over flexible *versus* rigid price supports. Farm leaders were outraged at moves by Secretary Benson that they interpreted as appeals for consumer support.

Finally, a special word should be said about the presidential veto power, even though it is one of the checks to which reference has just been made. Representing a national constituency, the President is generally in a better position that anyone else to resist the demands of particular interests. The same argument was cited in support of the view that it is to the interest of the Government in England to support a consistent policy, and one that does not give undue concessions to special interest. Applied to the presidency, this argument tends also to be subject to the same weaknesses. But here an important qualification is to be noted. A British Government desiring to remain in office is wholly dependent upon having its party continue to hold a majority of the seats in Parliament; hence it must consider the electoral situation in all of the constituencies. The President also has a large stake in having his party control the Congress. But it is not *so* large a stake. It is not all or nothing. He may remain in office even though his party is in the minority in both Houses of Congress and he may even continue to exercise very considerable power under such circumstances. To this extent the "general interest" base provided by the veto power is stronger than its equivalent under the cabinet system.

For examples from agriculture, we may go back to the spring of 1946. Wool production had been heavily subsidized during the war and was in excess supply. In spite of recommendations by the Secretary of Agriculture and a special committee established for the purpose, Congress failed to act. The Secretary of Agriculture then discontinued all support of wool prices, which had been provided under general war powers. Congress responded by passing a bill which included among its provisions a special fee on imported wool. This provision ran directly contrary to our postwar foreign trade policy and its enactment threatened to wreck the Geneva Trade Conference, then in session. In spite of the strong opposition of the Department of State, the bill passed both houses of Congress. The President vetoed the bill and Congress sustained his action. A new bill, omitting the import fee provision, was thereupon speedily enacted. A special interest that was threatening our foreign economic policy was successful in Congress, but was checked by action of the President.

Eight years later another President was able to take advantage of the special interest in wool to prevent the success of a move in behalf of high price supports for basic crops which he believed to be counter to the general interest. The President had recommended a system of production payments for wool, substituting this for commodity loans. He had also recommended reversion to a flexible price support system for basic crops, as already mentioned. The House Committee on Agriculture, apparently in a move to outwit the President, combined his wool bill with an extension of the then-existing price supports for basics at a fixed 90 per cent of parity. However, they had miscalculated. On the eve of the crucial vote, Secretary Benson himself is said to have carried the word to Congressmen from wool states that the President would veto a 90 per cent bill even though it carried the wool payments plan with it. Thus in the end Congressmen from wool states had to vote for flexible supports for basics in order to get their wool subsidy. Five out of a possible 32 did so. This is not a particularly strong case, but it at least suggests the possibility of a situation in which the threat of a veto might bring some pressure on one interest group to help check another.

Many cases can be cited when the bicameral system has tended to work in the same way—to obstruct the demands of special interest groups. In both 1948 and 1949 the House of Representatives first voted to prolong the operation of high price supports, ultimately acceding to the Senate's insistence on a downward modification. Only the Korean war prevented this action from being allowed to take effect. One may find other instances in which either one House of Congress or the other or both or the Administration has manifested a great—perhaps too great—sensitivity to agricultural interests and demands. Frequently, however, the requisite concurrence of all three is lacking.

In spite of what has just been said, it is often true that the inertia of government tends to favor the special interest. Where an emergency situation develops, Congress may act fairly quickly—especially if a well organized interest is prodding it; but, where legislation favoring a special interest is already on the books, it is difficult to get it removed even in the face of conditions that seem to call for such action. But for many situations there is a technique to counter this tendency, and Congress often sees fit to use it. This is simply the device of granting a demand for a limited period, requiring renewal if it is to be extended beyond the original grant. In this way the weight of governmental inertia is shifted. In the battles over flexible *versus* rigid price supports, the proponents of flexible (which in effect meant lower) supports always enjoyed the great advantage that inertia, and therefore the check and balance system, was on their side; for no action at all meant a return to an even lower level of price guarantees than they were proposing.

To summarize briefly what has been said: the purpose of this case study was to examine the commonly held belief that "responsible government," British style, is markedly superior to the system of separated powers in its ability to resist the demands of special interests—to examine this belief in the light of the evidence of postwar agricultural subsidies and price supports. From that evidence it appears that in Britain, the all-or-none nature of party competition may make leaders extremely sensitive to the demands of pressure groups, and party discipline may be used to suppress elements in the party that would like to resist the demands of those groups. The American system, it is true, may be less responsive to a clear popular majority, when such a majority exists. But, in the more common event that only minorities have clear positions, these minorities have more hurdles to cross, more roadblocks at points where their demands may be checked, than similar groups face in Britain. No single case establishes a general rule. But viewing the case of agricultural subsidies and price supports in combination with more general analysis, the writer concludes there are strong grounds, at least, for doubting that the American form of democracy is any more susceptible than the British to the pressures of minorities. . . .

POLITICIZATION OF THE ELECTORATE IN FRANCE AND THE UNITED STATES

PHILIP E. CONVERSE AND GEORGES DUPEUX

The turbulence of French politics has long fascinated observers, particularly when comparisons have been drawn with the stability or, according to one's point of view, the dull complacency of American political life. Profound ideological cleavages in France, the occasional threat of civil war, rather strong voter turnout, the instability of governments and republics, and the rise and fall of "flash" parties like the R.P.F. in 1951, the Poujadists in 1956, and the U.N.R. in 1958 have all contributed to the impression of a peculiar intensity in the tenor of French political life.

It is a sign of progress in the study of political behavior that such symptoms no longer seem to form a self-evident whole. We feel increasingly obliged, for example, to take note of the level in the society at which the symptoms are manifest. Most of our impressions of the French scene reflect only the behavior of French political leadership. Growing familiarity with survey data from broad publics has schooled us not to assume perfect continuity between the decision-making characteristics of a leadership and the predispositions of its rank and file. The extremism of the military elite in Algeria or ideological intransigence in the French National Assembly are in themselves poor proof that the shipyard worker in Nantes has political reflexes which differ from those of the shipyard worker in Norfolk. . . .

We intend in this paper to examine comparative data on the French and American publics in an effort to determine more precisely the locus of Franco-American differences in these matters. We shall consider the locus in qualitative terms, covering an extended series of political

From *The Public Opinion Quarterly*, 1962, Spring: 1–3, 9–23.

characteristics which run from expressions of involvement, acts of participation, and information seeking to orientations whereby the voter links party alternatives to the basic ideological issues in the society. We shall throughout maintain an interest as well in a vertical locus of differences. That is, we shall think of the two electorates as stratified from persistent nonvoters at the bottom, through the large middle mass of average voters, to citizens who engage in some further partisan activity, and thence by extrapolation to the higher leadership whose highly visible behavior is so frequently the source of our cross-national impressions. Such extrapolation is necessary, of course, because it is unlikely that the handful of "activists" whom we can distinguish at the top layer of both national samples include more than one or two persons who have ever had any direct hand in a leadership decision of even a parochial party organization or political interest group. . . .

Partisan Orientations

The gross similarities between the two publics in apparent political interest do not, to be sure, remove the possibility that the Frenchman in his interested moments may respond to politics in much different terms than his American counterpart. Actually, when we consider the character of partisan ties felt by citizens in the two countries, we strike upon some contrasts of great magnitude.

If Americans are asked to locate themselves relative to the American party system, 75 per cent classify themselves without further probing as psychological members of one of the two major parties, or of some minor party. In France, somewhat before the elections, less than 45 per cent of those who did not refuse to answer the question were able to classify themselves in one of the parties or splinter groups, while another 10 to 15 per cent associated themselves with a more or less recognizable broad *tendance* ("left," "right," a labor union, etc.). The cross-national differences of 20 to 30 per cent are sufficiently large here to contribute to fundamental differences in the flavor of partisan processes in the two electorates. For a long time, we wrote off these differences as products of incomparable circumstances or of reticence on the part of the French concerning partisanship, most of which was being expressed not as refusal to answer the question, but as some other evasion. As we grew more familiar with the data, however, these differences took on vital new interest.

The hypothesis of concealed partisanship was very largely dispelled by a close reading of the actual interviews. It is undeniable that nearly 10 per cent of the French sample explicitly refused to answer the question, as compared with a tiny fraction in the United States. However, we have already subtracted this group from the accounting. Beyond the explicit refusals, the remarks and explanations which often accompanied statements classified as "no party," or as "don't know which party," had a very genuine air about them which made them hard to read as hasty evasions. No few of these respondents were obviously embarrassed at their lack of a party; some confessed that they just hadn't been able to keep track of which party was which. The phrase "je n'y ai jamais pensé" ["I never thought about it"] was extremely common. Others indicated that they found it too hard to choose between so many parties; some indicated preferences for a specific political leader but admitted that they did not know which party he belonged to or, more often, had no interest in the identity of his party, whatever it might be. Others, forming a tiny minority of the nonparty people, rejected the notion of parties with some hostility.

It became clear, too, that people reporting no party attachments were distinct on other grounds from those who willingly classified themselves as close to a party. On our vertical involvement dimension, for example, they tended to fall in the bottom stratum of the least involved, just as the paper-thin stratum unable to choose a party in the United States consists heavily of the least involved. Demographically, these nonparty people were disproportionately housewives, poorly educated, young, and the other familiar statuses which tend to be uninformed and uninvolved.

Among actual party identifiers in France there was further interesting variation in the character of the party objects to which reference was made. A very few linked themselves with small new ideological splinter groups which had developed during the political crises of 1958. For these people, it was not enough to indicate that they felt closest to the Radical-Socialists, for example: they had to specify that they were Mendesists or anti-Mendesists, Valoisiens, and the like. Most identifiers suffered no difficulty in seeing themselves as "Radical-Socialists," completely shattered though the party was. Others, perceiving the system even more grossly, linked themselves only with a broad *tendance*. On involvement measures these groupings showed the expected differences: the grosser the discrimination, the lower the involvement.

In other ways as well it was clear that the extreme ideological fractionation of parties in France has few roots in the mass population, members of which simply pay too little attention to politics to follow the nicer discriminations involved. When asked whether the number of parties in France was too great, about right, or too few, 97 per cent of those responding said there were too many parties, and less than 1 per cent said there were too few. In response to an ensuing question as to the desirable number of parties, the mean of the number seen as optimal was 3.5 for the handful of adherents of the new ideological splinters, 3.0 for the partisans of the traditional mass parties, and less than 2.8 among those who had formed no party attachments. Perhaps the most apt expression of the problem of partisan fractionation and discrimination came from the naïve respondent who opined that France should have two or three parties, "enough to express the differences in opinion."

The fact that large proportions of the French public have failed to form any very strong attachments to one of the political parties should not be taken to mean that these people are totally disoriented in the French party system. In particular, a sensitivity to the gulf separating the Communist Party from the remainder of French parties does pervade the mass public. There seems to be less confusion as to the identity of the Communist Party than for any of the other parties; and for the bulk of non-Communists, the Communist Party is a pariah. There are some nonidentifiers who appear to shift from Communist to non-Communist votes with abandon, and were all of these votes to fall to the Communists in the same election, the Party would undoubtedly exceed its previous high-water mark in its proportion of the French popular vote. At the same time, however, one cannot help but be impressed by the number of respondents who, while indicating they were not really sure what they were in partisan terms, indicated as well at one point or another in the interview that they were not only non-Communist but anti-Communist. In other words, were the descriptions of party adherents to proceed simply in terms of a Communist, non-Communist division, the proportion of ready self-classifications would advance considerably toward the American figure, and would probably exceed that which could be attained by any other two-class division in France.

Nevertheless, the limited party attachments outside the Communist camp in France retain strong theoretical interest, as they seem so obviously linked to a symptom of turbulence which is clearly not an elite phenomenon alone—the flash party. With a very large proportion of the electorate feeling no anchoring loyalty, it is not surprising that a new party can attract a large vote "overnight," or that this base can be so rapidly dissolved. Furthermore, there is a problem here that is peculiarly French, in that the low proportion of expressed attachments cannot simply be seen as a necessary consequence of a multiparty system per se. Fairly comparable data from Norway, where six parties are prominent, show party attachments as widespread as those in the two-party United States.[1]

The French sample was asked further to recall the party or *tendance* which the respondent's father had supported at the polls. Here the departure from comparable American data became even more extreme. Of those Americans in 1958 having had a known father who had resided in the United States as an American citizen, thereby participat-

[1]Angus Campbell and Henry Valen, "Party Identification in Norway and the United States," *Public Opinion Quarterly*, 1961, *25*: 505–525.

ing in American political life, 86 per cent could characterize his partisanship, and another 5 per cent knew enough of his political behavior to describe him as apolitical or independent. Among comparable French respondents, only 26 per cent could link fathers with any party or with the vaguest of *tendances* (including such responses as "il a toujours voté pour la patrie" ["he always voted for his country"]), and another 3 per cent could describe the father's disposition as variable or apolitical. In other words, among those eligible to respond to the question, 91 per cent of Americans could characterize their father's political behavior, as opposed to 29 per cent of the French.

It goes without saying that differences of this magnitude rarely emerge from individual data in social research. And they occur at a point of prime theoretical interest. We have long been impressed in the United States by the degree to which partisan orientations appear to be passed hereditarily, from generation to generation, through families. It has seemed likely that such transmission is crucial in the stability of American partisan voting patterns. Therefore, we find it startling to encounter a situation in which huge discontinuities seem to appear in this transmission.

What do the French responses concerning paternal partisanship really mean? As best we can determine, they mean what they appear to mean: the French father is uncommunicative about his political behavior before his children, just as he is more reserved in the interviewing situation than Americans or Norwegians. It seems highly unlikely, for example, that Franco-American differences in recall represent French concealment: large numbers of the French willing to speak of their own party preference are unable to give the father's preference of a generation before, and explicit refusals to answer, while attaining 10 per cent or more where own partisanship is at stake, are almost nonexistent for paternal partisanship. . . .

Partisan attachments appear . . . to be very weakly developed within the less politically involved half of the French electorate. While undoubtedly a large variety of factors, including the notoriety which the French parties had acquired in the later stages of the Fourth Republic, have helped to inhibit their development, more basic discontinuities of political socialization in the French family appear to be making some persisting contribution as well. Of course, similar lack of party attachment does occur among people indifferent to politics in the American and Norwegian systems as well; but the strata of unidentified people are thinner in these systems and do not extend greatly above that layer of persistent nonvoters which is present in any system.

The link between an electorate heavily populated with voters feeling no continuing party attachments and a susceptibility to "flash" parties is an obvious one. It must be recognized at the outset, of course, that such phenomena arise only under the pressure of social, political, or economic dislocations occurring in some segment of the population, thereby generating an elite which wishes to organize a movement and a public which is restive. This means that even a system highly susceptible to such phenomena is not likely to experience them when it is functioning smoothly: their prevalence in postwar France cannot be divorced from the severe dislocations the society has been undergoing. Once misfortunes breed discontent, however, the proportions of partisans in an electorate is a datum of fundamental significance. One cannot fail to be impressed by the agility with which the strong partisan can blame the opposing party for almost any misfortune or deny the political relevance of the misfortune if some opposing party cannot conceivably be blamed. Hence, where partisans are concerned, misfortunes do relatively little to shift voting patterns. Independents, however, have no stake in such reinforcements and defenses and move more massively in response to grievances. In France, the institutions which conduce to a multiparty system make the organization of new party movements more feasible from an elite point of view than it is likely to be under two-party traditions. At the same time, the presence of a large number of French voters who have developed no continuing attachments to a particular party provides an "available" mass base for such movements. This available base is no necessary concomitant of a multiparty system, but is rather a peculiarity of the current French scene.

Parties and Policy Controversy

Whatever differences exist in partisan orientations, no assessment of politicization would be complete without consideration of the manner in which ideological conflict is worked out through the party system. If parties are recognized at all in the classical view of democratic process, they are relegated to a distinctly secondary position: they are means to policy ends, and should be judged by the citizen accordingly. In this light, the number of Americans with strong party loyalty and a poor sense of what either party stands for in policy terms represents a distinct perversion of the democratic process. In this light, too, weaker partisan orientations in the French populace might simply mean a relegation of party to second rank, with a primary focus on policy goals. . . .

Data have been collected in both countries concerning reactions to a variety of issues confronting the two systems. While both sets of items must be regarded as only the crudest samplings of hypothetical issue universes, selection on both sides was performed in an attempt to tap some of the most basic controversies of the period. In France, three items were devoted to the classic socio-economic left and right, with one concerning the role of labor and the other two the relative roles of government and private enterprise in housing; two more involved the clerical question; a sixth item had to do with military expenditures and national prestige; a seventh concerned the freedom of the press to criticize the government. Of eight American questions, two dealt with social-welfare legislation and a third with the relative role of government and private enterprise in housing and utilities, covering the classic right and left; two more dealt with the government's role in racial matters (FEPC and school desegregation); and three others were concerned with the internationalist or isolationist posture of the government in foreign affairs. All questions were in Likert scale form.

We shall focus upon three properties of these issues which we can more or less crudely measure in the two countries: (1) the degree to which public opinion is sharply crystallized on each issue; (2) the degree to which opinion within the two publics is polarized on each; and (3) for each issue, the degree to which individual opinion is associated with partisan preference. Assuming the items do give fair coverage to most primary issue dimensions in the two nations, we are interested to see if opinion in France at a mass level appears more sharply crystallized or polarized, and to assess the manner in which policy concerns are linked with party preference. As before, we shall distinguish layers of both populations in terms of partisan involvement. At the top, we isolate as political "actives" those people who were either party members or reported attending two or more political rallies in the respective election campaigns, a group which amounts to 5 to 7 per cent within each population and hence is sufficiently large for analysis. We also continue to distinguish between party identifiers (three quarters of the American population, but half of the French) and nonidentifiers.

In both nations, the issue items were asked again of the same respondents after an interval of time. We take as a measure of crystallization of opinion the rank-order correlation between the two expressions of opinion. There is a good deal of internal evidence to suggest that "change" in opinion between the two readings is almost never a matter of true conversion, but rather represents haphazard reactions to items on which the respondent has never formed much opinion. With minor exceptions, there is no significant change in the marginal distributions of the [data], despite the high turnover of opinion. There is a persistent relation between the proportions of people who confess they have no opinion on any given issue and the amount of turnover shown by those who do attempt an opinion. As one might expect, too, there is a tendency for high crystallization, high polarization, and high party-relatedness to co-occur, despite intriguing exceptions. Clearly both publics are more likely to have arrived at stable prior opinions on some items than on others, and this degree of crystallization has an obvious bearing on the vitality of the role the issue dimension may play in partisan choice.

. . . Actives in both countries show more highly crystallized opinions, and usually more polarized opinions as well, although American actives differ less sharply and consistently from their mass public than do French actives. In neither country do identifiers differ reliably from nonidentifiers with regard to crystallization or polarization of opinion. In both countries, however, there are quite reliable differences in party-relatedness, not only between actives and the remaining 95 per cent of the population, but between identifiers and nonidentified. In other words, while the partisan manner of relating to the political process makes little difference in basic opinion formation save for the extremely active, the translation of these attitudes to some kind of party choice seems increasingly haphazard as party attachments become weaker.

Throughout these comparisons, however, we may remain struck by the fact that the "slope" is steeper on the French side: the differences between actives and mass are large relative to those in the United States. From the upper end of this steep slope, one might wish to extrapolate to the sharp and rigid cleavages on policy matters for which French elites are noted; for our purposes, it is sufficient to observe that these cleavages blur rapidly and lose their tone in the mass of the French electorate.

Finally, it should be observed that the issues seem to sort themselves into two rough categories in both nations: (1) emotional-symbol issues involving some of the more gross group conflicts within the two societies (racial in the United States, religious in France, along with items which touch in a direct way upon labor as an interest group), which show relatively high crystallization and polarization; and (2) more complex questions of relations between the state and private enterprise which, along with all foreign policy issues, tend to be less crystallized.

These differences in crystallization are scarcely surprising, as the objects and means involved in the second group of issues are clearly more remote from the common experience of the man-in-the-street. Yet the pattern is ironic, for the issues which show a stronger resonance in both mass publics tend to be those which both elites make some attempt to soft-pedal, in favor of direct debate over such more "ideological" matters as arrangements between state and private enterprise. The more resonant issues are not dead, of course, and are used for tactical advantage by elites in both countries. Calculations of vote gain are made in the United States on the basis of the religion of the nominee, and the clerical question in France has been resuscitated repeatedly as a handy crowbar to split apart government coalitions. At the same time, however, there is genuine elite effort to keep such cleavage issues in the background: the American public is told that religion is not a proper criterion for candidate choice, and the battleground for elite debate on the racial issue is usually displaced quite notably from race itself in the modern period. Similarly, much sophisticated French opinion has for some time argued that even the secondary role which the clerical question has been playing in elite debate exaggerates its importance.

Given this common background, the different manner in which the two types of controversy weave into partisan choices in the two countries is fascinating. In France, there is fair coincidence between the ordering of issues in terms of party-relatedness and the ordering on the other two properties. The clerical questions, for example, are highly crystallized and polarized, and show high levels of party-relatedness as well. The structure of party competition is such that, elite values notwithstanding, these emotional cleavages achieve prominent partisan expression. Such is not the case in the United States: there is little coincidence between the party-relatedness of issues and the other two properties. Indeed, the racial issue finds little clear party expression, while the "elite" issue concerning government and private enterprise, one of the least crystallized issues, is at the same time one of the most party-related across the full electorate.

Where mass or elite control of issue controversy is concerned, then, the two systems have rather paradoxical outcomes. By conception, the French party system is geared to elites, encouraging them to a multi-faceted ideological expression which is too complex for most of the public to encompass. At the same time, the multidimensional clarity of party positions serves to return a measure of control to part of the public, for the more involved citizens can single out certain dimensions to reduce the system to manageable simplicity. These reductions are naturally made in terms of issues which are more resonant in the public, even if these are not the dimensions which the elites might wish to stress. The American system is less elite in conception; it is sufficiently simple in its gross characteristics that it is easier for the common citizen to follow it with only limited attention. But this simplification requires great blurring of party differences across most of the universe of possible issues, and the differences which are maintained are those which the competing elites select as battlegrounds. Hence, control of controversy which can be given partisan expression is, paradoxically, more nearly in elite hands.

Conclusions

We have attempted to sort through a number of those characteristics of French politics which add up to vague impressions of intense French politicization, in order to identify more precise loci for Franco-American differences. It appears likely that the more notable of these differences stem from the actions of elites and require study and explanation primarily at this level, rather than at the level of the mass electorate. While certain peculiarities reminiscent of French political elites are visible in the most politically active twentieth of the French population, these peculiarities fade out rapidly as one approaches the more "representative" portions of the broad French public.

It is unlikely that the common French citizen devotes any greater portion of his attention to politics than does his American counterpart, and he may well give less. His behavior is constrained within a much different set of political institutions, and these differences have important consequences for the character of his political behavior, including the opportunity of closer articulation between any crystallized opinions he may hold and an appropriate party instrument. However, the data give no striking reason to believe that the French citizen, either through the vagaries of national character, institutions, or history, is predisposed to form political opinions which are more sharply crystallized or which embrace a more comprehensive range of political issues than do comparable Americans. On both sides, opinion formation declines as objects and arrangements become more remote from the observer; and much of politics, for both French and Americans, is remote. Hence the proliferation of choices offered by the multiparty system is itself a mixed blessing: it is capitalized upon only by the more politically interested segments of the electorate, and appears to represent "too much" choice to be managed comfortably by citizens whose political involvement is average or less.

Over the range of characteristics surveyed, only one striking difference at the level of the mass public was encountered which seemed more uniquely French than the multiparty system itself. There is evidence of a widespread absence of party loyalties, a phenomenon which can be empirically associated with peculiarities in the French socialization process. This characteristic has obvious links with the major symptom of French political turbulence, which is based on the behavior of the mass population rather than that of elites—the current availability of a mass base for flash party movements under circumstances of distress.

SOCIAL RELATIONS AND POLITICAL CULTURE

Gabriel A. Almond and Sidney Verba

Because of the tendency to generalize from one social sphere to the other, we may reasonably expect some strain toward homogeneity among the authority relations to which an individual is exposed. But we do not expect complete homogeneity. There is a wide gap between family, school, and occupational participation and political participation. In the first place, an individual who has had ample opportunities to participate in a wide range of nonpolitical situations may live within a political system that affords few opportunities to participate. He may have the propensities for civic participation but little opportunity to perform a civic role. Conversely, his prepolitical experiences may give him little encouragement for participation, but other social characteristics or political characteristics may lead him into participation. Furthermore, participation in the more intimate situations of the family, the school, and the job (particularly in the family and perhaps the school) may differ markedly from participation in politics. The authority patterns within the smaller units may take a different form from those in politics and thereby inhibit the degree to which he will generalize from one social situation to the other. The authority patterns of smaller, more intimate units tend to be informal. Decisions may "emerge" from the group without ever having been "decided" in any formal sense. The channels of influence are less clearly articulated. Because of this, the political socialization that occurs within more intimate social units may be inadequate training for the performance of civic activities within the larger, secondary political system. Therefore, those institutions closer to the political realm and in which authority patterns become more similar in kind to authority patterns in the political system may be more crucial for the formation of political attitudes.

. . . Though the individual may not have much control over whether or not the structure of politics affords him many actual opportunities to participate, his expectations of whether or not he is able to participate (what we have called his "subjective competence") ought to be more amenable to influence from outside of the realm of politics. . . .

Participation in Family Decisions

The two most significant institutions for the socialization of the child are the family and the school. In both, authority patterns are important and salient. Within the family and the school the child is first exposed to authority relationships. And though the authority patterns of both are necessarily hierarchical, involving relations between adults and children, the institutions may vary substantially in the extent to which they allow some freedom for children to participate. This participation may begin implicitly at a very early age. But since we felt that patterns of activity closer in time to political participation would be of greater significance and more reliably remembered, we decided to ask about participation within the family during adolescence. Respondents [in Britain, Germany, Italy, Mexico, and the United States] were asked if they could remember how much influence they had had in family decisions that concerned them when they were about sixteen. . . . In all countries but Italy, more than half of the respondents remember having some influence in family decisions, and in Italy the proportion is close to one-half. Respondents in the United States and Britain most frequently report (73 per cent and 69 per cent, respectively) that they had some influence over family decisions; German, Italian, and Mexican respondents in roughly equal frequency report that they had no influence. Respondents were also asked if they had had opportunities to complain about decisions. Had they felt free to complain if decisions were made that they did not like? And could they remember actually complaining? Within the informal structure of the family this freedom to dissent may be considered a form of participation.

. . . In general, British and American respondents report the greatest ability to participate in family decisions in this way. British respondents report more frequently than others that they remember feeling free to complain, while the American respondents report somewhat more frequently than others that they remember actually complaining. At the other extreme, about one-half of the Mexican respondents report that it was better not to complain and that they in fact did not complain. The frequencies with which German and Italian respondents report family participation lie between those of the United States and Britain, on the one hand, and Mexico, on the other . . . .

Participation in School

The data on participation within the family roughly parallel much of the data . . . reported on participation within politics: a relatively greater frequency of participation in Britain and the United States, intermediate participation in Germany, and somewhat lower participation in Italy and Mexico. On the other hand, the data on remembered participation in the schools show sharp contrast between the United States and the other four countries. This is true for informal participation within the school, but especially true for the opportunities for formal participation in school political discussions.

Consider the remembered ability of our respondents to participate informally within the school. To what extent did they have the opportunity to express their opinions? . . . American respondents report most often that they felt free to complain of unfair treatment and report least often that it was better not to talk to the teacher. In the other nations the pattern is rather mixed. Italian respondents report least often that they felt free to complain, and the British respondents report most frequently that it was better not to speak up. . . . While equal proportions of American respondents remember having actually complained as remember having never complained, in each of the other four nations the proportion reporting that they never complained is substantially larger than the proportion reporting that they did complain.

But the sharpest difference in school participation is observed if one considers more formal opportunities to participate. Here the distinction between education in the United States and education elsewhere is immediately apparent. Respondents were asked whether children in their school were given the opportunity to discuss and debate political and social issues. If they reported that there were such discussions, then they were asked if they themselves took part. . . . In the United States 40 per cent of the respondents report that there were such discussions and that they took part. In the other nations the percentage so reporting is much smaller, ranging from 16 per cent in Britain to 11 per cent in Italy. Clearly, the amount of explicit training for political participation in the schools is much higher in the United States than elsewhere. . . .

Class and Early Participation

Our data suggest that authority patterns in the family and the school vary substantially among different social groups. Our survey unfortunately contained no index of the social status of the respondent's parents, and we must use certain information about the respondent to infer this. Perhaps the most useful though far from exact index is the respondent's educational level, for one may assume that the amount of education an individual receives is related to the social status of his parents.

In all five nations the frequency with which respondents report that they were able to participate in decisions within the family or at school—both their freedom to complain about decisions and the actual complaining they remember doing—rises with level of education. On the question of whether the respondent remembers ever protesting a family decision he did not like, the data . . . indicate how closely such remembered protest is related to educational level. The distinction is particularly sharp between those with primary education or less and those with secondary education; the difference between those with secondary education and those who attained some higher education is somewhat less; and in Britain and Italy the percentages of remembered protest decline as one moves from the secondary to the university level.

Due to their retrospective nature and to the fact that the measure of family social status is crude, the data must be interpreted with great caution; yet they do suggest strongly that experience with family authority patterns differs among the social classes. Those of higher social status are more likely to participate in family decisions. If such experience facilitates the growth of democratic political competence in later life, one of the many reasons for the generally lower political competence of those with low educational attainment may be that these people are usually raised in families that do not nourish the expectation that one can make one's voice heard in decisions.

A similar class difference is observable in school participation (see Tables 1 and 2). Respondents with higher education remember informal participation (complaining about unfair treatment) and formal participation (classroom discussion) much more frequently than do those of lower educational attainment. For example, 25 per cent of the Italian respondents who did not get beyond primary school report that they remember complaining about unfair treatment, in contrast with 44 per cent of those who reached secondary school. And the differences are as sharp within each of the nations. Even more striking are the differences among social groups in the frequency of remembered formal participation in classroom discussions (as reported in Table 1). In each nation the frequency of remembered participation is about three or four times as great among respondents with some secondary education as it is among those with only primary education.

At first glance one may wonder at this class difference in school participation. Don't individuals of varying social classes often attend

Table 1

PER CENT REPORTING ACTUAL DISCUSSION OF UNFAIR TREATMENT OR DISAGREEMENT WITH TEACHER, BY NATION AND EDUCATION

Nation	Total		Prim. or Less		Some Sec.		Some Univ.	
	(%)	(No.)*	(%)	(No.)	(%)	(No.)	(%)	(No.)
United States	46	(959)	32	(339)	52	(447)	55	(188)
Great Britain	36	(963)	31	(593)	44	(322)	58	(24)
Germany	31	(953)	26	(790)	52	(124)	81	(26)
Italy	32	(907)	25	(604)	44	(245)	57	(54)
Mexico	38	(783)	32	(656)	63	(103)	81	(24)

*Numbers in parentheses refer to the bases upon which percentages are calculated.

Table 2

PER CENT REPORTING ACTUAL PARTICIPATION IN SCHOOL DISCUSSIONS AND DEBATES BY NATION AND EDUCATION

Nation	Total		Prim. or Less		Some Sec.		Some Univ.	
	(%)	(No.)*	(%)	(No.)	(%)	(No.)	(%)	(No.)
United States	40	(970)	17	(339)	50	(442)	57	(188)
Great Britain	16	(963)	7	(593)	26	(322)	46	(24)
Germany	12	(953)	7	(790)	34	(124)	42	(26)
Italy	11	(907)	6	(604)	22	(245)	22	(54)
Mexico	15	(783)	9	(656)	37	(103)	54	(24)

*Numbers in parentheses refer to the bases upon which percentages are calculated.

the same schools, and isn't school policy often made for a geographic area and not for specific social groups? If this is the case, one would not expect children of various social classes to differ in their school experiences. But though this may be partially true (unlike the situation with the family), there are a number of ways in which class differentials might be introduced. In the first place, children of varying social classes do not attend the same schools; this may be due to neighborhood differences or to the fact that those in upper-status families will more often attend private schools. And the opportunities to participate may be uneven among the various types of schools. Furthermore, even if children from a variety of social backgrounds attend the same schools and are in the same classroom, the school may favor the participation of those of higher status. In life-history interviews, for instance, when respondents were asked to expound more fully on their school experiences, a large number of respondents from lower-status families in all five nations commented on the differential treatment that teachers gave to children of different social backgrounds. And lastly, children from higher-status homes may be better equipped and more highly motivated to participate within the school, if given the opportunity, than are children from lower-status homes. For if we can expect individuals to generalize from their family experiences to the political system—if their earliest attitudes toward authority determine some of their later attitudes toward political authority—the same pattern should hold between the family and the school. And higher-status children do have greater opportunity to participate within the family.

The implications of these data are significant. If experience with nongovernmental patterns of authority is indeed a source of political attitudes, then the sharp differences in political attitudes that one observes among respondents from various social backgrounds may originate in their early experiences with authority. We shall return to this question below.

One further point must be made about the distribution of school and family participatory experiences among those with varying educational backgrounds. In our earlier discussion of the national differences in the frequency with which respondents report remembered opportunities to participate within the family, we found a rough parallel between the frequencies of reported ability to participate in politics and remembered participatory family experiences. Both were most frequent in the United States and Britain and least frequent in Italy and Mexico. And within the schools we found the contrast between the United States and the other four nations to be the clearest pattern. But if one considers the data in Tables 1 and 2, it becomes clear that much of the difference in school and family experiences seems to be due to the differing distributions of educational attainment among the nations. . . . [T]he national differences in remembered family participation are only faintly mirrored in the data for respondents with no more than primary school education, and not mirrored at all at higher educational levels. The remembered informal participation in schools (reported in Table 1) shows little systematic national difference within each educational group. It is, in fact, only with formal participation in school debates (Table 2) that any sharp national difference persists —and this is the clear contrast between the frequency of participation in the United States and in other nations.

Thus those with higher education in all five nations seem to receive somewhat greater opportunities to participate in nonpolitical situations than do those with lower educational attainment. And when one considers respondents of similar educational backgrounds, cross-national differences in opportunities to participate become insignificant.

Age and Early Participation

Perhaps even more significant than the differences among social classes in the degree to which individuals have opportunities to participate in family and school decisions are the differences among generations. Our data strongly suggest[ed] that patterns of family and school participation have been changing over time, and, what is more important, that they have been changing in the same direction in all five nations. . . .

. . . The older the respondent, the less likely he is to report opportunities to participate. In almost every instance the two groups over fifty years of age report school and family participation least frequently. Despite the wide disparities in the recent histories of these nations, the differences in their social structures and in overall levels of participation and competence, all five appear to be experiencing a similar secular trend toward a less authoritarian school and family system.

Despite the general similarity of pattern in the five nations, there are some interesting differences in the regularity of change in family and school participation over time. In the United States one observes a relatively gradual increase in the frequency of remembered participation; the data seem to indicate that this change has been going on steadily over the last generations. A similar pattern of gradual change over time is apparent in the data about family participation for Great Britain and Germany and, to a lesser extent, Italy. Despite political and social vicissitudes, which at times may have slowed changes in family structure, there appears to be a relatively steady movement toward a participatory family in these three nations. Increases in school participation, on the other hand, seem to have occurred in two stages in Britain, Germany, and Italy: during the post-World War I period and again in the post-World War II period, with relatively little change for those respondents who attended school roughly from the mid-1920's to the end of the Second World War. This pattern is what one might expect in Germany and Italy, where institutional change was arrested by the Nazi and Fascist regimes. And indeed, the sharp changes in the postwar generation suggest the degree to which old, imposed forms of school training have been replaced by new forms. The similarity in the British pattern may be explained by the modifications in secondary education following both world wars.

In Mexico changes in family and school authority patterns appear to have been the slowest. There is a steady increase in the frequency of reported participation in school decisions as one moves from older to younger respondents, but the changes are much more gradual than in the other nations. And in relation to family participation, there appears to be little regular pattern in the responses. . . . Nevertheless, the cross-national uniformity is impressive. All the patterns of authority outside the realm of politics appear to be changing in the same direction: toward greater participation. Furthermore, they appear to change somewhat independently of the political system. This is at least the inference one can draw from the relatively steady change in patterns of family authority—especially in Germany—since the early part of the century. On the other hand, the arrested change in school authority patterns in Italy and Germany suggests that these patterns are more likely to be affected by the political system.

What we may be observing in this general trend toward greater participation in the school and family are certain aspects of the industrialization, urbanization, and modernization processes in Europe and the United States. The last century has seen a dramatic shift from agricultural to industrial employment, from rural to urban residence, and a sharp rise in educational levels. This has meant by and large a shift from the extended, patriarchal family to the nuclear family, the emancipation of women, and the development of greater individual autonomy. The striking point about these general changes in patterns of social authority and individual participation is that they do not immediately, or even necessarily, spill over into the political sphere. They do, however, have political consequences. . . .

Part V

Public Policies: A Reader's Guide to Education and Politics

The control of its educational systems has always been a matter of great importance to a society, since the character of formal and informal instruction profoundly affects the citizenship of students and adults. The selections presented in Part V focus on some critical political aspects of the educational system that is currently emerging in a period of social upheaval. The changes in the American educational scene are a result of the following factors:

1. The extension of education, including advanced education, to nearly all citizens, rather than merely to those who wish to perpetuate the dominance of an elitist minority. The equalitarian ethos of American culture, in its attempt to provide the best possible education for all, leads to the rapid expansion of secondary school and university facilities, creating growing administrative problems of coordination and control.

2. The demand for higher competence in scientific and technological fields, stimulated in part by the foreign policy of the United States since World War II.

3. Divided and constantly shifting control over the educational scene by national, state, and local agencies.

4. The rapid influx of culturally deprived populations into major metropolitan areas, which makes difficult the realization of mass education and the satisfaction of the needs of a post-industrial society for skilled professions.

5. The fluidity of ideas and social structures that invalidate such educational concepts as the "local citizen" and the "neighborhood school."

---

17. Allocation of Money, Power, and Knowledge

The formation of government policies concerning education is especially important because of the unique role of the schools. Schools not only transmit learning and job skills; they also impart to the student the broad cultural values held by professional educators, parents, and student peer groups. For this reason, school politics are often explosive—a point documented by William Dobriner's study of Levittown on pages 473-481. As Robert Wood suggests in the first selection, school politics constitute a special issue in suburban areas because of the ideological notions of education held by suburbanites and because of the natural tendency to local control of suburban schools.

Few institutions are as decentralized as those in education, and as a result there are often conflicts between local, state, and federal administrations. After establishing once and for all that education does involve politics, Thomas Eliot examines some major interests that determine "who gets what, when, and how" in the American public schools. He also defines four areas involving decision-making primarily at the local level: facilities, personnel, curriculum, and the units and organization of government.

Stephen Bailey and his colleagues outline the structure of educational politics at the state level and point out the diversity of educational systems even within the relatively homogeneous Northeastern states. While reading this selection, the student should keep in mind the historically weak position of state boards of education in light of current attempts in many states to strengthen that position. A suitable model for comparison with the American school system would be the highly nationalized and centralized French educational system, which is free from the many conflicts of the American federal system.

THE SPECIAL ISSUE OF THE PUBLIC SCHOOLS

Robert C. Wood

A sketch of suburban politics as the power relations of a relatively large number of personalities and of relatively few and generally harmonious interest groups operating under the cover of nonpartisanship needs to be qualified in at least one important respect. The program and expenditures of suburban schools are quite likely to engender a brand of active, if not frenzied, political behavior that stands in stark contrast to the more controlled decision-making in other parts of suburban government. Part of the pattern of school politics is explicable in universal terms and is likely to be found in all types and sizes of American communities; part seems to be peculiar to the suburbs. Regardless of its source and motivations, however, the operation of the public schools results in more extensive public participation in political affairs, more heat, and not infrequently less light than any other function.

The quantitative magnitude of the school problem is one aspect of school politics. Since the suburbs represent the growing edge of the American population, the provision of school facilities is their major public problem. The central cities wrestle with deteriorating land values, slums, and blight, and concentrate on renewal and redevelopment programs to restore physical and fiscal soundness. Rural areas find highways perhaps the most persistent and politically sensitive public function. But the suburbs grapple with the growing tide of children who invade their borders. Following the Pied Piper lure of better schools, family after family lists consideration of their young as a primary cause for the suburban trek, and they tumble over one another to find governments with "good school systems."

In this context, the relative youth of the suburban population, the social acceptability of large families in the growing middle class, the almost universal practice of the present generation to complete at least a high school education, all combine to raise enormous quantitative demands on public education. In all local American governments, educational expenditures account for almost one half of the total budget; for suburban governments it is frequently a good deal more. Metropolitan school systems spend considerably more per pupil, adopt advanced techniques in instruction more quickly, and expand curricula more readily. Because the schools have the largest bureaucracy, take the greatest part of the tax dollar, and represent the most rapidly growing public demand, they are the most important function suburban governments perform.

Viewed in these terms simply of quantitative pressures, the school problem exaggerates whatever conflicts and disagreements already exist. Cleavages between established residents and new, commuters and stay-at-homes, young residents and old, industrial and residential taxpayers, are naturally intensified. And new dimensions in the power pattern are likely to come to the fore, expressed by the sharply different attitudes of Catholics, Protestants, and Jews toward the proper role of public education. The conflicting pressures of population and finance are likely, in and of themselves, to ignite public debate.

Yet quantitative pressures alone do not generate the suburban school battles which are so evident at the present time. Americans, and particularly suburbanites, care deeply about the qualitative aspects of public education—how "good" the additional teachers and the expanded curricula are. In part, this strong popular interest results from the suburban preoccupation with family and children. In part, it arises from the demands for literary and technical skills in our highly developed economy. In part, too, it stems from the social responsibility education now provides.

But the qualitative aspect of school politics stretches back beyond the values of our contemporary culture. A full explanation of school politics, its emotionalism and agitation, lies buried in the American political tradition as it is interpreted in educational philosophy. The national commitment to education began with the eighteenth century belief in man's reason as a prerequisite for popular government. Given that conviction, it follows that the development of the power to reason deserves the most careful attention any democracy can manage. If man is perfectible, in the sense of becoming progressively more reasonable, then the schools are the critical force in guiding and shaping his advance.

The twentieth century emphasis on irrational and emotional factors in human nature—the discounting of pure reason as a major determinant in human affairs—does not diminish the importance of the school. On the contrary, as the educator interprets the new philosophies, they extend its responsibilities. No longer does the cultivation of rationally acquired skills suffice; the proper qualities of attitude and outlook, psychological balance and social poise, need also to be instilled. To reading, writing, arithmetic, and vocational training, modern educational doctrine adds instruction in social skills and group behavior, to ensure the development of the well-rounded personality. The "whole" child has to be considered, and his orderly adjustment to the world around him becomes a major function of the school. Even the techniques of teaching traditional subjects must be altered to ensure proper motivation and incentive for the student. In a curiously distorted way, the liberalism of Dewey has fused with the liberalism of Locke and the function of public education becomes no longer "schooling" in the restricted sense of imparting definite skills and knowledge. Now its responsibility is even greater: it is nothing less than the successful ordering of man's relationship to man, the happy adjustment of the individual to society.

Take the outright quantitative pressures on schools, add the requirements of modern culture, and mix philosophical assertions that raise fundamental issues about human nature, and an explosion is inevitable. A special type of politics emerges, and focuses on the suburb: the "politics of the particularists," a pattern isolated and divorced from other local public duties. Since education is of such unparalleled importance in making money, in the achievement of success, and especially in the well-being of a democratic society, it is a "unique" function. If it is unique, it has priority above all other governmental responsibilities. If it has such priority, it deserves special institutional arrangements and a special decision-making process. So the major public activity of suburbia is carefully set apart from the rest of suburban political life and wrapped in a shell peculiarly its own. The politics of the schools, rooted essentially in the educator's assertion of primacy, intensifies and exaggerates—almost to the point of burlesque—the features of suburban political behavior. . . .

Because the function is of such importance, it should demand the special attention of every resident in town. Further, it is not enough that school systems be local public institutions; they must be a particular type of local government. Since education is so vital a public activity, ordinary officialdom cannot be trusted with its management, and a special form of grassroots administration must be installed to isolate education from the more humdrum problems of land use, welfare, highways, police and fire protection.

Therefore, except in New England, an entirely separate government is provided for school management; and even in New England, the school board shares the limelight with the selectmen. Independent, popularly elected school boards and, quite frequently, elected school superintendents, take their places alongside—but apart from—other local officials. A separate tax levy is set aside for the school; generally, independent control of the budget is granted to the school government. Separate qualifications for the recruitment and advancement of the school bureaucracy are established; special arrangements are made with the state for financial aid.

Not only is the government divided . . . but the political man of suburbia is himself subdivided. He is already partly partisan and partly nonpartisan. Now the suburbanite must become a "school nonpartisan" as well. Education is too important to be left to ordinary political attitudes and actions; it must be "taken out of politics," and the last vestiges of group dissension and compromise must be erased. The all-wise, objective citizen assumes another burden. Responsibility and objective inquisitiveness are no longer sufficient for good citizenship; for the schools, positive support, open dedication and unquestioned allegiance are required. Patronage and favoritism cannot be allowed to enter the classroom in the way in which they are acceptable in granting highway contracts. No real debate can take place about the comparative needs of schools and other functions for no one can seriously argue that the building of a new fire station should be made possible by cutting the school budget. The essence of politics—compromise among competing needs, majority decisions between competing values—is ruled out. The school citizen must talk only about school.

Yet if politics is barred, who makes the decisions? Here an important shift in the relationship between expert and interest group takes place. In the case of the city manager, the professional might actively solicit support, but when he crossed over the line from administration to policy, he still had to convince his audience of the correctness of his views. In the schools, the expert looms even larger; the interest group exists to support the professional, almost without regard to his policies. The Parent-Teachers Association unites bureaucracy and the school public to work continually—if vaguely—for school "betterment," and in rapidly growing, predominantly Protestant suburbs, the PTA quite frequently can deliver a majority of the electorate.

The critical figure is the school superintendent. He has, in the words of Herold Hunt, the obligation not to defend his policies, as is the case with other professionals, but to "explain" them. Standards of administration and personnel performance have become the almost exclusive prerogative of the professional along with the substance of the school program, the curriculum. Even the school construction program may be put into the hands of the educators instead of into those of architects or builders, since each physical detail of the classroom intimately affects the attitude of the child. The "lobby of the good," the professional leaders mobilized to defend the basic principle of American education and their lay disciples, frequently becomes the most powerful force operative in the public affairs of the locality.

Of course, the declaration that schools must be above politics and that the professional's judgment must be accepted as the determining one is not an accurate summary of the actual state of affairs. It is too much to expect a public activity, equipped with a popular decision-making process that includes elections, to operate without politics. The school board and the superintendent are subjected, as numerous case studies testify, to all kinds of pressures and demands. Some are of the ordinary, garden-variety type of political action: petty intrigue on the part of school architects, connivance in the adoption of textbooks, building and equipment awards. More frequently the focus is on the philosophy of education adopted by the given school system. Is the program excessively "modern" or too old-fashioned? Should progressive techniques be encouraged or would a return to the discipline of vocational training be more appropriate?

On the critical issue of philosophy—of what the schools should do —the school officials are often curiously silent, except for defending the development of the curriculum as a professional matter. Generally, they concentrate solely on the quantitative aspects of the problem. They make a "bricks and mortar" defense: more buildings, more teachers and more money. When pressed, they exhibit the uncertainty in beliefs and the capacity to change dogmas in midstream which the investigators of Crestwood Heights discovered when they studied the objectives of school experts. As a rule, however, the educators strive either to keep the problem to themselves or to avoid participating in its public debate.

In terms of political realism, this position makes more sense than the Crestwood Heights analysis supposed. It is not so much a commentary on the unsettled doctrines of the educational profession as it is a tribute to that profession's recognition of the Pandora's box which is unlocked when the bricks-and-mortar position is abandoned. For when the slogan "betterment of schools" is directly examined, it becomes nothing less than a debate on fundamental principles—on the validity of the underlying assumption which makes education a prerequisite not just for democracy but, in modern dress, for the reform of society itself. There is nothing else really left to debate since the divorce of school government from other government removes the opportunity to compare the values received from other public services. The demands for school expenditures become insatiable, for the goal of the school system is as unspecific as the citizen's individual prescription for the ills of all mankind.

Thus the school electorate finds itself at the extreme end of the road that the logic of nonpartisanship has built. The conscientious citizen is called upon to determine not only ways and means, to decide not just between competing priorities in functions. He is required to define, year after year, the goals of government itself, and to resolve persistent philosophical disputes. School politics take on the color of a constitutional convention that is continually in session, always discussing the fundamentals of its political order. It operates, moreover, in the open atmosphere that prevailed in France after the Revolution rather than in the closeted, protected circumstances in which the American Constitution was prepared. The participants are asked to dig up their first premises by the roots and examine them anew, while constantly under public scrutiny. When debate of this nature occurs, it is violent; ardent Deweyites are asked to defend their prophet, and sometimes they may be forced to read him. The "Americanist" strand of liberalism thunders that current school philosophy is nothing less than subversion. The dwindling ranks of Horatio Algers call out for a return to practical education without frills and fads. Lay Catholics are brought again to the question of defining the boundaries between Church and State, in an atmosphere in which even Jesuits find an orderly discussion difficult.

Once the politics of the school particularists become really politics, one of Jefferson's least promising injunctions is pushed to an extreme that even he never intended. There is no longer just a revolution every generation, there is a revolution going on constantly. Divorced from the rest of the political process, suburban school government may avoid some of the unpalatable by-products of partisan politics, but it exposes itself to the dangers of ideological politics where no holds are barred, common beliefs rarely recognized, and where opponents can constantly hurl charges of infidelity to basic principles. In school politics, grass-roots democracy attains its ultimate promise: the citizens not only fully participate as individuals, but participate by laying bare their most fundamental convictions. And, since the goals of prevailing educational philosophy are open-ended, even agreement reached at one time in any one locality is unrewarding. The schools remain unsatisfactory, and the constitutional convention goes on unendingly.

TOWARD AN UNDERSTANDING OF PUBLIC SCHOOL POLITICS

THOMAS H. ELIOT

Mounting concern over the aims and achievements of American public schools emphasizes the need for continuing analysis of how the schools are run and who runs them. The general theory is simple enough: schools are objects of local control, the people of a local school district exercise that control through an elected school board, and the board appoints a superintendent to act as the chief executive of the district. There are variations from this pattern—in some places school boards are appointed rather than elected, in others the school system is formally a part of the city government, and in a few districts other officials, such as a business manager or building superintendent, share the top executive authority—but it is by far the most common arrangement among the nation's approximately 50,000 school districts.

I

The formal structure is based on state constitutions and statutes, and the latter have tended to confirm the historical development of education in the nineteenth century, especially in one respect: the district system of organization. The desirability of *local* control of the public

From *The American Political Science Review*, 1959 (December), *53*: 1032–1043, 1050–1051.

schools is an article of faith among most trained educators and many other Americans, including President Eisenhower. Laymen assume that local control means control by the people of the district, usually through elected representatives. Professional educators, however, are less clear about this. Their books and journals are rife with intimations that the people and even the school board members should keep their hands off the schools. Even James B. Conant's "report," after echoing the typical recommendation that school boards should confine themselves to "policy" as distinguished from "administration," says that they should refrain from interfering with curricular development.[1] But where is educational "policy" made, if not in the development of the curriculum? Doubtless Conant's remark was an inadvertent slip, for his book as a whole deals primarily with the curriculum and is addressed to "interested citizens," a category which surely includes more than educators; but many educators are insistent in urging, in effect, that the schools are the special province of the professionals, the voters being a necessary evil who must be reckoned with because they provide the money. In this view, the school board's primary functions, aside from directing the district's business affairs, are to hire and support a competent professional as superintendent, defend the schools against public criticism, and persuade the people to open their pocketbooks. . . .

The professionals consist of three groups. Numerically the largest, and politically today the least significant, are the school teachers. A hundred years ago, school teaching, in contrast to university teaching, law, medicine, and the ministry, was a vocation rather than a profession. A prime purpose of the National Education Association, originated in 1857, was to raise it to a professional status. By a kind of bootstrap operation, this was largely achieved, though it took eighty years to do it. The early normal schools, essentially vocational training institutes, were supplemented by colleges and graduate schools of education; and states were moved to pass certification laws prescribing educational qualifications for teachers. The second professional group is composed of the pedagogues' pedagogues—the faculties of teachers colleges and university departments of education. Their professional status was ready-made, but as the justification of their existence depended largely on the professionalization of school teaching itself, they naturally took a leading part in that process. They also were foremost in creating the third group, the professional school administrators. School administration, as a profession, is a latecomer, but in terms of understanding the politics of the public schools it is perhaps the most important of all. School administration is a decidedly hierarchical and disciplined business and the top administrator, the local school superintendent, holds

[1]James B. Conant, *The American High School Today* (New York, 1959), p. 43.

the key position in each school district. Indeed, there seems to be professional agreement that the most significant duty of the people's representatives on the local school board is the selection of the superintendent.

The thoroughly defensible assumption that school teaching and school administration are the specialized tasks of persons with professional training and status leads inevitably to a professional distrust of lay interference. This distrust has been accentuated by the frequency with which lay demands have conflicted with the convictions of the educators, seeming to them to be destructive of the very purposes of education. Even well meant lay suggestions that more emphasis should be placed on the "three r's" have caused flutterings of alarm, for too often such criticisms have been the softening-up forerunners of assaults on the freedom of the teachers and so on the whole professional concept. Such assaults have caused one writer to describe the politics of public education as "ideological politics," otherwise a comparative rarity on the American scene.[2]

But are we permitted to speak of the "politics" of education? To many educators the word seems abhorrent: not even the admonitions of George S. Counts[3] can overcome their aversion to it. Again, this is understandable. Whole school systems have been blighted by the intrusion of certain aspects of politics, especially the use of patronage in appointments and contracts in apparent disregard of the need to give children the best possible education. Yet because school districts are governmental units and the voters have ultimate responsibility, school board members and school superintendents are engaged in political activity whether they like it or not. The standard professional terminology for this—a semantic triumph—is "community relations"; a successful superintendent, particularly, must be skilled in community relations. Why not say frankly that he must be a good politician?

Surely it is high time to stop being frightened by a word. Politics includes the making of governmental decisions, and the effort or struggle to gain or keep the power to make those decisions. Public schools are part of government. They are political entities. They are a fit subject for study by political scientists.

Yet neither educators nor political scientists have frequently engaged in the examination of public education from this angle. Educators have shied away not only from the word "politics" but from political scientists as well. (The terminology of social scientists who deal with "power structures" and "communications" they find more acceptable.) Their suspicion of political science stems in part from the writings

---

[2]Robert C. Wood, *Suburbia* (Boston, 1958).

[3]"The profession should seek power and then try to use that power fully and wisely and in the interests of the great masses of the people." George S. Counts, *Dare the Schools Build a New Social Order?* (New York, 1932), p. 29.

of some public administration professors who have occasionally urged that school systems, being part of local government, should be merged with multi-purpose local units—namely cities and towns—thus losing their "independent" status; and at the state level, that a department of education, like other departments, should be headed by an appointee of the governor rather than a quasi-independent board. These proposals are in direct conflict with the passionate convictions of professional educators, and so have given political science a bad name in the teaching profession.

As for the political scientists, the running of the public schools —except for national defense the most extensive and expensive governmental activity in this country—has seldom seemed worth more than a chapter or two in a text on state and local government. There are honorable exceptions, but they are very few indeed. The taboo has worked both ways, almost as if by tacit agreement: if politics has been anathema to educators, the governing of the public schools has seemed inconsequential to political scientists. . . .

II

The most significant subjects for decision by whoever runs the public schools concern the curriculum, the facilities, the units and organization of government, and personnel; and partly shaping them all is the omnipresent issue of finance.

Since World War II a war of words over the *curriculum* has been waged at white heat. Because their professionalism seems to lack full public acceptance and because any attack may make it harder to raise the money needed for good schooling, educators tend to object vehemently to most lay criticism. The laity, of course, embraces most of us, including school board members and university professors (of everything but Education), so the inference might seem to be that no one but a professional educator has any business criticizing the methods or ideas of professional educators. This was a typical answer to the vigorous attack on the curriculum mounted by Arthur E. Bestor, professor of history at the University of Illinois. However, by stepping carefully even an outsider may win a hearing. Constructive suggestions so phrased as to avoid sensitive toes, especially if preceded by well-publicized and protracted study, are treated with respect: witness the generally deferential reception of the report of James B. Conant, who is just as much a "layman" as Bestor. Any citizen who wants to influence the conduct of the schools might be well advised to follow Conant's example. And the person seeking to portray the political process in relation to education must also resist the temptation to be drawn into the controversy over "progressive education," "life adjustment," whether Johnny can read and if not why not, and the curriculum generally. His task is not to say what should be in the curriculum, but how, by whom, and through whose influence that decision is or might be made.

It is hard to read professional pronouncements on this subject without concluding that in professional eyes, the curriculum is essentially the school superintendent's business. To be sure, a committee of the American Association of School Administrators, in a report addressed to school board members, did say that the school board had "general responsibility" for the curriculum. The emphasis, however, seemed to be on the word "general," as was indicated by the committee's statement that "Curriculum planning and development is a highly technical task which requires special training. . . . Board members do not have and cannot be expected to have the technical competence to pass on the work of expert teachers in this field. . . . Nor can the board pass upon specific textbooks."[4] Conant likewise assumes that "the school board will leave the development of the curriculum to the administrative officers and the teaching staff but will be kept informed of all developments."[5] Even this, however, leaves some doubt about the school board's role, or lack of it. Is curriculum "development" something different from educational "policy," and if so, what is the line that separates them? . . .

Although recent controversies give the impression that the professionals have made the curriculum "progressive" (whatever that may mean) and want the school boards to keep hands off, there are indications that in many districts the shoe is on the other foot. Through conviction, or perhaps through ignorance and indifference, school boards have often adhered to curricula which the superintendents consider sadly out of date. Neal Gross quotes as typical of a sizeable minority view among Massachusetts superintendents the following complaints: "The selectmen and the town finance committee take the attitude, 'What was good enough for me ought to be good enough for them (the children).' And so do some of my school committee members. How can you run a modern educational program with . . . a classical curriculum when 80% of the kids don't go on to college?"[6] And again: "My committee is primarily interested in keeping costs down. They don't want to discuss or even consider the need to revise the curriculum."[7] The burden is on those who want change: if the Bestors feel frustrated by the insistence on professional domination of curriculum-making, the professionals feel blocked by lay conservatism or apathy.

The question of whether board or superintendent should dominate is important, but nowhere near as significant as what the curriculum contains. The question is reminiscent of the excitement about balanc-

---

[4]*School Boards in Action*, (Washington, D.C.: American Association of School Administrators, 1946), p. 178. . . .

[5]Conant, *op. cit.*, p. 43.

[6]Neal Gross, *Who Runs Our Schools?* (New York, 1958), p. 10.

[7]*Ibid.*, p. 13.

ing the Federal budget before World War II. Many people in the 1930s were convinced that to save the country expenditures must be drastically cut—which meant, of course, the reduction or elimination of the relief programs that gave work and wages to millions of otherwise unemployed men and women. Came the war in Europe, and by 1940 many of these same economizers, fervently pro-British and anti-Hitler, enthusiastically favored vast increases in Federal expenditures for defense and aid to Britain. Whether the budget should be balanced was less crucial than what the money was spent for. In the same way, while a certain form of board-superintendent division of authority may, like budget-balancing, seem generally sound, the real question is what kind of school it produces. The basic problem, therefore, is not one of "school administration"; it is the political issue of what is to be taught or read in our schools. We may wish to leave this decision to the experts; we may wish to make it ourselves. This issue is decided chiefly at the local level, and to a lesser extent in the state capitols by legislatures and state education departments. For the last forty years it has also been affected by national legislation granting federal aid for vocational education.

The decisions concerning *facilities*—chiefly school buildings—are made very largely in the districts, with a comparatively high degree of popular participation. The people get engaged in school-building politics more than in any other phase of public school politics, for two reasons. First, a building program requires a major capital outlay, and in nearly all states the bond issues which such capital outlays necessitate are by law subject to popular approval. Second, buildings being tangible and the distance a child must walk or ride to school being measurable, most people feel more qualified to have opinions about the need, nature and location of the schoolhouse than about what goes on inside it.

Closely allied with the location and adequacy of buildings is the issue of *district organization*. Like the former, it is profoundly affected by finance: the Conant report, for instance, calls for reorganization of districts to eliminate small high schools because a really good small high school is, Conant believes, prohibitively expensive.[8] On the other hand, the problems of location cause Alvin Eurich of the Fund for the Advancement of Education to criticize this recommendation: in sparsely populated areas, a large high school would be too far from many children's homes.[9] The decisions on district size are sometimes made directly by state legislatures, or by state departments of education, but more often by the voters in the districts affected. The local voters' capacity to consolidate districts is, however, profoundly affected

[8]Conant, *op. cit.*, p. 37.
[9]*New York Times*, February 1959. Evidently, the question depends in part on how much the district is willing to pay for bus service.

by the kind of statutes enacted by the legislature. The internal organization of a district—its system of government, whether its board shall be elected or appointed, its budgetary connection with the municipality—is ordinarily decided at the state level, though some states permit a certain amount of local option.

Personnel decisions include one which, in most districts, is made directly by the people—the election of school board members. Here is politics at its plainest, despite the non-partisan ballot that prevails in the majority of such elections, yet few efforts have been made to analyze the nature of school board campaigns and patterns of voting behavior therein. The educators and such useful publicists for education as the National Citizens Council for Better Schools rightly emphasize the importance of choosing "good" school boards, but their hortatory efforts are seldom buttressed by information as to what factors actually decide school board elections. The next significant personnel decision is the selection of a superintendent by the school board. He is often the key figure (as the professionals wish him to be) on the local educational scene. Indeed, his selection or retention sometimes is the central issue in school board elections; the voters thus occasionally affect the choice directly, and their potential ability to do so influences board action. Also for local decision is the matter of appointment, retention, and promotion of the teachers. Here direct, official popular intervention via the ballot box is rare indeed, although it has happened, and although occasionally a school board election has revolved around the retention of a school principal or teacher rather than a superintendent. In the main the decisions, formally made by the board, are based on the superintendent's recommendations. Chiefly on the superintendent, therefore, beat the informal pressures for appointment, transfer, or removal of a teacher, often in an emotional context arising naturally out of the complex psychology of the teacher-parent relationship.

While these personnel decisions are made locally, in most districts they are constrained by state legislation, particularly laws prescribing minimum qualifications of superintendents, principals, and teachers, and governing the conditions of promotion and discharge. At the state capitols, more than anywhere else, the educators have fought and largely won their fight for professional status. Tenure laws are, in the main, protections against "politics," but a tenure system may enhance status as well as security. More important, as a recognition of professionalism, are the certification statutes. To be sure, state occupational licensing laws hardly confer professional status, in the traditional sense, on every occupation licensed, such as those of elevator operator or hairdresser. In the case of teachers, however, they have been accompanied—indeed, have often been preceded—by state provisions for substantial formal training. This gives an additional justification for the claim of professionalism, especially as certification requirements, which obviously influence teachers college programs, may also be to some extent geared to the courses offered by the teachers colleges. The establishment of teachers colleges, furthermore, has created an institutional pressure center which some critics claim has a dominant effect on state and local curriculum decisions and on the selection of superintendents.

Schools cannot be built, equipped, or staffed without money. The problems of *financing* are inherent in virtually all the issues just discussed. Indeed, they are so omnipresent and so grim that if we were required to give one general explanation of the behavior of professional educators, we might frame it in terms of a ceaseless search for funds. Here may well be the basic reason why educators react so emotionally to criticism: any adverse criticism may make it harder to raise money. When school board members are instructed to go out and "support the schools" in the community, it is not because the superintendents and teachers are thin-skinned or prefer praise to criticism. It is because schools, good or bad, cost money, which must be provided by vote of the people or of their elected representatives on the school board, in the city or county government, and in the state legislature. At each level, the issue of school finance is a focal point of several obvious and broad conflicts of interest. The desire for low taxes clashes with the wish for good schools, in a struggle which is waged not only in the community by organized groups but within the mind of the thoughtful householder. A conflict between the owners of real property, on the one hand, and retailers and consumers on the other becomes increasingly important as proposals are made to shift the growing burden from the real property tax to the sales tax. The interests of those who live in wealthy districts with low taxes and good schools clash with the need to provide good schooling in less fortunate districts, through consolidation or equalization formulae. The local taxpayer wants relief which can be provided by state or federal aid, yet fears such aid because it might open the door to state or federal control: he who pays the piper calls the tune. The professionals are apparently less fearful of dictation from distant seats of power,[10] perhaps because what they really distrust is dictation from any lay source, including the local citizenry: the people should pay for the schools but the professional educators should run them.

Financial decisions traditionally have centered in the districts. Studies have consistently shown that citizens who are interested in the substance of education and have some knowledge of what the schools are doing tend to support the educators' demands for money more than do the less informed voters: hence the great emphasis, in the train-

[10]For many years the National Education Association has led the fight for federal aid.

ing of the superintendents, on public relations and "communications." But the ways in which decisions are made are fixed by state laws, and often profoundly affect the decisions themselves. Thus in one state a school board may finally approve a budget which increases the property tax rate; in another the tax increase must be approved by the voters; in a third, the budget itself is the subject of a popular referendum. Bond issues may be voted by simple majorities in some states but require a two-thirds approval in others. The states, then, play a vital role in the local settlement of financial issues. They also are playing a more direct part, for state funds provide now an estimated 39.7 per cent of all money spent for public schools.[11] What new part, if any, the federal government will play remains a matter of conjecture. Today about 3.5 per cent of all school funds spent by school districts comes from federal sources. . . .

. . . The [education] profession is certainly not intellectually monolithic, as the debates and disagreements in journals and conventions show; but it may well be growing more unified in its devotion to agreed-upon professional standards and goals.

If this is so, what is the future for the "diversity" which justifies unimpaired local control? If local control in the most fundamental matters — curriculum and teaching — is largely in professional hands, are there even now fewer significant differences between districts than was formerly the case? Granted that state requirements differ, that local interests may differentiate programs in rural districts from those in urban districts, and that the curricula and teaching in particular schools or districts take account of the varying backgrounds and objectives of the student population; still, the classifications are broad. In thousands of districts the educational needs are similar. Conant may disclaim any intention to provide a blueprint, but his recommendations are not intended as the basis for a single district's experimentation: they are aimed at innumerable American high schools. And, significantly, the professional reaction to the Conant report has included little, if any, objection to the basic curricular uniformity which it implies. Perhaps, then, at least within broad urban-rural or socio-economic categories, local diversity is or will soon be significant only with respect to those matters where professional domination is weakest: school buildings (including site selection), transportation of pupils, and finance. Decisions as to the last, assuming any real public desire for improved schooling, will continue gradually to move out of local hands and into the state legislatures. Certainly the extent and nature of inter-district diversity in basic educational processes need prompt analysis. If, indeed, they are

[11]*Estimate of School Statistics, 1958–1959* (Washington, D.C.: National Education Association, 1958), p. 15; in southern states the percentage runs much higher, up to 75 or more.

minimal, then the lay proponents of complete local control must be prepared to defend their position in terms of their convenience and their pocketbooks rather than their concern for educational content.

This kind of inquiry seems best suited for specialists in education, checked by "lay" scholars from other disciplines who are free from any charge of bias. The latter might or might not include political scientists. Many of the other questions raised in this paper, dealing directly with governmental and political processes, more immediately challenge students of government and politics. They point to the need for research in the following areas:

(1) At the local level, (a) structural analysis, in terms of familiar public administration concepts, the forms of school district organization being relatively few in number and providing a manageable field of comparative study; (b) behavioral analysis, especially of the impact of professional and lay leadership and group pressures on the decision-making process—such analysis can provide helpful insights even though, as the writer believes, school districts are too numerous and too disparate for safe generalization in this field; and (c) the voters' responses in bond issue or consolidation referenda, under various but comparable conditions imposed by state law.

(2) At the state level, studies of (a) the organization and financial administration of the state's educational activities; and (b) the pressures on the legislatures and their response to those pressures. The view indicated in this paper is that state action, especially in the legislatures, is now significant and will soon have a crucial impact on educational development, and that useful findings can result from a comparative study of state influence, management or control.

(3) At the federal level . . . the history of school legislation since World War II needs searching analysis, down to and including the National Defense Education Act of 1958, which may point a way around the impediments to earlier federal aid bills but which raises anew the question of federal control.

Three other fields of study are also relevant to political science. One involves comparison with countries having unitary governments, central fiscal control, and many local school districts where curricular innovation may or may not be possible. Another, which should not be limited to the segregation issue, concerns the impact of the judiciary on the school systems: the questions here involve both federal and state courts, the conditions, values, or pressures which affect their decisions, and the ways in which the schools and their government have been influenced by those decisions. Finally, the speculative political scientist may find fruitful a field heretofore ploughed chiefly by professional educators: namely, the relationship of the school curriculum (and the interests and training of the teachers) to the values of American political society. Here the political philosophers, perhaps bemused by the mysteries of "education" or thwarted by the old taboos, have been silent. The leadership was taken by articulate professional educators who propounded social and political goals for the schools, and sometimes by lay pressure groups which stressed conformity to prevailing economic norms and the instillation of national and local patriotism.

In all such studies, the realization that public policy in education is the product of discernible professional-lay interaction (sometimes conflict) at different governmental levels, may serve as a unifying conception. The conception itself needs to be tested by acute political analysis. If it is valid, it can lead to the identification of the real sources of power and the main roadblocks to progress, however defined—and so to new concepts of organization and more productive leadership, professional or lay or both.

STATE EDUCATIONAL AND POLITICAL OFFICIALDOM

STEPHEN K. BAILEY, RICHARD T. FROST, PAUL E. MARSH, AND ROBERT C. WOOD

If the scribblers and consultants have the crucial role in designing new state aid programs [for education] and suggesting strategies for their legislative enactment, they cannot go it alone. They need contact and support from individuals and groups possessing greater political influence than academics and salesmen can muster. Typically, their first couplings are made with officials within the formal structure of those parts of state governments and of state political systems most intimately concerned with educational policy. In short, as proponents for state aid push forward, they soon touch base with state educational agencies.

. . . [I]n canvassing the behavior of these organizations, the similarities are impressive. But . . . differences in structure and program, with important implications for our understanding of educational policy-making at the state level in the northeastern part of the United States, need to be highlighted.

As to gross similarities, a glance at the basic structure of government in the eight states in the Northeast reveals substantial uniformities —in some cases, virtual identities. These patterns spring from a common constitutional heritage dating back to revolutionary times and from a common administrative heritage of more recent origin.

Each state of course has a governor. Each state has a bicameral legislature. Each state relates governor and legislature ambiguously to formal instruments of educational supervision: boards, commissioners, and departments of education. In each of the states there exists a board of education, although not always called by that title.

From *Schoolmen and Politics: A Study of State Aid to Education in the Northeast* by Stephen K. Bailey, Richard T. Frost, Paul E. Marsh, and Robert C. Wood (Syracuse: Syracuse University Press, 1962), pp. 26–35.

State School Boards

State school boards vary in size from thirteen in New York to seven in New Hampshire, Vermont, and Rhode Island. In all states except New York members are appointed by the governor, either with or without some form of legislative consent. In New York State alone, members of the Board of Regents are elected by the legislature.

Although the eight states vary widely in terms of office for board members (from five years in Vermont to thirteen years in New York), these terms uniformly extend beyond the terms of any one governor or legislator, and, perhaps more important, members are elected in every state for overlapping terms.

There is considerable variation in the formal responsibilities of state boards of education in the Northeast. In terms of the range and monolithic character of its operations, the Board of Regents of the State of New York is unique. The New York Board enjoys independent executive, legislative, and judicial power of such scope as to bring into question its consonance with American constitutional principles of separation of powers and checks and balances.

At the other extreme is the complicated maze of educational administration in the state of Massachusetts in which the Board of Education must compose itself into three overlapping structures in order to do legal business covering collegiate and vocational as well as elementary and secondary education. In addition, the State Board must live with autonomous units such as a School Buildings Assistance Commission, a Youth Services Board, a Board of Educational Assistance, and trustees of the Lowell Institute of Technology which have their own separate jurisdictions. Beyond this, two other technical institutes in Massachusetts have their own boards.

Other state boards of education fall somewhere between the administrative patterns of New York and Massachusetts.

But whatever the scope of legal power and concern, each state board, by constitutional and statutory provision, has a general mandate to encourage and supervise public education within the confines of the state, and to make recommendations to the governor and the legislature for the improvement of education. However formal and nominal the powers of state boards of education may be in reality, their place in the chain of legal authority makes them significant factors in the initiation and execution of state educational policy.

The state board's political role must be precisely understood, however. They are less independent forces in their own right than sympathetic responders to the executive and administrative officials they oversee. Rhode Island is an extreme case in point. A recent governor and a board member have both complained that the board "rubber-stamps" departmental action, and is a passive agent in school policy-making. The rule is that strong commissioners of education, exercising forceful professional leadership, have a ready sounding-board and supporting officialdom in their state boards.

These observations suggest that as the policy-making — or, at least, policy-sanctioning — state agency for schools, boards are best understood as a statutory link between government and schools. Any official position taken by the commissioner must carry the explicit or implicit stamp of his board's approval. After all, in law the commissioner is the board's executive secretary, acting on its behalf and at its discretion. While practice may construe the relationship differently, statutory formalities are not to be winked at.

But the basic fact is that the visibility of state boards of education as bodies politic is generally low. For the most part they act as sounding-boards for educational ideas and programs rather than as active partic-ipants in the political process of consent-building. Exceptions exist. In New Hampshire, the Board chairman has recently been so bold as to ask the legislature for 30 per cent more money for state aid, a fruit-less, if not quixotic, gesture. In Connecticut, many State Board members have testified before legislative committees and have spoken tirelessly before civic and educational groups. But, in Vermont, contrarily, public opposition by the State Board to a new aid formula helped to kill whatever slight hopes it had of passage. Most typically, board mem-bers can be expected to record on cue their support of the commis-sioner's program when it comes up for discussion before legislative committees. Members of state boards in the Northeast do not sit in the councils of the mighty in school politics.

Commissioners and Departments

The key educational official in each state is called commissioner. Except in New Jersey, the commissioner is appointed by the board. In New Jersey he is the direct appointee of the governor. A tradition of pro-fessionalism frequently attaches to this office in contrast to the lay back-grounds of state board members. In New Hampshire, for example, strong professional administrators — frequently from out of state — have characterized departmental leadership throughout most of this century. In the area as a whole, Allen, Morrison, Butterfield, Engleman, Fuller, Hill, Buley, McCaffrey, Ritch are names known as educators first, with or without the additional status of native sons which some of them enjoyed.

The commissioner in turn supervises the state department of edu-cation, which carries out the various functions which law and adminis-trative rulings mandate. Although departments of education in the

Northeast vary substantially in size, they all perform certain core functions. A comparison of organization charts of the various departments
reveals a recurring list of divisional and bureau titles: Instruction,
Vocational Education, Administrative Services, Teacher Certification,
Special Education, Higher Education, Finance, and Planning and
Research. The peculiar nomenclature in each state reveals the historical
development of legislation and of administrative reorganizations.
These, in turn, have often reflected the views and recommendations
of professional educators from university schools of education, and
of professional associations.

Perhaps of particular importance to this study is the fact that in
each state department of education there are at least a few individuals,
with varying titles and under varying administrative units, who have as
their special responsibility research, planning, and administration in
the general field of state financial aid to local school districts. It should
be noted, also, that there can be found in each state department one or
more key individuals (sometimes the commissioner, sometimes the
deputy commissioner, sometimes the departmental attorney, sometimes
others) who have as one of their special responsibilities the cultivation
of strategic and tactical relationships with the governor (and his budgetary staff) and with key legislative leaders concerned with matters of
educational finance policy. It is this political role of the department,
often working through the state board, as in New Hampshire and
Rhode Island, sometimes moving through other channels as in New
York, Connecticut, and New Jersey, which is the focus of attention
here.

This "political" orientation of the educational agencies is, of course,
not surprising. In spite of the relative independence of board, commissioner, and department of education in each state, there are scores
of ways in which the major constitutional instrumentalities of the state
impinge upon the activities of the state education agencies. This is most
particularly true in the field of educational finance. The amount that
a state spends on education is ultimately determined not by the recommendations of the education agencies, but by political decisions taken
at the level of the governor and the state legislature. So, although
activities of the key officials in the state education agency may be highly
relevant to the success of educational finance policies, the final, deter-
minative action is legislative and gubernatorial.

The Political Officialdom

This need for school agencies to engage in a broader arena than their
legally independent status would suggest indicates a second linkage

made among pro-school interests and introduces another set of actors: political officialdom or, more precisely, governors and legislators. Here the political flavor of the schoolmen becomes even more apparent. Whatever their role as chiefs of state, governors are partisan political figures. However harmonious legislative bodies may be, their capacity to do business and to insure even a modicum of political responsibility is heavily dependent upon the partisan political structure of the state and of the partisan leadership structure in the two houses of the state legislature. This is true even in the states of northern New England in which one-party domination is a long-standing item of state political life.

The cardinal political fact in the region is that partisan political machinery has been fused with a constitutional system of representation which has given inordinate power to rural, small-town, suburban and overwhelmingly Republican forces in parts of every state legislature save two. This fact produces special tensions in the states of Connecticut, New York, and New Jersey whose populations are either evenly balanced between the two major parties, or in which a largely big city, Democratic popular majority feels itself thwarted by the over-representation of suburban, small town, and rural Republican interests in at least one branch of the assembly.

These tensions are heightened by the frequent existence of Democratic governors in these states. These governors, elected of course at large, must somehow develop public policies in cooperation with politically divided or hostile legislatures. . . . [T]he politics of educational finance in the Northeast has frequently centered in the executive-legislative struggles of split partisan majorities. This drama is usually personalized in the relationships between key legislative leaders (majority and minority leaders in the upper houses; the speaker and floor leaders in lower houses; and strategically placed committee chairmen in both houses) on the one hand, and the governor and his party stalwarts on the other. Often, the struggle is quite as apparent when the governor and the legislative leaders are of the same party: a tribute to the differences in constituencies and historical habits between the two major branches, as well as to intra-party factionalism which so often builds around competing, strong personalities.

Out of this maelstrom of conflicting partisan and institutional interests, schoolmen nonetheless must co-opt some influential spokesman for their goals. This they do in the Northeast in several ways: working on party leaders to have their aims recognized in party platforms, joining hands occasionally with other interest groups, doing staff work for legislative and executive branches alike. But most typically, the procedure has been to persuade governors and key legislators to espouse their cause.

It would distort reality to suggest that leading politicians are always among the staunchest friends the schoolmen have. But over and over again our studies have shown the energizing influence of governors and the power and importance of key legislators. Furthermore, political parties in states where such organizations count have taken important stands on educational policy. Even in those cases where partisan reaction has been derivative, one must assign credit to political friends of schoolmen who have given priority to education's cause.

As far as gubernatorial support is concerned, a long list of the names of recent chief executives can be enscribed on the schoolmen's honor roll: in Connecticut, Chester Bowles; in Rhode Island, Dennis Roberts; Muskie for Maine; Bradford in Massachusetts; Smith, Harriman, and Rockefeller in New York. Each in his own way has provided assistance and leadership on critical occasions.

Cementing executive and legislative — and sometimes party — relations has been the role of legislative leadership. Again, a survey of the eight states results in a long list of names. Walter Mahoney and Joseph Carlino, majority leader and speaker in New York, are usually counted as schoolmen's friends for reasons at least in part explicable by their school-oriented suburban constituencies. E. O. Smith for Connecticut, Ralph Mahar in Massachusetts, Rhode Island's Florence Murray — the role can be extended for all states and in depth to include at least three or four dedicated friends of education. . . .

Special Commissions

Governors, legislators, party leaders, do not always move, of course, in ways the schoolmen desire and some of their acts of apparent friendship turn out to be ambiguous. A case in point is the use of special commissions as a favorite device for politicians to get themselves off the hook. On inspection, responsible decisions can be found to be politically unpalatable or perhaps enticing political movements may turn out to have irresponsible implications. In instances like these, the study commission has real virtue even if its friendship to schools may be not immediately apparent. The virtue lies both in delaying a commitment and in involving more people — the members of the commission — in reaching a solution. The ambiguity lies in the nature of commission recommendations which, almost by definition, must bridge some political impasse. Study groups may be set up as conscious "depressants"; others have been conservatively weighted so that strong recommendations for increases in state aid will get somewhere but at the same time will free the governor or the legislature from sole responsibility. School politics by study committee has flourished in just those northeastern states where forces at loggerheads with each other had to find common ground on which to proceed. New Jersey's strongly partisan politics, for instance, beset by keen urban-rural, low tax-high expectation, state-local splits, has for years leaned heavily on research commissions as vehicles for educational decision-making. But in whatever state, if their findings are not always all the schoolmen might hope for, at least they do open ways around political roadblocks.

Although most of the northeastern states since World War II have established special committees or commissions on school finance which would illuminate the above generalizations, a typical example has been the so-called Diefendorf Committee, which wound up its affairs early in 1962 in New York State.

Called a Joint Legislative Committee on School Financing, the committee has been popularly identified with its chairman, Charles H. Diefendorf, a Buffalo banker. The committee was established in 1960 in the full knowledge of Governor Rockefeller and his Republican legislative leaders that demands for increased state aid would continue to be insistent and that a special committee might well cushion the political impact of major increases in state aid.

The Diefendorf Committee issued a staff report on December 28, 1961. The committee itself modified the report in the direction of big city demands and issued a final statement on February 14, 1962.

Legislation based upon the Diefendorf recommendations was passed unanimously in the Assembly on March 30, 1962, but with substantial modifications. From the point of view of this essay, the most important modifications involved a substantial increase in state aid over the Diefendorf Committee's best judgment. Perhaps no better indication exists of the power of the schoolmen in New York State than their ability to convince the Governor and their legislative leaders of the inadequacy of the Diefendorf proposals. But it may also be stated that the existence of the Diefendorf proposals helped to establish an ideological benchmark which gave to the political leadership of the state a bargaining weapon with which to counter even greater demands by the schoolmen.

In states where schoolmen have been weak, one of course can find examples in which the reports of special committees or commissions have been filed away as too radical. But the classic use of the special commission seems to be to construct a conservative countervailing force to the schoolmen which will at the same time provide a rationale for prudent progress in aid to education.

An examination of the personnel appointed to special committees in the various states suggests the conservative bias of such committees. The dynamics of the special committee seems to start from this conservative bias but move toward a more liberal conclusion which is still short of the demands of the schoolmen but which at least presents an entering wedge for further legislative action.

Educational Associations and Their Satellites

The sum and substance of school politics is not restricted to inner groups of academics and professional politicians. A broader arena is inevitably involved, and a third set of actors perform the role of uniting the political actionists in government to the laborers in the educational vineyard and the public at large. The hard core of this group is the professional educational associations, and, to a much lesser extent, teachers unions, often reflective of the split personality of an occupation still unsure of its status. In these states, the more professionally oriented associations claim by far the majority of teachers as members, around 90 per cent. They have professional staffs, at least an executive director and a research "figure-gathering" person, and they are active at their respective state houses. Minimum salary laws, teacher retirement plans, teacher dismissal laws occupy their attention year in and year out. So do the publication of journals, the holding of conventions and workshops, and the organization of committees. The unions are limited to the large cities and are likely to be oriented more directly to such bread-and-butter issues as single salary schedules for elementary and secondary school teachers, higher pay without regard to differences in educational attainment, and better working conditions. Except in New York, the unions rarely figure at the state level except in a line of witnesses before a legislative committee. More typically they snap at the heels of associations, encouraging them to more hardboiled stands on benefits and privileges to keep the membership rolls intact. In New York, however, the United Federation of Teachers works intermittently with organizations like the United Parents Association and the Public Education Association in developing legislative policies, and it has a full-time legislative representative in Albany. On school aid legislation, although not a member of the Conference Board, the UFT backs Conference Board proposals while pressing for a larger diversion of grants to urban areas — especially to New York City where UFT has its strength.

Between the teacher groups and the state educational officials are the "hierarchical" associations of superintendents and sometimes principals. These may best be classified as administrative-oriented, for their concern is for education as a going enterprise. They keep the local school staffs together, meet payrolls, schedule school bus arrivals and departures, speak to parents, oversee school plants, keep school doors open, make budgets and present them to school boards. Unlike the teachers, they are sure they *are* professionals, on career ladders which, when duty, advancement, or better pay call, can take them out of their districts, out of the state or even the region to new positions. Theirs is the broader horizon and the greater sophistication. Their problems are not so much with routine concerns of teaching but with the management of schools and school systems. Their recognition of the importance of state action is clear and unwavering.

Following those for whom education is a livelihood come the more diverse assemblies of laymen who for one reason or another are drawn into school affairs. The distinction is perhaps a Weberian one: they live for the schools in their public lives and not off of them. True, in the case of school committeemen, the local popularly elected officials charged with the legal responsibility of determining local school policies and perhaps ultimately accountable for their quality, the line may be blurred. Especially in a large city, a position on the local school board is often a stepping stone to a grander political career. But local school board members do not belong to the professional in-group, and not infrequently they part company with the professionals on matters of salaries, the dismissal of superintendents, teacher qualifications, merit plans for promotions, and curriculum.

Less ambiguous are the roles of the Parent-Teacher Associations in these states, and the councils of citizens, variously named, organized for "school betterment." Here the distinction is the lack of any official responsibility for the conduct of school affairs and the absence of paid staffs or a permanent budget. As between the two groups, the difference is in orientation: the first are parents, discharging the age-old concern of how Johnny is actually faring, whether he can read, and whether the school product satisfies the customers. The second group, the citizen councils, are engaged in what they consider a "higher" calling. For them the schools are an agent in the national life, a prime source of strength in our world-wide battle with the Soviets, the underpinnings of our economic system, in short, a national resource. But both groups share the frustrations of amateurs. They are uncertain as to whether or not in the eyes of the Internal Revenue System they can lobby without losing a tax-exempt status. They are not clearly informed as to the details of how the school enterprise functions. They cannot commit major portions of their time and political capital to the cause and they are sporadic in their attention.

Supplementing these groups whose pronounced aim is better schooling are other civic associations which encompass education in their general agenda. School bills sometimes become the pets of organizations not exclusively concerned with education. While state Leagues of Women Voters from time to time back school legislation, they are not the only ones to do so. State branches of the American Association of University Women, Federations of Women's Clubs, Library Associations, Leagues for Mental Health have all been found involved with educational campaigns on occasion. Each with its own style—often social—and at its own best level—usually local—these groups and others like them can rouse considerable political influence for matters they care about. And professional politicians know it.

18. Allocation of Educational Opportunities

Equality of educational opportunity is a crucial norm in the democratic credo. Race, social class, and other ascriptive characteristics theoretically are irrelevant to a democratic education based on merit and achievement. Yet, unfortunately, equality of opportunity in the United States remains a norm, not a reality. The selections in this section illustrate the differences between the norm and its real world approximation.

Since Midge Decter wrote her article on integration in New York City schools, important structural changes have been made to help implement high-quality, integrated education in that city. Her analysis remains valid, however, because it illustrates the difficulties of realizing educational equality. As Miss Decter shows, these difficulties stem in large part from the rapid increase of nonwhite and culturally deprived populations in metropolitan areas. Today, social class background still plays an important role in determining educational opportunities, a fact that Natalie Rogoff validates in her interpretation of college mobility rates.

Important factors determining the degree of utilization of educational opportunities are the complex strands of student motivation and psychological sets affecting learning and perceptions of the formal educational apparatus. Edgar Friedenberg, in an impressionistic but sensitive piece, describes the motivations of school dropouts and points to institutional characteristics of education that repress youthful spirit and spontaneity in the lower classes.

THE NEGRO AND THE NEW YORK SCHOOLS

MIDGE DECTER

During the school year 1963–64, there were 1,038,516 children attending public school in New York City, of whom 264,616—or a fraction more than 25 per cent—were Negro, and 177,544—or about 17 per cent—were Puerto Rican. If one considers Puerto Rican children

Reprinted from *Commentary* (September 1964), by permission; copyright © 1964 by the American Jewish Committee.

to be non-white[1] — and despite the fact that the United States Census Bureau does not, there are good reasons for so considering them in discussing the New York City school system — then that school system must be judged to be suffering from an extremely high rate of racial segregation. Of the 581 elementary schools (kindergarten through sixth grade) operated by the Board of Education in 1963–64, 134 had a student body at least 90 per cent Negro and/or Puerto Rican, and 186 had a student body at least 90 per cent white; and of 136 junior high schools (seventh through ninth grades), 31 were at least 85 per cent Negro and/or Puerto Rican, while 39 were at least 85 per cent white. In other words, more than half of the elementary schools and half the junior high schools in New York can be said to be segregated.

Moreover, while the number of predominantly white schools has declined, both the number and proportion of the predominantly Negro/ Puerto Rican schools have been steadily growing. Seven years ago, in the school year 1957–58, only 64 out of 565 elementary schools, and only 16 out of 123 junior high schools, were at least 90 per cent Negro/ Puerto Rican (as compared with 134 and 31 respectively for 1963–64). Three factors are responsible for this deteriorating situation. First of all, there are now simply more Negro and Puerto Rican children in the schools — a number, in fact, considerably out of proportion to the percentage represented by these groups in the population of the city as a whole. Thus, while Negroes and Puerto Ricans combined constitute roughly 22 per cent of the city's population, they provide something over 42 per cent of the public-school population. This is not, as many people think, because they have a much higher birth rate than whites (it is only insignificantly higher), but because the majority of their recent immigrants have come to the city just as they were reaching the peak of their childbearing years. The second factor, of course, is the famous flight of the white middle class to the suburbs; and the third is the enormous increase in private- and parochial-school enrollment during the same period, which has further depleted the number of white children in the public schools. According to an informal survey conducted by the New York *World-Telegram & Sun*, in the area of Manhattan that extends on the West Side from Greenwich Village to 114th Street and on the East Side from 14th to 96th Streets alone, some 19,000 white children from kindergarten to the eighth grade are now enrolled in either private or parochial schools, as compared with 15,092 white children in the area's public schools.

These figures cannot wholly be interpreted as meaning that white

[1]Out of deference to the fact that children who are neither Negro nor Puerto Rican nevertheless represent a wide variety of racial backgrounds — e.g., Oriental, American Indian, etc. — they are usually referred to as "Others." However, both for convenience and clarity they will here be called "white" since that is what, in the particular context of school integration, they are indisputably taken to be.

parents have been pulling their children out of the public schools to keep them from contact with non-whites—although this has clearly been the motivation in some cases. The truth is that Manhattan, in the wake of a disastrous course of real-estate development and credit policy, has come more and more exclusively to be the home of the very rich on the one hand and the very poor on the other. The middle-class people currently missing from its precincts and from its schools did not so much flee to the suburbs as they were pushed out to them. In any event, from 1957 to 1963, almost exactly as many white children —about 54,000—disappeared from the public-school system as Negro children were added to it. And unless this process can be interrupted, it has been predicted that by 1980, from 70 to 75 per cent of the New York public-school population will be Negro and Puerto Rican.

Thus, more than a decade after the Supreme Court pronounced segregated education to be "inherently unequal," here is not only the largest and most cosmopolitan, but also most officially liberal city in America—with half its schools still segregated. It does not seem at all surprising, then, that this city's school system, and the Board of Education which administers it, should within the past three years have become the targets of an all-out drive for school integration. This drive has been conducted by a group of organizations, most of them Negro organizations, that have worked and responded enough in concert to merit being called a movement—the NAACP, CORE, the Urban League, Harlem Parents Workshop, Parents Workshop for Equality, and the Citywide Committee for Integrated Schools. Essentially what the integration movement has been demanding is that the Board of Education adopt some citywide program or combination of programs —involving the transfer of children out of their immediate neighbor-hoods and neighborhood schools—to achieve a significantly better racial balance in the schools, and that furthermore, the Board, as a mark of the seriousness of its intentions, set a more or less precise timetable for doing so. The operative word here is "citywide," for it is felt, and no doubt rightly, that any tendency by the Board to concentrate on specific problems of redistribution from district to district must defeat the possibility of genuine integration: any real solution of a problem affecting as many as half the schools is bound to affect all the rest.

But if there was nothing surprising about the fact of the drive itself, what did at first seem surprising to many New Yorkers, and certainly to the Board of Education, were the bitterness, anger, and obduracy of the protests that attended the drive. Indeed, so bitter and angry did the representatives of the Negro community grow that by winter

and early spring of 1964 the school problem had succeeded in destroying, probably for years to come, whatever illusion of civic harmony
New York City still entertained. Each succeeding summer the Board has
prepared for the opening of school under an ever-darkening cloud of
threatened demonstrations, school strikes, and general administrative
upheaval. It has been publicly charged with everything from incompetence to outright malingering. Its offices have been "sat in" on, and
its officials denounced. And on February 3, 1964, in a stunning one-
day demonstration of force—organized by the Citywide Committee
for Integrated Schools and finally, if somewhat reluctantly, supported
by the rest of the movement—a quarter of a million children stayed
out of school.

Now, however reasonable the raw statistics of school segregation
make such an exertion of pressure appear to be, it is also the case that
the issue between the integrationists and the Board of Education has
never been one of principle. New York is after all not Little Rock; nor
is it, as the figures show, even Chicago, Detroit, or Philadelphia. The
truth is that the determination of New York's Negro community to
integrate the schools was a determination arrived at several years
after the Board's own. On December 23, 1954, seven months after the
Supreme Court's desegregation decision and in explicit response to
it, the New York City Board of Education unanimously affirmed its
commitment to a policy of integration. This resolution was the first
such statement of policy to be issued anywhere, and is to this day one
of the very few to have been issued entirely voluntarily.

In the years from 1955 to 1961 the Board accordingly instituted
several programs to improve the status and condition of the Negro
schoolchild—most of them related directly or indirectly to the eventual
promotion of integration. The two most directly related were the creation (in 1957) of a Central Zoning Unit—whose function was to rezone
existing schools, and to locate sites for new ones, with an eye to achieving maximum racial balance—and the institution (in 1961) of Open
Enrollment. Open Enrollment, which began on a rather limited scale
and was later considerably liberalized, enables children from schools
designated as overcrowded to transfer (transportation paid by the
city) to one of the schools designated as "underutilized." Under the
Central Zoning Unit, one hundred changes were made in district and
school zones from 1959 to 1963; and as of February 1964, some 16,000
Negro children had elected to participate in the Open Enrollment program, 10,000 of them at the elementary school level.

To be sure, these programs, as the figures so dismally reveal, have
failed even to scratch the surface. Nevertheless, they were set in motion
by the Board after no very great pressure—and they represent a goal
that integrationists in other Northern cities are willing even now to
conduct their own angry and bitter demonstrations to achieve. Why

then should the push to integrate the schools in New York have assumed the proportions of a struggle which can without exaggeration be characterized as "life-and-death"?

Part of the answer has to do with the striking reversal that took place in American Negro life in the 1960's, when the Northern urban Negro ceased pitying the Southern Negro and began instead to envy him his new-found vigor and dignity. The result was that some of the energies, all of the rhetoric, and, wherever they could be made to apply, the issues of the Southern battle for civil rights began to be imported into Northern cities. And the issue which proved most readily transportable was the issue of segregated schools. . . .

But possibly a more important contributing factor to the recent short temper of the school integration movement than the spreading mood of militancy has been the discovery of how very difficult a task it has taken upon itself in the City of New York. The difficulty begins with the concept of integration itself: is it a particular proportion of race to race that is to be achieved in each and every school; or is it some general over-all balance which must correspond to the balance of the population as a whole? While it is reasonable for integrationists to insist that the Board devise some comprehensive plan for the entire city, the fact is that New York is not really one city but five, separated, all but two of them, by bodies of water. And the ratio of whites to non-whites in the schools is by no means everywhere the same. In Manhattan, for instance, in 1963–64 there were about 76,000 Negro/Puerto Rican elementary-school pupils out of a total of about 99,000; in Brooklyn, 111,000 out of 223,000; in the Bronx, 66,000 out of 114,000; but in Queens, only 29,000 out of 130,000; and in Richmond, only 2,000 out of 20,000. In June of 1963, James E. Allen, Jr., State Commissioner of Education, who has been something of a penniless Dutch uncle to the integration movement, issued a memorandum in which he defined a racially balanced school as one having a student body no more than 50 per cent non-white. By Allen's definition Manhattan, unless it were to be miraculously lifted from its granite underpinnings and superimposed on the borough of Queens, could never even approach an integrated school system. If, however, integration were to be defined as the balance which reflects the over-all ratio of Negro and Puerto Rican children to white, the schools in Manhattan would have to be a little more than 75 per cent, and those of Staten Island 10 per cent, non-white in their racial compositions. The question of what is numerically meant by integration may seem somewhat pettifogging in a situation where so many children are to be found in unquestionably segregated schools. But it has nonetheless remained in the background to haunt the calculations of the movement, which has never officially given a clear answer, preferring to leave the matter of numbers negotiable.

The question, moreover, has remained if only because it has inevitably opened up an even more difficult one. The majority of New York's Negroes live in seven segregated enclaves, or "ghettos," as they have come to be called. In 1953, many schools were found to have been deliberately zoned to keep whites and Negroes apart, but it seems fairly certain that racially motivated gerrymandering has by now been done away with. This means that the problem of segregation is a problem of the seven Negro ghettos—and to desegregate the schools in those ghettos, either the schools must be moved out of them, or the children out of the schools, or both. But out to where? Extending beyond most of the ghettos are neighborhoods that are themselves in a state of sociological flux. Transferring children to, or building new schools for them in, these "fringe areas"—the simplest and most obvious step for the Central Zoning Unit to have taken—usually brings little or no improvement; the fringe-area schools become more and more heavily Negro, and the ghetto schools left behind, while relieved somewhat of overcrowding, remain as segregated as ever. One junior high school, for example, was opened only seven years ago in a fringe area in Brooklyn with a student body 80 per cent white and 20 per cent non-white, and by now the proportion has been reversed to 40 per cent white and 60 per cent non-white.

Given this difficulty, the next logical step would appear to be to by-pass fringe areas altogether and move ghetto children directly into all-white schools, which—because of the patterns of urban settlement—often means moving them a considerable distance. As for the ghetto schools themselves, in order to desegregate these, white children must be transferred in, again from a considerable distance, for the nearby fringe-area schools cannot afford to give up any of their already declining number of white students.

Apart from closing down all ghetto schools (an unimaginably expensive and, to ghetto residents, unpopular alternative), and apart from the long-range possibility of "educational parks"[2] there is one other immediate possibility: school pairings. School pairing—which was first used successfully in Princeton, New Jersey, and is therefore called the Princeton Plan—operates by combining a predominantly white school district and a predominantly Negro one and dividing the schools horizontally rather than vertically: that is, all the children from the two districts attend kindergarten through third grade in one building, and fourth grade through sixth in the other. This device has worked

---

[2]Not much is known about the "educational park," since it is still largely an idea in the minds of enthusiasts. Essentially, as I understand them, educational parks are visualized as huge central campuses containing several schools of all levels. All the children will converge on these campuses and there be integrated, rather than in individual neighborhood schools.

well—at least so far as actual physical integration is concerned—in a small town like Princeton and in a few others, among them the Greenburgh school district of White Plains, New York, where distance and travel are minimal and entail no particular inconvenience or peril. Since New York City does not, except in a few cases, offer the same convenience of neatly divided neighborhoods and contiguous segregated school districts, any widespread application of Princeton Planning would once again involve transporting large numbers of children over considerable distances.

And so with the passage of time, and its attendant escalation of greater failure and greater demand, it has become ever more apparent that there can be no effective school desegregation in at least four of the five boroughs of New York City without the mass cross-transportation of children—what is popularly called "busing." No other issue has so roused the public passions on both sides of the tangled school problem nor lent itself so readily to polemical manipulation as this issue of busing children out of their neighborhood schools. It is around busing that white opposition to the integration movement has been galvanized, and it is in regard to busing that integrationists have at times seemed ready to take a stand of no return. Neither Negroes nor whites wish their children to be bused; yet this understandable reluctance has been cited triumphantly by whites as a proof of the Negro masses' indifference to the education of their children, and by Negroes as a proof of the white community's opposition to integrated schools. . . .

If even as early as 1954—and *a fortiori* as late as 1964—the problem of integration had been merely one of creating a particular racial balance in all the schools, it would sooner or later have been brought to a political settlement through the usual American process of accommodating group interests that come into conflict. But the problem in New York City is not and never has been primarily one of achieving racial balance. Nor—as even those who make the most extreme political gestures on both sides know—is the struggle one in which victories can be won by strictly political means.

In essence, most white parents are desperate about the prospect of having their schools paired with predominantly Negro/Puerto Rican schools for exactly the same reason that the Negro community is desperate to do away with non-white schools—because they are bad schools. They are bad schools because they have failed, because overwhelming numbers of their students have failed. And in their failure these schools constitute a threat not only to the level and morale of all public education in New York City, but to the very structure of the common belief in democratic education. Even in terms of the coldest expediency, these schools involve the interest of all.

It is ordinarily not so easy to say what one means by a bad school: theorists, after all, have found sufficient material with which to debate this question for decades. In 1953, when a delegation headed by Professor Kenneth Clark met with the Board of Education to complain about the condition of the schools in the Negro ghettos, their complaints had largely to do with such things as antiquated and inadequate facilities, understaffing, overcrowding, and other manifestations of general neglect. By now, after the Board has devoted a great deal of attention and money to the ghetto schools, and replaced twenty-six of them, these conditions have measurably (though not completely) improved. And still the schools are bad. They are bad simply by virtue of the fact that large numbers of their students are permitted to reach high school without having become more than technically literate.

Harlem may not be absolutely typical of all the city's Negro ghettos, but there is little reason to suppose that its schools are much different from those of the others. There are twenty elementary schools and four junior high schools in Central Harlem. On an average, the record of academic achievement in these schools shows a marked inferiority in the attainment of grade level; and what is worse, the children suffer a progressive deterioration with the passage of years. In reading comprehension, for example, from 13.2 to 39.6 per cent of the pupils in third grade are below grade level, while from 10 to 36.7 per cent are above, but by the sixth grade, from *60.4* to *93.5* per cent score below grade level, while a maximum of only 26.7 per cent score above. The figures are much the same for word knowledge and arithmetic.

When a student completes junior high school, he may receive a diploma, a certificate, or nothing. A diploma means that he has passed four major subjects, three minors, and has a reading level of 7. A certificate means that he has passed two majors, two minors, and has a reading level of 6. If he is very much over-age, he may go on to high school with neither. Only about half the students leaving the four Central Harlem junior high schools receive diplomas. These children are then thrust into high school—there being nothing else for them to do. And in high school, if the attitude of the surrounding society has conceivably left the matter to any further clarification, they must finally and forever experience their intellectual, and with it social, inferiority. So they will drop out—into a society already despairing to know what to do with even its educated youth—or remain to suffer, languish, make trouble, or all three.

Thus, it is perfectly clear that under the present educational system, poor Negro children in New York City have been largely unable to master the most basic academic skills—and it is just as clear that this cannot be attributed to any innate or natural inferiority. But how, one might ask, will a sixth-grader who cannot read or properly use his own language be served by being transported into another school where there are many more children who can? One answer of the integrationists—based on the highly dubious belief that the public schools really know how to teach this boy, and have just been unwilling to do so—is that in a "better" school he will improve. Another answer is that if he attends school with white children, society will no longer allow him to be neglected as it has in the past. But the very existence of the integration movement has already insured against such neglect: whether or not the Board of Education ever succeeds in enforcing a massive program of integration, Negro education has attained a point of absolute priority in the New York's public concern. Indeed, several integration spokesmen themselves have repeatedly asserted, although with ironic intention, that the demand for integration has everywhere resulted in intensive new programs to improve Negro schools.

We are, then, still left with the question of whether integrated schools can do better by the many children who are being failed so badly by their segregated ghetto schools. But the question cannot be settled without determining the causes of that failure. Integrationists tell us that the ghetto child's inability to learn is related to the fact that he has middle-class white teachers who, out of indifference or hostility, begin with low expectations of his ability which in turn give him low expectations for himself. Teachers or representatives of teachers, on the other hand, tell us that the school cannot begin to exert a counterforce against his chaotic family life, the indifference of his parents to his achievement, or the inimical values of his peer group. On both sides of the argument, the children themselves seem to be forgotten, abstracted into all but oblivion by polemic and rhetoric.

No one who has spent any time in an ordinary classroom in an ordinary slum school can have failed to see that only a rare teacher can cope sympathetically with children whose lives or behavior or even language are alien to her. (It is, after all, even a rare teacher who can cope imaginatively with bright children, or with physically restless ones.) Slum schools undoubtedly have their quota of rare teachers, but they have not—though the Board of Education is taking steps to remedy this—had anything like a normal quota of experienced ones: the average level of experience for teachers in Harlem is three years, as compared to an average for the city as a whole of seven years. How important experience is, especially to the qualities of sympathy and imaginativeness, one cannot know: teaching is a tiring profession. But the high degree of turnover among teachers in Harlem schools suggests a low degree of ambition for dealing with special problems.

And the special problems are very real indeed. Many Negro children have no fathers, being either illegitimate or members of families deserted by the husband. A huge number of them have working mothers. They live in desperately crowded households in which only a minimal amount of attention can be allotted to them. They play in streets where dirt, violence, petty criminality, and the widespread use of narcotics are apt to be all around them. Since kindergarten attendance is not mandatory, many of them arrive in school at the age of six having had none of that educational experience—toys, books, trips —that is built into the very foundations of middle-class infancy. If they are reasonably healthy and remain reasonably untroublesome within their own homes, little more is demanded of them. . . .

Somewhere there must be a key for the translation of what the Negro ghetto child sees and knows into what he can learn anew. Paul Goodman, for instance, would argue that the key is to be found in the streets of the city in which he lives. Perhaps it is. Perhaps it is even to be found in his own anxiety and bewilderment. "To argue that no classroom can be good without a white child in it," says the introduction to the report finally prepared by Commissioner Allen's office, "is inaccurate and cruel." It is probably still more cruel to fantasy that public education as it is now constituted—in any school—can give the "culturally deprived" Negro child what he needs to bring hope into his life.

Yet that is precisely what democratic public education must do —or lose its *raison d'être*. The question of the function of the public school has been somewhat distorted and confused, particularly in the big cities, by the peculiar history of modern American society. Because of the arrival and subsequent acculturation of immigrant group after immigrant group, the public school has come to be regarded as the instrument *par excellence* for Americanization: from which it has been thought to follow that the public school is the main agency for creating new members of the middle class. Yet while it has indeed taught successive waves of immigrants the language and official manners of the country, there is no evidence that the public school has ever succeeded in making anyone middle-class who was not already quite intensely involved in making himself so. There are no more immigrants to Americanize, except for the Puerto Ricans, who show every sign of going the way of their predecessors—more slowly perhaps, in a society no longer so open. The Negro challenge to the schools is a different, more primal one, transcending the accidents of a particular history and going straight to the heart of the original belief in mass education. This belief is based on the idea—to put it rather crudely—that innate talent and value are distributed among the rich and the poor in about equal proportions. The rich have always managed to educate themselves—and, of course, to provide some comfortable alternative for the ineducable among them. American society committed itself to undertaking this obligation to the poor. Now, as a result of the Northern metropolitan struggle for school integration, American society is being forced to confront that commitment directly.

This, in effect, was the message sent to the New York City Board of Education on May 12, 1964, when the State Education Commissioner's Advisory Committee on Human Relations and Community Tensions submitted the evaluation the Board had requested in February. The report has come to be known as the Allen Plan, and is an exciting document, rather more for its implications than its practical possibilities. The integrationists were certainly excited by it and instantly joined together, after months of disunity, to support it, even though it very flatly states that: "Total desegregation of all schools . . . is simply not attainable in the foreseeable future and neither planning nor pressure can change that fact," and even though it defines desegregation as anything less than a 90 per cent-10 per cent ratio on either side. The Plan makes several proposals, of which the three most immediately relevant are: (1) the establishment of pre-primary classes; (2) abolition of the junior high school and a division of the grades instead into three four-year schools—the primary school, the middle school, and the high school; and (3) the establishment of educational complexes, visualized as a cluster of elementary schools and one or two middle schools under a single administrator and sharing among them special staff, facilities, and programs. . . .

As a result of the Allen Plan and the integrationist enthusiasm for it, in 1964–65, 4,500 ninth-graders who would normally still be attending Negro junior high schools will this year be transferred into 36 integrated high schools. Their places in the junior high schools will be taken by 5,800 sixth-graders from 44 elementary schools. And these schools in turn will be able to reduce the size of classes, expand their kindergarten programs, and establish pre-kindergartens. (Even so unglamorous a beginning will be expensive. Apart from the additional special staff needed for shifts in arrangements, it costs the Board eighty-eight cents a day for the transportation of each child relocated, whether by Open Enrollment, school pairing, or any other kind of adjustment. The new arrangement for sixth- and ninth-graders alone, then, will cost $10,000 a day.) . . .

At the moment it is impossible to predict what will be the outcome of the Board's new struggle: it depends on court decisions yet unissued, accommodations and spiritual adjustments yet unmade, and perhaps on developments in the city's social life that have nothing to do with schools. But the question has been posed and will never again be dropped: can the American public-school system find the means to teach *all* American children, and can American society find the means to value all the children so taught for the particular kind of people they turn out to be? It is a question that, though framed for our time by integrationists, goes far beyond the demands most of them have had to make. It is a question that goes, too, beyond our shameful history of race relations; for this can be assuaged by laws and softened by time.

But nothing will ever assuage or soften the shame of wasting lively and vital children who get no chance at life but what society gives them.

PUBLIC SCHOOLS AND EQUALITY OF OPPORTUNITY

NATALIE ROGOFF

Diversity stands out as the quality best describing the American educational scene. But clear though the signs of diversity may be, the implications are not. What are we to make of all the variations we know to exist in our schools? As a touchstone, as a principle for organizing and evaluating the observations we make, the ancient but still unanalyzed idea of equality of opportunity has a great deal to recommend it. What do we mean by equality of opportunity? What social and educational arrangements make it easiest to realize? Does it ever conflict with other accepted social aims? These questions assert themselves as some of the keystones of social research on education. . . .

Let us confine our attention to the secondary schools in the United States today. Certainly one of the consequences of prolonging the years of compulsory education is to keep most of the children in the limelight, to increase their visibility to the "guardians" and to increase the number of guardians by whom they are observed—all of which conditions perhaps lead to more accurate and objective judgments of their worth. But the thousands of schools differ among themselves in bewildering fashion; do any of these differences lead to impairing the work of the guardians in their crucial role of seeing gold, silver, and brass wherever they are found?

How, for example, could the matter of a school's size, now more than ever under scrutiny since President Conant's emphasis on it, affect its capacity to observe and assign each student to his most appropriate role?

Are small schools in a better or a worse position than large ones to evaluate their students? Immediately a number of empirical questions come to mind: is the size of a school related to the frequency and objectivity of the performance tests its students take? Is size associated with the "clear-sightedness" of teachers, that is, their capacity to make sound judgments of students? Does a small school give a few teachers the opportunity to make many observations, while a large school gives many teachers the opportunity to make only a few observations of each student? If these are the most frequent patterns, which of them is the more effective?

Enlarging the problem, a school's size is not unrelated to other structural and institutional attributes. To consider only one, smaller

From *Journal of Educational Sociology*, 1960 (February), *33*: 252–259.

schools are more isolated from the great centers of population and from the larger society as a whole. This may lead to less awareness of the standards of performance by the average American student, so that no matter if teachers at small schools see a great deal more of their students, their evaluations may be less correct because of their remoteness from national norms.

No indictment of small American high schools is intended by these remarks, which are incidental to and illustrative of a more basic idea — that the structure of our schools may, in a totally unplanned way, lead to inequalities in the opportunities students have for being evaluated and selected for the roles in society for which they are well suited.

. . . [N]ot only do we live in a more than usually heterogeneous society, but the separate sub-groups in America have a noticeable impact on the schools and colleges here. On the one hand, the vast system of private schools, colleges, and universities has been spawned by this very sense of religious, ethnic, and regional separateness. On the other, the residential propinquity of sub-group members — Catholics, Jews, Negroes, lower class persons, or Swedes, for example, tending to live in settlements each with his own — gives to many public schools a membership of both students and teachers predominantly affiliated with one such social category, whether it be of a religious, ethnic, or class character. Not all public, nor indeed all private schools share this quality, which means that only some of our young people experience the pleasures and pains of attending schools that are socially heterogenous.

What influence does this quality of our schools have on the chances of each student to be seen for what he is and selected for an appropriate adult role? Does the evaluation of a lower class, or a Protestant, or a Japanese child, let us say, depend on whether he attends a school where lower class or Protestant or Japanese children predominate rather than a school where children from his background are mixed in equal or unequal parts with others? The current state of knowledge bearing on this question is such that we might be led to any one of the possible answers to it. That the problem is complex is undeniable; we need to know in detail, among many other things, how this structural attribute of schools is related to the behavior and the qualifications of teachers, how it affects informal relations among students, and how it bears on the interaction between students and teachers.

This only begins the program of studies that might be carried out, using equality of opportunity as an ethical, a theoretical, and a technical yardstick. To throw a few more coals on the fire, we need to distinguish between the role of schools in furnishing young people with equal chances of being *selected* for and of being *provided* with appropriate educational and other opportunities. We need to distinguish between our schools' performances in recognizing talent and in knowing how best to utilize it. And between deliberate and unanticipated barriers to equality of opportunity. And between those sources of inequality which are connected with other of the major institutions in society—the family, the church, and economic and political institutions—in contrast to those stemming primarily from schools and colleges themselves. The work will take us far outside the orbit of the classroom, as research on education always has done, but perhaps the connections with the outside world will be better apprehended and of more point if this compelling principle furnishes the motive power.

Specifying the Idea of Equality of Opportunity

To advocate such a program of research is gratifying; to initiate it is perilous and sobering. In the following remarks, the reader will find untested assumptions, oversimplifications, and arbitrary selection of problematic elements. Time, work, and the help of others will, hopefully, reduce these.

Here are some of the things that have to be specified in order to apply the concept of equality of opportunity. First, between whom should there be equality of opportunity? Presumably, between those who "deserve" it equally, or those of equal capacity to take advantage of given opportunities. So we must have some way of classifying individuals according to their capacities—a task that psychologists, at least since the time of Binet, have taken as a serious and continuing responsibility.

Next, we have to have some ideas about the major sources of *inequality*. This is necessary because we must be able to compare the opportunities available to those equal in capacity but unequal in some respect that we believe affects their chances of getting such opportunities. Here we are in a fortunate position, because there is so vast an amount of previous research all of which shows the central role of *social class* as one of the leading sources of inequality.

Finally, we should specify the nature of the opportunities most crucial to the life chances of individuals. What are the rewards which should be equally available to those of equal capacity? Once again, we do not have to rely on our own efforts to find an answer. *Higher education*, to an increasing extent, is perhaps the major gateway to the personal and social rewards available to the members of modern industrial societies. While in the past it was only one of several alternatives, more and more higher education preempts the part formerly played by inherited wealth, personal daring and energy, or the slow climb from job to next higher job.

We already know a great deal about the empirical relations among ability, social class, and access to higher education, and even something about the processes underlying these relations. But we have not yet looked at the facts in connection with various patterns and possibilities of equality of opportunity. Some of the patterns are sketched below.

A. The "Radical" Pattern

For centuries, men have dreamed of ideal societies wherein all persons of equal capacity would be treated alike, without respect to their social origins. A very crude translation into contemporary research language might be as follows:

Let R_{ij} be the rate of college-going among persons of ability level i and social class j.

Then, $R_{aa} = R_{ab} = R_{ac} = \ldots R_{an}$, and $R_{aa} > R_{ba} > R_{ca} > \ldots R_{na}$.

Equal ability would lead to equal rates of college-going, no matter what the social class background, and higher ability would always lead to higher rates, no matter what the social class.

B. The "Moderate" Pattern

Although not as readily put into ideological form, a moderate set of views on equality of opportunity would go about as follows:

To strive for a set of selection processes that puts every person in a social class according to his ability may be not only impossible, but perhaps not even desirable. Native ability is modified continuously by myriad social mechanisms. To overcome their force might lead to such disruptions of the social structure that, had we the knowledge, we might actually prefer not to pay so high a price. Therefore, not ability alone, but some combination of ability and its social "facilitators" and "detractors" (here represented by social class) should be taken into account to produce the following pattern of opportunity (college-going):

$R_{aa} > R_{ba} > R_{ca} > \ldots R_{na}$, and $R_{ab} -> R_{ba}$; $R_{ij} -> R_{ji}$, but $R_{aa} > R_{ab} > R_{ac} > \ldots R_{an}$.

The first condition specified is certainly the simplest: within a given social class, the college-going rate is higher at higher levels of ability. The third condition states, however, that the rate is higher in more favored social classes at every ability level. In other words, social class facilitates college-going, independent of ability. Finally, the second condition attempts to say something about the *relative* weight of ability and social class in affecting the college-going rate, and specifies that ability should have an effect equal to or greater than that of social class position.

C. The "Conservative" Pattern

The stance of the conservative toward equality of opportunity is easily discerned from what has been said before. It is his position that, in the long run, we delude ourselves if we believe that talent and ability observed among the lowest social classes should be taken seriously and encouraged. What really counts is the character of the social class into which the youngster was born. Society will be better off if it allocates opportunities according to social class and does not try to tinker with the biological and socially reinforcing mechanisms that have worked well enough for centuries.

In our crude terms, the conservative pattern is described by the following conditions:

$$R_{aa}=R_{ba}=R_{ca}= \ . \ . \ . \ R_{na}, \text{ and } R_{aa}> R_{ab}> R_{ac}> \ . \ . \ . \ R_{an}.$$

The pattern of opportunity would show no sensitivity to ability but would decrease at successively less favorable social class positions.

Though stated here in the optative mode, the radical, moderate, and conservative patterns of equality of opportunity will serve equally well as a crude research tool. In fact they are nothing more than a way of evaluating the relative effect of two "independent variables," i.e., social class position and talent or ability, as such evaluations are ordinarily made in multivariate analysis. There is one difference, however. Much of the time, survey analysis deals with a single "population" and attempts to discern the underlying links among various attributes concerning that population. But here, we have in mind a way of comparing one population with another, describing each by its relative position between the radical and conservative extremes. . . .

The criteria of equality of opportunity proposed here are unlike those generally invoked by others interested in the problem. It is customary, for example, for comparisons to be made of public expenditures for education, or of the training of teachers, the average size of classrooms, and so on, between different states or regions of the nation. Differences in such standards are then cited as evidence of "inequality of opportunity" between residents of the states or regions. But this seems to miss at least one aspect of the concept. Equality of opportunity refers to the way *individuals* are treated relative to one another; as T. H. Marshall has suggested, it stands for "the equal right to display and develop differences, or inequalities; the equal right to be recognized as unequal."[1] It is an empirical question as to whether one community or region with a high level of "opportunity," however we choose to indicate that term, allocates those chances more equitably, i.e., in closer correspondence to individual differences among its residents, than does a community or region with a low level of opportunity.

Empirical Application

The rather simple and crude patterns described above for evaluating equality of opportunity have already proved useful in organizing various sets of empirical data now under scrutiny at the Bureau of Applied Social Research. We were fortunate enough to gain access to information collected by the Educational Testing Service concerning the college-going and career plans of over 35,000 American high school seniors, who constituted the "Class of 1955" at over five hundred public secondary schools. Information concerning the schools (a fairly representative sample of the 20,000-odd senior public high schools in the United States) was collected from the principals at the time of the field work. This has since been supplemented by consulting national and state school directories, other listings and surveys, and census material pertaining to the towns and counties where the schools are located.

The key element in the design of the survey is the inclusion of over five hundred schools, representing almost as many communities. This permits the close study of communities and neighborhoods, both in their own right, and as contexts which may affect the behavior and orientations of the young people located in them. Among other things, we are in a position to see whether some types of communities conform to the "conservative" pattern of equality of opportunity, others to the "moderate" or "radical" patterns. Although this work is still in a preliminary stage, it is possible to report that communities *do* vary in this respect. Some towns—perhaps the smaller and less well-to-do, if the tentative evidence is later confirmed—are relatively close to the conservative pattern, allocating opportunities more on the basis of a youngster's class position than of his ability; others—again tentatively, wealthier and larger communities—appear to come closer to the radical pattern, showing more sensibility to their students' talents than to their social origins.

It is not too early, however, to suggest that inquiries into the state of affairs concerning equality of opportunity is a desirable field of social investigation, with serious implications for understanding schools, communities, and the stratification hierarchy.

[1]T. H. Marshall, *Citizenship and Social Class* (Cambridge: Cambridge University Press, 1950), pp. 65–66.

AN IDEOLOGY OF SCHOOL WITHDRAWAL

EDGAR Z. FRIEDENBERG

Compulsory school attendance in the United States has been justified from the beginning as essential to democratic polity. . . .

[Yet] for the types of students it is designed for, the public high school and junior high school curriculum serves, I believe, exactly the same purpose as [some] responsive reading[s]. Its function is liturgical. This is not as true of elementary school, because the basic skills really work. If you read as you are taught there, you will understand at least the words; if you write, your words will be understood; if you follow the rules of arithmetic, your calculations will check out and your books will balance, though you may never have the remotest conception of mathematics.

High school, however, is another matter. What would happen to the businessman, or just citizen, who attempted to apply what he was taught in high-school civics to the actual power structure of his community or his country? Who learns to love reading, or to find the kind of reading he can love among the classics and the bitty anthologies of the high-school English course? High-school history, by and large, is not even propaganda, because nobody is expected to believe it or to be moved by it; it is received as official myth. We tell youngsters that the Pilgrims came to New England searching for religious freedom not in order to give them an understanding of the actual root values of Colonial New England, but in order to provide them with the relevant cliché about the relation of church and state in America, and to let them know that a good middle-class American thinks of "my religious affiliation" or "the faith of my choice." This keeps the youngsters from getting hung up on religion, like an Italian peasant or rural Southerner. As for high-school science, it has, since Sputnik, increased its work load enormously and often tries to duplicate the content of college science courses. But essentially, it serves not as an introduction to science but to legitimate the American middle-class epistemology; science proves that Truth is an aggregate of general principles induced from empirical data that observers can agree on. The function of science is to protect people from odd-balls by setting up the rules so that subjective feeling is discounted. The scientific method, then, becomes a way of separating ends and means. When we want to win an election, or spy on the Soviet Union, or redevelop a slum, we go about it scientifically —i.e., by defining what we are trying to do as a technical problem. Naturally, we care about the feelings of the people affected; people's

Reprinted from *Commentary* (June 1963), by permission; copyright © 1963 by the American Jewish Committee. Reprinted by permission of Edgar Z. Friedenberg in cooperation with Beacon Press.

emotions are a very important factor. That's why we have psychologists on our team.

It is even truer than the progressives have always maintained that there is no valid distinction between the curriculum and the extra-curriculum. What counts is the total experience of the student, and what he learns in both the classroom and the playing field is a posture, a pattern of anxieties and a pattern of responses for dealing with it. There is seldom any pleasure in scholarship or ideas as such; the classroom and the playing field alike are places where you try to make it, and learn the techniques for making it that alienate you least from your peers. The over-all rules are the same in both: learn the ropes; don't get hung up; always be friendly, sincere, and creative. And win!

The important thing about this familiar picture is that it is a picture of a totally instrumental institution. Nothing about the institution is meant to be valuable, here and now, for its own sake. I don't mean that high-school students don't have any fun. Of course they do; in the sub-urbs, at least, the high school is a "fun place." But this sort of fun is a part of the social pattern to be learned; being "fun" helps you to make it as well or better than anything, and it takes a great deal of social skill which American adolescents, notably, do learn.

We have never had much interest in what education means and feels like to the youngsters who are subjected to it; only in what it might help them to make of themselves. Even the Supreme Court, in its de-cision against segregation, could not rest on the moral obloquy and insult that segregation imposes on Negro children; that was not enough. It had to support its position further by pointing out that a major rea-son why separate schools could not be equal even if they were identical was that the Negro students couldn't make the same contacts there that white students could in their school, and that this was what people really go to school for.

So it is: the Court has done our motives no discredit, but merely reaffirmed our tradition. The public school gives poor boys a chance to develop their potentialities, both by formal education and by pro-viding an opportunity to mingle with and learn from their social super-ordinates. The commonwealth is then the richer for the skills they later contribute, which would otherwise have been forever lost. This is exactly the opportunity our dropouts need, and which they ought presumably to welcome. So what has gone wrong?

What has gone wrong is pretty complicated; but basically I think one might locate it in the schools' perennial assumptions about the nature of what they have had to offer the children of the poor. These assump-tions were probably never valid; but both the school and the poor once believed them. Now, only the school continues to assert them, though no longer with much conviction.

The schools assumed that in order to get ahead in America the student had to learn not only a body of skills, but also a set of social conventions, increasingly subtle and refined as he climbed up the ladder. In school he was taught techniques for handling things and manners for getting along with people. The teachers were the transmitters of an alien culture—alien to them, too. Social mobility was a process like preparing to get a job as a rice farmer in China or a coffee-grower in Brazil. There was a strange language to be learned—from instructors who didn't speak it too well themselves; a strange body of techniques to be mastered—from teachers who had never practiced them at first hand. It would all have to be learned over again when he got there; but at the time it seemed relevant, and made the student feel that he was well on his way.

Now, there are three important ways in which this situation differs from the condition in the high school today. In the first place, the problem of dropouts did not then exist. Most of the students who drop out today would never have been in high school fifty years ago; the school-leaving age has risen irregularly over the past decades, and a more rigid and self-confident school policy would not have hesitated to keep students in grade school until they reached it, whatever it was, if they did not pass. A good many of these dropped out, and took unskilled jobs, which existed; and that was the last anyone thought of them till election day six or seven years later. They weren't a dropout problem; they were the working class.

But those who didn't drop out, even though they came from a working-class background, did not feel at the time that they were losing their identity. This happened later, after they had made it, in the classical discovery of the loneliness of the long-distance runner. In school you were still you: *striving* didn't separate you from other poor, immigrant boys; it was exactly what poor, immigrant boys were supposed to do. There was no intimation at the time that you were leaving yourself behind. It wasn't that you were becoming a different person; the old *you* was learning new tricks. Education was instrumental, all right —it has always been that in America—but the instruments were thought to be in the curriculum. The student didn't have to learn to think of *himself* as one.

And finally, nobody doubted what the norms were. It seemed very clear that the people in the next stratum up were the ones who knew what the student had to learn; he had to be able to do what they did. This wouldn't make them accept him willingly; but it would allow him to work his way in even if they didn't.

I don't mean to imply that the school actually delivered the social mobility it promised; sometimes it did, more often it didn't. But this was the way it was supposed to work, and why there was so little controversy over whether compulsory school attendance was good for the individual as well as for the commonwealth. As long as the students who stayed in school believed in education naïvely, it served—much better than religion could have in this heterogeneous country—as the opiate of the people. And opium vendors don't have dropout problems.

Apparently, however—to judge by the present situation—they can: the American poor are getting over their addiction. It takes more and more education every year to invoke the same dream; and reality breaks through too often, leaving them sick, mean, and edgy. The educational establishment, fearful of losing popular support, is naturally much concerned with the possibilities of a *rapprochement*, of which two have already been tried. The simplest of these is an effort to beef up the traditional, but paradoxically faltering, economic appeal of education. Students are reminded over and over that today, more than ever, you need a high-school diploma to get any sort of job and a college degree to get a good one. They are given the statistics on the fabulous return education, as an investment, brings in over a lifetime in increments of annual income. The unemployment data on adolescents and unskilled labor are stressed so that the youngsters will understand how hopeless things will be for them if they drop out of school. If they and their teacher are sophisticated enough, the demographic shift in job-type may be explained: how unskilled and blue-collar work has fallen off, while service and white-collar jobs, demanding a higher level of school achievement, have enormously increased in proportion.

All this is true enough; but the implication is false. It does not follow that most of the students now dropping out would have a better chance, even economically, if they stayed in school. As S. M. Miller and Frank Riessman have pointed out in a recent WBAI [radio] broadcast, the illusory success of some of these school-retention efforts in leading students to better jobs is based on the fact that they made hardly a dent in the number of school dropouts; if the programs had been successful in reaching the students they would inevitably have failed in delivering the jobs. In our economy, the demonstrable economic value of an education is partly a consequence of its scarcity. The blue-collar-white-collar figures are relative, and one loses sight of how much smaller the white-collar one was to begin with. The absolute increase in white-collar opportunity does not compensate for the absolute loss in blue-collar jobs—a discrepancy which is rapidly increasing in magnitude as automation proceeds. Today's dropouts are, perhaps fortunately, pretty skeptical kids; if they all believed that the school could deliver them to a brighter economic future we would soon have unemployed IBM operators and technicians hanging around the way India and Africa have lawyers.

The other, and more sophisticated, *rapprochement* is represented by the Higher Horizons Program, about which I wish I could bring myself to be less doubtful, for it is a program that seems to me characterized by much intelligence, ingenuity, enthusiasm, and sheer good will. Its appeal, moreover, is not purely economic. I understand it to be an attempt to convey to students that middle-class culture, *in toto*, is not beyond their grasp. It can be theirs, if only they do their work. As the title implies, the Higher Horizons approach seeks to make education appear more worthwhile to the student, and encourages him to remain in school to develop his potentialities, by raising his level of aspiration not just economically but culturally. As the boy lifts himself to gaze beyond the slum there comes into view the Museum of Modern Art.

It is heartening to find the middle class so generously willing to share its resources, and, for once, apparently confident of their value. It is also obvious that if the middle class cannot somehow make public education acceptable to the poor on its terms rather than theirs, middle-class dominance of public education—a long established fact of American life—is doomed. But if the effort is successful, it will remind me of a story that a very intelligent, very British, very working-class hospital orderly used to tell, in a sensitive effort to ease his middle-class patients' embarrassment at the services he was obliged to perform for them. This story concerned a small pharmaceutical firm that was facing bankruptcy. It had an established reputation as Britain's most reputable manufacturer of suppositories. But respect for craftsmanship, as is well known, was declining; their customers, apparently, were turning to other sources for satisfaction. Things looked black. Then the firm consulted one of Madison Avenue's most resourceful advertising agencies. And the agency, after much brainstorming, came up with a slogan that at once opened vast markets to the company by motivating the very segment of the population which had hitherto most successfully resisted its appeal. The slogan was, very simply, "If you don't like our suppositories, you know what you can do with them!"

The dropouts, by and large, don't like middle-class culture; and they know quite well what we can do with it. Dropping out is one way of telling us, and it is about time we turned our attention to the things about the school that are bugging them. The school is the arena in which these youngsters encounter middle-class life; this is where the dropouts fight the ten-year's ideological war that ends in their defeat and rout. In this warfare the core values of their culture and the values the school represents are at issue, and any one that we start by considering will lead to the others. I think the most fruitful might be the familiar question of deferred gratification, or impulse control, which is the source of so much conflict with the school authorities.

We all know the school's side of the question; and know that lower-class youngsters act out their conflicts. Retention programs try to face up to this by helping the youngsters learn more self-control and giving them some valid experience of being rewarded for it, so that they will discover for themselves that certain very desirable goals exist that can only be achieved by people who plan, save, and give a soft answer to wrath-provoking circumstances. In this way the kids learn that there may be more desirable rewards than the immediate pleasure of blowing up and shooting your bolt. "Now, Dionysus, let's think about what we're really trying to get done here," friendly Apollo is always urging; and of course he is right. The difficulty lies in getting Dionysus to listen. . . .

. . . I think the youngsters who drop out are probably, in many ways, a more promising moral resource than those who stay in, and I think they are driven out in part by moral revulsion from the middle-class life of the school. They could never, themselves, identify their feelings as moral repugnance because they view morality as being on the side of the enemy and therefore square; they imagine they dislike morality and have never been allowed to realize that they have morals of their own. They don't have a complete moral *system*, because they are not systematic; they are unprincipled in their behavior, because principles are too abstract for them to handle. But in a concrete situation they can be trusted more safely than their middle-class peers who are trying to make it.

. . . Time after time the world finds a nice, friendly American standing in the middle of somebody else's ruins, with no more to say for himself than a rueful "It shoulda worked, but somebody must have goofed!"

I have a name for this boy. I call him Edsel, and I think it is time we withdrew him from production and got out a more responsive and less hazardous model. Even the practical-minded may not have much use for him any more; the locals seem to be getting pretty tired of Edsel and are about ready to get him out of there, with a hammer and sickle if necessary. But if we are to grow anything better, the dropouts are the kids to start with, for they have come part way on their own, against heavy opposition, already. They are ill-disciplined. They have no basic skills. They are so sore that any place you touch them hurts, and when they are hurt they hurt back. They are extremely parochial, limited in their experience of the world to a few city blocks of desolate slum, and therefore both gullible and suspicious about anything beyond it. They are sometimes homeless, and never have any quiet place to study and think. They are inconveniently aware of their own sexuality and inconveniently skilled at bringing it to the attention of others. They live, their teachers sometimes say, like animals; and as they say it, a ghost sobs, harshly. But if these youngsters are trapped, it is not in their apprehensions of pseudo-events. They are not alienated from themselves. They still have access to their sense-data, and, on their own terms, they are accustomed to fidelity.

These are the qualities that, I believe, we hoped to preserve and continually renew by building an open society in which a sensitive, compulsively masculine boy could become an Ernest Hemingway and a poor but beautiful waif a Marilyn Monroe. But at this juncture, less fatal alternatives to mediocrity are needed. Can a school geared to success and social mobility help formulate them? Its traditions are against it, its staff is against it, its relationship to the community power structure is against it.

To reach the dropouts and give them a reason for staying, the school would have to start by accepting their *raison d'être*. It would have to take lower-class life seriously as a condition and a pattern of experience — not just as a contemptible and humiliating set of circumstances that every decent boy or girl is anxious to escape from. It would have to accept their language, and their dress, and their values as a point of departure for disciplined exploration, to be understood, not as a trick for luring them into the middle class, but as a way of helping them to explore the meaning of their own lives. This is the way to encourage and nurture potentialities from *whatever* social class. Talent, and genius, when real, are expressions of individual experience and the inner life. But success and higher status are not the first goal to which talent or genius is devoted — though they are sometimes the last.

I do not mean to imply that I accept Sitwell's Fallacy: that the poor are happier in their station in life and should be left to enjoy it. Most lower-class people of whatever age hate lower-class life, I am sure: the noise, and the filth, and the crowding, and the vulnerability to the police and illness; never feeling quite well or quite rested. Worst of all, perhaps, is the constant din of the mass media — including the school — telling them that if they were any good at all they would be middle-class like everybody else, and live in loveliness in Larchmont. But the fact that they have reason to hate their life of fear and deprivation does not give us the right to force ours on them as the only acceptable alternative to it. This is something they must work out for themselves, and the school's job is to help them understand most fully the meaning and nature of what they have to work with. Basically, the problem of reaching the dropout is analogous to that faced by the Peace Corps in reaching the peoples of underdeveloped countries. Can we — do we even really wish to — help them deal with their situation on their terms with our resources, while leaving our way of life aside till somebody asks for it?

Frankly, I doubt it. This is not how the teachers I know approach lower-status youngsters. They are afraid of them, for one thing. The principal is afraid of disorder which looks bad in his record and in the records of his teachers, and they each have their careers to think of, too. So they learn early to keep the kids in line; this comes first. Order *is* helpful to learning, but it doesn't come first, it grows out of the common task; and teachers who put it first are not enthusiastic allies in keeping disorderly youngsters in school till a basis for order can be created. Order is not, to be sure, the central issue, but it will serve to symbolize the sharpness of the issue between those whose security depends on the suppression of impulse, and those who depend on its expression.

In the urban public school today, the former predominate, and I don't think they can be easily changed, within the limits of personality and bureaucracy that characterize the school. If they can be, there is no fundamental reason why the kinds of youngsters who now drop out may not be well served. But this is a big *if*, for the public school, as it is, is profoundly expressive of our culture. And the fate of the "dropouts" is just one more expression of their actual status in our democracy.

The answer, then, may be "No; this plant makes only Edsels." But if it is, I see no dropout problem. Let them go, let them go, God bless them. They may pop up again. St. James (or Santiago, as this chiliastic figure is known in Spanish) is not merely more merciful than the school system; he is far more flexible and versatile. He can accommodate a wider range of talent; he has a great Court, as well as an Infirmary, and though no familiar avenue bears his name, he has, like James Madison, been thus honored by the inhabitants of certain cities. The nearest, unfortunately, in Cuba.

---

19. Educational Content and the Polity

The potential contributions of education to man's politics are enormous; however, simple relationships between economic and educational development, or between political freedom and academic freedom, are difficult to verify. As James Coleman reminds us, we have precious little empirical evidence about the political consequences of various educational philosophies. Nevertheless, Coleman presents some suggestive material noting three dominant patterns. First, the Communist bloc emphasizes science to the detriment of the humanities and the social sciences (the latter field of study asks "dangerous" ques-

tions about power and society). A second legal-humanistic pattern is concentrated in countries with Hispanic roots and an elitist monopoly of education; these countries also happen to be relatively undemocratic in their politics and sluggish in the utilization of their human and economic resources. Third, a more balanced educational content is characteristic of highly developed Western nations; this content gives much attention to those disciplines concerned with man's relationship with himself, his fellows, and his society—the social sciences.

Aristotle may have been more correct than his teacher Plato when he said that wisdom and virtue are two different properties of man that are not necessarily joined. Political stability and democracy are not always advanced by higher education, much less by the progress of science. As the second selection indicates, in a metropolitan area courses in civic education do help reduce prejudice and chauvinism and increase general agreement with democratic norms. However, such courses appear to have little effect on the propensity to engage in political activity, which is more closely associated with social class and community attitudes.

A graphic case of different subcultures clashing over proper education is provided in William Dobriner's study of the school system in Levittown. Some segments of the community opt for psychological and other ancillary services, higher tax sacrifices, and utilization of modern scientific findings in the schools. Other segments favor a strictly vocational attitude toward education: they would eliminate the "frills," reject the novel and the unfamiliar, and hold down the pressing burden of financial costs that eat away the savings of the large family recently liberated from the core city. Importantly, both groups value good education for their children in the abstract; but religious, ethnic, and class factors determine their ideas of just what constitutes a good education.

THE POLITICAL CONSEQUENCES OF EDUCATIONAL PATTERNS

JAMES S. COLEMAN

Deeper insights into the circumstances under which particular educational patterns lead to undesirable political consequences may also

Pages 523–534: Reprinted from *Education and Political Development* by James S. Coleman by permission of Princeton University Press. Copyright © 1965 by Princeton University Press. Title supplied by the editor.

provide guidelines for development planning, for determining what educational "mix," what educational pyramid, what curricular content, what timing and spacing of educational inputs, will best support the interrelated development of society, the economy, and the polity. . . . [W]e will confine our attention to a few of the issues involved in the minimization of destabilizing influences, and to a brief consideration of what educational content is most likely to aid political development.

Developing countries burdened with tensions created by educational imbalances are not necessarily destined for anarchy. Protracted political instability, as well as retrogression to authoritarian stagnation, is a clear possibility, and even, in some instances, a probability. In limiting ourselves to only one or two historical models, however, we may overlook the astonishing variety in the institutional configurations and developmental sequences that have actually existed at critical points in the modernization of many countries of the world. Moreover, there is merit in the suggestion that we begin to think about developing polities, not as pathological deviants, but as a particular type of polity with its own distinctive characteristics, possibly possessing a capacity to survive and adapt, despite all appearances to the contrary.

Many societies are able to develop self-corrective mechanisms for such imbalances as "overproduction of the educated." Despite the virtually uncontrolled expansion of higher education in Japan and the Philippines, for example, adjustments have been made and protective mechanisms (such as absorption of the educated into the private sector or the downgrading of exaggerated notions about "a job appropriate to one's education") have come into play. And the problem of educational overproduction, though admittedly serious, may eventually be resolved: "An education system may very easily produce more educated people than the economic system can currently absorb in the types of job or at the rates of pay which the educated expect. This is a short-period phenomenon. In the long run the educated learn to expect different jobs and to accept lower rates of pay. . . . As the premium on education falls, the market for the educated may widen enormously. Jobs which were previously done by people with less education are now done by people with more education. The educated lower their sights, and employers raise their requirements. . . . As a result of this process an economy can ultimately absorb any number of educated people. . . . [It follows that one] ought to produce more educated people than can be absorbed at current prices, because the alteration in current prices which this brings about is a necessary part of the process of economic development."[1] It is true, however, that "the long run may be very long," that the loss of privileges by the

[1] W. Arthur Lewis, "Education and Economic Development," *International Social Science Journal*, 1962 (4), *14*: 686–688.

educated through the depreciation of education "not infrequently has political consequences," and that the process of adjustment "is painful, and fraught with political dangers."[2] In reality, the "only assurance of a [politically] healthy situation is a dynamic economy."[3]

This statement brings us at once to the Great Debate over the relationship between education and economic growth. . . . Here we need only underscore the fact that in the past both educational planners and development economists have unrealistically tended to exclude political considerations from the dialogue as well as from their own plans. They may have been motivated by a compulsion for professional purity, deference to the hypersensitivity of the political elites whom they were advising, or sheer political ignorance. Political imperatives and constraints, however, as well as probable political consequences are integral parts of this extremely complex issue. They should be given explicit recognition and due weight in all development planning, whether the specific goal is educational advance or economic growth, or both. It serves no useful purpose to "suggest solutions to economic problems which are politically unfeasible. . . . The policy planner should identify not just the desirable or theoretically possible, but the realistic alternatives which exist in the light of known or expected pressures."[4]

Three additional observations on development planning are in point. First, whether the planning objective is economic growth or the minimization of political vulnerability, there cannot be a single educational strategy. . . . [T]he desired strategy is one that maximizes both goals, or at least does not seriously compromise either goal. A separate strategy must be devised for different *types* of developing countries, as well as for different *phases* in their development. Second, because statism characterizes both the political culture and the political process in many developing countries, governing elites have an extraordinary opportunity to employ various stratagems to minimize the politically destabilizing aspects of educational development. To take full advantage of this opportunity they need not only the professional advice of politically sensitive development planners, but also political courage of their own. Third, few guideposts for educational planning can be found in the historical experience of more highly developed countries. The findings of the few existing studies are ambiguous or inconclusive; and even if a comprehensive body of validated theory based on Western experience were available, its relevance would be questionable. . . . Indeed, a recent empirical study of the relationship between education and social mobility in a developing country points up several social and

[2]*Ibid.*

[3]C. Arnold Anderson, "Education and Political Development: Reactions to a Conference" (memorandum circulated to the participants in the Conference on Education and Political Development, held at Lake Arrowhead, California, June 24–29, 1962), pp. 16–17.

[4]Frederick Harbison and Charles A. Myers, *Education, Manpower and Economic Growth* (New York: McGraw-Hill, 1964), p. 20. . . .

historical features that are in striking contrast to Western experience.[5] Moreover, . . . in the West there was usually firm ground in either the economy or the polity from which to grapple with change in the other, whereas in the developing countries the simultaneity of institution building in all spheres demands more fundamental conceptions of just how educational, economic, and political developments intertwine in the absence of such an anchor base.

The second problem requiring brief examination here concerns the content of education. Education is not politically dysfunctional solely because of the overproduction of educated persons, but because of the overproduction of persons whose education makes them unemployable, owing either to their psychic disposition or to their lack of the requisite knowledge and skills. The problem of excess capacity in absolute quantitative terms exists mainly in the case of unemployed primary-school leavers, whose education has been essentially homogeneous. Educational content becomes differentiated and variable, and the resultant heterogeneity becomes politically consequential, mainly at secondary and higher levels of education. The type of post-primary educational content considered most productive of unemployable intellectuals and political instability, and most criticized by development planners, is that in which legal, literary, and humanistic studies predominate. Development economists in particular have a pronounced bias "towards subjects which appear to promote rational methods of thought, like mathematics and the natural sciences, towards subjects which break up accepted attitudes, like sociology and other social studies, and towards practical subjects—crafts and elementary agricultural skills which enable people to develop their capacity to earn their own living."[6]

The debate over what curriculum content contributes most positively to development reveals an unfortunate tendency to regard development as a homogeneous process. By now it is abundantly evident that developmental requisites are not necessarily the same or even congruent in the different institutional spheres—educational, economic, and political; indeed, they may be and frequently are at variance, and sometimes even conflict with one another. Rapid educational expansion does not necessarily give rise to either economic growth or political development; economic growth has occurred without extensive educational development, and, in many instances, it has been politically destabilizing. To be sure, these incongruities in development among the different spheres are regarded as transitional; it is assumed that in the long run some sort of adjustment or balance will be achieved. But the long run can prove to be very long indeed.

[5]Philip J. Foster, "Secondary Schooling and Social Mobility in a West African Nation," *Sociology of Education*, 1963 (Winter), *37*: 150–171. . . .

[6]John Vaizey, "Economics of Education," *International Social Science Journal*, 1962 (4), *14*: 627. . . .

In any event, the immediate point is that the subject matter emphasis in curriculum content required for rapid economic growth may not be compatible with stable and democratic political development.

Two interrelated issues affect the relationship between political development and curriculum content in post-primary education. One concerns the political consequences of a predominantly scientific and technological curriculum; the other, the role of the social sciences in political development. The proposition that a predominantly scientific and technological orientation in education is not only compatible with, but possibly supportive of, political authoritarianism has been argued very persuasively:

"Will not education produce a questioning spirit incompatible with autocratic rule? Can an educated society continue to be regimented? There can be little doubt that compulsory, universal education has a profound impact. It is doubtful, however, whether it inevitably produces liberalization, first because the questioning spirit may not suffice to bring about liberalization, and second because education does not necessarily have to foster an attitude that is critical of political life. . . . Education is or can be made largely vocational. It can be made to repeat the specialization of an industrial society. And specialization is purchased at the price of considerable ignorance of most other fields. . . . Even in the field of science, the correlation between scientific and political freedom is far from absolute. Studying Hegel or Kant or Locke produces reflection and concern about the nature of authority and freedom. The study of physics and chemistry need not. It is true that the scientific spirit requires a willingness to accept whatever results research may reveal. But this presupposes the autonomy of the scientific sphere, not freedom as such. In science there is a certain manipulative element which in a different social context than ours may prove by no means inconsistent with 'forcing men to be free.'"[7]

The existence of a link between scientific and specialized education and authoritarian propensities has been stated far more categorically by Alfred Cobban: "There is little evidence that scientists are more scientific in their thought outside their own particular fields than the rest of the community, nor indeed is it to be expected. The scientist is dependent on the possession of a large body of scientifically ascertained evidence: where he has not done this he must either take refuge in agnosticism, or base his opinions on prejudice and guesswork. Now the mere labour that the acquiring and maintenance of his expertness in his own subject demands, by itself prohibits the specialist from devoting the time necessary to the study, either in theory or practice, of the problems of government. Unguarded either by belief in an ancient creed, or by a rational study of the problems of social life, the

[7]Henry A. Kissinger, *The Necessity for Choice* (New York: Harper & Brothers, 1961), pp. 295–297. . . .

Table 1
SUBJECT MATTER ORIENTATION OF HIGHER EDUCATION IN SELECTED COUNTRIES[1]

			Per cent enrolled by subject matter[2]			
	Level of Human Resource Development[3]	Science and Technology[4]	Humanities, Arts, Law, Social Sciences			
Country			Humanities, Arts, Law[5]	Social Sciences[6]	Total	Other[7]
NON-COMMUNIST						
Africa						
Ghana	II	30	27	26	53	17
Nigeria	I	40	31	14	44	16
Senegal	I	25	61	1	62	13
Tunisia	II	16	66	2[8]	68	16
Asia						
India	III	27	58	8	66	7
Indonesia	II	23	31	21[8]	52	25
Japan	IV	22	27	26	53	25
Philippines	...	21	6	48	54	25
Middle East						
Egypt	III	24	35	22	57	19
Iran	II	16	47	—	47	37
Iraq	II	26	29	27	56	18
Israel	IV	42	50	...[9]	50	8
Latin America						
Argentina	IV	15	36	17	53	32
Brazil	II	19	39	11	50	31
Mexico	III	18	8	5	13	69
Peru	II	31	42	19	61	8
Uruguay	III	5	51	11	62	33
COMMUNIST						
Communist						
China	II	55.7	...	...	...	...
Czechoslovakia	III	46	6	11	17	37
Hungary	III	46	20	6	26	28
Poland	III	52	15	8	23	25
USSR	IV	45	8	9	17	38
WESTERN						
Democratic						
Australia	IV	28	23	7	30	42
France	IV	32	46	...[10]	46	22
West Germany	IV	25	29	13	42	33
Sweden	IV	30	49	5	54	16
United Kingdom	IV	34	35	6[11]	41	25
United States	IV	23	18[12]	29[12]	47[12]	...
Authoritarian						
Portugal	III	17	56	7	60	23
Spain	III	25	36	4	43	32

[1]Based on figures for 1957, 1958, or 1959.

[2]Rounded.

[3]I, Underdeveloped; II, Partially developed; III, Semi-advanced; IV, Advanced. Based on the composite index of Human Resource Development by Frederick Harbison and Charles A. Myers, *Education, Manpower, and Economic Growth*, New York, McGraw-Hill, 1964, pp. 31–34.

[4]Include agriculture.

[5]Humanities include archaeology, psychology, and history; arts include architecture.

expert is ready to fall a victim to any new heresy. He will seize on any gospel that has the appearance of providing a safe orthodoxy on which to base the crumbling state, so long as it is presented by demagogues sufficiently clever or by tyrants sufficiently powerful. . . . In these conditions it is not difficult to understand why the general acceptance of the principle of universal education, and the great advance of specialist studies, should have been accompanied by the rise of dictatorship and the development of the totalitarian state. . . . The really surprising development is the extent to which the new doctrines, however wild and irrational they may seem, have won the sincere adherence, not of the illiterate, poverty-stricken masses, but of the professional classes, the technicians, the lawyers, doctors, scientists, engineers, administrators — in short of the experts who tend the complicated machinery of modern civilization. It is the educated, not the uneducated masses, who form the real problem in the modern state. . . . [In the future] the ablest minds from all ranks will be drawn into the service of society as scientists, or technicians, or specialists in some form or other. In many ways this is an admirable development; but it has the result that education can no longer be regarded as a preparation for government."[8]

These two authorities have been quoted at some length because they state with pungent succinctness the essence of the proposition that a predominantly scientific-technological emphasis in education is not in conflict with—indeed, it possibly may be conducive to—a nondemocratic pattern of political development. Their thesis derives support from various studies made in different cultural milieus. The figures in Table 1 underscore the heavy emphasis placed upon science and technology, and the comparatively slight attention given to the humanities, law, the arts, and the social sciences in Communist totalitarian countries. Further evidence of a correlation between field specialization and political values is revealed by Dwaine Marvick's sample survey of students in an African university* . . . . He found . . . that students concentrating in science (in contrast with liberal arts or economics) tended to be markedly less concerned with party politics and public affairs, seemed only slightly interested in taking an active part

[8]Alfred Cobban, *Dictatorship: Its History and Theory* (New York: Charles Scribner's Sons, 1939), pp. 232, 235, 240–241. . . .

*Dwaine Marvick, "African University Students: A Presumptive Elite," in James S. Coleman (ed.), *Education and Political Development* (Princeton, N. J.: Princeton University Press, 1965), pp. 463–497. — *Editor's note.*

[6]Include banking and commerce.

[7]Includes education and medicine.

[8]1956.

[9]Included with humanities.

[10]Included with law.

[11]Part of social sciences included with humanities.

[12]Per cent of degrees earned in 1958.

Sources: Frederick Harbison and Charles A. Myers, *Education, Manpower and Economic Growth*, New York, McGraw-Hill, 1964, pp. 46–48; UNESCO, *World Survey of Education, III, Secondary Education*, New York, 1961, pp. 28 and 42; UNESCO, *Basic Facts and Figures*, 1961, Paris, 1962, pp. 56–60.

in community politics in later life, and appeared likely to "spend quiet lives, making useful contributions to the modernization of their country either as technicians or teachers, almost irrespective of what kind of political regime or civic life flourishes around them." It is a moot question, Marvick suggests, whether this orientation reflects earlier propensities that led to the choice of a scientific field, or is the result of the socializing impact of the students' preoccupation with purely scientific subject matter. Once again we are reminded, not only of the extraordinary complexity of the issue of causal relationships, but also of the limited number of systematic comparative studies which have been made of this phenomenon.

The crux of the issue is not whether educational content should be exclusively scientific and technological or exclusively humanistic and legal, but what is the best "mix." Most development economists in the Western liberal tradition, it is only fair to note, do not propose that the curriculum should be exclusively scientific and technological in character; rather, they press for curricular changes that will correct the present imbalance favoring the humanities, law, and the arts—a lopsidedness vividly brought out by the data in Table 1—and presumably producing large numbers of unproductive and destabilizing unemployables. A consideration of equal importance is that the most desirable mix is not one that turns out a certain percentage of persons trained exclusively in science and technology, and another percentage trained exclusively in the humanities and law; rather, the mix should be in the heads of all students without sacrificing, of course, "the rigorous standards of the discipline in depth which are the virtues of specialization."[9] The fact is, of course, that the dominant European educational traditions which have served as models for the developing countries have emphasized intensive specialization.

The "either-or" quality of the polemic over the relative developmental power of a scientific-technological versus a humanistic-literary-legal education has meant that the middle ground, occupied by the "modern" social sciences[10] (anthropology, economics, history, political science, psychology, and sociology), has suffered neglect. The social sciences, although occupying a "strategic place in the intellectual spectrum, between the poles of physics and the arts and literature,"[11] are least solidly established as a coherent whole, and therefore are the least

[9]Eric Ashby, *African Universities and Western Tradition* (Cambridge: Harvard University Press, 1964), p. 9. . . .

[10]By "modern" social sciences, we refer mainly to the "behavioral sciences," that is, to those of the six social science disciplines, or to tendencies within those disciplines, in which "the scientific imperative is explicit and aimed at establishing generalizations about human behavior that are supported by empirical evidence collected in an impersonal and objective way . . . [in order better to] understand, explain, and predict human behavior." Bernard Berelson, "Introduction to the Behavioral Sciences," in Bernard Berelson (ed.), *The Behavioral Sciences Today* (New York: Basic Books, 1963), p. 3.

[11]Pendleton Herring, "On Science and Polity," *Items*, Vol. 15, No. 1, March 1961, p. 4.

recognized among the four major branches of learning (physical sciences, biological sciences, social sciences, humanities). Their lack of coherence and the instability of their middle position are reflected in the fact that the subject matter, as well as the practitioners, of the six disciplines are classified differently in different academic traditions. Moreover, within each discipline there are markedly divergent intellectual tendencies, of which the polar extremes are the philosophical-humanistic versus the empirical-scientific. A marked shift from the former to the latter is occurring in all of the social science disciplines, however, as a consequence of the impact of the scientific revolution. Nevertheless, except for economics, the relevance of social science knowledge and theory for understanding and guiding the development process is still not generally comprehended or appreciated, least of all in the developing countries themselves.

CIVIC EDUCATION, COMMUNITY NORMS, AND POLITICAL INDOCTRINATION

Edgar Litt

"All national educational systems," observes V. O. Key, Jr., "indoctrinate the coming generation with the basic outlooks and values of the political order."[1] But this indoctrination is not uniform. Do different socio-economic communities, for instance, differ in the kinds of textbooks they employ in civic education? Do differing political attitudes and norms in these communities affect the process of indoctrination? To answer these questions, we analyzed textual material in civic education programs, attitudes of leaders in the school's political and educational milieu, and changes in political attitudes accompanying participation in civic education classes.

Procedure

The study was conducted in the major secondary school in each of three communities in the Boston metropolitan area (to be referred to as Alpha, Beta, and Gamma).[2] The three communities differ in socio-economic and political characteristics: Alpha is an upper middle-class community with much political activity; Beta is a lower middle-class community with moderate political activity; and Gamma is a working-class community with little political activity.

[1]V. O. Key, Jr., *Public Opinion and American Democracy* (New York: Knopf, 1961), p. 316.
[2]Course titles of civic education instruction vary in the three communities. A control group was available in the same schools of Alpha and Gamma where the civic education course was not required. For Beta, a control group was selected from a school in an adjoining, and comparable community. From *American Sociological Review*, 1963 (February), *28*: 69–75.

A content analysis, described in the Appendix, was made of all textbooks used in the civic education programs in Alpha, Beta, and Gamma schools over the past five years (ten texts were investigated in Alpha, eight in Beta, and seven in Gamma). A random sample of paragraphs was selected in each text and classified, where applicable, along one of the following five dimensions:[3]

1. *Emphasis on citizen political participation*—references to voting, norms of civic duty, political activity, and the effectiveness of citizen action in influencing the behavior of public officials.

2. *Political chauvinism*—references to the unique and nationalistic character of "democracy" or "good government" as an American monopoly, and glorified treatment of American political institutions, procedures and public figures.

3. *The democratic creed*—references to the rights of citizens and minorities to attempt to influence governmental policy through non-tyrannical procedures.

4. *Emphasis on political process*—references to politics as an arena involving the actions of politicians, public officials, and the use of power and influence contrasted with references to government as a mechan-istic set of institutions allocating services to citizens with a minimum of intervention by political actors.

5. *Emphasis on politics as the resolution of group conflict*—references to political conflicts among economic, social, and ethno-religious group-ings resolved within an agreed-upon framework of political rules of the game.

A second measure of civic education norms consisted of a series of interviews with a pool of "potential civic and educational influentials" in each of the three communities.[4] The interviews included a sample of all school administrators who were responsible for the school's civic education program; all teachers of civic education; the president and vice-president of each school's Parent and Teachers Association or Home and School Association over the past five years; and the current and most recent presidents and vice-presidents of ten major civic groups in each community. Interviewees included leaders of business, fraternal, labor, patriotic, religious, and civic betterment associations, and the chairmen of the local Republican and Democratic party organizations.

---

[3]Based on procedures developed in Bernard B. Berelson, *Content Analysis in Communications Re-search* (Glencoe, Illinois: The Free Press, 1952), and Lloyd Marcus, *The Treatment of Minorities in Second-ary School Textbooks* (New York: B'nai B'rith Anti-Defamation League, 1961).

[4]The distinction "potential civic and educational leaders or influentials" is used because we have no data on overt attempts to influence the school's civic education program. Our immediate concern is with their attitudes toward the political themes in the program. This distinction between manifested and imputed political influence is drawn in Raymond Wolfinger, "Reputation and Reality in the Study of Community Power," *American Sociological Review*, 1960 (October), 25: 636–644.

A total of 66 leaders were interviewed in Alpha, 57 in Beta, and 63 in Gamma.[5]

The interview schedule was designed to tap the intensity of the respondent's attitudes toward the proper orientation of the community school's civic education program in each of the five political dimensions. The content, reliability, and sources of the items are presented in the Appendix.

A third measure involved the effects of exposure to a formal course in civic education. A civic education class in each community was matched with a control group in age, academic attainment, parental social class, parental political affiliation, and ethno-religious affiliation. The control group, which did not take a course in civic education, was used to measure the changes in attitudes along the five political dimensions.

These dimensions were adapted for a questionnaire given to the three civic education classes, and their corresponding control groups, before and after a semester's exposure to the course (see Appendix). Thus we can compare attitudinal changes attributable to the school's "official version" of political phenomena, and the differential effects of the course in each community.

Findings

The content analysis of textbooks in the civic education programs of Alpha, Beta, and Gamma schools revealed no substantial differences in references to elements of the democratic creed, or in chauvinistic treatment of American political procedures and institutions. Few references in the material employed by the three schools connoted an insular view of American politics; the isolationist and jingoist orientation of civic education texts observed in Pierce's pioneer study were absent in this sampling.[6] Nor does the textual material differ in references endorsing the political rights of minorities and political procedures available to them. Indeed, the endorsement of the democratic creed far exceeds the other political dimensions. The blandness of the Gamma texts should be noted; they contain a large number of descriptive references (dates of major political events, anatomical presentations of political procedure) that could not be classified along one of the five political dimensions (see Table 1).

Differences do exist in the formal exposure to norms supporting political participation, in the view of politics as process, and in the functions of the political system. Unlike Alpha and Beta texts, Gamma texts

---

[5]Wherever possible, civic leaders were selected from comparable organizations in each community, such as the Chamber of Commerce and political party organizations. Differences in social structure made complete matching impossible. For example, labor union leaders were included in the Gamma sample, but not in the Alpha or Beta pools. There were 8 non-respondents or 12 per cent of the sample in Alpha, 7 (13%) in Beta, and 11 (18%) in Gamma.

[6]Bessie L. Pierce, *Civic Attitudes in American Schools* (Chicago: University of Chicago Press, 1930).

Table 1
REFERENCES ON SALIENT POLITICAL DIMENSIONS IN CIVICS TEXTBOOKS

Political Dimension	Alpha	Beta	Gamma
Emphasis on democratic creed	56%	52%	47%
Chauvinistic references to American political institutions	3%	6%	2%
Emphasis on political activity, citizen's duty, efficacy	17%	13%	5%
Emphasis on political process, politicians, and power	11%	2%	1%
Emphasis on group conflict-resolving political function	10%	1%	2%
Other	3%	26%	43%
(Totals)	100%	100%	100%
Number of paragraphs	(501)	(367)	(467)

contain only a few references to norms that encourage voting, feelings of political effectiveness, and a sense of civic duty. References to the political process as a conduit involving political actors and the use of political power — rather than the workings of an invisible hand of governmental institutions — are also sparse in the Gamma texts.

Both Beta and Gamma texts are short on references to politics as a mechanism for settling competing group demands. Table 1 reveals that only Alpha schools indicate to some degree a political process in which politicians and power are the main ingredients, and through which a political group struggle is periodically ameliorated.

How do the norms of civic education that prevail among the potential civic and educational influentials of each community compare with the formal classroom material designed to shape student political attitudes? Are salient themes in the curriculum reinforced, opposed, or ignored by community norms?

Potential community influentials do support the inculcation of basic democratic principles (the democratic creed) and the avoidance of chauvinistic references to American political institutions — attitudes that were stressed in the texts. They also support material encouraging political activity and competence in young citizens, an attitude that is less reinforced in the Gamma school texts.

[Other data] indicates, however, that the potential influentials in the three milieux differ about the presentation of politics as a process involving the resources of politicians and power, and the conflict-alleviating goal of politics. Alpha leaders endorse these "realistic" political themes; and attempts to impart elements of political reality are present only in the Alpha civic education program. In Beta and Gamma the low level of support for these themes reinforce the contextual material of their school programs which ignores or avoids these perspectives on political phenomena.

It would be useless to talk about the effects of civic education programs without considering changes in political attitudes as functions of different textual emphasis and norms of community leaders. Comparisons of attitude changes in the schools do not uncover any reversal of beliefs along the five political dimensions that can be attributed to the school's indoctrination.

Several patterns, however, relate the effects of the civic education program on student attitudes to its material and the community's potential political support. Based on the "before" and "after" questionnaires administered to the three classes and matched control groups, the data in Table 2 reveals that students in the civic education classes were more likely to endorse aspects of the democratic creed and less likely to hold chauvinistic political sentiments than students not exposed to the program. But none of the three "exposed" classes was more likely to favor political participation than their control group. And only in Alpha were perceptions of politics as group conflict involving politicians and political power strengthened through exposure to civic education.

In Alpha, Beta, and Gamma, we observe (Table 2) that exposure to the course strengthened support for democratic processes and negated chauvinistic sentiment, thus reinforcing the material presented in the civic education program and supporting attitudes of community leaders. The result is to level the socio-political differences among the communities and their school populations. Training in the tenets of democratic fair play and tolerance is sustained by civic education courses within a supporting educational and political milieu.

But civic education does not affect the varying positive attitudes toward citizen political participation manifested by the school population of the three communities. Despite the positive references of civic education material in Alpha and Beta, and the supporting community norms in all three communities, different attitudes—based on socio-political cleavages—remain about the citizen's role in public affairs. Apparently attitudes toward political activity are so strongly channeled through other agencies in each community that the civic education program's efforts have little independent effect.

Attitudes toward political process and function are related to other variables in the classroom and community climate.[7] In Alpha, where community attitudes and texts are supportive, a positive change in views of political process and function occurs among students in civic education. In Beta and Gamma, where attitudes and texts are rela-

---

[7] A comparable investigation of this problem in advancement to college has been made by Natalie Rogoff, "Public Schools and Equality of Opportunity," *Journal of Educational Sociology,* 1960 (February), *33*: 252–279.

Table 2
EFFECT OF SEMESTER COURSE IN CIVIC EDUCATION ON
POLITICAL ATTITUDES IN THREE COMMUNITIES (IN PERCENTAGES)

| | Alpha | | | |
| | Class | | Control | |
Political Attitude	Before	After	Before	After
Support of democratic creed	62*	89	57	61
Political chauvinism	23	8	19	18
Support of political participation	70	72	79	76
Politics a process of power, politicians	59	72	53	58
Function of politics to resolve group conflict	32	59	39	34
Number of cases	(38)		(44)	

| | Beta | | | |
| | Class | | Control | |
Political Attitude	Before	After	Before	After
Democratic creed	56	74	53	50
Political chauvinism	31	19	29	27
Political participation	55	56	54	49
Political process	23	21	27	26
Political group conflict	17	21	19	17
Number of cases	(51)		(46)	

| | Gamma | | | |
| | Class | | Control | |
Political Attitude	Before	After	Before	After
Democratic creed	47	59	38	44
Political chauvinism	29	10	33	38
Political participation	32	29	31	33
Political process	12	15	16	14
Political group conflict	9	12	8	6
Number of cases	(59)		(63)	

*Denotes per cent of sample strongly holding political attitude. See Appendix A for indices.

tively non-supportive little change in such views occurs; politics is treated
and learned as a formal, mechanistic set of governmental institutions
with emphasis on its harmonious and legitimate nature, rather than as
a vehicle for group struggle and change.

Conclusions

The civic education program does not simply reinforce the prevailing
sentiments and political climate of the community. Nor are attitudes

about political participation and varying levels of political activity affected by courses in civic education. Even a combination of numerous textual references and support from community leaders fails to result in attitude changes about the role of the citizen in public life.

Nevertheless, without some degree of reinforcement from its material and the political environment, the school system's effort at political indoctrination also fails. The materials, support, and effects of civic education differ in the three communities, and it is the nature of these differences that are crucial in evaluating the political role of citizenship training.

All three classes are instructed in the equalitarian ground rules of democracy. Agreement with the maxims of the democratic creed and rejection of political chauvinism are increased in the civic education programs of all three communities. But the material and effects of the working-class community, Gamma, and its civic education program, do not encourage a belief in the citizen's ability to influence government action through political participation. And only the texts and community support of Alpha are related through its civic education course to a developed awareness of political processes and functions.

In sum, then, students in the three communities are being trained to play different political roles, and to respond to political phenomena in different ways. In the working-class community, where political involvement is low, the arena of civic education offers training in the basic democratic procedures without stressing political participation or the citizen's view of conflict and disagreement as indigenous to the political system. Politics is conducted by formal governmental institutions working in harmony for the benefit of citizens.

In the lower middle-class school system of Beta—a community with moderately active political life—training in the elements of democratic government is supplemented by an emphasis on the responsibilities of citizenship, not on the dynamics of public decision-making.

Only in the affluent and politically vibrant community (Alpha) are insights into political processes and functions of politics passed on to those who, judging from their socio-economic and political environment, will likely man those positions that involve them in influencing or making political decisions.

Appendix

The content analysis of the 27 civic education textbooks was conducted in the following manner. A random sample of paragraphs, as the content unit, was selected from each text. The text was entered by use of a random table of numbers to select page and paragraph. Every twentieth paragraph was read and classified by the writer and two other judges. The criteria of classification are noted in the text. In case of disagreement among the judges, a paragraph was classified in the "other" category. Dominant emphasis, based on sentence counts within paragraphs, was determining when a paragraph contained more than one politically relevant theme. In this manner, 1,235 paragraphs were classified.

Five indices were used in the questionnaire administered to the student populations, and the interview with community leaders. Responses ran across a five-point scale from "agree strongly" to "disagree strongly." Unlike the students, the community leaders were asked whether or not each statement should be included in the civic education program. The content, reliability, and source of the political indices follow.

1.   *The Democratic Creed:* (coefficient of reliability=.911)
Every citizen should have an equal chance to influence government policy.

Democracy is the best form of government.

The minority should be free to criticize government decisions.

People in the minority should be free to try to win majority support for their opinions.

(Adapted from James W. Prothro and Charles M. Grigg, "Fundamental Principles of Democracy: Bases of Agreement and Disagreement," *The Journal of Politics*, 22 (1960), pp. 276–294.)

2.   *Political Chauvinism:* (cr=.932)
The American political system is a model that foreigners would do well to copy.

The founding fathers created a blessed and unique republic when they gave us the constitution.

Americans are more democratic than any other people.

American political institutions are the best in the world.

(Index constructed for this study.)

3.   *Political Activity:* (cr=.847)
It is not very important to vote in local elections.

It is very important to vote even when so many other people vote in an election.

Public officials do care what people like me think.

Given the complexity of issues and political organizations there is little an individual can do to make effective changes in the political system.

People like me do not have any say about what the government does.

Politics is often corrupt and the interests of the underworld are looked after by some public officials.

(Adapted from the civic duty and sense of political effectiveness measures of the Michigan Survey Research Center, and Agger's index of political cynicism. See Angus Campbell, Gerald Gurin, and Warren E. Miller, *The Voter Decides*, Evanston: Row-Peterson, 1954, pp. 187–204, and Robert E. Agger, Marshall N. Goldstein, and Stanley A. Pearl, "Political Cynicism: Measurement and Meaning," *The Journal of Politics*, 23 (1961), pp. 477–506.)

4. *Political Process*: (cr=.873)

The use of political power is crucial in public affairs.

Many political decisions are made by a minority of political activists who seek to secure the agreement of the majority to the decisions.

Politics is basically a conflict in which groups and individuals compete for things of value.

Differences of race, class, and income are important considerations in many political issues.

Governmental institutions cannot operate without politicians. (Index constructed for this study.)

5. *Political Function*: (cr=.919)

Politics should settle social and other disagreements as its major function.

Since different groups seek favorable treatment, politics is the vehicle for bargaining among these competing claims.

Politics is not a means of insuring complete harmony, but a way of arriving at temporary agreements about policies within agreed-upon rules.

The politician is the key broker among competing claims made within society.

(Index constructed for this study.)

THE SCHOOLS: CRISES IN GRASS ROOTS AUTONOMY

WILLIAM M. DOBRINER

If in economic and political affairs Levittown has had to look to the great society beyond its unincorporated borders, in school affairs it has had to look hard into itself.

In 1947–1948, 40 students were in daily attendance at the local school; the school budget was $22,550; the tax rate per $100 of assessed valuation was set at $0.73. In 1950 the enrollment had increased to 1549; in 1952, to 5076; in 1954, to 10,729. By 1960, over 18,000 students were registered. (See Table 1.)

The number of school buildings increased from one in 1947 to 15 in 1960; the number of teachers from 2 to 678; and the tax rate leaped from $0.73 to $6.45 by the spring of 1962. Garden City—old,

Pages 113–121 from: William M. Dobriner, *Class in Suburbia*, © 1963. Reprinted by permission of Prentice-Hall, Inc., Englewood Cliffs, New Jersey.

Table 1
LEVITTOWN SCHOOL ENROLLMENT, 1960

Kindergarten	2,319
Public	2,299
Elementary (1-8 years)	14,458
Public	13,837
High School (1-4 years)	3,439
Public	3,264
College	764
Total enrolled	**20,980**

Source: Prepublication copy of Table P-1, "General Characteristics of the Population by Census Tracts 1960," Nassau County, Bureau of the Census.

established, high income, and white collar—had a school tax set at $4.27 for 1962—about a third less than that of Levittown.

Since the community has no industry to tax and comparatively little business property, its main tax resource is the home owner. Year after year, the Levittowner has had to reach into his pocket to build the new schools and hire the new teachers that the soaring school population demands. Since the percentage of blue collar workers has increased, the burden has become proportionately more difficult each year. According to the special report on Levittown conducted by the National Education Association, "Levittown has the lowest ability to finance its schools of any school system with eight or more teachers in the New York City metropolitan area."[1] As a consequence, the community has had to request an increasing amount of funds from state aid. In 1948, local funds based on taxation contributed 56 per cent of the budget; in 1950, 70 per cent. By 1960 the contribution of local funds dropped to 39 per cent, and state aid had increased to 58 per cent.

The development of Levittown's school system has given rise to so much bickering and agitation that in 1961 the district became the subject of an impartial investigation by the National Education Association, authorized by the Commissioner of Education of New York.

In 1954 and 1955, Levittown's residents were sharply split over the issue of "The Lonesome Train." This was the title of a record used in the lower elementary grades to illustrate moods in music. It describes the journey of the train carrying Lincoln's body from the Capitol to Springfield, Illinois, for burial.

Two Levittown residents had heard that the cantata was written and scored by "known Communists" and that the music contained Communist propaganda—they asked that it be withdrawn from classroom use. While a group rallied to the cause of the two complaining residents, another group argued that "The Lonesome Train" was quite

[1]*Levittown, New York*, a report by the National Education Association of the United States and the Ethical Practices Committee of the New York State Teachers Association, January 1962, p. 12.

safe for their children and asked that it be retained. The controversy raged for more than a year.

In 1956–1957, the principal of one of the elementary schools sent a letter to the parents of his pupils. In the main, the letter dealt with routine school matters, but it also included the following paragraph:

> *We would hope that your child will be given some religious training in the church of his choice, so that he will understand the principles of honesty, obedience, truthfulness, and respect for authority at all times.*

The letter precipitated another controversy. Jewish groups were particularly concerned with the "church of his choice" reference. In addition, to some, the letter opened up the entire question of the separation of church and state. The liberals and intellectuals questioned the assumption that honesty and truthfulness could only be acquired within a religious context. The psychologically sophisticated were not sure if obedience and respect for authority, particularly "at all times," were always good things. The traditionalists rallied with the assertion that anyone opposed to the letter was against "morality."

In 1958, the soaring school population had led the school board to propose the construction of two new elementary schools, the conversion of an elementary school into a junior high school, and the addition of 59 classrooms to five existing elementary schools. Six members of the board backed these propositions. One member, backed by the Information and Education Committee (IEC) opposed the propositions even though, under the emergency construction legislation of the state, the entire cost of the program would have been paid by the state. The IEC stands for a traditional and conservative approach to education. It is opposed to what it terms "frills" in the public school system. It stands for larger classes rather than increased building. Generally it opposes the employment of additional staff and advocates the reduction of special services such as guidance counselors and psychologists. It hews to a basic "three R" view of education and its primary concern seems to be economy in order to hold the tax rate in check. The IEC took the position that the approval of the three propositions would result in an indirect burden in the form of increased state taxes. In early December more than 9000 residents voted on the proposals; more than half were in favor, but the necessary two-thirds majority was not obtained.

Aligned against the IEC is the Better Education League (BEL) and the District Five Education Association (EA). In the main, they stand for smaller classes, more buildings, and extension of extracurricular services and activities. According to the Social Profile of Levittown prepared for the National Education Association in the study of School District Five by the Department of Sociology and Anthropology of Boston University, the IEC is frequently identified as a Catholic group while the BEL is seen as a predominantly Jewish group by the Levittown leaders interviewed for the study.

Over the years, the situation within the schools has been steadily deteriorating. On Sunday, April 3, 1960, the citizens of Levittown first learned of a "placement bureau" that was operating within the Levittown Teachers Association. Its function was to find jobs in other school districts for the members. This advertisement appeared in the April 3 issue of the *New York Times*:

TEACHERS:

Situations Wanted

LEVITTOWN
TEACHERS ASSOCIATION

Teacher Placement Bureau

HAS AVAILABLE FOR 1960–61
QUALIFIED – CERTIFIED – EXPERIENCED
ELEMENTARY (K–8) TEACHERS
FEMALE & MALE

Teachers of Math and Science
Teachers of English
Teachers of Cit. Ed.
Teachers of Mentally Retarded
Teachers of all Special Subjects
I.A., Phys. Ed., Art, Music, Lang., Bus.

Interested School Districts Contact:
L.T.A. TEACHER PLACEMENT BUR.
P.O. Box 63
Levittown, New York

Source: *Levittown, New York: A Study of Leadership Problems in a Rapidly Developed Community,* National Education Association and the Ethical Practices Committee of the New York State Teachers Association, p. 20.

In addition, the following letter was sent to all school districts in Nassau, Suffolk, Westchester, and Rockland Counties:

Dear Sir:

The Levittown, N.Y., Public School system has an outstanding staff. Many school districts, perhaps your own among them, have in the past attracted many of our top personnel. Many more have stayed to strive constantly for a fine educational system, hoping always for a more professional climate in which to teach.

The Levittown Teachers' Association has been requested, by many of its members, for aid in seeking employment. We have therefore established a teacher placement service for our members in an effort to satisfy this demand.

If your district is in need of qualified, experienced elementary, junior, and senior high school teachers in all general and specialized areas, please contact us.

We will comply at all times with the New York State Teachers' Association Code of Ethics.

> Respectfully yours,
> Levittown Teachers' Association
> Placement Service
> P.O. Box 63, Levittown, N.Y.

P.S. The problem in Levittown is not basically financial but one of an unsound professional climate in which to teach.

The problem, too, is not localized, but one which has nation-wide implications. For this reason the teachers of Levittown called in the NEA Defense Commission by a vote of 548–44.

The school board was enraged. On June 30, 1960, the board voted 4 to 3 to terminate the services of the Superintendent. Bitterness against the board grew to such intensity that in September 1960, two former members of the board filed petitions with the State Education Department for the removal of two members on the grounds that the board members were involved in irregularities pertaining to district funds, personnel, and procedures. In the meantime, the Levittown Teachers' Association was still actively soliciting jobs for its members in rival school districts. On November 21, 1960, a weary superintendent of schools formally filed his resignation.

After many more months of squabbling, the state's Commissioner of Education on April 17, 1961 noted

> . . . that a number of appeals relating to the operation of Union Free School District No. 5 of the Town of Hempstead, Nassau County, have been filed with me over the last several years pursuant to Education Law, Section 310, the latest of which sought the removal of two board members; that petitions, charges and countercharges have characterized this school district during this same period; that unrest, dissension, and strife have permeated the relations between factions of the school board, superintendent, teaching, and supervisory staff and citizens and taxpayers of the community.[2]

²*Ibid.*, p. 28.

By the spring of 1961, it was apparent that the conflict between the formal components of Levittown's educational system—the superintendent, the school board, the teachers' organizations—along with the two dissident citizen groups, had imperiled the operation of the system. But teachers still met their classes and the business of educating the young went on. Levittown high school students continued to receive scholarships from substantial colleges and universities. Since then at least some of the tension within the system seems to have abated. The two warring citizen factions have attempted to work out their differences on the basis of the NEA report. However, it is too early to say whether the pattern of conflict in school affairs is about to change significantly for the better.

The Search for Community

Levittown is a suburban reflection of many of the immigrant groups who shaped the social history of New York City over the past 100 years. The impact of city culture, social relationships, and the significant role of ethnicity still prevail in Levittown. As in New York, it is sociologically crucial in the shaping of the destiny of an individual whether he be born a Russian Jew or Irish Catholic or German Protestant. Although formal class terms such as *middle class* or *working class* are not often found in the working vocabulary of Levittown, class is empirically recognized and religious and ethnic considerations underlie evaluations of friends and neighbors. In New York City, where the nation's minorities are majorities and Protestants and "old American stock" are relatively scarce, Levittowners, as former New Yorkers, still live in a world divided into religious and ethnic subcommunities.

Some members of the community have interpreted the school situation as arising from fundamentally differing views of public education among Catholics, Protestants, and Jews. Some Levittowners explain the school crises in terms of a "Jewish" or "Catholic" or "Protestant" vote. In 1961, a Boston University research team, commissioned to do a social profile of Levittown by the National Education Association, spent a considerable amount of time exploring the extent of this feeling. Here are some remarks by Levittown leaders characteristic of those gathered by the Boston study group:[3]

> *The Protestants and Jews are in the BEL, with a few outstanding exceptions, and the Catholics are associated with IEC, with a few exceptions.*

> *This is probably the only community in the United States where a Protestant child finds himself ostracized. He cannot join certain play groups because he's not Jewish and others because he's not Catholic.*

[3]Louis Orzack and Irwin T. Sanders, *A Social Profile of Levittown, New York* (Research Institute, Department of Sociology and Anthropology, Boston University), mimeo., pp. 17–24, *passim.*

A Catholic resident, regarded as an educational "liberal," explained the situation of Jews in Levittown in this way:

> It is not a question of the Jews wanting to take over the school, as so many of the upper-income Catholics apparently believe; it is a question of understanding the Jewish community and its attitude toward the problem of religion and education — or, putting it more typically, the question of church and state.

Another leader said:

> The Jews for their part resent the dominance of the Roman Catholics in the school system. Too many of the high positions of the past have been given to Catholics. The Jews fear from time to time that the public school, while remaining that in title, will actually become a parochial school for Roman Catholics, or rather will be under Roman Catholic domination.

Another maintains:

> The Protestants are not organized. They have no axe to grind; they are the most apathetic in the community. The Protestant-Catholic cleavage may be very deep but it is not overt. The only time it becomes overt is in the school board situation. Otherwise, the Catholics and Protestants are good friends. They visit each other's homes. Just like Republicans and Democrats, you can still be friends.

Still another says:

> The Catholic clergy are never quoted; they operate behind the scenes and through the Holy Name Society. I only know of one priest who actually told his people how to vote on the school issue. We must lick the animosity between the Catholics and the anti-Catholics. The Catholics have the initiative, and this creates reaction, with other people either fighting the Catholics or moving out of Levittown.

The answer to the role of religion in the school controversy lies in the ethnic and class factors that underlie the overt and apparent religious dimension. In a sense, religion shows handily on the surface of Levittown's social system and becomes a ready explanation in a community already sensitive to group differences. It is a convenient answer much in the same way that race "explains" the Negro crime rate. However, the answer to Negro crime, as in the school crises in Levittown, will be found in a less visible but more significant set of determinants—the ethnic and class factors. The general socioeconomic stratum characteristically occupied by Levittown's Catholic population is the blue collar group, the working class. Catholics probably constitute the bulk of the working class population in Levittown. In addition, the Catholic population still has strong ethnic attachments. . . . [C]lose to 20 per cent of the total foreign stock in Levittown was Italian and 8 per cent Irish.

The literature of class values and motivation consistently reveals that the working class in the United States is less involved with the issue of education than the middle class. Members of the working class want their children to go to school, but the drive to achieve excellence and the intense desire to build first-rate schools in which their children are to be star performers are not working-class characteristics. The almost emotional commitment to educationalism as a form of class-typed behavior shows most clearly in the upper-middle class and filters down in modified form to the lower-middle class. The reluctance of Levittown's Catholic population to demonstrate all-out support of the schools thus becomes an expression of class behavior and values rather than of Catholic behavior and values.

In addition to the press of social class in the shaping of educational ideology, Levittown's Catholics are, in the main, third- and second-generation New Yorkers reflecting rural Irish, Italian, Polish, etc., ethnic definitions of education. Neither the Irish nor Italians, in contrast to the Jews, had much of a commitment or incentive for education when they arrived in this country. It had to be acquired. Generally, it takes three generations to achieve full assimilation of the new culture. The new values which the immigrant groups first learned and accepted would be those of the "lower" urban classes in which the educational ideal was characteristically weak.

In the case of Levittown's working-class and still ethnically bound Catholic population, the values of education and the importance of education as an instrument of upward mobility and social status are not yet fully perceived. This relative lack of interest with only partial commitment to middle-class educational standards and values is then superimposed over the marginal economic position of Levittown's Catholic population, and the answer to Catholic conservatism stands revealed. Not only is there some doubt on the part of the working-class population in Levittown regarding education as the middle class sees it, but they have been called upon to spend an extraordinary amount of money, particularly when one considers their modest income levels, to get the schools even to their present state. The financial burden with which Levittowners—both working and middle class—have been struggling has been incredible. In the main, therefore, the class and ethnic factors prevail over the religious in Levittown's school situation. If you are doubtful about the importance of schooling in the first place, you could not reasonably be expected to pay for other people's educative "frills"—particularly when you can't afford them anyway.

The critical role of economic and ethnic factors in school matters appears to be a national pattern. In their study of "Springdale," a rural community in upper New York State, Vidich and Bensman found a tradition of "rural dominance" in the over-all administration and character of the village school.[4] Unlike Levittown, this was a highly Protestant community. Nevertheless, the authors maintained that business interests in the village and farm interests outside the town combined forces to sustain a ". . . low-tax, low-expenditure ideology. . . ." Springdale, like Levittown, has a group of educational liberals who are willing to spend more to improve the schools. And, as in Levittown, the prime interest of the conservatives is keeping down the tax rate. In this almost exclusively Protestant community the familiar push and pull of liberal-conservative forces seems remarkably to parallel the Levittown situation.

---

20. Education for What?

Criticism of American schools is not a new phenomenon. Indeed, in a society characterized by a large, highly educated professional class and a sensitive public opinion network, it is impossible to avoid references to the school's inadequacies in fighting racial injustice, promoting social skills, or meeting some nebulous formula of national goals. In the first selection that follows, Michael Walzer argues for an elitist culture in a nonelitist society; he believes that the best liberal education should be provided in all segments of the educational system. However, Walzer points directly to the problem of retaining some degree of quality in a society devoted to the education of almost all its younger citizens.

In the high school Edgar Friedenberg describes, school authorities practice a particularly rigid form of suppression of youthful expression; in so doing, Friedenberg contends, "the high school is permitted to infantilize adolescence." This kind of school (which may be more authoritarian and restrictive than most) attempts to force its students into acceptable channels of socialization rather than providing them with a political and cultural system worthy of emulation and giving them freedom to grow in the directions best suited to them.

[4]Arthur J. Vidich and Joseph Bensman, *Small Town in Mass Society* (Garden City, N.Y.: Doubleday, 1960), pp. 174–201, *passim.*

> *The rationale of democratic education is derived from the Enlightenment with its emphasis on reason and freedom. An analysis of the role of social science education in enhancing freedom and reason is provided by C. Wright Mills. Concerned about bureaucratic growth, about learning geared to the needs of the powerful and of the masses, and about the self-interest of the American educational apparatus, Mills contends that the issues of reason and freedom themselves must be squarely faced. Neither teaching techniques nor structural reorganization of schools is meaningful without a fundamental probing of the relation of knowledge and power and of the relevance of Western values, such as reason and freedom, in a post-Western era.*

THE AMERICAN SCHOOL

Michael Walzer

I

The rhetoric of equality is a staple of American speech; we devoutly abstain, however, from planning the practice of equality. The amazingly rapid expansion of American education in the past fifty years is indeed an occasion for pride: *it is better that children be in school.* But it is not entirely—or necessarily—a democratic achievement; expansion has been hardly less rapid in undemocratic countries. Even as we survey the gains, we need to note the cunning survival of old, and the unlooked-for development of new, forms of inequality. In general, the survivals result from the lack of perspicacity, energy and system so characteristic of liberal reformers facing a *class* society, as well as from the eternal resourcefulness of privilege. The novelties are more likely the result of an apprehension of the needs of a *mass* society and its bureaucratic elite.

For the purposes of our examination, American schools can be roughly divided into those which are, in class terms, integrated and those which are socially "pure." The grossest inequality is obviously manifest in the latter, in the exclusiveness often enjoyed or endured by both upper and lower class children. That so much of the current debate centers upon the problems of schools already integrated reveals a surprising disinclination to face the most immediate educational problems. American school districts are organized geographically and in largest part financed locally; this means that insofar as the geography

From *Dissent*, 1959, Summer: 223–236.

of our cities and countryside is a class geography, the schools — especially on the elementary level — will be socially unintegrated. It follows that they will be dilapidated or luxurious according to the state of the local economy. Our post-war school building program has been predictably spotty, hardly beginning work precisely in those areas where it is most needed. Despite the progress of consolidation and the possibility of federal loans, a large number of Americans attend schools understaffed by underpaid teachers, housed in buildings partially condemned or ugly, dirty and (often) unsafe. In surroundings such as these they quickly learn what one might think was the single intended lesson: that such as they need not dwell very long on the business of education. School does not long detain such children, and they have usually fled in spirit years before they escape in fact.

The "school retention rate" offers significant evidence of educational inequality in America today. This measurement indicates the holding power of the schools, or, conversely, the ability (or the willingness) of children to continue their education. From fifth grade to high school approximately 55 per cent of the student population is retained: of every 1,000 students in fifth grade in 1946–47 only 553 graduated high school in 1954. Although the number of students leaving school is highest in the two years directly before graduation, it is actually rather evenly distributed over all the years after sixth-grade: thus a considerable number of children never get beyond grade school; many more drop out during junior high school years.[1]

But these figures by themselves tell only a small part of the story: for school retention is not at all evenly distributed among social classes. Precisely how it is distributed is more difficult to discover. We may assume that retention through high school, being 100 per cent among upper class children, and probably not too far from that among the middle classes, must drop radically among the children of unskilled workers, slum dwellers, agricultural laborers, new immigrants, etc. — for otherwise a national retention rate of 55 per cent is hardly explicable. Such sociological surveys as are available confirm this, indicating, for example, that in families whose income is below the national average some 30 per cent of those students *whose indicated capacity is sufficient for college work*, fail to finish high school.[2] School retention through college similarly follows class lines: a study by Elmo Roper among high school graduates found that only 20.5 per cent of the sons of factory workers applied for admission to college; among the sons of men in professional or executive positions the figure was 73.4 per cent. College acceptance rates showed a similar bias, though it was far less extreme.[3]

---

[1]U.S. Department of Health, Education, and Welfare, *Statistical Summary of Education*, 1953–1954, p. 10. Also previous editions of the *Summary*.

[2]Warner, Havighurst, Loeb, *Who Shall Be Educated: The Challenge of Unequal Opportunities*, 1944, p. 52.

[3]Roper, *Factors Affecting the Admission of High School Seniors to College*, 1949, p. 17.

The children of different classes, of course, apply to different colleges; most working class students who go to college at all move on to state teachers' colleges, junior colleges, or the smaller technical institutes.

School retention figures, it should be noted, have been showing a steady improvement for over half a century; the rate of this improvement appears, however, to have slowed down in recent years. It is possible that the "revolution" in American secondary education is nearing its close (in the colleges, perhaps, it is only beginning). Although the number of high school students will continue to rise—automatically with the birth rate—the social range of the school may already have been extended to its "natural" limits, that is, to limits set by the comparative political and economic powerlessness of the groups still beyond the pale. To be beyond the pale does not mean that one does not get an education, but rather that one's education is incomplete, is experienced as something to be resisted and avoided, and is provided at the hands of teachers who often imagine themselves—whether in the spirit of idealism or of cynicism—to be in exile. Between such teachers, usually recruited from the middle classes, and the children they must teach there arise the most fundamental and difficult problems of communication. . . .

II

Probably most American high schools are socially integrated, though this may mean no more than that they include a fairly wide middle class range, losing the children of both social extremes. . . . It is possible first of all to attract better and happier teachers (there is, however, a frightening "attraction" in slum schools as well, for some teachers enjoy the comparative freedom from parental supervision and aspiration, and the opportunity to maintain an overt, stern, and sometimes para-military discipline). It is possible, secondly, to offer a wider range of subjects, academic as well as commercial and vocational, and to provide some semblance of a liberal education. What is most important, however, is the simple fact of social confrontation in the school; its possibilities may well include hostility and mutual avoidance as well as tolerance and friendship, but either of these seems better than isolation: in this case a similar principle should govern the social treatment of class and racial differences. The recognition of difference, though not always or even often its abolition, must be made a basic goal of democratic education. This suggests a significant argument, repeated below, against overly rigid sectioning or the siphoning off of talent.

These are the possibilities—long explored in this country—of what the English call a "comprehensive" school. But it must be said that these are possibilities only rarely realized. In socially integrated schools participation in carefully differentiated programs leading toward fairly explicit careers has tended to follow class lines; and then comprehension becomes little more than formal co-existence. It is only in the lower-middle classes—to use Lloyd Warner's terms (and his figures) —that approximately equal numbers of students opt for, or are guided into, the commercial-vocational program and the academic curriculum. Among upper-middle class students the figures in a Yankee City high school were 12 per cent for the first and 88 per cent for the second; among upper-lower class students the figures were 72 per cent and 28 per cent respectively.[4] There is no evidence available to indicate any significant change in these divisions since Warner's work. They probably demonstrate certain general truths about American high schools. Surely no one who has recently spent any time in an average school can fail to be aware that *the vocational and commercial programs on the one hand and the academic on the other are simply the names behind which different social classes receive their education and discover their divergent destinies.*

It has sometimes been suggested, not always tongue-in-cheek, that high school athletic programs are the most democratic features of American secondary education: football has even carried racial integration into the south. Talent tells on the field more immediately, possibly more decisively, than in the classroom. This is probably true because a common set of cultural tastes and aspirations stands behind American athletics, while learning is still culturally divisive. Athletics, to put it crudely, has become a part of mass culture, and motivation toward athletic achievement a matter of massive indoctrination; learning is still a part of class culture, its pursuit dependent upon family encouragement and pressure. The outcome of the current crisis in education may well be to alter the last half of this discouraging proposition: to make at least scientific achievement a common cultural aspiration and to increase the degree of talent selection and reward. Such a result would have to be judged in terms of its effects upon the unselected, as well as in terms of the definition and uses of talent. As for the first of these, it might be worthwhile to point out that the social effect of democratic selection on the basis of extraordinary athletic talent has been the slow erosion of activity and participation among the untalented. But this distinction, at least, is no longer based on social class.

The possibilities for individual mobility are probably the major virtues of a class-integrated school today. The 28 per cent of Warner's upper-lower class sample who chose an academic program and perhaps went on to a college of some sort were socially mobile, aspiring upwards. Some modern sociologists suggest that the discovery of such individuals is virtually the only task of the school: a push for the first-born, a smiling and presumably socializing glance at the stolid unmoving mass. High school principals often acknowledge that such is their

[4]Warner, *et al., op. cit.,* p. 61.

mission; they nudge students into a suitable place in the school program and this is a foretaste of the process by which they will someday be adjusted to their position in society at large. Many educators are quite frank about discouraging expectations in students who in their opinion are likely to be frustrated later on. Frustration is recognized not only as a personal problem, but also as a social danger.

Such a selection as the high schools claim to make, however, can rarely be made on the basis of talent alone; despite the plethora of tests, talent remains chiefly an attribute of performance, and the judgment of performance, as well as performance itself, is a matter of manners and mores. "The judgment of ability," write Havighurst and his associates, "is primarily a social class judgment and those children who conform to middle-class standards [are said to] have ability." Learning to be middle-class and not merely learning mathematics or history is obviously an important element in upward mobility. And insofar as this particular skill is family-taught, the educational system serves as "a mechanism which helps perpetuate our class order."[5]

III

In the years before the launching of Sputnik our schools were in the process of shaping their curriculums to fit the needs of a mass society. This process parallels, complicates and to a limited degree undercuts the effort to maintain class distinctions which has just been described.

The essential purpose of the new education, a group of its apostles have argued, is "to build common cultural backgrounds that many homes no longer supply." The school thus self-consciously assumes many of the educational tasks of the family, in effect short-circuiting an older learning process in which the student's cultural and moral directions were most often supplied by his parents. Since the class system is, at its socially most significant level, a system of family relationships, the newer educational processes tend to soften any very precise sense of class distinction. To a degree, the family is no longer able to send into the school a child already conscious of his social position, already filled with a particular set of attitudes and aspirations.

This construction of a "common culture" is enhanced by that broader trend which is slowly transforming a society oriented to production into a society absorbed in consumption. Insofar as the student is still trained for productive activity, for "opportunity" in the old sense of that word, invidious distinctions prevail; family expectations, class manners and mores guide the student toward a kind of manifest destiny. Consumption in America today tends to be more homogeneous: expectations and taste are not governed by the family but created outside it. The young child, recognized as a consumer, is appealed to through the mass media — and with this appeal the family often cannot compete. Indeed, father and mother, instead of themselves supplying the cultural images and values of their children, will often succumb to the child's more "educated," more contemporary, sense of the appropriate and fashionable.

It is not, however, in the school that the child attains his education in the appropriate; it is rather from a host of external influences, among which the mass media are increasingly important. For the discovery of the child as a consumer has proven one of Madison Avenue's major inspirations. Assiduously followed up, it has resulted in the creation of a new, more or less homogeneous teen-age culture in America. The ever-present need for some sort of cultural unity has been filled by men who stood to gain by pitching its level low enough to maximize the immediate sale of cultural commodities. The process is not conspiratorial; it is the natural adjustment of salesman and customer. In the world of culture, however, one might well wish at least to supplement this with the relationship of teacher and student. If that relationship is more authoritative, it is at the same time less manipulative; and it can be a relationship of deep mutual respect.

The new teen-age culture no longer supports the work of the school as did the older middle-class training in work and aspiration. The product of this training was the man David Riesman called "inner-directed," a man whose experience of authority and love in the family had fitted him, once he had left the home, to face the world as an individual. In the absence of such a man, it becomes imperative that the school itself be capable of "inner-direction," that it discover value in its curriculum and confront its students with this value. Both their resistance and their acceptance, it should be noted, will then be salutary.

In the past the American school has supplied some such direction to those of its students, at least, who were preparing for college. It has done so, however, in such an unimaginative and crotchety fashion, and with such an extraordinary absence of enthusiasm or concern, as to endanger the very idea of direction in learning. Since World War II, the trend in education has been steadily away from the "inner-directed" school. Educators have moved — despite an inevitable, and one would think a fortunate, inertia in the system — to fit the schools to the needs of the increasingly socialized child, and through him to the needs of society.

"It would seem not to require proof that education at any time and in any society should in its character and purposes conform to the dominant ideals as to form of organization held by that society."[6] Thus wrote

[6]Douglas, *Secondary Education for Life Adjustment of American Youth*, 1952, p. 58.

the director of an American college of education in 1952. But neither this man nor any of his colleagues would acknowledge conformity alone as a goal of education. Political and social adjustment, they would probably insist, is only the means to personal happiness. The greatest happiness of the greatest number remains the goal of educators calling themselves liberals and progressives. Unimpressed with the history of social change, very much impressed with the contemporary mechanics of socialization, they seek quite consciously to break down any lingering, recalcitrant "inner-direction" in order to develop the student's "adaptive flexibility" and to expand his "frustration tolerance." The happiness to which such a training points is the contentment of the bland, a kind of friendly mindlessness. The student *reacts*, as does the school: *his* is a passive nature, oriented mainly to the consumption of pleasure; the school's role tends increasingly to become passive, aimed at a training in the pleasures of consumption.

The school is more and more able to assume that the buying of goods and services is the most universal human experience. Consumption, appreciation and use: here are a new trio of human "needs" which the school, in its more modern moments, seeks to fulfill. A kind of self-salesmanship and a perennial patriotism round out what may well pass for an education. These presumed "needs" of the child, which are also the anticipated requirements of society, received classical expression in an extremely important book published by the National Educational Association in 1944 (revised edition, 1952) entitled *Education for ALL American Youth*. In the order in which they there appear—their expression is shortened but not caricatured—these are the ten "needs of youth" which the school is to meet:

1. To develop salable skills.
2. To maintain good health and physical fitness.
3. To understand the rights and duties of citizenship.
4. To understand the significance of the family for the individual and for society.
5. To learn how to buy goods and services.
6. To understand the influence of science on human life.
7. To develop an appreciation of literature, art, music, and nature.
8. To be able to use leisure time well and to budget it wisely.
9. To develop respect for other persons.
10. To grow in the ability to think rationally.

Now it is obvious that the fulfillment of most of these "needs" is the normal outcome of an education in history, literature, and science —supplemented as it must be by subsequent vocational or professional training. The authors of the NEA book, however, seek to wring from such subjects a more immediate gain than genuine learning is able to offer. Instead of approaching problems in taste, personal choice, and political duty through an established, authoritative body of knowledge, they tend to fragmentize the old curriculum and to present instead a series of problem-solving lessons. This is already apparent in the approach to literature recommended by the NEA: "some of the best things ever said on the solution of students' personal problems were written by poets, novelists and dramatists." Similarly, history is no longer to be studied "for its own sake," but rather "for the sake of becoming a good practicing citizen."

In undertaking to solve personal problems and to train the student in the practices of citizenship, educators are all too likely to forget their primary duties. They appear to move in frenzied circles attempting to teach everything, responding with unreflecting enthusiasm to each new "need": the reaction to Sputnik is only a more newsworthy example. One of the results of this enthusiasm has been a proliferation of courses in the high school, a phenomenon especially noticeable in those new schools which have been able to plan for the needs of *all* their students. This proliferation is perhaps not a necessary evil, even if it does absorb, as some critics have alleged, a considerable portion of a narrowly limited amount of educational time. Both young children and teen-agers have, in fact, a great deal of time—time enough to learn to dance, to drive a car, to play football, to train for a vocation; even—hopefully—time enough for unorganized play and unplanned idleness. The danger to education is only significant when any of these activities achieves intellectual parity with traditional academic subjects. But today this danger is a very real one. The incongruous series has long been a device of satire; it has now become a source of moral confusion in the curriculum, a confusion only occasionally funny. . . .

One of America's most influential writers on education, James B. Conant, has suggested that the schools should seek to reduce the "visibility" of social and economic (and intellectual) differences. He has argued that all education is essentially vocational, that history, foreign languages, and physics serve career purposes no less than do workshop and commercial English. If this view were widely accepted, the prestige of the liberal arts and sciences would be effectively reduced. But this would be obfuscation and not equality. *The true goal of educational equality is to make available to all students who are in any way capable of learning a single heritage of knowledge in art and science. In relationship to this heritage all vocational training—however necessary and beneficial—is extra-curricular.*

A false equalitarianism of ideas and purposes leaves the school utterly unable to choose among the myriad demands made upon it. It responds instead to the greatest pressure, and it is not the needs of individuals but the requirements of society which prevail. . . .

IV

This educational defeatism is related to the secret opinion many educators seem to have of democracy: they believe that it is not possible but that it can be counterfeited by a kind of ruse. The common learning is often one form of this ruse; the pseudo-ethic of cooperation and consensus is another. (In some genuinely progressive schools, it should be said, the core curriculum represents an extremely valuable experiment in teaching method and involves very little tampering with content.) A bulletin of the U.S. Office of Education (No. 22, 1951) first made clear the nature of the trick. It was devoted to an examination of the "neglected sixty per cent" of American students; of the other forty per cent, presumably, half are prepared for college and half are provided with technical skills. Neither of these courses are really possible for the "neglected sixty": "reading to comprehend newspapers and magazines reasonably well" is considered a worthy aim for them. Nor is this seen as any cause for sorrow: it is "in fact fortunate," says an article in the *Bulletin* of the National Association of Secondary-School Principals, "for a society having a large number of jobs to be done requiring no unusual aptitudes or interests" that so many children exist who have neither "aroused interests or pronounced aptitudes." These children too must be formed into citizens and consumers, though hardly by a process which will help them to make intelligent and rational choices. Their democratic right to an education is transformed into the inescapable duty of society to provide them with the appearance of knowledge.

"We shall be denying educational opportunity to many people," wrote the President's Committee on Higher Education, "as long as we maintain the present orientation of higher education toward verbal skills and intellectual interests." This is sheer ruse; translated it means: "We shall be depriving children of the right to go to school unless we can find some way of not educating them once they are there." Finding such a way is often a task which absorbs all the ingenuity of writers on education. Thus the author of one of the better texts on building the high school curriculum suggests such "instructional units" as Managing Money, Family Living, Prejudice, Learning to Enjoy and Appreciate Literature, How to Apply for a Job, Physics in the Kitchen.[7] Another text describes a "new" English program oriented towards: 1) letter-writing, 2) oral discussion, 3) daily speech needs, 4) interviewing, 5) group discussion, 6) conversation.[8] Everyday problems indeed!

[7]Romine, *Building the High School Curriculum*, 1954, *passim*.
[8]Carlsen, "Life Adjustment Through English," in Douglas (ed.), *Education for Life Adjustment*, 1950, pp. 94–96.

Such suggestions from educators are frightening enough; it is somewhat comforting to know that schools are usually "reactionary" about implementing them. The school's adjustment to the mass media themselves is probably more rapid, however, than to the programs of these educated middle-men of cultural levelling. Many educational textbooks today advocate a teaching program in listening and watching (just as many more urge an education in buying). Such a training, they suggest, would enable men to become "intelligent users" of the mass media. There is something of ruse here also, for the noun and adjective are wedded too hastily. An intelligent man might, after all, choose *not* to use the mass media, and intelligence at any rate precedes use and does not merely modify it.

A more realistic argument, not so much for a training in television-watching, as for the use of material from the mass media, is offered by those who would seek to make contact with students "on their own level," and to knit together their school-learning with what they learn on their own. This is something like stooping to conquer and is justifiable if one does not stoop too low — and if one remembers to conquer.

The essence of the democratic ruse is the equality of subject matter (stooping, then, is *really* as good as conquering). But this is supplemented by a spurious equality of persons, achieved through an odd and disturbing sort of group harmony. The general effort of the new education to shape students into adjustable citizens is made real in the school by joining the student to an interdependent, cooperating group. The purpose of this is indicated in a list of aims set forth by the writers on Evanston High School [in *New Schools for a New Culture*]; under the heading "Social Adjustment" appears the following: "Learning to make common decisions concerning common problems, not by compromise, but by consensus, the democratic process." Differences of opinion, the authors continue, are never real; the school should "discourage controversy, encourage fact-finding." One of the critics of the new learning has rightly pointed out that in this world of consensus the individual who holds a minority view "is treated like a backward child who must be brought to see the light . . . permanent disagreement is never tolerated." It is the essential characteristic of spurious equalitarianism that it does not recognize respect, tolerance or conflict as possible relationships of equal men, but only agreement and resemblance. This attitude in our schools, re-enforced a hundred times from the outside, is perhaps the greatest existing threat to that other — that genuine — equalitarianism for which socialists yearn. . . .

Finally, a threefold set of suggestions. First, the most immediate and most important educational task remains the attack upon class barriers. Major work must still be done, and not only in slums and the poorer agricultural districts where such work should inevitably begin. For the subtle tenacity of class is manifest even in our better high schools with their two-highway system, and even (or especially) in the new, extravagantly modern and luxurious vocational schools. Secondly, a genuinely democratic education is ultimately a matter of what is taught. We require a major rethinking of our curriculum, and eventually a (tentative, latitudinarian) redefinition of that body of knowledge which we value so highly that we would impose it upon every child. Thirdly, if the commitment to a common learning is genuine, then it must be accompanied by radical experiment with the methods of education. Perhaps this is the true test of a democracy: that a way be found to confront all its children with cultural excellence and to win from all of them an intelligent and active response. The least that can be said is that educators today have not had faith enough in the possibility of success.

THE MODERN HIGH SCHOOL: A PROFILE

Edgar Z. Friedenberg

Not far from Los Angeles, though rather nearer to Boston, may be located the town of Milgrim, in which Milgrim High School is clearly the most costly and impressive structure. Milgrim is not a suburb. Although it is only fifty miles from a large and dishonorable city and a part of its conurbation, comparatively few Milgrimites commute to the city for work. Milgrim is an agricultural village which has outgrown its nervous system; its accustomed modes of social integration have not yet even begun to relate its present, recently acquired inhabitants to one another. So, though it is not a suburb, Milgrim is not a community either.

Milgrim's recent, fulminating growth is largely attributable to the rapid development of light industry in the outer suburbs, with a resulting demand for skilled labor. But within the past few years, further economic development has created a steady demand for labor that is not so skilled. In an area that is by no means known for its racial tolerance or political liberalism, Milgrim has acquired, through no wish of its own, a sizable Negro and Puerto Rican minority. On the shabby outskirts of town, a number of groceries label themselves Spanish-American. The advanced class in Spanish at Milgrim High School makes a joyful noise—about the only one to be heard.

Estimates of the proportion of the student body at Milgrim who are, in the ethnocentric language of demography, non-white, vary enormously. Some students who are clearly middle-class and of pinkish-gray color sometimes speak as if they themselves were a besieged minority. More responsible staff members produce estimates of from 12 to 30 per cent. Observations in the corridors and lunchrooms favor the lower figure. They also establish clearly that the non-whites are orderly and well behaved, though somewhat more forceful in their movements and manner of speech than their light-skinned colleagues.

What is Milgrim High like? It is a big, expensive building, on spacious but barren grounds. Every door is at the end of a corridor; there is no reception area, no public space in which one can adjust to the transition from the outside world. Between class periods the corridors are tumultuously crowded; during them they are empty. But at both times they are guarded by teachers and students on patrol duty. Patrol duty does not consist primarily in the policing of congested throngs of moving students, or the guarding of property from damage. Its principal function is the checking of corridor passes. Between classes, no student may walk down the corridor without a form, signed by a teacher, telling where he is coming from, where he is going, and the time, to the minute, during which the pass is valid. A student caught in the corridor without such a pass is sent or taken to the office; there a detention slip is made out against him, and he is required to remain after school for two or three hours. He may do his homework during this time, but he may not leave his seat or talk.

There is no physical freedom whatever at Milgrim. Except during class breaks, the lavatories are kept locked, so that a student must not only obtain a pass but find the custodian and induce him to open the facility. Indeed Milgrim High's most memorable arrangements are its corridor passes and its johns; they dominate social interaction. "Good morning, Mr. Smith," an attractive girl will say pleasantly to one of her teachers in the corridor. "Linda, do you have a pass to be in your locker after the bell rings?" is his greeting in reply. There are more classifications of washrooms than there must have been in the Confederate Navy. The common sort, marked just "Boys" and "Girls," are generally locked. Then there are some marked, "Teachers, Men" and "Teachers, Women," unlocked. Near the auditorium are two others marked simply, "Men" and "Women," which are intended primarily for the public when the auditorium is being used for some function. During the school day cardboard signs saying "Adults Only" are placed on these doors. Girding up my maturity, I used this men's room during my stay at Milgrim. Usually it was empty; but once, as soon as the door clicked behind me, a teacher who had been concealed in the cubicle began jumping up and down to peer over his partition and verify my adulthood.

He was not a voyeur; he was checking on smoking. At most public high schools, students are forbidden to smoke, and this is probably the most common source of friction with authorities. It focuses, naturally, on the washrooms which are the only place students can go where teachers are not supposed to be. Milgrim, for a time, was more liberal than most; last year its administration designated an area behind the school where seniors might smoke during their lunch period. But, as a number of students explained to me during interviews, some of these seniors had "abused the privilege" by lighting up before they got into the area, and the privilege had been withdrawn. No student, however, questioned that smoking was a privilege rather than a right.

The concept of privilege is important at Milgrim. Teachers go to the head of the chow line at lunch; whenever I would attempt quietly to stand in line the teacher on hall duty would remonstrate with me. He was right, probably; I was fouling up an entire informal social system by my ostentation. Students on hall patrol also were allowed to come to the head of the line; so were seniors. Much of the behavior that Milgrim depends on to keep it going is motivated by the reward of getting a government-surplus peanut butter or tuna fish sandwich without standing in line.

The lunchroom itself is a major learning experience, which must make quite an impression over four years time. There are two large cafeterias which are used as study halls during the periods before and after the middle of the day. The food, by and large, is good, and more tempting than the menu. The atmosphere is not quite that of a prison, because the students are permitted to talk quietly, under the frowning scrutiny of teachers standing around on duty, during their meal—they are not supposed to talk while standing in line, though this rule is only sporadically enforced. Standing in line takes about a third of their lunch period, and leaves plenty of time for them to eat what is provided them. They may not, in any case, leave the room when they have finished, any more than they could leave a class. Toward the end of the period a steel gate is swung down across the corridor, dividing the wing holding the cafeterias, guidance offices, administrative offices, and auditorium from the rest of the building. Then the first buzzer sounds, and the students sweep out of the cafeteria and press silently forward to the gate. A few minutes later a second buzzer sounds, the gate is opened, and the students file out to their classrooms.

During the meal itself the atmosphere varies in response to chance events and the personality of the teachers assigned supervisory duty; this is especially true in the corridor where the next sitting is waiting in line. The norm is a not unpleasant chatter; but about one teacher in four is an embittered martinet, snarling, whining, continually ordering the students to stand closer to the wall and threatening them with detention or suspension for real or fancied insolence. On other occasions, verbal altercations break out between students in the cafeteria or in line and the *student* hall patrolmen. In one of these that I witnessed, the accused student, a handsome, aggressive-looking young man, defended himself in the informal but explicit language of working-class hostility. This roused the teacher on duty from his former passivity. He walked over toward the boy, and silently but with a glare of contempt, beckoned him from the room with a crooked finger and led him along the corridor to the administrative office: the tall boy rigid in silent protest, the teacher, balding and stoop-shouldered in a wrinkled suit, shambling ahead of him. The youth, I later learned, was suspended for a day. At some lunch periods all this is drowned out by Mantovani-type pop records played over the public address system.

What adults generally, I think, fail to grasp even though they may actually know it, is that there is no refuge or respite from this: no coffeebreak, no taking ten for a smoke, no room like the teachers' room, however poor, where the youngsters can get away from adults. High schools don't have club rooms; they have organized gym and recreation. A student cannot go to the library when he wants a book; on certain days his schedule provides a forty-five-minute library period. "Don't let anybody leave early," a guidance counselor urged during a group-testing session at Hartsburgh, an apparently more permissive school that I also visited. "There really isn't any place for them to go." Most of us are as nervous by the age of five as we will ever be, and adolescence adds to the strain; but one thing a high-school student learns is that he can expect no provision for his need to give in to his feelings, or swing out in his own style, or creep off and pull himself together.

The little things shock most. High-school students—and not just, or even particularly, at Milgrim—have a prisoner's sense of time. They don't know what time it is outside. The research which occasioned my presence at Milgrim, Hartsburgh, and the other schools in my study required me to interview each of twenty-five to thirty students at each school three times. My first appointment with each student was set up by his guidance counselor; I would make the next appointment directly with the student and issue him the passes he needed to keep it. The student has no *open* time at his own disposal; he has to select the period he can miss with least loss to himself. Students well-adapted to the school usually pick study halls; poorer or more troublesome students pick the times of their most disagreeable classes; both avoid cutting classes in which the teacher is likely to respond vindictively to their absence. Most students, when asked when they would like to come for their next interview, replied, "I can come any time." When I pointed out to them that there must, after all, be some times that would be more convenient for them than others, they would say, "Well tomorrow, fourth period" or whatever. But hardly any of them knew when this would be in clock time. High-school classes emphasize the importance of punctuality by beginning at regular but uneven times like 10:43 and 11:27, which are, indeed, hard to remember; and the students did not know when this was.

How typical is all this? The elements of the composition — the passes, the tight scheduling, the reliance on threats of detention or suspension as modes of social control are nearly universal. The usurpation of any possible *area* of student initiative, physical or mental, is about as universal. Milgrim forbids boys to wear trousers that end more than six inches above the floor, and has personnel fully capable of measuring them. But most high schools have some kind of dress regulation; I know of none that accepts and relies on the tastes of students.

There are differences, to be sure, in tone; and these matter. They greatly affect the impact of the place on students. Take, for comparison and contrast, Hartsburgh High. Not fifteen miles from Milgrim, Hartsburgh is an utterly different community. It is larger, more compact, and more suburban; more of a place. Hartsburgh High is much more dominantly middle class and there are few Negroes in the high school there.

First impressions of Hartsburgh High are almost bound to be favorable. The building, like Milgrm, is new; unlike Milgrim's, it is handsome. External walls are mostly glass, which gives a feeling of light, air, and space. At Hartsburgh there is none of the snarling, overt hostility that taints the atmosphere at Milgrim. There are no raucous buzzers; no bells of any kind. Instead, there are little blinker lights arranged like the Mexican flag. The green light blinks and the period is over; the white light signals a warning; when the red light blinks it is time to be in your classroom. Dress regulations exist but are less rigorous than at Milgrim. Every Wednesday, however, is dress-up day; boys are expected to wear ties and jackets or jacket-sweaters, the girls wear dresses rather than skirts and sweaters. The reason is that on Wednesday the school day ends with an extra hour of required assembly and, as the students explain, there are often outside visitors for whom they are expected to look their best.

Students at Hartsburgh seem much more relaxed than at Milgrim. In the grounds outside the main entrance, during lunch period, there is occasional horseplay. For ten minutes during one noon hour I watched three boys enacting a mutual fantasy. One was the audience who only sat and laughed, one the aggressor, and the third — a pleasant, inarticulate varsity basketball player named Paul — was the self-appointed victim. The two protagonists were portraying in pantomime old, silent-movie type fights in slow motion. The boy I did not know would slowly swing at Paul, who would sink twisting to the ground with grimaces of anguish; then the whole sequence would be repeated with variations, though the two boys never switched roles. In my interviews with Paul I had never solved the problems arising from the fact that he was eloquent only with his arms and torso movements, which were lost on the tape recorder, and it was a real pleasure to watch him in his own medium. This was a pleasure Milgrim would never have afforded me. Similarly, in the corridors at Hartsburgh I would occasionally come upon couples holding hands or occasionally rather more, though it distressed me that they always broke guiltily apart as soon as they saw me or any adult. One of my subjects, who was waiting for his interview, was dancing a little jig by himself in the corridor when I got to him. This was all rather reassuring.

It was also contrary to policy. There is a regulation against couples holding hands and they are punished if caught by the kind of teacher who hates sexuality in the young. The air and space also, subtly, turn out to be illusions if you try to use them. Hartsburgh High is built around a large, landscaped courtyard with little walks and benches. I made the mistake of trying to conduct an interview on one of these benches. When it was over we could not get back into the building except by disturbing a class, for the doors onto this inviting oasis can only be opened from inside, and nobody ever goes there. Since the courtyard is completely enclosed by the high-school building, this arrangement affords no additional protection from intruders; it merely shuts off a possible place for relaxation. The beautiful glass windows do not open enough to permit a body to squirm through and, consequently, do not open enough to ventilate the rooms, in which there are no individual controls for the fiercely effective radiators. Room temperature at Hartsburgh is a matter of high policy.

Teachers do not hide in the washrooms at Hartsburgh; but the principal recently issued a letter warning that any student caught in the vicinity of the school with "tobacco products" would be subject to suspension; students were directed to have their parents sign the letter as written acknowledgment that they were aware of the regulation and return it to school. Staff, of course, are permitted to smoke. At Hartsburgh a former teacher, promoted to assistant principal, serves as a full-time disciplinarian, but students are not dragged to his office by infuriated teachers, as sometimes happens at Milgrim. Instead, during the first period, two students from the school Citizenship Corps go quietly from classroom to classroom with a list, handing out summonses.

Along with having a less rancorous and choleric atmosphere than Milgrim, Hartsburgh seems to have more teachers who like teaching and like kids. But the fundamental pattern is still one of control, distrust, and punishment. The observable differences—and they are striking—are the result almost entirely, I believe, of *structural* and demographic factors and occur despite very similar administrative purposes. Neither principal respects adolescents at all or his staff very much. Both are preoccupied with good public relations as they understand them. Both are inflexible, highly authoritarian men. But their situations are different.

At Milgrim there is a strong district superintendent; imaginative if not particularly humane, he is oriented toward the national educational scene. He likes to have projects, particularly in research and guidance. Guidance officers report through their chairman directly to him, not to the building principal; and the guidance staff is competent, tough, and completely professional. When wrangles occur over the welfare of a student they are likely to be open, with the principal and the guidance director as antagonists; both avoid such encounters if possible, and neither can count on the support of the district office; but when an outside force—like an outraged parent—precipitates a conflict, it is fought out. At Hartsburgh, the district superintendent is primarily interested in running a tight ship with no problems. To this end, he backs the authority of the principal whenever this might be challenged. The guidance office is vestigial and concerned primarily with college placement and public relations in the sense of inducing students to behave in socially acceptable ways with a minimum of fuss.

In these quite different contexts, demographic differences in the student bodies have crucial consequences. At Milgrim, the working-class students are not dominant—they have not got quite enough self-confidence or nearly enough social savvy to be—but they are close enough to it to be a real threat to the nice, college-bound youngsters who set the tone in their elementary and junior high school and who expect to go on dominating the high school. These view the rapid influx of lower-status students as a rising wave that can engulf them, while the newcomers, many of whom are recent migrants or high-school transfers from the city, can remember schools in which they felt more at home.

The result is both to split and to polarize student feeling about the school, its administration, and other students. Nobody likes Milgrim High. But the middle-class students feel that what has ruined it is the lower-class students, and that the punitive constraint with which the school is run is necessary to keep them in line. In some cases these students approach paranoia: one girl—commenting on a mythical high school described in one of our semi-projective research instruments—said, "Well, it says here that the majority of the students are Negro—about a third" (the actual statement is "about a fifth").

The working-class students are hard-pressed; but being hard-pressed they are often fairly realistic about their position. If the Citizenship Corps that functions so smoothly and smugly at Hartsburgh were to be installed at Milgrim, those who actually turned people in and got them in trouble would pretty certainly receive some after-school instruction in the way social classes differ in values and in the propensity for non-verbal self-expression. At Milgrim, the working-class kids know where they stand and stand there. They are exceptionally easy to interview because the interviewer need not be compulsively non-directive. Once they sense that they are respected, they respond enthusiastically and with great courtesy. But they do not alter their position to give the interviewer what they think he wants, or become notably anxious at disagreeing with him. They are very concrete in handling experience and are not given to generalization. Most of them seem to have liked their elementary school, and they share the general American respect for education down to the last cliché—but then one will add, as an afterthought, not bothering even to be contemptuous, "Of course, you can't respect *this* school." They deal with their situation there in correspondingly concrete terms. Both schools had student courts last year, for example, and Hartsburgh still does, though few students not in the Citizenship Corps pay much attention to it. Student traffic corpsmen give out tickets for corridor offenses, and these culprits are brought before an elected student judge with an administrative official of the school present as adviser. But Milgrim had a student court last year that quickly became notorious. The "hoody element" got control of it, and since most of the defendants were their buddies, they were either acquitted or discharged on pleas of insanity. The court was disbanded.

The struggle at Milgrim is therefore pretty open, though none of the protagonists see it as a struggle for freedom or could define its issues in terms of principles. The upper-status students merely assent to the way the school is run, much as middle-class white Southerners assent to what the sheriff's office does, while the lower-status students move, or get pushed, from one embroilment to the next without ever quite realizing that what is happening to them is part of a general social pattern. At Hartsburgh the few lower-status students can easily be ignored rather than feared by their middle-class compeers who set the tone. They are not sufficiently numerous or aggressive to threaten the middle-class youngsters or their folkways; but, for the same reason, they do not force the middle-class youngsters to make common cause with the administration. The administration, like forces of law and order generally in the United States, is accepted without deference as a part of the way things are and work. Americans rarely expect authority to be either intelligent or forthright; it looks out for its own interests as best it can. Reformers and troublemakers only make it nervous and therefore worse; the best thing is to take advantage of it when it can help you and at other times to go on living your own life and let it try to stop you.

This is what the Hartsburgh students usually do, and, on the whole, the results are pleasant. The youngsters, being to some degree ivy, do not constantly remind the teachers, as the Milgrim students do, that their jobs have no connection with academic scholarship. Many of the teachers, for their part, act and sound like college instructors, do as competent a job, and enjoy some of the same satisfactions. The whole operation moves smoothly. Both Milgrim and Hartsburgh are valid examples—though of very different aspects—of American democracy in action. And in neither could a student learn as much about civil liberty as a Missouri mule knows at birth.

What is learned in high school, or for that matter anywhere at all, depends far less on what is taught than on what one actually experiences in the place. The quality of instruction in high school varies from sheer rot to imaginative and highly skilled teaching. But classroom content is often handled at a creditable level and is not in itself the source of the major difficulty. Both at Milgrim and Hartsburgh, for example, the students felt that they were receiving competent instruction and that this was an undertaking the school tried seriously to handle. I doubt, however, that this makes up for much of the damage to which high-school students are systematically subjected. What is formally taught is just not that important, compared to the constraint and petty humiliation to which the youngsters with few exceptions must submit in order to survive.

The fact that some of the instruction is excellent and a lot of it pretty good *is* important for another reason; it makes the whole process of compulsory schooling less insulting than it otherwise would be by lending it a superficial validity. Society tells the adolescent that he is sent to school in order to learn what he is taught in the classroom. No anthropologist and very few high school students would accept this as more than a rationalization; but rationalizations, to be at all effective, must be fairly plausible. Just as the draft would be intolerable if the cold war were wholly a piece of power politics or merely an effort to sustain the economy, so compulsory school attendance would be intolerable if what went on in the classrooms were totally inadequate to students' needs and irrelevant to their real intellectual concerns. . . .

The first thing the student learns . . . is that as a minor, he is subject to peculiar restraints; the second is that these restraints are general, not limited either by custom or by the schools' presumed commitment to the curriculum. High-school administrators are not professional educators in the sense that a physician, an attorney, or a tax accountant are professionals. They do not, that is, think of themselves as practitioners of a specialized instructional craft, who derive their authority from its requirements. They are specialists in keeping an essentially political enterprise from being strangled by conflicting community attitudes and pressures. They are problem-oriented, and the feelings and needs for growth of their captive and unenfranchised clientele are the least of their problems; for the status of the "teen-ager" in the community is so low that even if he rebels, the school is not blamed for the conditions against which he is rebelling. He is simply a truant or a juvenile delinquent; at worst the school has "failed to reach him." What high-school personnel become specialists in, ultimately, is the *control* of large groups of students even at catastrophic expense to their opportunity to learn. These controls are not exercised primarily to facilitate instruction, and particularly, they are in no way limited to matters bearing on instruction. At several schools in our sample boys had been ordered—sometimes on the complaint of teachers—to shave off beards. One of these boys had played football for the school; he was told that, although the school had no legal authority to require him to shave, he would be barred from the banquet honoring the team unless he complied. Dress regulations are another case in point. . . .

The effects on the students are manifold. The concepts of dignity and privacy, notably deficient in American adult folkways, are not permitted to develop here. The school's assumption of custodial control of students implies that power and authority are indistinguishable. If the school's authority is not limited to matters pertaining to education, it cannot be derived from its educational responsibilities. It is a naked, empirical fact, to be accepted or contraverted according to the possibilities of the moment. In such a world, power counts more than legitimacy; if you don't have power, it is naïve to think you have rights that must be respected . . . wise up. High school students experience regulation only as control, not as protection; they know, for example, that the principal will generally uphold the teacher in any conflict with a student, regardless of the merits of the case. Translated into the high-school idiom, *suaviter in modo, fortiter in re* becomes "If you get caught, it's just your ass."

Students do not often resent this; that is the tragedy. All weakness tends to corrupt, and impotence corrupts absolutely. Identifying, as the weak must, with the more powerful and frustrating of the forces that impinge upon them, they accept the school as the way life is and close their minds against the anxiety of perceiving alternatives. Many students like high school; others loathe and fear it. But even the latter do not object to it on principle; the school effectively obstructs their learning of the principles on which objection might be based; though these are among the principles that, we boast, distinguish us from totalitarian societies.

Yet, finally, the consequence of continuing through adolescence to submit to diffuse authority that is not derived from the task at hand

—as a doctor's orders or the training regulations of an athletic coach, for example, usually are—is more serious than political incompetence or weakness of character. There is a general arrest of development. An essential part of growing up is learning that, though differences of power among men lead to brutal consequences, all men are peers; none is omnipotent, none derives his potency from magic, but only from his specific competence and function. The policeman represents the majesty of the state, but this does not mean that he can put you in jail; it means, precisely, that he cannot—at least not for long. Any person or agency responsible for handling throngs of young people —especially if he does not like them or is afraid of them—is tempted to claim diffuse authority and snare the youngster in the trailing remnants of childhood emotion which always remain to trip him. Schools succumb to this temptation, and control pupils by reinvoking the sensations of childhood punishment, which remain effective because they were originally selected, with great unconscious guile, to dramatize the child's weakness in the face of authority. "If you act like a bunch of spoiled brats, we'll treat you like a bunch of spoiled brats," is a favorite dictum of sergeants, and school personnel, when their charges begin to show an awkward capacity for independence.

Thus the high school is permitted to infantilize adolescence; in fact, it is encouraged to by the widespread hostility to "teen-agers" and the anxiety about their conduct found throughout our society. It does not allow much maturation to occur during the years when most maturation would naturally occur. Maturity, to be sure, is not conspicuously characteristic of American adult life, and would almost certainly be a threat to the economy. So perhaps in this, as in much else, the high school is simply the faithful servant of the community.

There are two important ways in which it can render such service. The first of these is through its impact on individuals: on their values, their conception of their personal worth, their patterns of anxiety, and on their mastery and ease in the world—which determine so much of what they think of as their fate. The second function of the school is Darwinian; its biases, though their impact is always on individual youngsters, operate systematically to mold entire social groups. These biases endorse and support the values and patterns of behavior of certain segments of the population, providing their members with the credentials and shibboleths needed for the next stages of their journey, while they instill in others a sense of inferiority and warn the rest of society against them as troublesome and untrustworthy. In this way the school contributes simultaneously to social mobility and to social stratification. It helps see to it that the kind of people who get ahead are the kind who will support the social system it represents, while those who might, through intent or merely by their being, subvert it, are left behind as a salutary moral lesson.

ON REASON AND FREEDOM

C. Wright Mills

I

Nowadays men everywhere seek to know where they stand, where they may be going, and what—if anything—they can do about the present as history and the future as responsibility. Such questions as these no one can answer once and for all. Every period provides its own answers. But just now, for us, there is a difficulty. We are now at the ending of an epoch, and we have got to work out our own answers.

We are at the ending of what is called The Modern Age. Just as Antiquity was followed by several centuries of Oriental ascendancy, which Westerners provincially call The Dark Ages, so now The Modern Age is being succeeded by a post-modern period. Perhaps we may call it: The Fourth Epoch.

The ending of one epoch and the beginning of another is, to be sure, a matter of definition. But definitions, like everything social, are historically specific. And now our basic definitions of society and of self are being overtaken by new realities. I do not mean merely that never before within the limits of a single generation have men been so fully exposed at so fast a rate to such earthquakes of change. I do not mean merely that we feel we are in an epochal kind of transition, and that we struggle to grasp the outline of the new epoch we suppose ourselves to be entering. I mean that when we try to orient ourselves—if we do try—we find that too many of our old expectations and images are, after all, tied down historically: that too many of our standard categories of thought and of feeling as often disorient us as help to explain what is happening around us; that too many of our explanations are derived from the great historical transition from the Medieval to the Modern Age; and that when they are generalized for use today, they become unwieldy, irrelevant, not convincing. I also mean that our major orientations—liberalism and socialism—have virtually collapsed as adequate explanations of the world and of ourselves.

These two ideologies came out of The Enlightenment, and they have had in common many assumptions and values. In both, increased rationality is held to be the prime condition of increased freedom. The liberating notion of progress by reason, the faith in science as an unmixed good, the demand for popular education and the faith in its political meaning for democracy—all these ideals of The Enlightenment have rested upon the happy assumption of the inherent relation of reason and freedom. Those thinkers who have done the most to shape our ways of thinking have proceeded under this assumption. It lies under every movement and nuance of the work of Freud: To be free, the individual must become more rationally aware; therapy is an aid to giving reason its chance to work freely in the course of an individual's life. The same assumption underpins the main line of marxist work: Men, caught in the irrational anarchy of production, must become rationally aware of their position in society; they must become 'class conscious'—the marxian meaning of which is as rationalistic as any term set forth by Bentham.

Liberalism has been concerned with freedom and reason as supreme facts about the individual; marxism, as supreme facts about man's role in the political making of history. The liberals and the radicals of The Modern Period have generally been men who believed in the rational making of history and of his own biography by the free individual.

But what has been happening in the world makes evident, I believe, why the ideas of freedom and of reason now so often seem so ambiguous in both the new capitalist and the communist societies of our time: why marxism has so often become a dreary rhetoric of bureaucratic defense and abuse; and liberalism, a trivial and irrelevant way of masking social reality. The major developments of our time, I believe, can be correctly understood neither in terms of the liberal nor the marxian interpretation of politics and culture. These ways of thought arose as guidelines to reflection about types of society which do not now exist. John Stuart Mill never examined the kinds of political economy now arising in the capitalist world. Karl Marx never analyzed the kinds of society now arising in the Communist bloc. And neither of them ever thought through the problems of the so-called underdeveloped countries in which seven out of ten men are trying to exist today. Now we confront new kinds of social structure which, in terms of 'modern' ideals, resist analysis in the liberal and in the socialist terms we have inherited.

The ideological mark of The Fourth Epoch—that which sets it off from The Modern Age—is that the ideas of freedom and of reason have become moot; that increased rationality may not be assumed to make for increased freedom.

II

The role of reason in human affairs and the idea of the free individual as the seat of reason are the most important themes inherited by twentieth-century social scientists from the philosophers of The Enlightenment. If they are to remain the key values in terms of which troubles are specified and issues focused, then the ideals of reason and of freedom must now be re-stated as problems in more precise and solvable ways than have been available to earlier thinkers and investigators. For in our time these two values, reason and freedom, are in obvious yet subtle peril.

The underlying trends are well known. Great and rational organizations—in brief, bureaucracies—have indeed increased, but the substantive reason of the individual at large has not. Caught in the limited milieux of their everyday lives, ordinary men often cannot reason about the great structures—rational and irrational—of which their milieux are subordinate parts. Accordingly, they often carry out series of apparently rational actions without any ideas of the ends they serve, and there is the increasing suspicion that those at the top as well—like Tolstoy's generals—only pretend they know. The growth of such organizations, within an increasing division of labor, sets up more and more spheres of life, work, and leisure, in which reasoning is difficult or impossible. The soldier, for example, 'carries out an entire series of functionally rational actions accurately without having any idea as to the ultimate end of this action' or the function of each act within the whole.[1] Even men of technically supreme intelligence may efficiently perform their assigned work and yet not know that it is to result in the first atom bomb.

Science, it turns out, is not a technological Second Coming. That its techniques and its rationality are given a central place in a society does not mean that men live reasonably and without myth, fraud, and superstition. Universal education may lead to technological idiocy and nationalist provinciality—rather than to the informed and independent intelligence. The mass distribution of historic culture may not lift the level of cultural sensibility, but rather, merely banalize it—and compete mightily with the chance for creative innovation. A high level of bureaucratic rationality and of technology does not mean a high level of either individual or social intelligence. From the first you cannot infer the second. For social, technological, or bureaucratic rationality is not merely a grand summation of the individual will and capacity to reason. The very chance to acquire that will and that capacity seems in fact often to be decreased by it. Rationally organized social arrangements are not necessarily a means of increased freedom—for the individual or for the society. In fact, often they are a means of tyranny and manipulation, a means of expropriating the very chance to reason, the very capacity to act as a free man.

Only from a few commanding positions or—as the case may be—merely vantage points, in the rationalized structure is it readily possible to understand the structural forces at work in the whole which thus affect each limited part of which ordinary men are aware.

The forces that shape these milieux do not originate within them, nor are they controllable by those sunk in them. Moreover, these milieux

[1]Cf. Karl Mannheim, *Man and Society* (New York: Harcourt, Brace, 1940), p. 54.

are themselves increasingly rationalized. Families as well as factories, leisure as well as work, neighborhoods as well as states—they, too, tend to become parts of a functionally rational totality—or they are subject to uncontrolled and irrational forces.

The increasing rationalization of society, the contradiction between such rationality and reason, the collapse of the assumed coincidence of reason and freedom—these developments lie back of the rise into view of the man who is 'with' rationality but without reason, who is increasingly self-rationalized and also increasingly uneasy. It is in terms of this type of man that the contemporary problem of freedom is best stated. Yet such trends and suspicions are often not formulated as problems, and they are certainly not widely acknowledged as issues or felt as a set of troubles. Indeed, it is the fact of its unrecognized character, its lack of formulation, that is the most important feature of the contemporary problem of freedom and reason.

III

From the individual's standpoint, much that happens seems the result of manipulation, of management, of blind drift; authority is often not explicit; those with power often feel no need to make it explicit and to justify it. That is one reason why ordinary men, when they are in trouble or when they sense that they are up against issues, cannot get clear targets for thought and for action; they cannot determine what it is that imperils the values they vaguely discern as theirs.

Given these effects of the ascendant trend of rationalization, the individual 'does the best he can.' He gears his aspirations and his work to the situation he is in, and from which he can find no way out. In due course, he does not seek a way out: he adapts. The part of his life which is left over from work, he uses to play, to consume, 'to have fun.' Yet this sphere of consumption is also being rationalized. Alienated from production, from work, he is also alienated from consumption, from genuine leisure. This adaptation of the individual and its effects upon his milieux and self results not only in the loss of his chance, and in due course, of his capacity and will to reason; it also affects his chances and his capacity to act as a free man. Indeed, neither the value of freedom nor of reason, it would seem, are known to him.

Such adapted men are not necessarily unintelligent, even after they have lived and worked and played in such circumstances for quite some time. Karl Mannheim has made the point in a clear way by speaking of 'self-rationalization,' which refers to the way in which an individual, caught in the limited segments of great, rational organizations, comes systematically to regulate his impulses and his aspirations, his manner of life and his ways of thought, in rather strict accordance with 'the rules and regulations of the organization.' The rational organization is thus an alienating organization: the guiding principles of conduct and reflection, and in due course of emotion as well, are not seated in the individual conscience of the Reformation man, or in the independent reason of the Cartesian man. The guiding principles, in fact, are alien to and in contradiction with all that has been historically understood as individuality. It is not too much to say that in the extreme development the chance to reason of most men is destroyed, as rationality increases and its locus, its control, is moved from the individual to the big-scale organization. There is then rationality without reason. Such rationality is not commensurate with freedom but the destroyer of it.

It is no wonder that the ideal of individuality has become moot: in our time, what is at issue is the very nature of man, the image we have of his limits and possibilities as man. History is not yet done with its exploration of the limits and meanings of 'human nature.' We do not know how profound man's psychological transformation from the Modern Age to the contemporary epoch may be. But we must now raise the question in an ultimate form: Among contemporary men will there come to prevail, or even to flourish, what may be called The Cheerful Robot?

We know of course that man can be turned into a robot, by chemical and psychiatric means, by steady coercion and by controlled environment; but also by random pressures and unplanned sequences of circumstances. But can he be made to want to become a cheerful and willing robot? Can he be happy in this condition, and what are the qualities and the meanings of such happiness? It will no longer do merely to assume, as a metaphysic of human nature, that down deep in man-as-man there is an urge for freedom and a will to reason. Now we must ask: What in man's nature, what in the human condition today, what in each of the varieties of social structure makes for the ascendancy of the cheerful robot? And what stands against it?

The advent of the alienated man and all the themes which lie behind his advent now affect the whole of our serious intellectual life and cause our immediate intellectual malaise. It is a major theme of the human condition in the contemporary epoch and of all studies worthy of the name. I know of no idea, no theme, no problem, that is so deep in the classic tradition—and so much involved in the possible default of contemporary social science.

It is what Karl Marx so brilliantly discerned in his earlier essays on 'alienation'; it is the chief concern of Georg Simmel in his justly famous essay on 'The Metropolis'; Graham Wallas was aware of it in his work on The Great Society. It lies behind Fromm s conception of the 'automaton.' The fear that such a type of man will become ascendant underlies many of the more recent uses of such classic sociological conceptions as 'status and contract,' 'community and society.'

It is the hard meaning of such notions as Riesman's 'other-directed' and Whyte's 'social ethic.' And of course, most popularly, the triumph — if it may be called that — of such a man is the key meaning of George Orwell's *1984*.

On the positive side — a rather wistful side nowadays — the larger meanings of Freud's 'id,' Marx's 'Freiheit,' George Mead's 'I,' Karen Horney's 'spontaneity,' lie in the use of such conceptions against the triumph of the alienated man. They are trying to find some center in man-as-man which would enable them to believe that in the end he cannot be made into, that he cannot finally become, such an alien creature — alien to nature, to society, to self. The cry for 'community' is an attempt, a mistaken one I believe, to assert the conditions that would eliminate the probability of such a man, and it is because many humanist thinkers have come to believe that many psychiatrists by their practice produce such alienated and self-rationalized men that they reject these adaptive endeavors. Back of all this — and much more of traditional and current worrying and thinking among serious and sensible students of man — there lies the simple and decisive fact that the alienated man is the antithesis of the Western image of the free man. The society in which this man, this cheerful robot, flourishes is the antithesis of the free society — or in the literal and plain meaning of the word, of a democratic society. The advent of this man points to freedom as trouble, as issue, and — let us hope — as problem for social scientists. Put as a trouble of the individual — of the terms and values of which he is uneasily unaware — it is the trouble called 'alienation.' As an issue for publics — to the terms and values of which they are mainly indifferent — it is no less than the issue of democratic society, as fact and as aspiration.

It is just because this issue and this trouble are not now widely recognized, and so do not in fact exist as explicit troubles and issues, that the uneasiness and the indifference that betoken them are so deep and so wide in meaning and in effect. That is a major part of the problem of freedom today, seen in its political context, and it is a major part of the intellectual challenge which the formulation of the problem of freedom offers to contemporary social scientists.

It is not merely paradoxical to say that the values of freedom and reason are back of the absence of troubles, back of the uneasy feeling of malaise and alienation. In a similar manner, the issue to which modern threats to freedom and reason most typically lead is, above all, the absence of explicit issues — to apathy rather than to issues explicitly defined as such.

The issues and troubles have not been clarified because the chief capacities and qualities of man required to clarify them are the very freedom and reason that are threatened and dwindling. Neither the troubles nor the issues have been seriously formulated as the problems of . . . social science . . . . The promise of classic social science, in considerable part, is that they will be.

IV

The troubles and issues raised up by the crises of reason and freedom cannot of course be formulated as one grand problem, but neither can they be confronted, much less solved, by handling each of them microscopically as a series of small-scale issues, or of troubles confined to a scatter of milieux. They are structural problems, and to state them requires that we work in the classic terms of human biography and of epochal history. Only in such terms can the connections of structure and milieux that affect these values today be traced and causal analysis be conducted. The crisis of individuality and the crisis of history-making; the role of reason in the free individual life and in the making of history—in the re-statement and clarification of these problems lies the promise of the social sciences.

The moral and the intellectual promise of social science is that freedom and reason will remain cherished values, that they will be used seriously and consistently and imaginatively in the formulation of problems. But this is also the political promise of what is loosely called Western culture. Within the social sciences, political crises and intellectual crises of our time coincide: serious work in either sphere is also work in the other. The political traditions of classic liberalism and of classic socialism together exhaust our major political traditions. The collapse of these traditions as ideologies has had to do with the decline of free individuality and the decline of reason in human affairs. Any contemporary political re-statement of liberal and socialist goals must include as central the idea of a society in which all men would become men of substantive reason, whose independent reasoning would have structural consequences for their societies, its history, and thus for their own life fates.

The interest of the social scientist in social structure is not due to any view that the future is structurally determined. We study the structural limits of human decision in an attempt to find points of effective intervention, in order to know what can and what must be structurally changed if the role of explicit decision in history-making is to be enlarged. Our interest in history is not owing to any view that the future is inevitable, that the future is bounded by the past. That men have lived in certain kinds of society in the past does not set exact or absolute limits to the kinds of society they may create in the future. We study history to discern the alternatives within which human reason and human freedom can now make history. We study historical social structures, in brief, in order to find within them the ways in which they are and can be controlled. For only in this way can we come to know the limits and the meaning of human freedom.

Freedom is not merely the chance to do as one pleases; neither is it merely the opportunity to choose between set alternatives. Freedom is, first of all, the chance to formulate the available choices, to argue over them—and then, the opportunity to choose. That is why freedom cannot exist without an enlarged role of human reason in human affairs. Within an individual's biography and within a society's history, the social task of reason is to formulate choices, to enlarge the scope of human decisions in the making of history. The future of human affairs is not merely some set of variables to be predicted. The future is what is to be decided—within the limits, to be sure, of historical possibility. But this possibility is not fixed; in our time the limits seem very broad indeed.

Beyond this, the problem of freedom is the problem of how decisions about the future of human affairs are to be made and who is to make them. Organizationally, it is the problem of a just machinery of decision. Morally, it is the problem of political responsibility. Intellectually, it is the problem of what are now the possible futures of human affairs. But the larger aspects of the problem of freedom today concern not only the nature of history and the structural chance for explicit decisions to make a difference in its course; they concern also the nature of man and the fact that the value of freedom cannot be based upon 'man's basic nature.' The ultimate problem of freedom is the problem of the cheerful robot, and it arises in this form today because today it has become evident to us that *all* men do *not* naturally *want* to be free; that all men are not willing or not able, as the case may be, to exert themselves to acquire the reason that freedom requires.

Under what conditions do men come to *want* to be free and capable of acting freely? Under what conditions are they willing and able to bear the burdens freedom does impose and to see these less as burdens than as gladly undertaken self-transformations? And on the negative side: Can men be made to want to become *cheerful* robots?

In our time, must we not face the possibility that the human mind as a social fact might be deteriorating in quality and cultural level, and yet not many would notice it because of the overwhelming accumulation of technological gadgets? Is not that one meaning of rationality without reason? Of human alienation? Of the absence of any free role for reason in human affairs? The accumulation of gadgets hides these meanings: Those who use these devices do not understand them; those who invent them do not understand much else. That is why we may *not*, without great ambiguity, use technological abundance as the index of human quality and cultural progress.

To formulate any problem requires that we state the values involved and the threat to those values. For it is the felt threat to cherished values—such as those of freedom and reason—that is the necessary moral substance of all significant problems of social inquiry, and as well of all public issues and private troubles.

The values involved in the cultural problem of individuality are conveniently embodied in all that is suggested by the ideal of The Renaissance Man. The threat to that ideal is the ascendancy among us of The Cheerful Robot.

The values involved in the political problem of history-making are embodied in the Promethean ideal of its human making. The threat to that ideal is twofold: On the one hand, history-making may well go by default, men may continue to abdicate its wilful making, and so merely drift. On the other hand, history may indeed be made—but by narrow elite circles without effective responsibility to those who must try to survive the consequences of their decisions and of their defaults.

I do not know the answer to the question of political irresponsibility in our time or to the cultural and political question of The Cheerful Robot. But is it not clear that no answers will be found unless these problems are at least confronted? Is it not obvious, that the ones to confront them, above all others, are the social scientists of the rich societies? That many of them do not now do so is surely the greatest human default being committed by privileged men in our times.